PREFACE.

MANY of the explanations usually given in a preface will be found in the body of the following work.

This Biography has swelled far beyond our original contemplation. Mr. Jefferson was more than half a century conspicuously before the American people. His official positions were numerous, furnishing not only a large mass of facts which cannot be passed over in a history of his life aiming at any degree of fullness, but his discharge of these trusts caused him to do acts or express opinions which have the force of precedents throughout nearly the whole range of topics in our nationo-federative system.

During the seventeen years he survived his retirement from public life, he remained a close observer, and continued to express his opinions in his correspondence, on all the leading political questions which engaged public attention. We have, therefore, a complete record of his views for more than sixty years—from a period preceding our national independence to one which found our peculiar institutions tested, determined in their nature, and fixed in their prescribed channels.

When it is taken into consideration that Mr. Jefferson is the conceded founder of that party which soon obtained undisputed control in our General Government, and which consequently affixed its own interpretations to our federal Constitution ; when it is remembered that his example and opinions are still quoted as authoritative by a decided majority of the American people, the importance of having that example and those opinions clearly understood, must become obvious to all reflecting persons.

His correspondence also discloses his views on a great variety of important extra-political topics. Like his political ones, they betray vigorous thought. They are often, too, clothed in that felicitous diction which is apt to enlist the sympathy of the ear as well as that of the understanding ; nay, which *may* captivate the former at the expense of the free exercise of the latter. It would be unusual to converse half an hour on great political or social problems with an intelligent American—and particularly among the rural classes, who talk around their firesides of the Revolution, and of the august fathers of the Republic—without hearing some lofty thought or ringing phrase quoted from Jefferson. There was a sympathy between his heart and the great popular heart, which nothing ever did, ever can, shake. His mission was leadership. Without an effort on his part, expressions from his lips, that from other men's would scarcely have attracted notice, became thenceforth axioms, creeds, and gathering-cries to great masses of his countrymen. Thus far, at least, his ideas have been transmitted to succeeding generations without any apparent diminution of their influence. We are presented with the remarkable spectacle of a reputation more assailed by class and hereditary hate than any other, and all others, belonging to our early history—scarcely defended by a page where volumes have been written to traduce it—yet steadily and resistlessly spreading, until all parties seek to appropriate it—until not an American man between the Atlantic and the Pacific dare place himself before a popular constituency with revilings of Jefferson on his lips. Two great names are embalmed before all others in the hearts of the people. One belonged to the SWORD, and the other to the PEN of our country!

There was another field, hitherto nearly a blank, which we have felt bound to improve admirable opportunities for exploring before it should be too late; and we were not willing to throw away the results of our exploration from the apprehension of making too voluminous a work.

Mr. Jefferson has a number of surviving grandchildren, who lived from ten to thirty years under the same roof with him. They had ample opportunities for observing him in nearly every relation of private life—as the father, the master, the neighbor, the friend, the companion under all circumstances, the farmer, the business man, etc. From the lips of their parents—Mr. Jefferson's two daughters—they constantly heard him described as the son and the husband. Their recollections were generally rendered precise and minute by the intense interest with which, from infancy, they regarded everything connected with one revered as few men were ever revered in their families. And these recollections, whether their own or derived from their parents, were supported by contemporaneous memoranda made by Mr. Jefferson or themselves, by contemporaneous correspondence, and by various other family records.

None of Mr. Jefferson's descendants have ever chosen to write his biography. They preferred to leave that duty to those who could not have, nor be supposed to have, consanguineal attachments or hereditary hostilities to influence their pens.

In a few years death would quench personal recollections but in small part recorded, and scatter the manuscripts we have referred to among a multitude of inheritors. Some of these manuscripts would, in all probability, become destroyed in the ordinary train of casualties, and others would be hopelessly lost trace of, because no biographer would know of their existence, and consequently where to institute a particular search for them. Every writer of experience knows that any other search is seldom rewarded. And at best the manuscripts, books, papers, etc., far too extensive for transcription, and scattered over a continent, would be the subject of too many wills, to stand any probability of being all delivered up for scrutiny and collation by one person.

The materials we have collected from these sources comprise, we should say, not far from one-third of these volumes.

We have preferred in all cases to give Mr. Jefferson's words at least once on every important question—and oftener if he materially changed his views—instead of attempting to convey the substance in any briefer synopsis of our own.

We have pursued the same course towards his conspicuous adversaries, where we have given their opinions ; or we have distinctly cited the work and the page where those opinions are to be found.

We have desired in no case to take refuge from responsibility under loose generalities, and have sacrificed severely in ease and flowingness of style to make our important statements—especially those conveying censure—so definite in respect to time, place, and matter, that they will present a tangible issue to inquirers who would investigate, or to opponents who would refute our views. The leering, sneering, dodging way of making charges by implication, and insulting by innuendo—which has been so extensively practised by early and late calumniators of Mr. Jefferson—is not to our taste. A fair, straight-forward blow against an adversary is legitimate, and becomes sometimes an unfortunate necessity to convey the genuine lessons, and vindicate the truth of history. But he who strikes should manfully stand up, like Friar Tuck, and abide the counter buffet, whether the hand that deals it be gauntleted or not.

It is a pity, in our judgment, that the world would not agree to consider that witness—as he really is in four cases out of five—a conscious liar, who will not

"Aye free aff han' his story tell,"

so that every important adverse assertion he makes or insinuates can be specifically met, and specifically corroborated or refuted.

And he who brings forward old anonymous personal

charges or imputations made in partisan newspapers or pamphlets during periods of violent controversy, never proved, and scarcely credited by reasonable men of any side when made—gives them countenance by repeating them—presents them as quasi-historical allegations, without distinctly exposing the flimsiness of the authority on which they rest—adds the spirit of a slanderer to that of a falsifier.

In quoting, whether for praise or censure, we have not in all cases been able to give the entire context. Sometimes it would lead but to repetition or amplification, and sometimes to matter irrelevant to the particular point under investigation. It has been our anxious wish to avoid garbling either in the letter or spirit. But in common-placing extracts from a multitude of books, perhaps a sound judgment has not always been exercised, on the brief consideration allowed, as to what should be retained or what omitted. We have attempted to indicate chasms, or the bringing together of disconnected clauses, by marks which all readers understand. We have aimed to take no liberties with quotations beyond occasionally changing the person of a noun, or the tense of a verb, for grammatical convenience, or by introducing italicization. The latter is to be always considered our own unless it is otherwise stated.

Yet we cannot but sincerely hope the context of our quotations will be examined, as often as is practicable, by every reader. There may be errors. The weary hand and eye are not always true to their office. Typographical mistakes sometimes elude detection, and independently of this, there may be facts, or shreds of facts.

which though not sufficiently relevant, or separately important for quotation, would, on a general view, tend to somewhat modify conclusions. It is never to be forgotten that the accuser acts *ex-parte*, and that, however fair his intentions, he may be unconsciously warped by prejudice both in the selection and the conclusion. The reader owes it to the accused, and the intelligent reader owes it to himself, to thoroughly test the good faith and general accuracy of this important kind of evidence.

It may be unnecessary to say that we have diligently sought accuracy in all particulars, as a matter of policy, if nothing else. But on so broad a canvas, spread over with so much that is minute and specific, we can scarcely hope to have avoided errors. We expect to be held responsible for them in all cases. And if they intrinsically, or in the light of the spirit which pervades the work, fairly convey the impression that they were intentional, we take it for granted that our accountability will be made that to which the false witness everywhere deserves to be held.

Our deepest and warmest acknowledgments are due to the family of Mr. Jefferson,[1] for their countenance and aid, in preparing this work. They welcomed our undertaking with a prompt and graceful expression of cordial approbation. They laid before us their stores of private manuscripts, never before opened, without reserve —transferring to us a large and important collection of newly discovered ones,[2] without preliminary perusal. They furnished us their full recollections and opinions

---

[1] His decendants and their wives and husbands.

[2] See vol. 1, p. 16, note.

on every class of topics. They labored for us assiduously in collecting materials from Mr. Jefferson's surviving friends in Virginia ; and they asked his friends in other States to in like manner contribute their assistance. They permitted us to select purely at our own discretion from the materials of every kind they were able to furnish—and to use their statements, either in the words or in the substance, and quote the family, or our particular informant, as our authority. Even the younger generation, those not born until after Mr. Jefferson's death, have made themselves busy collectors, copiers, etc. where they could thus render us any assistance.

We cannot undertake to specify all the other personal sources from which we have received valuable aid in the communication of manuscripts, facts, opinions, explanations, or authorities not otherwise easy of access. Indeed, we do not even know who have been the indirect contributors of many valuable documents, and ancient printed records from Virginia, nor can we delay this volume to make the requisite inquiries of those through whom they have been received.

Special acknowledgments are due to the late Hon. Joseph C. Cabell, the Hon. Hugh Blair Grigsby, and Professor John B. Minor, of Virginia ; to Dr. Robley Dunglison, Hon. Edward Coles, Professor George Tucker, Hon. Henry D. Gilpin, Hon. George W. Woodward, and George M. Conàrroe, Esq. of Pennsylvania ; to the late Henry Clay, of Kentucky ; to Colonel Hayne, of South Carolina ; to Richard Randolph, Esq. of the district of Columbia ; to Hon. Jared Sparks, Hon. Edward Everett, and J. C. Gray, Esq. of Massachusetts ;

to the Rev. Dr. Francis Wayland, of Rhode Island; to General Tench Tilghman and General John Spear Smith, of Maryland; and to the late Hon. William L. Marcy, Hon. Daniel S. Dickinson, General John A. Dix, the late Dr. Theodoric Romeyn Beck, Hon. George W. Clinton, Hon. Addison Gardner, the late Hon. Henry P. Edwards, Rev. Mr. May, Hon. John J. Taylor, Dr. S. B. Woolworth, Dr. J. G. Cogswell, of New York.

Cortland Village, N. Y. }
September, 1857.

CONTENTS OF THE FIRST VOLUME.

[A complete analytical Index will be found at the end of the third volume.]

CHAPTER I.

1743—1764.

CHAPTER II.

1764—1773.

CHAPTER III.

1773—1775.

CHAPTER IV.

1775.

CHAPTER V.

1776.

CHAPTER VI.

1776—1779.

His Double Reasons—Leaves Congress—Appointed a Commissioner to France—
Reasons for declining—Takes his Seat in the Virginia House of Delegates—Leader of
the Reform Party—Principal Coadjutors, Mason, Wythe, and Madison—Principal
Opponents, Pendleton and Nicholas—Bills introduced by Jefferson, and their Fate—
Bill to abolish Entails—Effect of this on Virginia considered—Creates a Party hostile
to Jefferson—His Bill to naturalize Foreigners—Bill to remove the Seat of Government—That to abolish Entails passed—Bill for a General Revision of the Laws—This
passes, and the Revisors appointed—Bill to define Treason—Bill to regulate the Laws
of Succession—Bills on other Subjects—The Committee òn Religion—Their Proceedings—The existing Church Establishment—Its results—Jefferson reports his Bills to
establish Courts—Obtains Leave of Absence—Summary of further Proceedings—Project for creating a Dictator—Patrick Henry proposed for Dictator—Wirt's Exculpation
of him—How the Project was crushed—Jefferson's View of it—Meeting of the Law
Revisers—Their General Plan—Allotment of their Parts—Meeting of the General
Assembly in 1777—Parties—Jefferson's Legislative Dispatch—Brings in various Bills—
The Church Question—Called Home by Illness of his Wife—Contest of Parties—R. H.
Lee's Defeat—Subsequently vindicated—His Letter to Jefferson—Jefferson's Attitude
between the Parties—Adjournment—National Events—Fall Session of General Assem-
bly—Jefferson's Bills to establish Courts—Elections—Jefferson's Appointment on
Committees—Contest between the two Houses—Final Struggle on Bills to establish
Courts—Jefferson's Bill to sequester British Property—Report of the Law Revisers—
How and by whom the Work was executed—Anecdote of Mr. Wickham—Extent of
the Revision—How certain Principles in it were settled—A Sentimental Anecdote
exploded—Jefferson opposed to the Principle of Retaliation—His Bill for establishing
Religious Freedom—Original and amended Copy—His other Religious Bills—History
of Religious Bills continued—Washington's, Henry's, and R. H. Lee's opinions in favor
of Compulsory Church Levies—The Struggle completed—Jefferson's three Educational
Bills—Copy of Preamble of his Free School Bill—Analysis of its Provisions—Further
History of the three Bills—Slavery Laws—Jefferson's Penal Code—General Analysis
of it—His View of the effects of the Revision—Ultimate Fate of the Revision—Letter to
Franklin—Chasms in Mr. Jefferson's Correspondence explained—His warm Appeal for
British Prisoners—Correspondence with English and German Officers—Philips, de
Riedesel, de Geismer, etc.—Letter to Philips and to de Unger—Courtesies to the
Prisoners—The Baroness de Riedesel—How Jefferson was repaid by the English and
German Officers, ... 194

CHAPTER VII.

1779—1780.

Jefferson chosen Governor of Virginia—John Page his Competitor—Gloomy Condition of
Affairs—Particularly so in the South—Weakness of the three Southern States—Statis-
tical and Natural Causes therefor—The British Plan—War transferred to the South—
War changes in its Spirit—British Commissioners to Bribe Americans—Their Strange
Manifesto—Condition of Virginia—Her Natural Exposure to the Enemy—No Fortifica-
tions—Her Militia without Arms—A Nursery of Men and Provisions—How freely she
supplied these to the Cause—But wholly destitute of defensive Strength—Washington
Responsible for her Military Policy—Never was State so exposed to Invasion—General
Matthew's Invasion before Jefferson's Accession—Colonel Lawson's Account of it—
Dangers in the West—Hamilton, British Governor of Detroit—His Atrocities to American Prisoners—His projected Campaign of 1779—Colonel Clarke had taken Kaskaskias—His Winter March against Hamilton—Incredible Hardships—Takes St. Vincenne
and captures Hamilton—Randolph compares Clarke to Hannibal—Hamilton placed in
Irons—General Phillips interferes—Jefferson consults Washington—Washington's
Reply—Retaliations menaced on both Sides—Was Retaliation by Americans expedient?—Machinations in and out of Congress—Virginia ratifies French Treaties—Spain
declares War—Jefferson takes Possession of Western Country—Anecdote of Colonel

CHAPTER VIII.

1780—1781.

CHAPTER IX.

1781.

CHAPTER X.

1781—1784.

CHAPTER XI.

1784—1786.

CHAPTER XII.

1787.

CHAPTER XIII.

1788—1789.

CHAPTER XIV.

1789—1790.

CHAPTER XV.

1790—1791.

LIFE OF JEFFERSON.

CHAPTER I.

1743—1764.

Topography of Virginia—The Birth-place of Mr. Jefferson—Early Settlement of the State
—Large Estates acquired by the Lowland Proprietors—Their Style of Living, Manners,
Habits, and Character—Other Social Strata—Mr. Jefferson's Ancestors—His Grand-
father—Early History of his Father, Colonel Peter Jefferson—Colonel Jefferson's
Estate—He marries Jane Randolph—Genealogy of the Randolph Family—Its Settle-
ment and Great Success in Virginia—Isham Randolph, the Father-in-law of Colonel
Jefferson—Colonel Jefferson's first Civil Offices—Birth of Thomas Jefferson—Colonel
Jefferson's Removal to Tuckahoe—Assists in surveying Boundary Line and construct-
ing Map of Virginia—His Return to Albemarle—Appointed Colonel of his County—
Elected a Member of the House of Burgesses—His Death and Character—His Training
of his Son, and Influence in forming his Character—Mr. Jefferson's Mother—Her Cha-
racter—Family Record—Childhood of Mr. Jefferson—His Religious Training—His
Early Education and Amusements—First meets Patrick Henry—Enters College—His
Relatives at Williamsburg—His Habits of Study—His Morals and Standard of Action—
Influence of Dr. Small—Second Year in College—Attainments and Favorite Branches—
Branches which were not Favorites—Mental Characteristics—Favorite Authors—
Studies Law with Mr. Wythe—Intimacy with Governor Fauquier—Habits as a Law
Student—First Love—Personal Appearance, Accomplishments, Conversational Powers,
Temper, etc.—Becomes of Age.

A GLANCE at the map of Virginia shows that the territory of
that State is divided about midway by several ranges of mountains, collectively taking the name of Appalachians or Alleghanies, which extend through it from the southwest to the northeast, nearly parallel with its Atlantic shore. From the ocean,
about half the distance to the most eastern of these ranges—the
Blue Ridge—stretches the low, and often marshy Tertiary
plain, through which the tides extend up the sluggish rivers;

and hence it is called the " tide-water country." From its western limit, the surface rises more rapidly and brokenly, but still
very gradually, to the base of the Blue Ridge; and this second
plain, known in Old Virginia statutes as the " Piedmont Country," is more fertile and salubrious than the lower, and as it
nears the mountains, is excelled in these particulars by few
countries on earth. Detached hills of no great elevation occasionally break its surface ; and parallel with the Blue Ridge, and
about twenty miles east of it, a continuous chain, from six hundred to a thousand feet in height, known now as the Southwest
Range, extends from James River to the southern head-waters
of the Rappahannock. South of the village of Charlottesville,
the space between these outliers and the Blue Ridge, is mostly
filled with a cluster of irregular heights, still lower than the
former, called the Ragged Mountains ; but north of Charlottesville, the broad valley stretches away as far as the eye will
reach to the northeast, presenting a mixture of fields and wood-
lands and running streams, combined into a landscape of quiet
but uncommon beauty.

From the slopes of the Blue Ridge, west of Charlottesville,
spring two streams which unite to form the Rivanna, the principal northern tributary of the James ; and after their confluence, they find their way through a gap in the Southwest
Range, not far from the centre of the chain, in Albemarle
county. This opening through the hills is about a mile in
breadth. A little more than a mile from its eastern outlet, on
one of those gentle swells into which the river banks are here
everywhere broken—in the midst of a now cultivated field—
stand two plane and two locust trees; and hard by is (or was
in 1851) a cavity, nearly filled by the plow, indicating to the
passer, by the bits of broken bricks and plaster, and remnants
of chimney-stones, fire-cracked and vitrified, which lay in and
about it, that here once had been the cellar of a human habitation. A Virginia farm-house formerly occupied the site. It
was of a story and a half in height ; had the four spacious
ground rooms and hall, with garret chambers above, common
in those structures a hundred years since ; and also the usual
huge outside chimneys, planted against each gable like Gothic
buttresses, but massive enough, had such been their use, to support the walls of a cathedral, instead of those of a low, wooden

cottage.   In that house was born THOMAS JEFFERSON ; the plane
and locust trees were planted by his hand in his twenty-first
year.

The spot commands a delightful view.   On the east and
south, the eye wanders over a rolling plain, bounded only by
the horizon.   West and north, it rests on the wooded folds
and waving summit line of the Southwest Range.   The first of
these elevations south of the Rivanna—a hill six hundred feet
in height, and approaching nearer to a hemispherical than
conical form, overtopped on the south by Carter's Mountain,
and on the north dropping down in rocky cliffs to the river's
brink—is Monticello.[1]   Through the Rivanna gap, the eye,
after traversing a portion of the valley west of the hills,
encounters, on the left, the broken and picturesque summits
of the Ragged Mountains, while beyond, and to the right, the
Blue Ridge lifts up its towering barrier—as if typical of the
soil and climate, of the rich hue of the ripe blue wild-grape[2]—
against the western sky.

In the early settlement of Virginia, the inhabitants found
the river-bottoms of the tide-water region more fertile than the
intervening sandy ridges ; and the rivers themselves for a long
period furnished the only convenient means for transporting
heavy products to or from the seaboard.   The population,
therefore, clung to their banks, each new wave of foreign emigration, or younger and spreading generation of the inhabitants,
advancing higher towards their sources.   Lands were obtained
on easy conditions from the Government and otherwise; and
provident individuals secured vast estates.   This was particularly the case on James River, where the most enterprising and
wealthy of the earlier emigrants established themselves.   Some
of these, men of particular mark and energy, acquired possessions vying in extent with those of the proudest nobles of
their native land.   These were perpetuated in their families by
entails, the laws regulating which were ultimately rendered
more stringent in Virginia, than in England itself.   As their
lands rose gradually in value, the great lowland proprietors
began to vie with English nobles in wealth as well as in terri-

[1] From the Italian, signifying "Little Mountain."
[2] Beverly, the early historian of Virginia, speaking of the wild grapes, when left to
grow in the clearings, says: "I have seen in this case more grapes upon one single
vine than would load a London cart."—*History of Virginia*, Book ii. chap. 22.

tory. Many of them lived in baronial splendor. Their abodes,
it is true, were comparatively mean, as the country did not yet
furnish permanent building materials, except at vast cost, nor
did it furnish practiced architects to make use of them:[1] but
their spacious grounds and gardens were bravely ornamented;
their tables were loaded with plate, and with the luxuries of
the Old and New World;[2] numerous slaves, and white persons
whose time they owned for a term of years,[3] served them in
every capacity which use, luxury, or ostentation could dictate;
and when they travelled in state, their cumbrous and richly
appointed coaches were dragged by six horses, driven by three
postillions. But usually the mistress of the household, with
her children and maids, appropriated this vehicle. The Virginia gentleman of that day, with much of the feeling of earlier
feudal times, when the spur was the badge of knighthood,
esteemed the saddle the most manly, if not the only manly,
way of making use of the noblest of brutes. He accordingly
performed all his ordinary journeys on horseback. When he
went forth with his whole household, the cavalcade consisted
of the mounted white males of the family, the coach and six,
lumbering through the sands, and a retinue of mounted body
servants, grooms with spare led horses, etc., in the rear.

In their general tone of character, the lowland aristocracy of
Virginia resembled the cultivated landed gentry of the mother
country. Numbers of them were highly educated and accomplished, by foreign study and travel; and nearly all, or certainly much the largest portion, obtained an excellent education at William and Mary College, after its establishment, or

[1] Yet, if they lacked the baronial piles of England, they did not lack comfortable residences. Beverly (writing about 1720, we think) says that several gentlemen of Williamsburg have "built themselves large brick houses, of many rooms on a floor; but," he adds, "they don't covet to make them lofty, having extent enough of ground to build upon; and now and then they are visited by winds which would incommode a towering fabric. They love to have large rooms, that they may be cool in summer. Of late they have made their stories much higher than formerly, and their windows larger, and sasht with crystal glass; adorning their apartments with rich furniture. All their drudgeries of cookery, washing, dairies, etc., are performed in offices apart from the dwelling-houses, which by this means are kept more cool and sweet." This description would apply equally to the better residences on the James, except that many of the latter were constructed of wood.

[2] "The families," says Beverly, "being altogether on country seats, they have their graziers, seedsmen, gardeners, brewers, bakers, butchers, and cooks within themselves; they have a great plenty and variety of provisions for their table; and as for spicery, and other things the country don't produce, they have constant supplies of 'em from England. The gentry pretend to have their victuals drest and served up as nicely as the best tables in London."

[3] Being apprenticed, to pay their passage money.

respectable acquirements in the classical schools kept in nearly every parish by the learned clergy of the Established Church. As a class, they were intelligent, polished in manners, high-toned and hospitable—and sturdy in their loyalty and in their adherence to the national Church. Their winters were often spent in the gaieties and festivities of the provincial capital; their summers, when not connected with the public service, principally in supervising their immense estates, in visiting each other, and in such amusements as country life afforded. Among the latter, the chase held a prominent place. Born almost to the saddle and to the use of fire-arms, they were keen hunters;[1] and when the chase was over, they sat round groaning boards, and drank confusion to Frenchman and Spaniard abroad, and to Roundhead[2] and Prelatist at home. When the lurking and predatory Indian became the object of pursuit, no strength of the Red man could withstand, no speed of his elude, this fiery and gallantly mounted cavalry. The social gulf which separated this from the common class of colonists, became about as deep and wide, and as difficult to overleap in marriage and other social arrangements, as that which divided the gentry and peasantry of England. Such were the Carters, the Carys, the Burwells, the Byrds, the Fairfaxes, the Harrisons, the Lees, the Randolphs, and many other families of early Virginia.

Various social strata intervened between the great lowland proprietors and the lowest class of whites. Midway in this scale, of conceded respectability and of a fortune neither large nor mean, stood a gentleman by the name of Jefferson, residing at Osborne's, on the James, in Chesterfield county. His

[1] For animated pictures of these dashing riders, hunting bears, deer, and "vermine"—dragging captured wolves alive at their horses' tails, "none faltering in their pace"—see Beverly, Book iv. chap. 21.

[2] We do not propose to enter upon the question whether the Cavalier or Puritan *blood* predominated among the early lowland *aristocracy* of Virginia. It will not probably be disputed by any that *this class* were generally decided *loyalists*, whatever their *pedigree*. Perhaps we should state the question which has been raised more accurately by saying it is whether the "lowland grandees" of Virginia were sprung from the higher or lower classes in England. Our *opinion* is that there have been decided exaggerations in the extreme statements on both sides. If well-preserved and properly connected family traditions and records can be relied on, not a few of the earlier settlers belonged to English families of rank, particularly those which were reduced from affluence to comparative poverty in the civil wars of Charles I.'s time. On the other hand, we entertain no doubt that many of the most opulent and distinguished families of the Old Dominion sprung from enterprising emigrants without any such pretensions. But esteeming the subject of no sort of consequence, we will not stop to bestow investigation on it.

ancestors had, according to family tradition, emigrated from near Mount Snowden, in Wales; and they were among the first settlers of Virginia. One of them was a representative of Flower de Hundred in the Colonial Assembly convened by Governor Yeardley, on the 30th of July, 1619, in the choir of the church at Jamestown[1]—the first legislative body of Europeans, we think, that ever assembled in the New World. This was twelve years after the first colonization of Virginia, and one year before the Mayflower reached the " wild New England shore." Virginia contained at the time but six hundred white inhabitants, men, women, and children. The first Jefferson, of whom any particular accounts are preserved, residing at Osborne's as already mentioned, had three sons, Thomas, · Field, and Peter. Thomas died young. Field emigrated to a place on the Roanoke, a few miles above the point where the river enters North Carolina, where he lived and died. He had a numerous family, several of whom were competent and successful men in their avocations.[2] The third brother, Peter, was born February 29th, 1708. His early education had been neglected, but possessing a strong thirst for knowledge, and great energy of character, he subsequently made up for the deficiency by study and reading. Like a celebrated contemporary, twenty-four years younger, George Washington, he started his business career as a surveyor, and it was probably in this capacity he first became acquainted with the Randolph family. If so, business relations speedily ripened into the most intimate social ones, for he soon became the bosom friend of William, the young proprietor of Tuckahoe, and the preferred suitor for the hand of the oldest daughter of Isham of Dungeness, Adjutant-General of Virginia. In 1735 he prepared to establish himself as a planter, after the usual manner of younger sons, by " patenting " one thousand acres of land, at the east opening of the gap where the Rivanna passes through the Southwest Range. His tract lay mostly on the plain, but it

---

[1] The record of this assemblage only exists, so far as we know, in the British State Paper Office, where it was seen by Conway Robinson, Esq., of Virginia, in 185-. He copied the names of the burgesses. Ensign Rossingham also represented Flower de Hundred. This, we are informed, was Sir George Yeardley's settlement, next below (and on the opposite side of the James River) Shirley Hundred, which was next below Bermuda Hundred, at the confluence of the Appomatox and James.

[2] A short instrument, in the handwriting and bearing the signature of one, and we believe the oldest of his sons, Thomas, is before us. It betrays a practiced hand and has a family likeness—a very decided one in the signature and in the numerals—to the chirography of a more celebrated cousin of the same name.

also extended up the declivities of the hills, embracing the entire one afterwards named Monticello. His "patent" was joined on the east by another,[1] of two thousand four hundred acres, made a few days earlier by his friend William Randolph. Not long afterwards, Peter Jefferson "purchased," as the family land-rolls specify, four hundred adjoining acres of the other's tract—probably to obtain a preferred site for his residence, for it was on this portion of his land he subsequently constructed it. But an authenticated copy of the deed, now in the possession of a great grandson, shows that the consideration paid for the four hundred acres was "Henry Weatherbourne's biggest bowl of arrack punch!" This was somewhat characteristic of the times, and entirely characteristic of all the intercourse between these devoted friends. To his whole farm Peter Jefferson gave the name of Shadwell, after that of the parish in London, where his wife was born. He was married in 1738.

The Randolphs had been for ages a family of consideration in the midland counties of Warwick and Northampton, in England, and they claimed among their ancestors the powerful Scotch Earls of Murray, connected by blood or alliance with many of the most distinguished families in the English and Scotch peerage, and with royalty itself. Many were the eminent statesmen, warriors, churchmen, and scholars,[2] who sprung from this stock.[3] William Randolph of Warwickshire,[4] the son of a

---

[1] Now Edgehill, the seat of Colonel Thomas Jefferson Randolph.

[2] Among the latter the reader of early English poetry will not forget the wit and poet, Thomas Randolph, whom Ben Jonson thought worthy to be enrolled among his adopted sons. He was the great uncle of William Randolph, the founder of the Virginia family.

[3] Mr. Jefferson, in his autobiographical "Memoir," remarks: "They [the Randolphs] trace their pedigree far back in England and Scotland, to which let every one ascribe the faith and merit he chooses." We have learned, with some astonishment, that the playful fling at *long* pedigrees generally, contained in the close of this sentence (made obviously to prevent the impression that *he* attached any undue importance to the fact *just named by him*, that is, that *his* maternal pedigree extended far back in England and Scotland), has been construed into a serious intention to discredit the pedigree "traced" by his maternal relatives! Apart from the questionable taste there would be in selecting such an occasion to make this issue with his maternal relatives (when he could quite as easily have passed over the topic in silence), we chance to know that it was the common understanding of his family that, if he attached no special importance to his long maternal pedigree, he never dreamed of throwing any discredit on its accuracy in point of fact—though perhaps he thought *all* pedigrees running back through *ages*, a class of records to place implicit confidence in which required a pretty strong exercise of "faith!" This was what he meant to express, and all he meant to express, in the remark we have quoted.

[4] He was the third of three sons (John. Richard, and William), sons of William Randolph (a) born Oct. 18, 1607, and his wife Dorothy Law, widow of Thomas West and daughter of Richard Law. William Randolph (a) was the son of William Randolph (b) born 1572, and his wife Elizabeth Smith, daughter of Thomas Smith. Their issue were, 1. Thomas (the poet); 2. William (a); 3. Robert; 4. Elizabeth. William Randolph (b) was the son of Robert Randolph and Rose Roberts, etc., etc.

cavalier whose fortunes had been broken in the civil wars, on
arriving at man's estate, or a little earlier, emigrated to Virginia
about the year 1660, and established himself at Turkey Island,[1]
twenty miles below Richmond, in James River. He married
Mary, daughter of Henry and Catherine Isham of Bermuda
Hundred, Virginia, of the family of Isham in Northampton-
shire, England, baronets. He brought with him, it is believed,
some small remains of a former family fortune, and being a
man of sagacity and enterprise he rapidly increased it, and continued to add possession to possession until the day of his death,
which took place on the 11th of April, 1711. He was a man
of decided mark and consideration in the colony; was made
colonel of his county; was one of the Trustees named in the
charter to William and Mary College, granted by King William
and Queen Mary; and he is said to have held several other
public positions of consideration. While preparing to leave a
large fortune to each of his numerous children, he had the wisdom to confer upon them a more substantial benefit, in advance,
in that finished education, which, in addition to their natural
talents and their numbers, laid the foundation of the remarkable future celebrity and influence of his family. He saw
several of his sons established on their estates before his death,
and with the paternal solicitude and determined energy which
marked his character, went in person with his slaves to make
the commencement of their improvements, and even to aid
them in the erection of their buildings.

His children were William, of Turkey Island; Thomas, of
Tuckahoe; Isham, of Dungeness; Richard, of Curles; Sir John,
of Williamsburg, knight; Henry, who died unmarried; Edward,
who resided in England; Mary and Elizabeth. These held
many of the most distinguished offices in the colony, as did
their children and their children's children, in that and in the
Republican Commonwealth which succeeded it. The family
prolificacy also continued; and, until a comparatively recent
period, few distinguished families or individuals could be found
in Virginia who did not claim kindred with the Randolphs.[2]

---

[1] Now a point of land, rather than an island (says the Virginia Historical Register),
lying between the James and Turkey Island Creek, where they come together. The latter divides Henrico from Charles City County, " and Turkey Island" is in Henrico.
[2] 1. William Randolph (the second of that name of Turkey Island) was a Royal Coun-
cillor of State, and two, at least, of his sons held high official positions. 2. Thomas, of

The only traces now visible of this once proud race at Turkey Island—the headquarters of the ancient family—are a portion of the mansion-house erected by the first proprietor, and the family burial-place. The massive walls of the former (built of imported brick), originally two stories high, surrounded by porticos on three sides, surmounted by a large fine dome called "the bird cage," by the early navigators of the James, "from the great number of birds seen hovering and singing about it;" the whole of such choice construction that it required seven years to complete it, insomuch that a joiner commenced, and served his entire apprenticeship in one of its elaborately finished rooms, "learning more of his trade than one could now do in building or helping to build a hundred houses," is, at the present time, but an unsightly ruin, stripped by fire of its porticos and interior ornaments, reduced to a single story, and roughly furnished for a negro quarter![1] Such, or a more complete destruction, has been the mournful fate of nearly all the ancient mansions of the early great families of Virginia! And there are but few instances where those families themselves now

Tuckahoe, was the father of Colonel William (of Dungeness), the friend of Peter Jefferson, and his son, Colonel Thomas Mann, was a member of the House of Burgesses, of the Committee of Safety, etc., and his son of the same name, of Edgehill (who married Martha, daughter of Thomas Jefferson), was Member of Congress, Colonel of the 20th Regiment, in the war of 1812, Governor of Virginia, etc. One of Thomas of Tuckahoe's daughters married President William Stith, the historian; another, the Rev. William Keith, by whom she had Mary, grandmother of Chief Justice Marshall. 3. Isham, of Dungeness, was a Member of the House of Burgesses, and Adjutant-General of the Colony. Several of his male descendants held official positions, and he was grandfather, in the maternal line, of President Jefferson and Governor James Pleasants. 4. Colonel Richard, of Curles (married to Jane Bolling, great granddaughter of Pocahontas), was Treasurer of the Colony, etc. He was the grandfather of John Randolph, of Roanoke, and on the mother's side, of Governor Thomas Mann Randolph, of Edgehill. 5. Sir John of Williamsburg. He was sent to England in 1729, to obtain a renewal of the charter of William and Mary College, and returned knighted. He was Attorney-General, Speaker of the House of Burgesses, Treasurer, etc., of the colony. His eldest son, Peyton, was also Attorney-General and Speaker under the Crown, and first President of the U. S. Congress. His second son, John, was Attorney-General under the Crown, and went to England on the breaking out of the Revolution. This last John's son, Edmund, was Aide-de-Camp of General Washington, Governor of Virginia, Attorney-General, and Secretary of State of the United States, etc., etc. 6. Henry died unmarried. 7. Edward became a captain in the British navy, and married an English heiress of large fortune. 8. Mary married Captain John Stith, and their only child, William, Rector of Henrico parish, was made President of William and Mary College. He wrote the History of Virginia. 9. Elizabeth married Theodoric Bland, by whom she had Richard Bland, the celebrated revolutionary writer and leader, member of the first Congress, etc., and a daughter, who was the mother (we think) of Richard H. Lee.

This sketch does not probably enumerate half of the offices held by the first three or four generations of the Virginia Randolphs, or of the distinguished men who were offshoots of the family in the maternal line. We have merely seized upon the most accessible facts for the purpose of giving a clear impression of Mr. Jefferson's social starting-point, and to show his degree of consanguinity to a good many very dear friends, and a good many very bitter enemies.

[1] Virginia Historical Register.

occupy their original possessions, or retain any approach to their ancient importance!

Isham Randolph, the third son of William, of Turkey Island, married Jane Rogers, in London, England, in 1717. Their issue were five sons and six daughters. Jane, the eldest child, except a son who died in infancy, was born in London, in 1720, and at the age of nineteen married Peter Jefferson. Isham Randolph shared fully in the prosperity of his family. His seat, Dungeness, lay in Goochland, on the north bank of the James, a few miles below the mouth of the Rivanna; and it was the abode of refinement and elegant hospitality. A hundred servants, it was said, waited in and about it. Its possessor was a well educated, intelligent and generous man. As such, and as the friend and correspondent of men of science and merit in the Colonies and in England, honorable mention is made of him in the Memoirs of Bartram, the naturalist.[1] He died in 1742, and his monument is yet extant at the family burial-place at Turkey Island.

Peter Jefferson established himself at Shadwell, and com-

[1] Q. v. by Wm. Darlington. M.D. LL.D. Philadelphia, 1849. To give a glimpse of Mr. Jefferson's maternal grandfather, and of Virginia manners at that day, we will subjoin a few extracts from this work, principally written by Bartram's patron, the celebrated old Peter Collinson, who seems to have been a personal acquaintance and somewhat particular friend of Isham Randolph. He thus wrote Bartram in 1737, when he was about taking Virginia in his field of botanical explorations :

"When thee proceeds home, I know no person will make thee more welcome than Isham Randolph. He lives thirty or forty miles above the falls of James River, in Goochland, above the other settlements. Now, I take his house to be a very suitable place to make a settlement at, for to take several days' excursions all round, and to return to his house at night." P. 89.

Something of the style of the appointments of the wealthy Virginians of that day, as well as the supposed deficiencies of a portion of them in more important particulars, are thus hit off by this quaint old writer :

"One thing I must desire of thee, and do insist that thee oblige me therein : that thou make up that drugget clothes, to go to Virginia in, and not appear to disgrace thyself or me ; for though I should not esteem thee the less to come to me in what dress thou will, yet these Virginians are a very gentle, well dressed people, and look, perhaps, more at a man's outside than his inside. For these and other reasons pray go very clean, neat, and handsomely dressed to Virginia. Never mind thy clothes : I will send more another year." P. 89.

Bartram's reception by Isham Randolph seems to have been what his friend Collinson anticipated, for Collinson writes him :

"As for my friend Isham, who I am also personally known to, I did not doubt his civility to thee. I only wish to have been there, and shared it with thee." P. 113.

Bartram's subsequent impressions of his host, as well as a lively idea of the facilities of intercommunication between the different parts of the Colonies in that day, are given in a letter to Collinson, in 1738 :

"Our friend Isham Randolph (a generous, good-natured gentleman, and well respected by most who are acquainted with him), hath agreed with me to have a correspondence together ; but can't tell well which way to carry it on—whether back of the mountains by the way of Schenendoah, or below the mountains, we can't yet tell." P. 122.

After the death of Isham Randolph, we find Collinson writing Bartram, "that the good man is gone to his long home, and I doubt not he is happy." P. 166.

menced his preparations to make it his residence, two years anterior to his marriage. He was the third or fourth white settler within the space of several miles, and the trails of the hostile Monacans or Tuscaroras were yet fresh on his lands and through the adjacent hills. In a small clearing in the dense and primeval forest, he erected his house; and his young wife, bred up among surroundings so different, took up her abode in it soon after her marriage. Their oldest son and third child, Thomas Jefferson, the future President of the United States, was born on the second day of April, 1743, O. S.

Shadwell was then included in Goochland, but it fell within the limits of Albemarle when that county was erected in 1744. Peter Jefferson was appointed one of the three original Justices of the Peace for the new county. It was an office then only held by gentlemen of the first consideration, as the Justices composed the County Court, which exercised almost unlimited jurisdiction, and controlled various important county affairs. He was made County Surveyor, an office also of the first trust, as it was his duty to *survey and describe* the lands sold by Government, and to discharge certain important administrative functions in other cases.

In 1745, Colonel William Randolph, of Tuckahoe, died— entreating his early friend to assume the executorship and personal charge of his estate, and of his only and infant son, Thomas Mann Randolph. Peter Jefferson accordingly removed to Tuckahoe, on the north bank of the James, a few miles above Richmond, and he remained there seven years. With a chivalrousness of feeling which challenges our admiration, if not our surprise, he evinced his recollection of early kindnesses and the fervor of his friendship, by refusing to accept any other compensation for discharging this long and laborious trust, than his support while he lived on the estate. This distinctly appears from his account as an executor, lying before us. Thomas Jefferson was two years old when the family exodus took place, and he used to mention as his first recollection, his being handed up and carried on a pillow by a mounted slave, as the train set off down the river towards Tuckahoe.

In 1749, Joshua Fry, Professor of Mathematics in William and Mary College, and Peter Jefferson, were associated in a commission to meet a like one from North Carolina, to survey the line between their respective States, from the point where it had been left by Colonel Byrd and his associate commissioners, in 1728. They commenced at Peter's Creek, one of the upper tributaries of the Dan, and continued from thence west over the Blue Ridge, and through the wilderness beyond, to " Steep-rock Creek," a distance of ninety miles. They were subsequently employed to construct a map of the State—the first one founded on much beside mere conjectural data—and they completed it in 1751. A copy of it is before us, and though inaccuracies of course would be expected in a map not made exclusively from actual survey, and though a portion of it is only conjectural, it is a highly creditable production, all things considered.[1]

Soon after Peter Jefferson's return to his former residence in Albemarle, he was appointed to the Colonelcy of the county, an office always regarded as of the first honor and importance under the Colonial Government, and particularly so when, as in the present instance, it conferred military command over an extensive portion of Indian frontier, and when, we may add, a war for territorial dominion with the French, on this very frontier, was regarded as imminent. Several years after Colonel Jefferson's appointment, we find, among his manuscripts, accounts of disbursements by him to military forces sent " to range against the Indians in Augusta," the adjoining county on the west.

He was, however, regarded with peculiar respect and veneration by the Indians far and near, and his house was a favorite stopping-place for friendly chiefs, and for embassies on their way to and from the colonial capital. A great many years afterward (in 1812), his son, Thomas Jefferson, wrote a friend :

" So much in answer to your inquiries concerning Indians, a people with whom, in the early part of my life, I was very familiar, and acquired impressions of attachment and commiseration for them which have never been obliterated. Before the Revolution, they were in the habit of coming often and in great numbers to the seat of government, where I was very much with them. I knew much of the great Ontassetè, the warrior and orator of the Cherokees; he was always the guest of my father, on his journeys to and from Williamsburg. I was in his camp when he made his great farewell oration to his people, the evening before his departure for England. The moon was in full splendor, and to her he seemed to address himself in his prayers for his own safety on the voyage, and that of his people during his

[1] There is a copy of this map (numbered 112) in the New York State Library at Albany.

absence; his sounding voice, distinct articulation, animated action, and the solemn silence of his people at their several fires, filled me with awe and veneration, although I did not understand a word he uttered." [1]

In 1755, Colonel Jefferson was a member of the Virginia House of Burgesses. How long he retained this position does not appear, but in all probability until the time of his death. Already, as we may conclude from his civil and military commissions, the most prominent man of his county—and evidencing, by the celerity of his rise after his return to Albemarle, that ability, and standing both with the government and the people, which promised greater future honors and usefulness— he was suddenly cut off, August 17th, 1757, in the fiftieth year of his age.

Many well attested facts and anecdotes are yet extant of the life of the father of Thomas Jefferson, which, though too desultory, and separately unimportant, to be embodied into a connected narration, give, taken together, a clear insight into his character. They all show that he was no ordinary man. He owed none of his success to good fortune or ingratiating manners. He was a man of gigantic stature and strength—plain, and averse to display—he was grave, taciturn, slow to make, and not over prompt to accept, advances. He was one of those calmly and almost sternly self-relying men, who lean on none—who desire help from none. And he certainly had both muscles and mind which could be trusted! He could simultaneously " head up " (raise from their sides to an upright position) two hogsheads of tobacco, weighing nearly a thousand pounds apiece! He once directed three able-bodied slaves to pull down a ruinous shed by means of a rope. After they had again and again made the effort, he bade them stand aside, seized the rope, and dragged down the structure in an instant. [2] Traditions have come down of his continuing his lines as a surveyor through savage wildernesses, after his assistants had given out from famine and fatigue, subsisting on the raw flesh of game, and even of his carrying mules, when other food failed, sleeping in a hollow tree amidst howling and screeching beasts

[1] Letter to John Adams, June 11th, 1812.—Congress edition of Jefferson's Works, vol. vi. p. 59.
[2] Both of these facts were mentioned by Thomas Jefferson to his family.

of prey, and thus undauntedly pushing on until his task was accomplished.

His mind was of a corresponding texture. He had the same love of mathematics which afterwards characterized his son— and much, if not all, of the same remarkable facility in understanding its processes. His judgment was swift and solid. His neighbors sought his advice ; his friends soon learned to esteem it unerring. His mind once made up, no danger could turn him aside—no obstacles thwart his iron will, and calm, but resistless energy. And he acted for another, in these particulars, as he acted for himself. His probity was so conspicuous, that other wealthy friends besides William Randolph, desired him to act as their executor, and in one or two other instances he consented.

When the foregoing traits of character are considered, it becomes easy to understand the nature of that strong bond of alliance which subsisted, from the outset, between Colonel Jefferson and the Randolphs—to understand why that proud family so readily took the young surveyor, without fortune or finished education—a comparative adventurer—to their close family alliance and friendship. Those shrewd and practiced men of the world were not slow to discover that this stately young man would prove a tower of strength to friends, and a bulwark to be relied upon against foes. And the eye of woman rarely looks down with indifference on such a union of mental and physical power.

But so massively moulded, he had a gentler, softer side. He was a tender husband, a devoted father. His tastes approached to the elegant, in his own household. After the wearisome and often stirring events of a day of border life were passed, he spent the evening in reading historians, essayists, and even poets. Addison, Swift, and Pope were prime favorites with him—but Shakspeare was his great favorite ! His well-worn and fine old edition of the work is yet extant.[1] This speaks volumes concerning the tastes of the man.

Colonel Jefferson was a staunch Whig, and he adhered to certain democratic (using the word in its broad, popular sense) notions and maxims, which descended to his son. His leanings

---

[1] Also his copy of the Spectator, some of Swift's Works, etc.

as a magistrate were to the popular side. He was unpretending in his equipage and address. A cardinal maxim with him was, "Never ask another to do for you what you can do for yourself." He held that it is the strong in body who are both the strong and *free* in mind—a text his son often afterwards preached from. His attempts to form the character of his son corresponded with his theories. He died when the latter was fourteen years old, but he had already taught him to sit his horse, fire his gun, boldly stem the Rivanna when the swollen river was

> "Rolling red from brae to brae,"

and press his way with unflagging foot through the rocky summits of the contiguous hills in pursuit of deer and wild turkeys. But his attention was not limited to physical training. Though his son was kept constantly at school, in the evenings he put good books into his hands for reading, taught him to keep accounts, instructed him in his own beautiful penmanship,[1] and impressed upon his mind lessons of system, punctuality, energy, and perseverance. Thomas Jefferson always possessed a particular veneration for the memory of his father. Young as he was when the latter died, we think his mind had been obviously impressed with his instructions and example; for we trace a manifest analogy—a family likeness, modified only by circumstances and more in degree than kind—between their political, social, and domestic ideas. There was some physical resemblance between them. According to tradition, the calm, thoughtful, firm eye of the son, and the outlines of his face, were those of his father; his physical strength, too, was beyond that of ordinary men; but his slim form and delicate fibres were those of his mother's family. His mind, too, gave evidence of both parental stocks—of the auspicious combination of new strength with old courtly culture, of the solid with the showy, of robust sense with the glitter of talent!

It would seem singular that Mr. Jefferson spoke no more fully of his father and mother in his biographical Memoir. To the intellectual powers and judgment of the former, he pays a brief passing tribute; and of the latter, he but records the dates of her birth, marriage, and death. He mentions none of the

---

[1] There is a marked resemblance in the handwriting of father and son.

public employments of his father but those to run the boundary
line, and construct the map of Virginia; but as he mentions
them to show how much his father had made amends for his
early defective education, why did he not mention his colonelcy,
his election to the House of Burgesses, etc., in the same connection? We have sometimes conjectured that he might have *forgotten* those facts when he sat down at the age of seventy-seven to
write the Memoir.[1] But this would not be a *necessary* inference.
He was, as we shall have other occasions to observe, singularly
shy in speaking or writing of matters of family history, out of
his family. Where females were the subject, this shyness
reached to positive aversion. His silence about his mother was
unquestionably occasioned by this feeling, and will be found
consistent with his course on analogous occasions where other
near and dear female relatives are concerned. His mother was
every way worthy of his highest respect and deepest love, and
she received them.

She survived until 1776—a year so memorable in the history
of her son—but not long enough to witness his agency in
procuring the Declaration of Independence, and draughting
the manifesto by which it was published to the world. She
was an agreeable, intelligent woman, as well educated as the
other Virginia ladies of the day, of her own elevated rank in
society—but that by no means implying any very profound

---

[1] During a visit made to Edgehill by us in 1851, Colonel Thomas J. Randolph—Mr.
Jefferson's *oldest* grandson, and the legatee of his *papers*—discovered in a long unthought-
of receptacle, a pile of old books in manuscript, a part of which neither he nor any member of his family had any recollection of ever having seen before. Among them were various early memoranda and accounts of Thomas Jefferson, and account books of his father,
Peter Jefferson, kept in his capacity as executor of William Randolph, County Surveyor,
Colonel of the county, Member of the House of Burgesses, etc. The accounts are continuous, go into minute details, are drawn up with admirable precision, and in his own
clear beautiful chirography. Not one of his living descendants—though they had lived
variously from ten to twenty or thirty years in the family of his son Thomas (their
grandfather)—knew that their great grandfather had ever been Colonel of his county, or
a member of the House of Burgesses. And the manuscripts disclosed various *other* facts
equally unknown—some of which settled *long mooted* questions in family tradition—and
which the family think it almost certain that their grandfather (Thomas Jefferson) would
have mentioned to them, *had he himself known or remembered them.* Mr. Jefferson's father
died when he was *fourteen* years old. He was immediately sent *away from home* to
school; then followed college life—law studies, carried on half the time at the capital—
politics—office—a stormy and busy life. It is easy to suppose, therefore, that he retained few personal recollections of the offices, etc., held by his father. We shall find
that a fire occurred when he was a young man, which destroyed his library and most of his
professional and *private* papers. He wrote a friend at the time that *all* of them perished.
It is very probable, then, that these old account books were saved *without his knowledge*,
in the bottom of some trunk, or box, or drawer, or package, stowed away amongst
other old lumber, and there lay for years during his long absences and busy life, until
finally transferred without examination into the depository where they were found, and
where they slept wholly unknown until twenty-five years after his death.

acquirements—and like most of the daughters of the Ancient Dominion, of every rank, in the olden time, she was a notable housekeeper.   She possessed a most amiable and affectionate disposition, a lively, cheerful temper, and a great fund of humor.   She was fond of writing, particularly letters, and wrote readily and well.

In Colonel Peter Jefferson's Book of Common Prayer, yet in good preservation, are the following entries of the births, marriages, and deaths of his children, recorded in the handwriting of his son Thomas:

	Births.	Marriages.	Deaths.
Jane Jefferson	1740, June 27....	—	....1765, October 1.
Mary	1741, Oct. 1	....1760, June 24	—
Thomas	1743, April 2	....1772, Jan. 1	—
Elizabeth	1744, Nov. 4		....1773, Jan. 1.
Martha	1746, May 29	....1765, July 20	—
Peter Field	1748, Oct. 16	—	....1748, Nov. 29.
A son	1750, March 9....	—	....1750, March 9.
Lucy	1752, Oct. 10	....1769, Sept. 12	—
Anna Scott } Randolph }	....1755, Oct. 1....	{ 1788, October { —	— —

Thomas Jefferson's earliest recollection has been mentioned. His second, of a year or two later date, was of going out on one occasion when his dinner had been unusually delayed, and repeating the Lord's Prayer, in the hope that he might thereby obtain relief to his hunger.   This shows nothing, except that at three or four years old he was taught to repeat his prayers. His religious education was, in fact, never neglected during his boyhood.   It was that of the Church of England, to which his father and mother belonged, as had their ancestors before them, and into which he and all his brothers and sisters were baptized in their infancy. It was, perhaps, somewhat due to this early training that, during all periods of his life, he retained a familiarity with the Bible, with the prayers and collects of the noble Liturgy of the Church, and with its psalms and hymns, possessed by very few persons. And those who knew him best, believe the natural tendency of his mind was devotional.

At five years old, he was placed at the English school at Tuckahoe. At nine, on the return of the family to Shadwell, he went to the school of Mr. Douglass, a Scotch clergyman, who taught him in Latin, Greek, and French. His after-recollections of this place—what student has not such?—were of mouldy pies and excellent instruction.   During his fourth year here, his father died, leaving directions that his oldest son receive a thorough classical education.   Mr. Jefferson often spoke of this dying direction with deep feeling.   "I have often heard him say" (Colonel Thomas J. Randolph, his grandson, writes us), "that if he had to decide between the pleasure derived from the classical education which his father had given him, and the estate left him, he would decide in favor of the former."   This idea, too, is several times advanced in Mr. Jefferson's published correspondence.

After his father's decease, he was removed to the school of the Rev. Mr. Maury, fourteen miles from Shadwell, at the east base of Peter's Mountain,[1] the highest of the Southwest Range. Mr. Maury, whose distinction it is to have educated a number of the finest scholars that Virginia has ever produced, was himself an elegant classical scholar, and a zealous, thorough teacher.   His pupil had already formed habits of persevering application, and to his clear, rapid understanding, acquisition scarcely cost an effort.   Such a boy, if amiable and correct in his habits, is always the pride of a teacher's heart, and no pains are spared on him; and thus the wind and tide of school life work together to accelerate his progress.   Mr. Jefferson *was* singularly amiable and correct in his habits.   His proficiency accordingly wholly outran his years.   Colonel Jefferson had not forgotton his son's physical education, in his dying injunctions.   The latter spent his hours of recreation, daily, in hunting on Peter's Mountain; and he thus strengthened and knit his person, which was now rapidly shooting up tall and thin; and he fixed into a habit that love of walking which never afterwards deserted him, and to which he doubtless owed a good deal of the healthfulness and elasticity of his old age.   His favorite amusement, indoors, was playing on the violin, and he was already a proficient on that instrument for one of his years.

The cost of instruction in the classical schools kept at their parsonages, by most of the Virginia clergy, at that day, may be a matter of curiosity to antiquaries.   Colonel Jefferson's account

[1] The parsonage occupied the site of the present residence of General William F Gordon.

books show that he paid the Rev. William Douglass, sixteen pounds sterling per annum, for teaching and boarding his son. Those of his executor show that twenty pounds sterling were annually paid to the Rev. James Maury. The mere board was held in very little account, and as money went a good deal further then than now, these sums are not as pitiful as they would at first appear.

After being two years with Mr. Maury, Mr. Jefferson returned home, and it would seem that there was a little uncertainty about the time it would be proper for him to enter college. His own wishes on the subject, and his reasons for them, are disclosed in a letter to his then guardian, Mr. John Harvey, a copy of which we are favored with by Mr. Jefferson's grandson, Mr. George Wythe Randolph, of Richmond:

SIR,—[1]   SHADWELL, *January 14th*, 1760.

I was at Colo. Peter Randolph's[2] about a Fortnight ago, and my Schooling falling into Discourse, he said he thought it would be to my Advantage to go to the College, and was desirous I should go, as indeed I am myself for several Reasons. In the first place, as long as I stay at the Mountain, the loss of one-fourth of my Time is inevitable, by Company's coming here and detaining me from School. And likewise my Absence will in a great measure, put a Stop to so much Company, and by that Means lessen the Expenses of the Estate in Housekeeping. And on the other Hand by going to the College, I shall get a more universal Acquaintance, which may hereafter be serviceable to me; and I suppose I can pursue my Studies in the Greek and Latin as well there as here, and likewise learn something of the Mathematics. I shall be glad of your opinion,

And remain, Sir,
your most humble servant,
THOMAS JEFFERSON, Jr.

To
 Mr. John Harvey,
  at
  Bellemont.

It would be difficult to understand why "junior" is attached to his name, if we did not in some of the account books catch glimpses of another Thomas Jefferson, who had some business relations with the estate or its representatives, and who was therefore probably a resident in Albemarle at this time. It is very likely that it was his cousin already mentioned, the son of

---

[1] We preserve the *capitalization*, as the printers term it, of the original.
[2] His mother's cousin, the son of the second William, of Turkey Island.

Field Jefferson, and that Thomas, of Shadwell, being the younger, assumed the above distinction.

It was determined that he should enter college when he desired, and he did so in 1760. On his way there, he spent the Christmas holidays at the residence of Colonel Nathan Dandridge, in Hanover, one of those old-fashioned seats of Virginia hospitality, where, on these merry occasions, a circle of young and old often assembled to pass from a week to a fortnight—the seniors, in amusements becoming their years—the juniors, in junketing, dancing, and high-jinks of all sorts. Here Mr. Jefferson met for the first time a young man destined to act a conspicuous part in the future history of his country—with whom his own future relations were to be most chequered in all but personal good-will—at times a powerful coadjutor, at times advocating widely opposite views—possessing in some respects transcendent powers, and in all unquestionable integrity ; but, partly from the lack of all solid training, and a little perhaps from a natural want of stability, liable sometimes to mistake the impulses of his fervid nature for the promptings of settled views —yet with his inconsistencies and errors, one of the most brilliant, at one time useful, and at all times popular, men of whom Virginia has ever boasted. He was a near neighbor of Colonel Dandridge's, a broken merchant, who, at the age of twenty-three or four, had dissipated his patrimony by miscalculations and incorrigible idleness. His gaunt, slightly stooping figure was coarse and ungainly. His bloodless face lacked every curve of beauty ; but the deep-set grey eye gleamed like a diamond under the shaggy brow, and there was a play in its expression, and in the movements of the mouth, which bespoke a soul whose depths had not yet been either stirred or sounded. His manners, dress, and even his pronunciation were broadly provincial. He talked like a backwoods-man about men's *naiteral* parts being improved by *larnin*—about the *yearth*, etc.[1] But the voice which uttered these rustic sounds, without being musical, was deep and sonorous ; and when in the revels he raised it suddenly to its full leonine roar, the welkin rung again, and the whole air was filled with its tremendous vibrations. Men of profound knowledge were in the circle at Colonel Dan-

---

[1] Governor Page, of Virginia, used to relate, on the testimony of his own ears, that such was the pronunciation of the subject of this sketch.

dridge's, but he sought not their company. "His passion," said Mr. Jefferson, describing this scene afterwards, "was fiddling, dancing, and pleasantry." In the last he excelled. None could tell a story with so sly a humor—none act a practical joke so cleverly. There was no end to his overflowing good humor and rollicking gaiety. He was, therefore, the prime favorite with the youngsters; and oddly as it would seem, considering their almost total dissimilarity of character, he and Jefferson struck up an intimacy and friendship, the latter of which, we think, lasted their whole lives; at all events, it did on Jefferson's part. And this friendship most essentially modified the course of some important future events. Notwithstanding their disparities, there were points—some of those deep, under-lying ones which tinge the whole character—where they were closely alike. These will be alluded to hereafter. They formed the instant and mystic bond of union between them.

Not far from three months from this time, Patrick Henry— for the young broken merchant and boon companion was he— called on his friend Jefferson at Williamsburg, and informed him that he had *in the meantime* studied law, and was now at the capital to obtain his license!

Though but seventeen, Mr. Jefferson was entered in an advanced class at William and Mary College. Williamsburg was then the seat of the Colonial Court, which in Virginia affected peculiar splendor. It was filled in winter with government officials, and with the families of the lowland grandees. Among both, Mr. Jefferson's maternal relatives ranked in the first class. His own reception by his relatives was flattering; but it was somewhat noticeable that Colonel Archibald Cary, of Ampthill[1]—afterwards so celebrated in Virginia history—was foremost in his attentions, inasmuch as the fiery cavalier was at mortal feud with Colonel Peter Jefferson—as dauntless and unbending an antagonist as himself—at the time of his death. Cary immediately sought out the son, introduced him to the intimacy of his family and friends, and here another friendship

[1] Colonel Cary married Mary, daughter of Richard Randolph, of Curles (fourth son of the first William Randolph, of Turkey Island), and consequently a cousin of Mr. Jefferson's mother. One of Cary's daughters married Thomas Randolph, Mrs. Peter Jefferson's brother, and another, Thomas Mann Randolph, of Tuckahoe, the ward of Colonel Peter Jefferson, and the father of Thomas Mann Randolph, of Edgehill (who afterwards married Martha, daughter of Thomas Jefferson).

sprung up between widely dissimilar men, destined to be lasting, and to produce important public and private consequences.

The gay and elegant society of the capital, into which he was generally introduced, did not wean the young student from his books. Taste and habit bound him to them, and his application continued unremitting. A pleasant anecdote is preserved of him and his guardian, then, we think, Colonel Walker. When the sum of his first year's college expenses was ascertained, it struck him as large for one who was living for the time, in common with his brother and sisters, on the proceeds of an estate of which they had inherited less, and he therefore wrote Colonel Walker, requesting him to charge the entire amount of his expenses to his separate share of the property. That sensible man, reflecting, perhaps, that Thomas's portion was actually furnishing a proportionate share of the *proceeds*, made answer: "No—if you have sowed your wild oats thus, the estate can well afford to pay the bill!" These expenses were incurred in a little too showy style of living—particularly in the article of fine horses. His general habits and morals continued as at Mr. Maury's. In reference to this, and to the experiences of this period, he long afterwards wrote a grandson, who also was away from home at school, and no better occasion will occur than this to transfer this beautiful morsel of personal history and advice to these pages:

WASHINGTON, *November* 24, 1808.

MY DEAR JEFFERSON,

*   *   *   *   *   *   *   *   *   *

Your situation, thrown at such a distance from us, and alone, cannot but give us all great anxieties for you. As much has been secured for you, by your particular position and the acquaintance to which you have been recommended, as could be done towards shielding you from the dangers which surround you. But thrown on a wide world, among entire strangers, without a friend or guardian to advise, so young, too, and with so little experience of mankind, your dangers are great, and still your safety must rest on yourself. A determination never to do what is wrong, prudence and good humor, will go far towards securing to you the estimation of the world. When I recollect that at fourteen years of age, the whole care and direction of myself was thrown on myself entirely, without a relation or friend, qualified to advise or guide me, and recollect the various sorts of bad company with which I associated from time to time, I am astonished I did not turn off with some of them, and become as worthless to society as they were. I had the good fortune to become acquainted very early with some characters of very high standing, and to feel the incessant wish that I could ever become what they were. Under temptations and difficulties, I would ask myself—what would Dr. Small, Mr. Wythe, Peyton Randolph do in this situation? What course in it will insure me their approbation? I am certain that this mode of deciding on my conduct, tended more to correctness than any reasoning powers I possessed. Knowing the even and dignified line they pursued, I could never doubt for a moment which of two courses would be in character for them. Whereas, seeking the same object through a process of moral reasoning, and with the jaundiced eye of youth, I should often have erred. From the circumstances of my position, I was often thrown into the society of horse racers, card players, fox hunters, scientific and professional men. and of dignified men; and many a time have I asked myself, in the enthusiastic moment of the death of a fox, the victory of a favorite horse, the issue of a question eloquently argued at the bar, or in the great council of the nation, Well, which of these kinds of reputation should I prefer? That of a horse jockey? a fox hunter? an orator? or the honest advocate of my country's rights? Be assured, my dear Jefferson, that these little returns into ourselves, this self-catechising habit, is not trifling nor useless, but leads to the prudent selection and steady pursuit of what is right.[1]

Wise forethought this, " under temptations and difficulties," in " the enthusiastic moment" of the hunt and the horse race, in a young, uncontrolled, wealthy and *fluttered* orphan! Two of the individuals he refers to as the chosen models of his conduct, were indeed to exert a marked influence over his future life. Doctor William Small was Professor of Mathematics, and became, soon after Mr. Jefferson's entrance, Professor *per interim* of Philosophy in William and Mary. He was a Scotchman (*all* of Mr. Jefferson's previous instructors had been *Scotchmen*[2]) of elegant manners, general culture, and of a peculiarly liberal and comprehensive mind. As an instructor, he had the happy, if not rare, art of making the road to knowledge both easy and agreeable. Attracted by the correct and modest deportment of young Jefferson, struck with his singular proficiency and his energy of thought, he not only instructed him with peculiar zest from the professorial chair, but he made him the friend and companion of his leisure hours; and he did much to create, or rather to encourage, in him that thirst for a general culture—those enlarged views of " the expansion of science and of the system of things in which we are placed "—for which his pupil, sixty years afterwards, covered with honors and renown, poured out his fervid acknowledgments.[3] Indeed, Mr. Jefferson, with some, we cannot but think, of that exaggeration with which generous minds are prone to regard the services of early

[1] For the remainder of this admirable letter, see either the Congressional, or his grandson's edition of Mr. Jefferson's Works, at the date indicated.
[2] And we may add, clergymen of the Anglican Church.
[3] See Memoir.

benefactors, declared in his Memoir that it was Doctor Small's instruction and intercourse that "probably fixed the destinies of his life."

His second year in college was more diligently employed than the first. Company, the riding-horse, and even the favorite violin, were nearly discarded. He habitually studied, as he often afterwards declared, fifteen hours a day. The only time he took for exercise, was to run sharply a mile out of the city and back at twilight. He left college at the end of the second year, a profound and accomplished scholar for one so young. Few probably have been better educated at the same age; and he had a good and broad foundation laid for that super-structure of learning which he continued to erect on it through-out his life.

He united, what is not common among students, a decided taste for *both* mathematics and the classics. The first was perhaps at this period of life rather the favorite, and intricate must be that process in it which "he could not read off with the facility of common discourse."[1] He maintained his famili-arity with this science, kept up with its advances, and made a practical use of it in all the concerns where it is applicable, through life. In later years, we shall find him giving the most attention to the classics. He was a fine and even a critical Latin and Greek scholar. The most difficult authors in those languages were read by him with ease—were habitually read by him as recreations, snatched from official and other labors, and they became the most prized solaces of his old age. Of French, as a written language, he had a thorough knowledge. His acquaintance with Anglo-Saxon, Italian and Spanish, have been assigned to his college period; but this is a mistake, unless so far as mere rudiments are concerned. He studied the Anglo-Saxon during his law studies, to enable him to dip for himself into the ancient fountains of the English Common Law. The Italian was taken up immediately after. The impressions of his family were, that he did not study Spanish until he went to France in 1784; and confirmatory of this, we find an entry in one of his account books of the purchase of a Spanish dic-

---

[1] He wrote Colonel William Duane, October 1, 1812: "When I was young, mathe-matics was the passion of my life. The same passion has returned upon me, but with unequal power. Processes which I then read off with the facility of common discourse, now cost me labor and time and slow investigation."

tionary as he was on the point of embarking. He probably
found it necessary to *improve* his knowledge of Spanish at
that period ; but a remark in John Adams's Diary shows that
he was *thought* to understand it, when he was in Congress in
1775 ;[1] and, what is far more decisive, he repeatedly and
familiarly quotes Don Ulloa, in the original, in his Notes on
Virginia (written in 1781), which assuredly he would not have
done, if ignorant of the language.[2] This includes the list of
languages with which he ever became familiar; but he probably
picked up some knowledge of German, for among his manuscripts are several interwritten literal translations—apparently
student's exercises—like the following :

Falle	doch	auf	Doris'	augenlieder	
Fall	oh !	on	Doris'	eyelids	
Holder	schlaf	leicht	wallend	sanft	hernieder
Gentle	sleep	light		soft	down
Drucke	doch	du	geber	susser	ruhe
Shut	oh	thou	giver	soft	repose
Jetz das	paar	der	schönsten	augen	zu
Now the	pair	of	prettiest	eyes	up

Mr. Jefferson's attainments in belles-lettres appear in all his
early writings.   His early acquirements in natural, political,
and statistical science are indicated in his Notes on Virginia.
In a word, there was no grand department, and scarcely a
branch of liberal learning then taught, in which he was not
comparatively well versed ; and he seems to have relished them
all with two exceptions—ethics and metaphysics. He greatly
approved of reading works calculated to foster the moral sense,
and strongly recommended a favorite nephew to read Epictetus,
Xenophontis Memorabilia, Plato's Socratic Dialogues, Cicero's
Philosophies, Antoninus and Seneca. He repeatedly expresses
his unbounded admiration of the teachings of Christ, putting
them above all other written moral systems. But it must be
confessed that, as a *science*, he derided ethics. His theory on

[1] The remark is worth quoting. It occurs under date of October 25th, 1775, when
Mr. Jefferson was a subject of curiosity as a new member. Adams writes: "Duane
says, that Jefferson is the greatest rubber-off of dust that he has met with; that he has
learned French, Italian, Spanish, and wants to learn German."—*Life and Works of John
Adams*, by his grandson, vol. ii. p. 430.
[2] Because it would imply pretension, and because it would involve the absurdity of
supposing the mass of his readers better linguists than himself.

the subject was contained in a letter to the same nephew just
alluded to:

"Moral Philosophy. I think it lost time to attend lectures on this branch. He
who made us would have been a pitiful bungler, if he had made the rules of
our moral conduct a matter of science. For one man of science, there are thousands
who are not. What would have become of them? Man was destined for society.
His morality, therefore, was to be formed to this object. He was endowed with a
sense of right and wrong, merely relative to this. This sense is as much a part of
his nature, as the sense of hearing, seeing, feeling; it is the true foundation of
morality, and not the το καλον, truth, etc., as fanciful writers have imagined. The
moral sense, or conscience, is as much a part of man, as his leg or arm. It is given
to all human beings in a stronger or weaker degree, as force of members is given
them in a greater or less degree. It may be strengthened by exercise, as may any
particular limb of the body. This sense is submitted, indeed, in some degree, to
the guidance of reason; but it is a small stock which is required for this: even a
less one than what we call common sense. State a moral case to a plowman and
a professor. The former will decide it as well, and often better than the latter,
because he has not been led astray by artificial rules. In this branch, therefore,
read good books, because they will encourage, as well as direct your feelings. The
writings of Sterne, particularly, form the best course of morality that ever was
written. Besides these, read the books mentioned in the inclosed paper; and above
all things, lose no occasion of exercising your dispositions to be grateful, to be
generous, to be charitable, to be humane, to be true, just, firm, orderly, courageous,
etc. Consider every act of this kind, as an exercise which will strengthen your
moral faculties, and increase your worth." [1]

No one will probably complain of this manner of stating, or
applying a theory of the moral sense, already advanced, according to our recollections, not only by its proposer Shaftesbury, but
by Hutchinson and Reid, and which afterwards received the
endorsement of Stewart and Brown.[2] And if such an exalted
estimate of the author of Tristram Shandy, the Sentimental
Journey, and the Sermons of Yorick, as a moralist, is not concurred in, it will not at least be forgotten, that seventy years
ago the range of selection in this class of reading was much less
extensive than now.

Mr. Jefferson does not perhaps express himself so pointedly
on any occasion against the study of metaphysics, but he evidently had little relish for it. His mind was rather objective
than subjective in its tendencies. He was eminently perceptive.

[1] Letter to Peter Carr, August 10th, 1787.
[2] We *think* the publication of Reid's views preceded, and that of Stewart and Brown
followed the date of this letter. But the whole sentence, even to the views of the
writers named, we write merely from memory. We do not mean to say that all these
writers' theories of the moral sense *precisely* corresponded. Hutchinson's view is not,
for example, that of Stewart and Brown.

He studied the actual, and his philosophy had in it a strong dash of utilitarianism. Recondite speculation, having no connection with practical questions, and especially with practical interests, could not long interest his attention. Though not destitute of imagination, and even fond of its higher *objective* creations, as for example in the Greek poets, he could not tolerate its intrusion in systems designed to influence the sober realities of life, or the solemn questions of the hereafter. And from faculties so peculiarly sharp and alert, it was not easy to disguise the boundaries between the real and unreal—between the terra-firma of reason and the cloud-land of hypothesis. A great gulf separated them, which no fog of words could hide; and though the rainbow played on that fog, the stern practicalist looked through and spurned what, to him, was the abasement of self-delusion, or the criminality of intentional deceit. We may remark, in passing, that it was precisely for such reasons as these, that a fine Greek scholar and a profound intellect, was guilty of that heresy, in most scholars' eyes, which appears a score of times in Mr. Jefferson's correspondence—of expressing unmitigated contempt for Plato and his writings!

Mr. Jefferson's early reading[1] was wide and various, including, in chosen departments, most of the standards of the Greek, Latin, and English tongues, and, to a considerable extent, of the French and Italian. He was more partial to the Greek than the Roman literature; and among the Greeks, the Athenians were, in all respects, his chosen people. In the "dense logic" and burning declamation of oratory, he placed Demosthenes immeasurably above Cicero; but he ranked the philosophies of the latter with those of Socrates, and above those of Epictetus. Among the ancient historians he gave a decided preference to Thucydides and Tacitus. Plutarch was first disliked, but afterwards liked by him. Among the moderns, he admired Hume's style, but from his very first perusal of

---

[1] Our facts on this subject are drawn mainly from the recollections of his family, and especially of one of its members, who was for many years his frequent secretary and amanuensis, and his almost constant library companion. It was his wont to converse very freely with this companion on books; and as he shaped her education and reading, he often referred to his own at a parallel period of life, stating his early preferences, and how far he had retained or abandoned them. We have spent a good many hours in writing down from the mouth of the narrator, distinctly preserved recollections of these; and a rapid synopsis of them appears above. We prepared it much more fully for these pages, but have omitted it for fear that it would be considered tedious by the reader.

him detested his political sentiments, and therefore preferred the older and less elegant historians of England. For fiction, he had so little taste, that nearly every work he *ever* read of this class could here be stated. The list now embraced little, probably nothing, beyond the works of Sterne and Fielding, a part of those of Smollett, Marmontel's Tales, Gil Blas, and Don Quixote. The last was perhaps the only novel he ever read the second time, or ever very keenly relished. He disapproved of much novel reading for the young—but his own abstinence was founded on pure disinclination. He was afterwards wont to ridicule the morbid taste for the mysterious and horrid school, which rose in his day (Mrs. Radcliffe's school), by declaring that when a young man he often passed sleepless nights, until he hit upon the excellent expedient of mentally composing a "love and murder" novel—that whenever he was sleepless, he took it up where he had left it off, and that so capital an opiate was it, that before getting three pages he was always sound asleep!

In the cognate branch of poetry—somewhat strangely it might seem, in view of the preceding, and of his utilitarian tendencies—he was a pretty general reader. His particular favorites among the classics were Homer, the Greek Dramatists, and Horace; and of later times, Tasso, Molière, Shakspeare, Milton, Dryden, Pope, the old English ballad, pastoral and lyric writers, and lastly Ossian. He admired Virgil and Dante, but read them less. The same may be said of Corneille, in contrast with Molière. (He had a decided taste for pure comedy.) Petrarch, ever ringing his changes on Laura, was not to his taste. Metastasio was enjoyed by him in lighter moods, perhaps quite as often as Tasso. He loved the dulcet melodies of several of the minor Italian poets, and neatly written copies of some of their songs, in his early handwriting, are yet preserved. This song-copying seems not to have been an unusual amusement with him. Lying before us thus traced are "Lovely Peggy," "Tweedside," "Mary of Tweed," an English Pastoral,[1] etc., etc. Scraps of Shenstone are scribbled on some

[1] Commencing:

"It rains, it rains, my fair,
Come drive your white sheep past;
Let's to my shed repair,
Haste, Shepherdess, make haste."

of his early manuscripts, but he admired the author of the Leasowes more than of the pastorals!

Ossian may be thought in good company in the above list.
It was, we believe, the very year that Mr. Jefferson entered
college that Macpherson published his Remains of Ancient
Poetry. The second or third year after, appeared Fingal,
Temora, and the smaller Ossianic poems. The splendid career
of this bold imposture, as well as the actual merits of these
remarkable poems (Jonathan Oldbuck to the contrary notwithstanding) are well known. Productions which attracted the
marked admiration of Hume, and of some other of the finest
writers and scholars of England—which in Cesarotti's Italian
costume, "formed almost the whole poetical library of Napo-
leon"[1]—were hailed with deep enthusiasm by the young Virginia student. There was something in the high-wrought
objective descriptions, in the wild, grand imagery, that captivated him, and for once our practicalist and utilitarian came
almost to see like his Cherokee friend, Ontassetè, the forms of
heroes in clouds, and to hear their clashing shields in the
elemental strife! With a characteristic disregard of labor,
where a mental gratification was in view, he at once resolved to
study the Gaelic or Erse, to enable him to read the originals of
Macpherson's wonderful collection; and he actually wrote a
relative of that gentleman in Scotland, who had formerly
resided in Virginia, to procure him, if possible, a *Gaelic grammar and dictionary*, and to request the soi-disant translator's
leave to have a *manuscript* copy taken of the original poems!
He desired his correspondent to spare no expense, "the glow of
one warm thought" being "worth more than money." "He
was not ashamed to own that he thought this rude bard of the
North the greatest poet that had ever existed."[2] The reply, if
any ever reached him, has not transpired. This admiration of
Ossian—fairly outheroding Hector McIntyre's—was long in
cooling. As late as 1781 or 1782 we shall find Mr. Jefferson
and a celebrated French traveller (Major-General the Marquis
de Chastellux) reciting passages from it with particular gusto,
one evening round a punch-bowl at Monticello! Long enough

[1] So says Sir James Mackintosh.
[2] This curious letter, dated as late as Feb. 25, 1773, will be found in the Congress
edition of his Works.

before his death, however, he ceased to think it the production of " the greatest poet that ever existed "—or to often name it, or ever take it from the shelf.

Soon after leaving college, Mr. Jefferson entered upon the study of the law.   He says in his Memoir :

" He [Dr. Small] returned to Europe in 1762, having previously filled up the measure of his goodness to me, by procuring for me, from his most intimate friend, George Wythe, a reception as a student of law, under his direction, and introduced me to the acquaintance and familiar table of Governor Fauquier, the ablest man who had ever filled that office. With him, and at his table, Dr. Small and Mr. Wythe, his *amici omnium horarum*, and myself, formed a *partie quarrée*, and to the habitual conversations on these occasions I owed much instruction."

Mr. Wythe was one of the purest, ablest and most profoundly erudite lawyers ever produced by a State which has been particularly famous for good lawyers ; and probably there was something in the care he manifested in his students' progress and in the general regulations of his office,[1] which made Mr. Jefferson esteem studying under him so desirable—while Peyton and John Randolph, the sons of his great-uncle, Sir John, were also both practising law in Williamsburg—were both of sufficient distinction in their profession to become Colonial Attorney-Generals—and were both intimate and attached friends of his own, so there could have been no doubt of their willing reception of him as a law student, had he desired it.

Francis Fauquier, Governor of Virginia at this period, is thus described by the historian Burk: " With some allowance he was everything that could have been wished for by Virginia under a royal government.   Generous, liberal, elegant in his manners and acquirements, his example left an impression of taste, refinement, and erudition on the character of the colony, which eminently contributed to its present high reputation in the arts."[2]

There was something peculiar in a young law-student, not yet twenty-one years old, being made the chosen and habitual

[1] Our impression is that Mr. Wythe took extraordinary pains with the few students he received, having them make careful abstracts of all they studied—practising them in mock courts—freely giving his opinions to them and otherwise instructing them.
[2] Burk's Hist. of Virginia, vol. iii. p. 333.

fourth of *such* a "partie quarrée;" and Mr. Jefferson, in fact, understates his intimacy at "the palace," as the Governor's house was then styled. Not only was he invited to all its parties, little and large, but he belonged to a small band of musical amateurs, of which the Governor was one, who assembled weekly, to perform on their several instruments and indulge in the most familiar private intercourse. He was, therefore, the Governor's "friend of all hours"—serious and gay—even more literally than Dr. Small and Mr. Wythe. This would seem to show the estimate placed on his social and intellectual qualities, and probably the expectations formed of his future career, by an able and experienced observer and a practised man of the world. Apart from the intellectual improvement derived from such an intercourse, Mr. Jefferson, it is said, owed that polish of manner which distinguished him through life, to his habitual mingling with the elegant society which Governor Fauquier collected about him.

But with these good gifts, according to the late John Randolph of Roanoke, came more questionable ones. Governor Fauquier was a disciple of Shaftesbury and Bolingbroke, and he was passionately addicted to gaming.[1] While it is conceded that Mr. Jefferson escaped the contamination of his vices, Mr. Randolph conjectured that he did not that of his religious views.[2] But a far more impartial and discriminating witness— one vastly better acquainted with and capable of appreciating

[1] Burk, in stating the "allowance" to be made, in estimating Fauquier's high services to Virginia (see preceding page), draws the following melancholy picture: "It is stated, on evidence sufficiently authentic, that on the return of Anson, from his circumnavigation of the earth, he accidentally fell in with Fauquier, from whom, in a single night's play, he won at cards the whole of his patrimony; that afterwards, being captivated by the striking graces of this gentleman's person and conversation, he procured for him the government of Virginia. Unreclaimed by the former subversion of his fortune, he introduced the same fatal propensity to gaming into Virginia; and the example of so many virtues and accomplishments alloyed but by a single vice, was but too successful in extending the influence of this pernicious and ruinous practice. He found among the people of his new government, a character compounded of the same elements as his own: and he found little difficulty in rendering fashionable a practice which had, before his arrival, already prevailed to an alarming extent. During the recess of the courts of judicature and assemblies, he visited the most distinguished landholders in the Colonies, and the rage for playing deep, reckless of time, health, or money, spread like a contagion among a class proverbial for their hospitality, their politeness, and fondness of expense. In everything beside, Fauquier was the ornament and the delight of Virginia."—[*History of Virginia*, vol. iii. p. 333.] This picture of Virginia society sufficiently explains "the bad company," "the temptations and difficulties," to which Mr. Jefferson states he was early exposed, in the letter to his grandson, already quoted.
[2] Professor Tucker mentions this as an oral statement to himself by that gentleman.—[*Life of Jefferson*, vol. i. p. 41.] It was made, then, long after the fountains of John Randolph's bitter heart were turned to gall against his earlier friend and kinsman.

the particular structure of Mr. Jefferson's mind, as well as more familiar with his opinions—James Madison, "gave no credit to this supposed influence."[1]

During Mr. Jefferson's law course of five years, he usually spent the summer months at home, at Shadwell, where the rest of the family continued to reside. The systematic industry of his college life continued. Notwithstanding the time given to company, he contrived to pass nearly twice the usual number of hours of law students in his studies. He placed a clock in his bedroom, and as soon as he could distinguish its hands in the grey of the summer morning, he rose and commenced his labors. In winter, he rose punctually at five. His hour of retiring in the summer, in the country, was nine—in the winter, at ten. At Shadwell, his studies were very little interrupted by company. He usually took a gallop on horseback during the day, and at twilight walked to the top of Monticello. An hour or two given to the society of his family, and the favorite violin, completed the list of interruptions, and still left fourteen or fifteen hours for study and reading.

With Mr. Jefferson, the lover succeeded the schoolboy in the due and time-honored order, as laid down by the "melancholy Jaques." The only record of this affair is to be found in a series of letters addressed by him to his friend, John Page, commencing immediately after he left college, and extending, at intervals, through the two succeeding years. These are to be found at length in the Congress edition of his Works, and also in his Life, by Professor Tucker. They possess some interest, perhaps, in relation to their subject matter, but most, as the earliest specimens of their author's epistolary writing which have been preserved. Though they display something of that easy command of language—that "running pen"—for which he was afterwards so celebrated, they exhibit no peculiar grace of style, or maturity of thought. Perhaps, however, these would scarcely be expected in the careless, off-hand effusions of boyish intimacy. It causes a smile to see the future statesman "sighing like furnace" in a first love; concealing, after the approved fashion of student life, the name of his mistress under awkward Latin puns and Greek anagrams, to bury a secret which the world, of course, was supposed to have a vast interest in discovering; delightedly describing happy dances with his "Belinda" in the Apollo (that room of the Raleigh tavern where we shall soon find him acting so different a part); vowing the customary despairing vow, that "if Belinda will not accept his service, it never shall be offered to another;" and so on to the end of the chapter—in the well-beaten track of immemorial prescription. The object of his attachment was a Miss Rebecca Burwell (called Belinda, as a pet-name, or by way of concealment), whom tradition speaks of as more distinguished for beauty than cleverness.

His proposals seem to have been clogged with the condition that he must be absent for two or three years in foreign travel before marriage. He several times expresses this design, specifying England, Holland, France, Spain, Italy, Egypt, and a return through the northern British provinces in America, as his proposed route. Why he gave this up, does not appear. Whether for this, or because her preferences lay in a different direction, Miss Burwell somewhat abruptly married another man, in 1764.

Mr. Jefferson was generally, however, rather a favorite with the other sex, and not without reason. His appearance was engaging. His face, though angular, and far from beautiful, beamed with intelligence, with benevolence, and with the cheerful vivacity of a happy, hopeful spirit. His complexion was

ruddy, and delicately fair;' his reddish chestnut hair² luxuriant
and silken. His full, deep-set eyes, the prevailing color of
which was a light hazel (or flecks of hazel on a groundwork of
grey), were peculiarly expressive, and mirrored, as the clear lake
mirrors the cloud, every emotion which was passing through his
mind. He stood six feet two and a half inches in height, and
though very slim at this period, his form was erect and sinewy,
and his movements displayed elasticity and vigor. He was an
expert musician, a fine dancer, a dashing rider, and there was
no manly exercise in which he could not play well his part.
His manners were unusually graceful, but simple and cordial.
His conversation already possessed no inconsiderable share of
that charm which, in after years, was so much extolled by
friends, and to which enemies attributed so seductive an influence in moulding the young and the wavering to his political
views. There was a frankness, earnestness, and cordiality in its
tone—a deep sympathy with humanity—a confidence in man,
and a sanguine hopefulness in his destiny, which irresistibly
won upon the feelings not only of the ordinary hearer, but of
those grave men whose commerce with the world had perhaps
led them to form less glowing estimates of it—of such men as
the scholarlike Small, the sagacious Wythe, the courtly and
gifted Fauquier. Mr. Jefferson's temper was gentle, kindly, and
forgiving. If it naturally had anything of that warmth which is
the usual concomitant of affections and sympathies so ardent,
and it no doubt had, it had been subjugated by habitual control.
Yet, under its even placidity, there were not wanting those indications of calm self-reliance and courage which all instinctively
recognize and respect. There is not an instance on record of
his having been engaged in a personal rencontre, or his having
suffered a personal indignity. Possessing the accomplishments,
he avoided the vices, of the young Virginia gentry of the day,
and a class of habits, which, if not vices themselves, were too

---

¹ It had that peculiar ruddiness produced by a very thin skin filled with minute exposed veins. The cuticle was so thin and fragile that it peeled off after the slightest
exposure to sun or wind.
² It has been generally mentioned as *red*. It was not so—at least in the sense in
which that designation is ordinarily understood—though it had a decidedly reddish or
"sandy" tinge. Hair of its color is often denominated "auburn." In France, a few
rare white hairs intermixed with it; during his presidency, these became abundant
enough to considerably modify the original hue; at the time of his death, it was much
whitened, but retained the sandy tinge very perceptibly. A locket, containing his hair
at all these periods, lies under our eye as we write. These are but minutiæ, but whatever is worth telling is worth telling accurately.

often made the preludes to them. He never gambled. To avoid importunities to games which were generally accompanied with betting, he never learned to distinguish one card from another ;[1] he was moderate in the enjoyments of the table; to strong drinks he had an aversion which rarely yielded to any circumstances ; his mouth was unpolluted by oaths or tobacco !   Though he speaks of enjoying " the victory of a favorite horse," and the " death of the fox," he never put but one horse in training to run—never run but a single race, and he very rarely joined in the pleasant excitement—he knew it to be too pleasant for the aspiring student—of the chase. With such qualities of mind and character, with the favor of powerful friends and relatives, and even of vice-royalty to urge him on-ward, Mr. Jefferson was not a young man to be lightly regarded by the young or old of either sex.

He became of age in 1764.

[1] His grandson, Col. Thomas J. Randolph, informs us that cards were never played in his house.

CHAPTER II.

1764—1773.

THE misunderstandings with the parent country, which led to the Revolutionary struggle, though long accumulating, first began to wear an immediately menacing aspect at about the close of Mr. Jefferson's minority. Mr. Jefferson himself was a Whig both by inheritance and by the natural constitution of his mind. And when that transient gleam of joy which broke over the Colonies at the conclusion of the Peace of Paris (1763) faded into gloom; when the Colonists found that British triumphs were not their triumphs; when they found that new exactions were their only requital for bearing so much more than their proportionate share of the burthens of the late war, and contributing so essentially to its success; and when a few of their

36

bolder spirits determined to resolutely oppose those exactions by every constitutional method—their number did not include one whose views were more decisive and uncompromising than the young Williamsburg law student, whose biography we are writing.   In this, he went counter to the feelings of some of his most influential relatives and friends, and far ahead of those of them even who professed Whig principles.   Wealth and rank are usually conservative and slow to embark in violent opposition to constituted authority.   The political chasm between Mr. Jefferson and a portion of his kinsmen was destined to widen until it became one of total and permanent separation; but with another portion, it was destined to be obliterated—and though more cautious at the outset, those kinsmen were to nobly vindicate the fidelity of their patriotism at the council-board and in the battle-field.

When the news of the Declaratory Act—declaratory of the power of the British Parliament to tax the American Colonies—reached Virginia, in the spring of 1764, it called forth a remonstrance from the House of Burgesses in the form of an address to the King and a memorial to Parliament, in which the asserted right was denied, and its exercise deprecated in earnest though perhaps rather supplicatory terms.   The famous Stamp Act was advanced on its passage through Parliament, when these papers, and similar ones from several other Colonies, reached England; and they were not sufficient to prevent its consummation.   It became a law in January, 1765, to take effect the ensuing November.   The news of this, when it reached Virginia, produced a pause among the old Whig leaders.   There was a wide difference between remonstrating against an obnoxious proposition, or even taking theoretical grounds against its constitutionality, and making a factious opposition to *law*.   The spring session of the Burgesses was therefore within three days of its close, before the Stamp Act was mentioned on its floors!

The broken merchant whose acquaintance we have made at Colonel Dandridge's, was in the body, a representative from Louisa.   His appearance and manners were as rustic as ever.

———"The forest-born Demosthenes,[1]
Whose thunder shook the Philip of the seas,"

[1] Lord Byron so termed Henry, though the resemblance between the latter and the

sat with a burning heart to see if none of the old Whig leaders
would propose to the House to take some step to vindicate the
rights of their country. As the session was about closing, on
the 30th of May he took a blank leaf from "an old Coke upon
Littleton," and penned five resolutions. They assumed the
common ground that the colonists brought with them to America all the *rights of British subjects*—that the taxation of the
people by themselves or their representatives, was "the distinguishing characteristic of British freedom"—that all power to
lay taxes was in the Colonial Legislature—and they concluded
by spiritedly declaring "that every attempt to vest such power
in any person or persons whatsoever, other than the General
Assembly aforesaid, had a manifest tendency to destroy British
as well as American freedom." Henry offered these resolutions, and then broke suddenly upon the astonished House with
that torrent of burning and vehement declamation, thus described by Jefferson in his Memoir:

"When the famous Resolutions of 1765, against the Stamp Act, were proposed, I
was yet a student of law in Williamsburg. I attended the debate, however, at the
door of the lobby of the House of Burgesses, and heard the splendid display of Mr.
Henry's talents as a popular orator. They were great indeed; such as I have
never heard from any other man. He appeared to me to speak as Homer wrote.
Mr. Johnson, a lawyer, and member from the Northern neck, seconded the resolutions, and by him the learning and logic of the case were chiefly maintained."

In narrating the same scene to Mr. Wirt he gave these
further details:

"Mr. Henry moved, and Mr. Johnson seconded these resolutions successively.
They were opposed by Messrs. Randolph, Bland, Pendleton, *Wythe*, and all the old
members, whose influence in the House had, till then, been unbroken. They did
it, not from any question of our rights, but on the ground that the same sentiments
had been, at their preceding session, expressed in a more conciliatory form, to
which the answers were not yet received."

He then mentions that the last resolution was carried but by
a single vote—that the debate on it was "most bloody"—that
Peyton Randolph, the Attorney-General, coming to the door
where he was standing, said as he entered the lobby, "By God!

Athenian orator does not extend beyond their common power to move the *feelings* of their
auditors. It would be difficult indeed to mention two men, of what may be termed the
same vocation, more unlike.

I would have given five hundred guineas for a single vote," (for that would have made a tie, and the Speaker, Robinson, would have negatived the resolution)—that Mr. Henry left town that evening—that Colonel Peter Randolph,[1] then of the Council, came to the House next morning, and looked over the journals to find a precedent for expunging a resolution—that as soon as the House met a motion was made and carried to expunge it.[2] In another letter to Wirt, he said, in addition to the preceding enumeration, that the resolutions were opposed by Robinson "and all the cyphers of the aristocracy."

It was on this occasion that occurred the incident thus narrated by Wirt:

"It was in the midst of this magnificent debate, while he [Henry] was descanting on the tyranny of the obnoxious act, that he exclaimed, in a voice of thunder, and with the look of a god, 'Cæsar had his Brutus—Charles the First his Cromwell—and George the Third'—('Treason!' cried the Speaker—'treason! treason!' echoed from every part of the House. It was one of those trying moments which is decisive of character. Henry faltered not an instant; but rising to a loftier attitude, and fixing on the Speaker an eye of the most determined fire, he finished his sentence with the firmest emphasis)—'may profit by their example. If this be treason, make the most of it.' "[3]

When Mr. Henry sat down, the real leadership of the opposition had passed away from the Pendletons, the Wythes, the Blands, the Randolphs, and the Nicholases;[4] and the "forest-born Demosthenes" was the idol of the people—the head of that class of Whigs who (whether they had yet formed resolutions on the subject or not) were sure to make their opposition to tyranny commensurate with the necessity. Mr. Jefferson afterwards modestly and liberally said of the old leaders we have mentioned:

"These were honest and able men, had begun the opposition on the same grounds, but with a moderation more adapted to their age and experience. Subsequent events favored the bolder spirits of Henry, the Lees, Pages, Mason, &c., with whom I went in all points. Sensible, however, of the importance of unanimity among our constituents, although we often wished to have gone faster, we slackened our pace, that our less ardent colleagues might keep up with us; and they, on their part, differing nothing from us in principle, quickened their gait somewhat beyond that which their prudence might of itself have advised, and thus consoli-

---

[1] Son of the second William Randolph, of Turkey Island.
[2] For these statements, see Wirt's Life of Patrick Henry, 7th edition, New York, 1834, p. 78; and Jefferson to Wirt, in his published correspondence, Aug. 14, 1814.
[3] Wirt's Life of Henry, p. 83.   [4] Jefferson to Wirt, Aug. 1814.

dated the phalanx which breasted the power of Britain. By this harmony of the bold with the cautious, we advanced with our constituents in undivided mass, and with fewer examples of separation than, perhaps, existed in any other part of the Union." [1]

Mr. Nicholas P. Trist, who resided at Monticello the last two or three years of Mr. Jefferson's life,[2] kept daily memoranda of conversations held with the latter, always recording them the same day, and usually the same hour they took place. These jottings disclose an obvious attempt at that literal and precise fidelity which those who know the writer need not be informed marks his character. We are kindly favored with the use of these papers, and shall have not unfrequent occasion to quote them. Here is an extract giving some remarks of Jefferson in regard to Henry, which will be read with interest:

"Wirt says he [Henry] read Plutarch's Lives once a year. I don't believe he ever read two volumes of them. On his visits to court, *he used always to put up with me.* On one occasion of the breaking up in November, to meet again in the spring, as he was departing in the morning, he looked among my books, and observed, 'Mr. J., I will take two volumes of Hume's Essays, and try to read them this winter.' On his return he brought them, saying he had not been able to get half way into one of them.

"His great delight was to put on his hunting-shirt, collect a parcel of overseers and such like people, and spend weeks together hunting in the 'piny woods,' camping at night, and cracking jokes round a light-wood fire.

"*It was to him that we were indebted for the unanimity that prevailed among us.* He would address the assemblages of the people at which he was present, in such strains of native eloquence as Homer wrote in. I never heard anything that deserved to be called by the same name with what flowed from him; and where he got that torrent of language, is inconceivable.

"I have frequently shut my eyes while he spoke, and when he was done asked myself what he had said, without being able to recollect a word of it. He was no logician. He was truly a great man, however, one of enlarged views. (Oct. 11, 1824. This was said to Mr. Leavit Harris, U. S. Consul or ex-Consul at St. Petersburg, then on a visit to the United States.)"

Some interesting letters from Jefferson to Wirt, in respect to Mr. Henry, which are not included in either edition of Mr. Jefferson's published Works, will be found in Kennedy's Life of Wirt.

In the autumn of 1765, Mr. Jefferson was called upon to experience a severe domestic bereavement, in the death of his

[1] Letter to Wirt.
[2] He married Virginia Jefferson Randolph, a grand-daughter of Mr. Jefferson.

oldest and favorite sister Jane. She died on the 1st day of October, aged twenty-five. She had been her brother's constant companion when at home, and the confidant of all his youthful feelings. He ever regarded her as fully his own equal in understanding, and there was a depth, earnestness, purity and simplicity in her high nature which made an impression on his mind which was never effaced. More than half a century afterwards he continued to occasionally speak of her to his grand-daughters in terms of as warm admiration and love as if the grave had but just closed over her. It was listening to church music that oftenest struck the chord of these memories. She had been a singer of uncommon skill and sweetness, and both were particularly fond of the solemn music used by the Church of England in the Psalms. He carried through life a strong partiality for the Psalms and Psalm-tunes, regarding hymns as "far less suited to the dignity of religious worship." His sister Jane excelled in this description of music, to the execution of which she brought the fervor of a deep religious devotion; and many a winter evening, round the family fireside, and many a soft summer twilight, on the wooded banks of the Rivanna, heard their voices, accompanied by the notes of his violin, thus ascending together. Among some of his earliest memoranda,[1] are two different plans of a family cemetery, and two epitaphs—one intended for his sister. It runs as follows:

> "Ah, Joanna, puellarum optima,
> Ah, ævi virentis flore præpta,
> Sit tibi terra lævis;
> Longe, longeque valeto!"

The loss of this sister was more deeply felt, from vacancies which had already been made in the household. Mary, the second sister, had been married several years previously to Thomas Bolling; and Martha, the fourth, in the preceding July, to Dabney Carr, and both had moved away to their husbands' residences. There was nothing in the minds of Elizabeth or Lucy to commend them to the companionship of their gifted brother; and the two youngest children were not yet much advanced beyond the period of infancy.

In the spring of 1766, Mr. Jefferson commenced keeping a

[1] Hereafter to be given.

garden book which, escaping fire and other accidents, was continued, with the chasms occasioned by absence, to 1824. And we may as well here mention some other of the books found in the old receptacle mentioned in a preceding note, to which we shall have frequent occasion to refer. Among them was Mr. Jefferson's farm book, commenced in 1774, and which continued, with the same chasms as the preceding, down to the same date. The list also included pocket account books, containing all his personal expenses, and heads of his farm, official and all other accounts, covering, with the exception of two years, the period from 1771 to 1803; books of special accounts, as for example, expenses of the Presidential mansion, profits and losses in several manufacturing undertakings, accounts kept as an executor, etc.,—a law register (extending from 1767 to 1774) giving the titles of all the cases in the higher courts in which he was ever employed,[1] with memoranda of his proceedings in them—and some other books hereafter to be noticed.[2] All of these contain passing memoranda on other subjects than the principal one—many of them preserving important dates and incidents in Mr. Jefferson's life. The reader will understand them also as the source of a multitude of new minor facts, presented in these volumes, a separate citation of our authority for stating which, in every instance, would appear frivolous.

All the manuscripts of Thomas Jefferson present a striking and persistent coincidence in one particular—and it is one of the first ones which the examiner notices, partly from its own prominence, and partly because few out of the circle of his immediate friends are prepared for the fact it discloses. It is his remarkable *precision* down to minute details—his apparent *fondness for details*. Never was there a more methodical man from great matters down to the merest seeming trifles—never so diligent a recorder of them! We will present some specifications. In his garden book, for example, the times of planting, sprouting, coming to the table, or ripening of his multitude of esculents are severally noted; the plots of ground containing them, the rows of plants, and sometimes the separate plants in

[1] He occasionally gave professional *advice* subsequently. All such memoranda, and those in reference to inferior courts go into the pocket account books.
[2] It will not be understood that ALL these were entirely *forgotten* books, like Peter Jefferson's accounts. Some of them had found their way into the old dark receptacle later.

Oct. 1. put into church box 1/?
    2 p.d an Bartram the ironmonger
                for 12 sashbolts 36/
                2 small doorbolts 8/ } £ 2 – 4
        p.d Sparhawk for a purse 7/
        p.d Aitkin for an ivory book 12/
                for Military instructions for J Fleming 7/6
    3 rec.d Roberts for 4 sashbolts 16/
        p.d Hillegas a former debt 8/6
    4. p.d Humphries for pamphlets 4/6
        p.d a barber 1/?
    5. p.d for a Dutch blanket 14/
    6. p.d for pins 4/2
        p.d Bell for books 35/
        p.d my part for an express to Williamsburgh 10/
        commenced lodgings at Randolph's, Chesnut street.
    7. p.d mrs Maxfield one week's lodging &c £ 3 – 10
    9. p.d Brooks for sundries 10/6
        p.d for pins 5/3
        p.d postage 3/
    10. p.d postage 8/3
        put into Common stock for housekeeping 30/
    11. p.d E. Rutledge for whips for J m. Randolph 31/10½
        rec.d of J. Willing part of allowance from our assembly
                for Congress 100£ sterl = 165. Pennsylva currency
        p.d Smith in full 19/
    12 p.d Brinkhurst, ironmonger £ 36 – 15
    13. p.d for whetting penknife 4/?
        p.d Roberts for sundries £ 2 – 12 – 6
        p.d for walking stick 1/6
        PAGE OF POCKET ACCOUNT BOOK.

each row are numbered; diagrams, as neatly drawn as engrav-ings, present the different plots or beds collectively to the eye, and display their annual rotations. Meteorological observa-tions, recorded punctually at three different periods of the day, extend through a long course of years, and through some of the busiest ones of his life. The pocket account books include the minutest items of his daily expenditure, down to two or three pennies paid for a shoe string, or tossed into a beggar's hat in Paris—and we think we remember one or two entries of a single penny, to make the inexorable *cash book* balance *exactly*! The object of the disbursement is generally specified. Account books kept thus, present a curious history of a man's life; and Mr. Jefferson's tell where he went, and what he bought every day for thirty years. When he is away from home his monthly expenses are often tabularized, so as to separately exhibit the aggregate expenditure for each principal article—as for meat, bread, wine, etc.—and thic 's habitually done where official posi-tion required him to keep an expensive establishment. His regis-ter of law cases, and table of fees will be referred to hereafter. He makes memoranda of minute economical facts of every descrip-tion. Those in regard to farming and gardening are innumera-ble. Even household details do not escape his attention. We often find how much of this or that it will take to supply the wants of a person or family—how much oil will supply a lamp for a certain number of hours—comparative cost of lamps and candles, etc., etc.

In everything pertaining to natural history, we have a series of almost miscroscopic observations. Those condensed and generalized in his Notes on Virginia, are not, with the excep-tion of the meteorological observations, before us—but we have a multitude of new ones. They do not need to be here speci-fied; but we will name one, which in what may be termed the department of economico-natural history (a department in which he seems to have specially delighted), exhibits something which it is hard, at the first blush, to define. This is a *table* beautifully drawn up, giving the average earliest and latest appearance of *thirty-seven* varieties of vegetables in the Wash-ington market during the whole eight years of his presidency! To think of a leader of a great civil revolution—the founder of a new party and creed—the statesman engaged in the pressing cares of a nation—watching with a green-grocer's assiduity, and recording with more than a green-grocer's precision, the first and last appearance of radishes, squashes, cabbages, and cauliflowers in the market—suggests a curious train of reflections !

Those reflections, we confess, are not at first favorable to Mr. Jefferson. Some of these minutiæ might seem to show an over-solicitude on the subject of money. And taken together, we are disposed to ask if a mind so constantly intent on small subjects, can have much taste, or time, or *power*, to master large ones. We are inclined to feel as the visitor of a celebrated cardinal did, when triumphantly informed by him that he had done all his writing for a specified term of years, with the same pen he held in his hand. The visitor's reflection was, "after all, this man is a trifler." But nothing is more certain than that Mr. Jefferson had not even a leaning towards avarice, as will abundantly appear throughout the record of his life. That he thought great thoughts—that he embodied them in imperishable words—that he performed great achievements—will now scarcely be denied by his most illiberal foes. If, then, he was little and frivolous, he was also concededly great.

But on deeper reflection, do the facts involve that anomaly? Dr. Johnson said: "The truly strong and sound mind is the mind that can embrace equally great things and small." Does the most transcendent mind of which we can possibly form a conception—that mind which, while guiding rolling worlds in their orbits, suffers not a sparrow to fall to the ground without its notice—disdain *small* things? The ordinary great mind has only time and room for great things. The master mind, that comes but once in a century, is stamped with universality. It bids its servants, the senses, collect all knowledge that is good ! It will not overlook or throw away anything that is useful to humanity ! It has vigor to collect all, without becoming over-wearied or frittered away in the pursuit—it has capacity to embrace all, without being overloaded with its stores, or suffering them to fall into confusion—it has the exhaustless energy which can keep every physical and intellectual faculty constantly strained and in full play, each one a conduit which is pouring knowledge into the soul. The eye of such a man looks at nothing, his ear hears nothing, his hand touches nothing, without collecting some of those facts which finally are

a Statement of the Vegetable market of Washington, during a period of 8 years, wherein the earliest & latest appearance of each article within the whole 8 years is noted.

ance	Feb	Mar	Apr	May	June	July	Aug	Sep	Oct	Nov	Dec	Jan	Feb	Mar	Apr	May
sley.																
nach																
roots	22			20												
corn sallad	4		30													
radishes		20		31			13			11						
sorrel		2									30					
asparagus		6			26											
broccoli		7	24													
cucumbers		23						27								
cabbage			3													
strawberries			8		9											
peas			9					17								
turneps			30										18			
potato Irish				1												
snaps.				8			17									
artichokes				9	16											
carrots				14										16		
salsifia				12										8		
raspberries				10	4											
squashes				11			18									
windsor beans				12	6											
beets				14										15		
currants				17	6											
parsneps				29											2	
watermelons					7	4										
corn					8	26										
tomatoes					16		17									
melons						2	22									
mushrooms						11	19									
limabeans						27	16									
grapes						20										
endive						27							27			
celery						1									9	
eggplant						1	27									
cauliflower							7							16		
creses							11		4							

TABLE OF VEGETABLE MARKET &c

grouped into systems, to establish great truths in science or social economy.   If half the men who fret and bustle in brief importance in public or private, would each devote themselves for life to the constant observation of a single plant, or insect, or in perfecting the manipulations of the most trivial economic process, and record the result of their observations, they would unquestionably effect more good, and therefore live to better purpose, than they now do.   Any discovery that brings the smallest appreciable gain to the individual, brings a stupendous gain to mankind in the aggregate, and especially to the aggregate of mankind through all coming ages.   Who is above such labor?   And when he who performs well his part in every ordinary, social, political and other relation—nay, far surpasses most of his fellows in them—can still find time to add something useful to the stock of every-day human knowledge—though it be not making two blades of grass grow where but one grew before, but only making five grow where four grew before—shall his pursuit be ridiculed by those who spend the same time in vacuity or mere sensuous employment?   Above all, shall a man, whose great deeds fill the trump of fame, be pronounced a small man for condescending to be also useful in small things?

One source of Mr. Jefferson's small facts, not mentioned, calls for notice, for it discloses a persistent habit of his life. Col. Thomas J. Randolph writes us:

"His powers of conversation were great, yet he always turned it to subjects most familiar to those with whom he conversed, whether laborer, mechanic, or other; and if they displayed sound judgment and a knowledge of the subject, entered the information they gave under appropriate heads for reference, embodying thus a mass of facts upon the practical details of every-day life."

That this desire for information was blended, a little, with the desire to give pleasure to those he conversed with, by allowing each man to canter his own hobby, is very possible. A most intelligent and dignified Virginia matron of the old school, and famous for her *cuisine*—whose guest Mr. Jefferson often was, and whose acquaintance and friendship followed him through every step of his career—was wont to boast that he never failed to inquire with great particularity how her best dishes were compounded and cooked.   "I know this was half

to please me," she would smilingly say, " but he's a nice judge
of things, and you may depend upon it, he won't throw away
anything he learns worth knowing."

The remark about his entering information under " appropriate heads," suggests to us to say, that he observed this rule in
regard to *all* facts thought worthy of record. Thus his agricultural observations are ultimately arranged under seventeen
general heads, and these into upwards of fifty subdivisions.
Everything, even to his expense accounts, has a paged index,
made by himself. We look in vain for an illegibly scrawled
word or figure—though we shall find him on one occasion, by
and by, making all his entries, for two or three months, with
his *left* hand, owing to a broken wrist. He could, therefore,
turn at a moment's warning to any fact in his possession. It
was thus he combined his facts into systems, deduced rules and
made practical applications.

In May, 1766, Mr. Jefferson made a journey north to Annapolis, Philadelphia and New York. He was in Annapolis when
the people were celebrating the repeal of the Stamp Act. In
Philadelphia, he stopped to be inoculated for the small pox by
the celebrated Dr. Shippen. To this point, at least, he made
his journey, in a one-horse chair, and his adventures by field
and flood, equalling those which would now attend a trip to the
Rocky Mountains, are duly chronicled in a letter to Page. At
New York he put up at the same house with, and made the
acquaintance of, Elbridge Gerry,[1] a young man of about the
same age, a traveller from Massachusetts—destined to be a conspicuous co-actor in the drama of coming events.

In 1767, Mr. Jefferson, now twenty-four years old, was
introduced to the practice of the law, at the bar of the General
Court of Virginia, by " his faithful and beloved Mentor in youth,
and most affectionate friend through life," Mr. Wythe. If
sufficiently decisive indications of the attainments which he
carried with him into his profession, are not made to appear by
his success, they are furnished by his writings.

A partisan historian, who has as signally failed in depicting
the private as the public character of Mr. Jefferson, and who

---

[1] He mentions this in a letter to Gerry, June 11th, 1812, but erroneously places the
period of the visit in 1764. He cannot refer to another and *preceding* visit, for his
various memoranda in our possession clearly prove that he made none such.

apparently never hesitates to substitute a conjecture, or vague impression drawn from newspaper statements (and generally hostile ones) for facts, in regard to that private character, says : " He [Jefferson] had been educated to the law, but he had little taste for the technicalities and chicanery of that profession."[1] Literally, this is true. But the spirit of the remark, namely, that he had little taste for law practice as he found· it in the courts of Virginia, is unsupported by a particle of authority. And this conjectural compliment (for so it appears designed), at the expense of his profession, would have probably been quite as offensive to the subject of it, as those equally conjectural calumnies, from the same source, to which it was doubtless designed as some offset, in the way of establishing a claim to impartiality ![2] Mr. Jefferson was neither ignorant enough, nor prejudiced enough, to consider the fixed and adjudicated forms of English law, then practised in Virginia, " technicalities," as the same author elsewhere remarks, " in nine cases out of ten, obstacles to justice," nor fair practice under those forms, " chicanery." He loved his profession—keenly relished the study and the practice of it—and continued both with unabated zeal, until the Colonial Courts were closed by the Revolution.

His register of cases, already referred to, shows that he was employed in sixty-eight cases in 1767; in one hundred and fifteen in 1768; in one hundred and ninety-eight in 1769; in one hundred and twenty-one in 1770; in one hundred and thirty-seven in 1771; in one hundred and fifty-four in 1772; in one hundred and twenty-seven in 1773; in twenty-nine in 1774. On the 11th of August, the latter year, he gave up his business to Edmund Randolph.[3] The above being confined to the General Court, does not indicate the whole amount of his business. In one of the pocket account books, it appears, for example, that he was retained as attorney or counsel in no less than four hundred and thirty cases, in all, in 1771, and in three hundred and forty-seven in 1772. In the account book of 1771, the

---

[1] Hildreth's History of the United States, 2d series, vol. ii. p. 549.
[2] The curious reader who would see every contemporaneous, bitter, personal, and political attack on Mr. Jefferson, made in times of high party heat, as carefully preserved as the dead wasps in an entomological cabinet, will find it done *con gusto* in the pages of Hildreth.
[3] The son of Attorney-General John, and grandson of Attorney-General Sir John. Edmund was afterwards Governor of Virginia, Attorney-General and Secretary of State of the United States, etc.

annual amount of his fees to that year is given—the proportion of each fee-bill, paid and unpaid, stated—and each entry is carried out with characteristic exactitude to pence and half pence.   To enable "the profession" to catch a glimpse of the ante-Revolutionary scale of fees, we subjoin these: The "total profits" of 1767 were £293 4s. 5¼d.; those of 1768, £304 8s. 5d.; those of 1769, £370 11s.; those of 1770, £421 5s. 10¼d.   The increase during the remaining four years must have been proportionably rapid, for his executor informs us that his average annual profits, for his whole term of practice, reached three thousand dollars.   With the very low rate of fees then paid in Virginia,[1] this was a decidedly successful practice for a young lawyer, or indeed for a lawyer of any age, unless possibly with the exception of three or four of the greatest old luminaries of the bar, like Wythe, Pendleton, Peyton and John Randolph, and Nicholas.

Mr. Jefferson's marked position in his profession, admits of no question.   He was employed in important causes by the most distinguished citizens of the colony, and not unfrequently by gentlemen of standing in the other colonies and in England. Among his Virginia clients appear in the register such names as those of the Blands, Burwells, Byrds, Carters, Careys, Harrisons, Lees, Nelsons, Pages, and Randolphs.   The list embraces several Royal Councillors of State, and other crown officers— the foremost of the lowland grandees—the most prominent men of the colony in all particulars, who were not themselves lawyers.   We find him in various instances associated in the trial of causes with Mr. Wythe, Mr. Pendleton, or Peyton Randolph; and, in one case, retained as associate *counsel* with the Attorney-General, by Colonel Corbin (the Receiver-General), who himself acted as the *attorney*, in a suit brought by Ex-Governor Dinwiddie, then in England, against a citizen of Virginia.

Mr. Wirt, in his Life of Henry (page 95), says:

"I find that in January, 1773, Robert C. Nicholas, who had enjoyed the first practice at the bar, and who, by virtue of his office of Treasurer, was forced to relinquish that practice, committed, by a public advertisement, his unfinished business to Mr. Henry—a step which a man so remarkably scrupulous in the discharge

[1] The entries in the Register show this—and the same fact is stated by Henning, we think, in his Statutes at Large of Virginia.   At least there is no doubt of the fact.

of every moral duty, would not have taken had there been any incompetency on the part of his substitute."

This was not done, however, until two years after Colonel Nicholas had offered his unfinished business to Mr. Jefferson, and until the latter, after having actually taken it on his hands for a few months, relinquished it—probably from the pressure of his own practice, and, we make no doubt, in favor of, or recommending, Mr. Henry as his successor. The following is an entry from his register:

"1771, *Oct.* 31.—Robert Carter Nicholas, Esq., having retired from the bar, put his business into my hands, to be finished, about April last. Finding myself, however, under the necessity of declining it, I make no entries of cases, nor charge anything but what I actually received, which has been as follows: [Then follow the titles of a few cases, and the sums received in them.] See entries of these apart by themselves, on the cover of rough memorandum book for 1771."

It appears from this, that Mr. Wirt was mistaken as to the time of Colonel Nicholas's retirement—if he means to be understood that it took place in 1773—or else, and this is a very probable solution, Mr. Jefferson's relinquishment of Nicholas's business induced the latter to again take the closing up of it on his own hands, until he found a successor for Mr. Jefferson in Mr. Henry. The office of treasurer, which Mr. Wirt mentions as the *cause* of Mr. Nicholas's retirement, was conferred on him, we believe, in 1766.

Of Mr. Jefferson's erudition and ability as a lawyer, the most substantial proofs remain. They are to be found in his portion of the revision of the laws of Virginia—and, we may add, in the actual post of pre-eminence assigned him in that revision by such colleagues as Wythe and Pendleton—in his Reports of the Decisions of the General Court of Virginia—in his Notes on Virginia—in his written opinions and papers as Secretary of State—in his Parliamentary Manual—in his paper prepared for the use of counsel in the Batture case—in his correspondence—and in a multitude of citations and annotations, scattered through his books. Of several of the above productions, there will be occasion to speak more fully when they are reached, in the chronological order of this narrative. Taken together, no intelligent investigator will presume to deny that they show him to have been one of the most learned and discriminating lawyers of a period when wide and profound erudition was probably more common—or, at least, more universal—at the American bar than now. The law was then (Mr. Henry's case to the contrary notwithstanding) an aristocratic profession in Virginia, to which few aspired who did not possess education, if not also fortune; and to enter upon it without long and profound preparation—to expect eminence in it without Blackstone's "*lucubrationes viginti annorum*"—was a thing rarely dreamed of, unless by some such spirit as Henry, whose genius enabled him to trample on all ordinary rules. It is not to be understood, we suppose, that Mr. Henry was licensed to practise in the *superior* courts on the wonderfully short novitiate which has been named; nor is it to be supposed that even his genius, with his idle habits, ever placed him in a high rank at the Virginia bar, in any other department but that of an advocate.

Mr. Jefferson's mind and habits eminently fitted him for a great lawyer in (as the exact contrast of Henry) every other department but that of an advocate. With that grasp of understanding which at once led him to seize all the strong points in his case—with that mental discipline which taught him to readily combine them in proper order and marshal them for the best effect—with that portentous diligence in collecting and classifying facts down to a feather's weight, and in hunting precedents through whole wildernesses of books—who could be better fitted to prepare a cause for trial before bench or jury? He was disqualified from being a very successful advocate by a peculiarity in his articulation. His voice, if raised much above the loudness of ordinary conversation, began, after a few moments' effort, to "sink in his throat"—in other words, to become husky and inarticulate. Such was the reason assigned for his never speaking (beyond a few sentences at a time) before legislative and popular bodies, by Mr. Madison and Mr. Wirt.[1] The first declared that he had heard him address a court, and that he did it fluently and well. This all may be, and doubtless is true, as far as it goes; and this natural impediment may have increased a natural distaste, or incapacity, for addressing public bodies. But it was not half the physical difficulty that Demos-

[1] We have this from those who heard the declarations from their lips.

thenes, and a good many other orators, overcame—men who felt they had the gift of oratory in them (as much a *born* one as the poet's in our judgment, in spite of a great authority), and who were determined to bring it out. The structures of a great writer's and a great orator's mind, rarely coincide—or, to vary the expression, the qualities that fit for one do not fit for the other; and they rarely go together. The precision in matter and form, the sedulousness of accuracy, the condensed expression, which should belong to the former, would hang like clogs on the soaring wing of the latter. The man who has written much and well, finds it difficult to abandon himself to those careering impulses of thought and passion, without which oratory never rises to its true lyrical grandeur and its mastering sway—without which, it is but spoken essay, or reasoning thrown into declamatory forms. The powerful writer, with his pen out of his hand—his paper not spread before him—acting on a new physical base of operations, namely, his *feet*—may, after sufficient practice, state his case eloquently and reason profoundly; but few have been the instances, where he has reached the quality of true oratory.[1] And it often happens that the writer spoils the orator—that previously acquired reputation in the first line prevents its possessor from ever resorting to sufficient practice in the last. He is unwilling to speak against, or to speak down, his own reputation. A master of one of the methods of addressing men, he is not willing to exhibit himself among tyros, stammering and stumbling through a hundred or two preparatory efforts; for, but in one case out of ten thousand, does the throe end, or is the result brought forth, as many persons fancifully suppose, after half a dozen attempts.

We have wandered from the point, for Mr. Jefferson might have been an able and fluent public speaker, without being a great orator. But to the former, the same remarks apply in part—particularly those which refer to talking against one's

[1] Our definition of the word may be considered peculiar—and we will not stop to attempt it—but an example or two will sufficiently present our idea. Camille Desmoulins, when he sprang upon a table, and shouted, "brethren, shall we die like lambs in the hands of the butcher?" and led the roused populace over the Rubicon of civil war, was an *orator*. Mirabeau was an orator—and there were many such, whose names appear momentarily —now thought of like the phantasms of a terrible dream—glimmering over the black and surging wave of the French Revolution. James Otis was an orator: John Adams was, *sometimes*, and Patrick Henry *always* an orator. Logan and Red Jacket were orators. Fox was a great *debater*. The Pitts were magnificent *declaimers*. Daniel Webster was an *eloquent reasoner*.

own reputation. We shall see—we have already seen—that Mr. Jefferson became early conspicuous for marked ability, in more respects than one. He acquired an immediate reputation as an "office lawyer." His mental taste did not lie in the line of an advocate. His natural habits had not tended to fit him for it—and, in our judgment, his mental qualities were not suited to it. He was too mathematical, too precise in matter and form, too unimaginative to make a ready and felicitous public speaker—though we can conceive of particular topics on which, after the necessary training, he might have proved himself eloquent.

But for a fire, by and by to be alluded to, in which most of his books and papers perished, we should doubtless now have before us, among Mr. Jefferson's manuscripts, digests and syllabuses without number of legal authorities, beginning with his student life, and ending only when he threw up his profession. He kept a common-place book, and has himself preserved a remarkable sample of it written when he was a student, in a letter to Dr. Cooper, dated February 11th, 1814.[1] We would advise law students of the present day, who regard themselves as particularly well read in their profession, to consult that letter! His taste for the investigations of his profession—for tracing authorities—prompted him, in long after years, to do a most fortunate piece of service for his native State. To his zeal as a collector, Virginia owes the preservation of most of her earlier statutes, the records of which became scattered before, and especially during the Revolution. The diligence and labor required to make this collection—the great pains necessary to preserve its crumbling materials—and its extent and value, will be gleaned from a letter from him to Mr. Wythe, of January 16th, 1796, and from the preface to Henning's Statutes at Large of Virginia. Most of the earlier materials for the latter work were obtained from this source.

Before dismissing this topic, we are tempted to give the following letter, furnished us by Mr. George Wythe Randolph,[2] of Richmond, and believed by Mr. Jefferson's family to be hitherto unpublished. It appears in neither edition of his published

[1] And again in a letter to Major John Cartwright, June 5, 1824.
[2] A grandson of President Jefferson, being fifth son and tenth child of Gov. T. M. Randolph, of Edgehill, and his wife Martha Jefferson.

Works. The body of it was written ninety years since, and in its author's early practice. It will be read with interest by the legal profession, as furnishing the writer's idea of a proper course of law reading, and what he considered a "respectable" *starting point* in the profession ; and by others as marking out a proper course of reading for all young men. It comprises substantially the course which Mr. Madison, Mr. Monroe, and many other distinguished gentlemen pursued in their studies, under the directions of Mr. Jefferson :

MONTICELLO, *Aug. 30th,* 1814.

DEAR SIR,

I have at length found the paper of which you requested a copy. It was written near fifty years ago, for the use of a young friend whose course of reading was confided to me ; and it formed a basis for the studies of others subsequently placed under my direction, but curtailed for each in proportion to his previous acquirements and future views. I shall give it to you without change, except as to the books recommended to be read ; later publications enabling me in some of the departments of science to substitute better, for the less perfect publications which we then possessed. In this the modern student has great advantage. I proceed to the copy.

THOMAS JEFFERSON TO BERNARD MOORE.

Before you enter on the study of the law a sufficient groundwork must be laid. For this purpose an acquaintance with the Latin and French languages is absolutely necessary. The former you have ; the latter must now be acquired. Mathematics and Natural Philosophy are so useful in the most familiar occurrences of life, and are so peculiarly engaging and delightful as would induce every one to wish an acquaintance with them. Besides this, the faculties of the mind, like the members of the body, are strengthened and improved by exercise. Mathematical reasonings and deductions are therefore a fine preparation for investigating the abstruse speculations of the law. In these and the analogous branches of science the following books are recommended :

Mathematics.—Beyzout, Cours de Mathématiques—the best for a student ever published ; Montucla or Bossut, Histoire des Mathématiques.

Astronomy.—Ferguson, and le Monnier or de Lalande.

Geography.—Pinkerton.

Nat. Philosophy.—Joyce's Scientific Dialogues ; Martin's Philosophia Britannica, Muschenbroek's Cours de Physique.

This foundation being laid, you may enter regularly on the study of the law, taking with it such of its kindred sciences as will contribute to eminence in its attainment. The principal of these are Physics, Ethics, Religion, Natural Law, Belles Lettres. Criticism, Rhetoric, and Oratory. The carrying on several studies at a time is attended with advantage. Variety relieves the mind as well as the eye, palled with too long attention to a single object, but, with both, transitions from one object to another may be so frequent and transitory as to leave no impression. The mean is therefore to be steered, and a competent space of time allotted to each branch of study. Again, a great inequality is observable in the vigor of the mind at different periods of the day. Its powers at these periods should therefore be attended to, in marshalling the business of the day. For these reasons I should recommend the following distribution of your time:

Till Eight o'clock in the morning, employ yourself in Physical Studies.

Ethics, Religion, natural and sectarian, and Natural Law, reading the following books:

Agriculture.—Dickson's Husbandry of the Ancients; Tull's Horse-hoeing Husbandry; Lord Kames' Gentleman Farmer; Young's Rural Economy; Hale's Body of Husbandry; De Serres's Théâtre d'Agriculture.

Chemistry.—Lavoisier, Conversations in Chemistry.

Anatomy—John and James Bell's Anatomy.

Zoology.—Abrégé du Système de la nature de Linné par Gilibert; Manuel d'Histoire Naturelle by Blumenbach, Buffon, including Montbeiliard and La Cepède; Wilson's American Ornithology.

Botany.—Barton's Elements of Botany; Turton's Linneus; Persoon's Synopsis Plantarum.

Ethics and Natural Religion.—Locke's Essay; Locke's Conduct of the Mind in the Search after Truth; Stewart's Philosophy of the Human Mind; Enfield's History of Philosophy; Condorcet, Progrès de l'Esprit Humain; Cicero de Officiis, Tusculanae, de Senectute, Somnia Scipionis; Senecæ Philosophica; Hutchinson's Introduction to Moral Philosophy; Lord Kames' Natural Religion; Traité Elémentaire de Morale et Bonheur; La Sagesse de Charron.

Religion Sectarian.—Bible: New Testament, Commentaries on them by Middleton in his Works, and by Priestley in his Corruptions of Christianity and Early Opinions of Christ; The Sermons of Sterne, Massillon and Bourdaloue.

Natural Law.—Vattel, Droit des Gens; Rayneval, Institutions du Droit de la Nature et des Gens.

From Eight to Twelve read Law.

The general course of this reading may be formed on the following grounds. Lord Coke has given us the first views of the whole body of law worthy now of being studied; for so much of the admirable work of Bracton is now obsolete that the students should turn to it occasionally only, when tracing the history of particular portions of the law. Coke's Institutes are a perfect digest of the law in his day. After this, new laws were added by the Legislature, and new developments of the old law by the judges, until they had become so voluminous as to require a new digest. This was ably executed by Matthew Bacon, although unfortunately under an alphabetical instead of analytical arrangement of matter. The same process of new laws and new decisions on the old laws going on, called at length for the same operation again, and produced the inimitable Commentaries of Blackstone.[1] In the department of the Chancery, a similar progress has taken place.

---

[1] This must be understood, with some qualification, as applying to the skillful *manner* in which Blackstone handled his subject. He was not, as we shall again and again have occasion to see, a favorite of Mr. Jefferson as a law expounder—as authority—at least on certain great leading theories he maintains of the British Constitution. Mr. Jefferson looked upon him among law writers, as he did on Hume among historians—as a man who brought great abilities and an admirable style and manner to the support of *unsound political* principles. Mansfield, as a law writer, was included in the same category. Coke was his great favorite.

Lord Kames has given us the first digest of the principles of that branch of our jurisprudence, more valuable for the arrangement of matter than for its exact conformity with the English decisions. The reporters from the early times of that branch to that of the same Matthew Bacon are well digested, but alphabetically also in the abridgment of the cases in equity, the second volume of which is said to be done by him. This was followed by a number of able reporters, of which Fonblanque has given us a summary digest by commentaries on the text of the earlier work, ascribed to Ballow, entitled 'A Treatise on Equity.' The course of reading recommended then in these two branches of law is the following:

Common Law.—Coke's Institutes; Select Cases from the Subsequent Reporters to the time of Matthew Bacon; Bacon's Abridgment; Select Cases from the Subsequent Reporters to the Present Day; Select Tracts on Law, among which those of Baron Gilbert are all of the first merit; the Virginia Laws; Reports on them.

Chancery.—Lord Kames' Principles of Equity, 3d edition; Select Cases from the Chancery Reporters to the time of Matthew Bacon; the Abridgment of Cases in Equity; Select Cases from the Subsequent Reporters to the Present Day; Fonblanque's Treatise of Equity.

Blackstone's Commentaries (Tucker's edition) as the best perfect digest of both branches of law.

In reading the Reporters, enter in a common-place book every case of value, condensed into the narrowest compass possible, which will admit of presenting distinctly the principles of the case. This operation is doubly useful, insomuch as it obliges the student to seek out the pith of the case, and habituates him to a condensation of thought, and to an acquisition of the most valuable of all talents, that of never using two words where one will do. It fixes the case, too, more indelibly in the mind.

From Twelve to One read Politics.

Politics, General.—Locke on Government, Sidney on Government, Priestly's First Principles of Government, Review of Montesquieu's Spirit of Laws. De Lolme sur le constitution d'Angleterre; De Burgh's Political Disquisitions; Hatsell's Precedents of the House of Commons; Select Parliamentary Debates of England and Ireland; Chipman's Sketches of the Principles of Government; The Federalist.

Political Economy.—Say's Economie Politique; Malthus on the principles of Population; de Tracy's work on Political Economy, now about to be printed, 1814.

In the Afternoon read History.

History, Ancient.—The Greek and Latin Originals; Select histories from the Universal History; Gibbon's Decline of the Roman Empire; Histoire ancienne de Millot.

Modern.—Histoire moderne de Millot; Russel's History of Modern Europe; Robertson's Charles V.

English.—The original historians, *to wit:* The History of Edward 2nd, by E. F.; Habington's Edward 4th; More's Richard 3rd; Lord Bacon's Henry 7th; Lord Herbert's Henry 8th; Goodwin's Henry 8th, Edward 7th, Mary; Camden's Eliza-

beth, James, Ludlow; Macaulay [Catharine]; Fox; Belsham; Baxter's History of England; Hume republicanized and abridged; Robertson's History of Scotland.
American.—Robertson's History of America; Gordon's History of the Independence of the U. S.; Ramsay's History of the American Revolution; Burk's History of Virginia; Continuation of do., by Jones and Girardin, nearly ready for the press.

From Dark to Bedtime.

Belles Lettres; Criticism; Rhetoric; Oratory, *to wit:*

Belles Lettres.—Read the best of the poets, epic, didactic, dramatic, pastoral, lyric, etc.; but among these, Shakspeare must be singled out by one who wishes to learn the full powers of the English language. Of him we must declare as Horace did of the Grecian models, 'Vos exemplaria Græca nocturnâ versate manu, versate diurnâ.'

Criticism.—Lord Kames' Elements of Criticism; Tooke's Diversions of Purley. Of Bibliographical criticism, the Edinburgh Review furnishes the finest models extant.

Rhetoric.—Blair's Rhetoric; Sheridan on Elocution; Mason on Poetic and Prosaic Numbers.

Oratory.—This portion of time (borrowing some of the afternoon when the days are long and the nights short) is to be applied also to acquiring the art of writing and speaking correctly by the following exercises: Criticise the style of any book whatsoever, committing the criticism to writing. Translate into the different styles, *to wit,* the elevated, the middling, and the familiar. Orators and poets will furnish subjects of the first, historians of the second, and epistolary and comic writers of the third. Undertake, at first, short compositions, as themes, letters, etc., paying great attention to the elegance and correctness of your language. Read the orations of Demosthenes and Cicero; analyze these orations, and examine the correctness of the disposition, language, figures, state of the cases, arguments, etc.; read good samples also of English eloquence. Some of these may be found in Small's American Speaker, and some in Carey's Criminal Recorder; in which last the defence of Eugene Aram is distinguished as a model of logic, condensation of matter and classical purity of style. Exercise yourself afterwards in preparing orations on feigned cases. In this, observe rigorously the disposition of Blair into introduction, narration, etc. Adapt your language to the several parts of the oration, and suit your arguments to the audience before which it is supposed to be delivered. This is your last and most important exercise. No trouble should therefore be spared. If you have any person in your neighborhood engaged in the same study, take each of you different sides of the same cause, and prepare pleadings according to the custom of the bar, where the plaintiff opens, the defendant answers, and the plaintiff replies. It will further be of great service to pronounce your oration (having before you only short notes to assist the memory) in the presence of some person who may be considered as your judge.

NOTE.—Under each of the preceding heads, the books are to be read in the order in which they are named. These by no means constitute the whole of what might be usefully read in each of these branches of science. The mass of excellent works going more into detail is great indeed. But those here noted will enable the *student to* select for himself such others of detail as may suit his particular views *and dispositions.* They will give him a respectable, an useful and satisfactory degree of knowledge in these branches, and will themselves form a valuable and sufficient library for a lawyer who is at the same time a lover of science."

So far the paper, which I send you, not for its merit, for it betrays sufficiently its juvenile date, but because you have asked it. Your own experience in the more modern practice of the law will enable you to give it more conformity with the present course ; and I know you will receive it kindly with all its imperfections, as an evidence of my great respect for your wishes, and of the sentiments of esteem and friendship, of which I tender you sincere assurances.

THOMAS JEFFERSON.

As a sequel to this letter, the reader will do well to examine those of January 16th, 1814, to Dr. Thomas Cooper, and of February 26th, 1821, to Dabney Terrell (published in the Congress edition of Jefferson's Works), in regard to a course of law studies. Another course of reading—one intended particularly for *females*, will be found (in the same edition) in a letter to N. Burwell, March 14th, 1818. This last, however, will be published in this work, when reached in its chronological order.

Soon after Mr. Jefferson attained his majority, he had been put in the nomination of justices for his county, and at the first general election thereafter—namely, in 1769, was chosen a Member of the House of Burgesses. This body convened in May that year. Lord Botetourt had succeeded Governor Fauquier, and this was the first session called by him. On the reception of the Governor's speech, it was customary to move resolutions, as heads for an address in reply. At the request of Mr. Pendleton, Mr. Jefferson drew the resolutions, and the House accepted them. He was then placed on the committee with Mr. Pendleton, Mr. Nicholas, and some others, to prepare the address. His colleagues desired him to make the draft, and he did so; but Colonel Nicholas objected to it, that it "pursued *too* closely the diction of the resolutions, and that their subjects were not sufficiently amplified." Nicholas was then requested by his colleagues "to draw one more at large, which he did with amplification enough," and it was accepted. This afforded some mortification to the new legislator![1]

[1] Jefferson to Wirt, August 5, 1815.

The House proceeded to pass spirited resolutions in regard to the joint resolutions and address to the King which were adopted by the British Parliament, in February, on the subject of the proceedings in Massachusetts. The Burgesses re-asserted the exclusive right of self-taxation—a right to petition for a redress of grievances, and to procure the concurrence of other Colonies therein—the latter, the very measure on the part of Massachusetts, which had most particularly incurred the reprobation of Parliament. They also remonstrated in becoming terms against the recommendation of Parliament to the King to transport persons accused of treason in the Colonies to England for trial, under the provisions of the statute of 35th of Henry VIII.

Lord Botetourt, though liberal in his views as a politician, and a most amiable man, did not even wait for an official notification of these decided proceedings before he dissolved the Assembly. The following day the members convened at the Apollo—the long room of the Raleigh tavern—and entered into an association, pledging themselves, during the continuance of the act for raising a revenue in America, not to import, nor, after the ensuing 1st of September, purchase various kinds of British merchandise, which they specified ; and they recommended the same course to their constituents.[1] Among the signatures to this instrument were those of Washington, R. H. Lee, Henry, Jefferson, Peyton and Richard Randolph, R. C. Nicholas, and Archibald Cary. It affords a marked proof of the vigor with which the pulse of popular patriotism beat in Virginia, at this epoch, that every member of the dissolved House who signed the association, was reëlected.[2]

At this his first session, Mr. Jefferson introduced a bill giving owners the right, which the laws did not then allow them, to manumit their slaves. It was defeated, nor was such a right given before 1782.

On the 1st day of February, 1770, that accident occurred already hinted at, which deprived Mr. Jefferson of the books and papers of his early life. The family mansion at Shadwell, where he resided with his mother, brother, and unmarried sisters, was burned to the ground, with nearly all its contents.

[1] Burk's History of Virginia, vol. iii. p. 345, note.
[2] Jefferson's Memoir.

He wrote Page that he lost "every paper he had in the world, and almost every book."[1] He said the cost of the books *burned* was equal to two hundred pounds sterling, and he "would to God it had been the money, and then it had never cost him a sigh." But the letter is filled with quite the usual amount of those facetious sallies which mark his earlier correspondence with the same gentleman. Most of his father's little library, and his papers also, perished in the flames—a matter more to be deplored than the preceding, because the materials of *his* papers cannot be replaced. Mr. Jefferson used to tell, in after years, with great glee, an anecdote connected with this fire. He was absent from home when it occurred, and a slave arrived out of breath to inform him of the disaster. After learning the general destruction, he inquired: "But were none of my books saved?" "No, master," was the reply, "but" (with a look of truly African satisfaction), "*we saved the fiddle!*"

Mr. Jefferson had fortunately begun, the preceding year, the preparation of a residence for himself on the summit of Monticello. It appears from the garden book, that in the spring he had planted a great variety of fruit trees on the southeast slope of the hill, and towards fall erected a brick story and a half building, containing one good-sized single room—the same structure which now forms the southeastern "pavilion" (at the extremity of the south "terrace") of the mansion. On the destruction of Shadwell he removed thither, the rest of the family finding cramped quarters in the overseer's house.

In 1770, Lord North became First Lord of the Treasury, and he carried a bill through Parliament repealing the duties imposed by the Act of 1767 on American imports, except tea. The tea duty was retained by a decisive vote avowedly to maintain the principle of the right of Parliament to tax the Colonies. Yet this concession—perhaps construed into a permanent surrender of all but the principle—seems to have partially lulled to sleep in Virginia the heroic spirit which dictated the reso-

---

[1] Jefferson to John Page, Feb. 21, 1770. This, with all the earlier letters to Page, appear in the Congress, but not in his grandson's edition of his works. They were first given by Professor Tucker.

lutions of the House of Burgesses in 1769. Mr. Jefferson said of the events between 1770 and 1773, in his Memoir :

"Nothing of particular excitement occurring for a considerable time, our countrymen seemed to fall into a state of insensibility to our situation ; the duty on tea, not yet repealed, and the declaratory act of a right in the British Parliament, to bind us by their laws in all cases whatsoever, still suspended over us."

But according to the historian Burk, this "insensibility" was very far from being complete—and implied anything but acquiescence in the "principle" reässerted by Parliament.[1] · It would seem rather the sullen lull of the tempest, when the elements pause as if to gather strength for a fiercer struggle.

The pocket account book for 1771, shows that Mr. Jefferson was then busy in forming plans for his future residence and grounds—and that like most other young projectors at that precise point (particularly where they possess the means, and perhaps we should add, when they are on the point of marriage), he was tracing a good many fanciful schemes, sure never to be carried out. From the place (that is, in the book) where they appear, they were not probably written at home ; and it is easy to guess they were the cogitations of unfilled hours on circuit— perhaps to wear off a dull evening at a country tavern. Here are some specimens :

"BURYING PLACE.

"Choose out for a burying place some unfrequented vale in the park, where is 'no sound to break the stillness but a brook, that bubbling winds among the weeds ; no mark of any human shape that had been there, unless the skeleton of some poor wretch, who sought that place out to despair and die in.' Let it be among ancient and venerable oaks ; intersperse some gloomy evergreens. The area circular, about sixty feet diameter, encircled with an untrimmed hedge of cedar, or of stone wall with a holly hedge on it in the form below. In the centre of it erect a small Gothic temple of antique appearance. Appropriate one half to the use of my own family, the other of strangers, servants, etc. Erect pedestals with urns, etc., and proper inscriptions. The passage between the walls, four feet wide. On the grave of a favorite and faithful servant might be a pyramid erected of the rough rockstone ; the pedestal made plain to receive an inscription. Let the exit of the spiral at (a)[2] look on a small and distant part of the Blue Mountains. In the middle of the temple an altar, the sides of turf, the top a plain stone. Very little light, perhaps none at all, save only the feeble ray of an half-extinguished lamp."

[Here is inserted the epitaph for Mr. Jefferson's sister, already given.]

[1] See Burk's History of Virginia, vol. iii. p. 360, note.
[2] On margin is a spiral of two equi-distant lines just completing one volution.

"AT THE SPRING ON THE NORTH SIDE OF THE PARK.

"A few feet below the spring level the ground forty or fifty feet square. Let the water fall from the spring in the upper level over a terrace in the form of a cascade. Then conduct it along the foot of the terrace to the western side of the level, where it may fall into a cistern under a temple, from which it may go off by the western border till it falls over another terrace at the northern or lower side. Let the temple be raised two feet for the first floor of stone. Under this is the cistern, which may be a bath or anything else. The first story arches on three sides; the back or western side being close because the hill there comes down, and also to carry up stairs on the outside. The second story to have a door on one side, a spacious window in each of the other sides. The rooms each eight feet cube; with a small table and couple of chairs. The roof may be Chinese, Grecian, or in the taste of the Lantern of Demosthenes at Athens.

"The ground just about the spring smoothed and turfed; close to the spring a sleeping figure reclined on a plain marble slab, surrounded with turf; on the slab this inscription :

> ' Hujus nympha loci, sacri custodia fontis
> Dormio, dum blandæ sentio murmur aquæ
> Parce meum, quisquis tangis cava marmora, somnum
> Rumpere; si bibas, sive lavere, tace.'

"Near the spring also inscribe on stone, or a metal plate fastened to a tree, these lines : 'Beatus ille qui procul negotiis, Ut prisca gens mortalium, Paterna rura bobus exercet suis, solutus omni foenore; Forumque vitat et superba civium Potentiorum limina. Libet jacere modo sub antiqua ilice, modo in tenaci gramine : Labuntur altis interim ripis aquæ ; Queruntur in silvis aves; Fontesque lymphis obstrepunt manantibus, somnos quod invitet leves.' Plant trees of beech and aspen about it. Open a vista to the mill-pond, river, road, etc. *Quere,* If a view of the neighboring town would have a good effect? Intersperse in this and every other part of the ground (except the environs of the burying-ground) abundance of jessamine, honeysuckle, sweet-brier, etc. Under the temple, an Æolian harp, where it may be concealed as well as covered from the weather.

"This would be better.

"The ground above the spring being very steep, dig into the hill and form a cave or grotto. Build up the sides and arch with stiff clay. Cover this with moss. Spangle it with translucent pebbles from Hanovertown, and beautiful shells from the shore at Burwell's ferry. Pave the floor with pebbles. Let the spring enter at a corner of the grotto, pretty high up the side, and trickle down, or fall by a spout into a basin, from which it may pass off through the grotto. The figure will be better placed in this. Form a couch of moss. The English inscription will then be proper.

> ' Nymph of the grot, these sacred springs I keep,
> And to the murmur of these waters sleep ;
> Ah! spare my slumbers! gently tread the cave !
> And drink in silence, or in silence lave !'

"THE GROUND IN GENERAL.

"Thin the trees. Cut out stumps and undergrowth. Remove old trees and other rubbish, except where they may look well. Cover the whole with grass. Inter sperse jessamine, honeysuckle, sweet-brier, and even hardy flowers which may not require attention. Keep in it deer, rabbits, peacocks, guinea poultry. pigeons, etc. Let it be an asylum for hares, squirrels, pheasants, partridges, and every other wild animal(except those of prey). Court them to it, by laying food for them in proper places. Procure a buck-elk, to be, as it were, monarch of the wood; but keep him shy, that his appearance may not lose its effect by too much familiarity. A buffalo might be confined also. Inscriptions in various places, on the bark of trees òr metal plates, suited to the character or expression of the particular spot.

" Benches or seats of rock or turf.

"THE OPEN GROUND ON THE WEST—A SHRUBBERY.

" *Shrubs.*—(Not exceeding a growth of ten feet).—Alder—Bastard indigo—Flowering Amorpha — Barberry—Cassioberry—Cassine—Chinquapin — Jersey-tea, F. Ceanothus—Dwarf cherry, F. Cerasus, 5—Clethra—Cockspur hawthorn, or haw, Crataegus, 4—Laurel—Scorpion Senna, Emerus—Hazel—Althea F.—Callicarpa— Rose—Wild honeysuckle—Sweet-brier—Joy.

" *Trees.*—Lilac — Wild Cherry — Dogwood — Redbud—Horse-chestnut—Catalpa — Magnolia—Mulberry—Locust—Honeysuckle—Jessamine—Elder—Poison oak— Haw.

" *Climbing Shrubbery Plants.*—Trumpet-flower—Jasmine—Honeysuckle.

" *Evergreens.*—Holly—Juniper—Laurel—Magnolia—Yew.

" *Hardy Perennial Flowers.*—Snapdragon — Daisy—Larkspur — Gilliflower—Sunflower—Lily — Mallow—Flower-de-luce — Everlasting pea — Piony — Poppy — Pasque flower—Goldy lock, Trollius—Anemone—Lily of the valley—Primrose— Periwinkle—Violet—Flag.

On the 1st day of January, 1772, Mr. Jefferson was married to Mrs. Martha Skelton, widow of Bathurst Skelton, Esquire, and daughter of John Wayles of "The Forest," in Charles City county.[1] Mr. Wayles was born in Lancaster, England, in 1715. He was three times married, and his last wife was Mrs. Martha Epes (her maiden name was Eppes), widow of Lewellin Epes, of Bermuda Hundred. Martha Wayles, the issue of this union, was born in 1749, and was married to Bathurst Skelton, Novem-

[1] Mr. Lossing, in his very interesting Field Book of the Revolution (vol. ii. p. 443) gives a fac-simile of Mr. Jefferson's marriage license-bond, drawn up in his own handwriting, which the former found in a bundle of old papers in Charles City Court House, while searching for records of Revolutionary events. As a curiosity to a generation, to most of whom instruments of this kind (intended to prevent the solemnization of illegal marriages) are obsolete, we transcribe it :

" Know all men by these presents, that we, Thomas Jefferson and Francis Eppes, are held and firmly bound to our sovereign lord the king, his heirs and successors, in the sum of fifty pounds current money of Virginia, to the paiment of which well and truly to be made we bind ourselves jointly and severally, our joint and several heirs, executors and administrators, in witness whereof we have hereto set our hands and seals this twenty-third day of December, in the year of our Lord one thousand seven hundred and seventy-one. The condition of the above obligation is such, that if there be no lawful cause to obstruct a marriage intended to be had and solemnized between the above bound Thomas Jefferson and Martha Skelton, of the County of Charles City, widow, for which a license is desired, then this obligation is to be null and void, otherwise to remain in full force.

"FRANCIS EPPES."   "THOMAS JEFFERSON.

ber 20th, 1766. Mr. Skelton was born June, 1744, and died September 30th, 1768. John Skelton, their only issue, died in infancy.[1]

Mr. Wayles was a lawyer of extensive reputation and practice. Mr. Jefferson remarks, in his Memoir, that he was introduced to the latter "more by his great industry, punctuality, and practical readiness, than by eminence in the science of his profession"—that " he was a most agreeable companion, full of pleasantry and good humor, and welcomed in every society." By each of his wives he had a daughter; and these were married respectively to Francis Eppes (the signer of the preceding license-bond, father of John W. Eppes who married Maria, daughter of Thomas Jefferson) and Fulwar Skipwith, afterwards American Consul-General in France, etc. The youngest daughter, Mrs. Skelton, left a widow when scarcely advanced beyond her girlhood, was distinguished for her beauty, her accomplishments, and her solid merit. In person, she was a little above medium height, slightly but exquisitely formed. Her complexion was brilliant—her large expressive eyes of the richest shade of hazel—her luxuriant hair of the finest tinge of auburn. She walked, rode, and danced, with admirable grace and spirit—sung, and played the spinet and harpsichord (the musical instruments of the Virginia ladies of that day) with uncommon skill. The more solid parts of her education had not been neglected. She was also well read and intelligent; conversed agreeably; possessed excellent sense and a lively play of fancy; and had a frank, warm-hearted, and somewhat impulsive disposition. Last, not least, she had already proved herself a true daughter of the Old Dominion in the department of housewifery.[2] With such traits—with rank and wealth (if the last can be supposed to have had any influence on the men of the olden time!) it is not wonderful that Mrs. Skelton was a favorite

---

[1] We glean these details from records, lying before us, in the handwriting of Thomas Jefferson, and furnished by his family.

[2] We suppose very few need be told that nowhere on earth are these qualities so necessary, or do they display themselves to so good purpose, as in a great household of slaves; and in Virginia, anciently and to a considerable extent now, the mistress of the household supervises a certain class of affairs for the whole plantation. The sick slave, the unfortunate slave in any particular, relies on her intervention—her constant kindly offices—and he never fails to receive them. She is apt, therefore, to be practically the busiest slave on the plantation. Mrs. Skelton had been trained to be what is called a business woman. Even after her marriage, she methodically kept her household accounts. Many of these are yet extant, written out accurately, and in a neat hand.

with the other sex—that her hand was sought by wooers far and near.

Tradition has preserved one anecdote of the contest. It has two renderings, and the reader may choose between them. The first is, that two of Mr. Jefferson's rivals happened to meet on Mrs. Skelton's door-stone. They were shown into a room from which they heard her harpsichord and voice, accompanied by Mr. Jefferson's violin and voice, in the passages of a touching song. They listened for a stanza or two. Whether something in the words, or in the tones of the singers appeared suggestive to them, tradition does not say, but it does aver that they took their hats and retired, to return no more on the same errand! The other, and we think less probable version of the story, is, that the three met on the door-stone, and *agreed* that they would "take turns," and that the interviews should be made decisive; and that by lot, or otherwise, Mr. Jefferson led off; and that then, during his trial, they heard the music that they concluded settled the point!

Great were the festivities at the Forest at the bridal. It is to be supposed the Rev. Mr. Davis, the officiating clergyman, tied the knot effectually; but the Rev. W. Coutts (both of them being of the Established Church) was present, and shared, at least, in an equal fee! Douceurs to fiddlers and servants occupy a page of that never silent witness the pocket account-book! The bride and bridegroom soon set out for Monticello— and they were destined to meet some not exactly amusing adventures by the way. A manuscript of their oldest daughter (Mrs. Randolph), furnished us by one of her grand-daughters, says:

"They left the Forest after a fall of snow, light then, but increasing in depth as they advanced up the country. They were finally obliged to quit the carriage and proceed on horseback. Having stopped for a short time at Blenheim, where an overseer only resided, they left it at sunset to pursue their way through a mountain track rather than a road, in which the snow lay from eighteen inches to two feet deep, having eight miles to go before reaching Monticello.[1] They arrived late at night, the fires all out and the servants retired to their own houses for the night. The horrible dreariness of such a house, at the end of such a journey, I have often heard both relate."

[1] Blenheim was the seat of Colonel Carter, and was, as stated in the text, eight miles from Monticello, or, to emulate the accuracy of *Mr. Jefferson's* "table of distances," its gate was 8·01 miles distant from his house.

The only part of the house then habitable was the little pavilion already mentioned. These written recollections ought not to have stopped just at this point—and we will complete them from the oral ones of those who often heard the sequel from Mrs. Randolph's and Mr. Jefferson's own lips. Part of a bottle of wine, found on a shelf behind some books, had to serve the new-married couple both for fire and supper. Tempers too sunny to be ruffled by many ten times as serious annoyances in after life, now found but sources of diversion in these ludicrous *contre-temps*, and the "horrible dreariness" was lit up with song, and merriment, and laughter! An entry in the garden book, immediately after (January 25th), states that the snow was three feet deep, and mentions it as the deepest ever seen in Albemarle.

Mr. Wayles, Mr. Jefferson's father-in-law, died in May, 1773. The latter says, in his Memoir: "the portion which came on that event to Mrs. Jefferson, after the debts should be paid, which were very considerable, was about equal to my own patrimony,' and consequently doubled the ease of our circumstances." Colonel Randolph writes us these further particulars —some of them embracing a period considerably in advance:

"He [Mr. Jefferson] inherited from his father 1,900 acres of land, and some negroes. He commenced the practice of the law soon after he came of age. When he married in his twenty-ninth year, he had increased his estate to 5,000 acres, all paid for. His accounts show a receipt of $3,000 a year from his practice at the bar, and $2,000 from his farms, a large income at that day. The death of his father-in-law ensuing soon after his marriage, he acquired a large addition to his estate, but the share of debt which fell to him was £3,749 12s. He sold property immediately to pay it. The payments for this property were made in paper money which he deposited in the Loan Office, and received it back again at a depreciation out to him, of one to forty. He sold again in 1785² and 1792 to discharge the debt with its accumulated interest. This swept nearly half of his estate."

The nineteen hundred acres left him were among the finest lands in Virginia—embracing his father's home farm. He

¹ This word, to express the precise fact, ought to be *property* instead of *patrimony.* Mr. Jefferson was prone to underrate or keep out of sight his own success in business. Thus he wrote a gentleman in 1800: "that his property was all patrimonial, excepting about seven or eight hundred pounds' worth of land," purchased and paid for by himself. Now this was literally true in respect to his lands, and perhaps all his possessions. But in presenting such a view, he deducted all the *losses* of his life from *his earnings* (at least to the extent of those earnings), and then only gave the *balance* remaining on the side of the latter, to show what he had *acquired.*
² We think this should be 1787.

inherited probably about thirty slaves. The precise number in 1774 was fifty-two.[1] His wife inherited about forty thousand acres of land, and one hundred and thirty-five slaves. The land included Poplar Forest, in Bedford county, a favorite estate and occasional residence of Mr. Jefferson's to the time of his death—Byrd or Elk-Hill, on the James, near the junction of the Rivanna, which we shall hereafter find associated with some disagreeable Revolutionary memories—and other farms called Indian Camp, Angola, Guinea, Bridge-quarter, Liggon's, Forest, etc.

This seems a proper occasion to make some inquiry in respect to his early character as a business man, and to his early providence in money matters. That he could acquire has been seen; that he was precise and methodical in keeping accounts has also been seen. As would be expected from the latter trait, he was habitually punctual in all business engagements. But did he lack judgment in buying and selling property and making investments, as might certainly be suspected from the history of his British debts? This, too, has been a constant allegation or insinuation of a certain class of his foes, in his after-life. They dubbed him with the appellation of "Philosopher," and then of course, attached to him the popular derisive idea of a "philosopher," namely, a person of too sublimated mind to understand *common* affairs, or to possess any judgment in such every day practical matters as buying and selling. The ready anecdotists to be found in every political circle, and the ingenious newspaper paragraphists, did not fail to adduce practical examples of this want of what our countrymen generally comprehensively sum up in the words "common sense." Curious were the marvels narrated! Endless were the "Philosopher's" absurdities! To say nothing about *dry-docks*, he once fairly built a *dry* mill; that is, finding a convenient gorge, having a sufficient fall (as it was on a steep hill-side) and there being a nice place to build the dam and convenient materials, he did build a dam and an expensive mill, never once stopping to think that not a drop of water flowed through the gorge! Was this story a little incredible of any person not in the worst ward of a madhouse? Nothing is incredible of a "philosopher!"

---

[1] His brother, Randolph Jefferson, inherited an estate on the James, called Snowden, and some slaves.

If Mr. Jefferson ever did build a dry mill, or anything else as chimerical, we stipulate the reader shall be informed of it, and we beg him not to arrive at the conclusion that our subject was a fool or a madman, until he receives this proof! We have now but to do with his early life, though it must be conceded early business habits and capacity are apt to be lasting. We have seen that without the help of any "speculations," or a rise in property, he contrived to about double a handsome estate before he was thirty years old, and to put himself in the receipt of a regular income of $5,000. We shall hereafter see that his losses in paying his British debts grew out of inevitable circumstances, which no financial sagacity could foresee or avert. He was successful in farming and in his law practice, the only kinds of business in which he ever importantly engaged. No dollar of his gains was wasted or unwisely invested, unless adding to his lands at the common prices, was an unwise investment. He carried his accomplished and wealthy wife to a residence which would not be too large, or too elegant, in any particular, for the porter's lodge of a modern fine establishment. He drove as yet but two horses and a phaeton, though the grandees drove six, and the middlemen four. It was this modest vehicle that stuck in the snow when he was bringing home his bride! If, with his head full of the Leasowes, and Pope's grotto, and *marriage*, he devised some very fanciful improvements for his grounds, he did not carry them out. In a word, it is impossible for any one, up to this period, and for years to come, to point to any foolish venture or improper expense. His personal expenses of every kind for a period of upwards of thirty years, as exhibited in his account books,[1] afford a better criterion of his prudence, or the contrary, in that respect, than can be derived from marvellous stories floating through newspapers without the sanction of anybody's authority. Those expenses serve to confirm the impressions entertained by his family, and the entire circle of personal friends who knew him best: and these are, that he was generous and liberal without being profuse, and exact without a trace of sordidness. His friends always remarked that he was peculiarly a well-bred man in his expenses,

---

[1] And we have read *every entry* they contain.

that he intuitively adapted them with a nice discrimination to the occasion and to his own position.

We had like to have forgotten one expensive taste of his younger years—that for fine horses, and it lasted through his life—or rather it would have been an expensive taste, had he ruined his favorites often by mismanagement, or been afflicted with the mania for changing them, or neglected to breed a considerable portion of them for his own use. He rode and drove magnificent horses. When younger, he was finical in their treatment. When his saddle-horse was led out, if there was a spot on him that did not shine as faultlessly as a mirror, he rubbed it with a white pocket-handkerchief, and if this was soiled, the groom was reprimanded. His decided preference was for the Virginia race-horse; he did not ride, and was scarcely willing to drive, any other. Two or three pages of his farm book are devoted to the pedigrees of his choicer ones. He usually kept half a dozen brood mares of high quality: and we shall find among Lord Cornwallis's victorious achievements in Virginia, the carrying off of all his serviceable brood mares, and the butchering of their foals! Though Mr. Jefferson was no turfman, and though, as has been said, he never ran but a single race, he retained the partiality of a Virginian for this sport. He rarely lost a convenient opportunity of witnessing a promising race. When President of the United States, he was not a few times seen on the contiguous race-courses. As riding-horses, he desired not only powerful, but fleet and high mettled animals, even though the latter quality was obtained at the expense of a tameless temper. Colonel Randolph writes:

" A bold and fearless rider, you saw at a glance from his easy and confident seat, that he was master of his horse—which was usually the fine blood horse of Virginia. The only impatience of temper he ever exhibited, was with his horse, which he subdued to his will by a fearless application of the whip on the slightest manifestation of restiveness. He retained to the last his fondness for riding on horseback; he rode within three weeks of his death, when from disease, debility and age, he mounted with difficulty. He rode with confidence, and never permitted a servant to accompany him. He was fond of solitary rides and musing, and said that the presence of a servant annoyed him."

This aversion to the ordinary Virginia custom of being followed by a servant, will be found strikingly illustrated hereafter.

Until after mid-life, he rarely drew rein for broken ground; and when in haste, unhesitatingly dashed through the Rivanna, even when the usually quiet stream was swollen into a wide and rapid river by the rain. Instances of his fearless horsemanship, and anecdotes of his superb horses, "Cucullin," "The General," "Wildair," "Caractacus," "Tarquin," "Diomed," "Arcturus," "Jacobin," "Celer," "Eagle," etc., are yet rife in family recollection and tradition. The fleet, fiery, but gentle-tempered Eagle was the last, and was ridden by him when he was so feeble that he required assistance to mount him, even from the terrace side, which was on a level with the horse's back. Yet this animal was so spirited, that when a young kinsman of Mr. Jefferson's rode him with a company to meet Lafayette, at his visit to Monticello in 1825, the brave old horse became so ungovernably excited by the approaching roll of drum and trumpet—bounding and caracoling in the air—that the *young* rider was fain to fairly turn tail and retire.

On one occasion, when Mr. Jefferson was old and decrepit—after the last accident to his wrists—a messenger arrived to inform him that a grandson had met with a disaster, and lay seriously injured at Charlottesville. The weather was dark and lowering, night was setting in, and he was more than usually feeble. He directed Eagle to be brought to the door. His family entreated him not to set out, at least on horseback, at such a time; but his order was repeated in a tone which brooked no further opposition. The moment he was in the saddle, he struck the noble horse, which bounded forward at full run. His family held their breath with suspense, expecting he would draw bridle at the "notch," where the mountain begins to descend abruptly. But the clatter of hoofs from the rocky passes showed them that the fearful race was continued. He swept by the returning messenger like an arrow, and reached Charlottesville in a time that, over such ground, the boldest rider in Virginia might, without suspicion to his courage, have pronounced appalling.

On a beautiful day in the latter part of February (the opening of the Virginia spring), 1851—the author rode up Monticello, having for his cicerone an old manumitted slave, who had for forty-five years belonged to Mr. Jefferson. Wormley had been first a door-yard servant, and subsequently a gardener

He had dug the grave of his master and others of his household, and now was the oldest living chronicler of Monticello. Like most of his color, he had a strong attachment for horses. After a few minutes' inquiries, his taciturnity gave way to animation on this favorite theme. He could distinctly remember, and described the points, height, color, pace, temper, etc., of every horse as far back as Arcturus, which Mr. Jefferson brought home from Washington. A crag of serpentine jutting into the narrow road, built high on the sides of a steep ravine, was selected by the fiery stranger horse as a shying butt—as if conscious that his rider would feel it dangerous to administer correction in such a spot. Mr. Jefferson tolerated this once or twice, but on its being repeated, punished the rearing and plunging animal with whip and spur until he was " glad to put his fore feet on the rock and stand still." Higher up, Wormley pointed out the path, or rather the rough untrodden course, on the side of Carter's Mountain, where Mr. Jefferson rode away when a detachment of Tarleton's dragoons were sent to capture him, " but not till the white' coats were climbing the mountain." An inspection of the deserted and dilapidated stables, called forth other incidents; and finally we returned so as to pass Moore's Creek at the ford, where Mr. Jefferson was thrown over his horse's head into the stream, as there will be subsequent occasion to relate. We shall have more to do with old Wormley's recollections, on other topics, hereafter.

We perhaps cannot better close this chapter than by giving some specimens from the garden book, which will illustrate several of the mental peculiarities and habits which have been mentioned. Nothing is omitted from or changed in the copy. The entries to which an asterisk is prefixed, were thus marked by Mr. Jefferson, to show that they did not belong to the garden record proper, and were to be copied into another book—for this was before he had got all his memoranda classified into their several subsequent departments.

1772.   EXTRACTS FROM GARDEN-BOOK.

Jan. 26. The deepest snow we have ever seen. In Albemarle it was about three
            feet deep.
Mar. 80. Sowed a patch of later peas.

---

¹ Tarleton's cavalry wore white coats (faced, we think, with green) during their
service in Virginia.

Other patches were sowed afterwards.

July 15.   Cucumbers came to table.

Planted out celery.

Sowed patch of peas for the fall.

Planted snap beans.

22.   Had the last dish of our spring peas.

31.   Had Irish potatoes from the garden.

* Julius Shard fills the two-wheeled barrow in 3 minutes, and carries it 30 yards in 1½ minutes more.   Now this is four loads of the common barrow with one wheel.   So that suppose the 4 loads put in in the same time, viz., 3 minutes, 4 trips will take 4 × 1½ minutes = 6′, which added to 3′ filling, is = 9′, to fill and carry the same earth which was filled and carried in the two-wheeled barrow in 4½′.   From a trial I made with the same two-wheeled barrow, I found that a man would dig and carry to the distance of 50 yards 5 cubical yards of earth in a day of 12 hours' length.   Ford's Phill did it, not overlooked, and having to mount his loaded barrow up a bank two feet high, and tolerably steep.

Aug. 20.   * The wagon with four horses, and the driver without any assistant, brought about 300 yds. wood, which measured 4, 8, and 19½ feet, i. e., nearly 5 cords, calling a cord 4, 4, and 8, in one day.   It took 10 loads.

* The wagon brings 28 rails at a load, up a steep part of the mountain.

* By. Randolph's mason, cuts stone at 8*d.* the superficial foot, the blocks being furnished to his hand.   Provision found, but no attendance.

* Park paling, every other pale high, the tall pales to have 5 nails, the low one 4 nails, is worth but 30*s.* the 100 yards, out and out.   Calculated by Skip Harris.

* A coach and six will turn in 80 feet.

Oct. 8.   Gathered two plum-peaches at Monticello.

Nov. 12.   * William Gillum says it will take a bushel of lime-stone (which he says is equal to two bushels of slacked lime) to a perch of stone-work 18 inches thick.   But Anderson says 3 bushels of lime.

* In making the round-about walk, 3 hands would make 80 yards in a day in the old field, but in the woods where they had stumps to clear, not more than forty, and sometimes 25 yards.

1773.   * Gordon, the mill-wright, says where the workman is found, and everything brought into place, he should make a double-armed water-wheel for 12*s.* the foot, and the cog-wheel for 15*s.* the foot in diameter, and the shaft and gudgeon supporters into the bargain. And a single-armed water-wheel for 20*s.* the foot.

* Mrs. Wythe puts one-tenth very rich superfine Malmesey to a dry Madeira, and makes a fine wine.

Mar. 12.   Sowed a patch of early peas, and another of marrow-fats.

31.   Grafted five French chestnuts into two stocks of common chestnut.

Sent Patrick Morton the following slips of fruits from Sandy Point:

No. 1. Green-gage plum.

2. Almonds.

3. Carnation cherry.

    4. Duke cherry.

    5. Forward pear.

    6. Late   do.

    7. Fine late large pear.

    8. Newtown pippins.

    9. French chestnut.

    10. English mulberry.

    11. Broadnax's cherry.

    12. Very fine late cherry.

April 1. Both patches of peas up.

       Set out strawberries.

    2. Planted 50 vines of various kinds from the Forest.

    8. Sowed a patch of early peas, and another of marrow-fats.

May 22. First patch of peas come to table. Note, this spring is remarkably forward.

    * 2 hands grubbed the graveyard 80 feet square = 1·7 of an acre in $3\frac{1}{2}$ hours, so that one would have done it in 7 hours, and would grub an acre in 49 hours = 4 days.

    * By. Randolph's fencing chain, weight $\frac{1}{2}$lb. per foot, and is 3 feet 3 inches from the ground.

   * Articles for contracts with overseers:

      He shall let his employer have his share of grain if he chooses it at a fixed price.

      He shall not have his share till enough is taken out to sow, and then only of what is sold or eaten by measure.

      Allow one-half a share for every horse, and the same for a ploughboy.

      To have at the rate of a share for every 8 hands, but never to have more than 2 shares if there be ever so many hands.

      Provision 400lb. pork if single; 500lb. if married.

      To be turned off at any time of year if employer disapproves of his conduct, on paying a proportion of what shall be made, according to the time he has stayed.

      To pay for carrying his share of the crop to market.

      To pay for carriage of all refused tobacco.

      To pay his own levies.

      To pay his own share of liquor and hiring at harvest.

      And never to bleed a negro.

1774.

Mar. 10. Sowed a bed of early and a bed of marrow-fat peas.

    12. Planted in the S. W. border of the garden the following stones:

       No. 1. A Virginian almond. No. 2 to 13. Almonds from the Straits. No. 14, 15, 16. Apricots. No. 16. A Filbert.

    15. Sowed the following seeds, and distinguished them by sticking numbered sticks in the beds.

         Aglio di Terracina, Garlic.

      No. 15. Radicchio di Pistoia. Succory or wild Endive.

       26. Cipolle bianche di Tuckahoe. The Spanish onion of Millar.

      31. Savoys.
      33. Salsafia.
      34. Cabbage.
      35. Lettuce.
      36. Lettuce (different).
      38. Radishes.
      39. Peppergrass.
      41. Salvastrella di Pisa.
      42. Sorrel, Acetosa di Pisa,
      46. Cochlearia di Pisa (scurvy grass or perhaps horse-radish)
      47. Cavolo Cappuccio, Spagnolo di Pisa.
      56. Prezzemolo. Parsley.
      58.   Do.

Mar. 21. Peas of Mar. 10 are up.
    23. Sowed the following seeds distinguished by numbered sticks
        No. 12. Cluster peas, or Bunch peas.
        13. Windsor beans.
        14. Green beans from Colo. Bland.
        16. Vetch.
        37. Spinace. Spinach.
        45. Carote di Pisa. Carrots.
        48. Cavolo broccolo Francese di Pisa. Broccoli.
        49. Carote. Carrots.
        51. Beans. Dr. Bland.
        54. Lattuga. Lettuce.
        55. Cipolle. Col. Cary. Onions.
        57. Parsnips. Col. Cary.
        59. Parsnips. Mr. Eppes.
        60. Salmon radishes.
        61. Carrots.
        72. Siberian wheat.
    24. Sowed the following things distinguished by numbered sticks.
        No. 8. ⎫
           9. ⎭ Early and later peas from Col. Cary.
        28. Small lentils.
  25.   29. Green lentils.
        4. Black-eyed peas which yield two crops. Col. R. Randolph.
  26. Seven rows of Grano Estivo from Tuscany.
        No. 50. Nasturcium in 25 little hills. ⎫
        29. Cresses.   ⎬ in the meadow.
        23. Celery.   ⎪
        Radicchio, the same as No. 15. ⎭
  28   Solid celery in the meadow.
  29.   No. 18. Asparagus.
        5. Beans. Dr. Clayton.
    Peach trees at Monticello in general bloom.
  31. Laid off ground to be levelled for a future garden. The upper side is
    44f. below the upper edge of the Round-about and parallel thereto. It is
    668 feet long, 80f. wide, and at each end forms a triangle, rectangular and
    isosceles, of which the legs are 80 feet and the hypothenuse 113 feet.

Planted the following trees, seeds, etc.

Twenty-four apple trees, } from the mountain plains.
Nineteen cherry trees,

No. 3. A doz. sweet almonds with smooth rinds, 8 of which were cracked, the others not.

    5. A doz. do. with hairy rinds, 8 cracked, the others not.

    7. A dozen do. with hard shells, 8 cracked.

    10, 32. Bitter almonds, 20 cracked.

    13, 20. Meliache e Albicocche (2 different kinds of apricots), 12 of them cracked, the others not.

    8, 4. Ciriege corniole (a particular kind of cherry).

    1, 198. Cherries of different kinds from Italy.

    14. About 1,500 olive stones.

    44. Lamponi. Raspberries (the seeds) in 3 rows.

    30. Fragole Alpine. Alpine strawberries (the seeds), 3 rows.

    22. Fragole Maggese. May strawberries (the seeds), 3 rows.

    43. Fragoloni di giardino. Large garden strawberries (the seeds), 1 row.

    A bed of parsley.

    62. Red cabbage.

    Radishes.

Apr. 1. Sowed and planted as follows :

No. 53. Turnips. Dr. Bland.

    25. Fagiuoli d'Augusta.

    19. Do. verdi coll' occhio bianco. D. Hylton.

    71. Bonny-Bess. Colo. Bland.

    70. Snap-beans. Colo. Bland.

    2. Fagiuoli coll' occhio di Provenza.

    7.   Do.   bianchi di Parigi.

    6. Cetriuoli.   Webb, 9 monticini.

    5.   Do.   Eppes, 12 monticini.

4. The peas of Mar. 24 come up.

5. Cucumbers; the same as No. 6, only that these were steeped in water from Mar. 31 till this day when they were sprouted. 10 hills.

Do. Same as No. 5, only soaked as before. 17 hills.

No. 63. Piperone. John Wood,

    52. Cayenne pepper. Dr. Bland.

    24. Purple beans. Jas. Donald.

    17. White and purple do. Do.

    21. Sugar beans.

    1. Fagiuoli bianchi di Toscana.

    65. Hotspur peas. Monticello.

    66. Marrow-fat do.   Do.

Planted thirty vines just below where the negro garden wall will run, towards the westermost end; eight of them at the westermost end of the row were Spanish Raisins from Colo. Bland's; next to them were sixteen native vines from Winslow's, in New Kent; and at the eastermost end were six native vines of Monticello. They were planted by some Tuscan

Vignerons, who came over with Mr. Mazzei.[1] The manner was as follows :

April 6.   A trench 4 feet deep and 4 feet wide, was dug. At the bottom were put small green bushes, and on them a thin coat of dung and earth mixed, which raised the bed to within 2½ feet of the surface. The cuttings, which were from 3½ to 6 feet long, and which had been hitherto buried in the earth, were then produced. About 18 inches of their roots were dipt into a thick paste made of cowdung and water, and then planted in the bottom, the Raisins 3 feet apart, the rest about 2 feet, having a stick stuck by each, to which it was bound with bear-grass, in order to support it, while the earth should be drawn in. The earth was then thrown in, the mould first, and afterwards the other earth in the same order in which it was dug, leaving the bottom clay for the last. The earth was thrown in very loose, and care was taken to avoid trampling in it. The trench was not quite filled, but left somewhat hollowing to receive and retain the water, and the superfluous earth was left on each side without the trench. Then the supporting sticks were drawn out, and would have served for the other rows, had the plantation been to be continued. In such a case the rows are to be 4 feet apart, so that, in fact, the whole surface is taken up to the depth of 4 feet. The best way of doing it is to dig every other trench, and leave the earth which is thrown out exposed for a twelvemonth. Then the vines may be planted at any time from the middle of November to the first week in April. Afterwards dig the other alternate trenches, and leave the earth of these also exposed for a twelvemonth. When the latter trenches are planted, leave the superfluous earth in ridges between the rows of vines till by the subsidence of the earth it becomes necessary to pull it into the trenches. If any of your grapes turn out illy, cut off the vine and engraft another on the stock. An acre in vines where they are 2½ feet apart in the row will admit 4,316 in all.

 7. Sowed, planted, etc., as follows:

       No. 1. Cocomere di Pistoia.   Watermelons. 84 hills.

            2. Cocomere di seme Neapolitane. 87 hills.

          12. Zatte di Massa. Canteloupe melons. 18 hills.

          18. Poponi Arancini di Pistoia. Muskmelons. 11 hills.

          64. In the meadow. Rice.

8.   7. Zucche bianche.   White pumpkins. 22 monticini.

            8. Zucche nere.   Black   do.   42 hills.

Meadow.   9. Do.   di monacho. 8 monticini.

          10. Do.   Lauri. 9 monticini.

          11. Do.   da Pescatori. 8 do.

 11. * In making a stone wall in my garden, I find by an accurate calculation that 7½ cubical feet may be done in a day by one hand, who brings his own stone into place and does everything.

 25. Sowed four rows of forward peas.

      two do. of ————

---

[1] His gardeners at this period were from the same quarter, and this accounts for his frequent use of Italian names in the garden record.

April 30. Sowed No. 67. White beet } from England.
              68. Red beet }
              69. Scarlet radishes.   Tuckahoe.

May 2. Sowed No. 3. Carrots
          6. Spinach
        10. Curled parsley
        11. Peas
        20. Rape   } from Dr. Brown's.
        32. Savoys
        73. Coleworts
        75. Broccoli
        40. Ice lettuce

    4. The blue ridge of mountains covered with snow.

    5. A frost which destroyed almost everything. It killed the wheat, rye, corn, many tobacco plants, and even large saplings. The leaves of the trees were entirely killed, and all the shoots of vines. At Monticello near half the fruit of every kind was killed ; and before this no instance had ever occurred of any fruit killed here by the frost. In all other places in the neighborhood the destruction of fruit was total. This frost was general and equally destructive through the whole country and the neighboring colonies.

   14. Cherries ripe.

   16. First dish of peas from earliest patch.

   26. A second patch of peas come to table.

. une 4. Windsor beans come to table.

    5. A third and fourth patch of peas come to table.

   13. A fifth patch of peas come in.

July 13. Last dish of peas.

   18. Last lettuce from Gehee's.

   23. Cucumbers from our garden.

   31. Watermelons from our patch.

Aug. 3. Indian corn comes to table.
        Black-eyed peas come to table.

Nov. 16. This morning the northern part of the Blue Ridge is white with snow.

   17. The first frost sufficient to kill anything.

CHAPTER III.

1773—1775.

WHEN the Virginia Assembly met in the spring of 1773, an event had occurred to rouse them from their torpor. The intolerable insolence of an armed government vessel (the Gaspee), stationed in Narraganset Bay to enforce the revenue laws, had led to its being decoyed aground and burned.[1] This called out an Act of Parliament "for the better securing his Majesty's dockyards, magazines, ships, ammunition, and stores," by which the destruction of the least thing appertaining to the British navy, down, as the historian Gordon remarks, to the "button of a mariner's coat, the oar of a cutter's boat, or the head of a

[1] June 10th, 1772.

cask belonging to the fleet," was made punishable by death; and the accused might, at the pleasure of his Majesty, be transported to any county in England for trial.[1] In December (1772), a commission arrived from England, appointing several colonial officers whose servility to government could be relied on, as a Court of Inquiry in the Gaspee affair,[2] and intrusted with the power of deciding whether those whom they determined should be placed on trial should be transported to England.

We have seen that the claim of this power of deportation for trial, under an ancient statute, drew forth the indignant remonstrances of the Virginia House of Burgesses in 1769; and they now met incensed by the new statutory enactment and the attempted practical enforcement of a principle which, if allowed to go peaceably into execution, all foresaw would soon be extended far enough to place the liberty and life of every prominent colonist who should dare to render himself obnoxious to government, in the hands of packed and prejudiced foreign tribunals, and "judges predetermined to condemn." But, as usual, there was a difference between the old and young Whigs, in the House of Burgesses, as to the proper measures of opposition to be adopted. Mr. Jefferson (in his Memoir) thus describes the action of the latter:

"Not thinking our old and leading members up to the point of forwardness and zeal which the times required, Mr. Henry, Richard Henry Lee, Francis L. Lee, Mr. Carr, and myself agreed to meet in the evening, in a private room of the Raleigh, to consult on the state of things. There may have been a member or two more whom I do not recollect. We were all sensible that the most urgent of all measures was that of coming to an understanding with all the other colonies, to consider the British claims as a common cause to all, and to produce a unity of action: and, for this purpose, that a Committee of Correspondence in each colony would be the best instrument for intercommunication: and that their first measure would probably be, to propose a meeting of deputies from every colony, at some central place, who should be charged with the direction of the measures which should be taken by all. We, therefore, drew up the resolutions, which may be seen in Wirt, page 87.[3]

These resolutions, after premising that the minds of his Majesty's faithful subjects in the Colonies were disturbed by

---

[1] Gordon's History of the Independence, vol. i. p. 324.
[2] Holmes' Annals of America, vol. ii. p. 176.
[3] Page 105 in the 7th (M'Elrath, Bangs & Co.) edition, which we use.

rumors of proceedings "tending to deprive them of their ancient, legal, and constitutional rights," proceed to designate "a Standing Committee of Correspondence and Inquiry," to obtain the earliest and most authentic intelligence of all proceedings in England in regard to the Colonies; "to keep up and maintain a correspondence and communication with the sister colonies, respecting those important considerations," and report from time to time to the House; and specially instructing the Committee "without delay, to inform themselves particularly of the principles and authority on which was constituted a Court of Inquiry, said to have been lately held in Rhode Island, with powers to transport persons accused of offences committed in America, to places beyond the seas, to be tried." The designated Committee consisted of Peyton Randolph (the Speaker), Robert C. Nicholas, Richard H. Lee, Benjamin Harrison, Edmund Pendleton, Patrick Henry, Dudley Digges, Dabney Carr, Archibald Cary, and Thomas Jefferson. To Mr. Jefferson (who, it might therefore be inferred, drafted or suggested them) it was proposed to move the resolutions in the House; but he "urged that it should be done by Mr. Carr, his friend and brother-in-law, then a new member, to whom he wished an opportunity should be given of making known to the House his great worth and talents."[1]

Mr. Carr accordingly moved them on the 12th of March, in a speech remarkable for its force and eloquence, and was supported by Mr. Henry and Mr. R. H. Lee. There was nothing in the tenor of the resolutions that the moderate party could very well object to, and they passed without dissent. The Governor, the Earl of Dunmore—who had succeeded Lord Botetourt in 1772—immediately dissolved the House. The Committee of Correspondence met the next day, and prepared a circular to the other Colonies containing a copy of the resolutions, with a request that they might be laid before their assemblies, "and requesting them to appoint some person or persons of their respective bodies to communicate from time to time with the said [Virginia] Committee."

Mr. Jefferson persistently claimed for Virginia the honor of originating the Committees of Correspondence between *the legis-*

---

[1] Memoir.

latures of the different Colonies; but later developments seem
to render it certain that the Massachusetts Assembly appointed
a committee for the same object, in 1770. This last body, however, does not appear to have *acted*—no record of any proceedings by it, we believe, is preserved—and, indeed, Bradford,
the historian of Massachusetts, expressly declares, "it does not
appear that this committee wrote to the other Colonies, as a
former letter to them from Massachusetts had been so severely
censured in England." [1] The fact that it took so long a time to
prove the existence of such a committee in Massachusetts, and
that it was discredited by Jefferson, Wirt, and so many other
either actors or investigators in Revolutionary history, shows at
least that its appointment was not contemporaneously made
known in the other Colonies. Nor is it claimed that the Massachusetts resolution requested the other Colonies to appoint similar committees—though it authorized correspondence with
those "they had or might appoint." The distinction may look
like a narrow one, but, on consideration, it will be found important. It appears, therefore, that Virginia acted spontaneously
in this matter—that she went farthest—that she first actually
organized and put into practical execution a measure which
soon led to the call of a federative Congress. The Massachusetts
Committee halted on the threshold by reason of *English censures;* on the other hand, Jefferson always declared that he
and his co-actors saw that "the first measure" of *their* committee "would probably be to propose a meeting of deputies from
every Colony" [2]—and they consequently were appointed with
that for their primary object. Under all these circumstances,
every one will decide for himself where the honor of the
measure should principally rest.

But, in truth, there is little need for attempting to settle the
question nicely. These, as well as some other of the Colonies,
have no occasion to be tenacious about an occasional stray leaf
of the broad harvests of their Revolutionary laurels. We will
not aver that all the Colonies acted exactly alike in the opening
of that struggle. But it is safe to say, that the *Whigs* in all of
them *felt* substantially alike—and that the overt acts of resistance
were generally first made, when the practical encroachment

---

[1] History of Massachusetts from 1764 to 1775, pp. 237, 276.   [2] Memoir, *et al.*

was first attempted, and there was any actual capacity for resistance.   It was for this reason, that the curtain of civil war first rose in Massachusetts, and next in Virginia.   They were first attacked, as the oldest and strongest of the American brotherhood—and in the expectation, doubtless, that their over throw or submission would be decisive of the result.   And like brave older brothers, they advanced in front of the younger to the stern conflict.   We confess we sicken at arguments and arrays of facts to show *where* the credit of originating the idea of resisting English oppression belongs !   It originated in every manly Whig's bosom (as resistance to oppression has originated in every manly bosom from the foundation of the world)—it making not a particle of difference of what precise colony, or spot of earth in the thirteen Colonies, he chanced to be an inhabitant.   When the time came and the cry of war was sounded, the true-hearted went forth from the ocean border to the Alleghanies—amidst the green hills and valleys of New England— on the "bloody and debatable ground of the Mohawk"—from the shores of the Delaware and Chesapeake—from the princely seats on the James—from the Cape Fear and the Santee—from the sands of Georgia !   And we sicken no less to hear opprobrium thrown on this Colony or that, because in that strife some of its people sided with the mother country, and thus weakened its means of resistance.   If the "Tories" (loyalists) committed any crime in this (a question we may by and by ask) was it the crime of the Whigs ?   Nay, did not the latter require the more courage to take side against enemies without and enemies within ?   And is it not the silliest kind of child's play to personify a Colony or a subsequent State—that is, a certain number of square miles of insensate earth—and talk about *its* being disgraced, or *its* subsequent inhabitants being disgraced—by its having produced men who thought differently from the majority of their countrymen on a momentous occasion.   If this sort of clan pride and clan prejudice must ever prevail, let it, at least, spare the heroic age of the Revolution—let its foolish vaunts and more foolish recriminations postdate the glory and the shame which were, as our forefathers called their congresses and their armies, purely "continental."

We have indulged in this strain of remark to intimate, in advance, that these pages will deal with men and their actions, caring as little whether they were born or nurtured in this Colony or that, or on this continent or that, as whether they powdered their hair alike, or wore shoe buckles of a pattern!

Dabney Carr, the gifted young delegate, who made his first appearance in the Virginia House of Burgesses, in moving the resolutions for a Committee of Correspondence, was a lawyer, representing the county of Louisa. It appears from the repeated testimony of Mr. Jefferson, and from the investigations of Mr. Wirt into other sources of information, that he was an extraordinary young man. Mr. Jefferson thus described him : [1]

> "I well remember the pleasure expressed in the countenance and conversation of the members generally, on this *début* of Mr. Carr, and the hopes they conceived as well from the talents as the patriotism it manifested. * * * His character was of a high order. A spotless integrity, sound judgment, handsome imagination, enriched by education and reading, quick and clear in his conceptions, of correct and ready elocution, impressing every hearer with the sincerity of the heart from which it flowed. His firmness was inflexible in whatever he thought was right; but when no moral principle stood in the way, never had man more of the milk of human kindness, of indulgence, of softness, of pleasantry of conversation and conduct. The number of his friends, and the warmth of their affection, were proofs of his worth, and of their estimate of it."

Mr. Wirt says :

> "This gentleman, by profession a lawyer, had recently commenced his practice at the same bars with Patrick Henry; and although he had not yet reached the meridian of life, he was considered by far the most formidable rival in forensic eloquence that Mr. Henry had ever yet encountered. He had the advantage of a person at once dignified and engaging, and the manner and action of an accomplished gentleman. His education was a finished one; his mind trained to correct thinking; his conceptions quick, clear, and strong; he reasoned with great cogency, and had an imagination which enlightened beautifully, without interrupting or diverting the course of his argument. His voice was finely toned; his feelings acute; his style free, and rich, and various; his devotion to the cause of liberty verging on enthusiasm; and his spirit firm and undaunted, beyond the possibility of being . shaken." [2]

A school-boy intimacy between Carr and Jefferson had ripened into that firm friendship which is founded on kindred feelings, tastes, principles and pursuits. They were inseparable companions; read, studied, took their exercise, practised their music, and formed their plans together. They daily repaired to an oak near the summit of Monticello (under the

---

[1] Letter to Dabney Carr, the younger, Jan. 19, 1816.   [2] Wirt's Henry, p. 106.

branches of which they both now slumber), where they had
constructed themselves a rustic seat, and here, in the deep
woods, far away from the sight and hearing of man, they
together pored over Bracton, Coke and Matthew Bacon; read
their miscellaneous reading; discussed the present, and painted
the glowing visions of the future.

On the 20th of July, 1765, Carr married Martha, the fourth
sister of Mr. Jefferson. She was a gifted woman, and every
way worthy of her husband; and their married life was one of
peculiar felicity. Mr. Jefferson had written Page, in 1770,
(February 21) as follows; and the reader will understand that
"Currus" was the Latin nickname he was in the habit of
applying to Carr:

* * * "I too am *cœlo tactus, Currus bene se habet.* He speaks, thinks, and
dreams of nothing but his young son. This friend of ours, Page, in a very small
house, with a table, half a dozen chairs, and one or two servants, is the happiest
man in the universe. Every incident in life he so takes as to render it a source of
pleasure. With as much benevolence as the heart of man will hold, but with an
utter neglect of the costly apparatus of life, he exhibits to the world a new phenomenon in philosophy—the Samian sage in the tub of the cynic."

On the 16th of May, 1773, just thirty-five days after his
first and last speech in the House of Burgesses, Dabney Carr
died at Charlottesville, of bilious fever, in the thirtieth year
of his age. The course of the disease was violent and brief,
insomuch that he could not be moved home, nor could Mr.
Jefferson, who was absent (at Williamsburg, we think), be
summoned to return before his death and burial. He was
buried at Shadwell, but Mr. Jefferson caused his body to be
disinterred, and removed to a grave beneath their favorite oak
on Monticello, where it had been agreed between them that
the survivor should bury the first which died. The walls of the
family cemetery now surround the spot, and the bones of the
two friends lie not two yards asunder.

Carr's sudden death fell with stunning force on his wife.
She was ill, from recent confinement, when her husband set out
on his last journey, and her mind was perhaps therefore filled
with the most gloomy presentiments concerning him. After her
last farewell, she again raised herself on her sick couch, to catch
a parting glance of him as he rode past her window; but she
saw merely his moving hat. This object took strong hold of an

imagination rendered morbid by disease, and soon to be fearfully excited by an almost despairing grief. For weeks and months, whether in the blaze of noon-day or in the darkness of night, the moving, phantomy hat was ever passing before her eye. For a period, reason tottered on its throne. Carr left three sons—Peter, Samuel, and Dabney; and three daughters—Jane, Lucy, and Mary. Mr. Jefferson took his widowed sister, and her entire family, into his house. He brought up and educated the children as his own. Warmly they repaid his kindness and attachment, and there was not one of them that would not have laid down his or her life for their generous uncle.

Peter, to whom some of the finest letters in Mr. Jefferson's correspondence are addressed—gifted, accomplished, noble in bearing, like his father—died in his early prime. Colonel Samuel was a respectable planter, and once held a seat in the State Senate. Dabney—so well known, through the recently published correspondence of his intimate friend, Wirt (in Kennedy's life of the latter, published in 1850)—rose to be one of the Chancellors of Virginia, and he subsequently occupied a seat on the bench of the Court of Appeals. He died in 1837, in the language of Mr. Wirt's biographer, "leaving behind him the fame of an upright and learned judge and a truly good man." Jane married the only son of Colonel Wilson Miles Cary, of Carisbrook, Fluvanna county—a gentleman of large property, and of great social importance before the Revolution. Lucy married —— Terrell, and removed to Kentucky, where she and her husband died, leaving one son, Dabney, to whom, in his grand-uncle's, Mr. Jefferson's, correspondence, is addressed a letter recommending a course of law studies.[1] Mary died unmarried.

News of the Boston Port-bill reached the Virginia Assembly during its spring session, in 1774. What took place thereupon, we will leave Mr. Jefferson to describe in his Memoir:

"The lead in the House, on these subjects, being no longer left to the old members, Mr. Henry, R. H. Lee, Fr. L. Lee, three or four other members, whom I do not recollect, and myself, agreeing that we must boldly take an unequivocal stand in the line with Massachusetts, determined to meet and consult on the proper

[1] Dated February 26th, 1821.

measures, in the council chamber, for the benefit of the library in that room. We were under conviction of the necessity of arousing our people from the lethargy into which they had fallen, as to passing events; and thought that the appointment of a day of general fasting and prayer, would be most likely to call up and alarm their attention. No example of such a solemnity had existed since the days of our distresses in the war of '55, since which a new generation had grown up. With the help, therefore, of Rushworth,[1] whom we rummaged over for the revolutionary precedents and forms of the Puritans of that day, preserved by him, we cooked up a resolution, somewhat modernizing their phrases, for appointing the first day of June, on which the Port Bill was to commence, for a day of fasting, humiliation, and prayer, to implore Heaven to avert from us the evils of civil war, to inspire us with firmness in support of our rights, and to turn the hearts of the King and Parliament to moderation and justice. To give greater emphasis to our proposition, we agreed to wait the next morning on Mr. Nicholas, whose grave and religious character was more in unison with the tone of our resolution, and to solicit him to move it. We accordingly went to him in the morning. He moved it the same day; the first of June was proposed; and it passed without opposition."[2]

The next day, Governor Dunmore applied the usual remedy in such cases—a dissolution; and this time he did so in a curt message of half a dozen lines, basing his action on the ground that the order of the House was a high reflection upon His Majesty and the Parliament of Great Britain![3] The members also resorted to their usual course after a dissolution. They met at the Apollo; and they entered into an association, signed by their entire number, and by several clergymen and other prominent citizens, in which they denounced with proper spirit the aggressive course of England—declared it unpatriotic to purchase tea or other East-India commodities—avowed that they considered an attack on one Colony an attack on all—and recommended the Corresponding Committee to confer with the other Colonies on the expediency of holding a *general annual Congress*.[4] Before dispersing, they further agreed that a convention should be held at Williamsburg, on the 1st of August, to learn the result of the proposition, to the other Colonies, for a Congress, and should it be favorable, to appoint delegates thereto.

The Burgesses, on their return to their homes, invited the

---

[1] *i. e.* Rushworth's Collection of Documents relative to the Civil War between Charles the First and his people.

[2] The Preamble and Order or Resolution of the House will be found in Wirt's Henry, p. 112.

[3] For the Message, see Burk's Hist. of Va. vol. iii. p. 378.

[4] Burk, vol. iii. p. 380.

clergy of their counties to perform the religious ceremonies of
the Fast-day, and to address the people discourses adapted to the
occasion. The clergy appear to have discharged this duty in a
most patriotic spirit, for Mr. Jefferson declares that " the effect
of the day, through the whole Colony, was like a shock of electricity, arousing every man, and placing him erect and solidly
on his centre."

The freeholders of Albemarle met on the 26th day of July,
and chose Thomas Jefferson and John Walker members of the
House of Burgesses, and deputies to the Convention.[1] The
instructions to these gentlemen, passed on the same occasion,
are well worthy of notice, and from their identity in peculiar
views (as far as they go), and partly in language, with a celebrated production of Mr. Jefferson, which will presently come
under examination, no doubt whatever can exist that they were
written by the same hand. They were as follows :

" *Resolved,* That the inhabitants of the several States of British America are
subject to the laws *which they adopted* at their first settlement, and to *such others*
as have been *since made by their respective Legislatures, duly constituted and
appointed with their own consent.* That *no other Legislature whatever can rightly
exercise authority over them ;* and that these privileges they hold as the *common
rights of mankind,* confirmed by the political constitutions they have respectively
assumed, and also by several charters of compact from the Crown.

" *Resolved,* That these their natural and legal rights have in frequent instances
been invaded by the Parliament of Great Britain, and particularly that they were
so by an act lately passed to take away the trade of the inhabitants of the town of
Boston, in the province of Massachusetts Bay ; that all such assumptions of unlawful power are dangerous to the rights of the British empire in general, and should
be considered as its common cause, and that we will ever be ready to join with our
fellow subjects in every part of the same, in executing all those rightful powers
which God has given us, for the re-establishment and guaranteeing such their constitutional rights, when, where, and by whomsoever invaded."

Here the ground is explicitly taken that the colonists are
subject to no laws but those of their own creation—that Parliament has no authority over them in any case, or on any subject
—that they possess the power of self-government by " natural
right," or " the common rights of mankind "—that these rights

---

[1] Mr. Jefferson states, in Note C, to his Memoir, that " it had been agreed that the
Burgesses, who should be elected under the writs then issuing, should be requested to
meet in convention." This may have been the *understanding* at the time, for we believe
the delegates to each body were in all cases the same, but the proceedings of the meetings in various of the counties are before us, in which it appears that they made the
appointment to the *Convention* a separate act, though taking place immediately after the
other.

have been invaded by Parliament frequently, and particularly in the Boston Port Bill—that the inhabitants of Albemarle will ever be ready to join in executing and reëstablishing these powers " by whomsoever invaded !"

This is wholly different ground from that assumed, so far as we know, by any other constituency at that period. The proceedings and instructions, on the same occasion, in twenty-eight other Virginia counties, are before us. All of them are spirited, and some of them point as plainly as the foregoing towards forcible resistance. Several deny the right of Parliament to *tax* the Colonies under any circumstances ; but none other contains a hint, or the shadow of a hint, that the Colonies were wholly independent of Parliament—free, of natural right, to enact all their own laws, and subject to none other.[1] All the rest tacitly or directly take the position, then, indeed, universally assumed throughout the Colonies—and asserted, by the by, in Mr. Henry's resolutions against the Stamp Act—that the people of the American Colonies were subject to all the provisions, and entitled to all the benefits of the British Constitution, in like manner with native born subjects, and it was under that constitution, and from no other source, that it was claimed that Parliament could not *tax* those who were *unrepresented* in it. In other respects, the legal or constitutional right of Parliament to legislate for the general concerns of the Colonies was nowhere denied, however bitterly the abuse of that right might be complained of, or even resisted.

We shall presently find Mr. Jefferson declaring the doctrine of the Albemarle resolutions more pointedly, and on a more conspicuous occasion. He asserted in his Memoir that such were his views from the first dawn of the question, " but that he had never been able to get any one [*i. e.* any distinguished person] to agree with him but Mr. Wythe." He adds:

"Our other patriots, Randolph, the Lees, Nicholas, Pendleton, stopped at the half-way house of John Dickinson, who admitted that England had a right to regulate our commerce, and to lay duties on it for the purposes of regulation, but not of raising revenue. But for this ground there was no foundation in compact, in any acknowledged principles of colonization, nor in reason : expatriation being a natural right, and acted on as such by all nations, in all ages "

[1] The light in which the resolutions speak of the Americans as " fellow *subjects*," will by and by appear, and it will in no way conflict with the tenor of the resolutions.

The freeholders of Hanover county, the constituency of Mr. Henry, for example, in instructing their representatives, on this same occasion (the Burgess and Convention election of 1773), while they very pointedly declare against the right of Parliament to tax them, and foreshadow resistance, only demand the "privileges and immunities of their fellow subjects in England," that they be permitted to "continue to live under the genuine, unaltered Constitution of England, and be subjects, in the true spirit of that Constitution, to His Majesty and his illustrious house." [1]

The Fairfax meeting, presided over by George Washington, took substantially the same positions. Referring to the power of Parliament to regulate American trade and commerce, its resolutions declared:

"Such a power, directed with wisdom and moderation, *seems necessary* for the general good of that great body politic *of which we are a part*, although in some degree repugnant to the principles of the Constitution. Under this idea, our ancestors submitted to it; the experience of more than a century, during the government of His Majesty's royal predecessors, *have proved its utility*." [2]

A doubt is here suggested about the theoretical propriety of the Navigation acts, under the principles of the British Constitution, which is admitted paramount, but even this is waived on the plea of necessity and utility! These are sufficient specimens of the resolutions generally adopted.

The Virginia Convention met at the appointed time (Aug. 1st) at Williamsburg, a purely voluntary body, to exercise quasi legislative powers, and thus the germ of a Revolutionary government was planted. Finding that the other Colonies had concurred in the calling of a general Congress, this body proceeded to appoint delegates to represent Virginia in it: and they were Peyton Randolph, Richard H. Lee, George Washington, Patrick Henry, Richard Bland, Benjamin Harrison and Edmund Pendleton. This selection was controlled in part by considerations extraneous of the talents or individual qualifications of the delegates; in short, to conciliate different, and to some extent, conflicting interests, views, and feelings. Professor Tucker, we think, very fairly states these:

---

[1] American Archives (Force's), 4th series, vol. i. 616.   [2] Ibid., vol. i. 598.

"The deputies chosen to represent Virginia in the general Congress were selected with great care, and regard was had not only to their talents and weight of character, but also, it is said, to the diversity of their qualifications. Thus Peyton Randolph was recommended by his personal dignity and acquaintance with the rules of order; George Washington, by his military talents and experience; Richard Henry Lee, by his persuasive oratory; Patrick Henry, by his spirit-stirring eloquence, and because, moreover, he was the man of the people. Richard Bland was deemed the best writer in the colony. Edmund Pendleton was chosen for his consummate prudence, as well as thorough knowledge of law; and Benjamin Harrison, as fairly representing the feelings of the wealthy planters." [1]

The geographical distribution of the population of Virginia also had something to do with the selection. So much more densely (and we might add *influentially*) was the tide-water region then inhabited, that the most western delegate chosen was Mr. Henry, his county lying about midway between the Chesapeake and the Blue Ridge!

Mr. Jefferson was prevented from attending the Convention by a severe illness (dysentery) which seized him on his way thither. He had prepared a draught of instructions to be offered in that body, for the direction of the delegates who should be chosen to Congress. When he found himself unable to proceed, he forwarded two copies by express, one to Peyton Randolph, who he knew would be called to preside, and the other to Mr. Henry. He said of these proposed instructions in the Appendix to his Memoir:

"They were written in haste, with a number of blanks, with some uncertainties and inaccuracies of historical facts, which I neglected at the moment, knowing they could be readily corrected at the meeting."

He thus speaks of their fate:

"Whether Mr. Henry disapproved the ground taken, or was too lazy to read it (for he was the laziest man in reading I ever knew) I never learned; but he communicated it to nobody. Peyton Randolph informed the Convention he had received such a paper from a member, prevented by sickness from offering it in his place, and he laid it on the table for perusal. It was read generally by the members, approved by many, though thought too bold for the present state of things; but they printed it in pamphlet form, under the title of 'A Summary View of the Rights of British America.' It found its way to England, was taken up by the opposition, interpolated a little by Mr. Burke so as to make it answer opposition purposes, and in that form ran rapidly through several editions. This information I had from Parson Hurt, who happened at the time to be in London, whither he

---

[1] Tucker's Jefferson, vol. i. p. 63.

had gone to receive clerical orders; and I was informed afterwards by Peyton Randolph, that it had procured me the honor of having my name inserted in a long list of proscriptions, enrolled in a bill of attainder commenced in one of the Houses of Parliament, but suppressed in embryo by the hasty step of events, which warned them to be a little cautious. Montague, agent of the House of Burgesses in England, made extracts from the bill, copied the names, and sent them to Peyton Randolph. The names, I think, were about twenty, which he repeated to me, but I recollect those only of Hancock, the two Adamses, Peyton Randolph himself, Patrick Henry, and myself." [1]

And again :

" Of the former [copy] no more was ever heard or known. Mr. Henry probably thought it too bold, as a first measure, as the majority of the members did. On the other copy being laid on the table of the Convention, by Peyton Randolph, as the proposition of a member, who was prevented from attendance by sickness on the road, tamer sentiments were preferred, and, I believe, wisely preferred ; the leap I proposed being too long, as yet, for the mass of our citizens. The distance between these, and the instructions actually adopted, is of some curiosity, however, as it shows the inequality of pace with which we moved, and the prudence required to keep front and rear together. My creed had been formed on unsheathing the sword at Lexington " [2]

If the word "Lexington" is not substituted by typographical carelessness for "Boston"—which was undoubtedly the *meaning* of the author—we have here one of those curious slips of the pen which occasionally creep into the writings of the most accurate ; for the battle of Lexington was not fought until the 18th of April, 1775, about nine months after the date of the proposed " instructions !" To show how easy it would be for an author to thus casually substitute one word for another—or, if it was a typographical error, for even a careful proof-reader to overlook it, we may remark that of all those lynx-eyed critics who have sifted Mr. Jefferson's writings, almost sand by sand, to detect contradictions and errors, none, so far as we have observed, have ever noticed this one !

The proposed instructions were very long. They occupy six-teen closely printed pages in the first edition of his Works. [3] This document is a most remarkable one—more remarkable, considering the period when it was written, for its boldness of tone, than the Declaration of Independence—and though less carefully and ornately written than the latter paper, quite its

---

[1] Memoir.   [2] Note C, to Memoir.
[3] We take the type to be what printers term *long-primer*. In the Congress edition, the paper is printed in a size larger type, and covers twenty pages.

equal, in our judgment, in the ability it displays. For the body of the document, we must be content to refer the reader to Mr. Jefferson's Works.[1] It has usually been referred to principally as advancing the novel and startling doctrine (already presented in the Albemarle resolutions) of the entire independence of the Colonies, in all respects, of Parliament; and also that the *only* bond of connection between them and Great Britain (which shows wherein he spoke of the Colonists as " fellow-*subjects*," in the Albemarle resolutions) is declared to be that they are under the executive government of the same chief magistrate, in the same way that Great Britain and Hanover are. And even this right of chief magistracy on the part of the King is not admitted to rest on the basis of allegiance, because the Americans emigrated from Great Britain—or on any principle whatever of the British Constitution; but purely and nakedly on natural right—that is, because the colonists, in the possession of *all* their natural rights, as much so as if England did not exist, had seen fit to choose, or what amounted to the same thing, willingly acknowledge, the Kings of England for their Kings. We cannot forbear to give enough extracts to exhibit the tone, and a glimpse of the style of reasoning in this extraordinary paper:

" *Resolved*, That it be an instruction to the said deputies, when assembled in General Congress, with the deputies from the other States of British America, to propose to the said Congress, that an humble and dutiful address be presented to his Majesty, begging leave to lay before him, as chief magistrate of the British empire, the united complaints of his Majesty's subjects in America; complaints which are excited by many unwarrantable encroachments and usurpations, attempted to be made by the Legislature of one part of the empire, upon the rights which God, and the laws, have given equally and independently to all. To represent to his Majesty that these, his States, have often individually made humble application to his imperial throne, to obtain, through its intervention, some redress of their injured rights; to none of which, was ever even an answer condescended. Humbly to hope that this, their joint address, penned in the language of truth, and divested of those expressions of servility, which would persuade his Majesty that we are *asking favors*, and not *rights*, shall obtain from his Majesty a more respectful acceptance; and this his Majesty will think we have reason to expect, when he reflects that he is no more than the chief officer of the people, appointed by the laws, and circumscribed with definite powers, to assist in working the great machine of government, *erected for their use, and, consequently, subject to their superintendence.*"

[1] In Randolph's edition, vol. i. p. 100; in Congress edition, vol. i. p. 122.

The natural right of expatriation (with the concurrent implied one of abjuring personal allegiance) is then broadly asserted; the American emigration compared to that of their Saxon ancestors to England from the north of Europe—and the ground taken that the *parent* country retained the right of sovereignty in the one case, as much as in the other. It is claimed that America was conquered by the efforts and at the expense of individuals; that the government of Great Britain had rendered the colonists no assistance until they "had become established on a firm and permanent footing;" that having become valuable to Great Britain for commercial purposes, assistance had been lent them "against an enemy who would fain have drawn to herself the benefits of their commerce, to the great aggrandizement of herself, and danger of Great Britain;" that the Colonists did not thereby submit to the sovereignty of the latter, any more than did Portugal, or any other allied State which had received its aid; that Great Britain may be amply repaid by *giving* her people "such exclusive privileges in trade as may be advantageous to them, and, at the same time, not too restrictive to ourselves." Then follows the celebrated proposition that the adoption, by the Americans, of the "system of laws under which they had hitherto lived in the mother country," and their submission "to the same common sovereign," were purely voluntary acts on their part. The paper proceeds:

"A family of princes was then on the British throne, whose *treasonable crimes against their people*, brought on them, afterwards, the exertion of those *sacred and sovereign rights of punishment*, reserved in the hands of the people for cases of extreme necessity, and judged by the Constitution unsafe to be delegated to any other judicature. While every day brought forth some new and unjustifiable exertion of power over their subjects on that side of the water, it was not to be expected that those here, much less able at that time to oppose the designs of despotism, should be exempted from injury. Accordingly, this country, which had been acquired by the lives, the labors, and fortunes of individual adventurers, was by these Princes, at several times, parted out and distributed among the favorites and followers of their fortunes; and, by an assumed right of the Crown alone, were erected into distinct and independent governments; a measure which, it is believed, his Majesty's prudence and understanding would prevent him from imitating at this day; as no exercise of such power, of dividing and dismembering a country, has ever occurred in his Majesty's realm of England, though now of very ancient standing; nor could it be justified or acquiesced under there, or in any other part of his Majesty's empire."

The various aggressions and encroachments, now of King and now of Parliament, in granting lands, in setting up governments, in restricting free commerce, and even in controlling and prohibiting interior manufactures, are energetically enumerated. The act, in the 5th year of the reign of George II., imposing those various prohibitions on American manufactures, is pronounced " an instance of despotism to which no parallel can be produced in the most arbitrary ages of British history." And it is added :

"But, that we do not point out to his Majesty the injustice of these acts, with intent to rest on that principle the cause of their nullity; but to show that experience confirms the propriety of those political principles, which exempt us from the jurisdiction of the British Parliament. *The true ground on which we declare these acts void, is, that the British Parliament has no right to exercise authority over us.*"

The resemblance of a portion of the following extract to a sentence in the second paragraph of the Declaration of Independence, is obvious :

"Scarcely have our minds been able to emerge from the astonishment, into which one stroke of Parliamentary thunder has involved us, before another more heavy and more alarming is fallen on us. Single acts of tyranny may be ascribed to the accidental opinion of a day; but a series of oppressions, begun at a distinguished period, and pursued unalterably through every change of ministers, too plainly prove a deliberate, systematical plan of reducing us to slavery."

It is asserted that the usurpations of Parliament have not been even confined to matters where the people of England are concerned, but extended to those where only the inhabitants of the Colonies are interested ; and various examples are cited. The act suspending the functions of the New York Legislature is thus characterized :

"One free and independent legislature hereby takes upon itself to suspend the powers of another, *free and independent as itself;* thus exhibiting a phenomenon unknown in nature, the creator and creature of its own power. Not only the principles of common sense, but the common feelings of human nature must be surrendered up, before his Majesty's subjects here can be persuaded to believe that they hold their political existence at the will of a British Parliament. Shall these governments be dissolved, their property annihilated, and their people reduced to a state of nature, at the imperious breath of a body of men whom they never saw, in whom they never confided, and over whom they have no powers of punishment or removal, let their crimes against the American public be ever so great? Can any one reason be assigned, why one hundred and sixty thousand electors in the island of Great Britain, should give law to four millions in the States of America,

every individual of whom, is equal to every individual of them in virtue, in understanding, and in bodily strength? Were this to be admitted, instead of being a
free people as we have hitherto supposed, *and mean to continue ourselves*, we should
suddenly be found the slaves, not of one, but of one hundred and sixty thousand
tyrants; distinguished too, from all others, by this singular circumstance, that they
are removed from the reach of fear, the only restraining motive which may hold
the hand of a tyrant."

The Boston Port Bill is thus spoken of:

"There are extraordinary situations which require extraordinary interposition.
An exasperated people, who feel that they possess power, are not easily restrained
within limits strictly regular. A number of them assembled in the town of Boston,
threw the tea into the ocean, and dispersed without doing any other act of violence.
If in this they did wrong, they were known, and were amenable to the laws of the
land; against which, it could not be objected, that they had ever, in any instance,
been obstructed or diverted from the regular course, in favor of popular offenders.
They should, therefore, not have been distrusted on this occasion. But that ill-
fated Colony had formerly been bold in their enmities against the House of Stuart,
and were now devoted to ruin, by that unseen hand which governs the momentous
affairs of this great empire. On the partial representations of a few worthless
ministerial dependents, whose constant office it has been to keep that government
embroiled, and who, by their treacheries, hope to obtain the dignity of British
knighthood, without calling for a party accused, without asking a proof, without attempting a distinction between the guilty and the innocent, the whole of
that ancient and wealthy town is in a moment reduced from opulence to beggary.
Men who had spent their lives in extending the British commerce, who had invested,
in that place, the wealth their honest endeavors had merited, found themselves and
their families thrown at once on the world, for subsistence by its charities. Not
the hundredth part of the inhabitants of that town had been concerned in the act
complained of; many of them were in Great Britain, and in other parts beyond
sea; yet all were involved in one indiscriminate ruin, by a new executive power
unheard of till then—that of a British Parliament. A property of the value of
many millions of money, was sacrificed to revenge, not repay, the loss of a few
thousands. This is administering justice with a heavy hand indeed! And when is
this tempest to be arrested in its course? Two wharves are to be opened again when
his Majesty shall think proper; the residue, which lined the extensive shores of the
Bay of Boston, are forever interdicted the exercise of commerce. This little exception seems to have been thrown in for no other purpose than that of setting a precedent for investing his Majesty with legislative powers. If the pulse of his people
shall beat calmly under this experiment, another and another will be tried, till the
measure of despotism be filled up."

Thus, of the Act for the Suppression of Riots and Tumults in
the Town of Boston (14th Geo. III.), by which a murder committed there, might, at the option of the Governor, be tried in
the Court of King's Bench, England, by a jury of Middlesex:

"The wretched criminal, if he happen to have offended on the American side, stripped of his privilege of trial by peers of his vicinage, removed from the place where alone full evidence could be obtained, without money, without counsel, without friends, without exculpatory proof, is tried before judges predetermined to condemn. *The cowards who would suffer a countryman to be torn from the bowels of their society, in order to be thus offered a sacrifice to Parliamentary tyranny, would merit that everlasting infamy now fixed on the authors of the act!*"

The "wanton exercises" of executive authority by the King are enumerated with the stern energy, and often somewhat in the diction of the Declaration of Independence. Thus of vetoing laws:

"For the most trifling reasons, and sometimes for no conceivable reasons at all, his Majesty has rejected laws of the most salutary tendency."

Thus of slavery and the slave trade:

"The abolition of domestic slavery is the great object of desire in those Colonies, where it was, unhappily, introduced in their infant state. But previous to the enfranchisement of the slaves we have, it is necessary to exclude all further importations from Africa. Yet our repeated attempts to effect this, by prohibitions, and by imposing duties which might amount to a prohibition, have been hitherto defeated by his Majesty's negative: thus preferring the immediate advantages of a few British corsairs, to the lasting interests of the American States, and to the rights of human nature, deeply wounded by this infamous practice. Nay, the single interposition of an interested individual against a law, was scarcely ever known to fail of success, though in the opposite scale were placed the interests of a whole country. That this is so shameful an abuse of a power trusted with his Majesty for other purposes, as, if not reformed, would call for some legal restrictions."

Thus of withholding the royal assent, or negative to laws:

"With equal inattention to the necessities of his people here, has his Majesty permitted our laws to lie neglected in England for years, neither confirming them by his assent, nor annulling them by his negative: so that such of them as have no suspending clause, we hold on the most precarious of all tenures, his Majesty's will. *   *   *   *   And, to render this grievance still more oppressive, his Majesty, by his instructions, has laid his governors under such restrictions, that they can pass no law, of any moment, unless it have such suspending clause: so that, however immediate may be the call for legislative interposition, the law cannot be executed till it has twice crossed the Atlantic, by which time the evil may have spent its whole force."

Thus of certain recent royal instructions to the Governor of Virginia:

"But in what terms reconcilable to majesty, and at the same time to truth, shall we speak of a late instruction to his Majesty's Governor of the Colony of Vir-

ginia, by which he is forbidden to assent to any law for the division of a county, unless the new county will consent to have no representative in Assembly ?
*   *   *   Does his Majesty seriously wish, and publish it to the world, that his subjects should give up the glorious right of representation, with all the benefits derived from that, and submit themselves the absolute slaves of his sovereign will ? Or is it rather meant to confine the legislative body to their present numbers, that they may be the cheaper bargain, whenever they shall become worth a purchase ?"

Thus of dissolving and refusing to re-convene colonial legislatures, and the necessary result :

"But your Majesty, or your governors, have carried this power beyond every limit known or provided for by the laws. After dissolving one House of Representatives, they have refused to call another, so that, for a great length of time, the legislature provided by the laws, has been out of existence. *From the nature of things, every society must, at all times, possess within itself the sovereign powers of legislation.* The feelings of human nature revolt against the supposition of a State so situated, as that it may not, in any emergency, provide against dangers which, perhaps, threaten immediate ruin. While those bodies are in existence to whom the people have delegated the powers of legislation, they alone possess and may exercise those powers. But when they are dissolved, by the lopping off one or more of their branches, *the power reverts to the people, who may use it to unlimited extent, either assembling together in person, sending deputies, or in any other way they may think proper.* We forbear to trace consequences further : the dangers are conspicuous with which this practice is replete."

But we must hurry to the conclusion of this paper. It declares that "from the nature of things," lands "within the limits which any particular society has circumscribed around itself, are assumed by that society, and subject to their allotment," and hence that the King "has no right to grant lands of himself" in America: that the King "has no right to land a single armed man on our shores," and that those he sends are liable to our laws, or they "are hostile bodies invading us in defiance of law ;" that he has no right to subject the civil to the military power—and in view of the King's aggressions in this particular, the paper asks :

"Can his Majesty thus put down all law under his feet ? Can he erect a power superior to that which erected himself ? He has done it indeed by force ; but let him remember that force cannot give right."

It would be inexcusable to omit a word of the lofty peroration :

"That these are our grievances, which we have thus laid before his Majesty, with that freedom of language and sentiment which becomes a free people, *claiming their rights as derived from the laws of nature, and not as the gift of their chief magistrate.* Let those flatter, who fear: it is not an American art. To give praise where it is not due might be well from the venal, but would ill beseem those who are asserting the rights of human nature. They know, and will, therefore, say, that Kings *are the servants, not the proprietors of the people.* Open your breast, Sire, to liberal and expanded thought. Let not the name of George the Third be a blot on the page of history. You are surrounded by British counsellors, but remember that they are parties. You have no ministers for American affairs, because you have none taken from among us, nor amenable to the laws on which they are to give you advice. It behoves you, therefore, to think and to act for yourself and your people. The great principles of right and wrong are legible to every reader; to pursue them, requires not the aid of many counsellors. The whole art of government consists in the art of being honest. Only aim to do your duty, and mankind will give you credit where you fail. No longer persevere in sacrificing the rights of one part of the empire to the inordinate desires of another; but deal out to all equal and impartial right. Let no act be passed by any one legislature which may infringe on the rights and liberties of another. This is the important post in which fortune has placed you, holding the balance of a great, if a well-poised empire. This, Sire, is the advice of your great American council, on the observance of which may perhaps depend your felicity and future fame, and the preservation of that harmony which alone can continue, both to Great Britain and America, the reciprocal advantages of their connection. It is neither our wish nor our interest to separate from her. We are willing, on our part, to sacrifice everything which reason can ask, to the restoration of that tranquillity for which all must wish. On their part, let them be ready to establish union on a generous plan. Let them name their terms, but let them be just. Accept of every commercial preference it is in our power to give, for such things as we can raise for their use, or they make for ours. But let them not think to exclude us from going to other markets, to dispose of those commodities which they cannot use, nor to supply those wants which they cannot supply. Still less, let it be proposed, that our properties, within our own territories, shall be taxed or regulated by any other power on earth but our own. *The God who gave us life, gave us liberty,*[1] at the same time: the hand of force may destroy, but cannot disjoin them. This, Sire, is our last, our determined resolution. And that you will be pleased to interpose, with that efficacy which your earnest endeavors may insure, to procure redress of these our great grievances, to quiet the minds of your subjects in British America, against any apprehensions of future encroachment, to establish fraternal love and harmony through the whole empire, and that that may continue to the latest ages of time, is the fervent prayer of all British America."

This "Summary View of the Rights of British America," as it was named by Edmund Burke, and his associates who republished it "interpolated a little" in England[2]—and as we shall

[1] This is a free translation of the motto on Mr. Jefferson's seal, which bore his family arms, viz: "ab eo libertas a quo spiritus."
[2] Amusingly enough, we have found charges of plagiarism against Mr. Jefferson for afterwards, in the Declaration of Independence, copying the sentiments, and even diction, of this "*English* publication!" The "Summary View" passed through various editions, and, in fact, it furnished, to no little extent, if not the topics, the *phrases* of the Revolutionary controversy.

hereafter term it, to distinguish it from other " Instructions "—
contained every idea, we think, which is to be found in the
Declaration of Independence. It complained essentially, and
even literally, of the same grievances,¹ claimed the same " inherent " and " natural " rights, and, indeed, went decidedly farther
in its avowals in the latter direction. Sentiments so radical had
not yet fallen—*never* fell—from the burning tongues of James
Otis and Henry, those fiery torch-bearers of the coming Revolution! If Mr. Wythe entertained them theoretically, they
seem to have died in his bosom unuttered. Except in the particular of a well-limited and well-hedged about executive, the
" Summary View " was a declaration of independence nearly
two years in advance of the adopted one! and we are not at all
prepared to wonder, either from its import or the ability it exhibited, that it procured the certainly unusual " honor " of a bill of
attainder for a man thirty-one years old—who had held no office
more conspicuous than that of a burgess—who had hitherto made
no dangerous speech, or been concerned in any separate or known
act of hostility (more than all his colleagues in the House of Burgesses) to Government—among a few old leaders of the Revolution held particularly dangerous by reason of their commanding
position, like Peyton Randolph; their wealth and liberality, like
Hancock; or their popular influence, and talents to secure such
influence, like the two Adamses and Henry.

The instructions for their delegates actually adopted by the
Virginia Convention of 1774—the " tamer sentiments," which
" were preferred," and which Mr. Jefferson said, " he believed
[were] wisely preferred," in the existing condition of public
opinion—have indeed a very " sucking-dove " sort of a " roar,"
compared with his? They fall back in mild and velvety
phrase on the old ground of claiming " the same rights and privileges as their fellow subjects possess in Great Britain," etc.,
and do not in fact come up to the spirit of many of the county
resolutions. They are (as note D) included in the Appendix to
Mr. Jefferson's Memoir in both editions of his Works.

Congress assembled at Philadelphia on the 4th of September,
1774, and Virginia was honored with its presidency in the person of Peyton Randolph—that one of her statesmen adhering

---

¹ The reader will bear in mind that we have not quoted the whole paper.

to the patriotic cause, around whom clustered most thickly the honors of the royal government, and as much as around any other, the prestige of the old Virginia aristocracy—a man of great and varied accomplishments—incorruptible in public or private life—a wise, calm, experienced, and popular, if not great, legislator and statesman—possessing a large knowledge of law and a perfect knowledge of society and parliamentary forms.[1]

The history of the proceedings of the first Congress, as it is usually called (though delegates from seven Colonies met in Albany in 1754 to discuss a plan of Union for mutual defence and protection against French and Indians), world renowned for their wisdom and patriotism, does not fall within the province of this work. It adjourned in October, to meet again in May.

The Virginia counties soon began to organize Committees of Safety—those local administrations set up by the Revolution in the place of all previously constituted ones, and for a long period, and until regular government was again established, clothed with undefined powers, understood to be adequate to all necessary emergencies. Girardin, the historian of Virginia, remarks:

"The powers of the committees not being defined, were almost unlimited. They examined the books of merchants to see if they imported prohibited articles, or sold at a higher price than usual. They examined all suspected persons, disarmed, fined and published them; and from their decision there was no appeal. When necessary, they enlisted, trained, officered, and armed independent companies, and minute men in each county."[2]

Except the death penalty and the confiscation of estates,—which the Conventions of the entire Colony seem to have retained control over or shared in controlling,[3] it would be difficult to say where the power of these local tribunals stopped. We believe it really stopped only with the supposed necessity of the emergency; and if the emergency demanded, it extended to life and death.

Albemarle held its election of its Committee of Safety in

[1] We have already given his genealogy in that of his family. His wife was a sister of his colleague, Benjamin Harrison.
[2] History of Virginia, p. 6.
[3] We judge so, because in the records of the Convention, we find them repeatedly taking order in regard to the disposal of prisoners, and in regard to the confiscation of estates.

January, 1775, and the following gentlemen were chosen by the number of votes opposite their several names—the votes for each doubtless indicating the relative popularity of the individuals: [1]

Thomas Jefferson,	211	George Gilmer,	155
J. Walker,	200	Thomas Walker,	150
N. Lewis,	197	John Ware,	113
C. Lewis, N. G.,	188	James Quarles,	76
Isaac Davies,	183	James Hopkins,	71
John Coles,	175	Thomas Napier,	71
David Rhodes,	165	William Sim,	64
John Henderson,	156		

The second Convention of Virginia met in Richmond, March 20th, 1775. Mr. Jefferson was one of the representatives of Albemarle, his colleague being John Walker, whose name stands next his own in the Committee of Safety. We may here remark that as a member of the House of Burgesses, and also of the Convention, Mr. Jefferson was uniformly in the representation, after his first election, until chosen to Congress—and uniformly, it is believed, without opposition. His colleagues were once or twice changed.

The second Convention exhibited the usual division between moderate and decided men. On the whole, it acted with vigor. It approved of the measures of the Continental Congress, and passed a resolution of thanks to the Virginia delegates in that body. But in some complimentary resolutions to the Assembly of Jamaica (on account of its petition and memorial to the King in behalf of the claims of the Colonies) occurred expressions exhibiting such an absurd and adulatory spirit of conciliation towards England, considering the period when they were uttered, that they were, says Wirt, " gall and wormwood " to the impetuous Henry. He rose, therefore, and moved that the Colony " be immediately put into a state of defence, and that —— —— be a committee to prepare a plan for embodying, arming, and disciplining such a number of men, as may be sufficient for that purpose." This unexpected and, to the body of the Convention, startling proposition, produced a most painful effect on the

[1] This list, with the number of votes cast, we find in Mr. Jefferson's pocket account book for 1775. The number of voters (freeholders) shows how small yet remained this class of population, in the counties bordering the Blue Ridge.

minds of many members. The old moderate leaders, Nicholas, Bland, and Pendleton, the two last, members of the late Congress; Harrison, also a member of that Congress; and even the not, theoretically, over conservative Wythe, shrunk back from the yawning gulf of rebellion which thus suddenly opened before their feet. The resolution was supported on the floor by its mover and by Richard H. Lee, and earnestly pressed by Jefferson, Mason, Page, and the other leaders of what may be termed the movement party. It was practically a sort of test question—and warm was the struggle.

It was on this occasion that Henry poured out that glowing and burning outburst of eloquence, the burden of which was " *We must fight* "—so familiar to all Americans—and which, as rendered by Wirt, constitutes one of the most vehement and effective appeals to the passions to be found in the records of Revolutionary declamation, here or elsewhere. Wirt gives as the recollections of Judge Tucker, " one of the auditory," that the sentence : " I repeat it, sir, we must fight ! An appeal to arms and the God of hosts is all that is left us "—was " delivered with all the calm dignity of Cato of Utica."[1] A number of years since, a clergyman described, in our hearing, the delivery of this speech, as he had it from " an old Baptist clergyman," who was also " one of the auditory ;" and the account is so different in the whole coloring it throws over the scene, that we give it for what it is worth. Instead of the formal grandeur of the " Roman Senate," the " Assembly of the Gods," and the " calm dignity " of the stoical Cato, mentioned by Judge Tyler, the old Baptist clergyman described an assembly of men too terribly intent to regard their attitudes, or their looks, or their dignity in any respect. Henry rose with an unearthly fire burning in his eye. He commenced somewhat calmly—but the smothered excitement began more and more to play upon his features and thrill in the tones of his voice. The tendons of his neck stood out white and rigid " like whipcords." His voice rose louder and louder, until the walls of the building, and all within them, seemed to shake and rock in its tremendous vibrations. Finally, his pale face and glaring eye became " terrible to look upon." Men " leaned forward in their

[1] Wirt's Henry, p. 140, note.

seats," with their heads "strained forward," their faces pale,
and their eyes glaring like the speaker's. His last exclamation
—" Give me liberty or give me death "—was like the shout of
the leader which turns back the rout of battle !

The old clergyman said, when Mr. Henry sat down, he (the
auditor) felt " *sick* with excitement." Every eye yet gazed
entranced on Henry. It seemed as if a word from him would
have led to any wild explosion of violence. " Men looked
beside themselves."

Wirt thus scenically describes the succeeding effort :

"Richard H. Lee arose and supported Mr. Henry, with his usual spirit and
elegance. But his melody was lost amid the agitations of that ocean, which the
master spirit of the storm had lifted up on high. That supernatural voice still
sounded in their ears and shivered along their arteries. They heard in every pause
the cry of liberty or death. They became impatient of speech. Their souls were
on fire for action." [1]

The father of Judge Marshall described this speech of Mr.
Lee as an interesting review of the resources and means of
resistance of the colonists, and an appeal to the House to remember " that the race is not to the swift nor the battle to the
strong," [2] It was, doubtless, well worded, well in all respects,
but it seems remarkable that anybody should have chosen to
follow such a speech as that which had just preceded it.

Richard Henry Lee was the finest rhetorician, and next to
Mr. Henry, the most eloquent popular speaker of Virginia. He
was always ready to speak ; and unlike the latter gentleman,
industrious and indefatigable in business and in correspondence.
His person and voice were fine, his manners those of that patrician class in which his family had long stood. A finished education had developed to the utmost, talents of a handsome, but
rather showy than profoundly solid order. He neither made
any approach to the philosophic breadth of Cicero (to whom he
has often been compared), nor to the " dense logic " of Demosthenes.[3] Pendleton excelled him as a debater. Jefferson
immeasurably, and Bland decidedly, as writers. As a popular
speaker, Wirt gives a felicitous idea, above, of the relation he

---

[1] Wirt's Henry, p. 142.   [2] Ibid. page 142, note.
[3] Wirt says, "he *reasoned well*, and *declaimed freely and splendidly*." Perhaps it is not
too much to say that Mr. Lee " reasoned *well*," but we know of no specimen of *powerful
reasoning* of his extant, or that it is claimed for him by well supported tradition.

bore to Henry, when he contrasts dulcet melodies with the roar of the chafed ocean. But with his handsome talents, his finished culture, his imposing person and manners, his high social position, his place at the head of a brotherhood so distinguished for numbers and influence,[1] and, finally, his bold and ardent patriotism, Mr. Lee occupied, and justly occupied, a commanding position among his countrymen. And he was the more conspicuous, because he was the only one of the older leaders, or the older members of the aristocracy, who sided heartily and unflinchingly with the younger Whigs.

Mr. Henry's resolution for arming, passed by a decided majority. The Committee appointed to carry out its provisions included among others Patrick Henry, R. H. Lee, R. C. Nicholas, Benjamin Harrison, George Washington, Edmund Pendleton, and Thomas Jefferson. Well did events justify the confidence in the conservative minority implied in a portion of these selections! Colonel Nicholas, for example, earnestly opposed the resolutions; but the moment they passed, he rose and moved, that as resistance was now determined on, that instead of arming the militia (as proposed in one of the resolutions) it be made more effective, by raising ten thousand regulars *for the war.*[2] This, however, did not prevail.

The Committee, the next day after their appointment, reported a simple, and, circumstances considered, efficient plan of defence, which received the approbation of the Convention, March 25th.

Governor Dunmore, in pursuance of orders from England, had recently directed the vacant lands of the Colony to be sold at auction—the purchasers to hold them subject to a small annual quit rent. This was regarded as an unwarrantable attack on the resources of the Colony, as well as an attempt to establish a subservient crown tenantry. Mr. Henry moved a committee of inquiry with directions to report to the next Assembly or the next Convention. Messrs. Henry, Bland, Jefferson, Nicholas, and Pendleton were appointed the Committee.

The Convention chose the same delegates who had represented the Colony in the first Congress to also represent it in

[1] His brothers were Philip Ludwell, Thomas Ludwell, Francis Lightfoot. William and Arthur. And his father, Thomas, was a conspicuous man, and had been President of the Council.
[2] Wirt's Henry, p. 143, note.

the next.[1] But it being anticipated that Peyton Randolph would be called away to preside over the House of Burgesses, Mr. Jefferson was chosen to fill the vacancy which would thereupon ensue.

The Convention, before its adjournment, passed a resolution thanking Lord Dunmore for his conduct on a late expedition against the Indians. Whether particular thankfulness was really felt, or whether this was a concession to the peace party (that is, peace party with England)—"to keep front and rear together"— we are not informed. We only allude to the affair because one of the Mingo Chiefs, against whom the Governor's arms had been directed, was the celebrated Logan, whose speech to Lord Dunmore is quoted as a specimen of Indian eloquence in Mr. Jefferson's Notes on Virginia. Mr. Jefferson, afterwards, to defend himself against the charge of having *manufactured* this speech (to refute Buffon's theory of the degeneracy of men and brutes in America!) brought against him by the friends of Captain, or Colonel, Michael Cresap—to whom Logan in the speech attributes the murder of his family in cold blood—states, in a letter to Governor Henry (December 31, 1797), "that he learned it [the speech] in Williamsburg, he believed at Lord Dunmore's;" and that from somebody's lips—he does not remember whose—he transferred it to his pocket book, from whence he copied it into the Notes. It appears, as he states, in one of the pocket books of that period, now lying before us, which was drawn forth from the old forgotten receptacle, already mentioned,[2] in 1851.

In pursuance, undoubtedly, of a concerted scheme among the royal governors in America, to disarm the Colonies, the commander of a British armed vessel lying in James River, acting on the orders of Lord Dunmore, on the night of the 20th of April (1775)—two days after the battle of Lexington—entered Williamsburg, and carried off all the powder in the public magazine, except a few barrels placed in mine, for a purpose which could not be misunderstood. This abstraction of the public property, as well as the public means of defence from other foes besides

[1] With their order, however (priority being settled by the number of votes each received), somewhat changed. They now stood as follows: Peyton Randolph, George Washington, Patrick Henry, R. H. Lee, Edmund Pendleton, Benjamin Harrison, and Richard Bland.
[2] See page 16, note.

their own government, led to sharp altercations between the
city authorities and the Governor. Through the interposition
of Peyton Randolph, Colonel Nicholas, and other influential
citizens, these were temporarily quieted; but the passionate
threats and conduct of Lord Dunmore—who in temper, judgment, manners, and every other quality, was as little fitted as
possible to act his part well in such a juncture—kept up the
public apprehension and irritation. The smouldering fire burst
into a flame on the receipt of the news of the battle of Lexington.[1] The people of Virginia flew to arms, and a considerable
body of men assembled at Fredericksburg and menaced the
capital.

Among others, the volunteers of Albemarle, Mr. Jefferson's
constituency, assembled under arms at Charlotteville, and
through their officers addressed a communication to Colonel
George Washington, stating that "the county of Albemarle in
general, and the gentlemen volunteers in particular," were justly
incensed by the proceedings of Lord Dunmore; and they offered
to march on Williamsburg to enforce the return of the public
powder, or "die in the attempt." They remained long enough
under arms to receive Washington's reply—but this does not
appear to have been preserved, nor is its tenor known.[2] As
they quietly dispersed, the inference is that they were advised
so to do by the future Commander-in-chief. As Mr. Jefferson
was chairman of the Committee of Safety, which as yet controlled all the military,[3] as well as civil public business of
the county (and without the permission of which, by the by,
the gentlemen volunteers could not be supposed to be referring
their public action to any other authority)—as the muster took
place within a fraction over three miles of Mr. Jefferson's house,[4]

---

[1] Burk says (History of Va., vol. iii. p. 416), that the rising of the people, and the
advance of Henry on Williamsburg, presently to be narrated, took place " before the
battle of Lexington was ever talked of in Virginia." But this is obviously a mistake.
Wirt, certainly disposed to claim *all just* priority for Mr. Henry in Revolutionary affairs,
states the matter as we do.—*Life of Henry*, p. 153.

[2] See Sparks' Life and Writings of George Washington, vol. ii. p. 508.

[3] See Girardin's statement of the authority of these committees, quoted at page 99.
He also expressly says, when Dunmore removed the powder, the people " *looked up to
their Committees, assembled on the occasion, for directions how to act, and by what means to
obtain redress* (p. 8). This statement may be considered to be made on the authority of
Mr. Jefferson himself, for reasons which will be hereafter stated. Again, it distinctly
appears that Mr. Henry, on the same occasion, acted under the orders of the Committee
of his county, and when he offered, in writing, to escort the public treasury to a place
of safety, he exhibited his authority to the Treasurer, Colonel Nicholas, by stating that
he acted under the orders of the Hanover Committee.—*Wirt's Henry*, pp. 12–14.

[4] By Mr. Jefferson's precise table of distances, 3·06 miles.

and in plain sight of it—as in addition to the authority just named, he had long been the leading member of the county in the House of Burgesses, and in the two Conventions already held (elected to both without opposition)—as in both bodies he had made himself familiarly acquainted with Colonel Washington, and it can be supposed that few, if any, of the gentlemen volunteers[1] had enjoyed that privilege, as Washington resided in a remote county—we make no hesitation in assuming that the reference of their action to the latter, by the volunteers, took place under the direction, and, in all probability, at the suggestion of Mr. Jefferson. And this would coincide with his earliest known impressions of the military skill and strong practical sense of his subsequently illustrious countryman.

The troops assembled at Fredericksburg were dispersed by advice and some quieting assurances of Governor Dunmore's intentions, received from Randolph and Pendleton. But, according to Burk, their advice but barely carried the point. He says it was referred to one hundred military deputies, and on voting, the majority for acquiescence was but one.[2]

But another body proved less tractable. Mr. Henry, who, his biographer thinks, was anxious to precipitate a struggle which he foresaw was inevitable[3]—and whose dauntless and vehement temper renders the supposition every way probable—assembled the Independent Military Company of his county (Hanover), and placing himself at their head, advanced rapidly on Williamsburg. He utterly disregarded the messages of the old conservative leaders there, which met him on the way, and as he approached the capital, five thousand armed men were on their march to join him.[4] The Governor, having issued proclamation after proclamation in vain, began to make preparations for defence. The Countess of Dunmore and her family retired on board the Fowey man-of-war, and Montague, the commander of that vessel, landed a detachment to support the Governor, and sent notice to the President of the Council, that if his forces were molested or attacked, he would fire on the town. But the Governor seems to have doubted the result, or rather to have apprehended certain defeat, for he caused Mr. (or Captain)

---

[1] Their officers, we believe, were all young men. —— Lewis was captain, and George Gilmer and —— lieutenants.
[2] Hist. of Virginia, vol. iii. p. 411.   [3] Wirt, p. 155.   [4] Wirt's Henry, p. 159.

Henry to be met at Doncastle, sixteen miles from Williamsburg, about sunrise on the 4th of May, with the Receiver-
General's (Colonel Corbin's) bill of exchange for the value of
the public powder. This was borne by the Receiver-General's
son-in-law, Carter Braxton, a future signer of the Declaration of
Independence. This left no ostensible cause for Henry to
advance, though had the landing of the marines, and the insolent threats of Montague, been known at the moment, it is not
probable that a collision could have been avoided. Henry,
before retiring, wrote Colonel Nicholas, the Treasurer, expressing the apprehension that the "reprisal now made by the
Hanover volunteers" might "be the cause of future injury to
the treasury," and he therefore offered to escort it to a place of
safety." Nicholas replied that "he had no apprehension of the
necessity or propriety of the proffered service." [1] On the 6th,
by about the time Henry's forces had reached their homes, the
greatly relieved Governor issued a truculently worded proclamation, cautioning the King's lieges against aiding or abetting
"*a certain Patrick Henry*, of the county of Hanover, and a
number of deluded followers!"

Not long after these events, Lord North's "conciliatory
proposition" was received by the Governor, and he convened
the House of Burgesses, on the 1st of June, to take it into
consideration. This withdrew Peyton Randolph from Congress,
as had been anticipated, and Mr. Jefferson succeeded to the
vacancy. But the latter was not permitted to leave the Burgesses before an answer to the ministerial proposition was
framed. He says, in his Memoir:

* * * "The tenor of these propositions being generally known as having
been addressed to all the Governors, he [Peyton Randolph] was anxious that the
answer of our Assembly, likely to be the first, should harmonize with what he knew
to be the sentiments and wishes of the body he had recently left. He feared that
Mr. Nicholas, whose mind was not yet up to the mark of the times, would undertake
the answer, and therefore pressed me to prepare it. I did so, and, with his aid,
carried it through the House, with long and doubtful scruples from Mr. Nicholas
and James Mercer, and a dash of cold water on it here and there, enfeebling it
somewhat, but finally with unanimity, or a vote approaching it."

How much the answer was "enfeebled" by the doubts and

[1] Wirt.

scruples of the moderate members, we cannot say, but it rings true revolutionary metal, and it was a noble lead off for the Assemblies of the other Colonies. Archibald Cary, Mr. Jefferson's kinsman and friend, reported the paper as it was agreed on in committee,[1] June 10. It was in the form of a preamble and resolutions, of which the following are the heads, divested of their examples, citations of authority, and reasoning.

The House, after the customary expression of a desire for reconciliation, declare that they have examined it [the Ministerial proposition][2] minutely, viewed it in every light in which they are able, and that, "with pain and disappointment, they must ultimately declare that it only changed the form of oppression without lightening its burden." And they proceed to the following specifications:

"That the British Parliament has no right to intermeddle with the support of civil government in the Colonies.

"Because to render perpetual their [the Colonies'] exemption from an unjust taxation they must saddle themselves with a perpetual tax adequate to the expectations, and subject to the disposal of Parliament alone.

"Because various acts (which they specify), and the other numerous grievances of which themselves and sister colonies separately, and by their representatives in General Congress, had so often complained, would still continue without redress.

"Because at the very time of requiring from them grants of money, the ministry were making disposition to invade the Colonies with large armaments by sea and land, 'which was a style of asking gifts not reconcilable to their freedom.'

"Because on their agreeing to contribute their proportion towards the common defence, the ministry did not propose to lay open to them a free trade with all the world.

"Because the proposition now made to them involved the interest of all the other Colonies; that they were represented in General Congress by members appointed by their House; that their former union,[3] it was hoped, would be so strongly

---

[1] We rather suspect the main discussion between the moderate and the decided Whigs took place in the Committee. It consisted of Mr. Treasurer (Nicholas), Mercer, Jefferson, Henry, Lee, Munford, Dandridge, Nelson, Jones, Cary, F. L. Lee, Whitinge, and Charles Carter of Stafford.

[2] Contained in joint address of Lords and Commons on the 7th of Feb., 1775. His Majesty's answer, and a Resolution of the House of Commons, Feb. 27.

[3] Quere. Union of 1754? Or did he merely refer to that of 1774?

cemented, that no partial application could produce the slightest departure from the common cause; that they consider themselves as bound in honor as well as interest, to share their general fate with their sister Colonies, and should hold themselves base deserters of that Union to which they had acceded, were they to agree to any measures distinct and apart from them."

They then pointed to a plan, Lord Chatham's, which they said "though not entirely equal to the terms they had a right to ask, yet differed but in few points from what the General Congress had held out," and that it might have brought about a reconciliation of the difficulties, but that "a change of minister" produced " a total change of measures."

The paper closed in the following strain:

"These, my Lord, are our sentiments, on this important subject, which we offer only as an individual part of the whole empire. Final determination we leave to the General Congress, now sitting, before whom we shall lay the papers your Lordship has communicated to us. For ourselves, we have exhausted every mode of application, which our invention could suggest, as proper and promising. We have decently remonstrated with Parliament—they have added new injuries to the old; we have wearied our King with supplications—he has not deigned to answer us; we have appealed to the native honor and justice of the British nation—their efforts in our favor have hitherto been ineffectual. What then remains to be done? That we commit our injuries to the evenhanded justice of that Being, who doeth no wrong, earnestly beseeching Him to illuminate the councils and prosper the endeavors of those to whom America hath confided her hopes; that through their wise directions we may again see reunited the blessings of liberty, prosperity, and harmony with Great Britain."

In the meantime events had transpired which soon afterwards terminated the official career of the Earl of Dunmore, and with it the royal government in Virginia. On the 5th of June, three men who entered the public magazine were wounded by a spring gun placed there by the orders of the Governor; and on the 7th, a committee of the House, appointed to inspect the magazine, found the locks removed from the serviceable muskets, and they also discovered the powder which had been placed in mine. These things highly exasperated the multitude, and on a rumor getting abroad that the same officer who had before carried off the powder, was again advancing towards the city with an armed force, they rose in arms. The Governor's assurance that the rumor was unfounded restored tranquillity. He, however, left the city in the night with his family, and went on board the Fowey, lying at York, twelve miles distant. He left a message declaring that he had taken this step for *his safety*, and that thenceforth he should reside and transact business on board of the man of war! An interchange of messages, acrid and criminatory on his part, firm and spirited on the part of the House, was kept up until the 24th of June; when, on his final refusal to receive bills for signature except under the guns of an armed vessel, the House declared it a high breach of privilege, and adjourned to the 12th of October. But a quorum never afterwards attended.[1]

The further history of the overthrow of the royal government in Virginia belongs not in these pages. We have so much ground to pass over, in the long and varied life of Thomas Jefferson, that we can nowhere go beyond the most passing glimpses into any general history, with the events of which he is not personally or officially pretty directly connected.

Let it suffice on the present occasion to say, that we soon find the Earl of Dunmore carrying on a petty but barbarous predatory warfare against the people he has so lately governed; burning towns, declaring martial law, inciting servile insurrection, and finally, when the gang of miscreants[2] he commanded were wasted away by the sword, by tempests, and by pestilential diseases, flying back loaded with disgrace to that country which he, in conjunction with an ignominious band, the Bernards, the Hutchisons, the Gages, the Martins, etc., had first aided in robbing of the affections, and then of the allegiance, of the fairest portion of North America.

---

[1] Girardin's History of Virginia, p. 55.
[2] Wirt describes them as "a motley band of Tories, negroes, etc.," guilty of all kinds of atrocities. Girardin confirms this account.

CHAPTER IV.

1775.

MR. JEFFERSON set out from Williamsburg for Philadelphia, to take his seat in Congress, on the 11th of June, 1775. He

travelled in a phæton, and with two spare horses ; and it is curious to trace his slow progress of ten days, in a journey which
can now, probably, be accomplished in a less number of hours.[1]
Once between Fredericksburg and the Potomac, and again
between Wilmington and Philadelphia, there are entries in his
pocket account book of money paid to *guides !* This would
seem to argue that the public thoroughfares were in rather a
primitive state.   He reached the Pennsylvania capital on the
20th, and took lodging with " Ben Randolph," a carpenter, who
had handsome rooms to let in Chestnut Street. He dined at the
City Tavern.

The next day he took his seat in Congress, it being six weeks
after the opening of that body. He was the youngest member
but one.[2] His reputation as the author of " A Summary View
of the Rights of British America " (the proposed instructions to
the Virginia delegates in 1774), had preceded him ; and he now
brought in his hand the answer of Virginia to Lord North's
" Conciliatory Proposition," also written by himself.   This
paper was looked for with intense solicitude, as not only the
first legislative expression, but that of the first Colony in population, and, withal, the great leading Southern member of the
Confederacy, on a proposition well calculated to receive the
approbation of the timid and halting as a compromise between
the claims of the Colonies and the mother country.   And the
Virginia answer signally met the hopes and wishes of the
decided Whigs in Congress. This very young member, representing no particular interest—not favored by his locality, the
weight of his county, or any other extraneous consideration—
had been chosen, over the old statesmen of Virginia, to succeed

[1] His lodging-places were King William Court House, Fredericksburg, Port Tobacco,
Upper Malborough, Annapolis, Rockhall, and Wilmington. When he crossed the Maryland line, there occurs the following entry in his pocket account-book :
" *Maryland.*—The following articles in Maryland currency, where coins are as
follows :

Pistareen,	1s. 4d.	Guinea,	85s.
English Shilling,	1s. 8d.	Half Jo,	£3 00.
Dollar,	7s. 6d.		

" NOTE.—The true difference of exchange with Virginia is 100=125."

In Maryland, the accounts are kept in Maryland currency. On reaching the Pennsylvania line, the difference of exchange is again formally noted, and the accounts conformed to Pennsylvania currency. This was a persistent practice of his life, however
often he crossed the boundaries of States or foreign governments. We mention it as a
specimen of the inveterate precision and regularity which strikes the eye on every page
of his Memoranda of every description.
[2] So he says in note A, in Appendix to his Memoir. Who the younger member was
we are not informed.

the President of Congress and the representative of the colonial capital—purely on account of his talents and energy; nay, he had been detained in the House of Burgesses by Mr. Randolph, expressly to write and aid in carrying through that important paper, which would undoubtedly have the effect of closing the *door* to all present, if not all future, arrangement with England. The Southern Colonies were sure to follow the lead of Virginia. Massachusetts required neither leading nor urging, and only to be certain of Southern support, to take her place in the front line, and marshal the other New England Colonies there also. The middle provinces, whatever their inclinations, would not be able to withstand the pressure from the North and the South. When, then, the Virginia Burgesses voted on this question, the temple of Janus was opened for a decisive war. Henceforth, the only alternatives were a forcible and full redress of grievances, or subjugation.

Among circumstances so well calculated to confer *éclat*, it would be expected that Mr. Jefferson's entrance into Congress would not be an obscure one. He was received with open arms by the leaders of the party who favored decisive measures, and at once took his place among the most distinguished members of the House.

John Adams writes, in his Autobiography:

"Mr. Jefferson had the reputation of a masterly pen: he had been chosen a delegate in Virginia in consequence of a very handsome public paper which he had written for the House of Burgesses, which had given him the character of a fine writer." [1]

Again, Mr. Adams said in 1822:

"Mr. Jefferson came into Congress in June, 1775, and brought with him a reputation for literature, science, and a happy talent of composition. Writings of his were handed about remarkable for the peculiar felicity of expression." [2]

And, remarking on the manner in which Jefferson sustained these favorable impressions after his arrival, Mr. Adams added:

"Though a silent member in Congress, he was so prompt, frank, explicit, and decisive upon committees and in conversation—*not even Samuel Adams was more so*—that he soon seized upon my heart." [3]

[1] Life and Works of John Adams, by his grandson, vol. ii. p. 511.
[2] Letter to Timothy Pickering, in Life and Works, vol. ii. p. 513.   [3] Ibid.

" *Prompt, frank, explicit, and decisive !*" These were the very key words of Jefferson's whole political life and character! Mr. Adams, as his writings abundantly testify, was little prone to over-estimate the merits of those whom the public regarded as his rivals in renown, particularly his rivals in Revolutionary renown. When the preceding sentences were written, he had passed through a warm career of antagonism to Mr. Jefferson, and had not only been beaten by him, but the very party which professed his principles had been well-nigh exterminated by his victorious opponent. Years of personal alienation had separated them. Yet the great and brave heart of John Adams, in its stormy career, had met too few with whom it could sympathize in its own most marked qualities, not to rekindle to its early attachment when party strifes had died away. " Prompt, frank, explicit, and decisive !" In these words Mr. Adams also described himself—what he could best appreciate and least brook the absence of in others—what his own utter unguardedness at once drew forth from associates, or placed their opposite qualities in the strongest relief.

Five days after Mr. Jefferson took his seat in Congress, he was placed on the Committee to draw up a declaration of the causes of taking up arms. The Committee had been previously appointed, and it was on its making a report which was not satisfactory to the House, that a recommittal was ordered, and Jefferson and John Dickinson, of Pennsylvania, were added to its number. The former thus gives the sequel, in his Memoir:

" I prepared a draught of the declaration committed to us. It was too strong for Mr. Dickinson. He still retained the hope of reconciliation with the mother country, and was unwilling it should be lessened by offensive statements. He was so honest a man, and so able a one, that he was greatly indulged even by those who could not feel his scruples. We therefore requested him to take the paper, and put it into a form he could approve. He did so, preparing an entire new statement, and preserving of the former only the last four paragraphs and half of the preceding one. We approved and reported it to Congress, who accepted it."

Mr. Dickinson had been, from the outset, the leader of the conservative party in Congress—its leader by a long interval in talents, if we except the acute and unprincipled Galloway, who had already retired from that body.[1] He was a Whig at heart,

[1] Joseph Galloway, of Pennsylvania, served with great distinction, in the first Congress, but declined a reëlection. He became a decided Loyalist in 1776, and fled to Eng-

and though disposed to temporize and hang back—though he
shrunk with horror from the idea that ultimate disunion of the
British Empire, which his more ardent colleagues now only
shrunk from with aversion—there probably was never a moment
when his mind was not fully made up to cast his lot with his
countrymen, on whatever they should finally decide. Mr. Jefferson's uniform course in Congress was the same that it had
been in the Virginia Assembly on the subject of "keeping
front and rear together." While John Adams was making and
waging bitter quarrels with even undoubted Whigs who differed
with him,[1] Mr. Jefferson, we have strong reasons to think, never
had an enemy in Congress. His modesty captivated allies—his
suavity left opponents nothing to complain of. He had not a
particle of the mere vanity of authorship, of being at the head
of committees, or of bearing the name of leadership. In three
cases out of four, where, in his various writings, he mentions his
participation in the action of any celebrated committee of which
he was really chairman, he places his name last—and this,
oftentimes, in instances where it is not easy to find the records
which assign him his true position. We scarcely recollect an
example of a contrary kind, where a positive effort had not
been made (not to leave the thing in a state of equality where
he left it) but to directly take credit from him to give it to
another. And his reclamations, then, were usually something
of the latest, as in the instance just given in regard to the
Address on the Causes of taking up Arms. That production
was one of the most popular ones ever issued by Congress. It
was read amid thundering huzzas in every market place, and
amid fervent prayers in nearly every pulpit in the Colonies.
The commanders read it at the head of our armies. On the
heights of Dorchester (we think it was) amid booming cannon,

land. Just before his departure, he received, by a Delaware vessel, a trunk contaning
only *a halter*, a present which, perhaps, he regarded as significant. It was in allusion to
this that Trumbull says in his McFingal :

> Did you not, in as vile and shallow way,
> Fright one poor Philadelphian, Galloway,
> Your Congress, where the loyal ribald
> Belied, berated and bescribbled?
> What ropes and halters did you send,
> Terrific emblems of his end,
> Till, lest he'd hang in more than effigy,
> Fled in a fog the trembling refugee?"

[1] Mr. Adams's own writings give by far the best proof of this statement in nearly every
page of his Autobiography.

and under the folds of the banner bearing the ever green pine tree, and the sternly confident motto, " Qui transtulit, sustinet,"[1] Putnam proclaimed it to the applauding yeomanry of New England under his command.   It was quoted again and again admiringly in history.   It will not probably be denied that this celebrated production owed most of its popularity to the "last four paragraphs and half of the preceding one."   It would have been a very ordinary affair without these.[2]   This was the only part the admiring historians quoted.   Yet the " youngest member but one in Congress" never gave even a hint (we believe) of its authorship, suffering all the reputation of it to rest with Mr. Dickinson, until he mentioned it in a paper (the Memoir) destined never to see the light until Mr. Dickinson and himself had gone down to the grave.   Of this, as of various other reclamations which he really owed to himself, he made no memoranda until he was seventy-seven years old—showing how little precaution he took, or anxiety he felt on the subject.   And many of them, like this, seem rather accidentally or incidentally made in his simple narration of facts, than set down for any special purpose.   It may be truly said, and the remark is thrown out here somewhat in advance—that the reader may make it a standard to try Mr. Jefferson by on all occasions—that a conspicuous public man more utterly destitute of vanity than he was, never existed.   An amusing parallel, or rather contrast might be run between himself and his friend, Mr. Adams, in this particular.

The effect of this comity and deference towards men who were true-hearted, but whom age or different circumstances had rendered more tardy and timid than younger associates, was as strikingly illustrated in Congress as in the Virginia House of Burgesses.   When Nicholas was voted down, he moved to raise regular regiments to render the war more effective ; when Dickinson was voted down, and the die was irretrievably cast, he opposed his bosom to the enemies of his country as a soldier![3] And the effect of this course on Mr. Jefferson's personal rela-

[1] He who bore across (the ocean) will sustain.
[2] Q. v. in Am. Archives, 4th ser. vol. ii. 1865.
[3] He was made a general in the Pennsylvania militia, but our impression is that he actually first enlisted as a common soldier. See his life in Sanderson. He suffered a temporary eclipse of reputation for voting against the Declaration of Independence, but afterwards recovered it fully, and held the most important offices. A grosser caricature cannot be found than Mr. Adams's picture of him in his Autobiography.

tions, and perhaps we should add personal interests, is not less observable. While swimming on the front wave of revolution—so decisive that "even Samuel Adams was not more so"—he retained the respect, we might almost say the affection, of the most conservative *Whigs*. From their meeting in the second Congress to the day of their deaths, he and Mr. Dickinson remained warm personal friends—as their correspondence abundantly testifies. The same was as true of the Nicholases and Pendletons of Virginia. Indeed we shall find Dickinson and Pendleton (Nicholas did not survive) among the most ardent of his future supporters for the first office of the nation.

To return to our narrative of Congressional events. The report on the Causes of taking up Arms, written by Dickinson and Jefferson, was presented to the House on the 6th of July, and was received with the liveliest approbation. Dickinson's part (and name) prevented the conservatives from considering the close too animated, and the closing part, by Jefferson, reconciled the radical Whigs to the tone of what preceded it. We make no doubt that Mr. Dickinson's substitutions improved the adaptation of the paper to public feeling. It gave to it that combination of moderation of claims with firmness of purpose, which was better suited to the times than would have been any inkling of Jefferson's more radical theory of entire independence of Parliament. It must be confessed that our ancestors drew the sword, not to vindicate "natural rights," trampled down by the attempt of England to govern them, but as British subjects in every sense of the word, merely attempting to redress the wrongs inflicted by a legal, but an unjust government.

We give the peroration of the report, as a specimen of the first purely popular address prepared by Mr. Jefferson, and also to exhibit the strong desire for reconciliation still felt and avowed by the most radical party:

"We are reduced to the alternative of choosing an unconditional submission to the tyranny of irritable ministers, or resistance by force. The latter is our choice. We have counted the cost of this contest, and find nothing so dreadful as voluntary slavery. Honor, justice, and humanity, forbid us tamely to surrender that freedom which we received from our gallant ancestors, and which our innocent posterity have a right to receive from us. We cannot endure the infamy and guilt of resign ing succeeding generations to the wretchedness which inevitably awaits them, if we basely entail hereditary bondage upon them.

"Our cause is just. Our union is perfect—our internal resources are great, and, if necessary, foreign assistance is undoubtedly attainable. We gratefully acknowledge, as signal instances of the Divine favor towards us, that His providence would not permit us to be called into this severe controversy, until we were grown up to our present strength, had been previously exercised in warlike operations, and possessed of the means of defending ourselves. With hearts fortified with these animating reflections, we most solemnly, before God and the world, declare, that, exerting the utmost energy of those powers which our beneficent Creator hath graciously bestowed upon us, the arms we have been compelled by our enemies to assume, we will, in defiance of every hazard, with unabated firmness and perseverance, employ for the preservation of our liberties; being, with one mind, resolved to die free men rather than to live slaves.

"Lest this declaration should disquiet the minds of our friends and fellow subjects in any part of the empire, we assure them, that we mean not to dissolve that union which has so long and so happily subsisted between us, and which we sincerely wish to see restored. Necessity has not yet driven us into that desperate measure, or induced us to excite any other nation to war against them. We have not raised armies, with ambitious designs of separating from Great Britain, and establishing independent States. We fight not for glory or for conquest. We exhibit to mankind the remarkable spectacle of a people attacked by unprovoked enemies, without any imputation, or even suspicion of offence. They boast of their privileges and civilization, and yet proffer no milder condition than servitude or death.

"In our own native land, in defence of the freedom that is our birthright, and which we ever enjoyed until the late violation of it; for the protection of our property, acquired solely by the honest industry of our forefathers and ourselves, against violence actually offered, we have taken up arms. We shall lay them down when hostilities shall cease on the part of the aggressors, and all danger of their being renewed shall be removed, and not before.

"With an humble confidence in the mercies of the supreme and impartial Judge and Ruler of the universe, we most devoutly implore his divine goodness to conduct us happily through this great conflict, to dispose our adversaries to reconciliation on reasonable terms, and thereby to relieve the empire from the calamities of civil war."

On the 22d of July, Congress appointed a committee to consider and report on Lord North's "Conciliatory Proposition." All committees were chosen by ballot, the members taking priority according to the number of votes they received. This one comprised, preëminently, the strength of the House, and it was arranged in the following order: Benjamin Franklin, Thomas Jefferson, John Adams and Richard H. Lee. Mr. Jefferson was chosen by his colleagues to draft the paper, and he did so to their entire satisfaction. He modestly remarks in his Memoir, "The answer of the Virginia Assembly on that subject having been approved, I was requested by the Committee to prepare this report, which will account for the similarity of feature in the two instruments."

There was certainly an entire similarity in the positions of the two instruments, and a general one in their diction. But the last is amplified, and is statelier in tone. It being the final and formal rejection of the British ultimatum, like the solemn voice of the ancient herald denouncing authorized and avowed war, and committing the question henceforth to the sole arbitrament of the sword, we cannot forbear to exemplify its style and tenor by a liberal quotation:

"Desirous and determined as we are to consider, in the most dispassionate view, every seeming advance toward a reconciliation made by the British Parliament, let our brethren of Britain reflect what would have been the sacrifice to men of free spirits, had even fair terms been proffered, as these insidious proposals were, with circumstances of insult or defiance. A proposition to give our money, accompanied with large fleets and armies, seems addressed to our fears, rather than to our freedom. With what patience could Britons have received articles of a treaty from any power on earth, when borne on the point of a bayonet, by military plenipotentiaries? We think the attempt unnecessary to raise upon us, by force or by threat, our proportional contributions to the common defence, when all know, and themselves acknowledge, we have fully contributed, whenever called upon to do so, in the character of freemen.

"We are of opinion it is not just, that the Colonies should be required to oblige themselves to other contributions, while Great Britain possesses a monopoly of their trade. This, of itself, lays them under heavy contribution. To demand, therefore, additional aids, in the form of a tax, is to demand the double of their equal proportion. If we contribute equally with other parts of the empire, let us, equally with them, enjoy free commerce with the whole world: but while the restrictions on our trade shut to us the resources of wealth, is it just we should bear all other burdens equally with those to whom every resource is open?

"We conceive, that the British Parliament has no right to intermeddle with our provisions for the support of civil governments, or administration of justice. The provisions we have made are such as please ourselves, and are agreeable to our own circumstances. They answer the substantial purposes of government, and of justice; and other purposes than these should not be answered. We do not mean that our people shall be burdened with oppressive taxes to provide sinecures for the idle or the wicked, under color of providing for a civil list. While Parliament pursue their plan of civil government, within their own jurisdiction, we, also, hope to pursue ours without molestation.

"We are of opinion, the proposition is altogether unsatisfactory; because it imports only a suspension of the mode, not a renunciation of the pretended right, to tax us; because, too, it does not propose to repeal the several acts of Parliament, passed for the purposes of restraining the trade, and altering the form of government of one of our colonies; extending the boundaries, and changing the government of Quebec; enlarging the jurisdiction of the courts of admiralty and vice-admiralty; taking from us the right of a trial by jury of the vicinage in cases affecting both life and property; transporting us into other countries, to be tried for criminal offences, exempting by mock trials the murderers of colonists from punishment; and quartering soldiers upon us in times of profound peace.   Nor do they renounce the power of suspending our own Legislatures, and legislating for us themselves, in all cases whatsoever.   On the contrary, to show they mean no discontinuance of injury, they pass acts, at the very time of holding out this proposition, for restraining the commerce and fisheries of the provinces of New England; and for interdicting the trade of other colonies, with all foreign nations, and with each other.   This proves unequivocally, they mean not to relinquish the exercise of indiscriminate legislation over us.

"Upon .he whole, this proposition seems to have been held up to the whole world, to deceive it into a belief, that there was nothing in dispute between us but the mode of levying taxes; and that the Parliament having been now so good as to give up this, the Colonies are unreasonable if not perfectly satisfied.   Whereas, in truth, our adversaries still claim a right of demanding, *ad libitum*, and of taxing us themselves to the full amount of their demands, if we do comply with it.   This leaves us without any thing we can call property: but, what is of more importance, and which, in this pι ʽposal, they keep out of sight, as if no such point was now in contest between us, they claim a right to alter our charters, and establish laws, and leave us without any security for our lives or liberties.

"The proposition seems also to have been calculated, more particularly, to lull into fatal security our well-affected fellow-subjects, on the other side of the water, till time should be given for the operation of those arms, which a British minister pronounced would, instantaneously, reduce the cowardly sons of America to unreserved submission.   But, when the world reflects, how inadequate to justice are these vaunted terms; when it attends to the rapid and bold succession of injuries, which, during a course of eleven years, have been aimed at the Colonies: when it reviews the pacific and respectful expostulations, which, during that whole time, were the sole arms we opposed to them; when it observes that our complaints were either not heard at all, or were answered with new and accumulated injuries; when it recollects that the minister himself, on an early occasion, declared, 'that he would never treat with America till he had brought her to his feet,' that an avowed partisan of ministry has, more lately, denounced against us the dreadful sentence, ' delenda est Carthago;' and that this was done in presence of a British Senate, and being unreproved by them, must be taken to be their own sentiments, especially as the purpose has already, in part, been carried into execution, by the treatment of Boston and burning of Charlestown; when it considers the great armaments with which they have invaded us, and the circumstances of cruelty with which these have commenced and prosecuted hostilities; when these things, we say, are laid together and attentively considered, can the world be deceived into an opinion that we are unreasonable?   Or can it hesitate to believe with us, that nothing but our own exertions may defeat the ministerial sentence of death or abject submission?'"

This report was adopted by Congress, July 31st, and thus the last great measure of the session was consummated.   The House adjourned on the first of August.

Mr. Jefferson returned to Virginia by the same conveyance he left it, carrying in his carriage, until their roads diverged, his friend and colleague, Colonel Harrison.

On the 11th of August, the Virginia Convention, which had been taking the most efficient steps to carry on the war, balloted for delegates to the next Congress, and the vote stood as follows: P. Randolph, 89; R. H. Lee, 88; Jefferson, 85; Harrison, 83; Nelson, 66; Bland, 61; and Wythe, 58. Mr. Bland, now old and nearly blind, declined a reëlection, and F. L. Lee was chosen in his place (receiving 37 votes to 36 for Carter Braxton). General Washington and Mr. Henry had declined a reëlection.

During the recess, Mr. Jefferson wrote a letter, deserving our attention, to his friend and kinsman, John Randolph, who had succeeded his brother Peyton in the Attorney-Generalship of the Colony. Mr. Wirt thus describes this gentleman:

"Mr Randolph, it has been remarked, was in person and manners among the most elegant gentlemen in the Colony, and in his profession one of the most splendid ornaments of the bar. He was a polite scholar, as well as a profound lawyer, and his eloquence was of a high order. His voice, action, style, were stately, and uncommonly impressive."[1] * * *

When the struggle between the Colonies and England assumed the form of open war, Mr. Randolph sided with the latter, and made his preparations to remove thither. Before his departure, Mr. Jefferson addressed him an earnest appeal to use his efforts to produce a more truthful impression in England in regard to the objects and character of the American Colonists. As explanatory of the real feelings of the most decided class of Whigs, at this precise period, this letter possesses great interest:

TO JOHN RANDOLPH, ESQ.

MONTICELLO, *August* 25, 1775.

DEAR SIR,

I am sorry the situation of our country should render it not eligible to you, to remain longer in it I hope the returning wisdom of Great Britain, will, ere long, put an end to this unnatural contest. There may be people to whose tempers and dispositions contention is pleasing, and who, therefore, wish a continuance of confusion, but to me it is of all states but one, the most horrid. My first wish is a restoration of our just rights; my second, a return of the happy period, when, consistently with duty, I may withdraw myself totally from the public stage, and pass the rest of my days in domestic ease and tranquillity, banishing every desire of ever hearing what passes in the world. Perhaps (for the latter adds considerably to the warmth of the former wish), looking with fondness towards a reconci-

[1] Wirt's Henry, p. 93.

liation with Great Britain, I cannot help hoping you may be able to contribute towards expediting this good work. I think it must be evident to yourself, that the ministry have been deceived by their officers on this side of the water, who (for what purpose I cannot tell), have constantly represented the American opposition as that of a small faction, in which the body of the people took little part. This, you can inform them, of your own knowledge, is untrue. They have taken it into their heads, too, that we are cowards, and shall surrender at discretion to an armed force. The past and future operations of the war must confirm or undeceive them on that head. I wish they were thoroughly and minutely acquainted with every circumstance, relative to America, as it exists in truth. I am persuaded this would go far towards disposing them to reconciliation. Even those in Parliament who are called friends to America, seem to know nothing of our real determinations. I observe, they pronounced in the last Parliament, that the Congress of 1774 did not mean to insist rigorously on the terms they held out, but .ept something in reserve, to give up; and, in fact, that they would give up everything but the article of taxation Now, the truth is far from this, as I can affirm, and put my honor to the assertion. Their continuance in this error may, perhaps, produce very ill consequences. The Congress stated the lowest terms they thought possible to be accepted,[1] in order to convince the world they were not unreasonable. They gave up the monopoly and regulation of trade, and all acts of Parliament prior to 1764, leaving to British generosity to render these, at some future time, as easy to America as the interests of Britain would admit. But this was before blood was spilt. I cannot affirm, but have reason to think, these terms would not now be accepted. I wish no false sense of honor, no ignorance of our real intentions, no vain hope that partial concessions of right will be accepted, may induce the ministry to trifle with accommodation, till it shall be out of their power ever to accommodate. If, indeed, Great Britain, disjoined from her Colonies, be a match for the most potent nations of Europe, with the Colonies thrown into their scale, they may go on securely. But if they are not assured of this, it would be certainly unwise, by trying the event of another campaign, to risk our accepting a foreign aid, which, perhaps, may not be obtainable, but on condition of everlasting avulsion from Great Britain. This would be thought a hard condition, to those who still wish for reunion with their parent country. I am sincerely one of those, and would rather be in dependence on Great Britain, properly limited, than on any nation upon earth, or than on no nation. But I am one of those, too, who, rather than submit to the rights of legislating for us, assumed by the British Parliament, and which late experience has shown they will so cruelly exercise, would lend my hand to sink the whole island in the ocean.

If undeceiving the Minister, as to matters of fact, may change his disposition, it will, perhaps, be in your power, by assisting to do this, to render service to the whole empire, at the most critical time, certainly, that it has ever seen. Whether Britain shall continue the head of the greatest empire on earth, or shall return to her original station in the political scale of Europe, depends, perhaps, on the resolutions of the succeeding winter. God send they may be wise and salutary for us all. I shall be glad to hear from you as often as you may be disposed to think of

---

[1] We have no doubt that a period should take the place of a comma after the word "accepted," and the succeeding words of the sentence (as now printed) form the beginning of the next one. Mr. Jefferson was but a careless punctuator in his letters, and as often began a sentence with a small letter as a capital. Consequently, printers could not be expected always to avoid errors of this kind.

things here. You may be at liberty, I expect, to communicate some things, consistently with your honor, and the duties you will owe to a protecting nation. Such a communication among individuals, may be mutually beneficial to the contending parties. On this or any future occasion, if I affirm to you any facts, your knowledge of me will enable you to decide on their credibility ; if I hazard opinions on the dispositions of men or other speculative points, you can only know they are my opinions. My best wishes for your felicity attend you, wherever you go, and believe me to be assuredly,

Your friend and servant.

As late as the close of November, the same year, he " cordially loved a union with Great Britain," but more " blood had been spilt "—and his tone now is of loftier warning and sterner menace.   He wrote, from his seat in Congress, to Mr. Randolph, then in England (Nov. 29th) :

" In an earlier part of this contest, our petitions told him that from our King there was but one appeal. The admonition was despised, and that appeal forced on us. To undo his empire, he has but one truth more to learn ; that after Colonies have drawn the sword, there is but one step more they can take. That step is now pressed upon us by the measures adopted, as if they were afraid we would not take it. Believe me, dear sir, there is not in the British empire, a man who more cordially loves a union with Great Britain, than I do. But, by the God that made me, I will cease to exist before I yield to a connection on such terms as the British Parliament propose ; and in this I think I speak the sentiments of America. *We want neither inducement nor power, to declare and assert a separation. It is will, alone, which is wanting, and that is growing apace under the fostering hand of our King.* One bloody campaign will probably decide, everlastingly, our future course ; I am sorry to find a bloody campaign is decided on. If our winds and waters should not combine to rescue their shores from slavery, and General Howe's reinforcement should arrive in safety, we have hopes he will be inspirited to come out of Boston and take another drubbing : and we must drub him soundly, before the *sceptered tyrant* will know we are not mere brutes, to crouch under his hand, and kiss the rod with which he deigns to scourge us." [1]

This precisely accords with the tenor of a letter which John Adams wrote a friend two months and a half later (February 18th, 1776), which will be found in Force's American Archives, 4th ser., vol. iv., 1183. In this he said : " Reconciliation if practicable, and peace if attainable, you very well know would be agreeable to my inclinations ; but I see no prospect, no probability, no possibility."

[1] Since this portion of the work was written, Francis Eppes, Esq., of Tallahassie, Florida, a grandson of Mr. Jefferson, has found and kindly furnished for our use (among a multitude of other papers), six letters addressed by Mr. Jefferson to his maternal grandfather, Francis Eppes (Mr. Jefferson's brother-in-law), in the year 1775, while occupying his seat in Congress. These give interesting glimpses of the ideas prevailing at the period. We have concluded, instead of presenting extracts here, to give them entire in APPENDIX. No. 1.

Indeed, Mr. Adams retained his desire for conciliation to a much later period, as appears from the following remarkable passage in a letter he wrote George A. Otis in 1821 :

"For my own part, there was not a moment during the Revolution when I would not have given everything I possessed for a restoration to the state of things before the contest began, provided we could have had a sufficient security for its continuance." [1]

When the idea of striking for independence began to be seriously entertained by the more decided Whigs in Congress, does not very definitely appear. John Adams conveys the impression, in his Autobiography, that from the first reassembling of the Congress of 1775, after the August recess, that *he* incessantly and in speeches on the floor urged the measure.[2] He says that he avowed the same designs before the recess, and that they were "no secret in or out of Congress."[3] He refers to two letters of his, written in July (1775), as in corroboration of this.

Per contra, when Otis's translation of Botta's History of the North American Revolutionary War appeared, Chief Justice Jay wrote the translator, in strong reprobation of Botta's hypothetical assertion, that the Americans (or a portion of their leaders) *entered* the struggle aiming at independence. Judge Jay remarked :

"Explicit professions and assurances of allegiance and loyalty to the sovereign (especially since the accession of King William), and of affection of and for the mother country, abound in the journals of the Colonial legislatures, and of the congresses and conventions, from early periods to the *second petition of Congress,* in 1775. If these professions and assurances were sincere, they afford evidence more than sufficient to invalidate the charge of our desiring or aiming at independence. If, on the other hand, these professions and assurances were factitious and deceptive, they present to the world an unprecedented instance of long-continued, concurrent, and detestable duplicity in the Colonies. Our country does not deserve this odious and disgusting imputation. During the course of my life, *and until the second petition of Congress, in 1775, I never did hear any American of any class, or any description, express a wish for the independence of the Colonies.*"

After citing some testimony in a letter of Dr. Franklin's to the same effect, but only coming down to August, 1774, when the expression was made, he added :

[1] See Adams's letter in the Life and Writings of John Jay, by his son, vol. ii. p. 416.
[2] Life and Works of John Adams, vol. ii. pp. 503–510.
[3] Ib. pp. 407, 412, *et passim.*

"It does not appear to me necessary to enlarge further on this subject. It has always been, and still is, my opinion and belief, that our country was prompted and impelled to independence by *necessity*, and not by *choice*. They who know how we were then circumstanced, know from whence that necessity resulted." [1]

Otis forwarded these statements to John Adams and to Jefferson, and both fully concurred in their general tenor, without taking any exception to the date assigned for the first public broaching of independence ideas—or rather, down to which Mr. Jay declares he had heard no contrary ones broached—namely, the second petition to the King.

A moment's reflection will show that Judge Jay meant the period of the *rejection* of the second petition, and not that of its being *made* by Congress. It was made July 8th (1775). It contained such asseverations as this: "We solemnly assure your Majesty that we not only most ardently desire the former harmony between her [Great Britain] and these Colonies may be restored, but that a concord may be established between them upon so firm a basis as to perpetuate its blessings uninterrupted by any future dissensions to succeeding generations in both countries," etc. It was, indeed, the tamest document of the session. Its humility of *tone* disgusted the bolder Whigs,[2] though to suppose they did not subscribe to its main *doctrines*, would be to suppose them guilty of that "detestable duplicity" of which Mr. Jay speaks, and guilty not only collectively, but individually—because individually they each and all signed their names to that petition. Nearly half a dozen other addresses, subsequently agreed on by Congress, before the recess, either directly or impliedly repudiate the idea of aiming at independence. Even Jefferson's answer to the "Conciliatory Proposition" (adopted July 31, the day before the adjournment), does not lurkingly point to ultimate separation. Jefferson says expressly, in his Notes on Virginia (Query XIII.): "*It is well*

[1] For this letter, dated Jan. 13, 1821, see Life and Writings of John Jay, vol. ii. p. 410.
[2] Mr. Jefferson relates the following anecdote on the subject in his Memoir:
"Congress gave a signal proof of their indulgence to Mr. Dickinson, and of their great desire not to go too fast for any respectable part of our body, in permitting him to draw their second petition to the King according to his own ideas, and passing it with scarcely any amendment. The disgust against its humility was general; and Mr. Dickinson's delight at its passage was the only circumstance which reconciled them to it. The vote being passed, although further observation on it was out of order, he could not refrain from rising and expressing his satisfaction, and concluded by saying 'there is but one word, Mr. President, in the paper which I disapprove, and that is the word *Congress*;' on which Ben Harrison rose and said 'there is but one word in the paper, Mr. President, of which I approve, and that is the word *Congress*.'"

known that in July, 1775, a separation from Great Britain, and establishment of Republican Government, had never yet entered into any person's mind." This statement was published on Jefferson's authority while all the important actors in the Revolution were yet alive. None of them, that we have ever heard, challenged its accuracy. There was nothing certainly in the act of petitioning the King, the second time, or in the character of succeeding events, until the rejection of that petition, to make that the turning point in American feeling, of which Judge Jay was attempting to fix the date.

On the 9th of November (1775) a letter was received and read in Congress, from Richard Penn and Arthur Lee, who had been intrusted with the delivery of the second petition to the King, stating that "no answer would be given." This contemptuous refusal to notice so humble a document, satisfied the bolder leading Whigs—men of the stamp of the two Adamses, Jefferson, and Lee—that their only choice was between entire independence and entire subjugation ; and henceforth there is little doubt that they, and such as they, advocated it as openly and directly as the state of public feeling permitted ; though there is not a particle of good reason for supposing that yet, or *for several months to come*, avowed and unqualified independence ideas were put forth on the floors of Congress, by any member of that body. Such avowals would yet have shocked and alarmed the moderate and the timid ; and it was imperatively necessary to "keep front and rear together." [1]

Far be it from us to aver that for a period somewhat anterior to the 9th of November, 1775, a few of these bolder spirits—all the individuals named in the preceding paragraph, and perhaps as many more—did not in their own bosoms contemplate the possible necessity of separation—nay, did not anticipate that necessity. They probably, too, *talked* of this together in their little secret conclaves, for they trusted each other. We cannot

---

[1] It is easy enough now to see that the *bent* of a good deal that was said and done was *in that direction*, and undoubtedly disclosed the ultimate motive ; but as, in the case of Mr. Adams's often-quoted letters in July, 1775, which were intercepted and published by the English, there was always a *saving clause* expressed or distinctly implied. We were to raise armies and navies, nay, *to frame governments*, in view of a tremendous struggle—but our object, after all, was but to *conquer conciliation !* Such was the *language* necessary till a period very close on to the Declaration of Independence, for the purpose of "keeping front and rear together !" This was not *now* the deliberate and therefore the "detestable duplicity" complained of by Mr. Jay. It was the *necessary* resort of *self-defence* in *immediate, pressing and practical danger*, and was as justifiable, therefore, as any other wile of war.

doubt John Adams's assertions when he declares that he *felt* thus, or when he declares that the prompt, frank, explicit, and decisive Jefferson " went with him at *all* points." And certainly Samuel Adams, preëminently the Anarch of the Revolution— one of the most inflexible, uncompromising, and dauntless men that ever marched in the bloody van of civil war—could not have been a jot behind the most daring colleague. R. H. Lee belonged to the same personal and parliamentary set. He invariably acted with the Adamses.

But John Adams's mistake, in a record written thirty years afterwards (and after a century of events) was, undoubtedly, in supposing he talked openly in Congress throughout 1775, what he only talked among confidential associates. This mistake would be not an unnatural one to an accurate writer, under such circumstances : and for an unquestionably honest one, a more habitually inaccurate, careless, and contradictory writer, in regard to details, than John Adams, it would be difficult to find in the whole history of literature. Mr. Jay was in Congress during the whole period of which he speaks—from the first meeting of the first session down to May, 1776.[1] He was not probably in the secrets, any more than he was in the policy, of the ultra Whigs. But had Mr. Adams openly advocated independence on the floor of Congress when he says he did, the ear of the cautious and circumspect Jay would not have failed to catch the sound, and his not only scrupulous, but most accurate pen would never have made the unqualified assertions it did to the translator of Botta. Moreover, Mr. Adams himself drops into one of his customary contradictions, (in his letter to G. A. Otis) by acquiescing in all Judge Jay's statements.

The point we have discussed is not german to any necessary topic of this biography ; but we confess we are as tired as Judge Jay was, of hearing the intensity of our forefathers' patriotism and foresight vindicated at the expense of their decent regard for truth ; and we may add, of what was likely to have been the natural feeling of their hearts, as civilized, morally cultivated, and politic men. Even Mr. Wirt, it seems to us, fell into this stale error, when he recorded conversations of thirty or forty years standing (for all that appears to the con-

---

[1] He then returned home to take his seat in the Convention or " Congress " of New York. See his Life and Writings, vol. i. p. 42.

trary, till then unwritten), to show that his hero, Mr. Henry, even " before one drop of blood was shed in our contest," foresaw, predicted, and consequently, we are left to infer, labored for a declaration of independence, and all that followed it, with super-prophetic ken as to details !¹   Far be it from us to snatch a decoration from the laurelled bust of Henry.   With far more " blanks " than Mr. Wirt's *private* correspondence assigns to him,² he was a man both to be revered and loved.³   But is it at all probable that Mr. Wirt would have claimed for him such a remarkable prescience in regard to the Declaration of Independence, had he known that a letter would one day see the light which seems to conclusively show that Mr. Henry actually hesitated a little in regard to making that declaration, when it was finally proposed ?⁴

But why should we wonder, or deem it any way discreditable to our ancestors, that they threw away the scabbard with great hesitation and reluctance, in that stern struggle ? That sentiments of loyalty and affection towards the parent country could survive Lexington and Bunker's Hill, may now seem a matter of astonishment; but we forget, after almost a century of separation and self-government—after becoming accustomed to institutions and associations so different—after the formation of an entirely new class of ideas in the science of government, and an experience which has demonstrated the success of those ideas—the innumerable ties of blood, language, literature, legal and social institutions, which linked our forefathers to the land

¹ See Wirt's Henry, p. 111.
² For a very curious and amusing letter in regard to Mr. Henry, and to Wirt's *materials* for writing his biography, see Wirt's letter to Judge Dabney Carr, of Aug. 20, 1815, given in Kennedy's Memoirs of Wirt, vol. i. p. 344.
³ We confess that there is something irresistibly attractive to us in the lyrical genius and in the exquisite naturalness and *bonhomie* of his character. We think Mr. Wirt has *dressed him up* too much. Wirt was the embodiment of social cultivation—Henry of wild nature. The letter to Carr, referred to in the preceding note, satisfies us that Wirt did not fully *appreciate*, or *feel* his subject; and hence the *troubles narrated in that letter*. Yet we are fully satisfied that Henry, *without any dressing up*, would have stood forth more *attractively*, more *vigorously even*, to posterity. His very faults would have made him more *lovable*.
⁴ The letter referred to is one from General Charles Lee (then in Williamsburg) tc Mr. Henry, stating the objections to an immediate declaration made by the *latter*, in conversation, *the day before*, and attempting to convince Mr. Henry that he was in an *error*. The objection of Mr. Henry, however, seems to have been only one of time. He thought the "pulse of France and Spain" ought previously to have been felt. Lee's letter is dated May 7, 1776. Consequently the conversation took place *eight days* before the Virginia Convention instructed their delegates in Congress to move for independence, and *while that subject was under discussion*. As Mr. Henry did not *oppose* the resolution in the Convention, he probably did not allow the views expressed to General Lee to become public. But this, perhaps, explains why, on this *occasion of occasions*, his "supernatural voice" was not heard! For Lee's letter, see Am. Archives, 5th ser. vol. i. 96.

from which they sprung. The sentiment of loyalty to constituted authority, is ever strong in considerate, and perhaps is
natural to elevated, minds. And the warmer sentiment of
patriotism, common to all men, included in the bosoms of our
ancestors England as well as America. Great Britain was *their*
country as much as America. Many of them had been born
there; multitudes of them had been educated there; near and
dear relatives of all of them continued to reside there. They
felt that to separate themselves politically from it, was to separate themselves from the freëst as well as the most powerful
government on earth—and this for the purpose of plunging
into an unexplored and doubtful future. That future was not
then illumined by the broad lights which their own experience
and that of their posterity have since cast over it. Their pride,
their prejudices, and their affections were with the Anglo-Saxon
race—their fathers and brothers. They were equally inheritors
with those fathers and brothers in the long line of the military
triumphs and civic glories of England. Agincourt and Ramilies, Drake and Marlborough, Elizabeth and William III., were
words in their national history. They were the countrymen of
Alfred, of the men of Runnymede and of Hampden—of Bacon,
Locke, and Newton—of Shakspeare and Milton. Magna Charta
and the Bill of Rights, the legal and municipal institutions of
England, were a part of their inheritance. The ancient and
peerless abodes of learning on the banks of the Cam and the
Isis—the Bodleian, Westminster Abbey, the noble benefactions
and accumulations of ages in philanthropy and in art, in many
a priceless collection, were theirs. The ancient public and
private customs—the traditions and prejudices—the social maxims—the bravery and loyalty in man—the stainless faith in
woman—the happy and inviolable homes—which were the
birthrights of Englishmen, were theirs.

To what country were they to turn for efficient aid in the
unequal struggle, unless to France? France was the hereditary
enemy of their blood and name. It was a government seemingly little likely to foster that liberty abroad, of which it did
not tolerate a vestige at home. It was a country of different
language, religion, laws, social and domestic notions, physical
habits, and it might almost be said, of intellectual organizations.
France and the whole house of Bourbon had been recently

smitten and humbled by England in the four quarters of the globe. The American colonists had contributed their full share to this. On the savannas of the Ohio, and under the ramparts of Quebec, their bosoms had been pressed forward foremost under the banner of St. George. Equally then as Americans and as Englishmen, they hated Frenchmen. The traditional prejudices sucked in with their mother's milk, nurtured by their nursery songs, and fostered by their national literature, had been embittered by recent war and mutual injuries.

If not to France, to what country could the Americans then turn? To Spain, to Austria, to Prussia or to Russia? With each of these the prospect of obtaining aid was less—the alliance still more unnatural. Could they offer any induce-ments sufficient to tempt the States General of Holland into an alliance in which both parties would not be a match for the flushed might of England? Indeed, there was not any single power in Europe which, united with the American Colonies, could, at that precise juncture, be regarded as such a match.[1] It required a combination of European powers to produce it. What materials had the Americans out of which to construct and consolidate such a coalition of nations, unless they bartered for it all and more than they were fighting England to save?

The suggestions of rational caution, then, coincided with the pleadings of ancient affection against such views as M. Botta theoretically, and without any authority whatever, assigns to our forefathers as those which led them to begin the Revolution-ary struggle. They began that struggle to *redress grievances*, not expecting or desiring a permanent separation. They never struck for independence, until they saw the only remaining alternative was utter subjugation. Then outraged ancient affec-tion turned to hate—then caution was cast to the winds—then, armed with the weapons of despair, they resolved to be free, or to die!

A curious entry (to make a sudden descent in our theme) occurs in Mr. Jefferson's pocket account book, before the re-assembling of Congress. It runs thus:

---

[1] This was decidedly the opinion of M. de Vergennes, the celebrated foreign minister of France, of this period, in regard to his own country. He again and again afterwards assured the American Ministers that it would not be safe for France and America *both* to attempt to match England in this war—that the adhesion of *other* allies must also be pro-cured. England was never before or since so paramount in Europe as at that epoch.

" *Williamsburg, August* 17.—Delivered to Carter Braxton an order on the Treasurer in favor of J. Randolph, Atty. General, for £13, the purchase money for his violin. This dissolves our bargain recorded in the General Court, and revokes a legacy of £100 sterling to him now standing in my will, which was made in consequence of that bargain." [1]

This suggests to us to say that Mr. Jefferson retained his full schoolboy partiality for the violin. He did so, indeed, through all periods of his life. The following entry occurs in Mr. Trist's Memoranda :

"Mr. Jefferson said: 'Alberti came over with a troop of players and afterwards taught music in Williamsburg. Subsequently, I got him to come up here (Monticello) and took lessons for several years. I suppose that during at least a dozen years of my life, I played no less than *three hours* a day (!) But, at the breaking out of the Revolution, I laid aside my violin, and have never taken it up again. At first I carried about with me that little instrument which I've given to Lewis ; but my mind was too much occupied with other matters. I have heard Viotti often, but never derived the same pleasure from him that I have from Alberti.'—'You have two fine violins now?' 'Yes, I have two that would fetch in London any price—one a violin of Sir John Randolph's (N. P. T. thinks he

---

[1] Mr. Richard Randolph, of Washington (of the Tuckahoe family of Randolphs), copied. as a curiosity, this record of a bargain, from the minutes of the General Court, and it was included among more valuable papers, kindly furnished us by that gentleman. The violin was a magnificent one, and such instruments and the fine accompanying collection of music, were not very *comeatable* things in Virginia at that day, but the peculiarity of the terms of the bargain, as well as the portentous array of attesting witnesses, shows that there was as much of the jocose as the serious in the arrangement. Here is the paper :

"*October* 11*th*, 1771.

"It is agreed between John Randoph, Esq., of the City of Williamsburg, and Thomas Jefferson, of the County of Albemarle, that in case the said John shall survive the said Thomas, that the Exr's or Adm'rs of the said Thomas shall deliver to the said John 800 pounds sterling of the books of the said Thomas, to be chosen by the said John, or if not books sufficient, the deficiency to be made up in money : And in case the said Thomas should survive the said John, that the Executors of the said John shall deliver to the said Thomas the violin which the said John brought with him into Virginia, together with all his music composed for the violin, or in lieu thereof, if destroyed by any accident, 60 pounds sterling worth of books of the said John, to be chosen by the said Thomas. In witness whereof the said John and Thomas have hereunto subscribed their names and affixed their seals the day and year above written.

"JOHN RANDOLPH (L. S.)
"TH. JEFFERSON (L. S.)

" Sealed and delivered in presence of :
    " G. Wythe,
    " Tho's Everand,
    " P. Henry, Jr.
    '' Will. Drew,
    " Richard Starke,
    " Wm. Johnson,
    " Ja. Steptoe.
" Virginia, ss.

" At a general court held at the capitol on the 12th day of April, 1771, this agreement was acknowledged by John Randolph and Thomas Jefferson, parties thereto, and ordered to be recorded.

" Teste,
" BEN. WALLER, C. C Cur.'

said),[1] the other a Cremona more than a hundred years old.' (Monticello, March 22d, 1826.)"[2]

We suppose the Alberti here mentioned was Dominico, the celebrated Venetian musician—and more celebrated as a harpsichord player than a violinist. At all events, Mr. Jefferson's teacher was also his (future) wife's master on the former instrument. The "little instrument given to Lewis" (his fourth grandson, Lewis Randolph) was a "kit," or small fiddle—which, as he remarks, he "carried about" with him, in his younger days, on journeys, of almost all kinds. It took up but a trifle of room packed in its little case, and afforded, he used to say, a capital way of whiling away the time before the people were up where he was staying. It could even be played in doors, in thick walled houses, without disturbing the occupants of adjoining rooms.

Mr. Jefferson is not to be understood literally that he never took up his violin again, after the breaking out of the Revolution. He means that he ceased to make it a part of his daily and regular occupation; for he certainly continued to play, occasionally, for his own diversion, or that of others, until his right wrist was broken past (full) recovery, in France.[3]

---

[1] It was, instead, as just seen. John, the *son* of Sir John.

[2] Compare this with the following letter of Mr. Jefferson, dated June 8th, 1778, to a correspondent in France, whose address is lost :

"If there is a gratification, which I envy any people in this world, it is to your country its music. This is the favorite passion of my soul, and fortune has cast my lot in a country where it is in a state of deplorable barbarism. From the line of life in which we conjecture you to be, I have for some time lost the hope of seeing you here. Should the event prove so, I shall ask your assistance in procuring a substitute, who may be a proficient in singing, etc., on the harpsichord. I should be contented to receive such an one two or three years hence ; when it is hoped he may come more safely and find here a greater plenty of those useful things which commerce alone can furnish.

"The bounds of an American fortune will not admit the indulgence of a domestic band of musicians, yet I have thought that a passion for music might be reconciled with that economy which we are obliged to observe. I retain among my domestic servants a gardener, a weaver, a cabinet-maker, and a stone-cutter, to which I would add a *vigneron*. In a country where, like yours, music is cultivated and practised by every class of men, I suppose there might be found persons of these trades who could perform on the French horn, clarinet, or hautboy, and bassoon, so that one might have a band of two French horns, two clarinets, two hautboys, and a bassoon, without enlarging their domestic expenses. A certainty of employment for a half dozen years, and at the end of that time, to find them, if they chose, a conveyance to their own country, might induce them to come here on reasonable wages. Without meaning to give you trouble, perhaps it might be practicable for you, in your ordinary intercourse with your people, to find out such men disposed to come to America. Sobriety and good nature would be desirable parts of their characters. If you think such a plan practicable, and will be so kind as to inform me what will be necessary to be done on my part, I will take care that it shall be done. The necessary expenses, when informed of them, I can remit before they are wanting, to any port in France, with which country alone we have safe correspondence.

[3] Capt. Bibby, an aid-de-camp of General Frasier, taken prisoner at Saratoga, and

The memoranda of this period (the summer and autumn of 1775) show Mr. Jefferson busy in making additions to his house —improving the grounds and roads about it, and extending his kitchen garden. Of a somewhat fastidious appetite, and subsisting mostly on vegetables, he cultivated an extraordinary variety of esculents, and collected them with care from all parts of the country, and, on every opportunity, from Europe.

His family, in Albemarle, now consisted of thirty-four free persons and eighty-three slaves. His oldest child, Martha, was nearly three years old. His second, Jane Randolph, died in September, aged about a year and a half.

The illness and death of this child prevented him from setting out for Philadelphia to take his seat in Congress before the 25th of September, though that body had convened on the 5th, and obtained a quorum on the 13th of the month. Mr. Jefferson reached the seat of government, *this* time, in six days!

Congress continued to proceed with its usual mixture of caution and vigor, until the news arrived of the King's refusal to notice its second petition. That very day (November 9th) the members signed a written pledge " not to divulge directly or indirectly " anything in relation to incomplete proceedings, without leave, or anything determined, which the House should order to be kept secret, and that any violator of this pledge should be expelled, " and deemed an enemy to the liberties of America." On the 29th the House adopted a letter to the Colonies' Agents, in regard to the King's refusal to notice their second petition, and in regard to the Royal Proclamation of August 23d, in which, though they avow their determination " to rely to the last on Heaven and their own virtuous efforts for security against the abusive system pressed by the Administration for the ruin of America," they declare " there is nothing more ardently desired by North America than a lasting union with Great Britain on terms of just and equal liberty!" On the 6th of December, a spirited declaration was adopted in regard to the Royal Proclamation (declaring the Colonies in a state of

who remained with the other Saratoga prisoners for several years at Charlottesville, Virginia, and who subsequently settled in New York, informed a friend of ours (Gen. J. A. Dix), that in the frequent visits of the British officers at Mr. Jefferson's house, music was often introduced—all who could, playing on some instrument, or singing with their host and hostess. He said he (Bibby) often played duets on the violin with Mr. Jefferson, and he considered him the finest unprofessional player he ever heard on the instrument. Bibby himself was a fine player.

rebellion, etc.), in which a want of allegiance to "our King" is
expressly repudiated, and the "British Constitution." pronounced "our best inheritance!"

Mr. Jefferson set out for home on the 28th of December.
We are not able to state positively the occasion of this absence,
but the presumption would seem to be that it finds its explanation in the antecedents of the fact thus stated in his pocket
account book: "March 31, (1776). My mother died about
eight o'clock this morning in the 57th year of her age." He
did not take his seat again in Congress (the same record shows)
until Monday, May 13th, 1776, in the midst of exciting events!
This will account for his name not appearing in so many of the
preliminary steps which gradually prepared the way for the
Declaration of Independence.[1] Reasons for the prolongation
of his absence will be by and by mentioned.

Congress had kept continuously in session from his departure
until his return. We will not enumerate in detail those well
known historic events, in and out of that body, which had
occurred in the interval, but an allusion to some of the leading
ones is necessary to the continuity of our narration.

Disastrous news arrived from England before the close of
the winter of 1775-6. The King had opened Parliament with
a speech in which he had denounced the Colonists as rebels,
seeking, with deceitful pretences, to establish an independent
empire ; and his Majesty recommended decisive, coercive
measures against them. Enough members were found in Parliament selfishly anxious to retain America in a position of mere
convenience to British commercial and navigation interests, or
instigated by their high monarchical principles, or exasperated
by collision, or instigated by love of place and the smiles of a
Court, to constitute a decisive majority in that body as hostile
to the rights and liberties of the American people, as that
Sovereign whose bigoted love of prerogative and sordid obstinacy had been mainly instrumental in pushing matters to their
present pass. Accordingly, the answer to the Royal Address
(adopted by a vote of seventy-six to thirty-three in the Lords,
and two hundred and seventy-eight to one hundred and eight

[1] And it accounts also for the following remark in John Adams's Autobiography :
"Mr. Jefferson had been now [July, 1776,] about a year a member of Congress, but
had attended his duty in the House a very small part of the time, etc."—*Life and Works.*
vol. ii. p. 511

in the Commons) gave assurances of the firm support of Parliament to the proposed measures. The very moderately conciliatory propositions made by the Duke of Richmond, Mr. Burke, and the Duke of Grafton, were summarily voted down, and not far from the middle of December the atrocious "Prohibitory Act," as it was generally designated, passed. It was, in effect, a declaration of war, and a war unrestrained by the customs, and unmitigated by the decencies of civilization. It authorized the confiscation of American vessels and cargoes, and those of all nations found trading in American ports. It authorized British commanders to impress American crews into the British Navy, and to place them on the same footing with voluntarily enlisted seamen; that is, to give them a choice between parricide and being hung at a yard-arm! [1] Finally, it referred all future negotiations to two Commissioners, to be sent out along with a conquering armament, who were allowed to grant *pardons* to individuals and Colonies, on *submission*, thus leaving no future alternative opposed to the latter but the sword, and indicating that henceforth all appeals to King or Parliament were cut off. Against this measure, not exceeded in pure despotism by any in the history of the Plantagenet monarchs before Magna Charta, which nothing in the mad struggles of the Stuarts had equalled, the warnings and entreaties of a Chatham, a Fox, and a Burke, were lifted up in vain!

Concurrently with these legislative steps, the practical ones for carrying on the *war*, with a large army, were entered upon. Finding it difficult or impossible to obtain the necessary recruits at home,[2] and that the existing English and Irish regiments embarked with such reluctance that it was necessary to keep a guard upon the transports "to keep them from deserting by wholesale,"[3] the Ministry successively applied to Russia, the States-General, and finally, several of the German States for mercenaries. But the fierce semi-barbarous battalions

---

[1] It was in allusion to this, that the Declaration of Independence said : "He [the King] has constrained our citizens taken captive on the high seas to bear arms against their country, to become the executioners of their friends and brethren, or to fall themselves by their hands."

[2] Arthur Lee enclosed a confidential letter to Franklin, Feb. 13, 1776, in which it is declared : "They [the Ministry] have found it impossible to recruit in England, Ireland, or Scotland, though the leading people of the last are, to a man, violently against America."

[3] See same letter. Am. Archives, 4th ser. vol. iv. 1126.

which under Romanzoff and Suwarrow had carried the banners
of Catherine II. over the desolated fields of Poland and Moldavia,
through the horrors of Bender, were not to be sold to execute
the slaughters of the King and Government of "free and constitutional England." The States-General refused the price of
blood in terms of indignant scorn.' The infamy of filling up
the British armament was reserved for the Princes of three
or four petty German States—Princes and States destined in
a few short years, under the spurning heel of an invader, to
drain the bitter cup of retribution to the dregs—and thus a
foreign horde, unacquainted with the language of Englishmen,
as ignorant and uninterested in the merits of the controversy
as the horses they rode, or the cannons they pointed, were sent
by one to subjugate another portion of the British realm!'

As the news of these events successively reached the American Congress and people, in the winter and spring of 1775–6,
the contest took a new coloring. Not only the bold, but the
moderate began now to see the real alternative before them.
And at a critical moment the remedy, and the path to it, were
pointed out by a master hand. "Common Sense" was published by Thomas Paine, and a more effective popular appeal
never went to the bosoms of a nation. Its tone, its manner,
its biblical allusions, its avoidance of all openly impassioned
appeals to feeling, and its unanswerable *common sense* were
exquisitely adapted to the great audience to which it was
addressed; and calm investigation will satisfy the historical
student that its effect in preparing the popular mind for the

---

¹ See opinion given by JOHAN DERK Van der CAPELLEN, upon the request of the King
of Great Britain for the loan of the Scotch Brigade, in the Assembly of the States of
OVERYSSEL, December, 1775, in Am. Archives, 4th ser. vol. iv. 285. It reads George
III. as pretty a lecture on his conduct as can be found in the American manifestoes of the
period, and the writer declares he "thinks the Americans worthy of every man's esteem,
and looks upon them as a brave people, defending in a becoming, manly, and religious
manner, those rights which, *as men, they derive from God, not from the Legislature of
Great Britain.*" Well done, DERK! This was higher ground than was taken by most
of the American leaders! A single negative then sufficed *to defeat* a proposition before
the States of Holland, and the Scotch Brigade was not loaned!

² It is but justice, however, to these troops to say, that they generally came as reluctantly as did the British. Various letters of the period prove this. And no troops were
sent to America who conducted themselves more mildly, or who *continued* so sincerely
to bewail the nature of their service. When their blood got up, the *British* troops *forgot*
all their original misgivings! We shall have occasion to see more of this difference
hereafter.

But even this *forced* recruiting in Germany, stung to the quick the pride and feelings
of the German settlers of America, particularly in Pennsylvania. In some places (it is
recorded by the historian Grahame), the *old* and *superannuated* men formed themselves
into volunteer companies, expressly to meet those who by selling their swords to a
foreign tyrant, had brought disgrace on the German father-land.

Declaration of Independence, exceeded that of any other paper, speech, or document made to favor it, and it would scarcely be exaggeration to add, than all other such means put together.

John Adams, with a childish petulance, and with a rancor so vehement that it appears ridiculous, spares no occasion to underrate Paine's services, and to assault his opinions and character. We cannot attribute this to the sincere prejudices which might have influenced Mr. Adams's Puritan ancestors on the score of religion; for an attentive examination of Mr. Adams's own religious views, as developed in his later correspondence with Jefferson, will leave it difficult to say where he had vastly the advantage of Paine, on the score of orthodoxy, if tried by that Puritan standard.[1] In short, his transparent motive seems to be to decry the author of a paper which had too much the credit of preparing the public mind for the Declaration of Independence, a credit which Mr. Adams was more than anxious to monopolize.[2]

Let us be just. Paine's services in paving the way to the Declaration, are not to be mentioned on the same page with John Adams's. Moreover, Independence would have been declared, and, perhaps, nearly as early, had Paine never written. But he did, at a propitious moment, and with consummate adaptation, write a paper which went like the arrow which pierces the centre of the target. Its effect was instantaneous and tremendous where it was addressed. Nay, it reached elsewhere. The brilliantly intellectual General Charles Lee wrote General Washington, that this "masterly, irresistible performance," convinced *him* "of the necessity of separation."[3] General Washington wrote Joseph Reed (January 31, 1776): "A few more such flaming arguments as were exhibited at Falmouth and Norfolk, added to the sound doctrine and unanswerable reasoning contained in the pamphlet 'Common Sense,' will not leave numbers at a loss to decide on the propriety of a separation."[4] The work run through innumerable editions in America and France. The world rung with it.

[1] We do not, of course, here speak of Mr. Adams merely as a *Unitarian*—but, as stated in the text, *in the light of the religious views developed in his correspondence referred to.*

[2] Let the reader, as *one* instance, read his Autobiography for 1775. Commence at p. 503, vol. ii. of his Life and Works.

[3] For this letter, see Am. Archives, 4th ser. vol. iv. 839.

[4] See ibid. 4th ser. vol. iv. p. 889. The sentence we quote shows that General Washington *could* be guilty of a pun! Falmouth and Norfolk had been *set on fire* by the enemy!

We confess we have no sympathy with Mr. Paine's religious views. If his personal character was what it is most commonly alleged to have been (though it is now said that there has been a good deal of exaggeration, and even out and out invention, on this head), there was much in it that no man can admire. But concede all the allegations against him, and it still leaves him the author of " Common Sense," and certain other papers which rung like clarions in the darkest hour of the Revolution· ary struggle—inspiriting the bleeding, and starving, and pestilence-stricken, as the pen of *no other man* ever inspirited them. Whatever Paine's faults or vices, however dark and crapulous the close of his stormy career, when he is spoken of as the patriot, and especially as the Revolutionary and pre-Revolutionary writer, shame rest on the pen which dares not do him justice! And shame, also, ought to rest on the most cursory narrator of the events which heralded the Declaration of Independence, who should omit to enumerate the publication of " Common Sense" among them!

Congress continued to fully keep up with the public feeling in its enactments; nay, we think it was generally somewhat in advance (that is, taking all the Colonies together), and that its constant effort was to tone up and prepare the general mind (in some places it was not necessary) for the decisive step. It admits of no doubt that pretty early in 1776, all the true Whigs in Congress, moderates as well as ultras, became satisfied of the necessity and expediency of separation, and that henceforth it was only a question of time with them.

Enactments placing the struggle on the footing of open war, instead of mere insurrection—issuing letters of marque and reprisal against the enemies of our commerce—advising the local authorities to disarm the disaffected—opening the ports of the country to all nations but Great Britain—directing negotiations for foreign alliances to be undertaken—were successively made. Finally, on the 10th of May, a resolution, prepared by John Adams and R. H. Lee, passed the House, advising all the Colonies to form governments for themselves; and in this, unlike preceding instances of giving advice on the same subject, no limitation of the duration of the governments to be formed " to the continuance of the present dispute," was inserted. This, with a befitting preamble, written by John Adams, was adopted on the 15th (the day, or the day after, Jefferson again took his seat'), and was, obviously, a long and bold stride in the direction of independence, and must have been understood by all as its signal and precursor.

Meanwhile the Colonial Legislatures exhibited almost exact epitomes of the Federative one—only all had not yet advanced to precisely the same point. All were progressing more or less rapidly towards independence. In all, there were able men—in some, quite as able as their representatives in Congress. In some cases, as must ever happen in popular government, the representative was toning up his constituency; in others, the constituency their representatives, for the final leap. So it happened, too, between the local administrations and their representatives in Congress, or Congress collectively. They constantly acted and reacted on each other. Congress cheered on those whom peculiar circumstances had rendered more backward, and it tarried for them a little by the way; on the other hand, it prudently waited for the prompting of the more forward. Thus it avoided the appearance of dominating over public opinion—thus it "kept front and rear together."

"Early in April (12th), North Carolina "empowered" her delegates "to *concur* with the delegates of other Colonies in declaring independency." * At its "May session" (the day of the month not appearing in the record under our eye), the General Assembly of Rhode Island abolished its act of allegiance, and directed all commissions and legal processes henceforth to issue in the name and under the authority of the "Governor and Company." * The Connecticut General Assembly, which met on the 9th of May, before its adjournment (date not before us), repealed its act against high treason, and made the same order with Rhode Island in regard to legal processes.* On the 15th of May, Virginia took a still more decisive step, by instructing its delegates in Congress to move for a Declaration of Independence, etc.—and it, at the same time, passed the Rubicon for itself, by ordering an unlimited and unconditional Declaration of Rights, and "a plan of government," in other words, "a Constitution" to be framed. The resolutions were reported by Colonel Archibald Cary. The

¹ He reached Philadelphia on the 14th.   ² Amer. Archives, 4th ser. vol. v. 860
³ Amer. Archives 4th ser. vol. v. 1215.   ⁴ Ib. 4th ser. vol. v. 1604, 1605.

first, after an exceedingly appropriate and dignified preamble, was as follows :

> " *Resolved, unanimously*, That the delegates appointed to represent this Colony in General Congress, be instructed to propose to that respectable body to declare the United Colonies free and independent States, absolved from all allegiance to, or dependence upon, the Crown or Parliament of Great Britain ; and that they give the assent of this Colony to such declaration, and to whatever measures may be thought proper and necessary by the Congress for forming foreign alliances, and a confederation of the Colonies, at such time, and in the manner, as to them shall seem best : Provided, that the power of forming government for, and the regulations of the internal concerns of each Colony, be left to the respective Colonial legislatures." [1]

By the originally published proceedings of the Convention, lying before us, it appears that one of the delegates of Albemarle was George Gilmer, who sat for, or as the substitute of, Thomas Jefferson. Three other of the delegates in Congress, Harrison, R. H. Lee, and Wythe, were also members of the Convention ; but none of them left Congress to take a seat in it until after Mr. Jefferson's return, and subsequently two of them (Lee and Wythe) did. We find, by entries in Mr. Jefferson's account book, up to nearly the day of his setting out for Philadelphia, that he was collecting money, by voluntary subscriptions, to buy powder to be used in Virginia, and for the relief of the city of Boston. We cannot but suspect that in these facts we find a clue to Mr. Jefferson's long absence from Congress. There was probably a motive in four members of Congress allowing themselves to be elected to this convention, for none of them, beside Harrison, had a seat in that of 1775.[2] What was that motive? Was it not to keep up a communication between Virginia and Congress, as we have observed was done on a former occasion, when an all-important measure was on foot? We have seen Mr. Jefferson once before kept at home to frame and secure the passage of a paper *where Congress desired Virginia to set the pattern*, and desired it to solicit from itself (Congress) precisely what Congress had in the minds of the members pre-resolved to do. And in that case (the answer to Lord North's "Conciliatory Proposition"), the paper so

---

[1] The latter provision was also inserted in the North Carolina resolutions. This shows whether, at the *outset*, the American confederacy was desired to be a union of the *people* or of the *governments*.

[2] The originally published proceedings of the Convention of 1775 lie before us.

prepared was presented in the Virginiā Convention by the same person, Mr. Jefferson's kinsman and early and confidential friend, Colonel Archibald Cary. Our conjectures do not extend to the mere drafting of the Virginia resolutions of May 15th. Mr. Jefferson might or might not have had a hand in this; and we regard that question as of no sort of consequence. But we do believe, from the facts mentioned, and from several trifling corroboratory hints not perhaps separately worth specific mention, that Mr. Jefferson, being called home as stated, *remained* there, by some understanding probably with the whole or a part of his colleagues, to prepare the public mind for, and concert with the prominent men elected to the Convention, the step which was taken on the 15th of May. It might or might not have been 'foreseen that the "supernatural voice" of the old popular leader, in the Convention (Henry), would remain silent on this question. Mr. Jefferson did not take a seat in the body, but he remained at home until its session commenced. A second and concurrent object has been mentioned, the raising of money for the purposes specified. This is the only rational solution we can give of the long and remarkable absence from Congress, in such a period as the spring of 1776, of a member conceded on all hands to have been one of the most ardent, daring, and energetic of the Revolutionary leaders. His account books do not give an inkling of any business of his own during the period, but that of the most ordinary kind, and in truth there was less than the usual quantity even of such business. The death of his mother rendered no important settlements or other arrangements necessary. The family business was in so systematic a train, that this event did not make six hours' labor necessary to perfectly re-adjust it. And, finally, had Mr. Jefferson been lolling at home in inglorious ease for more than *four months* during this most eventful session, is it probable that almost as soon as he returned, a vote of Congress would have placed him in the chairmanship of the most important and most honorable committee to which the Revolution had given birth—that to draft the Declaration of Independence? We cannot but believe it was well understood he had been very patriotically employed! Nay, we more than half suspect that the nature of that patriotic service was understood, and that this actually had some connection with his being placed on the committee for drafting that Declaration which Virginia had called for.

Mr. Adams is the only one who has alluded to his absence, and he vaguely and without explanatory remark, showing that he had no very definite recollections concerning it, after a lapse of thirty years. But is it said that Mr. Jefferson makes no allusion to such a mission on his part, in his Memoir or his Correspondence? Neither does he allude to his *absence*. Neither does he mention his collection of money for Boston, which appears in black and white in his accounts. Neither does he anywhere hint that he was chairman of the Safety Committee of his county; or that he was chosen to the State Convention of 1776; or a hundred other facts that a small man would consider important, which immediately suggest themselves to our memory (and which the reader will constantly discover as we proceed). This criterion would be the last one on earth by which it would do to try Mr. Jefferson!

The Virginia delegates in Congress made choice of Richard H. Lee to move the resolutions contained in their instructions of May 15th; and he did so on Friday, the 7th day of June, John Adams seconding them. Their consideration was postponed until the next day, when they were referred to a committee of the whole, and debated throughout Saturday and the succeeding Monday. On the latter day (10th) Congress resolved:

"That the consideration of the first resolution be postponed to Monday, the first day of July next; and in the meanwhile, that no time be lost, in case the Congress agree thereto, that a committee be appointed to prepare a declaration to the effect of the said first resolution, which is in these words: That these Colonies are, and of right ought to be, free and independent States; that they are absolved from all allegiance to the British Crown; and that all political connection between them and the State of Great Britain is, and ought to be, totally dissolved."

For this delay of twenty days on the "first resolution," Mr. Jefferson assigns the following reason in his Memoir:

"It appearing in the course of these debates, that the Colonies of New York, New Jersey, Pennsylvania, Delaware, Maryland, and South Carolina were not yet matured for falling from the parent stem, but that they were fast advancing to that state it was thought most prudent to wait a while for them, and to postpone the final decision to July 1st."

The debate on the 8th and 10th had been earnest and animated—John Adams, R. H. Lee, Mr. Wythe, "and others," speaking in the affirmative—Mr. Wilson, Robert R. Livingston, E. Rutledge, Mr. Dickinson, "and others," in the negative. These speakers' names and a synopsis of their arguments, are given by Jefferson. He distinctly states, without any exception, that the opponents of the resolution declared "they were friends to the measures themselves, and saw the impossibility that we should ever again be united with Great Britain, yet they were against adopting it at this time."[1] Their principal arguments were that the people of the middle Colonies were not yet ripe for the step—that premature action might lead to dissension and even to secession—that this would not only produce its own direct disastrous consequences, but prevent us from obtaining foreign aid—that we had little reason to expect aid from those to whom, as yet, we had alone cast our eyes, France and Spain, because they "had reason to be jealous of that rising power which would one day certainly strip them of all their American possessions," and that, therefore, they would be more likely to side with England, the one to recover Canada, and the other the Floridas[2]—that at all events we should soon hear from France, and if our present campaign was successful (as was anticipated), we could make alliance, if at all, on better terms; and that thus no time would be lost, for aid from France during the present campaign would be out of the question—and, finally, that it was prudent to fix among ourselves the terms on which we would form an alliance before we irrevocably committed ourselves to one.

There was certainly nothing unmanly or unpatriotic in these positions, and Congress showed its respect for the most important of them, by giving time to hear again and finally from the doubtful middle Colonies, before it proceeded to a decision.

On Tuesday, June 11th, Congress resolved that the Committee for preparing a *Declaration* of Independence consist of five persons. The members were chosen, as usual, by ballot, and they stood in the following order: Thomas Jefferson, John

[1] Governor Johnson of Maryland, a leading member and *decided* Whig, confirmed this statement to the biographer of R. H. Lee. See Lee's Life of Lee, vol. i. p. 171.
[2] This was a shrewd view, and it is a curious subject of historic speculation what would have been the results to France and Spain had they pursued this policy. Nothing can be clearer than that the French and Spanish Bourbons wrought *their own* destruction in the part they took in the American War.

Adams, Benjamin Franklin, Roger Sherman, and Robert R. Livingston.

To explain why Mr. Lee, the mover of the resolution for independence, was not made chairman of the Committee for drawing up the *Declaration* of Independence, as Parliamentary etiquette would seem to dictate, Judge Marshall states that he "had been compelled by the illness of Mrs. Lee to leave Congress the day on which the Committee was appointed."[1] This was, probably, the publicly understood version of the affair at the time, as the grandson and biographer of Mr. Lee subsequently stated that the latter received intelligence, by express, of the dangerous illness of his wife, on the evening of the preceding day; and that he obtained leave of absence and set out for Virginia on the 11th.[2] Professor Tucker, in his life of Jefferson, makes a similar statement, and infers but for that fact, "Mr. Lee would, no doubt, have been placed on this Committee, and according to the established usage towards the mover of a resolution, have been made its chairman."[3] Mr. Jefferson does not in his Memoir, or, so far as we have observed, in any of his other writings, make any allusion to this topic, though we cannot doubt he had seen a contradictory statement to the preceding ones made by John Adams in 1822.

At any rate, in 1822, John Adams wrote a letter to Timothy Pickering, in which occurred the following statements:

"Mr. Richard Henry Lee might be gone to Virginia, to his sick family, for aught I know, *but that was not the reason of Mr. Jefferson's appointment.* There were three committees appointed at the same time. One for the Declaration of Independence, another for preparing articles of Confederation, and another for preparing a treaty to be proposed to France. Mr. Lee was chosen for the Committee of Confederation, and it was not thought convenient that the same person should be upon both. Mr. Jefferson came into Congress in June, 1775, and brought with him a reputation for literature, science, and a happy talent of composition. Writings of his were handed about remarkable for the peculiar felicity of expression. Though a silent member in Congress, he was so prompt, frank, explicit, and decisive, upon committees and in conversation—not even Samuel Adams was more so—that he soon seized upon my heart; and upon this occasion, *I gave him my vote, and did all in my power to procure the votes of others.* I think he had one more vote than any other, and that placed him at the head of the Committee. I had the next highest number, and that placed me second.[4]

[1] Marshall's Washington, 2d ed. vol. i. p. 79, note.   [2] Lee's Life, vol. i. p. 173.
[3] Life of Jefferson, vol. i. p. 87, note.
[4] See Adams's Life and Works, vol. ii. p. 513.

A part, we do not know how much, of the letter, in which this occurs, was published in 1823, and is commented upon by Jefferson, in a letter to Mr. Madison (August 30th, 1823.')

Nearly twenty years earlier (in 1804 or 1805), Mr. Adams set down the following statements in his Autobiography:

> "Mr. Jefferson had been now about a year a member of Congress, but had attended his duty in the House a very small part of the time, and, when there, had never spoken in public. During the whole time I sat with him in Congress, I never heard him utter three sentences together. It will naturally be inquired how it happened that he was appointed on a committee of such importance. There were more reasons than one. Mr. Jefferson had the reputation of a masterly pen; he had been chosen a delegate in Virginia, in consequence of a very handsome public paper which he had written for the House of Burgesses, which had given him the character of a fine writer. *Another reason was that Mr. Richard Henry Lee was not beloved by most of his colleagues from Virginia and Mr. Jefferson was set up to rival and supplant him.* This could be done only by the pen, for Mr. Jefferson could stand no competition with him or any one else in elocution and public debate."[2]

Again, in a sort of recapitulation on a subsequent page of his Autobiography, where Mr. Adams takes up separately the important measures of Congress, and describes the action on them, he says:

> "Jefferson was chairman because he had most votes; and he had most votes *because we united in him to the exclusion of R. H. Lee, and to keep out Harrison.*"

In justice to all parties, it should be premised that the remarks in the Autobiography were penned when Mr. Adams was deeply estranged from Mr. Jefferson, and when, we believe, he was writing his celebrated "Cunningham Letters!" On the other hand, his admiration and his affection for Mr. Lee had been most ardent, down to the period of that gentleman's death.

We should have been quite content to leave this matter where it was left by Judge Marshall and Mr. Lee's biographer; but these statements of Mr. Adams demand such explanation as we can offer. We have here a characteristic specimen of his

---

[1] Pickering published a portion of it pertaining to the same subject (Jefferson's connection with the Declaration of Independence), in a 4th of July address, that year. Whether he published the above quoted passage we do not know—or how many, or what other (if any) publications of it took place before Mr. Jefferson's death. We have not supposed the point involved of sufficient consequence to solicit research on the subject.
[2] Life and Works, vol. ii. p. 511.

method of telling a story. Always dashing off what was
uppermost in his mind, without pausing for consideration, he
contrives, in three different statements, to render three essentially different reasons for the same act, which, though they in
reality involve, perhaps, no material inconsistency with each
other, and might well all be true, yet taken separately, give
quite different colorings to the same transaction. The first
reason he assigns (in our order of statement, but really his latest
one in date), was that Mr. Lee was placed on another of the
three important committees raised "at the same time" (and
equally under *his* resolutions), and "it was not thought convenient the same person should be upon both." This is a slip of
Mr. Adams's careless pen, in two particulars. The Committees
on Confederation and Treaties were not chosen until the 12th—
after Mr. Lee had gone home—and his name was included in
neither of them. The Virginia member of the Committee on
Confederation was Mr. Nelson, and on Treaties, Mr. Harrison.
Mr. Adams's second version is, that Mr. Lee was not beloved
by most of his colleagues, and Mr. Jefferson was set up to supplant him. Finally, he conveys the idea that he (Adams) and his
friends voted together for Jefferson, and elected him, to keep
out Harrison. These two last statements are reconcilable, and
we have no doubt that, so far as practical action was concerned,
they are essentially true; though the motive, at least on one
side, may be a little discolored by Mr. Adams's personal
feelings.

Traces of parties or factions on several questions are clearly
discernible in the Congress of 1776; and that they ran into
bitter personal animosities, we want no better proof than Mr.
Adams's own autobiographical writings. One, and the most
obvious, line of division was between the Ultras and the Moderates, on the question of independence; and it became a personal one, also, by reason of the rough handling which the parties gave each other in debate, and in letters which got accidentally before the public. Thus, Adams and Dickinson did
not speak to each other, and the former constantly accuses the
latter, and also Harrison, Hancock (the President), Charles
Thomson (the Secretary of Congress), and others acting in concert with them, and against himself, of even going so far as
conniving to suppress and keep off from the records *his* impor

tant resolutions and propositions.¹ He represents them as equally hostile to R. H. Lee.² He habitually speaks of them as the party *against independence,* laboring to thwart all measures tending towards its declaration.

Mr. Adams also declares that there were deep-rooted jealousies and divisions between the Virginia delegates; a strong feeling on the part of a portion of them against R. H. Lee, owing—he says he learned from Mr. Wythe—to the fact that Lee, "when he was very young, and when he first came into the House of Burgesses, moved and urged on an inquiry into the state of the treasury, which was found deficient in large sums, which had been lent by the treasurer to "many of the most influential families of the country, who found themselves exposed, and had never forgiven Mr. Lee." Mr. Adams particularly specifies Harrison and Pendleton among the Virginia opponents of that gentleman. He says that he (John Adams) and Samuel Adams were very intimate with Mr. Lee—that Harrison, Pendleton, and some others, showed their jealousy of this intimacy—that Harrison "consequently" courted Mr. Hancock; but that having the majority now they (the Adamses and Lee) "gave themselves no trouble about their little intrigues!"³

There was another very serious ground of difference between Mr. Adams (and we suppose his personal set) and a part of the Virginia delegation. Mr. Adams and the Lees were accused of having already become hostile to General Washington. This impression widely prevailed in and out of Congress. On two or three occasions, present in our recollection, Mr. Adams himself mentions that allegations of this kind were made against *him,* though he denies the truth of them.⁴ General Knox heard these rumors in a sufficiently authentic form to cause him to visit Mr. Adams on the subject, when he was about embarking

¹ Broad insinuations (or charges) of this kind will be found in his Autobiography, Life and Works, vol. iii. pp. 38, 39, 45, 51, 69.
² Ib. p. 45 *et passim.*
³ If Mr. Adams supposed that such men as Harrison and Pendleton were jealous and fell into "little intrigues," by reason of R. H. Lee's favor with *him,* we can smile at the assertion: but if he means—and certainly the cursory reader, and one not familiar with the characters of the individuals, would draw that inference—that these men were of the number that were hostile to Mr. Lee, *because he exposed a pecuniary fraud* in the Virginia Legislature, it is proper that we say that never was a charge more unjust or more utterly preposterous. There was no pecuniary or public matter where either of these gentlemen's garments were not quite as unsullied as Mr. Adams's.
⁴ See Autobiography, Life and Works, vol. iii. pp. 35, 48, 92.

the first time for Europe.' Alexander Hamilton, when Mr. Adams was a candidate for the Vice-Presidency in 1788 (long before any misunderstanding had arisen between them) wrote Theodore Sedgwick of Massachusetts:

" The only hesitation in my mind with regard to Mr. Adams has arisen within a 1 day or two, from a suggestion by a particular gentleman that he is unfriendly in his sentiments to General Washington. Richard H. Lee, who will probably, as rumor now runs, come from Virginia,' *is also in this style. The Lees and Adamses have been in the habit of uniting,* and hence may spring up a cabal very embarrassing to the Executive, and of course to the administration of the Government. Consider this—sound the reality of it, and let me hear from you."

Sedgwick answered:

" Mr. Adams was formerly infinitely more democratical than at present, and possessing that jealousy which always accompanied such a character, he was averse to repose such unlimited confidence in the commander-in-chief as then was the disposition of Congress." '

Lafayette distinctly and decidedly entertained the belief, through life, that "the Lees" and "the Adamses" were enemies of General Washington, and he thus confidently and without qualification states the fact in his "*Mémoires de ma main,*" published by his family in 1837:

" Gates était à Yorktown, où il en imposait par son ton, ses promesses, et ses connaissances Européennes. Parmi les députés qui s'unirent à lui, on distingue *les Lees*, Virginiens, ennemis de Washington, et *les deux Adams.*"

Mr. Adams was conscious, it would appear, of no hostility to General Washington; but if he talked *then* as he *wrote* about it afterwards (and men are apt to talk more heatedly than they write), it is not wonderful that he was understood by the particular friends of General Washington to be anything but very partial to him. For example, he says in his Autobiography, when commenting on occurrences about the 1st of March, 1776:

" There was, however, still a majority of members who were either determined against all measures preparatory to independence, or yet too timorous and wavering to venture on any decisive steps. We therefore could do nothing but keep our

¹ See Autobiography, Life and Works, vol. iii. p. 92.
² That is, into Congress.   ³ See Hamilton's Works, by his son, vol. i. p. 482.

eyes fixed on the great objects of free trade, new governments, and independence of the United States, and seize every opening opportunity of advancing step by step in our progress. Our opponents were not less vigilant in seizing on every excuse for delay ; the letter from Lord Drummond, which seemed to derive importance from the transmission of it by General Washington, was a fine engine to play cold water on the fire of independence. They set it in operation with great zeal and activity. It was, indeed, a very airy phantom, *and ought not to have been sent us by the General*, who should only have referred Lord Drummond to Congress. *But there were about head-quarters some who were as weak and wavering as our members ; and the General himself had chosen for his private confidential correspondent a member from Virginia, Harrison, who was still counted among the cold party* This was an indolent, luxurious, heavy gentleman, of no use in Congress or committee, but a great embarrassment to both." [1]

It would be hard to construe the meaning of these remarks into anything but this—that the opponents of independence derived aid from "head-quarters"—that there was a controlling clique there as "weak and wavering" as the opponents of independence in the House—that the General himself had chosen for his private confidential correspondent in Congress a man of this stamp, as well as a dull and sensual one.

From the manner that Harrison is repeatedly spoken of, one cannot but suspect that he had committed a deeper sin than "courting Hancock"—and one is led to the speculation whether that sin was not the misfortune of forestalling General Washington's ear and confidence to the exclusion of another gentleman who considered himself far more competent to occupy that position. Adams, on one occasion, says:

"Although Harrison was another Sir John Falstaff, excepting in his larcenies and robberies, his conversation disgusting to every man of delicacy or decorum, yet, as I saw he was to be often nominated with us in business, I took no notice of his vices or follies, but treated him, and *Mr. Hancock too*, with uniform politeness." [2]

If Mr. Adams felt precisely thus towards Colonel Harrison, the friend of Washington—a signer of the Declaration of Independence—afterwards Governor of Virginia, and a man otherwise again and again honored by the people of his native State [3] —we confess, we think it would have been more magnanimous to have spared some of this "politeness" towards him living, and refrained from perpetuating so purely personal abuse or him when dead !

[1] Life and Works, vol. iii. p. 31.　　　[2] Ibid. p. 35.
[3] He was the father of William Henry Harrison, afterwards President of the United States.

We will not follow up and quote every casual word that Mr. Adams dropped in his writings, which would go to show that his feelings were not cordial towards General Washington. But we suspect that any one who diligently notices his very peculiar occasional expressions on the subject, even to the last days of his life (for example, in his later correspondence with Jefferson), will come to the conclusion that it is very difficult to reconcile them to any other hypothesis of his real (though perhaps not understood by himself) feelings towards the General, than the one entertained by his and Mr. Lee's Virginia opponents in the Congress of 1776, and which Knox, Hamilton, and Lafayette seem to have been so familiar with.

There were other feuds in that Congress, partly public and partly private in their character. For instance, Dr. Arthur Lee, says Mr. Adams,[1] had written home to his brother Richard Henry, from London, " insinuations against Mr. Jay as a suspicious character," and these had been " communicated" " too indiscreetly," and Mr. Jay spoken of " too lightly." Mr. R. H. Lee had expressed his doubts whether Mr. Jay wrote the Address to the People of Great Britain, ascribing it to his (Jay's) father-in-law, William Livingston; and these things (Mr. Adams remarks), " had occasioned some words and animosities, which uniting with the great questions in Congress, had some disagreeable effects."

Some years afterwards (January 9, 1818), John Adams wrote Mr. Jay :

"The question ' Who was the draftsman of the Address to the People of England?' however unimportant to the public it may appear at this day, certainly excited a sensation, a fermentation, and *a schism in Congress at the time, and serious consequences afterward, which have lasted to this hour, and are not yet spended.* I fear, but I do not know, that this animosity was occasioned by *indiscretions of R. H. Lee,* Mr. Samuel Adams, and some other of the Virginia delegates, by whom Adams was led into error." [2]

Mr. Jay replied (January 31, 1818), among other things :

"I was informed, and I believe correctly, that *one person in particular* of those you specify, had endeavored, by oblique intimations, to insinuate a suspicion that the Address to the People of Great Britain was not written by me, but by Governor Livingston. * * * Those persons are dead and gone. *Their design did not succeed,* and I have no desire that the memory of it should survive them." [3]

[1] See Life and Works, vol. iii. p. 5.
[2] See Life and Writings of John Jay, vol. ii. p. 380.
[3] Life and Writings of John Jay, vol. ii. p. 383. Jefferson, in his Memoir (p. 9 of

Irving, in his Life of Washington, says:

" The following anecdote of the late Governor Jay, one of our purest and most illustrious statesmen, is furnished to us by his son, Judge Jay:

" 'Shortly before the death of John Adams, I was sitting alone with my father, conversing about the American Revolution. Suddenly he remarked, 'Ah, William, the history of that Revolution will never be known. Nobody now alive knows it but John Adams and myself.' Surprised at such a declaration, I asked him to what he referred. He briefly replied, 'The proceedings of the old Congress.' Again I inquired, 'What proceedings?' He answered, '*Those against Washington; from first to last there was a most bitter party against him.*' As the old Congress always sat with closed doors, the public knew no more of what passed within than what it was deemed expedient to disclose."

In view of all the preceding facts, it is not very difficult to see on what grounds Mr. Lee (and Mr. Adams, too) had some very decided opponents in the Virginia delegation—and indeed from all the Southern Colonies—or why Mr. Jefferson was set up to "rival and supplant" the former—or why Mr. Jay's friends from the North, Mr. Dickinson's and Charles Thompson's from Pennsylvania, Mr. Livingston's from New Jersey—nay, nearly all the moderate men of the House—should have seized the occasion of drawing up the Declaration to make that manifestation of their feelings which prevented Mr. Lee's special friends from even making him their candidate, but induced them to go in a body, it would appear, for Jefferson. Mr. Adams seems to have been afraid, otherwise, that the hated Harrison would be chosen. But this was probably but a fear. The Harrison set— the especial friends of Washington—must have voted for Jefferson, or he could not have led all the other candidates. If, indeed, Harrison had been a candidate, and been *beaten*, Mr. Adams would have recorded the fact in scornfully jubilant phrases. Harrison was not a writing man, nor, so far as we can discover, at all ambitious in that direction. Finally, Adams himself imputes the setting up of Jefferson, *on this very occasion*, to supplant Lee, to Lee's enemies in the Virginia delegation; in other words, to Harrison and his friends!

It is worthy of notice that Mr. Adams nowhere, even by

Randolph's, and p. 11 of Congress edition), gives the particulars of Mr. Jay's correcting the misstatements of R. H. Lee on this subject, apparently with some feeling, on a particular occasion—and he says they "*continued ever very hostile to each other.*"

H. Lee (son of General Harry Lee), in a *work* written to attack Mr. Jefferson, treats this story with huge disdain, as, if we remember right, a *pure fiction* to injure Mr. R. H. Lee!!

a hint, includes Jefferson among Mr. Lee's enemies, or imputes to him any complicity with the design to "rival and
supplant" that gentleman, even though at the time (and only
time, which we have observed) that he distinctly recorded that
design, he was himself so estranged from, we might say inimical
to, Jefferson, that he was anonymously supplying a partisan
editor (Cunningham) with materials to attack him! And he
has read Mr. Adams's writings unobservantly, who would ever
suspect *him*, when occasion offered, of sparing the conduct or
motives of a foe, or even an unfriend. But there is better proof
still that Mr. Jefferson was not implicated in the effort to "supplant" Lee, even in the suspicions of Lee's set. *They went for
him.* Adams declares "he gave him his vote, and did all in his
power to procure the votes of others." He declares also that
Jefferson "went with him at all points," that he "seized upon
his heart," etc., etc. A particular attachment existed between
Samuel Adams and Jefferson, which lasted for their lives, as
we shall have occasion hereafter to see. Jefferson could not
very well have been the known or suspected tool of a hostile
set, in "little intrigues," and at the same time have been a
favorite with such men!

What, then, was the precise position of Jefferson as between
these factions? This question is easily answered. In the first
place, he was the decided friend of General Washington. A
thousand facts and circumstances might be arrayed to prove
this, were it necessary. How General Washington and his
particular friends and "confidants" in Congress regarded the
matter, if not made sufficiently to appear by Jefferson's being
"set up" by the latter to "supplant Lee," is conclusively
made to appear from the fact, that when General Washington
was subsequently elevated to the Presidency, he offered to,
nay, pressed on Jefferson (so far as he ever stooped to press
anybody) the first and most confidential office in his gift. And
if any one will point out an instance where the stately Father
of his Country ever preferred policy to self-respect on such an
occasion, ever appointed a confidential officer about his person
whose unreserved attachment (aye, personal attachment) and
respect he did not fully confide in, we will agree to admit that
Jefferson's appointment as Secretary of State does not make
out even a *primâ facie* case (as the lawyers say) in that direc-

tion. We have seen Jefferson familiarly carrying home Harrison in his carriage. He does not allude to him often in his writings, but always kindly. He speaks of him in the terms of an intimate acquaintance as "Ben Harrison." He recounts in his Memoir an anecdote (already given) of his nerve and bluff gallantry, on the occasion of the second Petition to the King; and, by the way, a more brave or a more determined man, or truer patriot than Harrison sat not in the Congress of 1776, John Adams's autobiographical statements to the contrary notwithstanding! Jefferson used orally to recount another characteristic anecdote of "Ben," which has found its way into print from other sources. When the "Signers" were attaching their names to "the Declaration," the tremendously corpulent Virginia grandee looked down on the little spare, withered form of Gerry, and remarked with a chuckle: "Gerry, when the *hanging comes*, I shall have the advantage; you'll kick in the air half an hour after it is all over with me!" Not only Jefferson's writings and conversation always implied good will to Harrison, but, so far as we can discover, all his public acts and measures also in Virginia State politics, imply the same thing. We have, indeed, never seen the fact questioned. And it is certain that Harrison and his friends went vigorously for Jefferson on the 11th day of June, 1776, when it was (in effect) determined which of the two most luminous Virginia Congressional stars should then and henceforth pale its fires before the other.

In the second place, there is not a reason for believing that at this period there was a shadow of personal alienation between Jefferson and R. H. Lee. The assumptions of this kind which have been ventured upon, or insinuated, are unsupported by a solitary fact.[1] Mr. Jefferson addressed and treated

<hr/>

[1] The grandson of John Adams, and the editor of his Works, in a note (vol. iii. p. 32) to the statements of his grandfather we have mentioned (to the effect that there were two Virginia parties in Congress, that Harrison and Pendleton were hostile to Lee, etc.) *lugs in* an expression of wonder that Jefferson, *between thirty and forty years afterwards*, in a letter to Wirt, ascribed to Henry instead of Lee the origination of that inquiry into the state of the Virginia treasury, already referred to. And John Adams's editor and commentator adds: "*Mr. Jefferson's inclination to disparage the Lees is obvious enough in his writings.*" Why this note and this remark find exactly the *place* they do, why they are arranged in *connection* with John Adams's account of the *quarrels of the Virginia Delegates in the Congress of* 1776, why, in referring to a statement *made in* 1814, by Jefferson, Mr. Charles Francis Adams should attach to it a remark so conveniently general, *in respect to time*, as that we have quoted, and sounding in its connection, very much as if he had said, "Jefferson's inclination to disparage the Lees was *always* obvious enough," it would be difficult to divine, unless on the supposition, that Mr. C. F. Adams

Mr. Lee as a friend. He wrote to him as such then, and for
a considerable period after the events under examination. He
forwarded to him, with respectful attention, an autograph
draft of the Declaration of Independence. If Mr. Lee's
grandson and biographer is a competent witness, Mr. Lee himself *regarded Jefferson as a personal friend* long after '76 ;
probably always.[1] It is certain that afterwards, when a most
mortifying disgrace was inflicted on Lee by the Virginia Legislature (throwing him summarily out of the Congressional delegation, and voting him down on every ballot, by reason of
accusations which had been made against him in some public
capacity) the particular personal friends of Jefferson were
among those who rallied round, vindicated, and reinstated him.
Jefferson was in the House at the time, and was its undisputed
leader. Nor is this all. We shall find when we come to record
those proceedings in detail (in our account of the spring session
of the Virginia Legislature, in 1777, which will be given in

was not *unwilling* that the *reader* should draw the *inference* that Jefferson belonged to
the hostile, anti-Lee faction in 1776 ! If Mr. Jefferson's inclination to "disparage the
Lees" was half as obvious as Mr. C. F. Adams's is, on all occasions, to disparage Mr.
Jefferson, it would require no round-about insinuations to prove it !
   We will not stop to debate whether in a statement to Wirt, in which R. H. Lee *was
not alluded to* (in the Virginia treasury case) which will be found in Mr. Jefferson's correspondence, dated August 14, 1814, the latter sought to *disparage* R. H. Lee, or whether
Mr. Jefferson was in the right or the wrong in giving the main credit to Henry. Let the
reader consult Jefferson's letter and Mr. Wirt on one side, and *per contra* Lee's Life of
Lee and C. F. Adams, and then form his own conclusion who is in the wrong, and
especially *form his conclusion what Jefferson's remarks in this case have to do with the events
of* 1776 !!
   Finally, if John Adams's editor felt so sensitively Jefferson's *disparagement of the
Lees*, we submit that *he* ought hardly to have quoted that *disparagement* subsequently in
proof (as he *does*, with the mere prefix "If Mr. Jefferson's evidence be trusted ") that
R. H. Lee's services on the occasion of the Declaration of Independence no more
equalled his *grandfather's* in *quality* than, as he shows, in *quantity!* Call you this back-
ing a friend ! (See Life and Works of John Adams, vol. iii. p. 57 note.)
   [1] Mr. Lee's grandson, we believe, *uniformly* assumes this. He says, R. H. Lee carefully preserved the autograph copy of the Declaration forwarded by Jefferson, "not only
for the interest he felt in its history, but for *the great respect and warm friendship he felt
for Mr. Jefferson.*"—(*Lee's Life of Lee*, vol. i. p. 175.) Jefferson, in the same letter that
inclosed the Declaration, expressed a hope *that R. H. Lee,* "*and not Wythe,*" *would be
his colleague* in the approaching specially important State Convention ! (See letter in
work just quoted.) Put these with the facts which follow in the text, and the conclusion
seems irresistible that at the time of the Declaration, and for at least a considerable space
afterwards, there was not a trace of ill will or misunderstanding between Jefferson and
R. H. Lee. Mr. Jefferson does say, *forty-seven years* after, 1776, that "R. H. Lee charged
it [the Declaration of Independence] as copied from Locke's Treatise on Government."
But he mentions no time ; displays no feeling on the subject; and imputes no particular
motive of any kind to his critic. Lee's remark may have been made in or near 1776, in
some passing twinge of jealousy at the laudations poured out on "the masterly pen"
which had superseded his own. If the remark *was* made *then*, to suppose a deeper and a
malevolent motive at the bottom of it, would be to suppose Mr. Lee guilty of both
ingratitude and *deception.* The remark may have been casually thrown out long after in
some flush of political heat, for they ultimately parted in politics. But whenever made,
the simple knowledge that it was made furnishes no basis broad enough to build a
hypothesis on, contrary to the conclusions derivable from the numerous substantial facts
we have stated.

Chapter VI.) that it was to Jefferson's "candor" and "know-ledge of his political movements," that Lee on this occasion made his appeal, and, so far as we can discover, his sole appeal for *aid.*   This, surely, ought to show in what light he viewed Jefferson.   John Adams's views, we have already seen.

Another significant fact suggests itself.   A glance at the persons and "parties" in the Virginia delegation in the Congress of 1776, will show that unless R. H. Lee voted for himself (a thing not presumable), it required one or both (probably both) of Jefferson's and his particular friend Mr. Wythe's votes, to choose R. H. Lee to move the Virginia resolutions in favor of independence, on the 7th of June, unless those who were determined to defeat him in the chairmanship of the Committee formed under it, purposely desired to humiliate him more deeply by allowing him to move it.   This is quite as improbable a supposition as that Mr. Lee would vote for himself on such an occasion.

That Jefferson always considered Mr. R. H. Lee an over-rated man in point of ability, we have even better reasons for knowing than are to be found in those remarks twice or three times (and possibly oftener) casually dropped in his published writings, to the effect that Lee was a "frothy" and "rhetorical," speaker, rather than a profound debater, or, like Henry, a genuinely great natural orator.   With this opinion we have nothing to do; and the reader, after getting hold of all that can be legitimately traced to the tongue or pen of Mr. Lee, can decide the question for himself.   To doubt his oratorical powers or profundity of intellect, was scarcely a *disparagement* which necessarily implied *enmity* at any period of life.   But it would not be frank to drop this topic just here.   The petulant, conceited, and eternally disputatious (but able and patriotic) Dr. Arthur Lee, who, as we have seen, with his usual headlong pugnacity,[1] attacked, on some silly rumor, the integrity and

---

[1] Tucker, in his Life of Jefferson (vol. i. p. 166), says that Arthur Lee "was singularly impracticable in his temper and disposition;" that "he seems to have been one of those who rarely lost an opportunity of complaint, or censure, or contradiction,".and he gives the following laughable illustration of his love of controversy:

"While he [Lee] resided in England, one of his early acquaintances having inquired about him of Dr. M——, who had recently returned to Virginia, the latter answered the inquiry by the following characteristical anecdote: Dr. Lee being once caught in a shower of rain in London, sought shelter under a shed, and a gentleman who had joined him, from the same motive, civilly remarking, 'It rains very hard, sir.' his difficult companion immediately replied, 'It rains *hard,* sir; but I don't think you can say it rains *very* hard?'"

patriotism of John Jay, and drew his brother Richard Henry
into the quarrel; afterwards (as all know who have read the
history of those times) waged a more bitter, and rancorous, and
open warfare against Benjamin Franklin. Mr. Jefferson wrote
Robert Walsh, December 4, 1818:

" Dr. Lee was his [Franklin's] principal calumniator, a man of much malignity,
who, *besides enlisting his whole family in the same hostility*, was enabled, as the
agent of *Massachusetts* with the British Government, to infuse it into that State
with considerable effect."

Mr. Jefferson's opinions of the merits of this controversy are
to be found in the same letter and elsewhere. In a word, he
was a warm admirer and reverer of Franklin; and he regarded
this attack on him with indignation. Nor did he feel disposed
to overlook Richard Henry Lee's constant tendency to hunt in
couples with his quarrelsome brother. We *know* that he drew
decidedly unpleasant inferences from it; but as he has not
chosen to *record* them, we do not regard it proper for us to do
so. The very fact that he did not record them when speaking
so plainly of Arthur—that, indeed, nowhere does he utter anything against the character of Richard H. Lee—shows that his
disapprobation of that gentleman's conduct never reached the
point of enmity. And this serious disapprobation long post-
dated the events of 1776.

The quietness with which Mr. Jefferson passed over, without
criticism, the super-florid delineations of R. H. Lee, in the portions of the life of Henry written by his (Jefferson's) warm and
deferential friend Wirt—and when he could have spoken as
confidentially as he chose on the subject—would seem to
exhibit the same intentional forbearance. The truth is, Jefferson's heart ever warmed to every member of that daring little
band, who swam with himself on the first wave of the Revolution—the devoted band WHOSE NAMES WERE WITH HIS OWN IN
THE BILL OF ATTAINDER! Towards such, it was hard to provoke
his enmity.

It is not at all difficult to assign Mr. Jefferson his true attitude in the Virginia delegation, and in Congress, in 1776. He
was the warm friend of Washington, and of those who *claimed*
to be *his* particular friends in the Virginia delegation, and who
claimed that a portion of their colleagues were hostile to him.

On the other hand, he pressed forward with as daring a foot as the fiery Adamses towards independence. He admired those stern champions; their ruggedness did not disgust *him ;* nay, it was never *shown* towards *him.* They loved[1] the gallant young warrior who ranged himself under the banner of no chief, but pressed ever forward, on Arab charger, and with flashing arms, where their own coarse but ponderous strength—their rude iron maces—were bearing down in the front of the battle.

Mr. Jefferson now, as through life, had no taste for personal cliques, or clique feuds. We shall find him in no one instance, in politics or elsewhere, ever tied to, or connected with, any mere personal set. He never allowed such combinations to trammel or even to influence his actions. If he unquestionably had his likes and dislikes, as other men have, he was not gregarious in them. He never held it any impeachment of friendship, that he was obliged to divide it with an ill-wisher of his own; and in that particular he always evinced the independence he was willing to tolerate in others. Here, again, the reader is invited to submit assertion to the test of the facts of a life, as they shall gradually unroll before the eye.

Mr. Jefferson's ability to preserve his disconnection with mere personal cliques had, were it necessary, been favored by circumstances. He had been absent in Virginia during the heat of those bitter heart burnings which fill so many pages in Mr. Adams's Autobiography. Then, we have already mentioned his extreme modesty and suavity, and his generous construction of the motives of early opponents. If he ever judged harshly and intolerantly of the last, the time had not come yet. For example, the men whom John Adams represents as enemies of independence—open opponents—thwarters and delayers by every disingenuous subterfuge—haters even of the advocates of independence merely as such, etc., etc.—Mr. Jefferson describes as good and true Whigs, moving forward to the same end, only with that degree of caution which their age, the condition of their particular constituents, or their natural tempers as men, suggested.

Finally, there was another very important consideration which we cannot flinch from uttering. Congress was made up of able men—a good portion of them being also scholarly and

---

[1] "*I always loved Jefferson*" were the words of John Adams, which terminated the only estrangement which ever took place between them.

accomplished men. Was there probably a single man in that body, familiar as he must have been with R. H. Lee's written productions, who would dream for a moment of comparing him, as a *writer*, either in polish or power, with the author of the Summary View of the Rights of British America, and of the Congressional Reply to Lord North's Conciliatory Proposition? If there was, the universal verdict of posterity has pronounced him egregiously mistaken. The tenor of John Adams's own declarations go to show that whatever else had an influence on the question, it was probably quite as much as any other cause the reputation of the " masterly pen" which induced a body of decorous men, and *gentlemen*, to determine to violate parliamentary etiquette in overriding Mr. Lee on this Committee.

Do we, then, assume that the illness of his wife was pretended, and that this was an excuse to leave Congress to avoid the humiliation of a defeat? By no manner of means. His family biographer declares the illness of his wife, and that is sufficient authority. But Mr. Lee lived in Westmoreland, near the mouth of the Potomac—neither a very distant nor a very inaccessible point from Philadelphia. No definite action could be taken on the *Declaration*, until the original resolution was disposed of, and its consideration was already postponed for twenty days. Who could very well know that Mrs. Lee's health would not permit her husband to return short of that time? And the printed records of the Virginia Convention, lying under our eye, show that at least as early as the 29th of June, R. H. Lee was present and acting in that body (of which we have already stated that he was a member), and that he continued so acting until the close of its session.

Our theory of explanation is probably obvious to all who have followed the facts thus far. It is, that John Adams's assertions in regard to the matter are substantially correct, and that the facts had their reasons or causes in what *we* have narrated. The illness of Mrs. Lee was wisely seized upon by Mr. Lee's friends, as a reason for withdrawing his name, and not exposing him to defeat on the Declaration Committee. If they declined to place him on either of the other Committees (assuming they could have done so[1]), they acted wisely, because consistently with their excuse in the other instance. We are inclined to be-

---

[1] And we cannot reasonably doubt this.

lieve such was the case, but whether this was so, or whether for the present the tide was too strong against Mr. Lee to be resisted, perhaps will never be known. But for Mr. Adams's unnecessary disclosures, no part of this transaction would have been, probably, ever ripped up.

But it having been thus reopened, we have felt it our duty to all the parties, not only in reference to this particular occasion, but more or less in reference to others which will come under our notice, and in which the same principal actors took part, to probe it to the bottom. He who shall think that we have been influenced by the shadow of a desire to "disparage" Richard Henry Lee, will do us an injustice. Truth is not "disparagement." It is no disgrace to this or that Revolutionary character to say either that there was a greater or wiser than he. It is not vilifying the other generals of the Revolution to say that General Washington excelled them. It is no more discreditable to R. H. Lee to say that he was utterly inferior to Jefferson as a writer, than it is to say (what is equally undeniable) that Jefferson was utterly inferior to him as a speaker. It seems to us that the habit of profuse and indiscriminate eulogy *on all points*, of every man and thing connected with our Revolution, is worn somewhat threadbare. And the most grotesque part of the affair is, that each of these national Romuluses and Theseuses, if we may trust their ardent biographers, did the whole. Each conceived, and brought forth, and carried on his shoulders, the American Revolution! Now, we suppose there was a division of talent, a division of wisdom, and a division of labor. We suppose there were a good many *cogs* in the mighty wheel, and if there was not an indispensable one (except the will of Heaven) there were a thousand of extreme, and (striking out three or four towering names) of not greatly disproportionate utility. The swords of Washington, Greene, and Lafayette[1]—the eloquence of Adams, Henry, and Lee—the pens of Franklin, Jefferson, and Jay—were equally necessary; and each list might be greatly swelled without going down much in the scale of ability. Nor was it warriors, orators,

---

[1] We place the name of Lafayette here for what we consider the *fruits* of his serving our country in his military capacity. He was too young in the American Revolution to match, as a *soldier merely*, some older American commanders whom we have not named.

and writers, who did the whole. Not a profession, nor scarcely a human occupation, could have been spared; and in each the good work was achieved, not by one individual, but by a multitude. Peyton Randolph was not the only eminent Crown officer who faced a bill of attainder; Hancock was not the only princely merchant who bade the batteries train their guns on his store-houses; Putnam was not the only farmer who left one horse in the furrow, and mounted the other, in his farmer's frock, to speed to the battle muster; King's Mountain was not the only earth that drank the blood poured forth like water, of gentlemen of family, and name and condition, fighting in the ranks as private soldiers: the mechanic who gave his all—his labor, and sat up night and day to forge the pike-heads, make the wagons, or manufacture any of the different habiliments or equipments of war (and what handicraft would this leave out?) was but one of ten thousand; the matron who sent her last tender son to the fray, and defended her hearth with gun and axe against Indian and British savages, and the maiden who stopped not to weep her slain lover, but handed up the cartridges and carried water to the dying soldiers on the skirts of the battle, were each but one among thousands. Away, then, with the trash of ascribing the whole American Revolution, its deeds and its fruits, to a few supernatural men, as fabulous in their conception as the Guys of Warwick, and Bevises of Hampton, or the Sir Rolands and Sir Otuels, of the metrical romances of the Middle Ages! Of the nine towering names in that struggle, which we have mentioned respectively as generals, orators, and writers, perhaps not one individual of them decidedly excelled in either of the departments except in that in which we have given his name.

Reducing these mythical characters to something like their natural proportions, is neither unjust *disparagement* nor is it unkindness. Biography should aim at the truth, or it should be silent. The warmed-up biographer may run into exaggerated eulogy on his hero, and be somewhat excusable; but if he deliberately converts biography into a " Mutual Admiration Society "—praises to draw praise for his subject, or avert criticism from himself—makes for this purpose Cæsar, Brutus, Cassius " and all," " honorable men "—he deserves, in our judgment, quite as much contempt as he who deliberately converts biography into a vehicle of personal or political, or other individual resentments. We conceive there is one plain rule to follow in all cases; and that is to be truthful in the expression of opinions formed on fair, and what is believed to be sufficiently full investigation. In other words, the writer should be fearlessly true to himself, to *his own* mind and conscience.

We much mistake the calibre of the Revolutionary leaders if they would not have scorned that claim to a monopoly in their single persons of all the shades of ability, and of a good share of the great exploits which the world witnessed in that remarkable struggle. We much mistake the men if they would not say, "save us from our friends." And, in very truth, faith fully delineated, they would in most instances be equally revered, and vastly better loved than now. A few admitted faults or foibles—a few piquant individualities—a few of the lackings of common humanity—would show them to be human, to be real. Nobody puts actual faith in human impersonations of the perfect, either in intellect or character. Instinct instructs every man when he gazes on such, that they are, like the allegoric personages, the Christians and the Mr. Greathearts of Bunyan's story—the Goody-two-Shoes of the nursery tale—the Sir Guyons or Britomartises of Spenser's "faerie" song—that is to say, personifications of an *idea*—symbols of a virtue, or of a crowd of virtues. They are as vague in outline, as unsubstantial, and have as little individuality, as the cloudy heroes of Ossian—they are as cold, as bloodless, as little human as the marble demigods of Greece! It is easy to affect, and perhaps feel, an abstract admiration for a myth. A mind "diseased of its own beauty," may invest a myth with such a halo of sentiment as to fancy a genuine love for it. But there are but few of these Pygmalions in the world to animate stone, few who, like Bulwer's German student, have "a system of dreams," and can fall in love and die for the princess of their dreams—that is, few who have the qualifications which the law demands on various occasions for a *whole* man—"that he shall be twenty-one years of age, of sound mind," etc. Animals of the class "Mammalia," do not congencrate (if we may be excused in a neologism)—do not sympathize with white-blooded and cold-blooded, and particularly no-blooded animals! The mind admires perfection in the abstract—but it does not admire *claimed human* perfection, for

it knows it to be false; and, moreover, we are not quite certain
that beings

> ——"Not too pure and good
> For human nature's daily food,"——

are not more agreeable *per se*—for common humanity likes to
be kept in countenance by knowing that if it errs daily, all err
sometimes. A perfect human being, could such an one be
found, would move like a lone planet in a distant sphere—its
solitary heaven not irradiated by another star!

On the score of *character*, we will not say we regret Mr.
Jefferson's scrupulousness of demeanor down to trifles, but we
regard it as a serious misfortune to the writer of his life! The
relish of the most exquisite biographies in our language (we do
not speak of mere histories sometimes called biographies)
depends upon their freely narrating personal incidents illustrative of character, and recording little faults and foibles,
absurdities, blunders, and even, on occasion, serious errors, as
frankly as specimens of nun-like fastidiousness of deportment.
Who would strike the perverse and unappeasable bearishness
of Johnson from the pages of Boswell? Who laments the sharp,
clear, dissecting exposure of every one of Sir Walter Scott's pet
foibles and melancholy misjudgments, by the pen of his profound admirer and son-in-law, Lockhart? And who, let us
ask, in these and parallel cases, regrets such revelations on
account of the real reputation of the subject of them? Who
whines about violating the grave? Do the great masters of
fiction, untrammelled by the biographer's *facts*, free to choose
both their traits and their incidents, represent their favorite
characters—those they mean to render most attractive to their
readers—either as icicles or prudes? Would any one have the
gallant, sparkling Mercutio transformed into a hum-drum gentleman, too precise to take snuff and sneeze for fear of violating
decorum? Would anybody mercilessly stretch or cut off
Uncle Toby by the Procrustean bed of a very different class
of deacons, from what we suspect to have been "my father the
deacon?" Would any person make the inimitable Antiquary
freër in the article of expense—less liable to be taken in by a
Prætorium—or more lenient to "woman-kind" and dogs?
Finally (and that is going the whole length), let us ask, who

would venture to strip Falstaff of his vices, for fear of spoiling one of the most consummate and *favorite* delineations of dramatic literature?

In a word, we all love better a character on paper, if not in actual life, which has a seasoning of piquant faults. For instance, there is not a more thoroughly jumbled mixture of good and bad qualities in any hero of the National pantheon than in John Adams. Yet we predict the Alleghanies will disappear before the name of old "Sink or Swim" will cease to be a household word, or will cease among liberal men to be *loved* wherever it is pronounced.

And another paramount advantage had by the biographer of a man out of the "Goody-two-Shoes" line, is, that he can cheaply win the credit of candor. A face viewed in a level front light has no shadows, and thus Elizabeth wished to be painted. The artist knows that shadows are necessary to throw out what should be prominent and give expression to his picture; and, consequently, he throws the light so on his subject as to *make shadows.* Without this all is flat and tame. Minor faults, in biography, are the painter's shadows! But what might well be only the result of pure art, in this particular, is regarded as such extraordinary candor, that the biographer, after dashing on a shadow or two, might (if he desired) purposely exaggerate in important particulars without bringing his sincerity under suspicion. We suppose every lawyer has heard sharp and finessing witnesses on the stand, ostensibly lean, in the unimportant details, strongly against the very man whom they have ascended the witness-stand to swear safely through thick and thin! This is a wonderfully plausible way of enlisting credulity for the *lie* which is to follow! If some such admissions will win credence for falsehood, it is a pity, when they can be truthfully made, that their corroboration of an honest intention to tell the whole truth should ever be thrown away; for we take it that the good sense of mankind generally, in the long run, will distinguish between the biographical witness who will not see faults, or will intentionally suppress them—the artful one who will give a penny and ask back a pound in change—and the fair one who will tell his story rose-colored or sable, straight or crooked, *just as he finds it.* But it is time we drop a digression, which has wandered wide of the precise question from which it started.

CHAPTER V.

1776.

THE Committee to prepare a Declaration of Independence "unanimously pressed" Mr. Jefferson "to undertake the draft." He did so, but before submitting the paper to the full Committee, communicated it separately to Dr. Franklin and Mr. Adams, requesting their corrections, "which were two or three only, and merely verbal." The report was then laid before the entire Committee, which made no amendments; and on the 28th of June it was presented in Congress by its author. It was immediately read, and ordered to lie on the table.

In the often-quoted letter of John Adams to Timothy Pickering, in 1822, a somewhat different version of this affair is given. He says:

164

"The Committee met, discussed the subject, and then appointed Mr. Jefferson and me to make the draft, I suppose because we were the two first on the list. The sub-committee met. Jefferson proposed to me to make the draft. I said, 'I will not.' 'You should do it.' 'Oh! no.' 'Why will you not? You ought to do it.' 'I will not.' 'Why?' 'Reasons enough.' 'What can be your reasons?' 'Reason first—You are a Virginian, and a Virginian ought to appear at the head of this business. Reason second—I am obnoxious, suspected, and unpopular. You are very much otherwise. Reason third—You can write ten times better than I can.'[1] 'Well,' said Jefferson, 'if you are decided, I will do as well as I can.' 'Very well. When you have drawn it up, we will have a meeting.' A meeting we accordingly had, and conned the paper over. [After stating what he really liked and disliked in it, Mr. Adams proceeds:] I consented to report it, and *do not now remember that I made or suggested a single alteration.* We reported it to the Committee of five. It was read, and I *do not remember that Franklin or Sherman criticised anything.* We were all in haste. Congress was impatient, and the instrument was reported, as I believe, *in Jefferson's handwriting, as he first drew it.*"

This statement was published in 1823, and Jefferson soon after (August 30th), wrote Mr. Madison:

* * "Mr. Adams's memory has led him into unquestionable error. At the age of eighty-eight, and forty-seven years after the transactions of Independence, this is not wonderful. *Nor should I, at the age of eighty, on the small advantage of that difference only,* venture to oppose my memory to his, *were it not supported by written notes, taken by myself at the moment and on the spot.*" [After giving the substance of Mr. Adams's statement, he continues:] "Now these details are quite incorrect. The Committee of five met; no such thing as a sub-committee was proposed, but they unanimously pressed on myself alone to undertake the draft. I consented; I drew it; but before I reported it to the Committee, I communicated it *separately* to Doctor Franklin and Mr. Adams, requesting their corrections, because they were the two members of whose judgments and amendments I wished most to have the benefit, before presenting it to the Committee: and you have seen the original paper now in my hands, *with the corrections of Doctor Franklin and Mr. Adams interlined in their own hand-writings.* Their alterations were two or three only, and merely verbal. I then wrote a fair copy, reported it to the Committee, and from them, unaltered, to Congress. This personal communication and consultation with Mr. Adams, he has misremembered into the actings of a sub-committee."

The notes "taken by himself at the moment," which Mr. Jefferson refers to as "supporting" his memory, contained the following passages:

"The Committee were John Adams, Dr. Franklin, Roger Sherman, Robert R. Livingston, and myself. * * * * * *The Committee for drawing the Declara-*

[1] Mr. Adams's "reason second" and "reason third" go very distinctly to corroborate the "reasons" *we* gave in the last chapter *for Mr. Jefferson's being made chairman of the Committee.*

tion of Independence desired me to do it. It was accordingly done, and being approved by them, I reported it to the House on Friday, the 28th of June, when it was read and ordered to lie on the table."

And the "original paper" transferred from Mr. Jefferson's "hands" to the State Department, in Washington (a fac-simile of which will presently appear in this work), exhibits the interlineations mentioned, supporting the accuracy of Mr. Jefferson's narration down to details; and, on the other hand, showing how vague and loose must have been the minute recollections of a man who did not even remember whether he "made or suggested a single alteration!"

It is due to Mr. Adams to say that he inserted substantially the same version of the affair in his Autobiography, written about eighteen years earlier than his letter to Pickering, and about twenty-eight years after the occurrences took place, whereas Mr. Jefferson's statement to Mr. Madison, above given, was not written until forty-seven years afterwards. But independently of the testimony of the contemporaneous notes, which ought to be considered as settling the question (unless some one is prepared to say that Mr. Jefferson falsely entered in those notes, "the Committee desired *me* to do it—it was *accordingly* done"—when, in truth, the Committee desired *two* men to do it, and it was *accordingly* done by *two*); independently of the corroboration of Mr. Jefferson's version offered on the face of the interlined draft, and notwithstanding the difference of time intervening between the facts and respective statements, we should feel justly authorized to pronounce Jefferson's recollections by far the most reliable.

We have already mentioned that Mr. Adams was a signally inaccurate writer; and, in this respect, it did not make a very great difference whether he gave recollections five or fifty years after the event. It is hardly necessary to repeat that we regard his integrity and veracity as wholly above suspicion. But he was careless, impetuous, and unstudied in his statements, following the drift of the impression and the feeling of the moment, without stopping for investigation, or minding whom he ran against. It was his misfortune to run oftener against John Adams than any other man! But little cared he. Conscious integrity, overweening self-esteem, and an utter want of that sensitive delicacy which generally influences high-toned and (in the expressive common phrase) "thin-skinned" men, combined to render him vastly independent in regard to consistency either with himself or others.

Jefferson, on the contrary, was a good deal of a precisian in all things. He observed the minute, and he recorded the minute with elaborate circumspection. On the score of accuracy, he was as much above as Mr. Adams was below the common medium standard of honest and observing men. We shall not say, now, how often he erred in the impressions he derived from facts, or in credulously believing, on the statements of others, what were not facts; but, in cases where he deliberately recorded actual occurrences as on his own personal observation or knowledge, we venture to assert, after a long and patient investigation of his writings, that the page of American history does not present a man who has written so much, or half so much, on whom fewer errors can be proved. It is true that he never prided himself on a peculiarly strong memory—he rather conveys the opposite idea—and long before 1823, he more than once spoke of his memory as being seriously shattered. But we never have run our eye over one of these characteristic disclaimers without thinking of an anecdote of Gifford's. He says, that in a discussion with Soame Jenyns, he quoted Doctor Johnson's confession that he "knew little Greek." "But how shall we know what *Johnson* would have called *much* Greek?" was the reply.

Mr. Jefferson relied much on "supporting" notes, and it is everywhere obvious that when he appealed to his memory in regard to past facts of any importance, he did so with peculiar care and consideration. But when we compare his statements in such cases with other men's—and especially when we compare his own with each other, made at twenty, forty, and even sixty years intervals, and observe their striking similarity not only in details, but in the very stand-point from which the subject is viewed, so that those details appear always about in the same scale of proportion (showing the perfect method of his mind), we confess his memory seems to us portentous.

In an unpublished letter from Mr. Madison to Mr. Trist (May 15, 1832), lying before us, the former, after suggesting a careful review of all of Mr. Jefferson's correspondence which would touch a particular topic, then attracting a great deal of public interest, remarked :

"Allowances ought to be made for a habit in Mr. J., as in all others of great genius, of expressing in strong and round terms impressions of the moment. It may be added, that a full exhibition of the correspondences of distinguished public men, through the varied scenes of a long period, would not fail, *without one single exception*, to involve delicate personalities, *and apparent, if not real, inconsistencies.*"

The "inconsistencies" Mr. Madison principally referred to, were probably those of *opinion* at different periods of life. But taking the remark in its other sense, it is true of all the extensive correspondences ever written. Yet we say, frankly and fearlessly, that a serious and not fairly explainable inconsistency in statements of facts does not exist in all the correspondence of Thomas Jefferson—perhaps the most voluminous, with one or two exceptions, preserved of any of our earlier American statesmen.

Of course we have not spent all this time in discussing this topic, simply in reference to the really insignificant question of whether or not the Committee to draft the Declaration of Independence chose a sub-committee of two, or directed their chairman to perform this duty. It being conceded on all sides that Jefferson alone drew up that immortal instrument, the other question scarcely rises to the dignity of a "curiosty of literature ;" and it would not have here been noticed, except that on the authority of Adams's letter to Pickering (Mr. Jefferson's reply in the letter to Madison, not being then published), Mr. Webster, Mr. Wirt, and other distinguished gentlemen who delivered addresses on the death of Adams and Jefferson in 1826, followed, of course, Mr. Adams's version of the affair, and thus, without due explanation, would appear, to the generality of readers in after times, to give the weight of their great names to assertions of Mr. Adams's where he was directly contradicted by Jefferson with the asserted support of contemporaneous "notes ;" and except, moreover, that in a work published by (or by the aid of) Congress, the facts in the case have been deliberately, though we hope not intentionally, misrepresented.'

1 We refer of course to the Life and Writings of John Adams, edited by his grandson, Charles F. Adams. After mentioning that Mr. Jefferson attributed his grandfather's

On the 1st day of July, Congress, pursuant to order, resumed the consideration of the original resolution, to declare the Colonies independent (that is, the resolution introduced by R. H. Lee, on the 7th of June, in accordance with the Virginia instructions), and having debated it through the day, the question was taken *in Committee of the Whole*, and the resolution passed by the vote of nine Colonies, namely, New Hampshire, Connecticut, Massachusetts, Rhode Island, New Jersey, Maryland, Virginia, North Carolina, and Georgia. In relation to the action of the other four, Mr. Jefferson says :

"South Carolina and Pennsylvania voted against it. Delaware had but two members present, and they were divided. The delegates from New York declared they were for it themselves, and were assured their constituents were for it; but that their instructions having been drawn near a twelvemonth before, when reconciliation was still the general object, they were enjoined by them to do nothing which should impede that object. They, therefore, thought themselves not justifiable in voting on either side, and asked leave to withdraw from the question; which was given them. The Committee rose and reported their resolution to the House. Mr. Edward Rutledge, of South Carolina, then requested the determination might be put off to the next day, as he believed his colleagues, though they disapproved of the resolution, would then join in it for the sake of unanimity."

And Mr. Jefferson writes in continuation :

"The ultimate question, whether the House would agree to the resolution of the Committee, was accordingly postponed to the next day, when it was again moved, and South Carolina concurred in voting for it. In the meantime, a third member had come post from the Delaware counties, and turned the vote of that Colony in favour of the resolution. Members of a different sentiment attending that morning from Pennsylvania also, her vote was changed, so that the whole

error, in the matter just considered, to the "failing memory of eighty-eight, the *assumed* age of Mr. Adams at the time" (a lamentable "assumption," as we believe Mr. Adams lacked two or three months of that age!) continues:
"Perceiving also the *awkward nature* of the *charge* made by one—himself—having, at the moment, nearly attained four-score, Mr. Jefferson *disclaims all reliance upon his recollection*, and appeals to the unequivocal authority of his notes, made at the time. This seemed conclusive testimony, sufficient to set the matter at rest forever. But if by those notes is to be understood no more than what has since been published under that name, in the first volume of his Correspondence, it is clear, on examination, that they present no evidence, excepting that which may be implied BY THEIR AFFIRMING NOTHING IN CORROBORATION."—*Life and Works of J. Adams*, vol. ii. p. 515, note.
This is a most extraordinary commentary! *Does* Mr. Jefferson, in the Madison letter, bring or imply any "*charge*" against Mr. Adams on the score of *age*, or any other score? *Does* he treat him otherwise than *kindly* and *respectfully*? *Does* he so far base a claim to superior accuracy on his own *juniority*, that it makes a reference to Mr. Adams's age "*awkward?*" *Does* he (in exact conflict with the preceding hypothesis!) 'disclaim *all* reliance on his recollection?" And, lastly, *is* it *true* that Mr. Jefferson's contemporaneous "notes" "affirm *nothing* in corroboration" of his statements in the premises? In *our* extracts from the Madison letter and the "notes," we need not say we have given Mr. Jefferson's language word for word and letter for letter; and the reader will be enabled to judge understandingly between him and the assailant, who has neither given that language nor *correctly stated its purport.*

twelve Colonies who were authorized to vote at all, gave their voices for it; and, within a few days,[1] the Convention of New York approved of it, and thus supplied the void occasioned by the withdrawing of her delegates from the vote."[2]

On the same day this resolution passed (July 2d), the House, in Committee of the Whole, took from the table the draught of the *Declaration* of Independence, which had been reported by Mr. Jefferson. The question, on its adoption, was debated throughout that and the two succeeding days. Several amendments were carried in committee. Of the causes which led to the two most important ones, Mr. Jefferson gives the following account in his Memoir:

"The pusillanimous idea that we had friends in England worth keeping terms with, still haunted the minds of many. For this reason, those passages which conveyed censures on the people of England were struck out, lest they should give them offence.[3] The clause, too, reprobating the enslaving the inhabitants of Africa, was struck out in complaisance to South Carolina and Georgia, who had never attempted to restrain the importation of slaves, and who, on the contrary, still wished to continue it. Our northern brethren also. I believe, felt a little tender under those censures; for though their people had very few slaves themselves, yet they had been pretty considerable carriers of them to others."

[1] July 9th; and the resolution in the New York Provincial Congress to that effect, was reported by John Jay. (See his *Life and Writings*, vol. i. p. 45.)
[2] The journal of Congress does not give anything but the general result. For all these details, the public are indebted *alone* (we believe) to Mr. Jefferson's contemporaneous "notes."
[3] Lord John Russell, in strong concurrence with a portion of these views, says in his Life of Charles James Fox: "The Declaration has one singular defect in it, but which only proves the lingering affection which the Americans still retained for the mother country. As Mr. Jefferson originally drew the Declaration of Independence, he charged the acts of which the Americans complained, in the first place to the King, but secondly to the people of Great Britain." After quoting several of Mr. Jefferson's expressions from the stricken out passages, conveying the latter idea, and repeating the opinion that this emasculation of the document by Congress was occasioned rather by the lingerings of "fond regard," than a fear of *breaking with friends*, Lord Russell continues:
"Be this as it may, the omission of these papers warped the truth of this memorable Declaration. George III. appears in it as a single and despotic tyrant; as Philip II. must have appeared to the people of the Netherlands. The fact was, that the Sovereign and his people were alike prejudiced, angry and willful."—*Life of Fox*, vol. i. p. 134.
We would here remark, in justification of our own former position, that the King was mainly instrumental in producing the Revolutionary struggle, that Lord Russell himself *prefaces* the preceding statement with the assertion that "it was the peculiar infelicity of George III. and Lord North that *they turned to gall* all those feelings of filial piety which had so long filled the breasts of the Americans." No fact is more clearly established than that the King was equally instrumental in "turning to gall" the feelings of the British nation in this controversy. Lord North was perhaps only *the more* censurable for carrying out measures of which he clearly saw the inexpediency, if not the impropriety; but George III. was repeatedly compelled to have recourse to entreaties, to appeals to his personal friendship, and even to *threats of abdication*, to induce the minister to persevere in turning a deaf ear to all propositions for putting an end to the barbarous struggle!—[*Brougham's Life of Lord North*.] If the Declaration of Independence, as adopted, failed to inflict just censure on the people of Great Britain, it certainly inflicted *no more than just censure* on their obtuse, violently prejudiced, and inveterately obstinate Sovereign. (See Brougham's confirmation of this view in his sketch of the Life of George III.)

On the evening of the 4th of July, the Declaration, as amended in Committee, was reported to the House and agreed to; and thus was consummated that legislation, which, sustained by subsequent years of struggle and suffering of which history affords few parallels, struck from the British realm a territory far exceeding its whole extent under its Plantagenets and Tudors—and to contain, even before the generation then living should pass entirely away, a population far outnumbering that which owned the sway of Henry V. or Elizabeth.

How little various persons whose names are attached to the Declaration had to do with preparing it, or paving the way for it, at least in Congress, is a matter of notoriety and need not be here recounted. Several delegates arrived only in time to vote for it, and others were allowed to attach their names who were not present at that vote.[1]

---

[1] In Mr. Jefferson's contemporaneous "notes," he says that on the 4th "the Declaration was reported by the Committee, agreed to by the House, and *signed by every member present*, except Mr. Dickinson." And again: "the Declaration thus signed on the 4th on paper, was engrossed on parchment, and *signed again on the 2d of August*."

In a letter to S. A. Wells, in 1819, he said:

"It was not till the 2d of July, that the Declaration itself was taken up; nor till the 4th that it was decided, and it was signed by every member present, except Mr. Dickinson.

"The subsequent signature of members who were not then present, and some of them not yet in office, is easily explained, if we observe who they were; to wit, that they were of New York and Pennsylvania. New York *did not sign till the 15th*, because it was not till the 9th (*five days after the general signature*), that their Convention authorized them to do so. The Convention of Pennsylvania, *learning that it had been signed by a minority only of their delegates*, named a new delegation on the 20th, leaving out Mr. Dickinson, *who had refused to sign*, Willing and Humphreys, who had withdrawn, re-appointing the three members *who had signed*, Morris, who had not been present, and five new ones, to wit, Rush, Clymer, Smith, Taylor and Ross: and Morris, and the five new members were permitted to sign, because it manifested the assent of their full delegation, and the express will of their Convention, which might have been doubted *on the former signature of a minority* only. Why the signature of Thornton, of New Hampshire, was permitted so late as the 4th of November, I cannot now say; but undoubtedly for some particular reason, which we should find to have been good, had it been expressed. *These were the only post-signers*, and you see, sir, that there were solid reasons for receiving those of New-York and Pennsylvania, and that this circumstance in no wise affects the faith of this Declaratory Charter of our rights, and of the rights of man."

The Congressional Journal speaks of but one signing. And we are informed that the paper copy which he so repeatedly and particularly mentions as signed on the fourth, and *as having been signed by the New York Delegation on the 15th* (such is his minuteness of specification), is not now in existence. Where, too, is that "*fair copy*" of the Declaration which, in his letter to Madison (August 23d, 1823), he says he made out *from his draft, after the corrections of Franklin and Adams*, and reported to the Committee, and from them "unaltered to Congress?" We have not searched the public archives at Washington for this *fair copy*—but we *suppose* it does not exist. At least we do not remember to have heard of it. If this supposition is correct, when that *fair copy* is found, *probably* the *first set of signatures* will be found attached to it. But were that copy found without the signatures, it would neither disprove nor render it improbable that another copy was made at the time by the Clerk of the House for the express purpose of the first signing. What was the object of two signings? Perhaps, when the first was begun, a second one was not contemplated—but was afterwards judged expedient to place the instrument on a single and less perishable sheet, and in a better form before the eye. Perhaps the first was signed immediately, as a full contemporaneous authentication of the validity of the instrument—for it will be observed, throughout, that

Herewith is given a fac-simile of Jefferson's draft now in the State Department—the parts stricken out by Congress being placed in brackets, and most of the amendments it made, interpolated in the hand-writing of the author of the instrument.

To facilitate a more convenient comparison between the document as it was reported, and in the shape in which it finally passed the House, a printed copy of the draft is given below with the parts which were stricken out inclosed in brackets *and in italics*—and the amendments placed in the margin, or in a concurrent column.

A Declaration by the Representatives of the Unite l States of America, in General Congress assembled.

When, in the course of human events, it becomes necessary for one people to dissolve the political bands which have connected them with another, and to assume among the powers of the earth the separate and equal station to which the laws of nature and of nature's God entitle them, a decent respect to the opinions of mankind requires that they should declare the causes which impel them to the separation.

We hold these truths to be self-evident: that all men are

Jefferson speaks of the signing not as a mere personal act, but as an authenticating and *binding* expression of the assent of the different Colonies to this great instrument. *The will of a majority of Congress could not bind any Colony to the Declaration; and it could only be bound by the express assent of its delegates.* Their signatures were the only decisive proof of such assent of the delegates. We doubt whether the Declaration was considered *made* or *executed*—whether it was proclaimed out of doors—until all the delegates present (except Dickinson) had come forward and signed their names. It would be rather preposterous to suppose that a month and a half elapsed before so important an instrument received any *binding* effect or authentication, when a day was as ample time as a month and a half for the preparation of the engrossed copy.

What became of the first signed copy? It was, in all probability, purposely destroyed when the second was made complete. It is not customary in any analogous cases to preserve two copies of the complete and executed instrument. In various important instruments a rough copy *is* often temporarily signed until the final one is ready; and when the last is executed, the first is destroyed. Why was the second signing delayed so long? To give an opportunity to New York to act on the question—to give other States, where there were dissentients, as in Pennsylvania, an opportunity of showing something better than a minority of their delegation in attestation of the assent of the State to the bill—and the formal second signing was delayed so that it might bear the appearance of a simultaneous and unanimous act of the States through their delegates.

We think we have been informed that the engrossed copy of the Declaration was not on *parchment*. Then Mr. Jefferson was mistaken in that unimportant particular.

When Mr. Jefferson speaks of "Post-Signers," in the above extracts from his letter to Wells, his reference to New York and Pennsylvania shows that he particularly referred to delegations or majorities of delegations, and not to individuals: for no one could have known better than he that neither R. H. Lee nor Mr. Wythe, of Virginia, were present in Congress on the 4th of July, 1776. We have given certain proof of Lee's absence; and that of an equally decisive character exists in Mr. Wythe's case. The records of the Virginia Convention of that year, show that he *acted* as one of the tellers to count the votes for Governor, in the Convention, on the 29th of June. His name appears daily in the proceedings until the 4th of July, and on that day he *presided* in a Committee of the Whole, and *reported* from it to the House.

A Declaration by the Representatives of the UNITED STATES

OF AMERICA, in General Congress assembled

When in the course of human events it becomes necessary for one people to dissolve the political bands which have connected them with another, and to assume among the powers of the earth the separate and equal station to which the laws of nature & of nature's god entitle them, a decent respect to the opinions of mankind requires that they should declare the causes which impel them to the separation.

We hold these truths to be self-evident, that all men are created equal, that they are endowed by their creator with inherent & inalienable rights, that among these are life, liberty & the pursuit of happiness; that to secure these rights, go-

+ Dr Franklin

+ abolishing our most ~~important~~ valuable laws

for taking away our charters, & altering fundamentally the forms of our governments,

for suspending our own legislatures & declaring themselves invested with power to legislate for us in all cases whatsoever:

he has abdicated government here, by declaring us out of his protection & waging war against us. [withdrawing his governors, & declaring us out of his allegiance & protection:]

he has plundered our seas, ravaged our coasts, burnt our towns & destroyed the lives of our people:

he is at this time transporting large armies of foreign mercenaries to compleat
the works of death, desolation & tyranny already begun with circumstances
Scarcely and other
of cruelty & perfidy unworthy the head of a civilized nation.
scarcely paralleled in the most barbarous ages, and totally
which he urges on us & has
excited domestic insurrections amongst us &
he has endeavored to bring on the inhabitants of our frontiers the merciless Indian

savages, whose known rule of warfare is an undistinguished destruction of

all ages, sexes, & conditions [of existence:]

he has refused his assent to laws the most wholesome and necessary for the pub-
- lic good:

he has forbidden his governors to pass laws of immediate & pressing importance,
unless suspended in their operation till his assent should be obtained,
and when so suspended, he has utterly neglected to attend to them.

he has refused to pass other laws for the accommodation of large districts of people,
unless those people would relinquish the right of representation in the legislature, a right
inestimable to them, & formidable to tyrants only:

he has called together legislative bodies at places unusual, uncomfortable & distant from
the depository of their public records, for the sole purpose of fatiguing them into compliance
with his measures.

he has dissolved Representative houses repeatedly [& continually] for opposing with
manly firmness his invasions on the rights of the people:
time after time, he has refused for a long space of time, to cause others to be elected;
whereby the legislative powers incapable of annihilation, have returned to
the people at large for their exercise; the state ...

nor have we been wanting in attentions to our British brethren. we have warned them from time to time of attempts by their legislature to extend a jurisdiction over [these our states] we have reminded them of the circumstances of our emigration & settlement here, [no one of which could warrant so strange a pretension: that these were effected at the expence of our own blood & treasure, unassisted by the wealth or the strength of Great Britain: that in constituting indeed our several forms of government, we had adopted one common king, thereby laying a foundation for perpetual league & amity with them: but that submission to their parliament was no part of our constitution, nor ever in idea if history may be credited: and] we [have] appealed to their native justice & magnanimity, [as well as to] the ties of our common kindred to disavow these usurpations which [were likely to] interrupt

created equal ; that they are endowed by their creator with [*inherent and*] inalienable rights; that among these are life, liberty, and the pursuit of happiness ; that to secure these rights, governments are instituted among men, deriving their just powers from the consent of the governed ; that whenever any form of government becomes destructive of these ends, it is the right of the people to alter or to abolish it, and to institute new government, laying its foundation on such principles, and organizing its powers in such form, as to them shall seem most likely to effect their safety and happiness. Prudence, indeed, will dictate that governments long established should not be changed for light and transient causes ; and accordingly all experience hath shown that mankind are more disposed to suffer while evils are sufferable, than to right themselves by abolishing the forms to which they are accustomed. But when a long train of abuses and usurpations [*begun at a distinguished period and*] pursuing invariably the same object, evinces a design to reduce them under absolute despotism, it is their right, it is their duty to throw off such government, and to provide new guards for their future security. Such has been the patient sufferance of these Colonies; and such is now the necessity which constrains them to [*expunge*] their former systems of government. The history of the present King of Great Britain is a history of [*unremitting*] injuries and usurpations, [*among which appears no solitary fact to contradict the uniform tenor of the rest, but all have*] in direct object the establishment of an absolute tyranny over these States. To prove this, let facts be submitted to a candid world [*for the truth of which we pledge a faith yet unsullied by falsehood*].

He has refused his assent to laws the most wholesome and necessary for the public good.

He has forbidden his governors to pass laws of immediate and pressing importance, unless suspended in their operation till his assent should be obtained ; and, when so suspended, he has utterly neglected to attend to them.

He has refused to pass other laws for the accommodation of large districts of people, unless those people would relinquish the right of representation in the Legislature, a right inestimable to them, and formidable to tyrants only.

He has called together legislative bodies at places unusual, uncomfortable, and distant from the depository of their public records, for the sole purpose of fatiguing them into compliance with his measures.

He has dissolved representative houses repeatedly [*and continually*] for opposing with manly firmness his invasions on the rights of the people.

He has refused for a long time after such dissolutions to cause others to be elected, whereby the legislative powers, incapable of annihilation, have returned to the people at large for their exercise, the State remaining, in the meantime, exposed to all the dangers of invasion from without and convulsions within.

He has endeavored to prevent the population of these States; for that purpose obstructing the laws for naturalization of foreigners, refusing to pass others to encourage their migrations hither, and raising the conditions of new appropriations of lands.

obstructed
by

He has [*suffered*] the administration of justice [*totally to cease in some of these States*] refusing his assent to laws for establishing judiciary powers.

He has made [*our*] judges dependent on his will alone for the tenure of their offices, and the amount and payment of their salaries.

He has erected a multitude of new offices, [*by a self-assumed power*] and sent hither swarms of new officers to harass our people and eat out their substance.

He has kept among us in times of peace standing armies [*and ships of war*] without the consent of our Legislatures.

He has affected to render the military independent of, and superior to, the civil power.

He has combined with others to subject us to a jurisdiction foreign to our constitutions and unacknowledged by our laws, giving his assent to their acts of pretended legislation for quartering large bodies of armed troops among us; for protecting them by a mock trial from punishment for any murders which they should commit on the inhabitants of these States; for cutting off our trade with all parts of the world; for imposing taxes on us without our consent;

in many cases

for depriving us [ ] of the benefits of trial by jury; for transporting us beyond seas to be tried for pretended offences; for abolishing the free system of English laws in a neighboring province, establishing therein an arbitrary government, and enlarging its boundaries, so as to render it at once an example and fit instrument for introducing

Colonies

the same absolute rule into these [*States*]; for taking away our charters, abolishing our most valuable laws, and altering fundamentally the forms of our governments; for suspending our own Legislatures, and declaring themselves invested with power to legislate for us in all cases whatsoever.

by declaring us out of his protection, and waging war against us.

He has abdicated government here [*withdrawing his governors, and declaring us out of his allegiance and protection*].

He has plundered our seas, ravaged our coasts, burnt our towns, and destroyed the lives of our people.

He is at this time transporting large armies of foreign mercenaries to complete the works of death, desolation, and tyranny already

scarcely paralleled in the most barbarous ages, and totally

begun with circumstances of cruelty and perfidy [ ] unworthy the head of a civilized nation.

He has constrained our fellow-citizens taken captive on the high seas to bear arms against their country, to become the executioners of their friends and brethren, or to fall themselves by their hands.

excited domestic insurrection among us. and has

He has [ ] endeavored to bring on the inhabitants of our frontiers the merciless Indian savages, whose known rule of warfare is an undistinguished destruction of all ages, sexes, and conditions [*of existence*].

[*He has incited treasonable insurrections of our fellow-citizens, with the allurements of forfeiture and confiscation of our property.*

He has waged cruel war against human nature itself, violating its most sacred rights of life and liberty in the persons of a distant people who never offended him, captivating and carrying them into slavery in another hemisphere, or to incur miserable death in their transportation thither. This piratical warfare, the opprobrium of INFIDEL *powers, is the warfare of the* CHRISTIAN *King of Great Britain. Determined to keep open a market where* MEN *should be bought and sold, he has prostituted his negative for suppressing every legislative attempt to prohibit or to restrain this execrable commerce. And that this assemblage of horrors might want no fact of distinguished die, he is now exciting those very people to rise in arms among us, and to purchase that liberty of which he has deprived them, by murdering the people on whom he also obtruded them: thus paying off former crimes committed against the* LIBERTIES *of one people with crimes which he urges them to commit against the* LIVES *of another.*]

In every stage of these oppressions we have petitioned for redress in the most humble terms:·our repeated petitions have been answered only by repeated injuries.

A Prince whose character is thus marked by every act which may define a tyrant is unfit to be the ruler of a [ ] people [*who mean to be free. Future ages will scarcely believe that the hardiness of one man adventured, within the short compass of twelve years only, to lay a foundation so broad and so undisguised for tyranny over a people fostered and fixed in principles of freedom.*]   **free**

Nor have we been wanting in attentions to our British brethren. We have warned them from time to time of attempts by their legislature to extend [a] jurisdiction over [*these our States*]. We have reminded them of the circumstances of our emigration and settlement here, [*no one of which could warrant so strange a pretension: that these were effected at the expense of our own blood and treasure, unassisted by the wealth or the strength of Great Britain: that in constituting indeed our several forms of government, we had adopted one common king, thereby laying a foundation for perpetual league and amity with them: but that submission to their parliament was no part of our Constitution, nor ever in idea, if history may be credited: and,*] we [ ]   **have** appealed to their native justice and magnanimity [*as well as to*] the   **and we have conjured them by** ties of our common kindred to disavow these usurpations which [*were likely to*] interrupt our connection and correspondence. They too   **would inevitably** have been deaf to the voice of justice and of consanguinity, [*and when occasions have been given them, by the regular course of their laws, of removing from their councils the disturbers of our harmony, they have, by their free election, re-established them in power. At this very time too, they are permitting their chief magistrate to send over not only soldiers of our common blood, but Scotch and foreign mercenaries to invade and destroy us. These facts have given the last stab to agonizing affection, and manly spirit bids us to renounce forever*

an unwarrantable us

*these unfeeling brethren. We must endeavor to forget our former love
for them, and hold them as we hold the rest of mankind, enemies in
war, in peace friends. We might have been a free and a great people
together; but a communication of grandeur and of freedom, it seems,
is below their dignity. Be it so, since they will have it. The road to
happiness and to glory is open to us too. We will tread it apart from
them, and]* acquiesce in the necessity which denounces our *[eternal]*
separation [ ]!

We must therefore and hold them as we hold the rest of mankind, enemies in war, in peace friends.

We therefore the representatives of the United States of America in General Congress assembled, appealing to the supreme judge of the world for the rectitude of our intentions, do in the name, and by the authority of the good people of these Colonies, solemnly publish and declare, that these united Colonies are, and of right ought to be, free and independent States; that they are absolved from all allegiance to the British crown, and that all political connection between them and the state of Great Britain is, and ought to be, totally dissolved; and that as free and independent States, they have full power to levy war, conclude peace, contract alliances, establish commerce, and to do all other acts and things which independent States may of right do.

And for the support of this declaration, with a firm reliance on the protection of divine providence, we mutually pledge to each other our lives, our fortunes, and our sacred honor.

We therefore the representatives of the United States of America in General Congress assembled, do in the name, and by the authority of the good people of these [*States reject and renounce all allegiance and subjection to the kings of Great Britain and all others who may hereafter claim by, through, or under them; we utterly dissolve all political connection which may heretofore have subsisted between us and the people or parliament of Great Britain: and finally we do assert and declare these Colonies to be free and independent States,*] and that as free and independent States, they have full power to levy war, conclude peace, contract alliances, establish commerce, and to do all other acts and things which independent States may of right do.

And for the support of this declaration, we mutually pledge to each other our lives, our fortunes, and our sacred honor.

The following particulars may be of interest to the curious. In answer to inquiries from Dr. John Mease, Mr. Jefferson (September 26, 1825) tells *where* he wrote the Declaration of Independence. He says:

"At the time of writing that instrument, I lodged in the house of a Mr. Graaf, a new brick house, three stories high, of which I rented the second floor, consisting of a parlor and bed-room, ready furnished. In that parlor I wrote habitually, and in it wrote this paper, particularly. So far I state from written proofs in my possession. The proprietor, Graaf, was a young man, son of a German, and then newly married. I think he was a bricklayer, and that his house was on the south side of Market street, probably between Seventh and Eighth streets, and if not the only house on that part of the street, I am sure there were few others near it. I have some idea that it was a corner house, but no other recollections throwing light on the question, or worth communication."

The account book, before us, shows that on reaching Philadelphia, he remained eight days at his old lodgings, with "Ben. Randolph," and that on the 23d of May he "took lodging at Graaf's." Entries of the payment of the weekly rent of his rooms (thirty-five shillings sterling) continued throughout the session. He appears to have taken most of his meals at "Smith's"—the keeper, we suppose, of the City Tavern.

The little writing desk on which he wrote the Declaration of Independence is yet in existence. A grand-daughter who, on her marriage, left Monticello for her future residence in Boston, intrusted most of her belongings to a packet sailing from Richmond, which was lost at sea. The most severely felt loss among her effects was a writing desk containing her grandfather's letters to her, and some other personal memorials of him. And there was another utterly bereaved party—John Hemmings, Mr. Jefferson's faithful old black, head-carpenter, joiner, etc., of whom we shall see more as our narration progresses. John had fondly lavished all his skill on the lost treasure, for the favorite young "Missus." Innumerable were the different kinds of veneers on it, and curious and (John thought) *recherché* their arrangement. "He could not make another like it for Miss Ellen." "He had no more such choice sticks laid away." "Besides, he was getting old, and couldn't see well enough," etc., etc. In a word, he was inconsolable. Whether Mr. Jefferson had any eye on him in sending a substitute, which the faithful old fellow had learned to look upon with a sort of mystical veneration, we cannot say; but he probably thought that a little reading and writing desk in his possession—some fourteen inches long, by about ten in breadth and three in depth —would almost make good to the other parties the place of John's beautiful handiwork; and accordingly, he sent it (to divide the compliment) to his grand-daughter's husband, with the following inscription attached to the under side of the leaf which is turned down, in writing:

"Thomas Jefferson gives this writing desk to Joseph Coolidge, Jr., as a memorial of affection. It was made from a drawing of his own, by Ben. Randolph, cabinet-maker at Philadelphia, with whom he first lodged on his arrival in that city, in May, 1776, and is the identical one on which he wrote the Declaration of Independence. Politics, as well as religion, has its superstitions. These gaining strength with time, may one day give imaginary value to this relic, for its associations with the birth of the Great Charter of our Independence.

"*Monticello, Nov.* 18, 1825."

So much for "*relics;*" and we trust the possessors of this will pardon us for giving its history.

To go back to Congress. "The Great Charter" did not pass that body without encountering a fiery ordeal. The steadiness and force of the resistance it encountered, Mr. Jefferson afterwards compared to "the ceaseless action of gravity weighing upon us by night and by day."[1] He did not attempt to say a word for it himself, thinking "it a duty to be on that occasion a passive auditor of the opinions of others, more impartial judges than he could be of its merits or demerits."[2] But this passiveness does not appear to have entirely embraced his feelings. Several passages in his writings show that he felt with natural sensibility the sharp attacks on both the matter and form of his intellectual progeny. In one of these, he says: "During the debate I was sitting by Dr. Franklin, and he observed that *I was writhing a little* under the acrimonious criticisms on some of its parts; and it was on that occasion that, by way of comfort, he told me the story of John Thompson, the hatter, and his new sign."[3]

---

[1] Letter to Madison, Aug. 30th, 1823.   [2] Ibid.

[3] This story is too illustrative of the Doctor's quaint humor and imperturbable *sang froid* to be omitted. It is thus (with a different preface) related by Mr. Jefferson in some anecdotes of Dr. Franklin, written to Robert Walsh in 1818 (see Jefferson's Works, Congress Ed. vol. viii. p. 497):

"When the Declaration of Independence was under the consideration of Congress, there were two or three unlucky expressions in it which gave offence to some members. The words 'Scotch and other foreign auxiliaries' excited the ire of a gentleman or two of that country. Severe strictures on the conduct of the British King, in negativing our repeated repeals of the law which permitted the importation of slaves, were disapproved by some Southern gentlemen, whose reflections were not yet matured to the full abhorrence of that traffic. Although the offensive expressions were immediately yielded, these gentlemen continued their depredations on other parts of the instrument. I was sitting by Dr. Franklin, who perceived that I was not insensible to these mutilations. 'I have made it a rule,' said he, 'whenever in my power, to avoid becoming the draftsman of papers to be reviewed by a public body. I took my lesson from an incident which I will relate to you. When I was a journeyman printer, one of my companions, an apprentice hatter, having served out his time, was about to open shop for himself. His first concern was to have a handsome sign-board, with a proper inscription. He composed it in these words, "John Thompson, *Hatter, makes* and *sells hats* for ready money," with a figure of a hat subjoined: but he thought he would submit it to his friends for their amend ments. The first he showed it to thought the word "*Hatter*" tautologous, because followed by the words "makes hats," which show he was a hatter. It was struck out. The next observed that the word "*makes*" might as well be omitted, because his customers would not care who made the hats. If good and to their mind, they would buy, by whomsoever made. He struck it out. A third said he thought the words "*for ready money*" were useless, as it was not the custom of the place to sell on credit.

But the calm pulse kept pretty good time! The pocket account book, the meteorological table, etc., all show that the usual precise routine of matters was neither overlooked nor disturbed, during the three days of the galling debate.[1]

John Adams was the great champion of the Declaration on the floor, indulging in none of the milk-and-water criticisms of his Pickering letter (about the "personality" of styling George III. a "tyrant," etc.), but fighting fearlessly for every word of it[2]—and with a power to which a mind masculine and impassioned in its conceptions—a will of torrent-like force—a heroism which only glared forth more luridly at the approach of danger—and a patriotism whose burning throb was rather akin to the feeling of a parent fighting over his offspring, than to the colder sentiment of tamer minds, lent resistless sway.

The meed of praise to the principal defender, comes, appropriately, from the author of the Declaration. No other pen has done, and all other pens have not done, half so much as Jefferson's to impress the public mind with the magnitude of John Adams's splendid services—with the glorious display of his, in some respects, preëminent abilities, on that memorable occasion. His written tributes to Mr. Adams are numerous and glowing—

Every one who purchased expected to pay. They were parted with, and the inscription now stood, "John Thompson sells hats." "*Sells hats!*" says his next friend: why, nobody will expect you to give them away; what then is the use of that word? It was stricken out, and "*hats*" followed it, the rather as there was one painted on the board. So the inscription was reduced ultimately to "John Thompson," with the figure of a hat subjoined.'"

[1] The following, for example, are the entries in the account-book :

      July 1. pd. ferriage of horses, 8d.
            8. pd. Towne for Dr. Gilmer, 7s. 6d.
               pd.   do.   for myself, 7s. 6d.
               pd. Smith in full, 15s. 6d
            4. pd. Sparhawk for a thermometer, £3 15s.
               pd. for 7 pr. women's gloves, 27s.
               gave in charity, 1s. 6d

The following are from the meteorological register :

FAHRENHEIT'S THERMOMETER.

			Philadelphia.	
1776			H. Min	
July 1	9	0	A. M.	81½°
	7	0	P. M.	82
2	6	0	A. M.	78
	9	40	A. M.	78
	9	0	P. M.	74
3	5	30	A. M.	71½
	1	30	P. M.	76
	8	10		74
4	6	0	A. M.	68
	9	0		79½
	1	0	P. M.	76
	9	0		73½

[2] Jefferson to Madison, August 30, 1823.

and that " he was the colossus in that debate," was a tribute he never withheld from him during the sharpest rivalries, or ensuing alienations. Collect all the instances of John Adams's faults, and foibles, and occasional insanities almost, and grave political errors, to be found in truthful records, and then expunge all the memorials of his great and good deeds and private virtues, except from the writings of Jefferson, and from the latter alone the reader who has a heart, would turn away from the dark strokes of the picture and exclaim, in the language of one of Mr. Jefferson's descendants, "Glorious old John Adams !" [1]

From a collation of all the accounts left of the debates on the resolution for declaring independence, and subsequently on the matter and form of the Declaration, we infer that Mr. Adams was often on his feet—that, in fact, like the Knight of Chivalry, at his *pas d'armes*, he was ready to encounter *all* comers. But we conjecture that his great effort—that, which by happily catching the tone of the man, and interweaving some contemporaneous expressions from his letters, Mr. Webster has so felicitously represented, or, as the naturalists say, *restored*— was made July 1st, in answer to Dickinson's powerful and final appeal on the other side, just before the question was taken in committee on the original resolution. It was made, says Mr. Adams, without " minutes " and without " preparation beforehand." [2] It was not reported at the time, nor written out afterwards, and consequently not an actual sentence of it is known to be perpetuated. The classic traveller sighs, at Mycene, to find the lion gateway, and a few vestiges of crumbling masonry, are all that remain of him whom Homer sung " the King of men." The classic traveller mourns on the banks of Alpheus, that no trace remains of the temple of the Olympian Jove, and the master-piece of Phidias. But what are such losses to posterity—to mankind—compared with those intellectual and moral ones, which ensue when debates like those which took place in the English Parliament in 1688, and in the American Congress in 1776, cease to live, except in a few traditionary recollections, and in their fruits?

---

[1] We deem it no impropriety here to say, and we do say of our own knowledge, that *this* descendant of Jefferson spoke but the *warm feelings* of *all* his descendants towards their *grandsire's* or *great grandsire's* ancient friend.
[2] For his account of this speech, see his Life and Works, vol. iii. pp. 54–58.

In the case of John Adams, as in that of Patrick Henry (and more especially in the last), we never have believed that the elegant pen of the *restorer* came up to the spirit and eloquence of the original. The oratory which, on a great exigency, flows molten from a mighty soul, and which fuses all that it encounters in its burning stream, cannot be manufactured, for the purposes of illustration, in a funeral oration, or in a biography ! The form may be pretty well caught, but the soul is wanting. We have so much of Mr. Adams—of his unstudied, energetic, abrupt diction—now putting the case to self-interest and common sense, with all the shrewdness of a New Englander, and now suddenly flashing into heroism, and into that exulting courage which seizes contagiously on the spirit of all that is permitted to bear even the outward form of manhood—that a master hand, like Webster's, may " manufacture" the strong semblance of the reality. But in the case of Henry, we would as soon think of now imitating eolian harps, and winds moaning through tree-tops, and anon the crash and roar of the rushing tornado ! [1]

It is to be regretted that Jefferson's contemporaneous notes are so meagre. They do not, avowedly, give the names of *all* the speakers ; they give a mere synopsis of the arguments used by each *side*, without specifying which were advanced by one speaker, and which by another; and (a fact which seems to be overlooked by most writers) they pertain only to the debate on the 8th and 10th of June, and have no reference whatever to that from the 1st to the 4th of July. Mr. Adams's Diary does nothing to supply this unfortunate chasm.[2] It is therefore wholly erroneous to assume (as many writers, indeed, if not most, have done) that Mr. Jefferson has given the names of the principal speakers, or of any speakers, on the latter occasions. The 15th page of the Memoir in Randolph's edition (18th and 19th in Congress edition), leads strongly to the inference that the objectors, particularly to the form and language of the Declara-

---

[1] Oh! that—as "the crowning glory"—the "supernatural voice" could have been heard in the debate on the Declaration of Independence, and that Henry's name could have been affixed to that instrument !

[2] John Adams's "Diary" does not include any part of 1776 but the month of January. His Memoranda of "Debates" are silent from May 10th to July 25. His "Autobiography," written about twenty-eight or twenty-nine years afterwards, attempts to supply the chasm from memory, but does it but generally and vaguely. He does not even remember on what day "the greatest and most solemn debate was had on the question of Independence." (See his *Life and Works*, vol. iii. p. 54.)

tion, were numerous; and there is no good reason to doubt that
supporters were equally numerous.   Short speeches were then
(fortunately) in vogue, and one extending beyond half an hour,
or, at the outside, three quarters of an hour, would have been
regarded as preposterously long.   And the debate on both
questions stretched through four days.   If we presume, what is
hardly presumable, that John Adams took the floor half a dozen
times, during those days, in a set speech, still there was room
for many others on the same side.   Who were they?   We are
not aware that even tradition pretends to answer this question.
But conjecture can be at no loss as to a part of them.   Mr.
Trist's Memoranda contain the following paragraph :

"*November 28th*, 1825.   At breakfast, again on the subject of R. H. Lee's Life.
Mr. Jefferson made several remarks—among others the following: ' If there was
any Palinurus to the Revolution, Samuel Adams was the man.   Indeed, in the
Eastern States, for a year or two after it began, he was truly the *Man of the
Revolution*.   He was constantly holding caucuses of distinguished men (among
whom was R. H. Lee), *at which the generality of the measures pursued were previously determined on—and at which the parts were assigned to the different actors,
who afterwards appeared in them.*'   ' John Adams had very little part in these
caucuses ; but as one of the actors in the measures decided on in them, he was a
Colossus' (written directly after)."

Mr. Jefferson wrote S. A. Wells (May 12, 1819):

"I can say that he [Samuel Adams] was truly a great man, wise in counsel,
fertile in resources, immovable in his purposes, and had, I think, a greater share
than any other member, in advising and directing our measures in the Northern
war.   As a speaker, he could not be compared with his living colleague and namesake, whose deep conceptions, nervous style, and undaunted firmness, made him
truly our bulwark in debate.   But Mr. Samuel Adams, although not of fluent elocution, was so rigorously logical, so clear in his views, abundant in good sense, and
master always of his subject, that he commanded the most profound attention,
whenever he rose in an assembly, by which the froth of declamation was heard with
the most sovereign contempt."

It is impossible to doubt that the rigorous logic of the stern,
immovable "Palinurus to the Revolution"—the man who was
usually content to guide, and let others wear the ostensible
trappings of command, and receive the laurels of victory—was
heard in the momentous debate on the 1st and 2nd of July, and
in all human probability, in defence of the high and vigorous
tone of the Declaration.

Is it probable that the high-spirited and patriotic Nelson

and bluff "Ben Harrison," left the voice of Virginia unheard on the floor, on the side of their *instructions ?* [1] Did the able and indomitable McKean remain silent? Did Gerry fail to support his older colleagues? Was the manly sense of Sherman unspoken? And were there not others, whose names every reading man's eye at once recognizes, as it glances over the list of the "Signers," who it cannot be supposed sat, during the four days' discussions, without getting up, and in set speech or shorter exhortation, manfully defining their position, and pledging their "lives, and fortunes, and sacred honor" to the cause?

We have hitherto passed over one transcendent name, because if Franklin was heard on the floor, as he doubtless was in his short pithy way, his influence on the decision of the pending questions was exerted principally in other quarters. That influence was truly great. If he lacked the eloquence and vehemence of John Adams, he greatly excelled him in other particulars. He was a more experienced, and undoubtedly a wiser man. He had a nice appreciation of the qualities of associates, and consummate tact in addressing himself to them. From the suavity of his temper and manners, from his respectful way of treating adversaries, from his entire want of that egotism which disgusts, and that dogmatism which offends all, and particularly equals in position—he was personally popular in and out of Congress.[2] In the step which he, in his own quiet and peculiar manner, was urging onward, he was apparently incurring greater risks, and certainly making greater sacrifices, than a comparatively young man, who, as yet, had attained to nothing like his general position. Franklin's ability as a statesman had been tested and established, in the most difficult positions. He was better acquainted with Europe, and especially

---

[1] The Virginia delegation were R. H. Lee, Wythe, Jefferson, Harrison, Nelson, F. L. Lee and Braxton. The two first were absent. Jefferson did not speak. We are not aware that F. L. Lee, or Braxton, were in the habit of addressing Congress. Nelson, said John Adams, "was a speaker."—(*Life and Works*, vol. ii. p. 422.) Harrison was in the habit of presiding in Committee of the Whole, and, we think, of making *short* offhand speeches.

[2] John Adams repeatedly declares that he (John Adams) was regarded with suspicion and aversion by the "outsiders," especially by the wealthy and conservative classes, and also by the *same class* in Congress. They (he says) looked upon both himself and Samuel Adams as *poor* and *ambitious* adventurers. And if the reader will be at pains after a careful perusal of J. Adams's Autobiography, to count up his recorded quarrels, and misunderstandings and dislikes *in Congress*, he will see how slight must have been his *personal* popularity with at least a large portion of that body. Jefferson, the Lees, and a few other determined spirits, rallied closely round him, loved him for his *services* and his *great qualities*, and, probably, quietly laughed at his foibles. *They* saw in him an enthusiast instead of a demagogue—a hero instead of an adventurer!

with England, than any of his colleagues. In science and philosophy, he enjoyed a reputation not before attained by any American. He possessed exquisite address as a writer. His "Poor Richard's Almanac" had made his shrewd sense familiar to every class of his countrymen. His style was adapted to all tastes and comprehensions. The scholar admired its compact and nervous simplicity; the uneducated fancied the limpid diction was like that which they themselves employed in familiar intercourse! It united some of the characteristics of Bunyan and Defoe, with some of those of Swift and Addison. There was an obvious common sense in its propositions—its illustrations were so inimitably apt and telling—its poignant but easily understood wit so surely exposed every weak point of an adversary, so surely carried the derisive laugh of the multitude along with it—that it may well be doubted whether a more effective popular writer, on a class of subjects (simple appeals to the understanding, in regard ,to the purely practical affairs of life) has written in the English tongue. If he lacked the deep earnestness and fiery enthusiasm of some natures—if he was proverbially cautious—if he was more disposed to surrender something than ask too much, and act a yielding than a stubborn part until deeply roused—if no one would suspect the cool, placid sage of loving danger for danger's sake—perhaps these negative qualities gave only the more weight to his opinions, when his reputation, his honors, and his life were staked on their accuracy. And all who knew that Franklin had cast off and severed every tie with an only and distinguished son, because he sided with the mother country, knew how implacable were his resolves when his line of action was determined on.[1]

---

[1] William Franklin was the last royal Governor of New Jersey. He was born about 1731 —was made Port Master at Philadelphia, Clerk of the Colonial Assembly, etc.—became a captain in the French war, and distinguished himself at Ticonderoga. Lord Fairfax, without solicitation from any quarter, appointed him Governor of New Jersey in 1763. When the difficulties arose between the Colonies and Great Britain, Gov. Franklin, from the beginning, acted the part of a determined Loyalist. In 1775 he was declared an enemy of his country, and sent a prisoner to Connecticut. In 1777 he applied to General Washington for leave to visit his sick wife, who was but a few miles distant. The Commander-in-Chief forwarded this request to Congress, and that body declined to give its permission. His wife, it would seem, attributed this rigor to his father, Dr. Franklin. She died in 1778, and it was recorded on her monumental tablet in St. Paul's Church, New York, that, "compelled to part from the husband she loved, and at length despairing of the soothing hope of his speedy return, she sunk under accumulated distresses, etc." Gov. Franklin was exchanged in 1778, and little is known of him for the rest of the war. In 1784 he made overtures of reconciliation to his father, and received the following reply:

And there was another member who it is certain uttered not a word in the debate, whose personal influence, off the floor, was probably equalled only by that of Franklin and Samuel Adams, and who, locally, commanded an influence superior to theirs. We have stated the causes of Jefferson's personal popularity. No other Southern advocates of the Declaration in Congress approached him in the reputation of ability but R. H. Lee and Wythe. Mr. Lee's standing in this particular and in some others, compared with his, had recently been submitted to a decisive test. Wythe, with the modesty of his manly and unambitious nature, saw that his true position was a secondary one to that of his former pupil, and he assumed it perhaps even more cheerfully than he would have assumed the first. Jefferson came from the great leading Southern member of the Confederacy, containing a larger population than any other two of those members—indeed, more than half the population south of the Potomac—and proportionably paramount in political influence and consideration. Its other

"I am glad to find that you desire to revive the affectionate intercourse that formerly existed between us. It will be very agreeable to me; indeed nothing has ever hurt me so much, and affected me with such keen sensations, as to find myself deserted in my old age by my only son; and not only deserted, but to find him taking up arms against me in a cause wherein *my good fame, fortune, and life, were all at stake.* You conceived, you say, that your duty to your King, and regard for your country, required this. I ought not to blame you for differing in sentiment with me in public affairs. We are all men, subject to errors. Our opinions are not in our power; they are formed and governed much by circumstances; they are often as inexplicable as they are irresistible. Your situation was such, that few would have censured your remaining neuter, though there are natural duties which precede political ones, and cannot be extinguished by them. This is a disagreeable subject; I drop it. And we will endeavor, as you propose, mutually to forget what has happened relating to it as well as we can."

Doctor Franklin, however, it seems could *not forget* what had happened. In his will, dated five years afterwards, after bequeathing his son certain lands in Nova Scotia, the book and papers of his father's in his possession, and the debts due to his father, the latter added : "The part he acted against me in the late war, which is of public notoriety, will account for my leaving him no more of an estate he endeavored to deprive me of." William Franklin died in 1813. He left a son, William Temple Franklin, who edited his grandfather's works.

To those who would judge harshly of Washington and Dr. Franklin for permission being refused to William Franklin to visit his sick wife, we would simply say they should study closely the inside history of that truly ho:rible struggle, before they pass rash judgments on those whom the world has never impeached of personal cruelty. Such refusals were *common.* They were regarded as imperatively *necessary* by *wise* men who *understood all the facts* ; and they will be so regarded now by wise men who go back to investigate all those facts. They were necessary to prevent unscrupulous and most dangerous abuses of parole, and they did not half retaliate the hellish severities and abuses of the same kind practised on the other side, principally through, and at the instigations of, "*Tories.*" No country can withstand, for any period, overwhelming and cruel invasion, where the rules of civilized warfare are not enforced by *retaliation.* But let no superficial judge of character, deceived by Dr. Franklin's *smoothness* and his *pliability* in *little matters,* again pretend that he lacked *iron resolve* when the occasion demanded it !

For the above particulars in Governor William Franklin's history, we are principally indebted to that very interesting work, Sabine's Biographical Sketches of American Loyalists.

already distinguished civic national leaders had all of them
touched their meridian. The new orb which was so steadily
and rapidly ascending the horizon had not yet culminated.
The political "wise men" are never blind to such signs, nor
slow in their "worship."

Of the real merits or demerits of the Declaration of Independence, as a literary production and as a State paper, it is
unnecessary now to speak. The voice of mankind throughout
the civilized globe has pronounced on this question, and it
would be useless for any man to attempt to alter or gainsay
that decision.

Its originality has been questioned. Even John Adams
wrote Pickering, in 1822:

"As you justly observe, there is not an idea in it but what had been hackneyed
in Congress for two years before. The substance of it is contained in the declaration of rights, and the violation of those rights, in the Journals of Congress, in 1774.
Indeed, the essence of it is contained in a pamphlet, voted and printed by the
town of Boston, before the first Congress met, composed by James Otis, as I suppose, in one of his lucid intervals, and pruned and polished by Samuel Adams." [1]

Jefferson, on seeing this, with characteristic forbearance to
Mr. Adams, replied, in a letter to Madison (August 30, 1823):

"Pickering's observations, and Mr. Adams's in addition, 'that it contained no
new ideas, that it is a common-place compilation, its sentiments hackneyed in Congress for two years before, and its essence contained in Otis's pamphlet,' may all be
true. Of that I am not to be the judge. Richard Henry Lee charged it as copied
from Locke's treatise on government. Otis's pamphlet I never saw, and whether I
had gathered my ideas from reading or reflection, I do not know. I know only
that I turned to neither book nor pamphlet while writing it. I did not consider it
as any part of my charge to invent new ideas altogether, and to offer no sentiment
which had ever been expressed before. Had Mr. Adams been so restrained, Congress would have lost the benefit of his bold and impressive advocations of the
rights of Revolution. For no man's confident and fervid addresses, more than Mr.
Adams's, encouraged and supported us through the difficulties surrounding us,
which, like the ceaseless action of gravity, weighed on us by night and by day.
Yet, on the same ground we may ask, what of these elevated thoughts was new,
or can be affirmed never before to have entered the conceptions of man?

"Whether, also, the sentiments of Independence, and the reasons for declaring
it, which make so great a portion of the instrument, had been hackneyed in Congress for two years before the 4th of July, '76, or this dictum also of Mr. Adams
be another slip of memory, let history say. This, however, I will say for Mr.
Adams, that he supported the Declaration with zeal and ability, fighting fearlessly
for every word of it."

[1] Adams's Life and Works, vol. ii. p. 514

Here we should be quite content to leave this matter, had not Mr. Adams—not in the hurry and ardor of writing a letter, but deliberately, and towards twenty years earlier, in his Autobiography—*founded* one of the above charges, in the following words: * * "these two declarations, the one of rights and the other of violations, which are printed in the journals of Congress for 1774, were two years afterwards *recapitulated* in the Declaration of Independence, on the Fourth of July, 1776." [1]

John Adams reminds us of certain enchanted personages in fairy tales. A part of the time they are glorious warriors, seeking high adventures. The wizard spell falls on them, and they become little, deformed dwarfs, filled with rage and spite against all that wears the fair proportions of humanity! When his country was solely in consideration—when a great and purely abstract question of right or wrong was to be met— Mr. Adams towered to heroic proportions; but touch his morbid vanity, by directly or indirectly bringing before his mind a parallel between himself and a rival in fame, and, presto! the grimacing, sputtering dwarf is at once before us!

Of course, Mr. Adams wrote the report, or a material part of the report, which Jefferson borrowed from! But here, as we believe in every instance wherein Mr. Adams has, in his splenetic moments, sought to detract from the reputation of his *friend* Jefferson, for his own benefit, he has proved signally unlucky. The Committee on Rights and Grievances made their report to the Congress of 1774—and, if we remember rightly, not till September. [1] The paper, as matured and adopted in the House, is an able one. But if it sets forth an important right or complains of an important grievance, or presents an important idea or hardly a fact of any kind, not equally distinctly and far more forcibly expressed in Jefferson's "Summary View of the Rights of British America," we are wholly unable to discover it. And the republication of the former in the Appendix to the Life and Works of John Adams

---

[1] Life and Works, vol. ii. p. 377. And the reader will find in the Appendix of the same volume (p. 535) copies of the draft and adopted form of the report of the Committee on Rights and Grievances (which Mr. Adams *has misremembered into two committees and two reports!*) to "facilitate a comparison" between the two, and (*we imagine*) to "facilitate" certain *other* "comparisons!"

[1] They reported, *in part*, on the 22d of September, and again soon after.

will readily "facilitate" a "comparison" which will enable
every reader to decide this question for himself! That "Summary View" was presented to the Convention of Virginia
before the Congress of 1774 assembled. It was published in
America and published and republished in England. John
Adams, a *devourer* of political literature, must needs have
seen it. Nay, Mr. Adams says, in his Autobiography (already
quoted), Jefferson "had been chosen a delegate [to Congress] in
Virginia in consequence of a very handsome public paper
which he had written for the House of Burgesses," etc. Again,
in the Pickering letter (also quoted), he says: "Mr. Jefferson
came into Congress in June, 1775, and brought with him a
reputation for literature, science, and a happy talent of composition. Writings of his were handed about remarkable for the
peculiar felicity of expression." Jefferson had written no other
conspicuous "public paper" before being *chosen* to Congress.
He had *preëstablished* a national "reputation" as a writer on
no other production. No other writings of his had been
"handed about." [1]

We have already mentioned that the "Summary View"
enumerated most of the *texts*, and furnished a goodly number
of the *phrases* of the Revolution. The texts existed in the
nature of things; and any broadly intelligent writer, who
brought a patriotic pen to the review of the whole subject,
must needs set them forth. And a writer having Jefferson's
"peculiar felicity of expression" (the "curiosa felicitas ver-
borum"), and being one of the first to handle the topic, would
almost inevitably furnish a large class of those happy collocations of words which are at once appropriated by society, and
used so familiarly that they are soon supposed to be the natural
expressions of the thought, and no more individual property
than the common body of definitive words in the language.

Mr. Adams's Report on Rights and Grievances does unquestionably smack a little of the Declaration of Independence, but
still more (except in the claim of entire independence of Parlia-

---

[1] And in a note, Mr. Adams's *Editor* himself specifies the "Summary View," as the
"handsome public paper" which Mr. A. refers to as procuring Jefferson's election to
Congress.

And if Newcastle wants another coal, be it known that one of Mr. Adams's colleagues
(after the 19th of September) on this identical Committee on Rights and Grievances, was
Patrick Henry, to whom one of the two original manuscript copies of the Summary View
had been sent by its author about two months before.

ment) of the "Summary View." We do not conceive there is sufficient identity between any of the papers (the texts being necessarily so near alike), to establish a fair charge of plagiarism against either, unless Mr. Jefferson plagiarized from himself. but we have felt it incumbent on us to show if Mr. Adams insists (in colloquial phrase) that the "boot be worn," that it go on the "right foot!" If anybody borrowed, *he* was the borrower!

The less specific allegation of Mr. Adams, that the "essence" of this great State paper was already contained in a pamphlet "composed by James Otis," in "one of his lucid intervals"—the far better-taken position of Lee, that "it was copied from Locke's Treatise on Government"—and all similar attempts to impeach its originality, because it contained many ideas already advanced by other writers, is met on precisely the proper ground in Jefferson's remarks on the subject in his letter to Madison. It is *not* any part of a statesman's duty (or of any writer's on a practical subject) to attempt "to invent new ideas altogether;" and he who should, at this age of the world, utter nothing (on such subjects) but that which was purely original, would keep pretty nearly silent, and if he did speak, would probably utter very little to the purpose! Jefferson undoubtedly repeated some of the ideas of Otis, if he wrote after him, on the same general or special subject, though he "never saw" Otis's "pamphlet." Jefferson, and we will venture to assert, Otis (though we will not stop to look up his "pamphlet"), repeated many ideas from Locke. Locke, in turn, might, and probably did, find not a few of his noblest ones in Hooker, Sydney, and even Harrington. And we would venture to undertake to find in his clear, solid paragraphs, threads even from the woof of Hobbes, who taught absolutism as an expediency; and of Filmer, who taught it as a divine institution!

Nay, if the game is to be run clean down, Mr. Adams and Mr. Lee but began the chase! The "essence of the Declaration," that is, the right of man to be a man—his right to his own, and to enjoy his own—was thought of and expressed, we fancy, very early in this world's history! It was heard in the wild whoop of the American savage, ages, probably, before Columbus's keels plowed the bosom of the Atlantic. It rung from the clashing shields of the Northmen, when the ancestors of Locke and Sydney were painted savages, performing Druid worship and under Druid government in Britain.[1] It was uttered in the orations and songs of early Greece, and *practised* in the better periods of its "fierce democraties." There are those who can draw it from the Sermon on the Mount, and, centuries earlier, from the Decalogue! Did ever a man stand upright, with "heaven erected face," not wholly perverted by ignorance or false education, and not feel it, as instinctively, as his right to breathe the air and receive the sunshine of heaven?

Another charge of want of originality, or rather, so far as it went, of direct plagiarism, was brought against the Declaration of Independence, forty-three years after its publication, in consequence of an alleged discovery then made. A paper, styled the Mecklenburg Declaration of Independence, said to have been adopted by the Committee of Mecklenburg county, North Carolina, May 20th, 1775, first appeared in print in the Raleigh (N. C.) Register, April 30, 1819. This contained peculiar collocations of words to be found in the National Declaration, amounting, when put together, to perhaps *three lines;* yet, in one or two of the coincidences, the language is so unusual, that it is difficult to believe those coincidences were accidental. Mr. Jefferson denied ever having seen or heard of this Mecklenburg paper, and much controversy ensued, even State Legislatures entering the field. But later discoveries—the discovery of the contemporaneously published and recognized Mecklenburg Declaration—has effectually disposed of the question. Those who would have a full account of the facts and arguments in the case, and see a full collection of *all* the Mecklenburg declarations, supposititious and genuine, will find them in the Appendix.[2]

We ought not to omit to mention the contemporaneous reception of the Declaration of Independence by the American people, and the fruits it produced. It is not to be denied that some, who hitherto had acted with the Whigs, considered it precipi-

---

[1] It would seem that even the word Britain was derived from the word *brith*—the *paint,* with which the early inhabitants of that country gave "an azure blue to their bodies and shields!" So says Sir William Temple; and if his authority is not the best on a question involving a knowledge of ancient languages, the really learned Camden gives the same derivation. adding that the suffix *Tania* signified a region of country.

The Druid worship of our English ancestors included a belief in the transmigration of souls and human sacrifices!

[2] See APPENDIX, No. 2.

tate—others, as impolitic at any period, or inherently improper.
Most of the first, like Mr. Dickinson, gave up their individual
views and determined to share the fate of their countrymen.
Many of the second class undoubtedly did the same.   But others
turned back into decided loyalism, and fled to Great Britain or
some of its possessions, or remained in the land of their birth to
inflict and to suffer those dire extremities of hate, which rendered the struggle between the American Whigs and American
Loyalists one of the most ferocious and relentless on the record
of wars between civilized men—far more ferocious and relentless
even than that waged between the most .desperate Whig partisan bands, aggregated by misery and despair, and under the
control of no regular officers, and the most depraved and brutal
scum of the British armies.

With a large majority of the American rural population,
even in the most loyally affected districts—with the middle
classes in city and country generally—the Declaration was the
turning point. The Loyalist was called upon to leave his
hearthstone, his property, his neighbor, his brother, and his son
—oftentimes his wife and his daughters, who were ready to abjure the parricide.   He was called upon to risk his whole property on the chances of a re-subjugation—to risk meeting neighbor, brother, and son in the battle's front—to consort with those
among whom he would be compelled to witness, if not to take
part in, outrages against his countrymen at which humanity
weeps.   Few, compared with the whole number of the class
mentioned, were determined, were sanguinary enough, to adopt
such an alternative.   The great body of the open and acting
Loyalists, or "Tories," of the Revolution,[1] were from the two
extremes—opulent men who could go where they pleased, or
the dregs of society who had no honest ties to bind them, who
had old injuries to avenge against the respectable portion of
their countrymen, and who, in any event, would take that side
in which plunder and licentious indulgence could be best obtained!   If the condition of things had been so reversed that
American armies were invading and plundering the fields and
homesteads and public property of England, these mis-

---

[1] We speak now more particularly of those who joined the acting Tories as late as
1776. In the *beginning* of the struggle, many reputable men of the middle class joined
them.

creants would have been the most indomitable of American soldiers!

To the Patriots, the Declaration gave strength and courage.
It gave them a definite purpose—and a name and object commensurate with the cost. When it was formally read by the
magistracy from the halls of justice and in the public marts,
by the officers of the army at the head of their divisions, by the
clergy from their pulpits, its grandeur impressed the popular
imagination. The American people pronounced it a fit instrument, clothed in fitting words. The public enthusiasm burst
forth—sometimes in gay and festive, sometimes in solemn and
religious, observances—as the Cavalier or the Puritan taste
predominated. In the Southern and middle cities and villages,
the riotous populace tore down the images of monarchs and
Colonial governors, and dragged them with ropes around their
necks through the streets—cannon thundered, bonfires blazed—
the opulent feasted, drank toasts, and joined in hilarious cele-
brations. In New England, the grimmer joy manifested itself
in prayers, and sermons, and religious rites. He who would
learn particulars, must go to the pictorial page of Botta, and to
contemporary publications.[1]

Before Congress adjourned, on the 4th of July, it resolved,
"That Dr. Franklin, Mr. J. Adams, and Mr. Jefferson, be a
Committee to prepare a device for a Seal for the UNITED STATES
OF AMERICA."[2] Henceforth, then, the American historian treats
of "STATES," and not of "COLONIES."

We had, with no little care, prepared a list of Mr. Jefferson's
appointments on committees during that portion of the Congress

[1] For the proceedings in Virginia, see Gerardin, p. 140.
[2] Each member of the Committee proposed a device and then combined their ideas,
but their report was not adopted. The same thing happened (the appointment of a
Committee and a failure to adopt its report) in several subsequent cases, nor was a
"device" agreed upon until 178-. Mr. Jefferson proposed, originally (said J. Adams),
"the children of Israel in the wilderness, led by a cloud by day and a pillar of fire by
night; and on the other side, Hengist and Horsa, the Saxon Chiefs, from whom we
claim the honor of being descended, and *whose political principles and form of government we have assumed.*" (Was this another *plagiarism?*) Jefferson (says an article in
Harper's Magazine, July, 1856, exhibiting considerable research on the point) was then
requested by his colleagues to "combine their ideas." He did so, and (says the same
writer) the paper is in the Secretary of State's office, Washington, in his handwriting.
This retained the children of Israel, etc., surrounded by the motto "*Rebellion to tyrants
is obedience to God.*" On the other side, the Goddess of Liberty and the Goddess of
Justice took the place of Hengist and Horsa as supporters of a shield with six quarter-
ings, denoting the countries (England, Scotland, Ireland, France, Germany and Holland)
from which the United States had been peopled. The motto was "*E pluribus Unum*"—
from many, one. The crest was "the eye of Providence in a radiant triangle, whose
glory should extend over the shield, and beyond the figures," etc. etc.

of 1776 when he was present. It extended over several manuscript pages ; and he was chairman of a good many of the committees. As it must always happen in war, many of the topics of the greatest contemporaneous legislative interest and importance were purely temporary or incidental in their importance. The long list would, therefore, now be a dry one; and it may be doubted whether, even in cases where the subject retains its interest, it is of any real use to specify Mr. Jefferson's connection with a committee, unless we are prepared (which, when we have the means, we have not the space for) to state his performances in it. It neither illustrates his character (further than to show what never was denied to him, indefatigable industry), nor does it add much to *his* fame, at this day, to tenaciously lay claim to all these minor honors of his earlier career !

Three heretofore unpublished letters, written by Mr. Jefferson to his brother-in-law, Mr. Eppes, during the short period which elapsed between the Declaration of Independence and his resignation of his seat, will be found in the Appendix.[1]

---

[1] See APPENDIX, No. 3.

CHAPTER VI.

1776—1779.

It will be remembered that when the Virginia Convention instructed their delegates in Congress to move for Independence, they also appointed a Committee to draft a "Declaration of Rights" and a "plan of government" for Virginia. While· this Committee were engaged in their duties, Mr. Jefferson found time to prepare and forward from Congress (by Mr. Wythe, returning to take a seat in the Convention), the outline of a plan for their consideration. He thus mentions the facts, and what resulted, in a letter to Judge Augustus B. Woodward (April 3, 1825):

"The fact is unquestionable, that the Bill of Rights, and the Constitution of Virginia, were drawn originally by George Mason, one of our really great men, and of the first order of greatness. The history of the preamble to the latter is this: I was then at Philadelphia with Congress; and knowing that the Convention of Virginia was engaged in forming a plan of government, I turned my mind to the same subject, and drew a sketch or outline of a Constitution, with a preamble, which I sent to Mr. Pendleton, president of the Convention, on the mere possibility that it might suggest something worth incorporation into that before the Convention. He informed me afterwards by letter, that he received it on the day on which the Committee of the Whole had reported to the House the plan they had agreed to; that that had been so long in hand, so disputed inch by inch, and the subject of so much altercation and debate; that they were worried with the contentions it had produced, and could not, from mere lassitude, have been induced to open the instrument again; but that, being pleased with the preamble to mine, they adopted it in the House, by way of amendment to the Report of the Committee; and thus my preamble became tacked to the work of George Mason. The Constitution, with the preamble, was passed on the 29th of June, and the Committee of Congress had only the day before that reported to that body the draft of the Declaration of Independence. The fact is, that the preamble was prior in composition to the Declaration; and both having the same object, of justifying our separation from Great Britain, they used necessarily the same materials of justification, and hence their similitude."

On the 20th of June, the Convention balloted for delegates to Congress for the ensuing year, commencing on the 11th of August. Five of the former delegates were re-chosen, but Colonel Harrison and Mr. Braxton were left off, and no others put in their places. Girardin says the reason assigned for this proceeding was "economy, and a wish to obtain the aid of the

¹ Girardin (p. 151, note) preserves the following letter from Mr. Wythe to Mr. Jefferson on this occasion. It is dated July 27th, 1776:

"When I came here the plan of government had been committed to the whole House. To those who had the chief hand in forming it, the one you put in my hands was shown. Two or three parts of this were with little alteration inserted in that; but such was the impatience of sitting long enough to discuss several important points in which they differ, and so many other matters were necessarily to be dispatched before the adjournment, that I was persuaded the revision of a subject the members seemed tired of, would at that time have been unsuccessfully proposed. The system agreed to, in my opinion, requires reformation. *In October I hope you will effect it.*"

supernumeraries in the arduous business of internal government;" but he intimates that this was but an excuse, and mentions causes that had temporarily injured the popularity of
Harrison and Braxton. We suspect our historian was not
informed of *all* the causes, and that they must be looked for, at
least in part, in the Congressional feuds heretofore described.
R. H. Lee was now in Virginia. If he had any direct agency
in the affair (a fact in regard to which we know nothing) the
account was ere long to be signally balanced, when Colonel
Harrison had the like advantage of being at home, and when
Mr. Lee was absent in Congress.

Mr. Jefferson had been re-chosen, notwithstanding he had
expressed to the Convention a desire to withdraw from his seat.
On receiving notice of his election, he wrote Mr. Pendleton,
President of the Convention :

" I am sorry the situation of my domestic affairs renders it indispensably necessary that I should solicit the substitution of some other person here, in my room.
The delicacy of the House will not require me to enter minutely into the private
causes which render this necessary. I trust they will be satisfied I would not have
urged it again, were it not unavoidable. I shall with cheerfulness continue in duty
here until the expiration of one year, by which time I hope it will be convenient
for my successor to attend."

He assigned an additional reason in his Memoir, which
could not have been, without some show of egotism, offered to
the Convention :

" Our delegation had been renewed for the ensuing year, commencing August
11th ; but the new government was now organized, a meeting of the Legislature was
to be held in October, and I had been elected a member by my county. I knew
that our legislation, under the regal government, had many very vicious points
which urgently required reformation, and I thought I could be of more use in
forwarding that work." [1]

He accordingly left Congress on the 2d of September,
resigned his seat, and on the next day set out for Virginia. On
the 10th of the ensuing October, the House of Delegates of Virginia (assembled under the new Constitution) chose Colonel
Harrison to supply the vacancy by a vote of sixty-nine, to five

---

[1] The " private causes " not mentioned in the first of these statements, were the
precarious situation of his wife's health. The family record contains the following
entry: " a son, born May 28th, 1777, 10h. P. M." Williamsburg (unlike Philadelphia)
was within a distance of Monticello which admitted of its being speedily traversed.

votes cast for Meriwether Smith; and the Delegates resolved, unanimously, "that the thanks of this House are justly due to the said Benjamin Harrison, for the diligence, ability, and integrity with which he executed the important trust reposed in him as one of the delegates for this country in the General Congress."[1] (See *Journals*, p. 8.)

On the 30th of September, Congress appointed foreign commissioners or ministers. Dr. Franklin and Mr. Jefferson were associated with Silas Deane to negotiate treaties of alliance and commerce with France. Deane was already in that country to procure military stores, and as a secret agent to its government; and this doubtless accounts for his unfortunate elevation to his present position. The same considerations which influenced Mr. Jefferson to decline a seat in Congress, operated with double force to compel him to decline this flattering appointment.

He took his seat in the Virginia House of Delegates, October 7th, 1776, the first day of the session. Four days afterwards, as anticipated by Mr. Wythe, he began vigorously to "effect" that "reform" which the civil system of Virginia still required to conform it to anything like broadly republican theories. While Mr. Jefferson found a body of younger or hitherto less distinguished associates, who seconded his efforts with great ability and zeal, the old conservative chiefs in the House, now as on a former field and occasion, drew steadily in another direction; where they could not defeat, impeded; and where they could not delay, by their adroitness, perseverance, and personal influence, made almost every important victory purchasable only at the price of some compromise which chopped away a valuable portion of its fruits.

Mr. Jefferson thus, in his Memoir, described his principal coadjutors :

"In giving this account of the laws of which I was myself the mover and draftsman, I, by no means, mean to claim to myself the merit of obtaining their passage. I had many occasional and strenuous coadjutors in debate, and one, most steadfast, able, and zealous, who was himself a host. This was George Mason, a man of the first order of wisdom among those who acted on the theatre of the Revolution, of expansive mind, profound judgment, cogent in argument, learned in the lore of our former Constitution, and earnest for the republican

---

[1] On the 12th of October a vote of thanks was also passed to Braxton.

change on democratic principles. His elocution was neither flowing nor smooth; but his language was strong, his manner most impressive, and strengthened by a dash of biting cynicism, when provocation made it seasonable.

"Mr. Wythe, while speaker in the two sessions of 1777, between his return from Congress and his appointment to the Chancery, was an able and constant associate in whatever was before a Committee of the Whole. His pure integrity, judgment, and reasoning powers, gave him great weight. Of him, see more in some notes inclosed in my letter of August 31, 1821, to Mr. John Saunderson.

"Mr. Madison came into the House in 1776, a new member and young; which circumstances, concurring with his extreme modesty, prevented his venturing himself in debate before his removal to the Council of State, in November, '77. From thence he went to Congress, then consisting of few members. Trained in these successive schools, he acquired a habit of self-possession, which placed at ready command the rich resources of his luminous and discriminating mind, and of his extensive information, and rendered him the first of every assembly afterwards, of which he became a member. Never wandering from his subject into vain declamation, but pursuing it closely, in language pure, classical, and copious, soothing always the feelings of his adversaries by civilities and softness of expression, he rose to the eminent station which he held in the great National Convention of 1787; and in that of Virginia which followed, he sustained the new constitution in all its parts, bearing off the palm against the logic of George Mason, and the fervid declamation of Mr. Henry. With these consummate powers, were united a pure and spotless virtue, which no calumny has ever attempted to sully. Of the powers and polish of his pen, and of the wisdom of his administration in the highest office of the nation, I need say nothing. They have spoken, and will forever speak for themselves."

He said, "our great opponents were Mr. Pendleton and Robert Carter Nicholas;" and he thus described the former:

"Mr. Pendleton, taken all in all, was the ablest man in debate I have ever met with. He had not, indeed, the poetical fancy of Mr. Henry, his sublime imagination, his lofty and overwhelming diction; but he was cool, smooth, and persuasive; his language flowing, chaste, and embellished; his conceptions quick, acute, and full of resource; never vanquished; for if he lost the main battle, he returned upon you, and regained so much of it as to make it a drawn one, by dexterous manœuvres, skirmishes in detail, and the recovery of small advantages which, little singly, were important all together. You never knew when you were clear of him, but were harassed by his perseverance, until the patience was worn down of all who had less of it than himself. Add to this, that he was one of the most virtuous and benevolent of men, the kindest friend, the most amiable and pleasant of companions, which ensured a favorable reception to whatever came from him."

We remember no particular delineation of Colonel Nicholas by the same pen, but there is not any difficulty in ascertaining his general character from the histories of the period. With less tact than Pendleton—with, indeed, a religious sincerity of character, which scarcely stooped to strategy of any kind—his sound, rather than brilliant, abilities and manly candor, derived additional weight from an honored family name, from long service in distinguished positions, and from the alacrity with which he had yielded up his convictions to those of a majority of his countrymen in the opening of the present struggle. He was thus fitted in every particular for a most efficient auxiliary to the more adroit and subtle Pendleton. In the questions to arise concerning the Church Establishment, his religious character gave him a weight equal, if not superior, to Pendleton's.

On the 11th of October, Mr. Jefferson was designated on various committees, but following the course already marked out, we shall cumber our pages with no mere lists, unless something is to be shown beyond the fact of the appointments. He judged it best to first try " the strength of the general pulse of reformation," by attacking in detail a few " vicious points " of legislation, " prominent in character and principle." [1] As soon as the Committees were organized, he asked and obtained leave to bring in a bill establishing Courts of Justice throughout the commonwealth. The next day—October 12th—he obtained leave to bring in a bill " To enable tenants in taille to convey their lands in fee simple," [2] and another, " For a revision of the laws." On the 14th, he reported the bill in regard to entails, sweeping them all away at a blow, and leaving property hitherto subject to them, to be conveyed or devised by the owner according to his inclinations, and subject to his debts.

The effect of such a change on the division of property and the social condition of Virginia, must needs be enormous. In all the lower counties of the State, a large portion of the lands was divided into great estates, held from generation to generation by the older sons, in the same way, and producing the same political and social consequences, that are now witnessed from the like causes, in England and some other European countries. The political and social framework was essentially aristocratic, producing the luxury, æsthetic culture, showy and apparently prosperous appearances incidental to such a condition, and which are often mistaken by superficial observers for the highest and best national development. But the few controlled the many in politics, lorded it over them in society,

[1] Memoir.
[2] We may, in various cases as in this, use the precise titles of bills as found in the Journals of the House, instead of following the language of the Memoir.

monopolized what was equally theirs by natural right, and, finally, by holding more than they could put to its best uses, diminished the aggregate resources of the State. An intelligent, socially cultivated and opulent class, must necessarily exercise more influence, and live more elegantly, than one destitute of all, or either of these advantages. No laws can prevent this. No laws, unless the fierce temporary edicts of a mob, have ever attempted to prevent it. No intelligent people ever objected to individual accumulations of property fairly won. But if a father has ten sons, is there any good reason why, having means to educate all, he shall educate only one, and that one, invariably, without any reference to talents or virtues, the oldest son ? Or, if he educate them alike, is there a good reason why nine, as able to act and to judge in public and private affairs as their older brother, and to enjoy the comforts of opulence, shall be denied property, political influence, and the elegances of life, for the purpose of lavishing them all on the one ? Is not the governmental structure which rests on this monstrous and unnatural decimation where, instead of one suffering for ten, nine suffer for one, however fair its outside, an artificial thing built on the sandy foundations of injustice and falsehood ? Is not its apparent strength its real ultimate weakness ? Can one man produce as much from his ten thousand patrimonial acres, as ten men could produce from them ? Can one man do as much in the battle-field or the senate for his country as ten, or the *pick* of ten ? We have been led involuntarily into this strain of remark by glancing our eye over the whining lamentations of a sentimental writer (Garland, author of Life of John Randolph) on the decadence of the " Old Dominion ;" and this is held to be mainly owing to " Jefferson's " abolition of entail and primogeniture ! The princely seats of the Old Dominion are, no doubt, in a good measure gone, or are woefully faded from their ancient splendor. It is possible that, owing to defective systems of tillage, and the constant lure to her population of new and fertile lands in the West, the aggregate wealth of Virginia in the tide-water region has diminished since the day of entails. If the great estates have degenerated faster since their cutting up, it is only because they have *produced faster and more.* Required to support the same aggregate number, they would have equally degenerated,

whether the legal ownership was in the hands of few or many.
Now, they have fed the ten brethren somewhat equally. All
have lived comfortably and pleasantly. In the other case,
eight-tenths of the aggregate expense would have been required
for the pampered one, and two-tenths would have been distributed between nine " poor relations," of the same name and
blood ! If it is alleged that the cutting up of the great estates
has been the cause of their deterioration, how happens it that in
the middle and western regions of Virginia, where the estates
were never generally large—where they, to this day, continue
smaller than the estates of the tide-water region—the deterioration has been far less than in the former ? The small possessor
has surely a greater interest (and the experience of the world
demonstrates that he acts on it) in keeping up his soils than the
larger one. Imperfect tillage will under no circumstances support a very dense population; or even a moderately dense population in a very profuse style of living. But it appeals to the
mind with the force of an axiom, that if a given piece of territory must continue to support ten thousand agriculturists and
their progeny, it will (their capacities and knowledge being
equal) support them *better collectively*, by being equally divided
among all, than it would divided into a small number of immense entailed estates.

Such were, doubtless, hard and unpalatable doctrines to the
nurselings of luxury in Virginia, and to those monomaniacs
on the subject of family importance, who are to be found
in all aristocratic, if not other, communities. With such,
their own decadence is the decadence of the State. The overthrow of an ancient seat is with such a dire public calamity,
though its place be supplied by ten as happy and equally intelligent, and, in the aggregate, more opulent homes! And he
who lays unholy hands on a privileged order is always, with
such, a brutalized fanatic or an unprincipled " demagogue."
The day that Mr. Jefferson brought his bill to abolish entails
into the House of Delegates, he banded for the first time
against himself a numerous and very influential body of enemies—a body of enemies who never forgave him, or lost a good
opportunity to wreak their bitter hate on him. The second
and third generation of older sons even, shorn of their ancestral
grandeur, often too proud to curtail expenses to curtailed

means, often broken-hearted, broken in means, and debauched, continued to regard him very much as the rakehelly young cavaliers of Charles I.'s time regarded the grim Lord Protector who had slain their sires and confiscated their patrimonial estates. But this was not the deepest and most inveterate hatred that early and late dogged the steps of Jefferson, and which yet seizes on every trivial pretence to desecrate his grave. Individuals and individual antipathies gradually die out. But *class* hate—the rage of a permanently injured *profession*—never dies! We will not, however, anticipate. Nor will we attempt to characterize Jefferson's motives in any of these changes. Let the tenor of his life speak on that point.

On the same day that Mr. Jefferson reported the preceding bill (October 14th), he obtained leave to bring in one for the removal of the seat of government, and another for the naturalization of foreigners. The last was reported the same day, and it recognized, in express language, the right of expatriation claimed in Mr. Jefferson's "Summary View" in 1774, and conferred citizenship on foreigners on the easy terms of two years' residence, after a declaration in court of their intention to reside within the State, and giving "assurance of fidelity to the commonwealth." The minor children of a naturalized father or mother, and all minors who migrated without father or mother, to the commonwealth, were to be deemed citizens, without any legal steps.

The act abolishing entails came up for its final reading October 23d, and passed—the title being changed to "A bill declaring tenants of lands or slaves in taille to hold the same in fee simple." Mr. Pendleton's resistance was, as usual, obstinate and adroit. Finding the tide too strong for him, he suddenly proposed a middle course—a fair-seeming compromise—that the holders of entailed property might convey it in fee simple "if they chose to do so." He came within a few votes of carrying this amendment! The Act passed the Senate November 1st.

The bill for a general revision of the laws passed October 26th, and both houses designated November 5th for the election of five Revisers. Ten gentlemen were put in nomination at the appointed time by the Senate. The House balloted, and its choice fell on the following persons, in the following order:

Thomas Jefferson, Edmund Pendleton, George Wythe, George Mason, and Thomas Ludwell Lee. The Senate then balloted, with the same result.[1] The same day, the subject of the disputed boundary line with Pennsylvania was referred to a committee of which Mr. Jefferson was chairman.

On the 28th of October, he was placed on committees to report bills "Declaring what shall be treason," and "For regulating the laws of succession, and subjecting lands to the payment of debts." And he reported, the same day, from a military committee, a bill "For raising six additional battalions of infantry," etc. On successive days he was appointed on committees for encouraging domestic manufactures, for altering the rates of certain coins, and for amending the ordinances in regard to naval affairs.

Among the originally appointed (October 11th) Standing Committees of the House, was one "Of Religion"—directed "to meet and adjourn from day to day, and to take under their consideration all matters and things relating to religion and morality," and clothed with powers, without further order of the House, "to send for persons, papers, and records for their information." This Committee consisted of Messrs. Braxton, Harwood, Richard Lee, Bland, Simpson, Starke, Mayo, Hite, Fleming, James Taylor, Watts, Lewis, Adams, Curle, Jefferson, Scott, Page, Nicholas, and McDowell. The different religious persuasions were represented in it, but in it, as in the House, the Established (Episcopalian) Church had a decided preponderance. Jefferson headed a determined minority, struggling for the same principles which were afterwards ingrafted into his Bill for Religious Freedom; but they could as yet make but partial headway against the settled convictions of the majority. He, in his Notes on Virginia and in his Memoir, gives the following succinct history of the nature and effects of the existing Establishment, the history of this first trial of strength between it and its opponents, and the substance of all the legislative action on the subject during the session of 1776:

"The first settlers in this country were emigrants from England, of the English Church, just at a point of time when it was flushed with complete victory over the

[1] Among the Senate's nominations had been Benjamin Waller, William Ellzey Thompson Mason, Robert Munford and Robert C. Nicholas.

religious of all other persuasions. Possessed as they became, of the powers of making, administering, and executing the laws, they showed equal intolerance in this country with their Presbyterian brethren, who had emigrated to the northern government. The poor Quakers were flying from persecution in England. They cast their eyes on these new countries as asylums of civil and religious freedom; but they found them free only for the reigning sect. Several acts of the Virginia Assembly of 1659, 1662, and 1693, had made it penal in parents to refuse to have their children baptized; had prohibited the unlawful assembling of Quakers; had made it penal for any master of a vessel to bring a Quaker into the State; had ordered those already here, and such as should come thereafter, to be imprisoned till they should abjure the country; provided a milder punishment for their first and second return, but death for their third; had inhibited all persons from suffering their meetings in or near their houses, entertaining them individually, or disposing of books which supported their tenets. If no execution took place here, as did in New England, it was not owing to the moderation of the Church, or spirit of the legislature, as may be inferred from the law itself; but to historical circumstances which have not been handed down to us. The Anglicans retained full possession of the country about a century.   *   *   *   *   *   *

At the common law, *heresy* was a capital offence, punishable by burning. Its definition was left to the ecclesiastical judges, before whom the conviction was, till the statute of the 1 El. c. 1 circumscribed it, by declaring, that nothing should be deemed heresy, but had been so determined by authority of the canonical scriptures, or by one of the four first general councils, or by other council, having for the grounds of their declaration the express and plain words of the Scriptures. Heresy, thus circumscribed, being an offence against the common law, our act of assembly of October 1777, c. 17, gives cognizance of it to the general court, by declaring that the jurisdiction of that court shall be general in all matters of the common law. The execution is by the writ *De hæretico comburendo.* By our own Act of Assembly of 1705, c. 30, if a person brought up in the Christian religion denies the being of a God, or the Trinity, or asserts there are more gods than one, or denies the Christian religion to be true, or the Scriptures to be of divine authority, he is punishable on the first offence by incapacity to hold any office or employment ecclesiastical, civil, or military; on the second by disability to sue, to take any gift or legacy, to be guardian, executor, or administrator, and by three years' imprisonment without bail. A father's right to the custody of his own children being founded in law on his right of guardianship, this being taken away, they may of course be severed from him, and put by the authority of a court into more orthodox hands.'·

Thus far the Notes, and now from the Memoir :

" In process of time, however, other sectarisms were introduced, chiefly of the Presbyterian family; and the established clergy, secure for life in their glebes and salaries, adding to these, generally, the emoluments of a classical school, found employment enough, in their farms and school-rooms, for the rest of the week, and devoted Sunday only to the edification of their flock, by service, and a sermon at their parish church. Their other pastoral functions were little attended to. Against this inactivity, the zeal and industry of sectarian preachers had an open and undisputed field; and by the time of the Revolution, a majority [1] of the inhabi-

----
[1] Mr. Jefferson states this stronger in his Notes on Virginia, viz., that two-thirds

tants had become dissenters from the Established Church, but were still obliged to pay contributions to support the pastors of the minority. This unrighteous compulsion, to maintain teachers of what they deemed religious errors, was grievously felt during the regal government, and without a hope of relief. But the first republican legislature, which met in '76, was crowded with petitions to abolish this spiritual tyranny. These brought on the severest contests in which I have ever been engaged. Our great opponents were Mr. Pendleton and Robert Carter Nicholas; honest men but zealous churchmen. The petitions were referred to the Committee of the Whole House on the state of the country; and, after desperate contests in that Committee, almost daily from the 11th of October to the 5th of December, we prevailed so far only, as to repeal the laws which rendered criminal the maintenance of any religious opinions, the forbearance of repairing to church, or the exercise of any mode of worship; and further, to exempt Dissenters from contributions to the support of the Established Church; and to suspend, only until the next session, levies on the members of that church for the salaries of their own incumbents. For although the majority of our citizens were Dissenters, as has been observed, a majority of the legislature were churchmen. Among these, however, were some reasonable and liberal men, who enabled us, on some points, to obtain feeble majorities. But our opponents carried, in the general resolutions of the Committee of November 19, a declaration that religious assemblies ought to be regulated, and that provision ought to be made for continuing the succession of the clergy, and superintending their conduct. And, in the bill now passed, was inserted an express reservation of the question, whether a general assessment should not be established by law, on every one, to the support of the pastor of his choice; or whether all should be left to voluntary contributions."

On the 25th day of November, Mr. Jefferson reported three bills in the House, "For establishing a Court of Appeals," "For establishing a High Court of Chancery," and "For establishing a General Court and Courts of Assize."

On the 29th, he obtained leave of absence for the rest of the session. He was, however, in his seat on the 4th of December, and introduced bills "For establishing a Court of Admiralty," and "For better regulating the proceedings of the County Courts." He then retired to prepare himself for a meeting of the law Revisers, presently to be held.

The subsequent events of the session (which extended to December 21st), do not require particular mention here. The bills defining treason, and establishing a Court of Admiralty,

---

of the inhabitants were Dissenters. We believe that the most moderate of the statements has been doubted; but the subsequent history of the struggle, the triumph of the Dissenters against a vast preponderance of *personal influence* arrayed against them, would seem to show that they must at least have had the strength of numbers.

Girardin, in speaking of the Dissenters' petitions to the House, says (p. 181):

"It was well known, they said, that in the frontier counties, which teemed with an abundant population, the Dissenters had borne the heavy burthens of purchasing glebes and supporting the established clergy, where few Episcopalians could be found either to assist in bearing the expense, or to reap the advantage."

passed. Those establishing Courts of Chancery, a General
Court, and Assizes, were put over to the next session. The
Naturalization law also went over. That for regulating succession was not acted on. That to change the location of the capital, and that to encourage domestic manufactures, were rejected.
The question of disputed boundary with Pennsylvania, was
referred to the Virginia delegates in Congress, by the House,
but we believe the Senate did not act on it.

We have passed over the warlike preparations of the session, there being nothing distinctive in their character. We
find Mr. Jefferson's name repeatedly and honorably connected
with them.

One affair occurred near the close of the session, after Mr.
Jefferson left, which would now appear incredible, were it not
supported by unquestionable authority, and had not Congress
once or twice during the Revolutionary struggle so far exceeded
their *delegated* trust as to resort to the same expedient in kind,
if not quite the same in degree. This was a proposition to
create a Dictator, in the Roman sense of the term, an officer
described by Mr. Jefferson when speaking of this affair (Notes
on Virginia, Query XIII.), as "invested with every power,
legislative, executive and judiciary, civil and military, of life
and death over our persons and over our properties;" and the
horror and indignation with which *he* regarded this revolting
proposition, finds burning expression on the same occasion.

Jefferson said this "was proposed in the House of Delegates;" and his declaration was *published* in less than ten years
from the alleged event, while a great proportion of the members
of that House were yet alive, and none of them (that we have
ever heard) called his statement into question.

The biographer of Patrick Henry does not dispute the fact,
nor that Mr. Henry (then Governor) was the contemplated
Dictator; "but that the project was suggested by him, or even
received his countenance," Mr. Wirt says "he has met with no
one who will venture to affirm.' Deep was the feeling the proposition engendered. "The members who favored it, and those
who opposed it," says Girardin,' "walked the streets on different
sides." But a Brutus, in the person of the fiery and indomitable

¹ Wirt's Henry, p. 222.   ² Page 190.

Cary, of Ampthill, stood ready to defend the outraged Constitution, if need be, by a desperate deed of violence. We will allow Mr. Wirt to tell the story in his own way:

"There is a tradition that Colonel Archibald Cary, the speaker of the Senate, *was principally instrumental in crushing this project;* that meeting Colonel Syme, the step-brother of Colonel [Governor] Henry in the lobby of the House, he accosted him very fiercely in terms like these: 'I am told your brother wishes to be Dictator: tell him from me, that the day of his appointment shall be the day of his death—for he shall feel my dagger in his heart before the sunset of that day;' and the tradition adds that Colonel Syme, in great agitation, declared, 'that if such a project existed, his brother had no hand in it, for that nothing could be more foreign to him than to countenance any office which could endanger, in the most distant manner, the liberties of his country.' The intrepidity and violence of Col. Cary's character renders the tradition probable; but it furnishes no proof of Mr. Henry's implication in the scheme. It is most certain that both himself and his friends have firmly and uniformly persisted in asserting his innocence; and there seems to be neither candor nor justice in imputing to him, without evidence, a scheme which might just as well have originated in the Assembly itself." [1]

If by "violence of character," Mr. Wirt meant to impute to Colonel Cary anything more than that fiery vehemence and stern resolution which may belong to a stainless gentleman, and may come most happily into play, in emergencies, in the patriot, he uttered more than the facts will sustain, or than Cary's position in the Senate, and his constant position before the Virginia public, would render presumable or admissible.

Jefferson declared, in his Notes on Virginia, that *most* of "the advocates of this measure" "meant well," for "he knew them personally, had been their fellow-laborer in the common cause, and had often proved the purity of their principles." He says, they "had been seduced in their judgment by the example of an ancient Republic, whose Constitution and circumstances were fundamentally different." He might have added, that it was a period of unexampled disaster. The rout of Long Island had recently taken place. The British held the city of New York. Fort Washington had fallen. The American Commander-in-chief, pressed by overwhelming numbers, was flying through the Jerseys. The gleam of success at Trenton had not yet lit up the gloom. Well might Paine exclaim, in his Crisis, "these are the times which try the souls of men!" The panic was not confined to the Virginia Legisla-

[1] Wirt's Henry, p. 223.

ture. Within a month of the project on the part of some of its members, just described, Congress actually invested General Washington, for a period, with *some* Dictatorial powers!

Soon after the adjournment of the Virginia Legislature, on January 13th, 1777, the Committee of Law Revisers met at Fredericksburg, to mark out their plan of procedure, and allot their parts to the different members. The first question to settle was, whether they should attempt an entirely new code, or an alteration and adaptation of existing laws. For once, Jefferson and Pendleton exchanged their habitual positions! Jefferson was for alterations, Pendleton for the sweeping change! The principal reason of the former—one that appeals with much more force to lawyers than to laymen—was,

"That to compose a new Institute, like those of Justinian and Bracton, or that of Blackstone, which was the model proposed by Mr. Pendleton, would be an arduous undertaking, of vast research, of great consideration and judgment; and when reduced to a text, every word of that text, from the imperfection of human language, and its incompetence to express distinctly every shade of idea, would become a subject of question and chicanery, until settled by repeated adjudications; and this would involve us for ages in litigation, and render property uncertain, until, like the statutes of old, every word had been tried and settled by numerous decisions, and by new volumes of reports and commentaries; and that no one of us, probably, would undertake such a work, which, to be systematical, must be the work of one hand."

Wythe and Mason concurred in this view, and the point was settled accordingly.

When the distribution of the work was reached, Mason and Lee, not being lawyers, declined taking any part. Mason resigned, and Lee died not long afterward, and their places were not subsequently filled. The three acting Revisers thus allotted their task among themselves: to Jefferson was assigned the Common Law and the Statutes to the 4th of James I., when a Legislature was established in Virginia; to Mr. Wythe the Statutes from that to the existing period; and to Mr. Pendleton the laws of Virginia. It needs but little professional knowledge to see that the department requiring by far the greatest labor and erudition, fell upon Jefferson. Before separating, he obtained from his colleagues their views on certain leading questions in his province, which will be adverted to when we take up the report of the Revisers.

The Spring session of the Virginia Legislature, in 1777, commenced on the 5th of May. Three candidates, Colonel Nicholas, Colonel Harrison, and Mr. Wythe, were put in nomination for the speakership. The last, nominated by Jefferson, was elected. We cannot help conjecturing that we have in this a hint that the Reformers, and those who, in reference to certain great personal divisions, may be termed the "armed neutrals," were in the ascendant.[1]

Mr. Jefferson was again placed on the most important standing committees, and again entered upon the great topics of the session with that promptitude and rapid dispatch which must now seem portentous to men accustomed only to observe legislative bodies which hardly commence bringing in or passing important bills until they have been at least a couple of months in session; and which afterwards, in debates made up of speeches of from one to three days in length, and on all topics but the one under examination, spin out more time on each important bill, than it would have required, under Jefferson's auspices, to carry it from its first mention in the House to the Executive for his signature! If all this modern delay in getting started is necessary (to allow committees to investigate, draw their reports, mature the provisions of bills, etc.) in what a dreadful state of unpreparedness our ancestors must have done up their legislative work—especially when they had such a headlong engineer as Jefferson to control the machine!

On the 9th—the next day after the attendance of a quorum permitted the organization of the House—he obtained leave to bring in bills "For regulating and disciplining the Militia," and "For providing against invasions and insurrections." He reported both bills on the 10th.

On the 12th (Monday) he asked leave to bring in a bill "For regulating the appointment of delegates to General Congress." He was appointed sole committee-man to do so, and reported the same day the "Act limiting the time for continuing the delegates to General Congress in office, and making provision for their support," which passed the House four days afterward, and in the Senate on the 21st, with amendments which did not alter its principle; and both houses finally concurred. This

---

[1] Nicholas was nominated by Richard Lee of Westmoreland, Harrison by his namesake of Prince George.

limited the continuous service of the delegates in Congress to
three years. One of the objects sought to be reached by this
law will be presently seen.

On the 15th the House agreed to a resolution, to the effect
that compulsory levies to support the established clergy should
again be suspended to the close of the next session, and a bill
was subsequently brought in and passed, carrying out the
provision.

On the 17th Mr. Jefferson was made chairman of a committee to determine the rank of the marine officers turned over to
the land service; and, on the 20th, to determine the rank of the
officers of the minute battalions transferred to the regular
service. On the 19th his act for regulating and disciplining the
militia passed the House.

On the 20th he was called home by an alarming indisposition of his wife,[1] and anticipating considerable detention, and
desiring time to prosecute his revision of the laws, he obtained
leave of absence for the remainder of the session.

Some occurrences took place after his retirement, which
require mention to throw light on preceding parts of this narrative. Two days after Mr. Jefferson left the House, it proceeded
to elect a delegate to Congress to fill the vacancy occasioned by
the resignation of Mr. Nelson; and five others to serve for the
full term (one year), from the 11th of August ensuing. George
Mason was elected to fill the vacancy; and Benjamin Harrison,
George Mason, Joseph Jones, Francis L. Lee, and John Harvie,
for the full term. Each member was balloted for separately.
Richard H. Lee was a candidate on every ballot for the full
term, and he received in them respectively ten, two, nine,
eleven, and ten votes. This was a most humiliating defeat.
Reports injurious to his reputation were in circulation. Girardin says, "what these reports were could not be precisely
ascertained."[2] Mr. Lee's grandson and biographer says, he had
refused to receive from his tenants the paper currency of the
State, requiring his rents in produce. This was regarded
unpatriotic in itself, and he was accused further of having done
it for the *purpose* of depreciating the currency. His biographer

---

[1] His wife gave birth to her third child, May 28th. She was always indisposed for
considerable periods, and sometimes alarmingly ill, before and after such events. The
account book contains the following entry: "June 14. Our son died 10h. 20m. P. M."
[2] Appendix, No. 17, in History of Virginia.

says he really did it to relieve his tenants—at a time when their products could find no market.[1] He further says he was accused " of having favored the interests of New England to the injury of the interests of Virginia." Here, doubtless, we have a vague allusion to the real or the main cause—the bitter Congressional feuds in which R. H. Lee sided with the Adamses, and possibly some other " New England " adjuncts, against Harrison, and, if report did not belie them, against a much more prominent Virginian.

R. H. Lee soon after this took his seat in the Virginia Legislature ; and on the 20th of June he called upon the House, says its journal, " to inquire into certain matters injurious to his reputation and public character, which, as he was informed, had in his absence been alleged against him." The Senate were invited into the House—" several witnesses were examined, and Mr. Lee was heard in his place." The Senate withdrew, and the House passed the usual vote of thanks to Mr. Lee for his " faithful services " as a delegate in Congress. Speaker Wythe then gave the thanks of the House to Mr. Lee, offering, in warm and something more than merely formal terms, his personal testimony to their justice, and to the official merits and abilities of the late representative. George Mason declined a seat in Congress for the full term ; and on the 24th of June, the Legislature proceeded to fill the vacancy. R. H. Lee was chosen, receiving sixty-seven votes, to twenty-three for James Mercer, and thirteen for Mann Page, Jr. Thus, as in Harrison's case, the reaction against what bore the aspect of persecution, was prompt and effectual.

We have seen that Jefferson was absent when Harrison was beaten, and present when he was replaced. There is no doubt he aided in that replacement. Yet it is certain that Mr. Lee did not regard him as *his* opponent. Lee wrote Jefferson as a friend, in the Virginia Legislature, asking his favorable personal testimony in his behalf, in respect to the calumnies which were circulated against him ; and if he wrote any other member on the subject, the fact has not, as we remarked in a preceding chapter, transpired. His letter was dated Philadelphia, November 3d, 1776.

" I have been informed that very malignant and very scandalous hints and

[1] This is, we think, a very obvious mistake, taking both of the assertions together.

innuendoes concerning me, have been uttered in the House. From the justice of the House, I should expect they would not suffer the character of an absent person to be reviled by any slanderous tongue whatever. When I am present, I shall be perfectly satisfied with the justice I am able to do myself. From your candor, sir, and knowledge of my political movements, I hope such misstatings as may happen in your presence, will be rectified." [1]

We have seen that at the election of Speaker, neither Harrison, nor a candidate nominated by Richard Lee, of Westmoreland, succeeded, but a third candidate, nominated by Jefferson, not identified in any way with either of the hostile factions, and personally friendly both to R. H. Lee and to Harrison.

We have seen that when Mr. Jefferson asked leave to report a bill in regard to the tenure of Congressional incumbents, the House promptly ordered him (a very unusual proceeding) to report it alone—that is, to act as a committee of *one* on the subject. Had this been objected to, or voted against by any set, we cannot presume that Mr. Jefferson or his friends would have desired that he should thus act alone, where (under strong objection) to urge it would have savored of assumption or indelicacy. The presumption is, in our mind, next to a certainty that the arrangement was universally concurred in. If so, he was voluntarily placed by all the parties, to some extent, in the position of an umpire; for the great object of the bill he brought in was, and it was probably understood it would be, in advance, to put an end to the Congressional factions of Virginia—to establish a rotation which would ensure more than one set a place—and remove the temptations to intrigues for a permanent situation on one side, or to attempts to surprise and overthrow the incumbents, on the other.

It is but a conjecture, but we have no doubt that had Mr. Jefferson been in his seat on the 22d of May, Richard H. Lee would have been then reëlected to Congress. George Mason wore no man's colors, but he generally acted closely with Jefferson. He made place for Mr. Lee. Wythe was one of the nearest and warmest friends of Jefferson. His sympathies were obviously all on Lee's side. Unless Mr. Jefferson's particular friends had supported Lee on the 24th of June, he could have obtained nothing like such a vote. Mr. Jefferson, and doubtless all his friends, felt that Mr. Lee had been indiscreet

[1] This will be found in Appendix, No. 17, of Girardin.

in some things, and seriously in the wrong in others. But he had been an early and steady and able friend of the Revolution. He deserved well of Virginia and the United States, in many particulars. With more faults, and guiltier of far greater errors, he was not the man whom it was either right or seemly to suddenly and humiliatingly eject from Congress, especially when it was ostensibly done on charges affecting his personal reputation.

The Legislature adjourned on the 28th of June, and great events occurred before it reassembled. Burgoyne drove St. Clair out of Ticonderoga. The battles of Hubbardstown, Oriskany, Bennington, Brandywine, Stillwater, Germantown, and Saratoga were fought, with varying success, between the parties; and, though Philadelphia had now shared the fate of New York, on the whole, the real preponderance of success was on the side of the Americans. The moral effects of the capture of Burgoyne and a British army at Saratoga, in raising the tone of American feelings and hopes, were incalculable; and its political bearings in other countries, particularly in France in making it thought worth while to furnish important aid to the Americans, were not less important.

The Virginia Legislature assembled October 20th, and it somewhat marks both the spirit and the necessity of the times, that upwards of fifty members were absent, and that all of them were promptly ordered under arrest for a contempt of the House; nor was one of them discharged until he had in his place made a formal excuse for his absence, and then been excused with or without the payment of costs, according to the absolute necessity of his absence.

Mr. Jefferson took his seat, and was placed on the important committees, as usual. On the first business day of the session (October 30th), he again brought in bills establishing a Court of Appeals, a Court of Chancery, and, on the 7th of November, a General Court, and Courts of Assize, which had not hitherto been acted upon.[1]

On the 12th of November, Mann Page, Jr., was chosen a delegate to Congress, in the room of Colonel Harrison, resigned; and James Madison was chosen a member of the Privy Council,

---

[1] The two last were *reported* by Nicholas, but *for* the Chairman (Jefferson) who was compelled to be absent three days.

or Council of State. Page declined, and John Bannister was chosen in his place.

We find Mr. Jefferson constantly placed on special committees in regard to laws, military arrangements, and, in short, all subjects affecting the immediate or ultimate interests of the State; but continual repetitions of this sort must, we judge, cease to interest the reader.

On the 1st of December, an incident occurred, insignificant in itself, but which led to some feeling and a protracted discussion, or rather contest, between the two houses. The House of Delegates had passed a resolution for paying a Captain Thomas Johnson "£15 15s. 6d." The Senate, on inquiry, with old fashioned scrupulousness, reduced this appropriation to £12 12s. The House considered this an invasion of their privileges in regard to a money bill, and sent Jefferson to ask a conference; and it appointed Messrs. Jefferson, Cary, Pendleton, Bullitt, and Meriwether a Committee "to draw up what is proper to be offered to the Senate at the said conference, and report the same to the House." The Senate appointed Messrs. T. L. Lee, Carrington, Holt, and Ellzey, managers on its part. The House appointed its managers, varying somewhat from its previous Committee, but retaining Jefferson at the head of it. It is not necessary to follow out here the particulars of conference on top of conference which ensued on a question of three pounds—but involving, it must be confessed, an important principle of legislative action and of constitutional law. All of Jefferson's papers on the subject took the ground that in legislatures acknowledging the Parliamentary law, the Senate had as little power to *alter* as *originate* a grant of money. One of his reports, embodying his arguments and authorities, will be found on the record of the proceedings of the House (January 9, 1778, House Journal, p. 115). Wherever the right of the case lay, the Senate Committee were obviously far overmatched on paper; but we think no ultimate disposition of the matter was made at the time.

On the 15th of December, the Articles of Confederation and Perpetual Union, which had passed Congress, were unanimously ratified by the Legislature.

On the 3d of January (1778), Mr. Jefferson's long delayed Judiciary Bills came up for final action. A motion was made to postpone the third reading of that for establishing a General Court and Courts of Assize to a day beyond the session—in other words, reject it. The previous question was ordered on this, and the yeas and nays to be entered on the Journal—the last a procedure (if we may trust to *our* examination of the Journal) having no precedent, at least since the adoption of the Republican Constitution; and we have no recollection of anything of the kind in the records of previous Conventions and Houses of Burgesses. The previous question, and the call for ayes and noes, is a comparatively modern invention. The motion to postpone came within six votes of prevailing, and the bill then passed by a majority of but two. These indications show that there was an extraordinary degree of feeling on the subject, and the complexion of the vote leaves little doubt that it must have been to *some* extent a test of strength between the conservative and popular parties; though if this be so, Mr. Pendleton was found again arrayed against his customary side. Other and extraneous considerations may or may not have had their influence.[1] The bill passed the Senate afterwards, with some amendments, and did not become a law until the 19th. The act establishing a High Court of Chancery also passed the House January 3d, and the Senate on the 9th.

Jefferson relates an anecdote of Pendleton, in connection with this Chancery Bill, highly illustrative of his tact in Parliamentary encounters. It occurs in the Memoir:

"In that one of the bills for organizing our judiciary system, which proposed a Court of Chancery, I had provided for a trial by jury of all matters of fact, in that as well as in the courts of law. He defeated it by the introduction of four words only—'*if either party choose.*' The consequence has been, that as no suitor will say to his judge, 'Sir, I distrust you, give me a jury,' juries are rarely, I might say perhaps never, seen in that court, but when called for by the Chancellor of his own accord."

On the 13th, Mr. Jefferson obtained leave to bring in a bill "For sequestering British property, enabling those indebted to British subjects to pay off such subjects, and directing the proceedings in suits where such subjects are parties."

On the 14th, both houses unanimously chose Edmund Pen-

[1] For the postponement (rejection), we find among others the names of Harrison, Nicholas, Tazewell, Syme, etc. Against: Jefferson, Pendleton, Mason, Richard Lee, etc. The division *may* have been purely on the details of the bill.

dleton, George Wythe, and Robert C. Nicholas, Judges of the High Court of Chancery just established; and on the 23d, Joseph Jones, John Blair, Thomas L. Lee, Thompson Mason, and Paul Carrington, were chosen Judges of the General Court. Richard H. Lee was the same day elected Delegate in Congress for the ensuing official year, receiving fifty-nine votes to twenty-six cast for James Mercer.

Mr. Jefferson's bill sequestering British property, and in regard to the payment of British debts, passed. It was a most liberal one, and contrasted favorably with that mean and mercenary spirit in regard to British debts afterwards attributed by a distinguished writer (Judge Marshall, in his life of Washington) to a large body of men who mostly became the political followers of Mr. Jefferson.

The Church levies were again suspended, and on the 24th of January, the General Assembly adjourned.

It is not deemed important to follow Mr. Jefferson further, in the details of his legislative career during 1778, and the part of the session of 1779 during which he sat. We will barely notice that, in the last, he again introduced and pushed through his "Bill declaring who shall be deemed citizens of this Commonwealth"—the most important provisions of which have been heretofore stated. His time was now principally occupied with the law revision.

The Revisers having completed their several tasks, met in Williamsburg, in February, 1779, and proceeded to examine and pass upon the whole, scrutinizing and amending sentence by sentence, until every part was conjointly agreed upon. This is Jefferson's statement in his Memoir, and he adds:

"We then returned home, had fair copies made of our several parts, which were reported to the General Assembly, June 18, 1779, by Mr. Wythe and myself, Mr. Pendleton's residence being distant, and he having authorized us by letter to declare his approbation."

We have here a characteristic avoidance of claiming merit at the expense of a friend—or of details calculated to reduce the attributed merits of a friend, unless drawn forth by necessity. In a letter in answer to certain inquiries of Skelton Jones, dated July 28th, 1809, Mr. Jefferson gives the *inside* history of Mr. Pendleton's participation in this revision:

"After completing our work separately, we met (Mr. W., Mr. P., and myself), in Williamsburg, and held a long session, in which we went over the first and second parts in the order of time, weighing and correcting every word, and reducing them to the form in which they were afterwards reported. When we proceeded to the third part, we found that Mr. Pendleton had not exactly seized the intentions of the Committee, which were to reform the language of the Virginia laws, and reduce the matter to a simple style and form. He had copied the acts *verbatim*, only omitting what was disapproved; and some family occurrence calling him indispensably home, he desired Mr. Wythe and myself to make it what we thought it ought to be, and authorized us to report him as concurring in the work. We accordingly divided the work, *and re-executed it entirely*, so as to assimilate its plan and execution to the other parts, as well as the shortness of the time would admit, and we brought the whole body of British statutes and laws of Virginia into 127[1] acts, most of them short."

A very celebrated Virginia lawyer, to whom we shall hereafter be introduced on an interesting occasion (the trial of Aaron Burr), was wont to say, if we may believe the assertions of a Virginia writer who made some noise in his time,[2] that the part of the Revision *performed by Pendleton* could be distinguished by its *superior precision!* If Mr. Wickham is not here belied, we have an amusing (and towards Jefferson, exceedingly characteristic) specimen of the ability of even grave, learned, and wise eyes, to see what they wish to see.

The report of the Revisers consisted of one hundred and twenty-six bills, which, as printed by the House, covered but ninety closely printed folio pages. This brevity was not attained by omissions, but by the remarkable succinctness with which the acts were drawn. In this particular, and in precision and clearness, they are models of legal style. Mr. Jefferson remarks in his Memoir:

"In the execution of my part, I thought it material not to vary the diction of the ancient statutes by modernizing it, nor to give rise to new questions by new expressions. The text of these statutes had been so fully explained and defined, by numerous adjudications, as scarcely ever now to produce a question in our courts. I thought it would be useful, also, in all new drafts, to reform the style of the later British statutes, and of our own Acts of Assembly; which, from their verbosity, their endless tautologies, their involutions of case within case, and parenthesis within parenthesis, and their multiplied efforts at certainty, by *saids* and *aforesaids*, by *ors* and by *ands*, to make them more plain, are really rendered more perplexed and incomprehensible, not only to common readers, but to the lawyers themselves."

The Revisers, at their first meeting, in 1777 (when the whole

---

[1] Misprinted, doubtless, for 126.   [2] H. Lee.

five originally chosen members were together), had settled some important principles for the revised code. The law of descents coming within Mr. Jefferson's share of the work, he proposed—in addition to the abolition of entails already accomplished—to also abolish primogeniture, and make real estate, like personal property, descendible equally to the next of kin. This would tear away the *last* prop of the ancient landed aristocracy of Virginia; and Mr. Pendleton made a strong stand against it. Finding, however, the majority of the Revisers against him, he proposed a compromise—namely, to adopt the Hebrew principle, and give a double portion to the older son. Jefferson demolished the proposition thus:

" I observed, that if the eldest son could eat twice as much, or do double work, it might be a natural evidence of his right to a double portion ; but being on a par in his powers and wants, with his brothers and sisters, he should be on a par also in the partition of the patrimony; *and such was the decision of the other members.*" [1]

The Revisers next agreed that the punishment of death should be abolished except for treason and murder ; and that other felonies should be punished by imprisonment, hard labor on the public works, and in some instances by retaliation in kind. Mr. Jefferson says in his Memoir: " how this last revolting principle came to obtain our approbation I do not remember." Here is another modest suppression of those details which would seem to claim for him superiority over his colleagues, for it distinctly appears that *he* was opposed to the "revolting principle," but was overruled. He wrote Mr. Wythe, his fellow-reviser, November 1, 1778:

" I have strictly observed the scale of punishments settled by the Committee without being entirely satisfied with it. The *Lex talionis*, although a restitution of the Common law, to the simplicity of which we have generally found it so advantageous to return, will be revolting to the humanized feelings of modern times. An eye for an eye, and a hand for a hand, will exhibit spectacles in execution whose moral effect would be questionable; and even the *membrum pro membro* of Bracton, or the punishment of the offending member, although long authorized by our law, for the same offence in a slave, has, you know, been not long since repealed, in conformity with public sentiment. This needs reconsideration." [2]

[1] Garland, in his Life of Randolph, represents George Mason as lamenting the overthrow of the ancient laws of descent in Virginia, and exclaiming that Jefferson, Wythe and Pendleton "*never had a son.*" He probably was not aware that George Mason was present when it was settled to overthrow these laws, and *voted for it*, as Jefferson above asserts. Jefferson was himself an older son. He *did* have a *son* born within four months of the time of this meeting. He *did* have *three children* born *afterwards*, and could not very well have known, in advance, that none of them would be *sons !*
[2] This letter is given in Note E to Jefferson's Memoir, in his Works.

That we should attempt anything like a description of Mr.
Jefferson's portion of the Revision will not be expected; but a
glance at the character and fate of a few of his most prominent
bills, introducing material changes, and changes of principle,
into the existing framework of legislation, will perhaps be
expected, for they illustrate *his* character as a lawgiver, and, to
some extent, as a statesman.

The bill for Establishing Religious Freedom was a splendid
example of the manner in which—at least on great subjects—
language, in all respects as appropriate and infinitely more dignified, may be made to take the place of the usual hard, dry,
tautological phraseology of legislation. This bill, as given in
the Notes on Virginia, and as commonly published, is *not* the
original, but the bill *amended*, as it passed the Virginia General
Assembly. The former not being very accessible to the mass
of readers, and being a good specimen of Mr. Jefferson's *law*
diction, we give it entire. The parts which the Virginia Legislature struck out are placed in italics; two inserted or added
words are placed in brackets; and three slight alterations are
indicated by placing the substituted words in the margin:

A BILL FOR ESTABLISHING RELIGIOUS FREEDOM.

Well aware *that the opinions and belief of men depend not on
their own will, but follow involuntarily the evidence proposed to their
minds;* that Almighty God hath created the mind free, *and manifested his supreme will that free it shall remain by making it
altogether insusceptible of restraint;* that all attempts to influence
it by temporal punishments or burdens, or by civil incapacitations,
tend only to beget habits of hypocrisy and meanness, and are a
departure from the plan of the Holy Author of our religion, who
being Lord both of body and mind, yet chose not to propagate it
by coercions on either, as was in his Almighty power to do, *but to
extend its influence on reason alone;* that the impious presumption of
legislators and rulers, civil as well as ecclesiastical, who, being themselves but fallible and uninspired men, have assumed dominion over
the faith of others, setting up their own opinions and modes of thinking as the only true and infallible, and as such endeavoring to impose
them on others, hath established and maintained false religions over
the greatest part of the world, and through all time: that to compel
a man to furnish contributions of money for the propagation of opinions which he disbelieves *and abhors*, is sinful and tyrannical: that
even the forcing him to support this or that teacher of his own
religious persuasion, is depriving him of the comfortable liberty of
giving his contributions to the particular pastor whose morals he
would make his pattern, and whose powers he feels most persuasive

to righteousness, and is withdrawing from the ministry those *temporary* rewards, which proceeding from an approbation of their personal conduct, are an additional incitement to earnest and unremitting labors for the instruction of mankind; that our civil rights have no dependence on our religious opinions, *any* more than our opinions in physics or geometry; that, therefore, the proscribing any citizen as unworthy the public confidence by laying upon him an incapacity of being called to [the] offices of trust and emolument, unless he profess or renounce this or that religious opinion, is depriving him injuriously of those privileges and advantages to which, in common with his fellow-citizens, he has a natural right; that it tends also to corrupt the principles of that very religion it is meant to encourage, by bribing, with a monopoly of worldly honors and emoluments, those who will externally profess and conform to it; that though indeed these are criminal who do not withstand such temptation, yet neither are those innocent who lay the bait in their way; *that the opinions of men are not the object of civil government, nor under its jurisdiction;* that to suffer the civil magistrate to intrude his powers into the field of opinion and to restrain the profession or propagation of principles, on [the] supposition of their ill tendency is a dangerous fallacy, which at once destroys all religious liberty, because he being of course judge of that tendency will make his opinions the rule of judgment, and approve or condemn the sentiments of others only as they shall square with or differ from his own; that it is time enough for the rightful purposes of civil government for its officers to interfere when principles break out into overt acts against peace and good order; and finally, that truth is great and will prevail if left to herself; that she is the proper and sufficient antagonist to error, and has nothing to fear from the conflict unless by human interposition disarmed of her natural weapons, free argument and debate; errors ceasing to be dangerous when it is permitted freely to contradict them.

We, the General Assembly, do enact, That no man shall be compelled to frequent or support any religious worship, place, or ministry whatsoever, nor shall be enforced, restrained, molested, or burthened in his body or goods, nor shall otherwise suffer, on account of his religious opinions or belief; but that all men shall be free to profess, and by argument to maintain, their opinions in matters of religion, and that the same shall in no wise diminish, enlarge, or affect their civil capacities.

And though we know well that this Assembly, elected by the people for the ordinary purposes of legislation only, have no power to restrain the acts of succeeding Assemblies, constituted with *powers* equal to our own, and that therefore to declare this act irrevocable would be of no effect in law; yet we are free to declare, and do declare, that the rights hereby asserted are of the natural rights of mankind, and that if any act shall be hereafter passed to repeal the present or to narrow its operation, such act will be an infringement of natural right."

The horror with which this proposed bill was regarded by the zealous friends of an Establishment, in Virginia, must have been somewhat mitigated by the next succeeding one in the Revision. This, entitled " A bill for saving the property of the Church heretofore by law established," provided that the glebes, churches, furniture, arrearages, etc., and all church property of every description of *private donation*, "should be saved in all time to come to the *members* of the English Church " resident in the parish—to be applied as they should see fit for the support of their ministry. The surviving vestry men in every parish were to have authority to carry into execution all legal contracts entered into before the 1st of January, 1777, even if a levy or tax, on all, should become necessary for that purpose. Where previous levies had exceeded the law, and surpluses above indebtednesses were on hand, at the same date, they were to be paid into the poor rates of the parish; but if the parish had no glebe, the surplus was to be applied to the purchase of one. This last liberal provision was doubtless based on the ground that until a glebe was purchased—anterior to 1776 a legal charge on the parish—no surplus could actually ensue.

The effect of such a law would have been to reserve to the Church all property legally in its possession; but the title and control would be transferred from the vestries to the members,[1] who would be bound to apply it to the support of *a* ministry, but would be left sole judges of the conditions of the application. This bill seems to have aimed to steer between a violation of vested rights, and using property for other purposes voluntarily devoted to religious objects by its owners—and the arming of a hierarchical body with perpetual power to use a fund contributed by *all* denominations for the exclusive support of a particular *class of tenets*.

Another bill exempted all clergymen from arrest while performing religious services, and provided severe punishments for disturbers of public worship.

The Revision, therefore, did not sanction that confiscation of the glebes which afterwards took place. Whether Mr. Jefferson changed his mind, and kept up with the demands of popular feeling in that particular, we have no means of know-

[1] *They* might still, we take it, constitute their vestries *their agents* for the management of their property.

ing. We remember no utterance of his on that subject, after reporting the bills we have described.

We might as well close what we have to say on this topic here. The General Assembly continued to suspend Church levies until the fall session of 1779, and then abolished them. This was not, however, acquiesced in; and after some preliminary legislation strengthening the Anglican Church, which we will not stop to describe, a determined move was made in 1784, to "establish a provision for teachers of the Christian Religion" by what was termed a "general assessment." This was a compulsory tax on all for the support of the clergy, but it allowed each person to decide to what denomination his contribution should go. This was the best arrangement the Anglican Church could now hope for, and most of the Dissenters, it would seem (the Baptists being said to be the only exception, as a church), were ready to join the former on this ground, and unite in a strenuous effort in favor of the measure.[1]

The struggle was tremendous. Jefferson was now in a foreign land. The massive strength of George Mason, the matchless logic of Madison, the dauntless nerve of George Nicholas were on one side, with such followers as such men and such a cause could command. On the other, were most of the churches, the landed gentry, and some such towering names as those of George Washington, Patrick Henry, and Richard H. Lee.

Pending the question in the House of Delegates, General Washington wrote George Mason (Oct. 3, 1785):

"Although no man's sentiments are more opposed to any kind of restraint upon religious principles than mine are, yet I confess that I am not among the number of those, who are so much alarmed at the thoughts of making people pay towards the support of that which they profess."[2]

"Mr. Henry," says his biographer, Wirt, "gave his warmest support" in the House of Delegates (November, 1784) to the approbatory resolutions on which the bill for a general assessment was founded; and that he did not vote for the bill itself when it came up for passage, was owing to his not being a member of the House, having been chosen Governor.[3]

[1] So Jefferson, Tucker and other Virginia writers declare.
[2] See Sparks's Washington, vol. xii. p. 404, in Appendix
[3] See Wirt's Henry, pp. 260-263.

Richard H. Lee wrote Mr. Madison from Congress, November 26, 1784:

"It is certainly comfortable to know that the Legislature of our country is engaged in beneficial pursuits, for I conceive that the *general assessment* and a digest of the moral laws are very important concerns; the one to secure our peace and the other our morals. Refiners may weave reason into as fine a web as they please, but the experience of all times shows religion to be the guardian of morals; and he must be a very inattentive observer in our country, who does not see that avarice is accomplishing the destruction of religion, for want of a legal obligation to contribute something to its support." [1]

The most that the opponents of the General Assessment Bill could obtain, was to procure a delay until the next session, on the avowed ground of submitting the question to the people. Mr. Madison then, at the solicitation of his principal colleagues, prepared the draft of a remonstrance for popular circulation. It was drawn up with consummate ability, and made such an unanswerable appeal to the good sense of reflecting men, that everything went down before it. At the next session, the remonstrants far outnumbered the petitioners. The assessment was abandoned; and in the session of 1786 Mr. Jefferson's bill to establish religious freedom passed, with the amendments indicated in the copy we have given.

In 1799, all laws made for the benefit of religious societies were repealed; and in 1801, the glebes, as soon as vacated by existing incumbents (excepting as to private donations before 1777), were ordered to be sold by the overseers of the poor.

To go back to the report of the Law Revisers: the statutes in relation to William and Mary College fell within Pendleton's part of the revision, but as its charter brought it also within Jefferson's, and as it was judged expedient to present a general plan of education for the State, which Jefferson would take up with peculiar relish, he was requested to undertake it. [2] He accordingly drafted three educational bills, "For the more general diffusion of knowledge," "For amending the Constitution of the College of William and Mary, and substituting more certain revenues for its support," and "For establishing a Public Library."

The preamble of the first distinctly assumes the principle that it is the right and duty of the *State* to make provision for

[1] Lee's Life of Lee, vol. ii. p. 51. See also vol. i. p. 237.   Memoir.

the proper education of the children of the "greater number," too indigent to so educate them themselves.[1] The bill provided for the election of three county officers (" Aldermen ") to divide their county into "hundreds;" and (the sites being selected by the inhabitants) to erect and keep in repair suitable school-houses. In the schools kept in these all free children were entitled to receive tuition gratis, for three years, and as much longer as desired at the expense of their parents. Reading, writing, and common arithmetic were to be taught in them; and the reading books were to be such " as would, at the same time, make them acquainted with Grecian, Roman, English and American History."

Over every ten of these schools the Aldermen were to annually appoint an Overseer, " eminent for his learning, integrity and fidelity to the Commonwealth," who was to appoint and remove teachers, visit the school as often as once each half year, examine the scholars, and see if the plan of instruction recommended by the visitors of William and Mary College was properly carried out. Every teacher was to receive a fixed annual salary from the county, and " his diet, lodging, and washing," be at the expense of the " hundred."

The bill then divided the State into twenty districts, directing the Overseers in each to procure one hundred acres of land centrally situated, and erect thereon suitable buildings of brick or stone for a school, each having a proper school-room, a dining hall, four rooms for a master and usher, and ten or twelve lodg

---

[1] This preamble is curious, and we transcribe it entire:

" Whereas it appeareth that however certain forms of government are better calculated than others to protect individuals in the free exercise of their natural rights, and are at the same time themselves better guarded against degeneracy, yet experience has shown, that even under the best forms, those intrusted with power have, in time, and by slow operations, perverted it into tyranny; and it is believed that the most effectual means of preventing this, would be to illuminate, as far as practicable, the minds of the people at large, and more especially to give them knowledge of those facts, which history exhibiteth, that, possessed thereby of the experience of other ages and countries, they may be enabled to know ambition under all its shapes, and prompt to exert their natural powers to defeat its purposes: And whereas it is generally true that the people will be happiest whose laws are best, and are best administered, and that laws will be wisely formed, and honestly administered, in proportion as those who form and administer them are wise and honest; whence it becomes expedient for promoting the public happiness, that those persons, whom nature hath endowed with genius and virtue, should be rendered by liberal education worthy to receive, and able to regard the sacred deposits of the rights and liberties of their fellow citizens, and that they should be called to that charge without regard to wealth, birth, or other accidental condition or circumstance; but the indigence of the greater number disabling them from so educating, at their own expense, those of their children whom nature hath fitly formed and disposed to become useful instruments for the public, it is better that such should be sought for, and educated at the common expense of all, than that the happiness of all should be confided to the weak or wicked."

ing rooms for pupils, and necessary offices. The site was to be paid for by the State. In these " grammar schools " were to be taught " the Latin and Greek languages, English grammar, geography, and the higher parts of numeral arithmetic."

A Visitor was to be annually appointed from each county by the Overseers, and these Visitors, in a district, were to have about the same powers and duties in regard to the Grammar Schools, that the Overseers did in those of the hundreds.

Each Overseer, " after the most diligent and impartial examination and inquiry," and after being *sworn* to act " without favor or affection,"[1] was to annually select from the schools under his charge, a pupil of at least two years' standing, " of the best and most promising genius and disposition," to be sent to the Grammar School of the district—to be there boarded and educated at the expense of the State for at least one year. At the end of that time the Visitors were to discontinue the attendance of one-third of the least promising. All were to be discontinued at the end of the second year, save one from each district of the greatest merit, who was then at liberty to remain four years longer on the public foundation, and was thenceforth deemed a " Senior." From these Seniors, the Visitors of the district were annually to choose one, and send him to William and Mary College, to be educated, boarded, and clothed for three years at the expense of the State.

The second of Mr. Jefferson's educational bills provided for almost entirely changing the organization of William and Mary College, and converting it into a University,[2] governed by five Visitors appointed by the Legislature in joint ballot.

The third educational bill provided for the annual disbursement of two thousand pounds from the State treasury, by three persons " of learning and of attention to literary matters," appointed by the Legislature, to purchase books and maps for a free State Library at Richmond.

All the provisions of each of these several acts, and especially

---

[1] Very stringent provisions were made otherwise to secure impartiality.

[2] Under the charter and other existing laws, the College of William and Mary had been organized into a school of sacred theology, with a professorship for teaching Hebrew and expounding the Holy Scriptures, and another for explaining the common places of divinity and the controversies with heretics : a school of philosophy, with a professorship for rhetoric, logic and ethics, and another for physics, metaphysics and mathematics ; a school for teaching the Latin and Greek tongues ; and lastly, a school (founded on a private donation by Robert Boyle) for teaching Indian boys reading, writing, vulgar arithmetic, the catechism and principles of the Christian religion. Mr.

of the great Free Common School Act, were guarded with the most minute and precise, as well as stringent provisions, to secure their full and impartial execution, both to the spirit and letter. In these respects the bills are legislative curiosities.

Mr. Jefferson thus gives a part of their further history in his Memoir:

"These bills were not acted on until the same year, '96, and then only so much of the first as provided for elementary schools. The College of William and Mary was an establishment purely of the Church of England; the visitors were required to be all of that church; the professors to subscribe its thirty-nine articles; its students to learn its catechism; and one of its fundamental objects was declared to be, to raise up ministers for that church. The religious jealousies, therefore, of all the dissenters, took alarm lest this might give an ascendency to the Anglican sect, and refused acting on that bill. Its local eccentricity, too, and unhealthy autumnal climate, lessened the general inclination towards it. And in the Elementary bill, they inserted a provision which completely defeated it; for they left it to the court of each county to determine for itself, when this act should be carried into execution, within their county. One provision of the bill was, that the expenses of these schools should be borne by the inhabitants of the county, every one in proportion to his general tax rate. This would throw on wealth the education of the poor; and the justices, being generally of the more wealthy class, were unwilling to incur that burden, and I believe it was not suffered to commence in a single county."

Jefferson's bill proposed, in the place of these, eight professorships (which it is believed the educated reader will feel interest in), as follows:

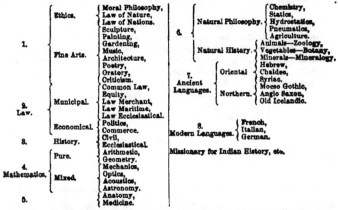

[We have here followed the bill as given in the original legislative publication. It is abundantly certain—and we shall hereafter have repeated occasions to show—that Mr. Jefferson considered Greek and Latin an indispensable part of a *liberal* education—of vastly more importance than any, or all, of those languages given above under the head of Ancient Languages. Their omission in the above list is probably to be attributed to the idea that a thorough knowledge of them was to be obtained in the long preparatory training of the Grammar School.]

The sequel will be mentioned hereafter, because it was closely connected with the events of another portion of Mr. Jefferson's life.

The course pursued by the Revisers in regard to the laws on slavery is thus mentioned by Mr. Jefferson:

"The bill on the subject of slaves, was a mere digest of the existing laws respecting them, without any intimation of a plan for a future and general emancipation. It was thought better that this should be kept back, and attempted only by way of amendment, whenever the bill should be brought on. The principles of the amendment, however, were agreed on, that is to say, the freedom of all born after a certain day, and deportation at a proper age; but it was found that the public mind would not yet bear the proposition, nor will it bear it even at this day. Yet the day is not distant when it must bear and adopt it, or worse will follow. Nothing is more certainly written in the book of fate, than that these people are to be free; nor is it less certain that the two races, equally free, cannot live in the same government. Nature, habit, opinion have drawn indelible lines of distinction between them. It is still in our power to direct the process of emancipation and deportation, peaceably, and in such slow degree, as that the evil will wear off insensibly, and their place be, *pari passu*, filled up by free white laborers. If, on the contrary, it is left to force itself on, human nature must shudder at the prospect held up. We should in vain look for an example in the Spanish deportation or deletion of the Moors. This precedent would fall far short of our case."

We find an outline of the proposed amendment in the Notes on Virginia:

"To emancipate all slaves born after passing the act. The bill reported by the Revisers did not itself contain this proposition; but an amendment containing it was prepared, to be offered to the Legislature whenever the bill should be taken up, and further directing, that they should continue with their parents to a certain age, then be brought up, at the public expense, to tillage, arts or sciences, according to their geniuses, till the females should be eighteen, and the males twenty-one years of age, when they should be colonized to such place as the circumstances of the time should render most proper, sending them out with arms, implements of household and of the handicraft arts, seeds, pairs of the useful domestic animals, etc., to declare them a free and independent people, and extend to them our alliance and protection, till they have acquired strength; and to send vessels at the same time to other parts of the world for an equal number of white inhabitants; to induce whom to migrate hither, proper encouragements were to be proposed."

The bill "For proportioning crimes and punishments in cases heretofore capital," has been made more familiar to the public than the others, by being included in the Appendix to the Memoir, in both editions of Mr. Jefferson's Works. It, as already mentioned, limited the death penalty to cases of murder and treason—a gigantic stride in ameliorating the bloody penal codes of the day. But the principle of retaliation (to which we have seen Jefferson himself was opposed) greatly marred the otherwise humane and admirable spirit of the bill. Among the "revolting features" were such as the following : The poisoner was to suffer death by poison ; the maimer was to be equally maimed ; and the body of the challenger who committed murder in a duel, was to be gibbeted after execution. And, by a peculiarly "Draconic clause," criminals condemned to die were to be executed the second day after sentence, unless it should be Sunday; and power to pardon was in all cases abolished, "that none might be induced to injure through hope of impunity." Labor on the public works was generally substituted when previous capital punishment was abolished. The principle of restitution entered pretty largely into the bill, sometimes awarding double and treble damages to injured parties, and extending the range of cases where the principle was made applicable beyond those recognized in the common law.

This new criminal code was not acted on in the Virginia Legislature until 1785. It was then brought forward by Mr. Madison, and lost by a single vote. The public mind was not yet ripe for such a mitigation in the scale of punishments. In 1796, the subject was resumed, and Mr. G. K. Taylor introduced a bill differently worded, but in substance principally the same, except that it substituted solitary confinement and labor in the place of labor on the public works—the latter having been meanwhile tried in a neighboring State, and not found to succeed. Experiments elsewhere had, however, now prepared the public mind in Virginia for the spirit of Jefferson's bill, and the one proposed by Mr. Taylor became a law.[1]

How Jefferson contemplated his legal scheme, as a whole— *his* great *aims* in it—are thus avowed by him :

"I considered four of these bills, passed or reported, as forming a system by which every fibre would be eradicated of ancient or future aristocracy; and a foundation laid for a government truly republican. The repeal of the laws of entail would prevent the accumulation and perpetuation of wealth, in select families, and preserve the soil of the country from being daily more and more absorbed in mortmain. The abolition of primogeniture, and equal partition of inheritances, removed the feudal and unnatural distinctions which made one member of every family rich, and all the rest poor, substituting equal partition, the best of all Agra-

See Jefferson's Memoir, and note G to Memoir.

rian laws. The restoration of the rights of conscience relieved the people from taxation for the support of a religion not theirs ; for the establishment was truly of the religion of the rich, the dissenting sects being entirely composed of the less wealthy people ; and these, by the bill for a general education, would be qualified to understand their rights, to maintain them, and to exercise with intelligence their parts in self-government ; and all this would be effected, without the violation of a single natural right of any one individual citizen. To these, too, might be added, as a further security, the introduction of the trial by jury, into the Chancery courts, which have already ingulfed, and continue to ingulf, so great a proportion of the jurisdiction over our property." [1]

Mr. Jefferson gave as one reason for declining the French mission in 1776, that he saw " that the laboring oar was really at home." We now understand what he meant by the " laboring oar !"

It remains to be stated what became of the main body of Jefferson's, Wythe's, and Pendleton's Revision of the laws of Virginia. Bills were taken from it and passed from time to time, as the public exigencies demanded ; but, beyond this, little was done until the war was over, and a subsequent breathing time had ensued. The final result is expressively recorded in the Memoir :

" The main body of the work was not entered on by the Legislature until after the general peace, in 1785, when, by the unwearied exertions of Mr. Madison, in opposition to the endless quibbles, chicaneries, perversions, vexations, and delays of lawyers and demi-lawyers, most of the bills were passed by the Legislature, with little alteration."

On the 13th of August, 1777, Mr. Jefferson wrote Dr. Franklin, in France :

" With respect to the State of Virginia, * * the people seemed to have laid aside the monarchical, and taken up the republican government, with as much ease as would have attended their throwing off an old, and putting on a new suit of clothes. Not a single throe has attended this important transformation. A half dozen aristocratical gentlemen, agonizing under the loss of preëminence, have sometimes ventured their sarcasms on our political metamorphosis. They have been thought fitter objects of pity than of punishment. We are, at present, in the complete and quiet exercise of well-organized government, save only that our courts of justice do not open till the fall. I think nothing can bring the security of our continent and its cause into danger, if we can support the credit of our paper * * * * I wish my domestic situation had rendered it possible for me to join you in the very honorable charge confided to you. Residence in a polite Court, society of literati of the first order, a just cause and an approving God, will add length to a life for which all men pray, and none more than," etc.

[1] Memoir.

In Randolph's edition of Mr. Jefferson's Works, this is the first letter given after the last one mentioned to John Randolph, of Nov. 29th, 1775. And after this (to Franklin) there is another chasm of towards two years—until March 27, 1779. In the latter year commences a scattering file of his *official* letters which continue through 1780 and part of 1781. Then there is another entire chasm for about *three years*, after which there are first meagre, but constantly swelling files, until they begin to diminish again towards the close of his life.

In the Congress edition these gaps are no further filled than by the following: a letter to R. H. Lee, July 8, 1776; to John Adams, August 21, 1777; to —— (address lost), June 8, 1778; to David Rittenhouse, July 19, 1778; to John Page, January 22d, 1779; to George Wythe, March 1, 1779. None of these are important.

Mr. Jefferson kept no files of his letters before 1779, when he occupied an official position which rendered the preservation of a part of them a matter of necessity. The major portion found in the files, however, during that official tenure (and now published in his Works), was some years afterwards recovered by him from the persons to whom they had been addressed. He never commenced keeping copies of *private* letters—excepting rarely on some special occasion—until he went to France, where he found copying machines.

The private letters occasionally preserved before that period, do not appear to have been ultimately thought worthy of preservation by him, because he did not place them in his files. He was exceedingly methodical and precise in the disposition of papers, and the following is an illustration of the trait by no means uncommon. A young gentleman once called on him, in his old age, to ask what steps had been taken in a certain law proceeding where Mr. Jefferson had acted for his father nearly half a century before. He made many apologies for the trouble he was causing. Mr. Jefferson immediately informed him that it would be no trouble at all, for if he had the paper which would supply the necessary information, he could put his hand on it in " less than one minute." He stepped to a case, opened the door, run his eye over the letters of the pigeon holes, drew forth a package of ancient papers, glanced at their " files," and in *less than a minute* put the paper into the hands of his astonished visitor.

For all his letters of any importance anterior to 1779, and especially for the four interesting ones given in Randolph's edition of his Works,[1] we are indebted to the care and wishes of others, not his own. The history of the recovery of the last four, is as follows: In March, 1828, a question of importance—turning on the general intention of the Statute of Descents, being before the Court of Appeals of Virginia, one of its judges, Dabney Carr, a grand-nephew of Mr. Jefferson, wrote Mr. N. P. Trist, then at Monticello, a letter (a copy of which is before us), asking him whether any notes or references concerning, or as to the sources from which he drew, had been preserved by Mr. Jefferson, in reference to that statute. Suffice it to say on this point, that Mr. Trist, with the permission of his brother-in-law, Mr. Randolph, sent Judge Carr extracts from the Memoir (not then published), which, the latter replied, were sufficient to dispel the doubts entertained by some of the judges, but which he (Carr) had never entertained. In a memorandum drawn up for us, Mr. Trist continues:

"Among Mr. Jefferson's papers (which, as left by him in his study, were in such perfect order that you could find at once any paper or letter you might be in quest of), I was unable to discover any 'notes or references,' such as Judge C. wished to obtain in regard to Mr. Jefferson's labors as a law-maker. It occurred to me to ascertain what might be the contents of a little trunk, evidently very old, which, on visiting a closet over the alcove containing his bed, I had noticed among the many old things collected there. Ascending once more the steep step-ladder which led to this *omnium gatherum*, I raised the lid of that little trunk, upon which lay a thickness of dust, indicating that it had not turned upon its hinges for a long period. It was filled with papers—law papers almost exclusively. Some related, so far as I can now recollect, to the subject which had occasioned the search; others to cases in which he had been engaged as a legal practitioner.

"The bundles were, of course, all examined by me—the tape around them giving way in the act of untying it. In one I found the epitaph of John Bradshaw; and, in its company, copies of several letters bearing date years before the earliest of those contained among his papers as arranged by himself, which, to the best of my recollection, began in 1779. Among them was one to his old preceptor Dr. Small, two to John Randolph, and one to Dr. Franklin; the three former written in 1775, the last in 1777. Their existence had evidently been forgotten by him, the only way of accounting for their not having been placed with the rest.[2] Delighted at

<hr/>

[1] That is, for the letter to Dr. Small, the two to John Randolph heretofore particularly mentioned, and the one quoted to Dr. Franklin four or five paragraphs back.

[2] It has been seen that our theory is a little different on this subject. And it is certain that Girardin, when writing his History of Virginia, came upon this old cast-aside receptacle of papers, for he *quotes* from two of the letters. This would have called them to mind if they had been forgotten by Mr. Jefferson. Their "noble utterances" were probably deemed by him too habitual and every day expressions of the times, to be matters of any importance or curiosity. Three were originally copied, doubtless, as a

this fortuitous rescue of such noble utterances of the spirit of the Revolution—of which their writer was so preëminently the incarnation—I forthwith made it known to Mr. Jefferson Randolph, and made copies of them, to occupy the place where they now stand, at the head of the selection from his correspondence then preparing for publication. These MSS. were in Mr. Jefferson's hand-writing of that period; the most beautiful, to my taste, I have ever seen." [1]

These facts will be sufficient to answer an inquiry which has been several times made, why Mr. Jefferson's grandson, inheriting all his manuscripts, saw fit to publish the three letters, mentioned by Mr. Trist, anterior to 1779, and no others.

Early in 1779, events occurred, connected with the public service and defence, in which Mr. Jefferson took a particular interest, and acted a part worth remembering. Here commenced his *personal* account current with the enemy, which is said (with what justice we shall see as our narrative advances) before it closed to have left him so bitter a personal foe of Englishmen and England. The four thousand British troops captured at Saratoga had been ordered by Congress to Charlottesville, Virginia. Their march, in the dead of winter, was accompanied with terrible hardships; but they had reached their destination, erected spacious barracks about five miles north of Charlottesville, and, as the spring opened, they had, by the aid of their officers and particularly the German ones, planted extensive gardens and even fields, procured domestic animals, and were in a fair way to make their further sojourn an extremely comfortable one. The officers had rented houses of neighboring proprietors, in many instances had repaired and furnished them at considerable expense, and had generally paid rents for a year. Just at this point, came one of those foolish panics which sometimes unaccountably get rife in the public mind. It was suddenly rumored among the rural population of Albemarle, that a scarcity of food was about to ensue—that the four thousand additional mouths were producing a famine. Governor Henry was applied to, to remove a part of the prisoners to another position, where, it was claimed, supplies would be more accessible and desertion less practicable.

From Governor Henry's known disinclination to refuse a

matter of prudence, because they were *political* letters addressed to citizens of an enemy's country, or to Tories.
[1] For an interesting continuation of this memorandum in regard to the epitaph on Bradshaw, and for the epitaph itself, see APPENDIX, No. 4.

popular demand, and from the energetic and argumentative tone of the communication of Jefferson to him on the subject, to which we are about to call attention, we *infer* that the removal of the prisoners was understood to be determined on. On the 27th of March, Jefferson addressed the Governor a long and almost vehement remonstrance against a measure which he pronounced unnecessary, cruel, and contrary to the public faith. An article in the "Convention of Saratoga" (from which the prisoners were known as "the Convention prisoners," in all the letters and publications of the period) had provided that the officers should not be separated from their men. The prisoners could not possibly be divided without separating a part of them from their general officers. Nor was this a mere technical objection. The general officer is, of course, more deeply responsible to his government for the welfare of his men, and he has superior means both to control and to aid them. The Baron Riedesel, for example, had given two hundred pounds to his German troops, solely to purchase garden seeds. If the general officer is the leader of his troops elsewhere, he is their father when in captivity. We would like to publish the whole of Mr. Jefferson's letter on this occasion, but space does not permit. The following extracts, showing its tone, must suffice:

"Congress, indeed, have admitted of this separation; but are they so far lords of right and wrong as that our consciences may be quiet with their dispensation? Or is the case amended by saying they leave it optional in the Governor and Council to separate the troops or not? At the same time that it exculpates not them, it is drawing the Governor and Council into a participation in the breach of faith. *   *   *   *   As an American, I cannot help feeling a thorough mortification, that our Congress should have permitted an infraction of our public honor; as a citizen of Virginia, I cannot help hoping and confiding, that our supreme Executive, whose acts will be considered as the acts of the Commonwealth, estimate that honor too highly to make its infraction their own act.   *   *   *   *   If the Commonwealth of Virginia cannot furnish these troops with bread, I would ask of the commissariat, which of the thirteen is now become the grain Colony? If we are in danger of famine from the addition of four thousand mouths, what is become of that surplus of bread, the exportation of which used to feed the West Indies and Eastern States, and fill the Colony with hard money? When I urge the sufficiency of this State, however, to subsist these troops, I beg to be understood, as having in contemplation the quantity of provisions necessary for their real use, and not as calculating what is to be lost by the wanton waste, mismanagement, and carelessness of those employed about it. If magazines of beef and pork are suffered to rot by slovenly butchering, or for want of timely provision and sale; if quantities of flour are exposed by the commissaries intrusted with the keeping of it, to pillage and destruction; and if, when laid up in the Continental stores, it is still to be embezzled and sold, the land of Egypt itself would be insufficient for their supply, and their removal would be necessary, not to a more plentiful country, but to more able and honest commissaries.   *   *   *

"Their health is also of importance. I would not endeavor to show that their lives are valuable to us, because it would suppose a possibility, that humanity was kicked out of doors in America, and interest only attended to.   *   *   *

"But is an enemy so execrable, that, though in captivity, his wishes and comforts are to be disregarded and even crossed? I think not. It is for the benefit of mankind to mitigate the horrors of war as much as possible. The practice, therefore, of modern nations, of treating captive enemies with politeness and generosity, is not only delightful in contemplation, but really interesting to all the world, friends, foes and neutrals.   *   *   *   *

"Having thus found the art of rendering captivity itself comfortable, and carried t into execution, at their own great expense and labor, their spirits sustained by the prospect of gratifications rising before their eyes, does not every sentiment of humanity revolt against the proposition of stripping them of all this, and removing them into new situations, where, from the advanced season of the year, no preparations can be made for carrying themselves comfortably through the heats of summer; and when it is known that the necessary advances for the conveniences already provided, have exhausted their funds and left them unable to make the like exertions anew?   *   *   *   *   *   *

"To conclude. The separation of these troops would be a breach of public faith, therefore I suppose it is impossible; if they are removed to another State, it is the fault of the commissaries; if they are removed to any other part of the State, it is the fault of the commissaries; and in both cases, the public interest and public security suffer, the comfortable and plentiful subsistence of our own army is lessened, the health of the troops neglected, their wishes crossed, and their comforts torn from them, the character of whim and caprice, or, what is worse, of cruelty, fixed on us as a nation, and, to crown the whole, our own people disgusted with such a proceeding."

This will probably be regarded as bold and manly, and none the less so that within two or three months a Governor of Virginia was to be elected in the place of Mr. Henry, whose term permitted by the Constitution would then expire—and that Mr. Jefferson was regarded as the most prominent candidate for the place. The effect of the letter on the really kind-hearted Henry, and on the Council, was decisive. Not a further lisp, as we understand it, was heard of removing the prisoners.

Jefferson's course drew forth the gratitude and unbounded plaudits of the British officers. Major General Phillips, represented by the Baroness of Riedesel, in her entertaining letters from America, as an amiable and agreeable man in private life—but certainly characterized by intense pride and insolence in all his communications with "the Rebels"—on this occasion became gracious and " emphatically extolled Mr. Jefferson's delicate proceedings." [1] Major General the Baron de Riedesel " repeatedly and artlessly poured out his thanks, and those of his wife and children," and, says Girardin, " his effusions, which flow from the heart, irresistibly engage our sympathies." Brigadier General Specht, and some inferior officers, the Baron de Geismer, De Unger, and others, wrote most grateful expressions of their thanks. Jefferson's courteous and liberal replies are quoted from by Girardin. He wrote Phillips:

"The great cause which divides our countries is not to be decided by individual animosities. The harmony of private societies cannot weaken national efforts. To contribute by neighborly intercourse and attention to make others happy, is the shortest and surest way of being happy ourselves. As these sentiments seem to have directed your conduct, we should be as unwise as illiberal, were we not to preserve the same temper of mind."

This is the close of a letter to the young and polished De Unger, who, we believe, was but a lieutenant in a German regiment :

"When the course of events shall have removed you to distant scenes of action, where laurels not moistened with the blood of my country may be gathered, I shall urge my sincere prayers for your obtaining every honor and preferment which may gladden the heart of a soldier On the other hand, should your fondness for philosophy resume its merited ascendency, is it impossible to hope that this unexplored country may tempt your residence, by holding out materials wherewith to build a fame, founded on the happiness, and not on the calamities of human nature ? Be this as it may—a philosopher or a soldier—I wish you personally many felicities."

We have before mentioned Jefferson's playing duets on the violin with another young officer, Bibby, aid-de-camp of Frasier, who fell at Saratoga. His house, his library, his philosophical apparatus, his musical instruments, his table, were thrown open to the foreign officers. His beautiful and attractive wife, when her health permitted, contributed a brilliant share to the amusement of these captive strangers.

General Riedesel rented and lived at Collé, the seat of Philip Mazzei, a short distance from the eastern base of Monticello. Himself and the Baroness were frequent visitors of Mr. Jefferson—the latter, especially, who in every domestic strait (not an

So says Girardin, who wrote with all the letters before him ; and he gives the facts which we further narrate in regard to the other officers (pp. 326, 327).

extraordinary thing with an ill-regulated commissariat and four thousand extra mouths), applied to him with the freedom of an old neighbor. Her Amazonian stature and practice of riding like a man, greatly astonished the Virginia natives; but tradition represents her as a cordial, warm-hearted, highly intelligent, and, withal, handsome woman, whose moderate penchant for gossip, and not unfrequent blunders in talking and pronouncing English, only contributed to the amusingness of her lively conversation. Were we a *raconteur*, we could give some specimens of those blunders with which, in after years, Mr. Madison was often " wont to set the table on a roar."

With the warm-hearted Germans, Mr. Jefferson was an unbounded favorite. His disregard of official rank—his putting a lieutenant on equal terms of respect and cordiality with a general where, as in the case of De Unger, his personal claims were equal—was incomprehensible to them. His philosophic tastes, his fine scholarship, his warm and cultivated love of art, his easy hospitality, were the theme of letters to all parts of Germany, and these letters, in some instances, found their way into the gazettes, and Jefferson's name became a known and honored one among the reading men of Europe. A pleasing proof of this, and of the gratitude of his present guests, occurred some years afterwards (1788), during a trip of his from Paris through some of the German States. Stopping at a town where a Hessian regiment was in garrison, he unexpectedly encountered the Baron de Geismer (who had written him once or twice since his return to Europe), and who was now delighted to see him, and at once announced his arrival to his brother officers. Many of these had not been in the American war, but they had heard the regimental traditions of this kind-hearted and munificent stranger; and they now flocked about him; enthusiastically welcomed him to the Father-land; "spoke, as Girardin quaintly observes, "of Virginia with sensibility," and pressed upon him a series of attentions which it would have taken a month to accept.

These are pleasant pictures. But the tapestry, unfortunately, has another side. Very soon after Mr. Jefferson's noble stand against the feelings and prejudices of his neighbors in favor of the Convention Prisoners—his kindly attentions to their officers —we shall find his property consigned not only to plunder,

but to wanton devastation—his " roofs " given " to the flames,"
and if not his " flesh to the eagles," that of his servants to the
more terrible talons of the pestilence—a particular and studied
attempt made to seize his own person—and all this, not by some
fierce partisan out from under the eye of his superiors, but by the
orders, and a good share of it under the immediate eye, of the
British Lieutenant General in America! But, we gladly add,
no *German* hand, it is believed, applied the torch, no *German*
spur urged the hot pursuit !

CHAPTER VII.

1779—1780.

On the first day of June, 1779, Mr. Jefferson was chosen Governor of Virginia. He was the second Republican incumbent of that office, taking the place of Patrick Henry, who, having served three years, was disqualified by the Constitution for a reëlection for the space of the next three years.   Mr. Jefferson's early friend, John Page, was his competitor on this occasion.   He had served at the head of the Privy Council, and in that capacity had acted as Lieutenant Governor.   He was a gentleman of ability, an active patriot, and belonged to a family of great influence in the State.   The competition between him and Jefferson was involuntary on the part of both; and was followed by explanations between them evincing a high sense of delicacy and mutual respect.

Mr. Jefferson was thirty-six years old when he entered upon the chief magistracy of Virginia.   The period, in the opinion of General Washington,[1] was more gloomy in the affairs of the whole country than any by which it had been preceded.   The last campaign had been productive of few important results on either side.   But the French alliance, without yet introducing into the country anything like a counterpoise to the British strength, had infused a fatal security into the public mind. Enlistments were far more difficult to be procured.   Men were not so willing to leave their all, when it was no longer urged by necessity and despair.   The State legislatures reflected the public feeling, and their efforts were proportionably languid.

For the South, a new and gloomier era was opening. Hitherto, the active operations of the war, and consequently its direct and desolating ravages, had been principally confined to the North.   But the unexpected degree of resistance made by the Colonies, or States, as a whole, and the now open adhesion of France, compelled the British Government to change its policy.   That government had become convinced that the prospect of reconquering the entire country was all but desperate. The fertile Southern provinces had fewer natural or artificial defences than the Northern, and they were far more thinly populated.   Georgia contained but about twenty-seven thousand white inhabitants, South Carolina about ninety-three thousand, and North Carolina about one hundred and eighty-three thousand.   The three together did not contain, by nearly fifty thousand,[2] the number of whites in Massachusetts alone, while

[1] See his Correspondence of the year.
[2] U. S. Census of 1850, folio edition, p. xxxi. We have followed its estimate for

their territory was more than double that of New England entire.' The scattered agricultural population of the South could not be easily concentrated for military purposes; the low level country where most of its population then resided, was unfavorable for defence by irregular troops, and was particularly accessible to a foe by means of its rivers; while the remote and isolated position of these States, with respect to most of the stronger parts of the Confederacy, cut them off from the chance of speedy succor except by sea. But notwithstanding the strong fleets sent from France, the British had generally, thus far, maintained an incontestable superiority in the North American waters. They could strike a sudden and serious blow, from New York, at any point south of Cape Charles—in fact, south of Cape May—before an efficient resistance could be matured out of the provincial militia, necessarily intent most of the time on their occupations as husbandmen, and long before reinforcements of regulars could arrive from those northern points, where the presence of the main force of the enemy and the consequent policy of the American commander-in-chief, kept them principally concentrated.

The British plan—adopted some time in 1778, and just entered upon before the close of the campaign that year—was, therefore, to seize and utterly subjugate Georgia and the Carolinas, restoring them by one decisive effort to the Crown, and returning the people to their allegiance by reëstablishing royal governments. This point gained, the career of reconquest north was to be governed by circumstances. The control of the Chesapeake, the natural outlet of such an immense region of country, was a prize worth a determined struggle. In any event, then, Virginia was to become, ultimately, the debatable ground, for the three Southern States were certain not to be given up without a protracted and bloody struggle to save them by their northern sisters. Virginia, particularly, lying next them, would fiercely put forth her last and most desperate efforts for their protection.

The war was to change as much in its character as in its the-

1775, in regard to the three preceding States. In the same, the whole population of Massachusetts is given at 352,000.
' Georgia, South and North Carolina contain, according to the best authority, 131,500 square miles; New England, entire, 58,280, of which Maine (then but little inhabited) comprises 35,000.

atre. Hitherto, some moderation had been observed by the invaders, because they did not regard conciliation as utterly hopeless. Parliament sent three Commissioners (Carlisle, Eden, and Johnstone), to offer terms to the Colonies, in the spring of 1778. They reached Philadelphia, then in the hands of the English, in June. Congress refused to negotiate on any other basis than that of a recognition of American independence and the withdrawal of the British forces. The Commissioners thereupon made an effort—perhaps the real one for which they were sent—to divide and disaffect the Americans, and to seduce over their officers and prominent men, by direct bribes and by munificent promises of influence, titles, and estates in the country when it should be brought back to its allegiance. This attempt produced very little effect, and Congress finally forbade all further communication with these emissaries. The latter, therefore, on the 3d of October, issued a manifesto, which they sent to Congress, the State legislatures, and scattered as widely as possible among the people, containing this remarkable avowal of the future spirit in which the war would be carried on:

"The policy, as well as benevolence of Great Britain, have thus far checked the extremes of war, where they tended to distress a people still considered as our fellow subjects, and to desolate a country shortly to become a source of mutual advantage: but when that country professes the unnatural design, not only of estranging herself from us, but of mortgaging herself to our enemies, *the whole contest is changed;* and the question is, how far Great Britain may, *by every means in her power, destroy or render useless a connection contrived for her ruin,* and for the aggrandizement of France. Under such circumstances, the laws of self-preservation must direct the conduct of Great Britain; and *if the British Colonies are to become an accession to France, will direct her to render that accession of as little avail to her as possible.*"

If these extraordinary declarations were intended for the purpose of intimidation, none the less was it also intended they should be literally and fearfully executed!

Let us now pause a moment to glance at the condition of Virginia, and her preparedness for the part which she would be soon called upon to play. The Chesapeake gave her, practically, as extended a line of sea-board to be defended, as any other State —while a superior naval power could, with a few ships at the mouth of that great estuary, blockade her entire coast, except in the unimportant matter of transit between the ports within the bay. Her numerous navigable rivers gave an enemy easy and rapid access to all her principal towns, and to nearly all her portable or destructible resources beyond those of mere agriculture. Her great artery of population, trade, and wealth, was the James. A forty-gun ship could ascend this as far as Jamestown, and by lightening herself, to Harrison's bar. Vessels of two hundred and fifty tons could proceed to Warwick, and those of one hundred and twenty-five tons to within a mile of Richmond. The State had but four armed vessels, mounting, in all, sixty-two guns, and two or three armed boats, of little consequence, and this flotilla was not manned well enough to make it fit for serious service. It would have required more means than the United States had at their disposal, to put the Virginia waters in a state of efficient defence; and there was not yet a fortification on them, probably, sufficient to beat off, and certainly not to stop one or two frigates.

The militia of the State consisted, nominally, of the able bodied male freemen between sixteen and fifty years old—comprising about fifty thousand able bodied persons, being less than one for each square mile of territory within the limits of the *present* State.[1] These were required by law to provide themselves with the arms used in regular service—but this had been but very imperfectly done before the Revolution; and the serviceable arms which the opening of the Revolution had found in the country, had been to a most serious extent withdrawn to supply the troops sent out of the State. At the present time (1779), the lower portion of the State was nearly disarmed; the middle portion was almost as destitute, except of guns provided to destroy game, and therefore of little value for military service.[2] West of the Blue Ridge, the hardy borderers were better armed, and they bore the deadly rifle.

No part of the militia was thoroughly disciplined—and not a man in a hundred of them had ever seen the face of an armed enemy. It was mostly composed of husbandmen, who owned real estate, and whose presence was all-important at home, in the summer, to plant, cultivate, and secure their crops. Being thinly scattered over an immense extent of country, they could neither be collected suddenly, nor called from home without a

[1] There are 61,352 square miles in Virginia—about 3,000 more than in all New England.
[2] Jefferson, a little later, computed there was *one such* gun only to *four* or *five* militiamen!

vast loss to themselves, and to the store of provisions throughout the United States. There were about two hundred and seventy thousand slaves[1] in the State. These were actuated by no general desire to escape, or join the enemy—and not a few would have borne arms bravely for their native land. But the threats or promises of a present foe, scrupling (as we shall see) at no immediate deception or subsequent cruelty, was sufficient to induce multitudes of this simple people to make, what proved to themselves, an unfortunate change of masters; and they, therefore, required to be watched and removed to places of security, in case of an invasion.

Virginia was strong in a class of resources. She was a nursery of raw soldiers, horses, and provisions. She poured these forth liberally during the war. But from the circumstances already mentioned, she had no defensive strength. A small hostile fleet, favored by the wind, could suddenly ascend any of her navigable rivers, and seize any of her towns almost without the shadow of opposition. Her regulars were fighting out of the State. Her militia could not be kept gathered for protracted periods for the defence of towns. There was not money to pay them—and the loss of their crops would bring on famine. They could not be collected soon enough to oppose a sudden descent of shipping, nor could they, of course, anything like keep up with the movements of shipping. And supposing a few hundred of them could first throw themselves into an unfortified town, what were they against one-half the number of well-armed regulars? Yet an enemy having, like England, the necessary forces and shipping, could always suddenly throw more than man for man upon a given point. The *defensive* strength of Virginia, then, within her own borders, was but a shadow—a name. It was wonderful that this fact was so little understood—so slowly seized upon, by the enemy. But the fatal want of arms in Virginia was probably unknown to the enemy. From the men and supplies she sent out, she wore the appearance of being a great magazine of both. The State which could spare so much to the others, must needs be, it would seem, abundantly supplied at home. They did not understand

---

[1] Jefferson, in his Notes on Virginia (Query VIII.), computes the free inhabitants in 1782 at 296,852, and the slaves at 270,762. We are inclined, from the examination of later data, to think that he placed the estimate of freemen too low, and of slaves too high—but we have not here departed from his authority.

that the lioness was meeting the hunter on the skirts of the wood—making battle for her young as far as possible from her lair, instead of *in* that lair! Whether this was good or bad policy, will be an after question. But whether good or bad, neither Governor Henry, nor Governor Jefferson, nor any other *civil* officer or officers in Virginia, was accountable for it. The responsibility rests solely on the best and greatest soldier of the Revolution. A Virginian himself, he was bound to feel for her as much as the common good would permit. If Virginia suffered for the common good, in the dreary scenes soon to unroll before us, she suffered well and wisely!

We have mentioned that the portions of the extreme Southern States then principally inhabited were not naturally adapted to defence by irregular troops, or by the weaker force. The same remark applies equally to Virginia. The lower country stretches away in broad plains, for immense distances, unbroken by undulations sufficient to prevent the most efficient operation of cavalry. There were unbridged rivers which those acquainted with the fords could sometimes take advantage of to gain on the pursuer—there were, occasionally, difficultly threaded morasses, which might be lurked in—there were bodies of forest dense enough to impede the free and rapid action of armies. But these were temporary and limited conveniences to fugitives. The assailant, if master of the streams, received, on the whole, far more benefit than injury from them even in pursuit. And a runaway slave or a tory soldier was generally found to point out the ford, or furnish the key to the morass. For many days' march there would scarcely be found a hill steep enough to break a charge of cavalry—to check or turn aside the steady onward roll of the wave of war. We have no intimate local knowledge of Eastern Virginia, but we doubt if there is in the whole tide-water region, a single strong natural fastness—a single dark defile, where the determined few could give bloody welcome to the many—where hunted men could safely lurk to pounce like birds of prey on exposed detachments, and carry terror and conflagration into the surprised midnight camp.

In a word, regarded in every point of view, never was there a state or country where the aggregate inhabitants were so numerous—where they stood physically and intellectually on the same footing with the invader, and employed the same arms and systems of war—which lay more completely at the mercy of a comparative handful of well-disciplined and well-provided assailants.

When Governor Jefferson took the chair of State, the British scheme for conquering the three Southern States had been entered upon and partly carried out. Savannah was taken, near the close of December, 1778, by an overwhelming force. Sunbury soon after surrendered; and thus Georgia, wholly incapable of resistance, had fallen, at a blow, at the foot of the invader. South Carolina had been also entered, and Charleston severely menaced; but the hot weather had caused a lull in operations. In the last month of Governor Henry's term, a detachment of two thousand men from Sir Henry Clinton's forces at New York, commanded by General Matthew, had made a short inroad into Virginia, captured Fort Nelson, burnt Suffolk, destroyed an immense amount of public and private property, committed every species of atrocity on their march, and then retired, without encountering beyond a shadow of opposition—without the loss, so far as appears, of a man.[1]

Colonel (afterwards General) Lawson wrote Governor Henry, May 13th:

"The cruel and horrid depredations and rapine committed on the unfortunate and defenceless inhabitants who have fallen within their reach, exceed almost anything yet heard of within the circle of their tragic display of savage barbarity—household furniture, stock of all kind, houses, and in short almost every species of perishable property are effectually destroyed, with unrelenting fury, by those devils incarnate: *murder, rapine, rape, violence,* fill up the dark catalogue of their detestable transactions. * * * * I met numbers of the unfortunate and distressed inhabitants flying from the rapid approach of the enemy, with such circumstances of distress as language cannot paint."

While the preceding events were taking place on the seaboard, Virginia was also very seriously menaced from the west. Detroit was the headquarters of some active British partisans, who, descending easily, by means of the Maumee and Wabash rivers, into the heart of the Indian territories, constantly stirred up the fierce and restless tribes on the Ohio and Mississippi to attack the frontier settlements of the United States. The British military commanders at Detroit provided the

[1] See Girardin, pp. 333–338.

Indians with arms, and usually sent with them, on their
important expeditions, enough British or Tory soldiers to give
system and breadth to their depredations—to impart permanency and thorough effect to them, without mitigating any of
their horrors. They had erected a fort at Kaskaskias, on the
river of that name, near its junction with the Mississippi,
planted some other posts further north, and were now making a
formidable head for further operations. What those operations
would be, unless vigorously arrested, the scenes at Wyoming,
Wilkesbarre, and Cherry Valley, in the preceding campaign,
fearfully attested. In truth, the whole western frontier, north
of Virginia, was now a region of utter desolation—its little
towns of white settlers and pioneer farms depopulated—every
evidence of the hand of civilization reduced to ashes or black-
ened ruins—its inhabitants slain, carried into a barbarous captivity, or driven, stripped of all their property, within the
denser settlements. The next wave of this savage inundation
was to break over Western Virginia—the present State of Kentucky—"the dark and bloody ground"—as it became appropriately called.

Henry Hamilton was military Governor of Detroit, and he
was well fitted, by his activity and his strong relentlessness of
temper, for the prime mover in an Indian border war. Mr.
Tucker, in his Life of Jefferson, makes a liberal effort to rescue
the memory of this man from the imputations which rest on it.
When a boy, he had personally known Hamilton, and shared
his hospitality; and he avers that he possessed all the qualities
of a gentleman, and that "there was nothing to show that he
wanted humanity." We doubt not these facts, nor the sincerity
of the beliefs expressed by the writer. But the testimony is
at best but negative. It is said "the Prince of Darkness is a
gentleman!" Not the voice of direct tradition alone fixes
ineffaceable stains on Hamilton's name. His own manifestoes
and proclamations offering a reward for scalps and none for
prisoners, were afterwards made to confront him. It was afterwards made to appear to the entire satisfaction of the Virginia
Council of State—a body made up of as good lawyers and
elevated men as there were in that State—that in the prison of
the then little village of Detroit, under the direct command and
eye of Hamilton, cruelties had been practised on American

prisoners which were only outdone by those of the Indians themselves. One American prisoner had been thrown, in the depth of a northern winter, loaded with irons, into a dungeon, and been denied fire or bedding. To add mental to bodily torture, he had it constantly held out to him that he was, sooner or later, to be given up to the Indians, to be put to death by torture. When brought so low by his sufferings that he appeared about to die, he was taken out and better cared for; but before he recovered ability *to walk*, he was returned to his dungeon and irons. Having lain there from January to June, with the short reprieve already mentioned, and being brought a second time to death's door, he was again taken out. It was in proof that war parties of the Indians who had brought prisoners to the neighborhood of the fort, finding no reward offered for captives, there put them to death, and then carried in their reeking scalps to the Governor, "who welcomed their return and success by a discharge of cannon!" It was in proof that, where a prisoner already bound to the stake, and "the fire already kindled," was dexterously withdrawn and secreted, a large reward was offered for his recovery, and that a servant being tempted by this to betray the place of his concealment, Philip Dejean, a justice of the peace, of Detroit, was sent with a party of soldiers to take him; that they threw him into prison, where the agonized man "soon expired, under the perpetual assurances of Dejean that he was to be again restored into the hands of the savages." His deliverer from the savages, when enlarged, "was bitterly reprimanded by Governor Hamilton." The Virginia Council of State at the same time declared:

"Their prisoners with us have, on the other hand, been treated with humanity and moderation; they have been fed, on all occasions, with wholesome and plentiful food, suffered to go at large within extensive tracts of country, treated with liberal hospitality, permitted to live in the families of our citizens, to labor for themselves, to acquire and enjoy profits, and finally to participate of the principal benefits of society, privileged from all burdens."

All the preceding facts were officially found by as high and dignified a tribunal as ever sat in Virginia[1]—and on testimony

[1] The decision of the Council of State, formally attested by their Clerk, will be found in Jefferson's Works. (See Appendix, Note A, vol. i. p. 451, of Randolph's edition. We have not looked it up in the Congress edition.)

collected by as brave and as honorable a man as ever belonged to that State.[1] And we are not aware that any attempt has been made to impeach its accuracy by counter. *proof.* Mere negative testimony, in such a case, is wholly out of the question. It is very probable that the English military officers, within whose particular jurisdiction lay the Sugar House, and the Jersey Prison Ship, and the vaults of the dead crammed with prisoners at Charleston, were "gentlemen." Tarleton was an accomplished gentleman in his address, and so was the far more fell Marquis of Cornwallis. Had any one met these "gentlemen" at their (usually) patrician homes, before the war, it is by no means unlikely he would have been delighted with their accomplishments, their liberality, etc.; and it is not probable that he would have heard among their associates, or their dependents, anything "to show that they wanted humanity."

Hamilton was preparing for a great move against Virginia in the spring of 1779. Colonel George Rogers Clarke—well termed by Randolph, of Roanoke, the Hannibal of the West—had, in the autumn of 1778, advanced with two or three hundred Virginia borderers into the wilderness, to prevent the tragedies of Wyoming and Cherry Valley being reënacted in Virginia before the close of that year. He had descended the Monongahela and Ohio to the great falls of the latter river, and then struck across the country for Kaskaskias. His troops subsisted mostly on ground-nuts until the wilderness was traversed. They entered and surprised Kaskaskias. The fiery partisan did not permit his famishing troops to stop to *eat* till the other posts were also surprised! He was now in a position to bridle the neighboring savages, by striking them in detail, and breaking up their combinations before they were matured. To dislodge him, therefore, was all-important to the enemy. Hamilton resolved on this, and then to ascend the Ohio, and by the aid of an.Indian army to sweep the whole country as far east as Fort Pitt—now Pittsburg. This would make the Alleghanies the western limits of the possessions of the United States—and *all* the territory drained by the Mississippi and its affluents would be reconquered. To be ready for prompt action in the spring, Hamilton descended the Wabash to St. Vincenne (now Vincennes)—repaired and fortified its dismantled fort—commenced

[1] Colonel George Rogers Clarke.

his arrangements with the savages—and made his dispositions to attack Kaskaskias as soon as the weather would permit.

Fortunately, he was matched against a far better and more decisive soldier than himself. Learning from a Spanish trader who arrived at Kaskaskias, in the dead of winter, that Hamilton, in his fancied security, had weakened himself by dispatching his Indian allies to prevent reinforcements from reaching Clarke, by the Ohio, and also to commence the work of destruction on the frontiers, the American commander immediately determined to strike the first blow. "He was sensible the resolution was as desperate as his situation, but he saw no other probability of securing the country." [1] Sending a small galley, mounting two four-pounders and four swivels, to force her passage up the Wabash, to await further orders a few miles below St. Vincenne, he commenced his own march across the country for that place, on the 7th of February, at the head of one hundred and thirty men. A portion of this force were volunteers—the "young men of the country." The rest, young and old, turned out to guard their towns, which might be fallen upon in Clarke's absence.

It required no less than sixteen days for the little band to traverse the comparatively narrow space between them and the foe—now the southern apex of the conically-shaped territory of the State of Illinois—and they suffered incredible hardships in their march. Clarke said in his dispatches:

"Although so small a body, it took me sixteen days on the route. The inclemency of the season, high waters, etc., seemed to threaten the loss of the expedition. When within three leagues of the enemy, in a direct line, it took us five days to cross the drowned lands of the Wabash River, having to wade often, upwards of two leagues, to our breast in water. Had not the weather been warm, we must have perished. But on the evening of the 23d, we got on dry land, in sight of the enemy; and at seven o'clock made the attack, before they knew anything of us."

The town being well affected towards the United States, "immediately surrendered with joy, and assisted in the siege." The fort contained eighty British soldiers, three cannon, and some mounted swivels. Clarke had no "expectation of gaining it until the arrival of his artillery." The firing continued eighteen

---

[1] Clarke's dispatch to the Governor of Virginia. This singularly modest and interesting document will be found in Jefferson's Works. Randolph's edition, vol. i. p. 451.

hours. When the moon set, the second night, he threw up an entrenchment within rifle-shot of their strongest battery, and "in fifteen minutes" (he does not specify—we suppose when it became light enough to see in the morning) the sheeted volleys of the border rifle had silenced two of the cannon. It had now become impossible for the cannoniers to serve their guns, for men accustomed to hit the eye of the panther crouching to spring, found no difficulty in marking an exposed hand's-breadth of a man's person through the port-holes. Seven were thus instantly disabled; and it was found in vain to continue the struggle. Hamilton and his men surrendered as prisoners of war. What further happened let Clarke relate:

"In the height of this action, an Indian party that had been to war, and taken two prisoners, came in, not knowing of us. Hearing of them, I dispatched a party to give them battle in the commons, and got nine of them with the two prisoners, who proved to be Frenchmen. Hearing of a convoy of goods from Detroit, I sent a party of sixty men, in armed boats well mounted with swivels, to meet them, before they could receive any intelligence. They met the convoy forty leagues up the river, and made a prize of the whole, taking forty prisoners and about ten thousand pounds worth of goods and provisions; also the mail from Canada to Governor Hamilton, containing, however, no news of importance. But what crowned the general joy, was the arrival of William Morris, my express to you, with your letters, which gave general satisfaction. The soldiery, being made sensible of the gratitude of their country for their services, were so much elated that they would have attempted the reduction of Detroit, had I ordered them."

Clarke "got only one man wounded! Not being able to lose many, he made them secure themselves well."

John Randolph afterwards said: "The march of that great man (Clarke) and his brave companions in arms, across the drowned lands of the Wabash, does not shrink from a comparison with the passage of the Thrasymene marsh."[1] The mere battle of St. Vincenne dwindles to the proportion of a mote, compared with that of Thrasymenus. But it was the turning point which probably settled the possession (the *uti possidetis*) at the Peace of Paris, of a territory vastly larger than that—all Italy—which was the stake between the Carthaginian and the Roman. The Carthaginian won the battle, but lost the stake. Clarke won both. If Hannibal was four days and four nights in the Clusian marsh, in summer, the Virginians were five days

[1] See his letter to a New England Senator, etc., Dec. 15, 1814.

in the wintry torrents of the Wabash![1] Randolph's comparison of the men was not, therefore, so very absurd !

The mention of the exploits of this favorite border hero, has seduced us into a somewhat disproportioned prolixity; but we cannot promise not to repeat the offence where Clarke's name occurs. There is a romance in his deeds more captivating than that of fiction.

Hamilton's men were, of necessity, mostly released on parole; but himself, his tool Dejean, who was in the fort, and a Captain Lamothe, who was the next most prominent instrument in the atrocities committed on Americans—who had commanded volunteer scalping parties, which had spared neither age nor sex—were sent prisoners to Williamsburg, where they arrived in June, soon after Mr. Jefferson's accession to the Chief Magistracy. The "murders, rapines, rapes, and violence" of General Matthew's invasion, the preceding month, had not tended to soften public feeling on the subject of these men's enormities; and the Governor, by the unanimous advice of his Council, after a full examination of the facts, and after the finding heretofore mentioned, ordered all three to be put in irons, confined in the dungeon of the public jail, debarred from writing, and excluded from conversation, except with their keeper. There was nothing secret, however, about the affair, the Executive order being published in the Virginia Gazette.

General Phillips (of the Convention prisoners) on seeing this order, addressed Governor Jefferson a long letter, claiming that the charges against Hamilton were not sufficiently proved,[2] doubting the right of the *State* authorities to enter upon measures of retaliation, and assuming that having been admitted to a capitulation, the prisoners were entitled to all the rights and privileges of prisoners of war. He entreated the Governor, therefore, to review his decision. And remembering Mr. Jefferson's prompt and efficient interposition for himself and his companions, in March, "the proudest man of the proudest country on earth " (as Mr. Jefferson once termed him), continued thus:

[1] Clarke says the weather was "warm." We are again reminded of Gifford's anecdote. Who knows what *Clarke* would have called *warm* weather in February? The *water* up to their armpits could not have been warm at that time of the year! And if we were instituting a comparison between the personal sufferings of the commanders, we would not omit to state that Hannibal kept *himself* out of the water by riding his *last* elephant!

[2] General Phillips had not, we suppose, a line of the *testimony* before him !

"From my residence in Virginia, I have conceived the most favorable idea of the gentlemen of the country; and from my personal acquaintance with you, sir, I am led to imagine it must have been very dissonant to the feelings of your mind to inflict such a weight of misery and stigma of disgrace upon the unfortunate gentleman in question."

The last question raised by General Phillips was a very grave one. Governor Jefferson, therefore, immediately forwarded a copy of the capitulation to General Washington, asking his opinion. He said: "There is no other person whose decision will so authoritatively decide this doubt in the public mind, and none with which I am disposed so implicitly to comply."

The General answered, that when he first received an account of the proceedings, he had no doubt of their propriety, "as being founded in principles of a just retaliation;" but that on consulting with some of his officers, it seemed to be their opinion that the capitulation, "even in the manner in which it was made," should protect Hamilton from any uncommon severity. Whether it was expedient to continue his confinement, "from motives of policy, or to satisfy our people," the General professed himself unable to determine; but if it *was done*, he thought a particular account of Hamilton's conduct ought to be published to the world. He thought he might "unquestionably, without any breach of public faith, or the least shadow of imputation, be confined to a room," and he added: "I should not hesitate to withhold from him a thousand privileges I might allow to common prisoners."[1]

This letter seems to show that General Washington had no doubts as to the prisoner's guilt, that he was disposed to make Hamilton's rigorous confinement a question of policy, and not one turning on the effect of a capitulation, and finally, that he indirectly advised a course which did not admit Hamilton to the usual privileges of a prisoner of war. In effect, then, he settled the principle in conformity with the action of the Virginia Executive.

This answer reaching the Council in the Governor's absence, they ordered the irons to be removed from the prisoners; and, on the Governor's return, it was further determined to send the prisoners to Hanover Court House, and allow them there to

---

[1] See Sparks's Washington, vol. vi. p. 315.

remain at large, within certain reasonable limits, taking their parole in the usual manner."[1] Hamilton and his associates refused to subscribe the portion of the parole requiring them to utter nothing to the prejudice of the United States—and they were remanded to their confinement, but not again placed in irons. Dejean and Lamothe soon yielded, and were enlarged. Hamilton, "aspiring to the fame of a martyr," held out until advised by Phillips (now exchanged and in New York) "that his sufferings would be perfectly gratuitous."[2]

The British commanders highly resented these proceedings, and blustered in proportion. Their Commissary of Prisoners declared no more Virginians would be exchanged until the affair was satisfactorily adjusted. As if in retaliation of Hamilton's treatment, Capt. Willing, an American officer, was placed in close confinement in irons; but the British commanders, not quite liking to make a direct issue on Hamilton's conduct, accused Willing of cruelties towards British subjects at Natchez. This was not known to the Virginia Executive until after the determination to parole Hamilton and his associates; and as the information of Captain Willing's confinement and release came to them together, their former action was not revoked. But immediate measures were taken to prove to the enemy that their menaces were scorned—and that henceforth, in Virginia, the outrages which were perpetrated or sanctioned by British officers on Americans, would be fully retaliated. A prison-ship was at once prepared; a cartel about to proceed to New York was stopped; a Virginia officer on parole at Williamsburg, who expressed his fears that his parole would be revoked, was exhorted to face like a man menaces likely to end in empty words. Yet the Governor sternly added:

"Their officers and soldiers in our hands are pledges for your safety; we are determined to use them as such. Iron will be retaliated by iron, but a great multiplication on distinguished objects; prison-ships by prison-ships, and like for like in general."[3]

Jefferson was now thoroughly roused. He wrote General Washington, October 8th:

"I am afraid I shall hereafter, perhaps, be obliged to give your Excellency

---

[1] Council Minutes. [2] Girardin, p. 357.
[3] Jefferson to Colonel Matthews, October, 1779.

some trouble in aiding me to obtain information of the future usage of our prisoners. I shall give immediate orders for having in readiness, every engine which the enemy have contrived for the destruction of our unhappy citizens, captivated by them. The presentiment of these operations is shocking beyond expression. I pray Heaven to avert them; but nothing in this world will do it, but a proper conduct in the enemy. In every event, I shall resign myself to the hard necessity under which I shall act."

Here the contest appears to have dropped. The British commanders did not receive a shadow of concession from the Virginia Executive, but they did not, according to promise, think it expedient to make the least discrimination, in any respect, against present or future Virginia prisoners.

It would be a piece of assumption to undertake to decide that the leaders of our Revolutionary armies, with all the facts before them, judged erroneously in resorting so slowly and unequally to the terrible code of retaliation. It seemed to be feared that with a foe usually superior in the field, and in the heart of our country, it would not do to incur so frightful a risk. But in our second war with Great Britain, under precisely analogous circumstances, and when we had twice or three times as many prisoners in the hands of the enemy, as they had in ours, on a memorable occasion,[1] the Executive of the United States unflinchingly resolved to carry out retaliation to the letter—though it appeared at the time that it must lead to such an execution of prisoners, as was never before heard of in civilized war—nay, practically, to giving no quarter in future on either side. In that case, the aggressor was glad to retreat, with ill-disguised humiliation, from his attitude. We are apt to think that when the weaker power makes up its mind to fight for its rights, it is the path of true prudence as well as honor, to fight for *all* of them, and throw everything into the scale! Mankind have learned that despair is a dangerous antagonist! The wise man does not willingly throw himself upon the feeblest animal that turns desperately at bay, resolved to sell its life dearly!

Again, we say, far be it from us to reproach the wise and gallant men of the Revolution for not resorting to this dread extremity; but we cannot but believe, had they done so—had iron been retaliated with iron—prison-ship with prison-ship—

---

[1] When the British Government threatened to hang for high treason twenty-three Irishmen captured in the American army at Queenstown.

crammed charnel-vault with crammed charnel-vault—rape, murder of non-combatants, arson, and the like, with a military execution for every offence—that though the horrors of an unnatural contest might have been for a little while increased, they would have been sooner ended; that the aggregate of woe would have been lessened; and that half of what did occur would have fallen on the heads of the aggressors. And then the American soldier would have marched against the foe feeling that he had a guaranty against any but the necessary contingencies of war, in the fact that his country held "pledges for his safety" against others, and would "use them as such;" and with the sweeter solace that the vengeance of his country hung like a guarding thunderbolt over his home.

We shall not attempt a history of the disgraceful factions in Congress, and some other circles, in 1779—the machinations against Washington—the base proposals to patch up a separate peace with England, leaving France to shift for herself—the effort to defeat the treaties of alliance and commerce with the latter power—the spread of rumors in New England that France would ultimately sacrifice its fisheries for concessions to herself elsewhere, and in the southern States, that she would certainly enforce all the claims of the Spanish Bourbons on the Mississippi—and many other equally unprincipled suggestions—a portion of which emanated in personal ambition, another portion in local interest, and another portion still in British emissaries, and in that concealed disaffection which had been roused into greater virulence by its ancient prejudice against France, and by the prospect that the American and French arms combined would probably ultimately triumph in the struggle.

On the second day of Mr. Jefferson's administration, the legislature which elected him to office formally ratified the French treaties, declaring them "binding on the commonwealth" of Virginia. This separate and unconditional action, showing that in no event could a separate peace be patched up with England without at once dividing the Union, was censured very warmly as arrogant and anti-federal by those whose hopes or prospects it suddenly and effectually blasted!

Spain declared war against England in June. Her previous offer of mediation between that power and her opponents, had, in the United States, led to a general expectation of speedy peace. That was one of the principal proximate causes of those languid preparations to continue the war, already mentioned, which so discouraged General Washington, and which exercised so disastrous an influence throughout the campaign of 1779.

Before hearing of the Spanish declaration of war (though really after it was declared) Governor Jefferson, sharing in the general opinion that peace was near at hand, felt it incumbent on him to take a formal possession of that vast territory extending westward from the south line of Virginia to the Mississippi, and northward to the great lakes—claimed to belong to the State originally by charter, and now by the additional title of conquest.[1] The object was to secure it to Virginia and to the Union in the approaching treaty of peace—the impression then being universal that the principle of *uti possidetis* (that each retain the possessions they had acquired, or were in actual possession of) would prevail in the formation of that treaty. Persons were therefore dispatched, under a military escort, to ascertain by celestial observations where a continuation of the southern boundary line of Virginia (latitude 36° 30′) would intersect the Mississippi; to erect a fort near that point; to measure the distance from the intersection to the mouth of the Ohio; and to extend a chain of forts from thence northward towards the great lakes. Colonel George Rogers Clarke was intrusted with the latter duty. All these measures were performed; and, as foreseen from the outset, the most important of them—the military occupation—proved a measure as well adapted to a continuance of the war as for an advantageous peace.

The establishment of Fort Jefferson in the southwest angle of the claimed territory (now Kentucky) gave serious offence to the friendly tribe of Chickasaws, who, inhabiting the northern portions of the present States of Mississippi, and Alabama, and Western Tennessee, claimed the regions lying on the lower waters of the Ohio, the Tennessee, and the Cumberland Rivers (in other words, Western Kentucky), as their hunting grounds. Colonel Clarke, as dashing a diplomatist as soldier, so far

[1] "That country was ours," said John Randolph, "by a double title, by charter and by conquest."

changed their views on the subject, that they subsequently advanced to the relief of the fort when it was pressed by hostile northern tribes. He had more difficulty, however, with the fierce clans who resided on the Missouri, the Illinois, the Des Moines, and the Upper Mississippi. But he played them off with consummate dexterity against each other, and none of them were very anxious for a direct rupture with the terrible soldier whose name was now pronounced with awe in the wigwams of the Iroquois, on the upper waters of the St. Lawrence—and in those of the Algonquins, on the western shores of Lake Superior.

A striking instance of Clarke's ascendency over the minds of the Indians, and of the characteristics which gave him that ascendency, is recorded in the "Notes of an Old Officer," an eye-witness of what he describes:

"The Indians came in to the treaty, at Fort Washington, in the most friendly manner, except the Shawahanees, the most conceited and warlike of the Aborigines, the first in at a battle, the last at a treaty. Three hundred of their finest warriors, set off in all their paint and feathers, filed into the council-house. Their number and demeanor, so unusual at an occasion of this sort, was altogether unexpected and suspicious. The United States stockade mustered seventy men. In the centre of the hall, at a little table, sat the Commissary General Clarke, the indefatigable scourge of these very marauders, General Richard Butler and Mr. Parsons. There was also present a Captain Denny, who, I believe, is still alive, and can attest this story. On the part of the Indians an old council-sachem and war-chief took the lead. The latter, a tall, raw-boned fellow, with an impudent and villainous look, made a boisterous and threatening speech, which operated effectually on the passions of the Indians, who set up a prodigious whoop at every pause. He concluded by presenting a black and white wampum, to signify they were prepared for either event, peace or war. Clarke exhibited the same unaltered and careless countenance he had shown during the whole scene, his head leaning on his left hand, and his elbow resting on the table. He raised his little cane, and pushed the sacred wampum off the table with very little ceremony. Every Indian, at the same time, started from his seat with one of those sudden, simultaneous, and peculiarly savage sounds, which startle and disconcert the stoutest heart, and can neither be described nor forgotten. At this juncture Clarke rose. The scrutinizing eye cowered at his glance. He stamped his foot on the prostrate and insulted symbol, and ordered them to leave the hall. They did so, apparently involuntarily. They were heard all that night debating in the bushes near the fort. The raw-boned chief was for war, the old sachem for peace. The latter prevailed, and the next morning they came back and sued for peace."

The representatives of the other States in Congress did not view with favor these extensive territorial claims of Virginia. They urged some very sensible reasons against the pretensions of that State, and some excessively absurd ones. Among the latter was the one that the sovereignty and all appertaining rights of the Crown had descended—been transferred by the Revolution—to Congress; a doctrine more repugnant to the Articles of Confederation than even to the present Constitution. And Congress showed some disposition to legislate in regard to the claims of Companies (the Vandalia and Indiana Companies) which had acquired such title as they had—Indian purchases—in express contravention of the laws of Virginia.

Virginia had already made propositions which she regarded as liberal, in offering to unite with the States having unappropriated lands, in furnishing, without compensation, the Continental soldiers of those States which had not such lands, as much as she gave to her own, if Congress saw fit to make that standard general—and to leave it to Congress to decide the quota of lands to be thus furnished by the contributing States. But fortunately for the future welfare of the Republic, she firmly met, at the threshold, the absurd pretence, or tendency to a pretence of sovereignty in Congress, and planted herself firmly on the doctrine of a pure State sovereignty, except so far as the States had expressly conferred that sovereignty on the Government of the Confederation. Virginia, and indeed various other States, never for a moment, in their history, took any other ground than this. The inhabitants of the United States have often acted as one *people*, as in the Declaration of Independence—and may they often do so again! But they never did act as one *nation*, in the political sense of the term—nor was there any approach to such action in their earlier history. The Declaration of Independence itself clearly preserves the distinction. It declared the thirteen united Colonies not a free and independent nation or State, but "thirteen free and independent States," clothed with every power of sovereignty. And the Articles of Confederation which post-dated this act, equally recognized the doctrine of State Sovereignty, except so far as it was voluntarily relinquished by the terms of that instrument. And nobody claimed, then, that any Sovereign State was bound by those articles (though it should be but a minority of one State in thirteen), until it had itself expressly adopted them.

The Virginia Legislature, in its fall session of 1779, in a firmly but temperately worded paper, protested against the

right of Congress to assume any jurisdiction, or right of adjudication, on the claims of the Vandalia and Indiana Companies.[1]

Besides the events already narrated, the participation of
Virginia in the warlike campaign of 1779, was confined to furnishing her quotas of different kinds to the Continental army,
and in sending her militia to succor the invaded Southern provinces. The war no further came within her own immediate
borders.

We have seen the British scheme of subjugating the three
Southern States arrested temporarily by the hot weather. The
arrival of Count d'Estaing on the Southern coast with a powerful French fleet, produced a further diversion. Clinton, the
British Commander-in-chief, believing New York threatened,
cautiously drew himself within his lines there, leaving a full
opportunity to the combined French and Americans to strike a
blow for the recovery of Georgia, and to cut off the British
army in Savannah. The latter place, accordingly, was invested
in September by three thousand French and one thousand
Americans, the latter under General Lincoln. The siege was
pushed with vigor for three weeks; but the danger of the
French West India possessions, and also the insecurity of the
fleet in the autumnal months on a coast so exposed, rendered
D'Estaing impatient of the delay. An assault took place on
the 9th of October, gallantly led by the French admiral and
American general; and the allied standards were planted upon
the parapet. But a part of the army mistook its way in a fog,
and a desperate sally—in attempting to stem which Pulaski fell
mortally wounded—drove back the shattered columns, and the
day was lost. Count d'Estaing and several of his principal
officers were wounded. Scarcely had the French troops reëm-

[1] It said:
"When Virginia acceded to the Articles of Confederation, her rights of sovereignty
and jurisdiction within her own territory, were reserved and secured to her, and cannot
now be infringed or altered without her consent. * * * *
But although the General Assembly of Virginia would make great sacrifices to the common interest of America (as they have already done on the subject of representation),
and will be ready to listen to any just and reasonable propositions for removing the
ostensible causes of delay to the complete ratification of the Confederation, they find themselves impelled by the duties which they owe to their constituents, to their posterity, to
their country, and to the United States in general, to remonstrate and protest, and they
do hereby, in the name and on behalf of the Commonwealth of Virginia, expressly
protest against any jurisdiction or right of adjudication in Congress upon the petitions
of the Vandalia and Indiana Companies, or on any other matter or thing, subversive of
the internal policy, civil government, or sovereignty of this or any of the United American States, or unwarranted by the Articles of the Confederation."

barked, before they were, as feared, scattered by a tempest, and thus the campaign was closed.

The leader of the British sally was Lieutenant-Colonel Webster—one of the best and most determined soldiers that ever drew a sword—to be the terrible, but, so far as we know, honorable, scourge of the South, until he met a soldier's death. Indeed, a close student in the campaigns of the South cannot but be struck with the remarkable ability of several of that cluster of officers who were hands and feet, and, we might add, staff and sword, to the British Lieutenant-General.[1] We will not say that they overmatched their commander, for the cold, stern, and, as he ultimately proved himself, ruthless Cornwallis, was every inch a soldier. But we can pick out at least three British Lieutenant-Colonels, in the Southern service (the nominal colonels of their regiments being usually absentee lords), either of whom, in Sir Henry Clinton's position, would have made the war doubly dangerous to America. And foremost among these, to our eye, stands Webster.

Clinton, relieved of his fears for New York, or, for a period, of the French forces anywhere, resolved to lose no time in prosecuting the suspended Southern scheme of his government. He embarked with a strong force for Georgia, near the close of December, but his fleet being dispersed and injured in a storm, was some time in collecting at its destination, Tybee. He reëmbarked for South Carolina, February 11th, and landed not long afterwards, without opposition, on John's Island. From thence he slowly and circumspectly approached Charleston. Lincoln, who commanded there, was unwilling to risk the capture of his force of regulars, called the "Southern Army," as it was the only considerable body of Continental troops in the Southern States, cooped up by greatly superior numbers in a place so indefensible. But the entreaties of the inhabitants, and the promises of the Legislature, overcame his better judgment. Clinton, already strong enough for an attack, soon received large reinforcements. Webster and Lieutenant-Colonel Tarleton cut off or dispersed the American reserves and militia approaching the town. Lincoln having exhausted every effort, and having lost nearly all his defences, capitulated on the 12th of May,

[1] Webster, Simcoe, Cambell, Tarleton, etc.

rather than withstand the final assault. The surrender included about two thousand regulars, and a considerable body of militia,[1] by far the severest disaster, thus far, of the war.

Virginia suffered severely in this unfortunate event. About half the captured regulars belonged to her Continental line. Her Colonel Parker and Captain Peyton had the good fortune to fall on the ramparts. General Woodford perished in that miserable captivity to which the prisoners were subjected. Never were the terms of a capitulation so shamefully violated. Eight hundred of the prisoners died within a year! He who is solicitous for the horrible details—he who has found his sentimentality painfully disturbed by the placing of irons on two or three prisoner-torturers and scalp-takers, will do well to consult the pages of the historian Ramsay.[2]

One of the parties surprised and routed by Tarleton (at Monk's Corner, April 14th), in attempting to succor the town, comprised the remains of Baylor's Virginia cavalry regiment, under Lieutenant-Colonel Washington. The blow, therefore, which swept the last vestige of a regular army from the South, fell far more heavily on Virginia, so far as the loss of men was concerned, than on the State whose capital passed thereby into the hands of the enemy.

Sir Henry Clinton lost no time in improving this decisive advantage. He immediately put three columns in motion, two of which were to sweep the interior of Georgia and South Carolina, to make their subjugation utter, and the third was to advance on North Carolina. The last, soon swelled to five thousand men, was commanded by Lord Cornwallis. He advanced on Camden, and learning that Colonel Buford was retreating with about four hundred Virginia regulars towards Salisbury, he dispatched Tarleton after him. The latter, pushing forward a hundred miles in two days, came upon his game at the Waxhaws; and if Judge Marshall's authority (always candid and liberal towards the English) can be relied on, under circumstances of unauthorized craft, little better than the violation of the whole spirit of a truce,[3] he fell upon an unprepared oppo-

---

[1] Clinton returned his prisoners at 5,618. But this, according to Judge Marshall, included the adult male inhabitants of the town, many of whom had not borne arms.
[2] History of South Carolina.
[3] Namely, putting things carefully in order for instant attack while the flags were passing, and on *the second* the truce had expired, charging like a thunderbolt on his wholly

nent, and *gave no quarter.* Three-fourths of Buford's command were believed to have been put to the sword.

We shall have often to record the exploits of this remarkable commander, and may pause a moment to speak of him and his terrible "legion"—which almost every American has heard his Revolutionary ancestors describe with as lively horror and detestation as if they had been a legion of fiends commanded by the arch-fiend in person. We have said that Cornwallis had subordinates who were foot, and hand, and staff, and sword to him. Tarleton was his hunting leopard, glossy, beautifully mottled, but swift and fell—when roused by resistance, ferocious. Even this does not give an adequate idea of the velocity of his movements. He was the falcon, which, when unhooded and cast off, darts with arrowy swiftness on its prey. Few were the commanders opposed to him whom he did not at one time or another *surprise*—and among them were Colonel Washington, Sumpter,¹ and some others—the very men more accustomed than all others in the American army to study and practise this line of soldiership. Tarleton was a man of imposing, and, when necessary, dignified manners—his conversation that of a soldier and well bred man of the world. There was not an appearance of bloodthirstiness about him, and he knew how to be studiously courteous to a foe. We cannot convince ourselves that he was cruel by nature, or took any pleasure in the atrocities committed by his band. We take him to have been one of those smooth, hard, unfeeling men, often met with, who have no positive cruelty of disposition, no brutalized taste for mere blood or crime, but who are not easily overcome by human distress—who, with the decisive promptitude of their energetic natures, do what they regard as necessary to their end with little ceremony or compunction—who, as principals, would not perhaps commit a gratuitous crime, but who, as subordinates, would unhesitatingly wade through seas of blood to obey the very letter of their orders. And commanding a band well supplied with those desperadoes, whose prowess in battle and reliability in deadly extremity so often make commanders very blind to their crimes inflicted on a foe, we should not wonder if Tarleton

unprepared opponents. This was, in lawyer's phrase, "too sharp practice" for an honorable soldier.

¹ Both of the officers here named, however, quit scores with him effectually in the long run.

bought their devotion and desperate services by indulging, to a certain extent, their licentious excesses. Why Buford's men were refused quarter, it is hard to see. If Cornwallis did not directly order that summary disposition of the matter, he certainly tolerated it; he certainly made himself an accessory after the act. Probably it was thought expedient, following up the Charleston blow, to intimidate all further effort at opposition. The slaughter of these men was nothing to the system of purely cold-blooded cruelty that Cornwallis soon after entered upon, and for a considerable period rigidly practised. The soldier's sword in the battle front, or even cleaving down the routed and flying, is surely mercy compared with the slow, deliberate movements of the hangman! How can we explain these things? Colonel (afterwards General) Harry Lee's Memoirs of the Southern War, are perhaps not very reliable authority where he had either a debt of love or enmity to pay, but he was a soldierly man, and appreciated the qualities of a soldier. We cannot conceive what feeling or prejudice should have biased him in favor of the British officers he was so often brought in conflict with. His coloring of Tarleton's deeds is infinitely milder than that, not only of tradition, but of most American history. If we remember aright, he generally represents Cornwallis as not personally cruel or vindictive, and as disposed to prevent the licenses of his troops. He traces everything, we believe, to the army principle, that orders must be obeyed—that Cornwallis and his subordinates were but carrying out the commands of the British Commander-in-chief. Was Sir Henry Clinton a particularly sanguinary man? What proof is there of this? Was *he* not acting under the orders of *his superiors?* In short, was it not the foolish and wicked plan and system of the British Government—as explicitly avowed by the published and never disavowed manifesto of its three Commissioners in 1778?

But we have wandered from Tarleton. Personally, he was an admirable soldier. He fared with his men. In the farm-house occupied for the night, he usually slept on his cloak on the floor, while subordinates crept into the feather beds. He was sudden as thought in determination and movement—and always as placidly and inexorably cool as sudden. We shall have a signal instance of this within sight of Monticello.

He reminds us not a little of the picture drawn by Sir Walter Scott, in "Old Mortality," of James Grahame, of Claverhouse. And scarcely darker and stranger were the pictures drawn of that terrible warrior by the hunted Covenanters, than our forefathers drew of Tarleton. Stripped of all exaggeration, there was enough, in both cases, to condemn and detest. If neither bore the features of a common ruffian, it would require a romantic imagination to find in either of those callous and prompt instruments of wicked power anything to deliberately admire.

Tarleton was Lieutenant-Colonel (Lord Cathcart being Colonel) of the "British Legion"—a cavalry corps. Their uniform was white, faced with green; and the people of the South soon learned to look with peculiar horror on this ominous color when a clump of horsemen was seen approaching—and the fugitive to put forth more desperate efforts to escape. Tarleton often, perhaps generally, combined a body of picked infantry with his legion, when on action, and this seems to have been the case even when he made his remarkable advance on Buford. We do not generally find any statements on the point, but it is probable that when we hear of his swift movements with a part infantry force, the latter were also mounted until brought into battle. Such were the troops pouring gradually towards the "debatable ground" of Virginia.

The British columns sent into the interior of Georgia and South Carolina found nothing to oppose them in regions so thinly settled, and without any army—and the only wonder is, that time was wasted in sending them there. The advancing summer of 1780 arrested further active movements in all three of the British divisions.

Congress had as early as March (1780) made preparations to strengthen the Southern army. The Marquis de Kalb led the Maryland and Delaware lines, and the first regiment of artillery, into North Carolina in July; but in the meantime the fatal blow had been struck at Charleston. General Gates was appointed to succeed Lincoln, and he reached the camp of De Kalb on the 25th of July.

The Virginia Legislature had opened the same spring with energetic measures; and their efforts were redoubled when the fall of Charleston, and the almost annihilation of their own Con-

tinental line, became known. The broken cavalry regiments, and
the State quota in the regular army, were ordered to be refilled
by drafts from the militia. Twenty thousand militia were placed
at the disposal of the Executive, if the State should be invaded,
and provisions made to succor the other States with militia. The
Governor was authorized to impress articles necessary for the
public service—to lay an embargo on the ports—to increase the
manufacture of arms—to provide magazines and public stores—
and new emissions of paper money were ordered to meet the
expenses, and new taxes devised. The Board of War and Trade
was reorganized—severer penalties were imposed on desertion,
on seditious writing or preaching, and on attempts to dissuade
enlistments. The fugitive citizens of the Carolinas and Georgia
were received into the State and authorized to bring and leave
their slaves therein until a year after the expulsion of the
enemy.

In preparations so imposing—so admirable on paper—there
was a fatal lack, which no power in the State could possibly
supply. This was money. There were property, and raw materials of every kind, but no money. The paper emissions, called
by that name, in spite of every effort to prevent it, rapidly depreciated towards worthlessness. There was little use of making
the pretence of basing them on a tax—for everybody knew a
tax could bring nothing to the treasury better than its own older
paper, unless it was made payable in lands and goods! A currency of the precious metals could by no contrivance be established, where precious metals were both absent and unattain-
able. We have heard it stated on good authority that there
were men in Virginia of some property, who had not possessed
a shilling, or *seen* a shilling in coin, for months—perhaps a year
—until the gold and silver brought over by the French began
to creep into circulation! He knows little of war who does
not know that money forms its " sinews "—aye, and its bones as
well as its sinews. Without it, the art of man cannot collect
and keep in use the means of efficient warfare. A citizen soldiery, with arms in their hands, and provisions in their knap-
sacks and wagons, may rush together and do efficient service for
a short period. But if the arms are wanting, what can be done
without money? How can arms be " manufactured " when
there are no considerable number of domestic artificers, and no

money to bring in others, or to provide them with materials to work with—and no commerce with foreign nations to exchange surplus commodities for them?

In this emergency, the ladies of Virginia came forward with loyal devotion, and contributed their ornaments and their pocket-money to the public cause. The heirlooms of ancestors, the tokens of old friendship, the symbols of the bridal altar, and even the souvenirs of the dead, were made merchandise of to arm levies to repair to the standard of Gates—to furnish forth another Charleston holocaust of victims, which the infatuation of this henceforth unlucky commander was preparing to sacrifice. The ladies' offering was well as far as it went; and the moral was still better than the physical effect. But such aids to the practically bankrupt State stopped but a leak, when the foundering vessel was taking in brine at every seam!

Governor Jefferson urged forward the measures enacted by the Legislature with untiring assiduity. He wrote General Washington, June 11th:

"There is really nothing to oppose the progress of the enemy, northward, but the cautious principles of the military art. North Carolina is without arms. We do not abound. Those we have, are freely imparted to them, but such is the state of their resources, that they have not been able to move a single musket from this State to theirs. All the wagons we can collect have been furnished to the Marquis de Kalb, and are assembled for the march of twenty-five hundred men, under Gen. Stevens, of Culpepper, who will move on the 19th instant. I have written to Congress to hasten supplies of arms and military stores for the Southern States, and particularly to aid us with cartridge paper and boxes, the want of which articles, small as they are, renders our stores useless. The want of money cramps every effort. This will be supplied by the most unpalatable of all substitutes, force. *
* * Could arms be furnished, I think this State and North Carolina would embody from ten to fifteen thousand militia, immediately, and more if necessary."

He already, then, saw clearly that nothing stood between Virginia and the foot of the ravager "but the cautious principles of the military art"—nay, that Virginia herself had little to stop the still further northward progress of the invader. He speaks of finding a substitute for money in force—that is, in impressment. But in a free State—in any State without an army extraneous of the people, and strong enough to curb them—the power of impressment is, in a great measure, nominal. It amounts to a *tax* of *articles*, collected in a short way, and to little more. It may take what men can spare, and patriots, in emergency, will submit to that point—but it cannot proceed much further. Nor is there an object to carry it further. A people cannot be *defended* by *starving* them. Governor Jefferson tried his "substitute" with rigorous impartiality. Among the first "impressments" in Albemarle were the horses and wagons of Thomas Jefferson, of Monticello! Everything went but what absolute necessity required should be kept to sustain the human beings on the plantation. Wagons and horses were the first need to carry supplies to Gates, and to forward them with the Virginia levies. Yet it would not do to cut off the very source of the supplies, by not leaving the farmers horses and wagons to secure their present crops and make preparations for the next. The quantity was therefore limited—many were destroyed on the rough roads—others were not promptly returned for new loads, but kept to serve the purposes of the army. Again and again we find Jefferson writing Gates, urging and imploring him to see to the return of the not half adequate number of teams. The "substitute" proved as imperfect in some other particulars—and far more so in still others—and in those of the very first magnitude. Could arms be impressed when not one militia man in five had a serviceable gun? Could powder and ball be impressed, when they could not be found in greater proportion? Could tents, medical supplies, etc., be impressed where they did not exist? Yet Virginia made noble efforts, under the circumstances—all that could of possibility be made—more, the fair investigator of the facts will decide, than could have been reasonably anticipated.[1]

The purely unselfish and unsectional character of Governor Jefferson's patriotism was repeatedly illustrated. He wrote General Washington, in the letter already quoted from:

"Your Excellency will readily conceive, that, after the loss of one army, our eyes are turned towards the other, and that we comfort ourselves, if any aids can be furnished by you, *without defeating the operations more beneficial to the general union*, they will be furnished. At the same time, *I am happy to find that the wishes of the people go no further*, as far as I have an opportunity of learning their sentiments."

To the same, a few weeks later (July 2d):

"I have with great pain perceived your situation; and, the more so, as being

[1] Such investigator is referred to Jefferson's official correspondence of the period

situated between two fires, *a division of sentiment has arisen both in Congress and here, as to which the resources of this country should be sent. The removal of General Clinton to the northward, must, of course, have great influence on the determination of this question; and I have no doubt but considerable aids may be drawn hence for your army,* unless a larger one should be embodied in the South than the force of the enemy there seems to call for."

He wrote General Edward Stevens, the commander of the Virginia militia in Gates's army, August 4th:

"You wish to know how far the property of this State, in your hands, is meant to be subject to the orders of the Commander-in-chief. Arms and military stores, we mean to be perfectly subject to him. The provisions going from this country will be for the whole army. * * * * The money put into your hands was meant as a particular resource for any extra wants of our own troops, yet, in case of great distress, you would probably not see the others suffer without communicating part of it for their use."

To the same, September 12th:

"We approve of your accommodating the hospital with medicines, and the Maryland troops with spirits. They really deserve the whole, and I wish we had means of transportation for much greater quantities, which we have on hand and cannot convey. This article we could furnish plentifully to you and them. What is to be done for wagons, I do not know. We have not now one shilling in the treasury to purchase them. We have ordered an active quarter-master to go to the westward, and endeavor to purchase on credit, or impress a hundred wagons and teams. But I really see no prospect of sending you additional supplies, till the same wagons return from you, which we sent on with the last."

These are but samples of constant expressions, and of the spirit of every letter addressed by him to the Virginia or to the Continental officers.

The italicised expressions, in the extract to General Washington, of July 2d, are very noticeable. The extreme Southern members in Congress were opposed to General Washington's retaining the main army in the North, and suffering the Southern States to be overrun by the enemy without effectual opposition. They insisted that it was absolutely necessary for the South, and better for the whole, that he should take the field in the South in the summer of 1780.[1] And this feeling had *now*, as

[1] The miserable factional spirit was yet rife in Congress. Opposed to these Southern members, were a class of Northern ones, who urged that the North should not be jeoparded to render aid to those who, it was with flagrant injustice asserted, had done so little for themselves!
On this subject, see the French Minister's (the Marquis de la Luzerne's) letter to the Count de Vergennes, and Mr. Duane to General Schuyler—both quoted in Sparks's Washington, vol. vii. pp. 92, 93—notes.

Governor Jefferson intimates, extended to Virginia. It was the starting point of a party there, which was to give serious trouble to Governor Jefferson, and inflict humiliations on him before he left the chief magistracy.

General Washington was placed in a most embarrassing attitude—literally " between two fires." He had always believed the fate of the war must be settled in the North. He had strongly and fervidly hoped, " by one great exertion " of the French and American arms, in the summer of 1780, to recapture New York, crush Clinton, and thus " put an end to the war." His letters to Lafayette, Mesech Weare (the President of New Hampshire), General Greene, and others, distinctly disclose that such was his plan of policy.[1] General Washington, we may presume, felt keenly enough for his native South, and the unfounded murmurs of her representatives and citizens must have given him intense pain—but he knew his duty, and had the firmness to undeviatingly pursue it. Gladly we record Jefferson's unshaken adhesion to him and to his policy, *whatever it was*, in this crisis ; and his noble offer—while Virginia was making such exhausting efforts for the South—still to raise additional aid for General Washington's army in the North, if the latter desired it ! This was not the act nor the offer of a private citizen, but of the Governor of the State which had more political and physical strength than the other Southern States put together—of Washington's own Virginia ! Is it probable or not probable that this devotion to his opinions and wishes, coming from such a source, was balm to the feelings of the immovable but always deeply-sensitive Commander-in-chief ? Let the reader keep another point distinctly in view, that Governor Jefferson steadily took General Washington's views as his standard and his guide of official military action.[2] We shall have more on this subject presently.

We will not follow out the particulars of Gates's failure to obtain the proper material of an army, or of his unfortunate advance on Camden. He met Cornwallis before that town, August 16th, and again the American " Southern Army " was

[1] For which see Sparks's Washington, vol. vii. pp. 39, 96, 106, 109, 112, etc.
[2] We have omitted to mention that in one of the letters quoted, he desired General Washington to perform a duty confided to himself—to fill up the offices in the New Virginia battalions sent north—and he directed General Muhlenburg to send lists of the Virginia line officers, out of command, for General Washington to choose from.

annihilated. The American regulars fought with heroic determination. The veteran de Kalb, leading on foot the iron 2d
Maryland brigade, fell covered with wounds. But the militia
of both Virginia and North Carolina (excepting Dixon's regiment of the latter), comprising two-thirds of Gates's force, fled
in a shameful panic at the opening of the action, actually throwing away their loaded guns, and sweeping along the officers
who attempted to rally them—and Gates among the number.

The Virginia militia-who thus disgraced themselves were
about seven hundred strong. They were commanded by General
Stevens, a brave officer, who had served two campaigns under
General Washington in the regular line. He made every possible effort to stop his men, and their conduct stung him to the
quick. Colonel Porterfield, of the Virginia regulars, fell in the
first skirmishing, with his leg broken, but his corps stood fast
with the two brigades whom Colonel Williams blames, in his
Journal, "for remaining too long on the field * * after all
hope of victory must have been despaired of!"   •

A few days afterwards (August 28th), Colonel Sumpter, who,
just before the battle of Camden, had struck a handsome blow
on the Wateree, was surprised near Catawba Ford by Tarleton,
and his whole force was cut to pieces or utterly dispersed.
Between three and four hundred were killed and wounded.
This left North Carolina defenceless; and had the season of the
year permitted Cornwallis to immediately act, it could have presented 'no resistance to him. But his unacclimated troops,
called into action at the hottest period of the year, had suffered
severely, and his camp now became almost a hospital. Moreover, his military stores had not yet been transported from
Charleston. He was therefore reduced to complete inaction.

In this dark hour of gloom and despondency for the South,
we do not find a fact, nor the trace of a fact, to show that Governor Jefferson for an instant relaxed his exertions, or for an
instant abated "a jot of heart or hope." The smoke had
scarcely risen from the fatal field of Camden, before Virginia
was again sending forth her sons to that shattered standard
which Gates had raised at Hillsborough. Governor Jefferson
wrote General Washington, September 3d :

"Our new recruits will rendezvous in this State between the 10th and 25th
instant. We are calling out two thousand militia, who, I think, however, will

not be got to Hillsborough till the 25th of October. About three hundred and fifty regulars marched from Chesterfield a week ago. Fifty march to-morrow, and there will be one hundred or one hundred and fifty more from that post, when they can be cleared of the hospital. This is as good a view as I can give you of the force we are endeavoring to collect; but they are unarmed. Almost the whole small arms seem to have been lost in the late rout. There are here, on their way southwardly, three thousand stand of arms, sent by Congress, and we have still a few in our magazine. I have written pressingly, as the subject well deserves, to Congress, to send immediate supplies, and to think of forming a magazine here, that in case of another disaster, we may not be left without all means of opposition."

The same day, he wrote thus calmly, considerately, and manfully, to General Stevens:[1]

"I sincerely condole with you on our late misfortune, which sits the heavier on my mind as being produced by my own countrymen. Instead of considering what is past, however, we are to look forward and prepare for the future. I write General Gates and Governor Nash as to supplies and reinforcements. Another body of 2,000 militia are ordered to you to rendezvous at Hillsborough, on the 25th of October. They come from the middle and north counties, beyond and adjoining the Blue Ridge. I am told, also, that a spirit of raising volunteers is springing up. The truth of this, however, is not certainly known, nor can its success be depended on. Governor Nash writes me that 400 wagons were lost. An officer here, however, thinks they are not. This, indeed, would be a heavy loss, as well as that of the small arms. We shall exert every nerve to assist you in every way in our power, being, as we are, without any money in the treasury, or any prospect of more till the Assembly meets in October."

Efforts in another direction are thus stated in a letter to General Gates, September 11th:

"Your bill for £54,712 in favor of Mallette, has been duly honored; that for £95,288 we shall also discharge; another bill (which being delivered back to be presented at the end of the ten days, I cannot recollect either the name of the holder or the sum) has been accepted. We are now without one shilling in the treasury, or a possibility of having it recruited till the meeting of the Assembly, which takes place on the 15th of the next month. In this condition Mr. Duncan Ochiltree found us when he delivered your letter of the 5th instant, and draft for £100,000 in favor of Colonel Polk. The only thing in our power, after stating to him our situation, was to assure him that it should be paid as soon as we should be enabled to do it by the Assembly, which I flatter myself will be as soon as they meet."

___

[1] General Stevens, in writing the Governor of the conduct of his men at Camden, had said: "Their conduct has mortally wounded my feelings," and again: "I never shall be reconciled with these fellows till I get them all together again, and put them into a situation where they may wipe off the stain they have brought on themselves and their country, and made some atonement for the distresses their disgraceful behavior has occasioned; and at a time, too, when if they had behaved like men, they might have relieved thousands, and immortalized their own names."

A new mortification awaited Stevens. He had collected again nearly all his fugitives at Hillsborough, and arms were again put in their hands. But their first panic had completely demoralized them. Being ordered to advance to Guilford Court House, four hundred deserted; and soon after reaching their destination, their number was further reduced to one hundred and fifty men. They were now so near the Virginia line, that the temptation to return home was stronger, and where the disaffection was so general, attempts to stop it were out of the question. Stevens informed Governor Jefferson of the facts, and avowed his determination to remain, and oppose, at least, his own body to the enemy. The Governor replied, September 12th:

"I have sent expresses into all the counties from which those militia went, requiring the county lieutenants to exert themselves in taking them; and such is the detestation with which they have been received, that I have heard from many counties they were going back of themselves. You will of course hold courts martial on them, and make them soldiers for eight months."

He again wrote General Gates, September 23d:

"I have empowered Colonel Carrington to have twelve boats, scows or batteaux, built at Taylor's Ferry, and to draw on me for the cost. I recommended the constructing them so as to answer the transportation of provisions along that river, as a change of position of the two armies may render them unnecessary at Taylor's Ferry; and I am thoroughly persuaded, that, unless we can find out some channel of transportation by water, no supplies of bread, of any consequence, can be sent you from this State for a long time to come. The want of wagons is a bar insuperable, at least, in any reasonable time.   *   *   *   *   Unless Congress furnish small arms, we cannot arm more than half the men who will go from this State. The prize you mention of tents and blankets is very fortunate. It is absolutely out of our power to get these articles, to any amount, in this country, nor have we clothing for our new levies. They must, therefore, go to you clothed as militia, till we can procure and send on supplies."

To General Washington, the same day, he communicated the following summary of his operations:

"The numbers of regulars and militia ordered from this State into the Southern service, are about seven thousand. I trust we may count that fifty-five hundred will actually proceed; but we have arms for three thousand only. If, therefore, we do not speedily receive a supply from Congress, we must countermand a proper number of these troops. Besides this supply, there should certainly be a magazine laid in here, to provide against a general loss as well as daily waste. When we deliver out those now in our magazine, we shall have sent seven thousand stand of our own into the Southern service, in the course of this summer. We are still more destitute of clothing, tents, and wagons for our troops. The Southern army suffers for provisions, which we could plentifully supply, were it possible to find means of transportation. Despairing of this, we directed very considerable quantities, collected on the navigable waters, to be sent northwardly by the quartermaster. This he is now doing, slowly, however."

These particulars might be indefinitely multiplied; but it would be to no purpose, if those already given have not shown the zeal and efficiency of Governor Jefferson at this trying crisis of Southern affairs.

In truth, General Gates was obliged to write him, requesting him to send no more *men*, unless they came provided with suitable military equipments. Virginia was ready to give all she had—her *blood* and her raw commodities—but she could not send what she neither had nor possessed the power of purchasing! The Governor's reply to Gates (October 15th) presents gloomy details:

"Your request (as stated in your letter of the 7th) that we will send no men into the field, or even to your camp, that are not well furnished with shoes, blankets, and every necessary for immediate service, would amount to a stoppage of every man; as we have it not in our power to furnish them with real necessaries completely. I hope they will be all shod. What proportion will have blankets, I cannot say: we purchase every one which can be found out; and now I begin to have a prospect of furnishing about half of them with tents, as soon as they can be made and forwarded. As to provisions, our agent, Eaton, of whom I before wrote, informs me in a letter of the 5th instant, he shall immediately get supplies of beef into motion, and shall send some corn by a circuitous navigation. But till we receive our wagons from the western country, I cannot hope to aid you in bread. I expect daily to see wagons coming in to us.   *   *   *   *   I inclose, by this express, a power to Mr. Lambe, quarter-master, to impress for a month, ten wagons from each of the counties of Brunswick, Mecklenburg, Lunenburg, Charlotte, and Halifax, and direct him to take your orders, whether they shall go first to you, or come here. If the latter, we can load them with arms and spirits. Before their month is out, I hope the hundred wagons from the westward will have come in."

Meanwhile, operations in Western Virginia were not overlooked. Colonel Clarke, the hero of the frontier, had steadily urged that it was the true, and, in the end, the cheapest policy, to make the war there an offensive one. He thought Detroit, the fountain-head of all the Indian irruptions, should be torn from the enemy. It was the day-dream of the resolute borderer to lead such an expedition, and thus save the keeping of six or eight hundred men at least, constantly on the alert, at different points, to watch the Indians, and give permanent repose to the

long-harassed frontiers. Before the close of 1779, Clarke had
collected an Indian army at St. Vincenne, for this object, but
he was disappointed in receiving a proper number of white
soldiers from the settlements, and it was in vain to rely on
Indians to oppose an equal body of Indians, and also to reduce
a fortified place defended by whites. Again, in the spring of
1780, he renewed his preparations. Governor Jefferson reinforced him, and placed it at his option whether to advance on
Detroit, or, as a preparatory step, to give "vigorous chastise-
ment to those tribes of Indians whose eternal hostilities had
proved them incapable of living on friendly terms with us."
The Governor immediately communicated his measures to General Washington (February 10th). Clarke spent the summer in
chastising the fiercest clans, and deeds innumerable, we doubt
not, of Spartan nerve, were enacted on the "dark and bloody
ground," of which no record, or even tradition, has preserved a
trace. Clarke, though never wantonly or unnecessarily cruel,
wrote *his* records with steel and flame, and left paper ones to
those more anxious to commemorate their own exploits. And
no traditions excepting those pertaining to very unusual, or very
important events, will take root in a new, unsettled country,
where nothing keeps the same place long but the solid ground,
the hills, the rocks, and the rivers. Traditions are like rooks—
they build their nests only amid the stable and the ancient.
Well might John Adams exclaim that the History of the
American Revolution never had been written—never could be
written! Deeds of as fierce daring as that which took place

"In bleak Thermopylæ's sepulchral strait,"

took place every month on the American borders! It was
there that the stern determination of the Saxon blood, kindled
into a more chivalrous warmth by its Norman infusion, properly
displayed itself. Courage, except in a few fiery natures, is a
thing of habit. It would be hard to point to an instance on the
whole American frontier where the pioneers exhibited an approach to cowardice, or failed to fight with a courage which
rose to the full point of the horrors with which it was called
upon to grapple. The borderers were used to this. They had
been trained to it. The same men brought into half the danger

in a novel position—in formal lines, and opposed to formal lines of trained soldiery, called upon to withstand a charge of horse— might act as ingloriously as the militia did at Camden, and on scores of other Revolutionary fields, North and South.   We take it that no sensible man believes the raw troops who fought so desperately at Bunker's Hill, would have made an equivalent resistance on an open plain.   It is no impeachment of their courage, and no detraction from their renown, to say this.   The Swiss peasants who annihilated the mailed chivalry of Bur- gundy at Granson fought amidst the crags and fastnesses of their native Alps.   Without pushing this digression by an enumeration of instances, it will be found a rule that purely raw troops never did, never can, withstand regulars, other things being equal, except in instances of enthusiasm or fury, so rare that they do not exceed the number of exceptions which are said to be necessary to prove a rule.   And the raw soldier is often panic-stricken at the outset, who, after a little discipline and practice, would be a choice man in a forlorn hope.

Clarke, having given the nearest hostile tribes a taste of war which would be likely to induce them to remain at home for a few months, renewed his projects against Detroit in autumn. His plan was to collect all the necessary force and equipments in the winter, and as soon as the Wabash broke up in the spring, ascend it, and strike Detroit before the navigation of the lakes opened to allow the British garrison to receive reinforcements or effect their own escape.   Governor Jefferson at once laid the plan before General Washington (September 26th), and stated that Virginia could furnish men, provisions, and every necessary except powder, if it had the money, "or could the demand from it be so far supplied from other quarters, as to leave it in its power to apply such a sum to that purpose."   The sum esti- mated to be requisite was about two million pounds of the existing currency.   As matters were then situated, it could not be undertaken, except at Continental expense, and the Governor referred the whole enterprise to the judgment and determina- tion of the Commander-in-chief.   He hinted that it was the more reasonable that the Confederacy sustain the expense, as, "speaking his private opinion," he " verily believed " Virginia was about to make a cession of a part of her western claim, "if the quantity demanded was not unreasonably great," to secure the general ratification of the Articles of Confederation, which was ostensibly made to depend on that cession.

No reply to this letter appears in General Washington's published correspondence. It reached him, if at all, when absorbed in the events growing out of the recent treachery of Arnold; and the Southern campaign soon afterwards assumed a shape which rendered the reduction of Detroit, for the present, a secondary consideration to the public, or to Virginia.

In September, Governor Jefferson employed engineers to make careful surveys about the mouth of the James, on its south bank, to the Dismal Swamp, and from Cape Henry to the Nansemond River; on the north bank of "the line of country from Portsmouth, by Hampton and York, to Williamsburg." Colonel Senf was, a little later, directed to take soundings of the important waters, and make drawings of the particular places.

On the 23d of September the Governor proposed to General Washington, that the French fleet winter in the Chesapeake, and he assigned the following reasons:

"Unapprised what may be proposed by our allies, to be done with their fleet in the course of the ensuing winter, I would beg leave to intimate to you, that if it should appear to them eligible that it should winter in the Chesapeake, they can be well supplied with provisions, taking their necessary measures in due time. The waters communicating with that bay furnish easy, and (in that case) safe transportation, and their money will call forth what is denied to ours."

According to Girardin, there seems to have been a reason for this request, not here expressed. Gates, he says, had learned from spies that Cornwallis was pressing Clinton for reinforcements, for the purpose of embarking his forces "to take possession of Portsmouth in Virginia, and establish there a strong post;" and therefore both General Gates and Governor Jefferson applied to Congress and to General Washington to have the French fleet winter in the Chesapeake.

We ought to have stated earlier that Mr. Jefferson, in his Memoir, gives no account of himself or his measures while Governor of Virginia, for which he assigns the following reasons:

"Being now, as it were, identified with the Commonwealth itself, to write my own history, during the two years of my administration, would be to write the public history of that portion of the Revolution within this State. This has been done by others, and particularly by Mr. Girardin, who wrote his Continuation of Burk's History of Virginia, while at Milton, in this neighborhood, *had free access to all my papers while composing it, and has given as faithful an account as I could myself.* For this portion, therefore, of my own life, I refer altogether to his History."

This is strong endorsement, and no doubt was generally merited. Notwithstanding, we believe that Girardin was mistaken in the last statements we have quoted from him, and that Mr. Jefferson chanced to overlook that mistake. Otherwise, the letter we have quoted from Jefferson to General Washington contains a suppression of the most important reason of all for the very request he was making, that the French fleet winter in the Virginia waters! Nor do we find a word in this or any other letter of the period, to justify Girardin's inference. Gates might possibly have picked up such a statement, and transmitted it to the Governor; but it is clear that nobody credited it, or attached serious importance to it. Jefferson continued to push on aids to enable Gates to again make head against Cornwallis in North Carolina, and Gates continued to call for such aids, from all directions, and to make every practicable effort for a fall and winter campaign in North Carolina.

The Virginia Legislature, at its fall session (commencing October 16th), made a strong effort to replenish the treasury. New bills for six millions of pounds were emitted, and the public faith solemnly pledged for their redemption. Each county was required to furnish a proportionable quota of clothes, military stores, and wagons. Three thousand men were ordered to be drafted for the Continental service. Even the pensioned invalids of the State were called upon to do garrison duty. New and more efficient provisions were made for the pay of soldiers and seamen, and for the relief of the widows and orphans of the fallen. Vessels were armed against "the predatory cruisers in the Chesapeake." This substantially coincides with Girardin's summary of the legislative proceedings, and the quoted words are his; but we do not find here, a measure hinting towards an anticipated invasion, by Cornwallis, or any other British commander, at the mouth of the Chesapeake. Can we suppose that all preparation, or direct attempts at preparation, would have been omitted by this body, had such a thing been really in expectation? Of course, such an idea is preposterous.

Let us now go back to Cornwallis, whom we left with his sick army at Camden, in the northern part of South Carolina

Pausing until the cooler weather had restored health to his troops, and made it possible to again act without the immediate loss of that health, he (October 8th) advanced on North Carolina. But a dangerous foe had, meanwhile, been waked up in his rear.

Sir Henry Clinton had, in less than a month after the capitulation of Charleston (June 3d) issued a proclamation declaring:

"All paroles given to prisoners not taken by capitulation, and not confined at the time of the surrender of Charleston, to be null and void after the 20th June; and calling upon the holders of such paroles to resume the character of British subjects, and to take an active part in forwarding military operations, under pain of being considered and treated as rebels against his Majesty's government."

Paroles had been extorted from the unarmed inhabitants generally; and as an equivalent for releasing them from these (or to save the trouble of continuing that system) the body of the inhabitants of South Carolina were, by a stroke of the pen, reconverted into British subjects, and not merely required (as a parole would have done) to remain neutral, but now to become active parricides, or be executed for treason! This was going far beyond any preceding assumptions of Great Britain. In the very opening of the Revolution, she had not tried and executed the rebellious colonists taken in arms as traitors, but had treated them, exchanged them, etc., as prisoners taken from another power. Now she proposed to execute non-combatants, if they would not take arms against their country!

These "bloody instructions" were carried out by Cornwallis. There is scarcely an old South Carolina family that has not its tradition of ancestors imprisoned, plundered, otherwise outraged, or executed by this relentless soldier. If better proof were wanting than this, that Clinton's proclamation was not an empty menace, but was executed with terrible literality, it is furnished by an intercepted letter from Cornwallis to Lieutenant-Colonel Balfour, written soon after the battle of Camden, the authenticity of which has never, we believe, been questioned. He wrote:

"I have given orders that all the inhabitants of this province, who have subscribed and taken part in this revolt, should be punished with the greatest rigor; also, that those who will not turn out, may be imprisoned, and their whole property taken from them and destroyed. I have also ordered that satisfaction should be made for their estates, to those who have been injured and oppressed by them I have ordered, in the most positive manner, that every militia man who has borne arms with us and afterwards joined the enemy, *shall be immediately hanged.* I desire you will take the most rigorous measures to punish the rebels in the district in which you command, *and that you will obey, in the strictest manner, the directions I have given in this letter,* relative to the inhabitants of this country.

"CORNWALLIS.

"*August,* 1780."

Yet the soldier acting on his own impulses, and as the instrument of official orders (if that was the distinction) were so different, that Gates thanked Cornwallis for his kindness to the prisoners captured by him at Camden! Perhaps the *esprit de corps* of the soldier prevailed in one case—while the aristocratic Marquis, who had commenced his career as an aid-de-camp of a king, did not regard unarmed countrymen as entitled to any such privileges or consideration. Whatever the motive of this contradictory conduct, his cold-blooded cruelties are equally detestable. If an unwilling instrument, he deserves hardly the respect of that fanatical royalist who plundered, imprisoned, and hung men on perverted principle. No man could be compelled to become an executioner under the British constitution and laws, even as administered by George III. He who committed sins against nature and against decency to obtain or preserve military rank, put himself morally, and in the eye of true honor, on a par with a paid executioner, or any other paid miscreant.

But the "instructions" returned to "plague the inventors." Forced to choose between active parricide and outlawry, men who would otherwise have remained quiet, fled desperately to the forests and morasses, to issue forth at midnight under the leadership of Marion and Sumpter, and strike terrible blows for liberty and vengeance. We cannot here deny ourselves the pleasure of quoting some of Bryant's felicitous lines on the subject:

> "Our band is few, but true and tried,
>   Our leader frank and bold;
> The British soldier trembles
>   When MARION's name is told.
> Our fortress is the good green wood,
>   Our tent the cypress tree;
> We know the forest round us,
>   As seamen know the sea.
> We know its walls of thorny vines,
>   Its glades of reedy grass,
> Its safe and silent islands
>   Within the dark morass.

" Woe to the English soldiery
    That little dread us near !
On them shall light at midnight
    A strange and sudden fear ;
When waking to their tents on fire,
    They grasp their arms in vain,
And they who stand to face us
    Are beat to earth again ;
And they who fly in terror deem
    A mighty host behind,
And hear the tramp of thousands
    Upon the hollow wind.

*   *   *   *

" Well knows the fair and friendly moon
    The band that MARION leads—
The glitter of their rifles,
    The scampering of their steeds.
'Tis life to guide the fiery barb
    Across the moonlight plain ;
'Tis life to feel the night-wind
    That lifts his tossing mane.
A moment in the British camp—
    A moment—and away
Back to the pathless forest
    Before the peep of day."

*   *   *   *

When Cornwallis put his troops in motion from Camden for
North Carolina, as already mentioned, he ordered Major Ferguson to advance from Ninety-Six with his troops, and a body of
Tories whom he had been disciplining, along the western skirts
of the same State, for the purpose of embodying the Tories on
their route, and ultimately to join himself at Charlottestown.   To
cut off an American force which had recently attacked Augusta,
and thence retreated northward, Ferguson deviated from his
prescribed line of march towards the mountains, and he also
made some delays which weighed fatally against him.   Bands
of Virginia and North Carolina mountaineers were in motion in
this region, and they immediately resolved to concentrate and
attack him.

The epithet " mountaineer" is usually associated with the
idea of a simple, hardy, poor peasantry.   Those of whom we
speak were men of an entirely different class—mostly men of
property and family—as conspicuous citizens as any in their
counties.   They were well mounted, armed with rifles—accustomed from childhood to the use of their weapons, and to des-

perate riding. They chose Colonel Arthur Campbell, of Virginia, for their leader, and on the 26th of September opened hotly on the chase. They were soon joined by a band of outlawed fugitives from South Carolina, whose eagerness equalled their own. It is probable that the Tories under Ferguson understood the character of their pursuers. That officer, at all events, retreated as fast as possible toward Charlottestown, and sent different messengers to Cornwallis to apprise him of his situation. All these were intercepted. At the Cowpens, nine hundred men were picked from the whole body of pursuers, and they dashed forward all night and through a heavy rain. At about three o'clock in the afternoon, October 7th, they came in view of Ferguson's force, drawn up to receive them on King's Mountain, a wooded eminence a few hundred yards long, and about seventy wide. The Americans dismounted, and advanced in three divisions to the assault—but pursuing the border custom, in such situations, of making covers of trees. The British officer made a heroic defence, again and again bearing back his assailants in front by charges with the bayonet—but while one division thus gave way, the other two poured in a flanking fire too deadly to be withstood. As he turned on one of these, the column before driven back would immediately advance, and he was again hemmed in. Fortunately for his troops, Ferguson soon fell mortally wounded, and they immediately surrendered. One hundred and fifty had been slain, an equal number wounded, and eight hundred were made prisoners, and fifteen hundred stands of choice arms taken. The American loss was trifling, except in the death of Colonel Williams, of South Carolina.

Of the eight hundred prisoners, about seven hundred were Tories. In the pockets of some of the slain or captured officers were found lists of executions, by hanging, of American soldiers, for violating the terms of Sir Henry Clinton's proclamation. Tories who had been forward in these proceedings, were among the prisoners. The victors selected ten of the most active and obnoxious of these parricides, and hung them on the trees which grew on the field of battle.

Cornwallis made loud complaints and threats on hearing of this execution. General Gates, in transmitting those complaints to Congress, aptly observed :

" For what has been done by our people after the battle at King's Mountain, I have nothing to say. It is my private opinion no person ought to be executed, but after legal conviction, and by order of the supreme civil or military authority, in the department where the offence is committed; but I must confess my astonishment at Lord Cornwallis's finding fault with a cruelty he and his officers are constantly practising. This is crying rogue first."

"Supreme civil or military authority," was not much better than a name, in the locality and exigency; and was quite as well represented, in our judgment, as it could elsewhere have been, in the intelligent and responsible gentlemen—for emphatically they were such—who by their own danger and exertions had done what no formally constituted "authority" was able to do; and if the victors of King's Mountain hung fewer men than the documents found on British officers clearly proved had been executed of Americans, by their orders, they enforced less, we believe, than the full measure of rightful and proper retaliation. And there is not a doubt that the practical effect of the measure was good, not only on the British Lieutenant-General, but on the parricides who were so keen to scent out, among their countrymen, the breakers of enforced and withdrawn paroles. The hunt became less intensely amusing, when it was understood that the hunter placed the noose that had strangled his victim round his own neck, in the event of his capture!

The battle of King's Mountain not only weakened Cornwallis physically, but it proved to him that a dangerous spirit was rising behind. Its effect on the Americans was everywhere visible. It taught them what even undisciplined men could do, if courage and effort were not wanting. It was the beginning of a new era, in the Southern war, in the conduct of raw troops, and also in the event of battles. The British General-in-chief, instead of continuing his march in North Carolina, fell back to Wynnsborough, a point from which he could protect his posts, and awaited reinforcements from the North.

General Gates was suspended by Congress, and General Washington was directed to select his successor. The choice most fitly fell upon Greene—an officer second only in experience, and in the wise forecast of a great general, to the illustrious Commander-in-chief of the American armies. He arrived at Hillsborough on the 2d of December, and the next day assumed command of the Southern Department.

CHAPTER VIII.

1780—1781.

As the autumn of 1780 approached, Sir Henry Clinton found himself so far in a position of superiority, in the North, that he felt able to make a considerable detachment from his army to reinforce Cornwallis in the South. Having heard only of that commander's successes, and not yet apprised of the disaster of King's Mountain, he had little doubt North Carolina was to be easily overrun; and now, with extended views, he anticipated making a permanent lodgment on the Chesapeake before the close of the fall and winter campaign. He judged that Cornwallis would require little or no assistance south of Virginia, and that, therefore, it would accelerate matters to dispatch his reinforcements directly to the mouth of the James, with orders to erect a strong post on the Elizabeth River.[1] This would give the Virginians employment at home, enable an easy coöperation with Cornwallis as he approached from the South, and prepare for him, in advance, a reliable base of operations, in easy communication with New York, provided the opposition from Virginia, on the arrival of the French aids, should render it desirable. And it was Clinton's intention to send a further reinforcement, and make the post a permanent one.

In accordance with these views, General Leslie was dispatched from New York, on the 16th of October, with three thousand men. The fleet entered Hampton Roads on the 23d, and took possession of Hampton; but it passed, immediately after, up Elizabeth River, and Leslie disembarked at Portsmouth and commenced the erection of fortifications at that point. This, the principal Virginia post occupied by the invaders in the subsequent stages of the war, lies on the south bank of Elizabeth River, opposite Norfolk—and at the head of the bay which the whole river actually forms. At common flood tide, there were eighteen feet of water to Norfolk; and sixty-gun ships had reached it by lightening to cross a bar at Sowel's point. Leslie also occupied Suffolk on the Nansemond, and thus controlled the pass between it and the Dismal Swamp, which formed the avenue of communication between the country east of that great morass and the interior of the State.

The British allowed it to get out that after drawing the forces of the State to Suffolk, they intended to sail up the Chesapeake for Baltimore. Governor Jefferson, however, at once divined

---

[1] The commanding officer of the reinforcement (Gen. Leslie) was ordered " to enter the Chesapeake, and establish a post on Elizabeth River, with the design of creating a diversion in favor of Lord Cornwallis's operations in North Carolina. General Leslie was to be under the command of Lord Cornwallis, and to act on James River, towards the Roanoake, but not to pass this latter river without orders from his commander. Should Lord Cornwallis meet with serious opposition in crossing the Yadkin, it was recommended to General Leslie to move upon Cape Fear River, but this was left to his discretion. Should a post be established on the Chesapeake, it was Sir Henry Clinton's intention to reinforce it with more troops."—*Substance of MS. letter from Sir Henry Clinton to Lord George Germain, November 10th, quoted in Sparks's Cor. of General Washington,* vol. vii. p. 269, note.

their true object, and apprising General Washington of the situation of things (November 3d), he intimated that the fate of Leslie's army hung "on a very slender naval force." He had already proposed to Gates to send a swift boat from some of the inlets of Carolina, "to notify the French Admiral that his enemies where in a net, if he had leisure to close the mouth of it."

The Governor had first got intelligence of the arrival of the British fleet within the Capes, on the 22d of October. He immediately ordered out all the force in the lower counties which could find arms, and stopped such of the detachments intended for the Southern army as had not yet marched; but to compensate Gates (yet in command) he exempted the counties lying nearest to him from the present levy. Generals Weeden and Muhlenburg of the line, and Generals Nelson and Stevens of the militia, were directed to take command of the State troops.

The arrival of General Leslie probably hurried forward arrangements which seem to have been already concerted with General Washington[1] for the removal of the "Convention prisoners" to Fort Frederick, in Maryland, where barracks were being prepared for them. On the 20th, the British portion of them (they being inclined to desert and to correspond with disaffected persons, while the Germans remained quiet) were ordered forward, with the expectation that the remainder would follow as soon as sufficient structures were prepared for their reception. The Governor assigned as a reason for temporarily doing now what he had a year before so warmly remonstrated against—namely, separating these troops—that safety demanded their movement in two bodies, and that it would be improper to crowd the whole into barracks not more than sufficient for half of them. But he says, if their officers complain at this, the second division can be moved speedily, and in that case their exposure "to a want of covering would be justly imputable to themselves only." The transfer of these troops, at all, to Maryland, was, we take it, a measure directed by Congress, as we know not on what other authority it could have been done, or preparations made for them in their new situation.[2]

General Leslie, on learning the course that affairs had taken

---

[1] See Jefferson's letters to General Washington, Nov. 3d and 8th.
[2] And their *General* officers had now been mostly, if not entirely, exchanged.

further South, dispatched a vessel to Charleston for orders, and
in the meantime entered upon no offensive movements. He
obtained a reply November 12th, and immediately embarked,
without even delaying to destroy his unfinished fortifications.
In marked contrast with General Matthew, and with all the
British commanders afterwards in the State, Leslie, during his
short stay in Virginia, had not only conducted with scrupulous
humanity and propriety, but actually thought it worth his while
to punish his soldiers who were guilty " of wanton and unnecessary devastations." [1]

Thus the dangerous storm blew over temporarily, but the
affair presented another warning that fell chillingly on the feelings of intelligent Virginians. If three weeks had not sufficed
to collect a force sufficient to offer the least molestation to three
thousand invaders—whose inaction had been entirely voluntary
—what would, what must be the result, when the British Commander-in-chief so far discovered his true policy as to send a
strong force to operate directly against the State; or when
Cornwallis should put down North Carolina, and then take
Virginia in its turn? Governor Jefferson wrote General Washington on the first appearance of the late enemy:

" We are endeavoring to collect as large a body to oppose them as we can
arm; this will be lamentably inadequate, if the enemy be in any force. It is mortifying to suppose that a people, able and zealous to contend with their enemy,
should be reduced to fold their arms for want of the means of defence. Yet no
resources, that we know of, ensure us against this event.   *   *   *   *
As to the aids of men, I ask for none, knowing that if the late detachment of the
enemy shall have left it safe for you to spare aids of that kind, you will not await
my application. Of the troops we shall raise, there is not a single man who ever
saw the face of an enemy."

This picture proved not to be overdrawn. General Nelson,
the most popular military commander in the State, possessing
great weight among one class by reason of his wealth and position at the head of one of the most distinguished families of the
State, and among another for his zealous devotion to the patriotic cause, flew rapidly from point to point in the lower counties, exerting himself, as a first step, to secure the important pass
at Great Bridge. Even this comparatively inconsiderable undertaking had not been accomplished when Leslie sailed for

---

[1] Jefferson to Washington, Nov. 26.

South Carolina. An almost unarmed people, in an open country, without any advantages for defence, or for the concealment of their families, is necessarily (however much authors in safe garrets may prate to the contrary) a people without courage against assailants known to be invincible by any force they can oppose to them, and believed to be regardless of all the rules of civilized warfare. The robbery of all valuable portable property, and the wanton destruction of most other; the "murder, rapine, rape, and violence,"[1] which had accompanied the desolating march of the first invader, a few months before, was very fresh in the memory of the people who lived in the region where these scenes had been enacted! Was it to be expected that the only gun in a household, and the strong arm to wield it, would, under such recollections, be divided from the *women* and *children* of the family, while they were wildly flying to places of security? Are there not natural duties to mothers, to wives, and to daughters, which take precedence even of duty to one's country?

An important question, deeply affecting Governor Jefferson's reputation for energy and sagacity, thrusts itself at this point upon the thinking reader. He was now fairly forewarned of the defencelessness of his State. He could not but see that the tide of war from both extremities was rolling rapidly towards the centre. It would appear that he ought to have seen that the least intelligent foe, after two such experiments, could no longer misunderstand the real situation of Virginia; and that such a foe would not long omit to plant his blows where they would tell almost equally on the Carolinas, and where they would far more effectually tend to break up the principal Southern nursery of raw soldiers and its principal storehouse of army supplies. And besides the attainment of so much additional territory to the British re-conquest, the possession of the mouth of the Chesapeake and of the lower streams which empty into it, especially James River, could not but be the most tempting lure to an enemy possessing common sagacity.

Why, then, did not Governor Jefferson at once set about preparing his State for future invasion? Why did he not stud her navigable waters with fortresses? Why did he not discipline regiments and keep them at suitable points for prompt

[1] See p. 245.

action? Why did he not hoard up munitions of war? In a word, why did he not put Virginia in the bristling attitude of defiance that an old and warlike European country would assume under like circumstances—that England herself assumed a few years afterward, when threatened with a French invasion? —every art of warlike defence exhausted—the whole yeomanry of the land instantly armed and constantly trained—beacons and watchmen on every headland—and when their fires should light up the sky, a nation prepared to convert itself into an army, and to rush on the disembarking invader?

If these questions have not been already in a great measure answered, we know not how to answer them. Less than one militiaman—that is, less than one citizen between sixteen and fifty years old—to the square mile! Less than one serviceable gun to five militiamen (and consequently to five square miles) in the best armed region east of the mountains! Men owning lands and tenements, who had not seen a shilling in coin for a year! An exposure to external and interior invasion, by water, practically equal to that of all England, without a fortress or fleet capable of withstanding a single frigate! An open border hundreds of miles in length without a particle of defence, and a conquering foe roaming at will on the other side of it! Fifty or a hundred million of dollars requisite to make a thorough system of river and border defences, and scarcely as many thousands attainable by any human device!

Would there have been any use in exhausting what little money the State could raise in erecting two or three fortifications, which, unless defended by the whole disposable force of the State, could not withstand for an hour either the naval or land force of the invader—and certainly not both, acting in concert? And if the whole troops and means of the State would be required to man two or three strong fortresses, what was the rest of the State to do at the same time for protection? For example, inasmuch as the defence of the mouth of the Chesapeake could not have been dreamed of in face of hostile fleets, with ten or twenty times the resources Virginia could then control, the next most important works which could be erected would be, most clearly, those which would command the entrance of the James. Let us suppose this effectually done, and the treasury of the State drained in the effort. What then would prevent Cornwallis, or some other British commander, from entering the State far inside of, or behind, such lower defences of the James—at any point of the open and undefended country between the Cumberland Mountains and the Roanoke? Or what would prevent any fresh expedition from New York literally sailing round those defences, by means of the York and Rappahannock rivers—or if their mouths were also defended, landing at fifty exposed points, which may be readily named, and at once penetrating behind all these coast defences? If the strength of the State was concentrated in the latter, what would then be left to protect that vast interior which they were designed to protect? Of what use, then, would they practically be? How far would a foe dread leaving them behind him (and leaving behind him French fleets into the bargain), who, in case of unforeseen casualties, had, for three hundred miles, a perfectly accessible conterminous province to fall back upon, which, if not entirely subjugated, could at no single point make head against the British forces already in it? Any idea, therefore, of defending Virginia by *fortifications* was in more respects than one wholly out of the question.

One inquiry remains. Did Virginia, at this epoch, make every practicable effort to raise and discipline troops and provide military stores? for, certainly, nothing could furnish any excuse for remissness here. Her Governor and Council believed every effort they were authorized by law to make in that direction was expended. The Legislature, too, seems to have believed it had passed all the laws which the circumstances rendered expedient—and the Legislature was made up principally of that class of citizens which was to suffer most deeply in case of invasion.

There was not a county in Virginia where there was not a recruiting station, and bounties and inducements of every kind were held out for enlistments.[1] These failing, resort was had to drafts or conscriptions.

A few figures at this point will be worth a good deal of

---

[1] An Act was passed in 1779 appointing a recruiting officer in every county, and giving him a premium of $150 00 in paper, equivalent to $12 50 in specie for every enlistment obtained by him; and a bounty of $750 00 in paper, or $62 50 in specie to each recruit—*with privilege of laying out his paper money in the public store at hard money prices.* He also received the usual donation of clothes and lands. (Jefferson to President of Congress, quoted by Girardin, p. 425.)

declamation. It appears by official records that in the beginning of the year 1780 Virginia had four thousand five hundred
regulars in the field. In May, the Assembly ordered one-fif-
teenth of the militia to be drafted into the regular service, equal,
after all deductions, to three thousand men. Twenty-five hundred additional militia were also ordered into Continental service. Thus the State had ten thousand troops (seven thousand
five hundred of them being regulars) in the army of the United
States, and not one of them was retained within her own boundaries, but the handful which guarded the Convention prisoners
at Charlottesville.[1]

An incomplete collection of vouchers showed that from May
21, 1779, to July 19, 1780—about fourteen months—Virginia
had answered for the Continent $13,681,368 56, it being an
excess over the requisitions of Congress during that period of
$4,081,368.[2] This did not include large disbursements made by
the State on its own account. It will be understood, however,
that the preceding sums were in paper money, then greatly
depreciated. But the specie standard would not be the true
one by which to estimate the real expenditures of the State.
Take one example. The State gave a recruit who enlisted for a
certain term $750 in paper money—we believe only equivalent
to $62 50 in specie—yet that recruit could buy goods in the
public store with his bounty money, at its par value. And the
State had, of course, to procure such goods with hard money, or
paper money at merely its commercial value.

We will here remark, that a paper purporting to be an
official statement by General Knox, when Secretary of War,
and giving the number of regulars and militia called into service or brought into service by the different States in the Revolution, does not, we believe (we have not the statement before
us), approach accuracy in regard to Virginia, and we presume not, in regard to many other States. It could only have
been made on very imperfect, and in many respects conjectural
data, as we need scarcely show; and *official conjectures*, are not,
we suppose, more conclusive than individual ones, other things
being equal. General Knox, though a capital soldier, was
not famous for profound and pains-taking research. The means

---

[1] See Governor's Returns to President of Congress, July 27th, 1780.
[2] See Table No. 2, appended to Returns mentioned in preceding note.

for making reliable estimates are still deficient, but they are far fuller than they were during General Knox's secretaryship. We suppose the impression has obtained that his statements were based on full and correct returns in the War Department, and therefore we have noticed them.

Beyond raising and doing its share towards equipping ten thousand troops, the Government of Virginia felt it could do no more at present, except to hold its militia in the best practicable state of efficiency. Strenuous efforts were made in this direction, but they, in reality, wholly failed. What could be done towards disciplining a militia until those weapons could be placed in their hands, the use of which it was the business of discipline to teach them?

Governor Jefferson, as we shall see, had Virginia critics, who blamed him for the *use* he (and his adherents in the Legislature) made of the State troops and militia—but if they blamed him for remissness in organizing and disciplining either kind of force, it is a fact of which not a trace of contemporaneous evidence is left, so far as we have been able to learn. They, on the other hand, blamed him for *doing too much*—and, especially, for doing it in a way which, they claimed, unjustly and perilously sacrificed the particular interests of Virginia.

What they found fault with was that the lioness continued to rush on the hunters before they reached her lair! Virginia continued to pour every enlisted soldier she could raise into the Northern and Southern armies, leaving her own bosom naked to the blow when it should be struck. Was this just to herself —was it expedient? So thought the Commander-in-chief of the American armies, and so thought Congress. The Confederacy had determined to stand or fall together. The war was equally for the whole—as much for Georgia or New Hampshire as for Virginia—and the only question was where could blows be best struck, and danger best averted, for the interest of the whole, no matter what State's bosom was temporarily gored in carrying out this heroic policy.

History presents constant examples of nations giving up a portion of their territories temporarily to uninterrupted ravage, for the purpose of best husbanding their means to ultimately save the whole. Nay, the patriot has been called upon to himself apply the torch to *his* all, to voluntarily cover *his* province with the blackness of desolation, for the purpose of placing famine between the invader and the more defensible parts of his country—and the patriot has responded to that call.

From the first opening of the Revolution to that moment when Virginia was herself (as we shall by and by have occasion to describe) wholly overwhelmed under the tide of actual invasion, General Washington and Congress never ceased to call upon the Virginia Executive to send men and supplies north and south, out of her own borders, as fast as they could be raised. Was this a want of penetration into the enemy's designs by the Commander-in-chief? Was it unfeelingness or misjudgment? Or was it the part of the mariner who throws overboard his treasures, and clears away the driving wreck, whatever the sacrifice, to save the vessel and the remnant of lives intrusted to his charge? Again we say, that if there is a fact in Jefferson's history that we record with real pleasure, it is his unwavering support, amidst lamentations and denunciations at home, of the national and self-sacrificing plan of action of General Washington. And if there is a feature in her Revolutionary history which Virginia has more reason to be proud of than all others, it is this.

Yet candor obliges us to say that the actual difference to her between the results of this policy and that which a natural, though, perhaps, a narrow selfishness would dictate and did dictate, was vastly less than would at first sight appear. If Virginia resolved to make common cause with the other twelve States, there was no way for *her* to escape her share of danger and sacrifice. The enemy that was pressing on the extremities, would, if successful, soon press on the centre. If Georgia and the Carolinas were subjugated, Virginia would come next in the path of conquest—and the easier they fell the more would the enemy be encouraged to urge forward to her overthrow. And, finally, it really cost far less to fight off from her own soil, than to have her resources not only employed to support her own troops but those of the enemy—wastefully, and oftentimes wantonly destroyed in addition, as always happens where an invader is his own purveyor—and, lastly, dried up, for years to come by having her producing classes driven from their occupations.

Be all this as it may, it has been purely an after-thought to accuse Governor Jefferson of remissness. And let the preceding question be decided as it may, on a cool calculation afterwards of the dollars and cents, none the less unselfish and noble was the action of Virginia and its Executive. There are some things besides dollars and cents staked in a war such as was that of the Revolution, as Colonel Lawson's dispatches to Governor Henry had testified! That man who stops to save nothing from his own house, but resolutely stands at the handle of the engine and fights the conflagration as it nears his dwelling, practically aids his neighbor. He, doubtless, keeps in view that if he is successful, he saves his own property—saves it entire, as he would not, if he carried off his goods and surrendered his house to the flames. So, in one sense of the word, he is controlled by the most exacting selfishness. But in that same sense, we apprehend that patriotism, and religion, and all that is good, are but manifestations of selfishness.

And at about the close of 1780, Virginia made another enormous practical sacrifice—a sacrifice of property which her citizens believed as much hers as her capital—for the benefit of the Confederation. She ceded to the United States that great territory northwest of the Ohio River, out of which are formed the present States of Ohio, Indiana, Illinois, Michigan, and Wisconsin. Governor Jefferson wrote the President of Congress on the occasion.[1]

"I do myself the honor of transmitting to your Excellency the resolution of the General Assembly of this Commonwealth, entered into in consequence of the resolution of Congress of September the 6th, 1780, on the subject of the Confederation. I shall be rendered very happy if the other States of the Union, equally impressed with the necessity of that important convention, shall be willing to sacrifice equally to its completion. This single event, could it take place shortly, would overweigh every success which the enemy have hitherto obtained, and render desperate the hopes to which those successes have given birth."

Another incident of the year deserves to be mentioned. Colonel Clarke came to Richmond in December—burning to execute his long deferred project against Detroit. Governor Jefferson fell in with it, and now for additional reasons to those which had urged, the year before. They were thus stated in a letter to General Washington, December 15th; which also shows how clearly the writer understood the dangers which impended over the State in other quarters:

[1] Jan. 17, 1781.

"The army the enemy at present have in the South, the reinforcements still expected there, and their determination to direct their future exertions to that quarter, are not unknown to you. The regular force, proposed on our part to counteract those exertions, is such, either from the real or supposed inability of this State, as by no means to allow a hope that it may be effectual. It is, therefore, to be expected that the scene of war will either be within our country, or very nearly advanced to it; and that our principal dependence is to be on militia, for which reason it becomes incumbent to keep as great a proportion of our people as possible free to act in that quarter. In the meantime, a combination is forming in the westward, which, if not diverted, will call thither a principal and most valuable part of our militia. From intelligence received, we have reason to expect that a confederacy of British and Indians, to the amount of two thousand men, is formed for the purpose of spreading destruction and dismay through the whole extent of our frontier in the ensuing spring. Should this take place, we shall certainly lose in the South all aids of militia beyond the Blue Ridge, besides the inhabitants who must fall a sacrifice in the course of the savage eruptions."

This "militia beyond the Blue Ridge" was by far the best armed in the State, and it was composed of the material which, with Clarke, had waded for days the drowned lands of the Wabash, in the frosts of February; and which, under Campbell, had tested the relative capacities of the border rifle and bayonet, at King's Mountain.

Believing there was no time to be lost, Governor Jefferson determined to wait no longer for the Confederation to assume the expense—but to leave that question for subsequent determination. "To save time and an immense expense of transportation," however, he asked General Washington for the loan of certain articles from Fort Pitt, which lay in the proposed route of the expedition. The express which bore this request returned with a prompt compliance, with an order to the commandant at the fort to reinforce Clarke with a detachment of artillery, and with the Commander-in-chief's warm plaudits on the undertaking. He said, "he had ever been of the opinion that the reduction of the post at Detroit would be the only certain means of giving peace and security to the whole western frontier," and that "he had constantly kept his eye on that object," but had been deterred from acting by "the low ebb of our funds."[1] Events soon transpired which again prevented the advance of this judiciously concerted expedition.

It is probable that General Philips's return to New York had made Sir Henry Clinton still better aware of the defence-

[1] Sparks's Washington, vol. vii. p. 341.

less condition of the interior of Virginia, than had been learned from the invasions of Matthew and of Leslie; and it is impossible to say how far the traitor Arnold supplied him with information on the same point, but we may conjecture he had something to do with it, from the fact that burning as he was to strike some blow to gratify his own vindictive hate, and to satisfy his present employers that they had not purchased his defection too dearly, he received the command of a flying expedition which Clinton determined to send to make a sudden inroad up the James River and then fall back on reinforcements with which, under another commander, a more deliberate and formidable invasion of Virginia was to be carried on.

The preparations for embarking the first detachment could not be entirely concealed. On the 9th of December, General Washington addressed a circular to the governors of all the States on the seaboard, apprising them of the fact that such an expedition was supposed to be preparing at New York, and that it was "destined for the southward, as was given out there."

This circular was not intended to produce any particular alarm in Virginia, and it did not.[1] "There never had been a

---

[1] See Jefferson to —— (H. Lee), May 15, 1826—Congress edition of Mr. J.'s Works, vol. vii. p. 444, also answers to George Nicholas, presently to be quoted.

Judge Marshall, in his Life of Washington, says: "So early as the 9th of December, 1780, a *letter* from Gen. Washington *announced to the Governor* [Jefferson] that a large embarkation, *supposed to be destined for the South*, was about taking place at New York." This statement is so worded that it conveys an entirely erroneous impression. It would *seem* from it that General Washington, instead of sending a circular to several Governors North and South, only addressed Jefferson, and that instead of communicating a mere rumor in relation to the destination of the expedition, he conveyed a *supposition* (or opinion) *of his own* on that point. Such a supposition, addressed to Jefferson alone, would lead clearly to the inference that General Washington believed, or strongly suspected, that Virginia was particularly menaced. And then again, Judge Marshall's remark that "*so early as the 9th* the letter *announced to the Governor*, etc.," has generally been construed to mean that on that day Jefferson *received the letter*—whereas, it was only written on that day from New Windsor (we think), in the interior of New York: and if it reached the Governor before eight or ten days afterwards, it made an unusually quick passage.

Nothing can be more unfounded than the impression that General Washington either conveyed or sought to convey a shadow of an impression to Jefferson that *he* supposed Virginia was *specially* threatened. Such circulars were often sent, as a matter of reasonable precaution, when unusual movements of the enemy were discovered, or reported with any show of truth; and they had often ended in empty alarms. And there are very strong reasons for believing that General Washington actually supposed Virginia *was not* menaced on this occasion. He wrote Baron Steuben, *then raising Continental forces in Virginia*, the *next day* after dispatching his circular to Governor Jefferson, and after alluding to some affairs of no moment to Virginia, he *closed* (as if almost casually) by saying :

"It is *reported* from New York that the enemy are about to make another detachment, consisting of one battalion of grenadiers, one battalion of light infantry, one battalion of Hessian grenadiers, Knyphausen's regiment, the forty-second British, a draft of five men from each company in the line, and two troops of light dragoons under Generals Knyphausen and Phillips; their destination *conjectured to be southward*. I should be glad to hear from you often, being, dear Baron, etc."

Is this the way in which the Commander-in-chief would have addressed the trusted

time since 1777 when such intimations had not been hanging
over the heads" of the Governor and Council. "General
Washington always considered it as his duty to convey every
rumor of an embarkation." Had "similar informations" from
him "and Congress been considered as sufficient ground at all
times for calling the militia into the field, there would have
been a standing army kept up "—a thing wholly impracticable.
The Virginia authorities had, "for some time past," "never
thought anything but actual invasion should induce them to the
expense and harassments of calling the militia into the field,"
and accordingly they had not done so, except in a particular
instance in 1779, "when it was thought proper to do this in
order to convince the French of their disposition to protect their
ships." It had been "inattention to this necessary economy, in
the beginning, [which] went far towards that ruin of their
finances which followed." Such were the reasons subsequently
assigned by Mr. Jefferson to George Nicholas,[1] for taking no
unusual steps on the receipt of General Washington's circular.
Had he not been addressing a contemporary Virginian, to
whom the fact would be a necessary inference, he might have
added that were the militia ordered out at each of these constantly recurring alarms, they would soon cease to obey such har-
assing requisitions, and thus the State incur the risk of being
left entirely without defenders when the actual danger came.
"Crying wolf" too often is everywhere a dangerous policy.

He might also have added, that General Washington perfectly understood what had been the usual course in Virginia
in regard to such intimations—that they simply led to greater
watchfulness, and nothing more—and that consequently, had he
really believed Virginia was specially menaced, it would, of
course, have been his duty not to content himself with barely
sending a circular so generally worded that he had every reason
to believe it would induce no departure from the usual course.

On the 30th of December, a fleet of twenty-seven sail
entered the capes of Virginia, bearing Arnold and a force
variously estimated from sixteen hundred to two thousand men.

Steuben, the highest officer in command in Virginia, and who would, as a matter of
course, be intrusted with its defence in case of immediate invasion, had he *supposed* or
even *strongly suspected* that an expedition was *on the point* of embarking to *invade that
State ?*
[1] This paper will be found in Randolph's edition of Jefferson's Works, and in the
Congress edition at vol. ix. p. 215.

The next day the Governor was apprised, through a letter from a private gentleman to General Nelson, of the appearance of the fleet,[1] but not whether it was a French or English one, its force, or any other circumstances. Even if English, there was nothing yet to show whether it purposed advancing up the bay in the direction of Baltimore, or up the James. The letter promised further intelligence in a few hours. The Governor, however, *immediately* dispatched General Nelson to the lower country, "with powers to call on the militia in that quarter, or act otherwise, as exigencies should require;" but he "waited further intelligence before he would call for militia from the middle or upper country." It is proper here to mention the following fact, afterwards stated by the Governor to George Nicholas:

"In the summer of 1780, we [the Executive] asked the favor of General Nelson to call together the county lieutenants of the lower counties, and concert the general measures which should be taken for instant opposition, on any invasion, until aid could be ordered by the Executive, and the county lieutenants were ordered to obey his call."[2]

The Legislature was now in session, and the Governor availed himself of "the counsel and information of the members." No further intelligence came until the 2d, when it was ascertained that the fleet was hostile, and that it had advanced up the James to Warrasqueak Bay. Acting on the "general advice," the Governor instantly ordered out the militia, one half from the nearer, and one-third from more remote counties —a requisition considered sufficient to bring four thousand and seven hundred men into the field, in addition to those called out by General Nelson in the lower counties. This was the number asked for by Baron Steuben, the superior Continental officer commanding in the State, and who, intrusted by the Governor with the defence of the State, was now present in Richmond, acting in concert with the Executive for that object. On the same day (Monday, January 2d,) the Legislature adjourned and every member went home.

Arnold had embarked his troops in the lighter vessels of the

---

[1] Jefferson to Washington, January 10th. Professor Tucker, by mistake, says that the Governor received his information on the 30th of December, and that the fleet entered the Chesapeake the day before.—*Life of Jefferson*, vol. i. p. 136.

[2] Jefferson received his information of the appearance of the fleet on Saturday, 31st, at 8 o'clock, A.M., and the "first moment" of receiving it, Nelson started for the lower counties. (See *Answers to Nicholas*.)

fleet; and being remarkably favored by wind and tide, he soon
began to ascend the river about as fast as the expresses dispatched to the Governor could ride. At eight o'clock on the
evening of the 3d, the latter received information that the
enemy were at anchor a little below Jamestown, and accordingly Williamsburg was supposed to be their object. At five
o'clock on the morning of the 4th, it was ascertained that
instead of this, they had ascended the preceding evening to
Kennon's. This evinced a design to penetrate towards Petersburg or Richmond, and the whole militia of the adjacent counties was ordered out, and they were ordered to come on individually, without waiting for any regular array. On passing
Hood's, two or three of the enemy's vessels received some
damage from military works there, but on the enemy landing
to invest them, the garrison, consisting of but fifty men,
retired. At five o'clock in the afternoon of the 5th, the Governor learned that the enemy had landed, and were drawn up
at Westover. This showing that Richmond was their object,
every nerve was now strained to accelerate the removal of the
public stores from that town which had been going on since the
2d. The place of deposit had been the foundry and other
public buildings near Westham (seven miles above Richmond,
and also on the north bank of the James), but now orders were
issued to convey what remained at Richmond directly across
the river. Corresponding orders were dispatched to Westham,
and Captains Brush,[1] and Irish, and Mr. Hylton, sent to drive
forward the work, without intermission, throughout the night.
The Governor went to the last-named place in the evening, and
having, by his presence, urged on the transportation until a late
hour, he rode on, seven or eight miles higher up the river, to
Tuckahoe, the seat of Colonel Thomas Mann Randolph, where
his family had been sent that day. He reached there at one
o'clock at night, and very early the next morning, took his wife
and three little children—the youngest about two months old—
across the river; and having started them off under the charge
of his servants for a place eight miles higher up, he mounted
his horse, and spurred to Britton's, opposite Westham. Having
given some orders for the better security of the public property,
he pushed on at full speed for Manchester, directly across the

[1] Or Boush. It is printed both ways.

river from Richmond. Before reaching there, his powerful horse, worn out by the severe exertions of the last thirty-six hours, sunk dying in the road.[1] The Governor carried his saddle and bridle on his back till he reached a farm-house, where he could only obtain an unbroken colt, and thus mounted, he reached Manchester. The enemy were already in possession of Richmond, and were accordingly in full view on the opposite bank of the river.

Arnold had marched from Westover (the seat of the late Colonel Byrd, twenty-five miles from Richmond) on the afternoon of the 4th, and encamping that night at Four-mile Creek, he reached the Capital about noon on the fifth. So suddenly had these events taken place—and for so short a time had Baron Steuben considered it proper, on military principles, to regard Richmond as the most probable destination of the enemy —that but about two hundred militia, under the command of Colonel John Nicholas, had assembled near the Capital; and they were mostly from the city and its immediate vicinity. They were not strong enough to offer any opposition, and did not attempt it. Richmond was at that time a very moderate-sized village, undefended by any military works.

Having entered the town, Arnold sent forward Lieutenant-Colonel Simcoe to the Public Foundry and Laboratory near Westham, who destroyed such property as had not been sent across the river, and also the public buildings. But the bulk of the arms and more valuable articles had been saved.

The Governor having remained long enough at Manchester to make as good provisions as were practicable for the preservation of the public property and arms there deposited, rode to Chetwood's to meet Baron Steuben, who had appointed that as a rendezvous and as his headquarters. Finding the Baron had proceeded to Colonel Fleming's,[2] four or five miles above Britton's, the Governor followed him thither, and remained there that night. Here he was waited on in the evening by two citizens of Richmond, who bore an offer from Arnold not to burn that town, provided the British vessels should be allowed to come to it and remove the tobacco collected in its warehouses

[1] Mr. Jefferson's Diary of these days would *seem* to make the dying of his horse subsequent to his arrival at Manchester, but there *must*, we think, be some mistake about this, or some carelessness of expression. We follow the account of those who had a hundred times heard the facts from his lips, and those of others.

[2] This is printed "Colonel Henry," in the Congress copy of Mr. Jefferson's Diary (See Congress edition of his Works, vol. ix. p. 213.) This is a misprint.

without molestation. This proposition was contemptuously rejected. And at the very time the traitor was sending it, Simcoe was burning the public buildings near Westham!

On the forenoon of the 6th, Arnold burnt some public and private buildings, and a large amount of private property, consisting of rum, salt, and such tobacco as could not be carried off. He also destroyed such of the public property as was left within his reach—but which was not very considerable.¹ He commenced his retreat at noon, and the next day again reached Westover.

The Governor returned to Westham on the morning of the 6th, and took measures to secure the public papers. He then repaired to the place (Fine Creek) where he had sent his family. On the 7th, he continued the same duties at Westham and Manchester, and passed the night at the latter place. At seven o'clock the next morning he crossed the river, and "resumed his residence" at Richmond.

He had been about eighty-four hours in the saddle, except during short periods devoted to rapid meals and scanty rest. He had been constantly within observing distance of the enemy, and had been making strenuous and successful efforts to save the public property. The remark is not made invidiously, but in the light of some subsequent events, justice demands that we add that in this "crisis of trial," Governor Jefferson "was left alone, unassisted by the coöperation of a single public functionary—for with the Legislature, every member of the Council had departed to take care of his own family."²

When Arnold got back to Westover, on the 7th, Colonel Nicholas had three hundred men six miles above; General Nel-

---

¹ The public loss has been so violently exaggerated by many writers that we publish the Governor's list, which no one, we believe, has either contradicted or attempted to *make additions to,* in specified details. Even Judge Marshall omits to mention that any part of the public property was *saved!*

"*Loss sustained by the Public.*

"The papers and books of the Council since the Revolution. The papers of the Auditors, but not their books. Five brass field-pieces, four pounders, which had been sunk in the river, but were weighed by the enemy. About one hundred and fifty arms in the Capitol loft. About one hundred and fifty in a wagon on the Brook road. About five tons of powder, and some made ammunition at magazine. Some small proportion of the linens, cloths, etc., in the public store. Some quarter-masters' stores; the principal articles were one hundred and twenty sides of leather. Some of the tools in the artificers' shops. Foundry, magazine, four artificers' shops, public store, quarter-masters' store, one artificer's shop, three wagons."

A great part of the powder thrown in the canal was saved by re-manufacturing.

² These are Mr. Jefferson's words in a letter to H. Lee, which is published, without any address, in the Congress edition of his Works, vol. vii. p. 444. This was republished by H. Lee in his (the 2d) edition of his father's "Memoirs of the War in the Southern Department of the U. S." (p. 204), and has never, so far as we know, been disputed

son two hundred at Charles City Court House, eight miles below : two or three hundred at Petersburg had put themselves under General Smallwood, of Maryland, " accidentally there on his passage through the State;" Baron Steuben had eight hundred, and General Gibson a thousand on the south side of James River, pressing forward to reach Hood's before the enemy should pass it.   But the wind, which had been due east to help Arnold up the river, now blew a strong breeze from the west, and sent him down with such speed that he distanced pursuit. Thus, within five days from the first summons, upwards of twenty-five hundred men were in the field, in the dead of winter; and had not Arnold been signally favored by fortune, he would not have escaped without at least a battle. The only blood shed was at Hood's, where Arnold, being out of the reach of pursuit, landed his men.   Colonel George Rogers Clarke being near with an advanced party, drew some of the enemy into an ambuscade, and killed seventeen and wounded thirteen at the first fire; but he was compelled to retreat in confusion.

Such are the minute facts of an expedition, none of which have ever been disproved, or perhaps ever in detail denied,[1] though suppressions and unfriendly colorings have often been employed to give them, in the mass, a very different aspect.

Perhaps no work has gone so far, or had so wide an influence, particularly among military men, in this direction, as Henry Lee's (" Legion Harry's ") "Memoirs of the War in the Southern Department of the United States."   Jefferson used to speak of this book as an amusing "historical novel."   "Legion Harry " was a dashing soldier, a man of considerable ability, and had attractive qualities. Partly, intimates Irving, from General Washington's early partiality for Lee's mother, "the lowland beauty," who was his first love, and who actually (we believe) drew forth his first and only *poetry;* and partly, perhaps, from Lee's really soldierly qualities, he was for a long period a sort of favorite with the Commander-in-chief, and this undoubtedly gave him a success and a standing that he would never have otherwise attained.   Unbiased by his feelings,

---

[1] We have taken all the particulars of this invasion thus far (except one or two unimportant facts given on unquestionable living authority) from Jefferson's contemporaneous Diary, from his letter to General Washington, Jan. 10, 1781, from his answers to the objections of George Nicholas in the Virginia Legislature of 1781-2, from his Letter to H. Lee, May 15, 1826. (See also Girardin, pp. 453, 457.)

we have no doubt that Lee's historical statements of what he
saw or learned directly from reliable authority, may be trusted;
he could be excessively magnanimous to foes who were not personal ones; but that he could be proportionably unscrupulous,
the history of his life, and the tenor of his writings, equally
show. The former we leave to pens, if there are any such,
which can find gratification in the record. With the latter, we
should have nothing to do, did we not regard them as the principal fountain head of those misrepresentations and misconcep-
tions concerning this period of Mr. Jefferson's life, which have
not even yet died away.

The tenor and spirit of his representations are, that Virginia
was easily defensible from Arnold and its subsequent invaders;
that the people of Virginia were ready and willing to do everything that was necessary to this end; but that the public spirit
and public efforts were all paralyzed by the " timidity and
impotence of rulers." " In them " [the rulers] exclaims this
moralizing gentleman, " attachment to the common cause is
vain and illusory, unless guided in times of difficulty by courage, wisdom and conduct!" [1]

This writer's calibre, and his knowledge of the facts in Virginia (where he was not in service at the time), will be readily
estimated by stopping to investigate almost any of his separate
assertions. He declares: " the face of our country [Virginia],
intersected in every quarter by navigable rivers, unprotected by
floating batteries and undefended by forts, manifested the propriety of resorting to this species of defence, as better calculated
than any other within our command to curb the desultory
incursions under which we had so often and severely suffered "
(p. 194.) The conclusion, here, would hardly seem a *sequitur*
from the premises, unless Virginia had from twenty to fifty
millions of dollars to at once expend on the erection of floating
batteries and forts, for no one would think of placing lower the
cost of thus efficiently defending all the navigable rivers " inter-
secting" the State in " every quarter!" That Virginia could
make any approach towards raising so large a sum for her separate defence, above what she was required to do for the Confederacy, is a preposterous proposition.

But in the very next paragraph, "Legion Harry" finds,

---

[1] Lee's Memoirs, 2d edition, pp. 194–196, *et passim.*

certainly, a vastly cheaper substitute. He says: "One single legionary corps of three hundred horse and three hundred musketry, with a battalion of mounted riflemen, accompanied by a battalion of infantry, under a soldier of genius, would have been amply sufficient to preserve the State from insults and injuries," etc. A "soldier of genius" would have been a very desirable acquisition, if he could have made the maintenance of one or two thousand men answer the same purpose as an expenditure of so many millions of dollars for forts and batteries (just pronounced the *best* species of defence " within our command "), and an annual sum probably exceeding five times the annual revenue of the State, for manning and providing those forts and batteries! And it would have been a feat for that number of men to put 99,032 square miles of territory (or 61,352, exclusive of Kentucky), " intersected in every quarter by navigable rivers," above " insults or injuries," from a foe generally paramount at sea, and who could, if he chose, place two, or even three such armies, at the same moment, in Virginia, at points a couple of hundred miles apart from each other !

Mr. Lee seems (on the same page) to point to the regular officers in the State, " bred under the eye of Washington," and now out of command by reason of the " diminished number of rank and file," as capable of supplying such "soldiers of genius." Jefferson tried them all! He placed these regular officers at the head of nearly all the State troops, to the disgust and serious offence of some very influential militia officers.[1] This was his persistent policy. It was not his good fortune to find among them any one who could dispose of enemies after the manner of Captain Bobadil, though he found good and faithful officers who received his full approbation and that of their country. If he had sought among the Virginia commanders out of the State, for this prodigy, it is very difficult to say where he could have found him. The search would have had to be guided by conjecture, for although Virginia had many fine officers, and " Legion Harry " among them, none of them had performed and, we may add, never afterwards did perform any approach to such exploits as Mr. Lee mentions !

To merely dispose of such an invasion as the late one, com-

---

[1] This was one of the strong ingredients in the growing opposition to him.

manded by a couple of such soldiers as Arnold and Simcoe, Mr. Lee concludes: "Six or seven hundred militia," called out from the neighborhood, would have amply sufficed, if the Governor had only "fortunately prepared," by calling them out, "on the receipt of General Washington's letter, early in December." (Here we have Judge Marshall's omissions converted into affirmations! There were, Mr. Lee feels assured, several points between Westover and Richmond, where this militia, after less than its month of training, could stop the largely superior body of regulars commanded by Arnold, and "could hardly fail to bring him to submission." [1]

It is unnecessary to follow further an author who has furnished the principal staple of the facts and opinions on which an extensive class of later writers and readers have formed their estimates of the military efficiency of Mr. Jefferson's administration. It was very fortunate that, at Guilford Court House and elsewhere, Mr. Lee did not fight with the instrument with which he wrote!

Arnold being beyond interception, after leaving Hood's, dropped more slowly down the James, touching at Cobham, Smithfield, and Mackay's Mills, to plunder and destroy. He reached Portsmouth on the 20th, and commenced intrenching himself immediately on the site of General Leslie's abandoned works. By this time, full four thousand Virginia militia were in the field. But they were in no condition to attack a fortified place defended by shipping, nor was it expedient to leave the country uncovered to another sudden blow, if reinforcements from New York should put Arnold in a condition to hazard it. The militia, therefore, were divided into three principal encampments, for the purpose of covering important points, and of being ready to act as circumstances should require. They were placed at Cabin Point, Williamsburg, and Fredericksburg, respectively under the command of Generals Steuben, Nelson, and Weedon.

Governor Jefferson felt that the danger had just begun. His painful sense of this, and of the actual helplessness of his State, found various expressions in his official communications at this period. In answer to a requisition of Congress to send

---

[1] If the curious reader will turn to the description of the ground by which Mr. Lee demonstrates this proposition (p. 195), he will probably be profoundly amused!

provisions to feed the Convention prisoners in Maryland, he wrote the president of that body, January 15th:

"You cannot be unapprised of the powerful armies of our enemy, at this time, in this and the Southern States, and that their future plan is to push their successes in the same quarter, by still larger reinforcements. The forces to be opposed to these, must be proportionably great, and these forces must be fed. By whom are they to be fed? Georgia and South Carolina are annihilated, at least as to us. * * * * Instead of sending aids of any kind to the northward, it seems but too certain that unless very timely and substantial assistance be received from thence, our enemies are yet far short of the ultimate term of their successes."

* * * *

"I am far from wishing to count or measure our contributions by the requisitions of Congress. Were they ever so much beyond these, I should readily strain them in aid of any one of our sister States. But while they are so far short of those calls to which they must be pointed in the first instance, it would be great misapplication to divert them to any other purpose; and I am persuaded you will think me perfectly within the line of duty, when I ask a revisal of this requisition."

He wrote the Virginia delegates in Congress, January 18th:

"The loss of powder lately sustained by us (about five tons), together with the quantities sent on to the southward, have reduced our stock very low indeed. We lent to Congress, in the course of the last year (previous to our issues for the Southern army), about ten tons of powder. I shall be obliged to you to procure an order from the Board of War, for any quantity from five to ten tons, to be sent us immediately from Philadelphia or Baltimore, and to inquire into and hasten, from time to time, the execution of it. The stock of cartridge paper is nearly exhausted."

To General Washington, February 8th:

"The fatal want of arms puts it out of our power to bring a greater force into the field than will barely suffice to restrain the adventures of the pitiful body of men they have at Portsmouth. Should any more be added to them, this country will be perfectly open to them, by land as well as water."

To the same, February 12th:

"Baron Steuben transmits to your Excellency, a letter from General Greene, by which you will learn the events which have taken place in that quarter since the defeat of Colonel Tarleton by General Morgan. These events speak best for themselves, and no doubt will suggest what is necessary to be done to prevent the successive losses of State after State, to which the want of arms and of a regular soldiery, seems more especially to expose those in the South."

To General Gates. February 17th:

VOL. I.—20

" I have been knocking at the door of Congress for aids of all kinds, but especially of arms, ever since the middle of summer. The speaker, Harrison, is gone to
be heard on that subject. Justice, indeed requires that we should be aided powerfully. Yet, if they would repay us the arms we have lent them, we should give
the enemy trouble, though abandoned to ourselves."

In this moment, when the future lowered so portentously
over Virginia, " abandoned to herself," Governor Jefferson
received intelligence from General Greene soon after the battle
of Cowpens, that he (Greene) was flying before Cornwallis, who
was furiously pressing on his rear to drive him to an unequal
battle. The Governor immediately ordered seven hundred
mountain riflemen from the region which had furnished troops
for King's Mountain, five hundred common militia, and five
hundred recruits assembled at Chesterfield Court House, to
advance at once to North Carolina for the succor of Greene.[1]

During the month of January, Governor Jefferson concerted
an attempt, with General Muhlenburg, to seize the person of
Arnold, and the former offered five thousand guineas[2] to the
party which should bring him off alive. (Our ancestors did not
hire assassins!) But the miserable parricide seems to have
anticipated some such attempt. He kept close in his quarters
at Portsmouth, or moved forth only when strongly guarded.
During his further stay in Virginia, the daring courage which
had appeared to court death under the walls of Quebec and
before the British intrenchments at Saratoga, seems to have
given place to an excessive caution.

Perhaps there was some reason for it. The attempt of
Sergeant Champe, of Lee's Legion, who, with the approbation
of his commander and of General Washington, apparently fled
to the British camp as a deserter, to bring off Arnold, is familiar
to all readers. If taken, Arnold's shrift would have been a
short one. When Lafayette was sent (as we shall presently see)
to Virginia, he was directed by the Commander-in-chief, in
case of the capture of Arnold, " to execute him in the most
summary way." [3]

Before the close of January, 1781, the southern mountaineers of Virginia, and their confederates in the adjoining regions

[1] Girardin, p. 480.
[2] A large share, if not the whole, of this sum was doubtless to be furnished by
Congress.
[3] Washington to Lafayette, Feb. 20, 1781.

of North Carolina, had struck one of their usually decisive
blows on the Indian border. The Cherokees, occupying extensive regions on the head waters of the Cumberland and Tennessee rivers, and further south, had been alienated from the
United States by British emissaries, and a season of uncommon
distress had ripened this feeling into one of active hostility.
Governor Jefferson dispatched an officer to them to propose that
a deputation of their chiefs visit the national capital and lay
their supposed grievances before Congress. But the message
arrived too late. The barbarous rites had been performed
which announced that they would immediately take the war
path. The Virginia and Carolina borderers did not wait to be
attacked in their homes. Assembling under Colonel Campbell,
the hero of King's Mountain, they suddenly descended upon the
Indian territory. Their success was complete. Few of the
Cherokees were killed or taken, as they fled before their assailants. But all their towns and stores on the Upper Tennessee
were destroyed; and Colonel Campbell, in dictating terms of
peace to them, by the directions of Governor Jefferson retained
the right to erect a fort at the junction of the Holston and
Tennessee rivers. It was necessary to obtain the permission of
Congress for its erection, the spot being out of the limits of Virginia. As soon as this was done, the fort was built, and it
proved an effectual bridle on the Indians, and preserved henceforth an uninterrupted communication between Eastern Virginia and the Mississippi.[1]

Soon after succeeding General Gates in the command of
the Southern Department, General Greene had directed that
movement of General Morgan's which brought on the battle of
Cowpens, between the latter and Tarleton, on the 17th of January. The Virginia troops bore a conspicuous part in this
brilliant and successful action. Both joyfully and sadly,
General Stevens wrote Governor Jefferson concerning it (January 24th):

"In my former letters, I informed you what troops Morgan's command was
composed of. They, in general, behaved well; though it adds greatly to my satisfaction that the detachment of Virginia militia under the immediate command of
Triplet, are spoken of with the greatest applause for their behavior on that day.

[1] Jefferson to Washington, Feb. 17; to Colonel Campbell, Feb. 17; and see Girardin
p. 472.

This I hope will wipe off some of the stain of the 16th of August. I am truly unfortunate, as I could not partake in the doing of it; and am rendered now much more so, as I have not the smallest glimpse of hope left of doing anything in that way with those men, who are under my immediate command, as their time is just about expiring, and I am ordered to march in the morning to take charge of the prisoners, and conduct them to Virginia. I must endeavor to reconcile myself to my hard fate. Colonel Washington, of the cavalry, distinguished himself in a particular manner. He, with only fifty horse, charged the enemy's cavalry and drove them."

Cornwallis, reinforced by Leslie, was but twenty-five miles from the Cowpens when the battle took place, and he pressed rapidly forward in pursuit of Morgan. His van reached the west bank of the Catawba at nightfall, but two hours after the Americans had passed over. A heavy fall of rain in the night rendered the river unfordable for two days, and Morgan made good his retreat. Greene soon took command of his detachment, Morgan retiring on account of ill-health;[1] and he employed himself actively in effecting a junction between the divisions of his army. It was with Morgan's prisoners, taken at the Cowpens, that Stevens was ordered to Virginia by Greene, when he wrote Governor Jefferson the letter just quoted from. But he was subsequently recalled, and the prisoners were escorted onward by a body of North Carolina militia.

Cornwallis forced the fords of the Catawba, February 1st, and Greene then commenced that retreat of two hundred miles, conducted in the depth of winter, before an entirely superior force, and commaded by as energetic a soldier as Britain ever sent to America, which is so celebrated in the annals of the Southern war. It was a miracle in the military art that he escaped; and it required almost physical miracles in the action of the elements, to save him. The van and rear-guards of the hostile armies were often in sight, and twice, at least, a sudden torrent of rain and a sudden rise of a river the moment Greene had crossed it—as happened in the case of Morgan on the Catawba—gave the Americans time to gain on their better provided pursuers. The shoes of Greene's men were worn out, their clothes were in tatters, and there was not more than one blanket for four.[2] On the night of the 14th of February, he threw his exhausted troops over the Dan into Virginia, with

[1] He appears to have been suffering from rheumatism. (See *Lee's Memoirs*, etc. on this subject, p. 139.)
[2] Lee's Memoirs, etc., p. 148.

the feelings with which the dweller amidst wildernesses, chased by furious beasts of prey, finally reaches the door of his own habitation.   And here Cornwallis's pursuit terminated.

Some of the Virginia militia, and particularly the rifles, had performed most effective service at the passage of the Yadkin, but soon after that stream was crossed, Stevens's corps gave evidence of their former demoralization.   Their time was now out, and though Greene, says Girardin, could scarcely muster eight hundred men fit for action—including Stevens's corps—and though Stevens paraded them and implored them to remain for a few days until a junction could be formed with General Huger's division—they sullenly refused.   They were accordingly marched to Pittsylvania Court House, and discharged after their arms were secured.   Stevens, therefore, did not, from the Yadkin, share in the honorable dangers of Greene's retreat.

The people of Halifax—the Virginia county entered by the Southern army on its retreat over the Dan—received the fugitives with open arms, and lavished on them every hospitality. Volunteers from that and the neighboring counties (where Stevens, since his return, had also, by the orders of the Virginia Executive, been organizing and disciplining forces), prepared to join Greene's standard.   "There was no restraint on the numbers that embodied," wrote Jefferson to Washington (February 26th), "but the want of arms."

Cornwallis, after resting one day, turned his army towards Hillsborough. North Carolina was now apparently substantially subjugated. Its numerous Tories were rising in all directions. Seven independent companies of these were raised in a day, and large bodies were organizing on Haw River.[1] To give time to complete these movements, and to formally reëstablish a royal government, was the object of the British commander.

Greene determined to follow, and for the reasons set forth in the following letter to Governor Jefferson:

"When the enemy first took their departure from the Dan, they had every prospect of great reinforcements from the Tories of Carolina; and I reflected that, if they were permitted to roam at large in the State, it would indubitably impress the idea of conquest upon the minds of the disaffected, and, perhaps, occasion those who were wavering in their sentiments, to take a decisive and active part

[1] Marshall.

against us   I instantly determined (as the most effectual measure to prevent it) to advance into the State without waiting for those reinforcements which the spirit of the Virginians at that time seemed to promise me. It was necessary to convince the Carolinians that they were not conquered; and by affording imme- diate protection to their property, to engage the continuance of their confidence and friendship."

Candor compels us to add that the enthusiasm of the Vir- ginia militia, mentioned by Governor Jefferson to General Washington—and on which, it would seem, General Greene had founded many expectations—proved very evanescent. On the 10th of May, the latter again wrote Jefferson :

"Every day has given me hopes of being stronger, but I have been as con- stantly disappointed. The militia, indeed, have flocked to me from various quar- ters, and seemed to promise me as much as I could wish; but they soon get tired with difficulties, and go and come in such irregular bodies, that I can make no calculations on the strength of my army, nor direct any future operations that can ensure me the means of success."

These remarks were applied equally to the Virginia and North Carolina militia. There was, doubtless, greatly too much truth in them—for Greene's statements are always perfectly reliable; but few of the commanders in the regular line, had much patience with the desultory movements of militia, or could make sufficient allowances for them. Very soon after the above letter was written, Greene *was* reinforced by upwards of a thousand Virginia militia who did not get " tired with diffi- culties," and who proved themselves men on the field of battle.

The first affair of consequence between the hostile forces took place on the 25th of February. Lee's legion, two Mary- land companies, and between three and four hundred North Carolina militia, under Brigadier Pickens, were sent to act against a body of Loyalists who had risen on the Haw, and against Tarleton, who had gone to escort the former to the British camp. Lee came upon these Tories four hundred strong, and was mistaken by them for Tarleton. He kept up the delu- sion, listening to their loyal professions until his dispositions were completed, and then instantly charged. Ninety of the Loyalists were killed, and most of the survivors wounded. The Americans lost not a man, and only one horse. Lee was accused of cruelty, and of having imitated the conduct of Tarle- ton at the Waxhaws, in refusing quarter. Steadman declares that the Loyalists " called out for quarter, but no quarter was granted, and between two and three hundred of them were inhumanly butchered while in the act of begging for mercy." We have followed Lee's statement of the number slain, and he justified his conduct on the plea of necessity.[1] His countrymen, generally, we believe, have accepted that justification. Whether they have stopped to nicely weigh the "necessity" of the case, we cannot say; we suspect they have usually put their decision on the broader ground of a merited retaliation.[2]

Greene, having at length received reinforcements which

---

[1] Lee says in his Memoir (p. 156):

"During this sudden rencontre, in some parts of the line the cry of mercy was heard, coupled with assurance of being our best friends; but no expostulation could be admitted in a conjuncture so critical. Humanity even forbade it, as its first injunction is to take care of your own safety; and our safety was not compatible with that of the supplicants, until disabled to offend."

[2] Lee does not (so far as we have observed) give the *numbers* engaged. It would appear from Girardin that the *Tories* numbered four hundred (p. 483). Marshall says the North Carolina militia, which formed a part of the American force, numbered "between three and four hundred" (vol. i. p. 409). He gives no further numbers, and pronounces this "terrible carnage" an "unavoidable one." He puts the Loyalist loss at "more than one hundred." Lee says the North Carolina militia were "of the best sort," and were riflemen. He speaks of them as "*half* of our *infantry*" on this occasion. In addition to them, were the infantry of the legion and "two companies of the veterans of Maryland, under Captain Oldham." And finally, there was the cavalry of the Legion. If we may trust these several accounts, then, the Tories were probably opposed to as many or more than their own number of *regulars*, and nearly as many more militia. They were "mounted like our militia," and armed with "rifles and fowling pieces." They were carefully hemmed in on every side, while Lee was passing "along the line at the head of the column with a smiling countenance, dropping, occasionally, expressions complimentary to the good looks and commendable conduct of his loyal friends." From Lee's saying that their guns were on their shoulders, with the muzzles opposite his cavalry—and that "in the event of discovery, they must have changed the direction before they could fire—*a motion not to be performed, with a body of dragoons close in with their horses' heads, and their swords drawn*," we are led to infer that they were *charged* in this situation. They were completely surprised, and if they had offered any serious resistance, the other side would have hardly escaped without the loss of a single man.

It is very difficult, therefore, to see how this "terrible carnage" was "*unavoidable;*" and we have no doubt whatever that our countrymen, in justifying the transaction, have pronounced it a necessary retaliation, instead of a necessary carnage, without waiting to ask nicely whether retaliation should have been inflicted by Lee or by a superior officer near by, in efficient command, and from whose army Lee's force was a detachment, sent out with no such orders. In this respect, there was, morally, a broad line of distinction between this case and the execution at King's Mountain. But at King's Mountain the "execution" was *formally* such; while the "carnage" of *these* Loyalists was, ostensibly, in battle.

Lee declares that he had concluded, after completing all his arrangements, to make known his real character to the Loyalists, and then give them "solemn assurance" of safety, "with the choice of returning to their homes or of taking a more generous part, by uniting with the defenders of their common country against the common foe." "Grasping Pyle [the Loyalist leader] by the hand, Lee was in the act of consummating his plan," he says, when the enemy's left, discovering Pickens's militia in ambush, "began to fire upon the rear of the cavalry commanded by Captain Eggleston," and "this officer instantly turned upon the foe, as did immediately after the whole column!" The fire on Eggleston does not appear to have been a very *fatal* one! It does not seem to have produced any "conjuncture so critical," that "humanity forbade" "cries of mercy" to be answered in any other way than by the sabre, the bayonet, and the rifle until scarce an enemy was left unkilled or unwounded!

In a word, it seems to us the most transparent nonsense to attempt to put in any other plea or pretence for this occurrence, than the terrible though sometimes necessary plea of *retaliation*.

considerably increased his army, determined to offer battle to
Cornwallis. The armies met a few miles from Guilford Court
House, on the 15th of March. The Virginia regulars and
militia appear to have comprised more than half of Greene's
army,¹ and, with the exception of one Maryland regiment, to
have done nearly all the fighting.² Stevens here had the inexpressible satisfaction to see his militia stand firm, until over-
powered. Then himself severely wounded, he ordered a retreat.

Greene had double the force of the foe, his choice of ground,
fresh troops, and entirely the superiority in firing. The British
loss was double, and included about one-third of its entire force.
Cornwallis had, however, the best material, his troops being
veteran, while of Greene's four regular regiments, three were
late recruits, only sprinkled with a few old soldiers.

It is but doing the British commander justice, however, to
say, that in rushing as he did to the attack (as if he supposed
his opponent might change his mind and decline the battle) and
in the undaunted gallantry with which he fought on with his
troops reduced to a handful, until he drove the Americans from
the field, he emulated the best feats which the stubborn courage
and admirable physical stamina of Englishmen have placed in a
record, which is full of glorious exploits. He exhibited no
exquisite manœuvring—seems to have aimed at none—but simply laid on with the iron will and unflinching muscle, with
which the followers of Edward III. and the Black Prince laid
on at Cressy. But he would have purchased his victory most
dearly if only one man he lost here had fallen. Lieutenant-
Colonel Webster was mortally wounded.

It is difficult for a mere "layman" to see exactly why it
was necessary for Greene to lose this field. He fought with
his usual courage and conduct, and neither of these have ever
been doubted by his countrymen. Had his regulars formed
his first line, flanked with the same deadly sharp-shooters and
cavalry—his militia forming the reserve—it would seem to an

¹ Greene's army was formed into three lines, the first, two North Carolina militia regiments; the second, two Virginia militia regiments (under Stevens and Lawson); the third,
two Virginia and two Maryland regiments of regulars. Strong corps of observation,
composed principally of Virginia regular cavalry and rifle militia, were posted on each
wing.
² The first line acted over the scene of Camden—the second fought well, and until
ordered to retreat—and of the third line, one of the Maryland regiments most unaccountably fell into a panic and fled. The parties on each flank fought desperately to the
last.

inexperienced eye that Cornwallis must have been crushed at the outset. Why the militia should have been drawn out in front here, as at Camden, and so many other Revolutionary fields—merely to be dispersed like chaff and demoralized as soldiers for the future'—their very arms often being thrown away and lost—(and it is wonderful that this constantly recurring scene did not oftener shake the regulars in reserve)—it surpasses one ignorant of military affairs to say.

It is not our province to follow the career of Greene further. Whether the Virginia Executive supported him efficiently let such facts as we have given declare. Lee (or his editor and commentator) conveys the idea, we think, that Greene himself thought differently. This must be a mistake. The distinguished biographer of General Greene (Judge Johnson), who, from his careful investigation of the facts of Greene's military career, and from (we suppose) a full inspection of his papers, ought, certainly, to be quite as well apprised of his opinions as any other man, thus speaks of Jefferson's official action at this period :

"Never did an officer of the United States experience more cordial and zealous support than that which Greene received at this time from Governor Jefferson. That the Governor's office in another quarter[2] should have been less ready, less judicious, or less efficient, it is difficult to conceive. Every requisition of the commanding general was promptly complied with ; the militia of the neighboring counties ordered into the field, and several active and spirited measures pursued for replenishing Washington's corps of horse. *Indeed, it is a well-known fact that his popularity was at this time greatly affected by charges of his having done too much ;* and if we suppose his efforts in other quarters to have been met with the same querulous spirit, it is not difficult to assign a cause why there was not sufficient preparation made for repelling the incursions of Arnold."[3]

If better proof is desired of General Greene's views, it is furnished in a letter of General Washington to General Greene, not long after the battle of Guilford Court House (April 18th), in which he says : "I am much pleased to find, by your letter, that the State of Virginia exerts itself to your satisfaction."[4] This would appear to be decisive on the point.

---

[1] It is true that the second line of militia did very well at Guilford Court House, but it was known they could not withstand the bayonet, and when that was to be resorted to, they were ordered to retire. Yet they fought well enough to have composed an admirable reserve to pour fresh on a broken enemy.
[2] That is, in Virginia, under the invasion of Arnold.
[3] Judge Johnson's Life of General Greene.   [4] Sparks's Washington, vol. viii. p. 17

We have already seen that Governor Jefferson understood perfectly the danger of his own State—that he anticipated that Arnold's invasion was only the forerunner of a more serious one—but that in face of these things, he continued those exertions out of the State, which the biographer of General Greene justly states, as a notorious fact, "greatly affected" his popularity at home. A strong party at home arrayed themselves against the Governor's policy and line of action. But, as already said, their complaint was not that he did too little; it was that he "did too much." They wanted him to content himself, if not entirely, at least to a much greater extent, with efforts to defend Virginia on her own soil.

We have already more than once asserted that in following the opposite policy—in throwing away the shield as well as the sword and spear of Virginia, in defence of her weaker Southern sisters—in presenting her own bosom naked and defenceless to the blow which he saw was impending—Governor Jefferson acted on the direct advice of that great soldier to whom the United States had committed their military destinies.

The whole tenor and spirit of General Washington's military orders, correspondence, and acts, from the breaking out of the war, prove this. And we are prepared to show, by the same evidence, that towards the close of 1780, and through a part of 1781, he distinctly appreciated the defencelessness of Virginia—anticipated invasion—was not in the least surprised at the result of Arnold's invasion—foresaw that it would prove the precursor of other invasions—yet still, with a marvellous firmness, called upon his native Virginia to persist in a policy which those who did not dare to attack him were bitterly denouncing in the Executive of their State!

He wrote Governor Jefferson, February 6th, 1781—in allusion to Arnold's recent incursion:

"It is mortifying to see so inconsiderable a party committing such extensive depredations with impunity; *but, considering the situation of your State, it is matter of wonder that you have hitherto suffered so little molestation.*[1] *I am appre-*

---

[1] There was another eminent Virginian who *wondered* as little as the Commander-in-chief. James Madison, then in Congress, wrote Edmund Pendleton:
"The enterprise against Richmond, at this season, was certainly an audacious one, and strongly marks the character which directed it. Having been long sensible that the security of the country, as high up as tide-water reaches, has *been owing more to the ignorance and caution of the enemy* than to its own strength and inaccessibleness. I was much less astonished at the news than many others. To those who are strangers to the sparse manner in which that country is settled, and the easy penetration afforded by its long

hensive you will experience more in future; nor should I be surprised if the enemy were to establish a post in Virginia till the season for opening the campaign here."

And he magnificently added:

"But as the evils you have to apprehend from these predatory incursions *are not to be compared to the injury of the common cause*, and with the danger to your State in particular, from the conquest of the States to the southward of you, I am persuaded the attention to your immediate safety will not divert you from the measures intended to reinforce the Southern army, and put it in a condition to stop the progress of the enemy in that quarter. The late accession of force makes them very formidable in Carolina, too powerful to be resisted without powerful succors from Virginia; and it is certainly her policy, *as well as the interest of America, to keep the weight of the war at a distance from her*. There is no doubt that a principal object of Arnold's operations is to make a diversion in favor of Cornwallis, and to remove this motive, by disappointing the intention, will be one of the surest ways of removing the enemy." [1]

General Washington wrote Baron Steuben, then in command in Virginia, February 20th:

"THE EFFECT OF DERANGING THE MEASURES OF THE STATE FOR SUCCORING GENERAL GREENE WAS TO BE EXPECTED. It is however an event of the most serious nature; and I am persuaded, if the enemy continue in the State, as their force is not large, *you will do everything in your power to make the defence of the State as little as possible interfere with an object of so much the more importance, as the danger is so much the greater*. From the picture General Greene gives of his situation, *everything is to be apprehended if he is not powerfully supported from Virginia*."

We do not remember a suggestion from General Washington to Governor Jefferson, during this whole period, to do more or to do anything for the special defence of Virginia except that in a letter in the autumn of 1780 (November 8th) he proposed the construction of some boats, on account of the extreme exposure of Virginia by means of her numerous rivers.[2] Attempts were made to provide the recommended boats, but no legislative action enabled an efficient provision to be made in this direction; and the superior swiftness and strength of the invader

navigable rivers, the rapid and unopposed advances of the enemy appear unaccountable, and our national character suffers imputations which are by no means due to it."—*Madison Papers*, vol. i. p. 79.

[1] For this letter see Sparks's Washington, vol. vii. p. 402.

[2] General Washington's remarks seem to us to strongly corroborate some views we have heretofore expressed.

"Should the enemy continue in the lower parts of Virginia, they will have every advantage by *being able to move up and down the rivers in small parties, while it will be out of our power to molest them* for wanting of the means of suddenly transporting ourselves across those rivers to come at them."

on the water to anything Virginia could have effected, rendered what was done of little use, and showed how completely ineffi- cient and powerless was this means of defence.

It will be observed that General Washington bases his habitual advice to the Virginia Executive on two grounds. He distinctly holds out that the " common cause " demands every sacrifice—but then he even goes so far as to aver that the immediate safety and policy of Virginia requires her to spend her last effort " to keep the weight of the war at a distance from her !" We will not undertake to decide whether the Com- mander-in-chief and Governor Jefferson took the soundest and broadest view of these questions. Their motives, at least, were such as we should expect from the men. No " pent up " Vir- ginia confined their patriotism or their sympathies ! Of the absolute and practical accuracy of their conclusions let connois- seurs in military affairs judge.

The British Lieutenant-General, at least, appears to have seen the full force of their policy, and to have deemed it neces- sary to propose as decisive a policy for its counteraction. Corn- wallis wrote Clinton, April 10th (1781) :

" I cannot help expressing my wishes that the Chesapeake may become the seat of the war, even, if necessary, at the expense of abandoning New York. *Until Virginia is in a manner subdued, our hold upon the Carolinas must be difficult, if not precarious.*"

Clinton, at the same time, was looking for the same results, by a movement north of Virginia, on the Chesapeake. (See his letter to General Phillips, April 11th, in Sparks's Washing- ton, vol. 7, p. 458, note.)

The campaign of 1781, concerted between General Washing- ton and the Count de Rochambeau, was based on the same general plan with that of the preceding year. Again it was decided that the reduction of New York " ought to be preferred to every other object," if France sent reinforcements enough to justify an attack. Failing in this, " as a secondary object, the reduction of Charleston—and Savannah, Penobscot, and other places might come successively into contemplation." [1] But at present the Northern army, weakened by the insurrection of

[1] Washington's "Instructions" to Knox, Feb. 10, 1781.

the Pennsylvania and New Jersey lines, was in a condition to attempt nothing—and scarcely sufficient to hold Sir Henry Clinton in check, though weakened by his recent detachments to the South.

The Chevalier Destouches, in command of the French fleet blockaded at Newport by the English fleet, under Admiral Arbuthnot, was so far relieved of the superiority of the latter by a storm, that he was enabled (February 9th) to dispatch a ship of the line and two frigates, under M. de Tilley, against Arnold at Portsmouth. The Virginia delegates in Congress had, through the French Minister, De la Luzerne, earnestly solicited such an expedition, and they had represented the force now sent as adequate to the object.

De Tilley entered the Chesapeake on the 14th of February. His ships were found wholly unsuitable for the object in view. His largest could not reach the British vessels drawn up in shallow water, and his frigates were not sufficient to cut them out from under the guns of Portsmouth. Having blockaded the mouth of the river a few days, he set sail for Newport, and off the capes of Virginia fell in with and captured the British man-of-war Romulus, 44, from Charleston. Aboard of her, says Girardin, " were persons formerly residing in Virginia, some of whom [were] traitors, who deserved exemplary punishment —and others, vindictive enemies of the State. For these persons it was fortunate that the allies thought it unworthy of their arms to imitate the cruel policy adopted by Clinton and Cornwallis in South Carolina."

The expedition of De Tilley had been communicated to General Washington, at its inception, for his advice. The latter at once foresaw the importance of a much more powerful armament, and proposed that the whole French fleet undertake it, carrying a land force and a siege train; and he offered to send Lafayette at the head of twelve hundred American troops to coöperate by land. To gain time, he immediately ordered the latter forward. Rochambeau's first letter, proposing the expedition, was unfortunately from February 3d to February 14th in reaching General Washington, and the latter did not send his reply until the 19th, so that De Tilley had been gone ten days when it arrived. General Washington did not, however, recall Lafayette, for reasons that will presently appear. The French were entirely cordial to General Washington's plan, and on the return of De Tilley, being placed on about an equality with the English, avowed their willingness to undertake it. General Washington proceeded to Newport, aided in arranging the expedition, and on the 8th of March it sailed.[1] Arbuthnot followed two days after, overtook the French off the mouth of the Chesapeake, and an engagement ensued, in which both sides claimed the victory. In the thanks voted to Destouches by Congress, it was stated that the English had the superiority in force. General Washington declared the same in a letter to Colonel Laurens.[2] Mr. Sparks (whom we regard as an extremely well informed and fair writer) states the English had the superiority in guns, and the French in men. A French council of war determined that it was expedient to return to Newport.

General Washington had written Governor Jefferson on the 21st of February, desiring him to call out a strong force of militia to coöperate with the expedition. The letter reached the Governor in seven days. He immediately ordered four thousand militia into the field; and ten or twelve hundred began to assemble in North Carolina. Early in March the Virginia militia had moved down in the vicinity of Portsmouth, cutting off Arnold's supplies, and greatly distressing him, until it was learned the French fleet had retired. This bootless movement of the Virginia militia was (General Washington wrote Colonel Laurens) attended with "much inconvenience" to that State.

It becomes evident that about as the spring opened General Washington penetrated the intention of the British commanders to exert their principal force, during the ensuing campaign, against the South, and his own views, therefore, underwent some modifications. His detaching Lafayette to Virginia is, we think, the first indication of this. A British expedition, which sailed south under General Phillips in March, showed that Virginia was becoming very seriously menaced. On the failure of the French expedition against Portsmouth, General Washington

[1] The particulars of the arrangement of the two expeditions, of the conduct of the French, and of the spirit they manifested towards General Washington throughout, will be found in Sparks's edition of his correspondence, supported by the letters on *both sides*. In Marshall's Washington, a very different version of the affair is given.
[2] Letter of April 9th. Sparks's Washington, vol. viii. p. 6.

evidently became deeply alarmed. He wrote General Lincoln April 4th :

"Every day convinces me, that the enemy are determined to bend their force against the Southern States, and that we must support them powerfully from this quarter or they will be lost. Unless such support is given in time, it will be ineffectual."

He wrote Lafayette April 6th :

"Since my letter to you of yesterday, I have attentively considered of what vast importance it will be to reinforce General Greene as speedily as possible ; more especially as there can be little doubt that the detachment under General Phillips, if not part of that now under the command of General Arnold, will ultimately join, or in some degree coöperate with Lord Cornwallis. I have communicated to the general officers, at present with the army, my sentiments on the subject ; and they are unanimously of the opinion, that the detachment under your command should proceed and join the Southern army.   * *   It will be well to advise Governor Jefferson of your intended march through the State of Virginia ; or perhaps it might answer a good purpose, were you to go forward to Richmond yourself, after putting your troops in motion, and having made some necessary arrangements for their progress."

The same fixed opinion that Southern affairs had arrived at a most critical pass, and that reinforcements must be hastened to that quarter, is expressed to General Wayne and other correspondents at this period. We have not the remotest hint that the Commander-in-chief dreamed that Virginia ought to, or possibly could, with such aid as she could derive from the Carolinas, withstand the hostile forces now collecting in the South.[1] If he speaks about pushing *through* Virginia, to support Greene in the Carolinas, it was only carrying out the old policy, because he hoped to give the enemy occupation there, and confine them to regions already ravaged, without blackening another and a new State with the fires of desolation.

Perhaps we have clung too long to this period of Mr. Jefferson's official history, and gone into a detail which may appear tedious to some readers. But his history and the history of his State have, through this epoch, been, according to our view of the facts, most singularly misunderstood, in some very important and in some unimportant, but still coloring particulars, which have conveyed wholly false impressions in regard to the character

---

[1] And especially have we no twaddle about a few hundred State troops "under a soldier of genius," or a handful of militia, devouring hostile armies *more Bobadiliano!*

and progress of the Revolutionary war in the South. We have seen no better way to do what we conceived exact justice to his administration (which is substantially the history of the State during its continuance) than to give the facts, and in that definite and tangible form which admits of ready correction in case of error. Mere opinions, or loose generalities, we have supposed, would not be sufficient to carry that conviction to unprejudiced minds, which it has been our object to convey.

CHAPTER IX.

1781.

THE Virginia General Assembly re-convened March 1st, 1781, while Arnold continued lying at Portsmouth, and while, on the requisition of the Governor, the militia were mustering to coöperate with the expected French expedition from Newport against that place. Richard H. Lee was chosen Speaker by the House of Delegates.

The events of the session we give in the' language of Girardin's summary of them:

"The session was short, and almost exclusively devoted to the exigencies of the moment. Legislative provision was made for raising two legions, each of which should consist of six companies of infantry and one troop of horse. The rules of Continental service and all the articles of war were extended to the militia, and martial law established within twenty miles of the American and the hostile camp. The recruiting service was invigorated by further encouragements. The Governor was empowered to call into the field such numbers of militia as circumstances might require; to impress provisions, horses, clothing, accoutrements, boats, vessels, wagons, and negroes to serve as pioneers; to apprehend disaffected persons; to send non-jurors into the enemy's lines; and to punish opposition to military laws with the loss of all civil rights. For the speedy trial of certain offenders, the establishment of commissions of Oyer and Terminer was directed; and the Executive were authorized to discontinue, if necessary, State quarter-masters and commissaries, and to place the resources of the Commonwealth in the hands of Continental staff-officers. The certificates given to citizens for impressed property were made receivable in lieu of specifics to be contributed, according to law, by those citizens. The resource of paper emissions was again recurred to, because no other method of providing for the exigencies of the times could be devised; the treasurer was consequently directed to emit 20,000,000 pounds, and the Governor authorized to issue 5,000,000 in bills to be redeemed in 1792 by means of an assessment on property. The depreciation had nearly reached its acme, and we will see the paper currency expire in the course of the present year."

In a note to the above, Girardin states that the "depreciation" in the paper money when the Legislature was passing these enactments, "was about ninety for one;" and that it was still going on so rapidly, that it soon reached "a thousand for one," and "became extinct!" It will be seen, therefore, how much the "resource of paper emissions" amounted to, and how deplorable was the condition of affairs, when there was "no other method of providing for the exigencies of the times!" How "legions" were to be raised—how the "recruiting service" was to be "invigorated"—or any other efficient provision made against an invader then in the State—beyond using the present militia and seizing necessary supplies by force, so far as it would be safe to resort to that alternative—does not appear. The Legislature had done perhaps all it could; and besides arming a few officers with additional powers—which would not bring a gun, or a pound of powder, or a cartridge box into the

State, or scarcely a dollar into the wholly bankrupt treasury—
had done, substantially, nothing.   We have already shown why
the power of impressment, in men or specifics, was, to a considerable extent, but a nominal resource ; that at best it was no
approach to an adequate resource against the merest handful of
bold and active invaders.

On the 21st of March, Sir Henry Clinton detached two thousand men, under General Phillips, from New York, for Virginia.
They soon landed at Portsmouth, where Phillips assumed the
principal command.

On the 28th, not yet informed of the arrival of the British
forces in the State, Governor Jefferson wrote the President of
Congress :

" I observe a late resolve of Congress, for furnishing a number of arms to the
Southern States ; and I lately wrote you on the subject of ammunition and cartridge
paper.   How much of this State the enemy, thus reinforced, may think proper to
possess themselves of, must depend on their own moderation and caution, till these
supplies arrive.   We had hoped to receive by the French squadron under Monsieur
Destouches, eleven hundred stand of arms, which we had at Rhode Island, but
were disappointed.   The necessity of hurrying forward the troops intended for the
Southern operations, will be doubtless apparent from this letter."

To the same, March 31st:

" The amount of the reinforcements to the enemy, arrived at Portsmouth, is
not yet known with certainty.   Accounts differ from fifteen hundred to much
larger numbers.   We are informed they have a considerable number of horse.
The affliction of the people, for want of arms, is great; that of ammunition is not
yet known to them.   An apprehension is added, that the enterprise on Portsmouth
being laid aside, the troops under the Marquis Fayette will not come on.   An
enemy three thousand strong, not a regular in the State, nor arms to put in the
hands of the militia, are, indeed, discouraging circumstances."

To the same, April 7th :

" Hearing that our arms from Rhode Island have arrived at Philadelphia, I have
begged the favor of our delegates to send them on in wagons immediately,
and, for the conveyance of my letter, have taken the liberty of setting the continental line of expresses in motion, which I hope our distress for arms will justify,
though the errand be not purely continental."

Phillips remained strengthening the fortifications at Portsmouth, and preparing boats for an expedition, until the 18th of
April, when he embarked twenty-five hundred men, and commenced ascending the James.   He landed near Williamsburg

compelling Colonel Innes, in command of a body of militia there, to retire. One of his divisions entered Williamsburg on the 20th, and the other proceeded to the State shipyard on the Chickahominy, and burnt the small amount of shipping and stores found there. He reëmbarked on the 22d, and two days after again landed at City Point, on the south bank of the Appomatox at its confluence with the James. The next day he advanced on Petersburg. The place was defended by Baron Steuben with a thousand militia. By a series of skillful movements, the latter contrived to hold the enemy in check for a couple of hours, and he then retired over the Appomatox, taking up the bridge to prevent immediate pursuit. Phillips destroyed here a large quantity of tobacco, a considerable amount of other stores, and some small vessels. On the 27th, he marched with one division to Chesterfield Court House, and burnt the barracks and stores there. Arnold was dispatched with the other to Osborne's, where he destroyed a large quantity of tobacco, and then ascended the river to a place where most of the small marine force of the State had been collected. Arnold's artillery entirely commanding the river, the crews were speedily compelled to retire, which they did after scuttling and setting fire to their vessels.[1] Phillips and Arnold reunited and advanced to

[1] It may be a matter of some curiosity to Virginia readers to compare the statements of this affair given by several Virginia writers, with the following, by a participator in the action, who was subsequently Consul-General of the United States to the Barbary Powers. "Commodore O'Brien" is honorably mentioned in the diplomatic papers of the period. He became, on his return, a respected citizen of Pennsylvania, represented his county in the legislature, etc. His letter (the original of which is before us) is addressed to Andrew Monroe, residing near Milton, Albemarle county, Virginia :

- "TO MR. MONROE, ETC.
"*Washington City, February,* 1842.

" SIR—It is nearly forty years since we have been shipmates, or that I have seen you. I was first-lieutenant of the State Brig Jefferson, under Captain Traverse, and had the command of said vessel when we destroyed her at Osborne's, below Richmond. I believe the date was, in 1781. Mr. Jefferson was Governor of Old Virginia.

" I had been at Princess Anne and Norfolk counties when the British Arnold, Simcoe and Dundas ravaged those counties, and found the citizen militia under the orders of Col. Matthews Thoroughgood, Robinson Walker and Weeks Lawson, etc.; and when we were drove out to Blackwater Bridge, I then had the command of the artillery, when all came under the orders of General Gregory of North Carolina. I quitted the same with dispatches for Richmond, crossed from Lynhaven Bay, after burning the bridges in Norfolk County; and from the eastern shore crossed to York, forwarded on the letters, and entered the State navy service at the request of the Honorable James Maxwell ; and was first-lieutenant superintending the building of the State frigate, the Thetis, at Chickahominy.

" [On] the hostile appearance of the British from Norfolk and Portsmouth, I was ordered on board the State Brig Jefferson, and proceeded up James River where we considered with Mr. Maxwell, Markham, Steele, Saunders and yourself, that at Osborne's was the best place to take a stand, the militia to secure the land position under Steuben. But the militia gave way on the advance and fire of the British, and the State ships under Capt. Markham, Steele, etc., in trying to bring across the river, the current drove them

Manchester, lying on the opposite bank of the river from Richmond. Here the tobacco suffered its usual fate.

In Richmond, there was a quantity of public stores again collected, and considerable tobacco, and therefore it was important to again capture the town![1] Nelson was in it with a corps of militia; Muhlenburg higher up on the other side, and Steuben advancing. Lafayette, learning at Baltimore the critical condition of Virginia, had left his artillery and tents to follow him, and hurried forward by forced marches to Richmond.[2] He reached there with nine hundred men April 29th, the day before Phillips entered Manchester. The latter had addressed Lafayette from his camp at Osborne's, April 28th, demanding certain persons alleged to have fired on a flag of truce, and a public disavowal of their conduct, under pain of desolating the towns and villages lying at the mercy of the King's troops; and

---

under the battery and shore of [at?] the spot occupied by the British, and said State ships surrendered.

"This circumstance left the State brig Jefferson [alone], for you well know the ship Letter of Marque, commanded by C. Lewis, was soon abandoned, and we had to resist all the British force of cannonading and in firing at the enemie; and that shortly after all the other vessels had been evacuated by their crews.

"You will remember, Monroe, I sent you to scuttle and set fire to several vessels, to prevent their falling into the power of the British; and I well remember you, a youth, performing that arduous duty, under the fire from the British battery, and also the additional fire of the surrendered ships, which Markham had a few minutes before commanded; and that the State brig Jefferson covered your exertions, until you, with Sailing-Master Nicholson, accomplished this requisite service.

"When between us, with Nicholson, Saunders, and our doctor, and I believe young Mococke, we did determine after all that the State brig should not fall into the power of the invading foe, [but] to set said vessel on fire fore and aft, and to blow her up by a fire placed near the powder magazine. You well know that you and O'Brien were the officers in the last boat prior to the burning and blowing up of said State brig The Jefferson.

"That we saved nothing but the clothes we had on.

"That after this, next day we were employed at Manchester removing stores and provisions to Richmond; and I shall never forget but with my last breath, the desolate manner in which the officers and seamen left Richmond, steering on to the N. E.—when before we came to Bowling Green we parted—and after 41 years navigating the world by land and water, we again come, I believe, in these letters, [within] hailing [of] each other. How fare you, friend? My left knee and leg was injured by the splinters, when covering your exertions in destroying the vessels.

"I was 19 years on the Algerine coast, and was negotiator in Commodore Preble's fleet in the attacks on Tripoli; and latterly [have] resided at Carlisle, in Pennsylvania.

*   *   *   *   *   *   *   *

"I shall always hold you my old friend, Monroe, in kind remembrance.
"Your most obt. servt.
"R. O'BRIEN.

"P. S.—You know by the event to Capt. Markham that I was [left] the senior officer on the event at Osborne's."

[1] It is singular that among the Revolutionary doggerels, the exploits of the "*Tobacco War*" were not fitly commemorated! The banner which, under *Cœur de Lion*, unfurled to the breezes of Palestine, in the Crusades—which waved proudly on the fields of Agincourt and Cressy, of Blenheim and Ramilies—now glancing fitfully through the dun clouds, not of battle but of *tobacco smoke*, would be an inspiring theme!

[2] Lafayette to Washington, April 18th. (Memoirs, Correspondence, etc., of General Lafayette, published by his family, vol. i. p. 403.)

further demanding that no vessels or public stores be destroyed
at Richmond, inasmuch as they were driven "beyond a possibility of escaping," and were consequently "in the predicament
and condition of a town blockaded by land, when it was contrary to the rules of war that any public stores should be destroyed."[1] The next day his insolence took a still higher flight.
He wrote that if any persons holding his protections were put to
death under the pretence of being spies, or friends to the British
government, "he would make the shore of James River an example of terror to the rest of Virginia," and he added: "It was
from the violent measures, resolutions of the present House of
Delegates, Council, and Governor of Virginia, that he was impelled to use this language, which the common temper of his
disposition was hurt at."[2] The reply of the Marquis was tart
and sarcastic, and closed by informing the British General that
should his future communications be wanting in the "regard due
to the civil and military authority in the United States," he
"should not think it consistent with the dignity of an American
officer, to continue the correspondence."[3]

Phillips prepared to cross the river to Richmond on the 30th,
and issued his orders for the attack. The number and size of
his boats gave him facilities for a quick passage. But after
reconnoitering the imposing force on the opposite heights, he
concluded to raise his "blockade by land," dropped quietly
down to Warwick, and attacked the *tobacco* there. Here
Arnold crossed the river with six hundred men, but his troops
being charged by a patrol of sixteen horse, under Major Nelson,
fled precipitately to their boats. It would seem that Arnold's
shadow was becoming terrible to him! Phillips proceeded to
Bermuda Hundred, and reëmbarking, May 5th, fell down the
river.

Lafayette sent a party to Hood's to annoy the retiring foe,

[1] Phillips to Lafayette. (Lafayette's Memoirs, etc., vol. i. p. 412.)
[2] Lafayette's Memoirs, vol. i. p. 413.
Phillips here, we suppose, had reference to an official proclamation of the Governor
(in pursuance of authority vested in him by the Legislature), in regard to citizens giving
paroles and accepting protections, which will presently be mentioned.
[3] Lafayette's Memoirs, vol. i. p. 414.
Phillips's Letters do not sustain the impressions of him that would be drawn from the
Baroness of Riedesel's statements. They do not read like the letters of a man of breeding, written, to borrow the General's phrase, in *any* "temper of his disposition." They
are marked by gasconade, and by that inflation and inaccuracy which distinguish the
attempts of an uneducated man to use lofty language.
Lafayette's reply is broadly, contemptuously sarcastic, showing that he felt little
respect for his correspondent.

and detaching General Nelson to Williamsburg, advanced himself between the Pamunky and Chickahominy to be in a
position to rapidly succor Williamsburg or Richmond, as circumstances might require.

Phillips, after passing Burwell's ferry, received a dispatch
from Lord Cornwallis, informing him of his own rapid approach
towards Petersburg, and ordering him to join him at that place.
Phillips immediately crowded all sail to reascend the river.
He anchored at Brandon on the 7th of May, disembarked, and
commenced his march.

After the battle of Guilford Court House, Cornwallis
retired in the direction of Wilmington, and Greene kept
within striking distance of him, until he reached Ramsay's
Mills.　Here the American commander came to his celebrated
determination to turn his back on Virginia—leave it uncovered
—and carry the war into South Carolina.　His reasons for the
step, assigned to the Commander-in-chief, were that it would
compel Cornwallis to follow him, and thus free North Carolina
from invasion, or else to sacrifice all his posts in the interior of
South Carolina and Georgia.　This measure has been compared
to Scipio's leaving Hannibal in Italy, to carry the war into
Africa.[1]　Scipio left Italy filled with soldiers and means, and
Hannibal himself reduced to the defensive.　Greene left Virginia unarmed to the grasp of foes able at once to crush her.
He left the centre to defend the outskirt—a hitherto unsubju-
gated State, to recover subjugated ones.　He broke up the
communication between the northern and southern American
armies—uncovered the southern approaches of the middle
States—and placed himself beyond relief, unless the plan
hitherto acted upon by the Commander-in-chief should be
departed from.　But the result was *success*.　Previous plans
were departed from.　The northern and French army were compelled to come to the rescue of Virginia.　The capture at Yorktown was the consequence.　In military affairs, " all is well
that ends well."

But a flood of woes was to precede this auspicious result.
When Greene turned the heads of his columns south on the
banks of Deep River, he gave up the most populous and largely

---

[1] General Alexander Hamilton used this comparison in his funeral eulogy on General
Greene, before the Cincinnati.

producing State in the confederacy to the ravage of a foe bent on drying up all the sources of resistance in ruin and desolation. He gave up the cities and rural homes of Virginia to insult, her public buildings, her warehouses, mills, manufactories, and collected products of agricultural industry, her horses, plate, and valuables of almost every description, to the pillager and incendiary. True, all these evils had fallen quite as heavily on the States which Greene went now to rescue. South Carolina had been called upon to suffer even more than Virginia suffered. In no State in the Union, during the war of the Revolution, was there anything like a proportionable number of executions, and confiscation of the property of the patriots, to what took place in South Carolina under the iron rule of Cornwallis. But the fiery storm had passed over. Things were now settled. Murder had glutted itself, and rapacity was comparatively dormant, for nothing was left unconcealed for it to prey upon. Greene, merely to accelerate the recovery of these States, or rather as a stroke of military policy, devoted a *new* region to the same woes. But the officers in the army justified him, in a military point of view. The nation justified him in a moral and political point of view. Posterity justifies him on both grounds.

Cornwallis, in choosing between the alternatives left to him by Greene, acted quite as decisively as his opponent. Leaving the American general to march forward unopposed in the Carolinas, he fell upon Virginia. Halting a few days necessarily to recruit his shattered army, he, on the 25th of April, took up his line of march for Petersburg, dispatching orders to Phillips to join him there. Traversing North Carolina where the State is broadest—during a march of many days—he received a significant proof of the opposition he was to expect from militia and yeomanry where they had the coöperation of no regular troops. No portion of the Union furnished a more patriotic and hardy race than the Whigs of North Carolina. Yet in Cornwallis's long march across the State, his van was hardly driven in by a skirmish! Resistance was not made where resistance was wholly unavailing. He reached Petersburg on the 20th of May, where he found Arnold in the command. When Phillips had landed at Brandon on the 7th, a bilious fever was preying upon him. Lafayette was attempting to reach the point of destination first. But the sick general pressed forward with such impetuosity that he reached Petersburg earliest, and even seized a couple of American officers in the town sent forward to procure boats for Lafayette's passage of the Appomatox. He died on the 13th.

Major-General Phillips was an active and able soldier. But from the moment he set his foot in Virginia, on this expedition, his naturally fiery and haughty temper seems to have been roused to a pitch resembling the phrensy of intoxication. In the expressive language of Girardin, "he held the torch of the incendiary rather than the sword of the soldier." Even the bearing of the gentleman and British officer seems to have habitually given place to undignified insolence and puerile gasconade.[1]

It is worthy of remark that immediately after the death of his superior, Arnold attempted to open a communication with Lafayette by dispatching a letter to him (in regard to prisoners) by a flag. The latter refused to receive any communication from him, but offered to receive a letter from any other British officer.[2] Two days after, Arnold sent back a flag from General Nelson, with its dispatches unopened on the ground that Nelson was not Commander-in-chief, and he threatened that "all the officers and soldiers" of the American army should be sent to the West Indies, unless a cartel for the exchange of prisoners was "immediately granted," "as General Arnold had repeatedly demanded."[3] But before any measures of this kind were

---

[1] He showed as much insolence to Baron Steuben and Gov. Jefferson as to Lafayette. An incident between him and the Governor—whose kindness to him and his fellow prisoners at Charlottesville had formerly been so strongly acknowledged—deserves relating. The Governor applied to him to supply an omission in the necessary formulas of a passport for a vessel to carry supplies to the American prisoners at Charleston. Phillips addressed his answer "to Thomas Jefferson, Esq., American Governor of Virginia." The latter paused before opening a letter bearing on its outside an intended disrespect to his *official* position, but the starving condition of the prisoners overruled every other consideration; and, besides, he knew he would soon have the opportunity of returning the compliment under corresponding circumstances. Soon after, the Governor received a permit from the Board of War for a *British* supply vessel to carry stores to Alexandria for *British prisoners,* and in forwarding it to Phillips, addressed his letter "To William Phillips, Esq., commanding the British forces in the Commonwealth of Virginia." He, at the same time, wrote the flag-master, that no necessaries should be carried through Virginia to the British prisoners, if they perished for want of them, "till General Phillips either swallowed this pill of retaliation, or made an apology for his rudeness." The "proudest man of the proudest nation on earth," *swallowed the pill,* perforce !

Phillips was probably irritated by the circumstances attending Hamilton's imprisonment and final exchange, and possibly somewhat by some not very agreeable circumstances attending his own exchange. He had taken great offence at a threat of retaliation in the treatment of prisoners, recently made. He was rendered giddy, perhaps, by the prospect of winning as much at a blow, as other British commanders had won by years of struggle. And it is not improbable that he became contaminated by listening to the suggestions of the fierce and implacable parricide, who was his second in command.

[2] Lafayette to Captain Emyne. (Lafayette's Memoirs, etc., vol. i. p. 415.)

[3] Arnold to Captain Ragedale. (Lafayette's Memoirs, vol. i. p. 415.)

entered upon by the parricide, the occasion of the dispute was
removed by the arrival of Lord Cornwallis.

During the whole progress of this invasion, the British commanders had carried out the practice previously so extensively
introduced further south, of laying all the unarmed inhabitants
of the country they passed through under paroles. This was a
custom wholly unjustified by the usual or honorable usages of
war. It practically disarmed the country then and in future, or
compelled every man to fight for his own native land with a
halter about his neck. It afforded the timid and secretly disaffected, or the purely venal, an excuse to wait, unharmed on
either side, and not serving either side, to take advantage of
circumstances, and ultimately join the strongest. Governor
Jefferson resorted to a decisive and what proved an effectual step to put an end to this abuse, in Virginia. In May,
he issued a proclamation declaring the nullity of all such
paroles, but requiring those who had signed them and considered them binding :

* * " forthwith to repair to some of the posts, encampments, or vessels of the
forces of his Britannic Majesty, and by surrender of their persons to cancel such
engagements, and thereafter to do as themselves, and those in whose power they
should be, should think fit, save only that they should not rejoin the Commonwealth, but in a state of perfect emancipation from its enemies, and of freedom to
act as becomes good and zealous citizens."

The Legislature of the State had again met at Richmond,
pursuant to adjournment, on the 7th day of May. " But," says
Girardin, " the movements of Phillips and Cornwallis evidently
threatening the metropolis, the members present on the 10th,
adjourned the House until the 24th, then to meet at Charlottesville." When the House so adjourned on the 10th, enough
members had not collected to proceed to business.

During the entire period of Phillips's invasion, and during
the one we are about to record so long as the Americans were
in possession of the capital, the Governor remained at his post,
moving about the country and sleeping repeatedly within from
three to six miles of the enemy without a single guard or
attendant.

On the 28th of May, the Governor addressed General Washington a letter, which is very noticeable in various particulars

After describing the movements of the two armies up to that date, he said :

" The whole force of the enemy within this State, from the best intelligence I have been able to get, is, I think, about seven thousand men, infantry and cavalry, including, also, the small garrison left at Portsmouth.[1] A number of privateers, which are constantly ravaging the shores of our rivers, prevent us from receiving any aid from the counties lying on our navigable waters: and powerful operations meditated against our western frontier, by a joint force of British and Indian savages, have, as your Excellency before knew, obliged us to embody between two and three thousand men in that quarter. Your Excellency will judge from this state of things, and from what you know of our country, what it may probably suffer during the present campaign. Should the enemy be able to produce no opportunity of annihilating the Marquis's army, a small proportion of their force may yet restrain his movements effectually, while the greater part are employed, in detachment, to waste an unarmed country, and lead the minds of the people to acquiescence under those events, which they see no human power prepared to ward off. We are too far removed from the other scenes of war to say, whether the main force of the enemy be within this State. But I suppose, they cannot any where spare so great an army for the operations of the field. Were it possible for this circumstance to justify in your Excellency a determination to lend us your personal aid, it is evident from the universal voice, that the presence of their beloved countryman, whose talents have so long been successfully employed in establishing the freedom of kindred States, to whose person they have still flattered themselves they retained some right, and have ever looked up, as their dernier resort in distress, would restore full confidence of salvation to our citizens, and would render them equal to whatever is not impossible. I cannot undertake to foresee and obviate the difficulties which lie in the way of such a resolution. The whole subject is before you, of which I see only detached parts: and your judgment will be formed on a view of the whole. Should the danger of this State and its consequence to the Union, be such, as to render it best for the whole that you should repair to its assistance, the difficulty would then be, how to keep men out of the field. I have undertaken to hint this matter to your Excellency, not only on my own sense of its importance to us, but at the solicitations of many members of weight in our Legislature, which has not yet assembled to speak their own desires.

" A few days will bring to me that relief which the Constitution has prepared for those oppressed with the labors of my office, and a long-declared resolution of relinquishing it to abler hands, has prepared my way for retirement to a private station : still, as an individual, I should feel the comfortable effects of your presence, and have (what I thought could not have been) an additional motive for that gratitude, esteem, and respect, with which I have the honor to be," etc.

General Washington's reply should be read in the same connection :

---

[1] This includes a reinforcement under General Leslie, presently to be mentioned.

To GOVERNOR JEFFERSON.

NEW WINDSOR, 8 *June*, 1781.

DEAR SIR;

The progress which the enemy are making in Virginia is very alarming, not only to the State immediately invaded, but to all the rest; for I strongly suspect, from the most recent European intelligence, that the enemy are endeavoring to make as large seeming conquests as possible, that they may urge the plea of *uti possidetis* in the proposed mediation.[1] Your Excellency will be able to judge of the probability of this conjuncture from the circular letter of the President of Congress.[2]

Were it prudent to commit a detail of our plans and expectations to paper, I could convince you by a variety of reasons, that my presence is essential to the operations which have lately been concerted between the French commanders and myself,[3] and which are to open in this quarter, provided the British keep possession of New York. There have lately been rumors of an evacuation of that place, but I do not put confidence in them. Should I be supported by the neighboring States in the manner which I expect, the enemy will, I hope, be reduced to the necessity of recalling part of their force from the southward to support New York, or they will run the most imminent risk of being expelled, with great loss of stores, from that post, which is to them invaluable while they think of prosecuting the war in America; and should we, by a lucky coincidence of circumstances, gain a naval superiority, their ruin would be inevitable. The prospect of giving relief to the Southern States, by an operation in this quarter, was the principal inducement for undertaking it. Indeed we found upon a full consideration of our affairs in every point of view, that, without the command of the water, it would be next to impossible for us to transport the artillery, baggage, and stores of the army to so great a distance; and besides we should lose at least one-third of our force by desertion, sickness, and the heats of the approaching season, even if it could be done.

Your Excellency may probably ask whether we are to remain here for the above reasons, should the enemy evacuate New York and transfer the whole war to the southward. To this I answer without hesitation, that we must in such case follow them at every expense, and under every difficulty and loss; but that, while we remain inferior at sea, and there is a probability of giving relief by diversion, and that perhaps sooner than by sending reinforcements immediately to the point in distress, policy dictates the trial of the former.

Allow me, before I take leave of your Excellency in your public capacity, *to express the obligations I am under for the readiness and zeal with which you have always forwarded and supported every measure, which I have had occasion to recommend through you,* and to assure you that I shall esteem myself honored by a continuation of your friendship and correspondence, should your country permit you to remain in the private walk of life.

I have the honor to be, etc.

---

[1] The Empress of Russia and the Emperor of Austria had proposed to act as mediators for a general peace. See Diplomatic Correspondence of the American Revolution, vol. xi. p. 33. (Sparks's note.)

[2] See this letter in the Secret Journals of Congress, vol. i. p. 221. (Sparks's note.)

[3] The reduction which Clinton had made in his forces by his southern detachments, and the anticipated arrival of another French fleet, under the Count de Grasse, had led to the resumption of the long cherished hope and plan of capturing New York.

How well this closing tribute was earned, we have not done relating!

Cornwallis, with his accustomed energy, halted but three days to refresh his weary troops at Petersburg, before he put them again in motion. He crossed the James at Westover, where he met a reinforcement of three regiments from New York, under General Leslie. Two of these were sent back to garrison Portsmouth, as he was already strong enough to overcome all opposition, even after making detachments to execute any collateral objects which might present themselves. With these returning troops, to the great satisfaction of the British officers, went the parricide Arnold; and he soon after embarked for New York.

Cornwallis was now on the field he had long coveted, and if Clinton should continue to give occupation to Washington and Rochambeau in the North, his prospects of triumphant success in crushing Virginia, as he had the Carolinas, and crushing it even more rapidly, seemed to be certain. This would make *him* the principal executor of the ministerial plan for dividing North America, south of the great lakes, with the United States and France. This would make him the preserver to the Crown of a good deal more than half of the territory of the revolted States! The cold soldier was flushed! He wrote home: "The boy [Lafayette] cannot escape me!"

Lafayette was lying at Wilton, and he retreated northwesterly in the direction of Fredericksburg, with the double object of covering the manufactory of arms at Falmouth, and of effecting a junction with General Wayne, who had been ordered south with a body of troops to reinforce him. Cornwallis followed Lafayette in a parallel line of march, a little further to the east; and their forces were often not twenty miles distant. Tarleton's legion formed the British van, and it was now rendered more effective than usual by plundering, by means of runaway negroes, the stables of the country gentlemen of their fine blood horses. These added the wings of the eagle to the ferocity of the vulture. Even the couriers bearing letters to Lafayette were overtaken and captured by their speed.[1]

Near the fords of the Pamunky, a large patrol pressed upon the American rear; and Lafayette, believing the British

---

[1] Lafayette's Memoir. vol. i. p. 418—note.

main body was upon him, faced about, and despairing but resolute, formed his line of battle. At this critical moment, Lieutenant Colonel John Mercer rode up with a finely armed and
mounted party of Virginians. Mercer had been one of the aids
of General Lee on the field of Monmouth, and had retired from
the army in disgust, on the suspension of his commander. But
at the intercession of General Weedon, he had, in the present
crisis, called upon the young gentlemen of his neighborhood to
arm and mount, at their own cost, and rush to the succor
of Lafayette. It was precisely the kind of force the latter
most needed, and proved invaluable on his further retreat.[1] He
had now scouts and rear guard as fleet as Tarleton's best
mounted dragoons, and the latter was not strong enough, unless
by surprise, to strike a dangerous blow except in conjunction
with the slower moving main body.

Mercer's horse, on their first appearance, soon discovered
that the British main body was still at some distance behind
Lafayette, and the latter, therefore, immediately resumed his
retreat. Compelled by Cornwallis's superiority to give up all
idea of protecting Falmouth, he pushed more westerly in the
direction of the fords of the Rapidan, at which he expected to
meet Wayne. Widening the distance between himself and his
pursuers by incredible exertions, he reached his destination,
formed the anticipated junction on the 7th of June, and thus
" the boy " escaped.

Cornwallis followed as far as a point on the banks of the
North Anna, in the northwestern part of Hanover county.
He here gave over the pursuit, and resolved to turn back into
the more thickly settled regions and destroy stores and harass
the unprotected country until the Americans should venture to
meet him in the field. But before leaving his present camp, he
made two detachments—one southerly to the Point of Fork
under Lieutenant Colonel Simcoe, to destroy a collection of arms
and stores destined for Greene's army—the other westerly,
under Tarleton, to capture or disperse the Legislature and officers of government, assembled at Charlottesville.

Simcoe's expedition was completely successful. The Point

---

[1] Lafayette says in his Memoir (vol. i. p. 263), "The richest young men of Virginia
and Maryland had come to join him as volunteer dragoons, and from their intelligence,
as well as from the superiority of their horses, they had been of essential service to
him."

of Fork is the point of land between the mouths of the Rivanna and James—or Fluvanna, as the latter is often called above this junction. Baron Steuben lay here with about five hundred recruits for Greene's army (for recruiting Greene's army from Virginia had not *yet* stopped!) covering the stores. The Baron obtained no intelligence whatever of Simcoe's approach, so careful were the arrangements of that remarkably able and wily soldier. But he did hear of the more distant, rapid movement of Tarleton, and believing himself the object of it, he removed his stores to the south bank of the James. He had just effected this, and got all but a handful of his men over, when Simcoe reached the opposite bank. The river was unfordable, and the Americans had all the boats of any size in the vicinity. Simcoe, unable to reach his opponent, resorted to a stratagem to put him to flight. Kindling camp fires as if for a large force along the heights, and scattering his troops so as to favor the illusion, he succeeded in convincing Steuben that the whole British army lay encamped opposite. The latter, therefore, retreated in the night, abandoning what he could not carry. In the morning, Simcoe sent over four or five dragoons in a skiff with their saddles and bridles, who caught loose horses and patroled after the retreating Americans. This *ruse*, also (says Girardin), completely succeeded, and the Baron was " confirmed [in] the belief " " that the whole British army was close in his rear." " His object was to resume his original destination and join General Greene," and he continued in rapid retreat in the direction of North Carolina, until " he received fresh orders not to leave the State, so long as Cornwallis should continue there." Simcoe destroyed what the Americans left behind—a considerable amount of property, though vastly magnified by British accounts—and retired without the loss of a man !

Tarleton, meanwhile, advanced swiftly towards Charlottesville. He reached Louisa Court House at eleven o'clock P.M. on the first day (June 3d), and halting but three hours, again put his troops in motion. He came upon and burnt a train of twelve wagons carrying clothing to Greene's army. His route lay near the residences of Doctor Walker and Mr. John Walker, where he understood some distinguished persons were stopping.[1] He divided his troops, surrounded both houses at

---

[1] The Messrs. Walker, Colonel Simms, a senator, William and Robert Nelson, brothers

once, and paused long enough to parole the prisoners, and, it would seem, for breakfast.[1]

A citizen of Charlottesville, named Jouitte, was in the Cuckoo tavern in Louisa, when the legion swept past on the main road. Suspecting their destination, he mounted his horse—a very fleet Virginia blood horse—and rode on at full speed "by a disused and shorter route, and made known the approach of the British several hours before their arrival."[2]

On his way, Jouitte stopped at Monticello, a little before sunrise, and gave information of Tarleton's approach to Governor Jefferson. The Speakers of the two Houses of the General Assembly, and several other members were lodging with him. They "breakfasted at leisure," and the members then proceeded to Charlottesville. The House assembled, and resolving that thenceforth forty members should form a quorum, adjourned to meet on the 7th, at Staunton, west of the Blue Ridge. They then dispersed, and had hardly done so before Tarleton rode at full speed into the town. The retiring members were pursued, and seven of them captured. General Stevens, who had been compelled to retire from the army by his wound at Guilford Court House, belonged to the House of Delegates. Attired as usual in the plain dress of a Virginia farmer, and mounted by chance on a shabby horse, he was soon overtaken by the dragoons. But a little way ahead was more attractive game— a horseman in a scarlet coat, and military hat and plume, and

of General Nelson, Francis Kinlock, a delegate in Congress from North Carolina, and some other gentlemen fell into his hands. Captain Kinlock commanded the party which surrounded Mr. John Walker's house, and the captured delegate to Congress of the same name was his relative.

[1] Professor Tucker, on the authority of a gentleman who, he says, had it from Dr. Walker, relates the following anecdote: Tarleton, on his arrival, ordered a breakfast to be prepared for himself and his officers. Unusual delay occurring, he became impatient, and Dr. Walker proceeding to the kitchen, ascertained that his cook was now getting a *third* breakfast, two having been seized and carried off by the dragoons. Tarleton then placed a guard over the kitchen, and thus saved his breakfast!

Perhaps there is nothing very surprising in this illustration of the wild license of Tarleton's dragoons—for this was not the vulnerable side of their commander's temper; but there is something so exceedingly uncharacteristic in Tarleton's stopping when on the very point of swooping on his prey, for a *third* breakfast *for himself and his officers*, that we cannot but believe that some strokes have been added to the story. The probability is (in our opinion) that Tarleton's troops had received nothing to eat since the day before, and having ridden a good share of the night, he judged it necessary to allow them some repast before coming upon a town where resistance might be offered, and fresh men and horses, at all events, wanted for pursuit. There might have been *something*, too, on which to found the story of a delayed breakfast for the officers.

It is quite certain that this delay did not, as Professor Tucker's informant supposed, save the Legislature from capture. They were warned of their danger *several hours* before Tarleton's arrival at Charlottesville.

[2] Girardin, p. 499.

probably, therefore, an officer of rank. The soldiers spurred on without noticing Stevens, who soon turned aside and escaped. The showy gentleman in front was no officer, but the same Mr. Jouitte recently introduced to the reader, who had an eccentric custom of wearing such habiliments. After he had coquetted with his pursuers long enough, he gave his fleet horse the spur, and speedily was out of sight.

Some distance back from Charlottesville, Tarleton had dispatched a troop under Captain McLeod, to proceed directly to Monticello to capture the Governor, and to remain in *vidette* on this lofty look-out. As soon as Mr. Jefferson's guests had retired, he directed his family to make ready for a journey, and commenced securing his most important papers. He continued thus occupied for nearly two hours, when a Mr. Hudson rode up, and declared that the British were ascending the mountain. He then sent off his wife and children in a carriage, under the care of a young gentleman who was studying with him (and escorted by his servants) with directions, after stopping at a friend's, intermediately, to proceed to Enniscorthy, the seat of Colonel Coles, fourteen miles and a half distant. Ordering his favorite riding horse to be brought from a distant smithy [1] (where he had been shod since Jouitte gave the alarm), to a designated point in the road between Monticello and Carter's Mountain, he remained a little while longer among his papers, to give time for the execution of this order, and then taking his telescope in his hand, proceeded by a cross path to the place where his horse was. Hearing no tramp of approaching cavalry, he walked a short distance up Carter's Mountain, to a rock from which he could obtain a good view of Charlottesville. Observing nothing unusual in the streets of the town, he was induced to think the alarm premature, and concluded to return to his house to complete the care of his papers. After proceeding a few rods, he observed that in kneeling down to level his telescope, his light walking sword had slipped from its sheath. Returning for this, another glance through the glass showed him the streets of the town swarming with dragoons. He then mounted his horse for the first time, and followed after his family. Within five minutes of the time he left his house, McLeod entered it, and was actually there when Mr. Jefferson

[1] At Shadwell Ford.

commenced that return which the loss of his sword hindered. McLeod had crossed the Rivanna at Secretary's Ford, and ascended the hill from that side.

Two faithful slaves, Martin and Cæsar, were left in the house, and were engaged in secreting plate and other valuables under the floor of the front portico, when McLeod's party arrived. The floor was then of planks. One of these was raised, and Martin stood above handing down articles to Cæsar in the cavity. As about the last piece went in, Martin either heard the clang of hoofs, or caught a glimpse of the white coats through the trees, and down went the plank, shutting Cæsar into the dark hole below. And here he remained eighteen hours without light or food. He was a powerful, determined fellow, six years younger than his master, and having been brought up with him, was sufficiently attached to him to have endured fast and darkness for another eighteen hours, rather than make apparent the cause of his concealment. Martin was but twenty-six—one of those sullen and almost fierce natures, which will love and serve *one*, if worthy of it, with a devotion ready to defy anything—but which will love or serve but one. He was Mr. Jefferson's "body servant," as far as the latter would ever permit a slave to bear the relation to him which these words, by custom, technically imply. Martin would voluntarily suffer no fellow-servant to do the least office for his master ; he watched his glance and anticipated his wants, but he served any other person with reluctance, and received orders from any other quarter with scarcely concealed anger.

He received Captain McLeod as he rode up, with as much courage, if not with as much dignity, as the seneschal of a surrendered mediæval castle, and showed him through the house. On reaching the study, the depository of the Governor's papers, McLeod gazed about him a few moments, and then locking the door gave Martin the key, and bade him refer any of his soldiers inquiring for it to *himself*. Not a thing was touched in the house excepting some articles in the cellar, where a few brutal soldiers contrived to get out from under the eye of their commander. One of these fellows, to try Martin's nerves, clapped a pistol to his bosom, and threatened to fire, unless he would tell which way his master had fled. "Fire away, then," retorted the black, fiercely answering glance for glance, and not receding a hair's breadth from the muzzle of the cocked pistol.

McLeod remained about eighteen hours, keeping an outlook on the surrounding country, and then retired. To the extraordinary moderation of this detachment of a legion which has been so infamously celebrated in the annals of the Revolution, Governor Jefferson was undoubtedly indebted, in no small measure, to the gentlemanly feelings as well as the firmness of its commander, whose whole conduct shows that he was a man of breeding and delicacy. But he was also indebted to Tarleton's own "strict orders to suffer nothing to be injured." [1]

The details above presented of this whole affair, in addition to those which have before appeared in Girardin, Tucker, and Mr. Jefferson's own writings, are given on the statements, oral and written, of several members of Mr. Jefferson's family, who repeatedly heard all the particulars from his lips, and from those of other actors in the scene. The stern Martin died so early that nothing of him but infantile recollections of his gloomy, forbidding deportment, is preserved by any of the living generation; but Cæsar lived to a good old age to fight over his battles as clearly, and far more *veraciously* than some contemporaries of a different complexion.

A characteristic incident marked Tarleton's stay at Charlottesville. He retired from the town the day he entered it, and encamped for the night at the house of Mr. Lewis, on the west bank of the Rivanna. As usual, he slept on the floor in his horseman's cloak, and rose early to shave himself. A saddled horse stood for him at the door. He had on but his pantaloons, shirt and boots. His lathered face was about half shaved, when a shot broke on his ear. It came from the direction of Monticello, and was so reëchoed as to sound like an irregular fire from several muskets. The sound had not *half* died away, before Tarleton, bareheaded, his face as the razor had left it, was, with drawn sabre, fiercely spurring in the direction of the sound, and shouting to his dragoons to mount and follow. A more soldierly man, on action, never drew a blade in battle.

The next day he fell down the river to rejoin Cornwallis,

---

[1] These are Mr. Jefferson's own words in a letter to the historian Gordon, July 16, 1788. They have been *singularly overlooked* by most of those who have given an account of the transaction. Let Tarleton at least have his *due*, for the credit of an old adage !

who had advanced with his main body to the Point of Fork. Mr. Jefferson had a plantation there, called Elk Hill, lying opposite Elk Island, in the James. The British lieutenant-general's encampment extended from the junction of the rivers to this place, and the treatment which Mr. Jefferson's property received at his hands, was thus described, some years afterwards, by its owner:

"He remained in this position ten days, his own headquarters being in my house, at that place. I had time to remove most of the effects out of the house. He destroyed all my growing crops of corn and tobacco; he burned all my barns, containing the same articles of the last year, having first taken what corn he wanted; he used, as was to be expected, all my stock of cattle, sheep and hogs, for the sustenance of his army, and carried off all the horses capable of service; of those too young for service he cut the throats; and he burned all the fences on the plantation, so as to leave it an absolute waste. He carried off also about thirty slaves. Had this been to give them freedom, he would have done right; but it was to consign them to inevitable death from the small pox and putrid fever, then raging in his camp. This I knew afterwards to be the fate of twenty-seven of them. I never had news of the remaining three, but presume they shared the same fate. When I say that Lord Cornwallis did all this, I do not mean that he carried about the torch in his own hands, but that it was all done under his eye; the situation of the house in which he was, commanding a view of every part of the plantation, so that he must have seen every fire. I relate these things on my own knowledge, in a great degree, as I was on the ground soon after he left it. He treated the rest of the neighborhood somewhat in the same style, but not with that spirit of total extermination with which he seemed to rage over my possessions."

And he added:

"Wherever he went, the dwelling-houses were plundered of everything which could be carried off. Lord Cornwallis's character in England would forbid the belief that he shared in the plunder; but that his table was served with the plate thus pillaged from private houses, can be proved by many hundred eye-witnesses.[1] From an estimate I made at that time, on the best information I could collect, I suppose the State of Virginia lost under Lord Cornwallis's hands, that year, about thirty thousand slaves; and that of these, about twenty-seven thousand died of

[1] Girardin gives a *specification* on this subject, which it would be difficult to believe, were it not, as he avers, supported by the statements of persons whose information and veracity were beyond question—and were it not strictly in keeping with other facts in his Lordship's career in America, which, sixty years ago, could have been proved by hundreds, if not thousands, of as respectable persons as there were in America. This is Girardin's account (p. 504, note):

"Lord Cornwallis slept one night at the house of a Mr. Bates, some distance from the South Anna. In the morning, when his Lordship sat down to a rural, yet neat and comfortable breakfast, he observed an elegant piece of plate, not, indeed, heavy, but of exquisite workmanship and great value. He took it in his hands, looked again and again at every part of it, expressed his admiration of its beauty, and *unceremoniously consigned it to one of his pockets*. The family had religiously preserved this little relic of the original opulence of their ancestors who had emigrated from England to avoid the persecutions of Church and State."

the small pox and camp fever, and the rest were partly sent to the West Indies, and exchanged for rum, sugar, coffee, and fruit, and partly sent to New York, from whence they went at the peace, either to Nova Scotia or England. From this last place, I believe they have been lately sent to Africa. History will never relate the horrors committed by the British army, in the *Southern* States of America. They raged in Virginia six months only, from the middle of April to the middle of October, 1781, when they were all taken prisoners; and I give you a faithful specimen of their transactions for ten days of that time, and on one spot only. *Ex pede Herculem.* I suppose their whole devastations during those six months amounted to about three millions sterling." [1]

In Mr. Jefferson's farm book, there is a list of "Deaths, etc.," and in another column, "Other losses by the British, in 1781," carrying the preceding statements, to Dr. Gordon, into their minute details. The name and particular fate of each slave carried off—the number of horses, cattle, sheep, and hogs taken—the number of barrels of grain of each kind in the house consumed or destroyed, and the estimated quantity of each kind of product destroyed on the ground—the buildings, utensils, and the number of "panels of fence" burnt—are set down in this melancholy record. We will give a few examples: Nine "blooded mares" and farm horses were carried away—the colts of the former having their throats cut! Fifty-nine cattle, thirty sheep and sixty hogs were eaten. The loss of the farm in corn (maize) was two hundred barrels in the house, and five hundred and eighty barrels growing; of tobacco, ten hogsheads in the house, and nineteen growing; a sowing of three hundred and fifty bushels of wheat (towards two hundred acres), and a sowing of seventy-five bushels of barley, destroyed growing, etc.

These sickening details are nothing, when we turn into the adjoining column, headed "Deaths, etc." Mr. Jefferson's statements to Gordon, being written from France, without the record before him, are not arithmetically accurate, and it is very easy to see how the numbers became confused in his memory. "Twenty-seven" was the whole number of slaves carried off by Cornwallis. "Three" of these were never heard from. Five of them returned home and recovered. But five others who had never left home, "caught the camp fever from the negroes who returned, and died." But not all of those who died, in consequence of being carried off, perished on the hands of those who had infected them with the pestilence. Stricken with

---

[1] Letter to Doctor Gordon, July 16, 1788.

small pox and camp fever, and left behind, some of the miserable wretches crawled home to die, and giving information where others lay perishing in hovels, or in the open air, by the wayside, these were sent for by their generous master; and the last moments of all of them were made as comfortable as could be done by proper nursing and medical attendance.[1] Five of the unfortunate nurses—slaves who had never left home—as we have seen, took the fever from them and died. What with the losses by death, and the number engaged in bringing home and taking care of the sick, and those who were temporarily ill, but subsequently recovered, and who therefore do not come into the above catalogue, and all this in the harvest time, a considerable share of Mr. Jefferson's crops on his other farms, which escaped Cornwallis, were "lost for want of laborers."

Be it remembered that not an allusion (so far as we recollect) to his own losses—at least, not to the particulars of his losses—was made by Mr. Jefferson until in answer to the inquiries of Gordon in 1788. No man was less a complainer of personal wrongs from friend or foe. The contemporaneous statements we have given from the farm book, were not intended for the public eye, and are mingled among records of the births and deaths of slaves, of overseers and stewards arrangements, etc. Two or three erasures and entries with another pen appear in the account, showing that it was corrected from time to time through the year, to make it (with Mr. Jefferson's invariably minute accuracy) conform to the exact facts. Thus, the names of two, who were first entered simply as having "joined the enemy," are erased and added to the list of those who "caught small pox from enemy and died." There is no escape for Lord Cornwallis from such testimony as this!

What had Mr. Jefferson done to draw such vengeance on his head? Was it the confinement of Hamilton, or the petty misunderstandings with Phillips? Were these sufficient to cancel the memory of his energetic and unpopular interference in behalf of the Convention prisoners—of his kind hospitalities and attentions to British officers of every rank from major generals

---

[1] Among the items, our eye falls on the following : "Expenses seeking and bringing back *some*"—twenty pounds sterling in specie ; "paid Doctors attending sick"—sixty-five pounds sterling in specie. It would appear from the first entry that this was only a *part* of the expense of bringing home the sick. Some of them were brought on blankets and mattresses in the last stages of disease, but feebly imploring that they might see Monticello again before they died.

down to lieutenants? Was it because of his "violent" measures in concert with the Council and Legislature, which Phillips had complained of in his correspondence with Lafayette, and for which he threatened to "make the shores of James River an example of terror?" What were those violent measures? Were the non-combatants who were ordered to give up their paroles or go within the British lines, and who refused to obey this order, executed or otherwise punished? We find no record, or trace of a record, of any execution on this ground. But it was true that secretly disaffected persons had remained in the country, and had made their paroles the excuse for not serving their country when called upon, while they were covertly acting for the enemy as spies and instigators of disaffection. If any such refused to obey the Executive mandate, we venture to presume they were punished according to law. If any of them were clearly proven to be spies, or to have committed overt acts of high treason, we should hope they suffered the penalty the law inflicted for such offences; and unsanguinary as was Governor Jefferson's disposition, we do not think he would have hesitated any more for Phillips's threats, than he did for the British Commissary's for prisoners in Hamilton's case, or for Arnold's at Richmond. He certainly, in other particulars, as for example, in impressment, carried the very ample powers vested in him to their last prudent limit. It was, past all doubt, his decisive course in regard to "non-jurors"—his compelling the whole body of the people to act for or against their country—which roused against him the vindictive hostility of those who had made such fatal use to America of the paroling system in the Carolinas.

We can give no minute particulars of the Governor's action in regard to non-jurors, having noticed nothing on the subject in any authorities in our possession. But one thing may be regarded as certain, that had Governor Jefferson, by any official act or order, caused a hair of an innocent man to fall to the ground—acted in a single instance either arbitrarily, in the least degree irregularily, or even too summarily, we should, in all probability, have found him accused of it by the English! And if they had spared him, he afterwards had political opponents in Virginia who would not have spared him! A hint of an act of official injustice on his part, would have set the latter ransacking

heaven and earth for everything and anything tending to substantiate the charge ! If Mr. Jefferson stands accused of a solitary act of official or personal injustice or cruelty, in his capacity
of Governor of Virginia, we never have heard of that accusation.

The truth is, the barbarities practised in Virginia, were in no
proper sense retaliatory. They were part of the British system
towards America, as avowed by the British Commissioners in
1778. And especially were they a part of the system which
had from that period been exercised by the cold, inexorable
Cornwallis. It is easy enough now to deny a good share of the
personal atrocities—that is, atrocities committed under the eye
and sanction—of this British General, Peer of the Realm, future
Commander-in-chief and Governor-General of India, Master-
General of the Ordinance, Member of the Privy Council, Lord-
Lieutenant of Ireland, British Plenipotentiary to conclude the
Peace of Amiens, etc., etc., on the ground that the facts now
exist only in tradition, or in the statement of writers who did
not see what they describe. This would be a good defence before a legal tribunal, but it is not so at the bar of history. There
were hundreds and thousands of contemporaneous witnesses—
men known to their neighbors and the public as of unquestionable veracity—who, in the hearing of those neighbors and of
their attesting children, did again and again, to their dying day,
with nearly as much precision as Mr. Jefferson's farm book,
declare that with their own eyes, they had seen Cornwallis, or
those under his immediate eye and command, commit a multitude of similar atrocities to that which marked his stay at Elk
Hill, and not a few like that at the house of Mr. Bates, recorded
in the last preceding note. Had wantonly burning every building but that necessary to cover his own head, on a farm where
not a shot had been fired on him—the malicious destruction of
growing crops—the butchering of sucking colts—the pouching
of a piece of plate, the last heirloom of a family, from the table
where he was breakfasting (thus adding the vulgar brutality to
the rapacity of a common robber)—we say, had these things
been actionable offences in British courts, this Peer of the Realm
could have been convicted of all of them on the finding of a
manly British jury, on a tithe of the testimony which could at
the time have been readily adduced ! This testimony was not,
of course, put into legal forms, for there was no occasion for it.

Unless in court, no respectable man's affidavit is worth a particle more than his deliberate assertion. The generation who could have testified to the facts in a court of law, have passed away. But their life-long assertions are yet in the distinct recollection of their posterity.

Is it said that religion, philanthropy, or other considerations, require these things to be unmentioned and forgotten. So judge not we. And those who solicit this forbearance towards England have never solicited it towards other nations, and especially towards that nation who in this very struggle was our faithful and efficient ally against England! To preserve the memory of national injuries merely to excite antipathies against the descendants of our cruel oppressors—against a particular land or its institutions—would be worse than merely silly; it would be impolitic and wicked. But we hold that every American should be made to clearly understand that national liberty is not a matter of course—is not a fruit of any civilization yet developed, ready to drop, like over-ripe plums, into the mouth without shaking the tree—that if we were to cast away the institutions which our forefathers bled for, others just as good, or a little better, would not come inevitably and without cost. Our fabric, such as it is, is a blood-cemented one. Groans, and tears, and woes unutterable, accompanied every step of its foundation. Let every coming generation of Americans understand these facts. Let the lesson acquire additional force from the circumstance that our unparalleled wrongs came from a nation, politically the freëst, and personally as good and as brave as any on earth. Let youth (slow to learn such lessons) learn that it was the noble, the cultivated, the talented, and the truly brave, that lent themselves to be the personal inflicters and coldly systematic perpetrators of these wrongs. Then shall the youth of America understand what the nation which does not rely on itself—which separates to unite its fragments with foreign protectors—has to expect from the best foreign protectors, when their interests are crossed and their passions roused!

Our narrative has already followed Mr. Jefferson to the close of his gubernatorial term, and beyond. His office, by the terms of the Constitution, expired on the 2d of June 1781, two days before Tarleton entered Charlottesville, and before the attempt was made to capture him. Anterior to the invasion of Cornwallis or Phillips, and when the French fleet was daily expected to rid Virginia of Arnold, confined to his intrenchments at Portsmouth, Governor Jefferson had distinctly intimated to a member of the French Legation in Philadelphia, that intention to retire at the close of his present (his second) term, which was also announced to General Washington in the letter of May 28th, which we have quoted. The reasons for this determination are thus given in his Memoir:

"From a belief that, under the pressure of the invasion under which we were then laboring, the public would have more confidence in a military chief, and that the military commander, being invested with the civil power also, both might be wielded with more energy, promptitude and effect for the defence of the State, I resigned the administration at the end of my second year."

It is believed that Governor Jefferson carried with him to the last hour of his official term the respect, good will, and approbation, for his official conduct and energy, of every one of the superior Continental officers in command in the South. We have given Washington's and Greene's views; Steuben's and Lafayette's we understand to have been of the same tenor. Lafayette immediately imbibed for him that deferential respect and sincere attachment which, as we shall have many occasions to see, continued unabated through his long life.

Both of the last named officers—particularly Baron Steuben, who soon got embroiled with the civil authorities of Virginia[1]—

[1] Frederick William Augustus, Baron von Steuben, had acquired his notions of men and military affairs in the armies of Frederic the Great, to whom he was an aid-de-camp and afterwards, we think, a lieutenant-general. Consequently they were absolute enough. He was a good soldier, a martinet in discipline, and hot and testy as he was, at bottom generous in temper. Little had the good Baron been accustomed in the camp of the "Great Frederic," to see high military dignitaries dancing attendance on *civil* officers to know what they should do or not do—or standing on *legal* ceremonies with every trumpery fellow who approached them! He was hardly in Virginia, therefore, before he was in "hot water." He knocked off a militia colonel's spurs, and forced him into the ranks as a common soldier, for attempting to impose a boy on him for a proper recruit by artificially adding to his height by, if we remember right, stuffing his boots! Then came talks of awkward interferences by intermeddling magistrates, who impertinently pretended to think that a general might not do what he pleased with the men under his command! What would one of Frederic's marshals have thought of a writ of habeas-corpus, and a half a dozen Justice Shallows, and a squad of Catchpoles to teach *him* of *his* duty? And with higher magnates than these the impetuous temper, and exacting etiquette of the fiery old soldier embroiled him. He stormed in good German and bad English, and was answered with new provocations. He wrote letters very unflattering to the magnates and to the system of things in Virginia. He had, however, one steady friend—in Governor Jefferson. The latter contrived to mollify the degraded colonel—and partly by laughing, and partly by management, prevented extremities between the Baron and his tormentors. It is clear that the Governor believed that the Commander-in-chief would not have left Steuben in Virginia at this period if not entitled to full confidence as a *soldier*. He accordingly gave him, until superseded by the arrival of Lafayette, the control of the military defences of the State. There is nothing to show that the Baron did not well execute the trust.

complained of the inefficiency of the *government*. This was the common complaint throughout the Union, during the whole of the Revolution, with the younger officers, and indeed all but a few great and ripe men, in whom the civilian was as prominent as the soldier, and who, with broad views, appreciated not only the purely military difficulties, but all the difficulties of our unprecedented national position. The machinery of republicanism was yet new. Perhaps, in a few instances it wrought blunderingly. And the State authorities could not at least obtain men and money half fast enough to suit these prompt gentlemen of the sword. Accustomed to army discipline, and the summary processes of martial law, such were struck with wonder that where there were people, there should be wanting troops! that when there were food, and raiment, and money in the country, the army chest should lack them! That there were such things as rights of persons and rights of property which ordinary legislation did not invade, and which extraordinary legislation could not safely too far invade, did not enter their imaginations. In a word, these men were fighting for liberty, and yet complaining that practical liberty existed! Some of them seemed to imagine that because they were fighting for the State, nobody else had a right to exercise any judgment whatever in regard to the conduct of the war, or in regard to raising means to carry it on. And accustomed to a military gradation which ascended to one supreme head, they had the less patience with this exercise of the right of controlling military affairs by State legislatures. Three fourths of the officers of the Revolution came out of the war political consolidationists!

We will not pretend to say that there was not often justice in their complaints of the dilatory or incomplete action of States. But the civil officers knew as well as they, what their respective States ought to endure, and they generally knew far better what they would endure. We suppose the patriotism and the real sacrifices of each of these classes were equal. Probably it is no more than just to say that the cautious dilatoriness of the one was as little out of the way as the uncalculating impetuosity of the other.

It will not be understood that these remarks are applied particularly to the case of Virginia—for perhaps she was as little complained of as any other State—nor particularly to

Lafayette and Steuben. Lafayette was now very young, but a wiser, cooler head rarely sat on young shoulders. He was not long in seeing the true situation of things. Nor did the fiery German, unless under the irritation of the moment, betray halt so much want of consideration and of knowledge in this direction, as certain native Hotspurs!

We have seen that the Legislature of Virginia adjourned on the 4th of June, on Tarleton's approach to Charlottesville, to meet again on the 7th, at Staunton, west of the Blue Ridge. Wirt, in his Life of Henry,[1] thus mentions what followed their reassembling:

"On the 10th of June a false report of his [Tarleton's] approach produced *another panic;* and the House having merely taken time to resolve that they would meet at the Warm Springs, if it should be found dangerous to meet in Staunton, on the next day and on their failure so to do, that the speaker might call a meeting, when and where he pleased, again broke up and dispersed."

It was in this last "panic," that gentlemen, hot from the saddle and grimed with the dust of recent flight, booted and spurred for new flight, and listening momentarily to hear the hoof-clang of pursuing cavalry, undertook to legislate for what seemed to them some radical disorder in the State! And of course to men in their condition of feeling, no remedy appeared decisive enough that was not as radical as the disease, and instantaneous in its effects. The plan pitched upon to save the Republic was the one already presented and exploded in Governor Henry's administration—namely, to show that republican government was worthless, in time of war, and constitutions but a mere fair-weather contrivance, by the appointment of a Dictator! Patrick Henry was again the proposed Dictator; and again his biographer asseverates "his entire innocence."[2]

This repeated selection of Mr. Henry, by the Dictator party, might seem to show that it was some peculiar talent or fitness which he was supposed to possess for the exigency, which lay at the bottom of their move. But if he had exhibited any particular military capacities, or indeed had any military experience, history has not very carefully preserved the fact. If he had prepared his State any better, or differently, for invasion than his successor, or repelled invasion any more success fully, history then belied and now belies the facts. Moreover, he was himself Governor, when it was the first time proposed to make him Dictator. It would seem, then, that there was a party who really believed that Dictatorial *powers* were necessary to save the State. Mr. Henry was a man of unbounded popularity with the masses of the people. Their confidence in him would lead them to believe that no office which he would accept would be used dangerously to the Commonwealth, and their love for him would be a vast makeweight in giving the office popularity at the outset, and in silencing opposition. Finally, we venture little in asserting that of the other very conspicuous and popular men in the State, at least of those who had been thought of in connection with the office of Governor, not another besides Mr. Henry could probably have been found who any body believed would accept the office of Dictator, or under any circumstances give their countenance to the project.

In regard to Jefferson, the Dictator party in the Legislature well knew that he and his particular friends were affirmatively and irrevocably hostile to their plan. It was his kinsman—his earliest and warmest friend—Cary, of Ampthill, who (to use Mr. Wirt's phrase) "crushed" the project, the first time it was started, by threatening to resort to the dagger of Brutus. Mr. Jefferson has preserved an almost impenetrable reserve in regard to both of these transactions, never giving the name of an individual directly implicated in them, and in general terms absolving the motives of "most of them." We doubtless owe his silence to his tenderness for some of these individuals. But there are unmistakable reasons for believing that he and his friends would have forcibly resisted the overthrow of the Constitution. He substantially declares so.[1] Girardin imitates Mr.

---

[1] Writing this same year (1781) the Notes on Virginia, Mr. Jefferson said of this last project of creating a Dictator:

"The very thought alone was treason against the people; was treason against mankind in general; as riveting forever the chains which bow down their necks, by giving to their oppressors a proof, which they would have trumpeted through the universe, of the imbecility of Republican government, in times of pressing danger, to shield them from harm. Those who assume the right of giving away the reins of government in any case, must be sure that the herd, whom they hand on to the rods and hatchet of the dictator, will lay their necks on the block when he shall nod to them. But if our assemblies supposed such a resignation in the people, I hope they mistook their character. I am of opinion, that the government, instead of being braced and invigorated for greater exertions under their difficulties, would have been thrown back upon the bungling machinery of county committees for administration, till a convention could have been called, and its wheels again set into regular motion. What a cruel moment was this for creating such an embarrassment, for putting to the proof the attachment of our countrymen to republican government." [See Answer to Query XIII.]

Jefferson's reserve; going into the fewest details on this subject necessary to record the main fact; giving no clue to names, or the manœuvres which preceded the vote in the House. But he does significantly say: "to introduce" this office, "it was necessary to place Mr. Jefferson *hors de combat.*" He also says the project finally failed, from the anticipation of a "*violent* opposition."[1]

It was necessary, for several reasons, to "place Mr. Jefferson *hors de combat.*" It was not yet known that he had determined to decline a reëlection. He and his confidential friends resolved not to make known that fact until the question of the Dictatorship was settled. The weight of his name was doubtless regarded by them as necessary against the weight of Mr. Henry's. It was therefore indispensable to the success of the Dictator party not only to demonstrate the necessity of their plan, by showing how inextricably Governor Jefferson had involved the affairs of the State, but to practically get him out of the way, and crush all danger from him by crushing his popularity and influence.

To effect this, all the misfortunes of the period were charged upon him. He was blamed for not making preparations for invasion, which Governor Henry, the proposed Dictator, had never thought of making. He was held accountable for Arnold's success and escape, with so small loss, in his sudden inroad, when Matthew, in the governorship of the proposed Dictator, did more actual damage in the State, committed far greater atrocities, was longer about it, and retired without the loss of a man! But what history has failed to show that in periods of extreme disaster and panic, enough are always found ready to charge public calamities—even those imposed by Heaven—on their rulers? How many chiefs and statesmen have, under such circumstances, been banished, torn in pieces by mobs, or judicially murdered, to satiate the least reasonable and cruellest of all human passions, fear! Rage may spare, but abject panic is

---

Mr. Jefferson states (under the same head in the Notes) that the proposition for a Dictator "wanted *a few votes only* of being passed." This would seem to show that the question was actually brought to a vote in the House; and we here repeat what we said when speaking of his statements in regard to the first proposal to create such an officer in 1776—that they (Mr. Jefferson's statements) were *published* soon afterwards—before any number of the members of the Legislature of 1781 were dead—and *were never denied.*

[1] Girardin, Appendix, p. xi. These passages passed, of course, under Mr. Jefferson's eye, and we have seen his pointed endorsement of the author's accuracy in all that pertained to himself.

unsparing! And then what shame and remorse have often
been extorted by the retributive future—what restitutions and
ovations to the living, and what funeral honors, and proud
monuments, and public deifications of the dead martyr!

To give point and shape to the attack on Mr. Jefferson—to
give it popular effect—charges were thrown out against his
official conduct, on the floor, at the legislative meeting at Staunton, and an inquiry into his conduct was demanded. George
Nicholas, one of the members from Mr. Jefferson's own county,
a very honest, but at that time a very young and impulsive man,
was the spokesman on this occasion. Quite unexpectedly, the
proposal met the prompt acquiescence of Mr. Jefferson's friends.
No vote was taken, but a day of hearing, at the next session,
was unanimously agreed upon. Having reached this point, the
Dictator party were no nearer their object than before. They
had not made a new proselyte to it; they had not deprived
Mr. Jefferson of a friend or supporter, and the rumbling of the
coming storm began to be heard in and out of the House. There
were a good many Carys of Ampthill in Virginia. Girardin
thus gives the sequel:

"The pulse of the Assembly was incidentally felt in debates on the State of the
Commonwealth, and, out of doors, by personal conversations. Out of these a
ferment gradually arose which foretold a *violent opposition* to any species of
Dictatorship, and, as in a previous instance of a similar attempt, *the apprehension
of personal danger produced a relinquishment of the scheme.*" [1]

Whether the danger now, as before, particularly menaced
Mr. Henry, or whether the storm of public indignation threatened all engaged in the affair—in other words, civil war between
the Constitutional party and the Dictator party—we are not
specially informed. We infer from Jefferson's remarks, already
quoted, that the Constitutionalists intended at once to resist the
authority of the Dictator, reorganize the county committees of
safety, and call a convention to form a *legal* government.

As soon as the Dictator party avowedly relinquished their
project, Mr. Jefferson's resignation of the government (that is, his
refusal to serve a third term) was made public, and his friends
proposed General Nelson as his successor. We are not apprised
that Mr. Jefferson had personal objections to any candidate;

Girardin, Appendix, p. xii.

but it was particularly to secure the election of a military man
—an officer combining civil and military functions—that he
had originally made up his mind to retire; and nothing had
occurred to shake his belief that such a selection would be more
expedient, and better secure the public confidence.   This
announcement took both parties by surprise, and it called out a
burst of feeling among the body of Mr. Jefferson's friends in the
Legislature. They insisted on reëlecting him. His confidential
friends (those who understood his feelings and unalterable determinations) strenuously opposed this, on the ground that he had
patriotically divested himself of his office to heal divisions in the
Legislature, and that he ought to be allowed to carry out his
wishes; and that now, accusations having been brought against
him and a hearing agreed upon, his honor required him to meet
his assailants without the advantage of official position. These
considerations induced a considerable body of his friends to vote
for General Nelson, and it required their votes, in addition to
those of the recent advocates of another man, to elect Mr. Jefferson's candidate over himself. But for his resignation, there
is no question he would have been triumphantly reëlected.
This was owing to no objection to General Nelson. He had
not an enemy in the Legislature, and was probably, at the
moment, the most popular man in the State. It was indignation at the farce of charges having been preferred against the
late Governor.[1]

During all these occurrences Mr. Jefferson remained quietly
at Poplar Forest, remote from the Legislature, and not interfering with or attempting in any way to influence its proceedings. On being driven from home by Tarleton, on the 4th
of June, he had accompanied his family one day's journey, and
then returned to Monticello. Learning, probably, the topic
agitated, or to be agitated in the Legislature,[2] he repaired again
to Bedford.

[1] Girardin (Appendix, p. xii.) gives the same general version of the facts stated in this
paragraph. We have added slightly to the details—or rather we have stated some minor
conclusions which he does not *express*, though his facts would lead the observing reader
to infer them. We have, we suppose, proceeded on *as good*—probably *the same*—
authority as Girardin; and *we* have not been restrained, as he was, by the delicacy
and the scruples of *third persons* still living, in making an exposition full enough for *all* to
understand.

[2] We are not, strictly speaking, *authorized* to give this as his *reason*. But from the
tenor of one or two of his own remarks, and from Girardin's speaking (evidently by
authority) as if Mr. Jefferson *chose* to remain in Bedford and *chose* not to interfere with
the proceedings of the Legislature, our statement becomes a necessary inference.

Passing over, for the present, intermediate events, we will here follow the history of the Legislative inquiry to its close. It has been common to speak of the proceedings as in the nature of an "impeachment." Girardin says, "he was impeached in some loose way." This is a "loose" use of terms, which has led to very unfounded impressions. To that solemn and serious legislative proceeding, which is technically termed impeachment, where the legislative body decide there are sufficient grounds for putting an important public functionary on his trial, and where the penalty extends to deprivation of office, no proceeding had in this case bore any analogy. No resolution to impeach was passed by the House—no articles drawn up —indeed, not a solitary vote of any kind was taken directly or indirectly in reference to the matter. A member simply rose in his place, and claimed verbally that Mr. Jefferson had not done his duty, in some particulars, at the time of Arnold's invasion, and asked or demanded an inquiry into the facts. Mr. Jefferson's friends took him at the word—met him rather more than half way—and after some conversation the parties informally agreed on a day for a hearing. Meanwhile, not a word was entered on the subject in the journal of the House, and no copy of any charges sent to the accused functionary. Here was not one feature of an impeachment, and we shall presently see that the affair closed without one such feature.

No injustice will be done George Nicholas in the assertion that his precipitate action in this matter was the source of deep mortification to many of his best friends and nearest kindred. He had not been present at the session at Richmond, during Arnold's invasion—did not know what was then done—and stung by the result, and incited by the designing misrepresentations then rife, he exhibited his naturally resolute, daring temper, by taking a step which his prompters would have shrunk from. Mr. Jefferson asked a copy of his intended charges, that he might have his witnesses ready to meet them without any delay, and to prevent all excuses for delay on the other side, he sent back the heads of what he would prove in his own justification. Some part of the paper has been anticipated, but we choose to give the "objections" and "answers" entire, in connection with each other:

1st Objection.—That General Washington's information was, that an embarkation was taking place, destined for this State.

Answer.—His information was, that it was destined for the southward, as was *given out* at New York. Had similar informations from General Washington, and Congress, been considered as sufficient ground at all times for calling the militia into the field, there would have been a standing army of militia kept up; because there has never been a time, since the invasion expected in December, 1777, but what we have had those intimations hanging over our heads. The truth is, that General Washington always considered as his duty to convey every rumor of an embarkation; but we (for some time past, at least) never thought anything but actual invasion should induce us to the expense and harassment of calling the militia into the field; except in the case of December, 1779, when it was thought proper to do this in order to convince the French of our disposition to protect their ships. Inattention to this necessary economy, in the beginning, went far towards that ruin of our finances which followed.

2d Objection.—Where were the post-riders established last summer?

Answer.—They were established at Continental expense, to convey speedy information to Congress of the arrival of the French fleet, then expected here. When that arrived at Rhode Island, these expenses were discontinued. They were again established on the invasion in October, and discontinued when that ceased. And again on the first intimation of the invasion of December. But it will be asked, why were they not established on General Washington's letters? Because those letters were no more than we had received upon many former occasions, and would have led to a perpetual establishment of post-riders.

3d Objection.—If a proper number of men had been put into motion on Monday, for the relief of the lower country, and ordered to march to Williamsburg, that they would at least have been in the neighborhood of Richmond on Thursday.

Answer.—The order could not be till Tuesday, because we then received our first certain information. Half the militia of the counties round about Richmond were then ordered out, and the whole of them on the 4th, and ordered not to wait to come in a body, but in detachments as they could assemble. Yet were there not on Friday more than two hundred collected, and they were principally of the town of Richmond.

4th Objection.—That we had not signals.

Answer.—This, though a favorite plan of some gentlemen, and perhaps a practicable one, has hitherto been thought too difficult.

5th Objection.—That we had not look-outs.

Answer.—There had been no cause to order look-outs more than has been ever existing. This is only in fact asking why we do not always keep look-outs.

6th Objection.—That we had not heavy artillery on travelling carriages.

Answer.—The gentlemen who acted as members of the Board of War a twelve-month can answer this question, by giving the character of the artificers whom, during that time, they could never get to mount the heavy artillery. The same reason prevented their being mounted from May, 1780, to December. We have even been unable to get those heavy cannon moved from Cumberland by the whole energy of government. A like difficulty which occurred in the removal of those at South Quay, in their day, will convince them of the possibility of this.

7th Objection.—That there was not a body of militia thrown into Portsmouth, he Great Bridge, and Suffolk.

Answer.—In the summer of 1780, we asked the favor of General Nelson, to call together the county lieutenants of the lower counties, and concert the general measures which should be taken for instant opposition, on any invasion, until aid could be ordered by the Executive; and the county lieutenants were ordered to obey his call; he did so the first moment, to wit, on Saturday, December the 31st, at eight o'clock, A.M., of our receiving information of the appearance of a fleet in the bay. We asked the favor of General Nelson to go down, which he did, with full powers to call together the militia of any counties he thought proper, to call on the keepers of any public arms or stores, and to adopt for the instant such measures as exigencies required, till we could be better informed.

Query.—Why were not General Nelson, and the brave officers with him, particularly mentioned?

Answer.—What should have been said of them? The enemy did not land, nor give them an opportunity of doing what nobody doubts they would have done; that is, something worthy of being minutely recited.

Query.—Why publish Arnold's letter without General Nelson's answer?

Answer.—Ask the printer. He got neither from the Executive.

Objection.—As to the calling out a few militia, and that late.

Answer.—It is denied that they were few or late. Four thousand and seven hundred men (the number required by Baron Steuben) were called out the moment an invasion was known to have taken place, that is on Tuesday, January 2d.

Objection.—The abandonment of York and Portsmouth fortifications.

Answer.—How can they be kept without regulars, on the large scale on which they were formed? Would it be approved of to harass the militia with garrisoning them?

This amounts to but an informal memorandum on both sides.

It will be observed, that among the "objections" there are none which even hint at an unmanly, or in any respect improper flight before Arnold at Richmond, or before Tarleton at Monticello—afterwards favorite themes of party detraction—and which the representations of newspapers, and even of works bearing the names of histories and biographies, have led a considerable portion of the public to suppose was the very gist of the imaginary "impeachment."[1] It would have hardly been expected, indeed, that any member of a Legislature which had no less than *four* times adjourned and dispersed *to a man*, on the near approach of a foe,[2] which perfectly well knew, on the other hand, that on two of those occasions (the only ones where there was anything left to save or accomplish) the Governor

---

[1] For example, the Life of Alexander Hamilton, by his son.

[2] Namely, on the 2d day of January, when Arnold was known to be ascending the James and was within two days' sail of Westover; again on the 10th of May, when Cornwallis threatened Richmond; again on the 4th of June, when Tarleton approached Charlottesville; and again on the 10th of June, when Arnold was reported to be approaching Staunton!

remained, executing his duties, in close proximity to the enemy, until the latter retired—we say it would have hardly been expected, that any member of that body would impute cowardice to the Governor! Not one of the Privy Council even had remained to stay up his hand—to watch when he slept—during Arnold's incursion to Richmond. And we infer from a statement of Girardin, that but one member of the Privy Council—William Fleming—remained on duty, when the second and third legislative adjournment (in the face of an advancing foe), took place.[1]

Let us not do injustice to repel injustice. We by no means assert that it was the absolute duty of the members of the Legislature, either in their official or personal capacity, to remain to sustain and aid the Executive in public crises so trying. The members of the Executive Council may have had imperious demands on their time, which prevented them (by their offices as much a part of the executive head of the government, as the Governor himself) from staying and sharing with the latter, dangers and responsibilities which pressed so undividedly on him that he was compelled to personally supervise the execution of his own orders, day and night, even to the ferriage of arms across a river, and to ride horses to death to gain time. There may have been reasons, and good reasons, for these things. But surely those who *retired* when the Governor *did not retire*, would not have accused him of cowardice!

In regard to the flight both of the Governor and Legislature before Tarleton's dragoons, common sense would have taught any person that there was nothing in this in the least degree discreditable to either, and nothing that, on the score of pride or honor, Don Quixote or a Knight of the Round Table could have found fault with! Both the Legislature and Governor were apprised that a strong body of horse—Tarleton's dreaded legion—was close upon them, and they had not defences which were adequate to withstand a single company of that legion.

---

[1] Girardin, speaking of that *legal* interregnum which the Legislature had permitted to occur between the 2d of June and the election of General Nelson, says:

"Mr. Jefferson, although, as before observed, his constitutional term of office had now expired, still continued to devote to his country that zeal and those capacities for which he had been uniformly distinguished. The crisis was too extraordinary, too imperious for technical formality. The exertions of Mr. William Fleming, the only acting member of the Executive Council *for some time before the appointment of Mr. Jefferson's successor*, were likewise of the highest service to the State."

Richard Henry Lee does not appear to have felt it incumbent on him to urge the members, in imitation of the superannuated officers of Rome, on the approach of Brennus, to devote themselves to the Infernal Deities, and passively await death or captivity from the foe.   General Stevens, whose courage had never been impeached under Washington, or at Camden, or at Guilford Court House, condescended to ride off on the shabbiest horse he could catch.   Even the brave Steuben had retired as precipitately before Simcoe as anybody did before Tarleton. The Governor had not a solitary soldier or guard at Monticello —a wholly indefensible house—not weapons enough to arm more than three servants—and he knew, of course, that Tarleton would not send a detachment to take him, not able to at once put down all resistance.   He remained in his house, taking care of public and private papers, until the enemy were within *five minutes* of entering it, and then retired with all the evidences of remarkable deliberation which have been narrated.   And not a specific fact in that narration has ever been denied, nor will one ever be denied on respectable authority.

The editor of the Congress edition of Mr. Jefferson's works (Professor Henry A. Washington) has fallen into a serious error in regard to this legislative inquiry, and especially in regard to George Nicholas's objections.   In a note appended to a letter from Jefferson to Lafayette, August 4, 1781, the editor says:

"In 1781, the depredations of the enemy, and the public and private losses which they occasioned, produced the ordinary effect of complaint against those who had charge of the public defence, and especially against Mr. Jefferson (the Governor of Virginia).   A popular clamor was excited against him, and, under the impulses of the moment, Mr. George Nicholas, a member from Albemarle, moved his impeachment.

"The charges were: 1. That he had not, as soon as advised by General Washington of the meditated invasion, put the country in a state of preparation and defence.   2. That during the invasion, he did not use the means of resistance which were at his command.   3. That he too much consulted his personal safety when Arnold first entered Richmond, by which others were dispirited and discouraged.   4. That he ignominiously fled from Monticello to the neighboring mountain on Tarleton's approach to Charlottesville; and 5. That he abandoned the office of Governor as soon as it became one of difficulty and danger.

"Mr. Jefferson has long since been acquitted of these charges by the almost unanimous voice of his countrymen."

A comparison of the language will show that these supposed charges were, by an error, copied from those on which Professor

Tucker says Mr. Jefferson "was arraigned before the bar of *public opinion*, for he never was required to answer before any other tribunal."[1] But the latter writer labored under no error, for four pages later he says: "It is worthy of remark, that among the charges, 'the flight' from Richmond and from Monticello, the favorite grounds of party censure many years afterwards, were not included."

Mr. Washington's mistake was, obviously, unintentional. If the spirit of the note we have quoted does not sufficiently show that he aimed to treat Mr. Jefferson fairly, the general tenor of his work amply establishes that fact.

If Mr. Tucker meant to be understood that contemporaneously with the events (that is, in 1781), Mr. Jefferson was arraigned even at "the bar of public opinion," in the manner indicated, we think *he* accidentally also fell into an error. We think, as his own subsequent remark in part would seem to imply, that it was "many years afterwards" when this became a favorite ground of "party censure." We believe no Virginia gentleman of that day expected the Executive of his State to emulate the exploits of Sir Bevis of Hampton, by mounting some trusty "Arundel," drawing his terrible "Morglay," and putting to death, single handed, ten or twelve hundred infantry, or even a cavalry legion—and we doubt whether any Virginia gentleman desired the Executive of his State to make a melodramatic exhibition of "dying in the Senate chamber!" Our Revolutionary ancestors appear to have been unromantic, every-day sort of men. None of them, from General Washington down to the last appointed corporal, appear to have had souls above retreating, when they were overmatched in the proportion of fifty, or even five to one! No; we suspect that this imputation on Mr. Jefferson's courage was a long-after thought, when the facts had become dim enough in the public memory to be readily interwoven with the fabulous. At all events, it is very difficult to see why, if such an impression did contemporaneously prevail, the spirit which dictated the attack on his official career and character, omitted this from the list of its "charges!"

Before the Legislature again convened in the fall, Mr. George Nicholas's colleague from Albemarle county resigned his seat, "to place Mr. Jefferson on an equal ground for meet-

[1] Tucker's Jefferson, vol. i. p. 152.

ing the inquiry," and the latter received the *unanimous* vote of the electors. He accepted the place "with a single object," and determined "to withdraw when that should be accomplished."[1] When the day for the hearing in the Legislature (December 19th) arrived, he rose in his place and avowed his readiness to meet any charges or inquiries. Not a word was heard in reply. Mr. George Nicholas was absent.[2] Mr. Jefferson then read the "objections" received from him and his own answers. Nearly every member present had been a witness of their truth, and knew that "all was done which could have been done" by the Governor. The House of Delegates then, *at once*, without a word of opposition, and by a *unanimous* vote, passed the following resolution:

"*Resolved*, That the sincere thanks of the General Assembly be given to our former Governor, Thomas Jefferson, Esquire, for his impartial, upright, and attentive administration of the powers of the Executive, whilst in office; popular rumors giving some degree of credence by more pointed accusations, rendered it necessary to make an inquiry into his conduct, and delayed that retribution of public gratitude so eminently merited; but that conduct having become the object of scrutiny, tenfold value is added to the approbation founded on a cool and deliberate discussion. The Assembly wish, therefore, in the strongest manner, to declare the high opinion which they entertain of Mr. Jefferson's ability, rectitude, and integrity, as chief magistrate of this Commonwealth, and mean, by thus publicly avowing their opinion, to obviate *all future* and remove all *former* unmerited censure."

The Senate struck out the words printed in italics, thus vastly improving the phraseology and good taste of the resolution, without in the least abridging its previous substance; and then *unanimously* adopted it. The House concurred, and thus on the 19th day of December, the following resolution was *unanimously* adopted by both houses of the General Assembly:

"*Resolved*, That the sincere thanks of the General Assembly be given to our former Governor, Thomas Jefferson, Esquire, for his impartial, upright, and attentive administration whilst in office. The Assembly wish, in the strongest manner, to declare the high opinion which they entertain of Mr. Jefferson's ability, rectitude, and integrity, as chief magistrate of this Commonwealth, and mean, by thus publicly avowing their opinion, to obviate and to remove all unmerited censure."

It is due to George Nicholas to say that his failure to push the inquiry arose solely from the deliberate conviction that he

[1] Jefferson to Edmund Randolph, Sept. 16.
[2] Jefferson's Works, Congress edition, vol. ix. p. 218.

had acted hastily and in the wrong. With the manly frankness which characterized him, he made no secret of this, and he afterwards declared it in a published letter to the world.

Such was the rise, progress, and termination of an affair—still trumpeted to the world as an " impeachment "—but which did not even amount to an ordinary legislative inquiry. Nor is the difference we have pointed out merely technical, or one only of words. A legislative inquiry or investigation into the conduct of a government official is generally considered a matter of course, if demanded by respectable opponents. The upright officer can have no fear of fair scrutiny into his conduct. But the resolution of a legislative body to "impeach," and their agreement upon charges to that end, is somewhat analogous to the finding of a grand jury. It presupposes that the evidences of guilt are strong enough to make public justice demand that the accused be put upon his *trial*. The House then makes itself an accuser, and the Senate tries. We are not aware that the Virginia Senate had anything to do with *this* case, but to pass a joint resolution of thanks, and proclaim their unanimous opinion, " in the strongest manner," not only of the rectitude but official "ability" and "attentive administration" of their late Chief Magistrate. Never did an official accusation end more abortively—stand more self-condemned and disowned in every quarter—and never was a vindication more triumphantly complete. George Nicholas did more than make a retraction. He became one of the staunchest and most efficient of that band of devoted personal and political friends who, long before Mr. Jefferson's star rose to the ascendant, stood by him through good and through evil report, proud to acknowledge him as their leader. No Virginia family contributed more to Mr. Jefferson's personal success, than the powerful family of the Nicholases— powerful in talents, powerful in probity, powerful in their numbers and their union. On every page of Mr. Jefferson's future political history, the names of George, John,[1] Wilson Cary, and Philip Norborne Nicholas, are conspicuous.

<hr/>

[1] Never to be confounded (as has been done by several writers) with a cousin John Nicholas, for a time the Clerk of Albemarle, and hence often designated popularly as "Clerk John " to distinguish him from a man of ten times his capacity and standing. The latter was sometimes popularly designated " one-eyed John," he having lost one of his eyes.

CHAPTER X.

1781—1784.

PENDING the last described proceedings in the Virginia Legislature, the national Legislature evinced in a decided manner how little Mr. Jefferson's standing had been impaired in the minds of his countrymen generally, by the events we have described. Congress, on the 15th day of June, 1781, associated him with the four American Plenipotentiaries already in Europe (Adams, Franklin, Jay, and Laurens), to appear and treat for peace on behalf of the United States, at the proposed Congress of Vienna.

But, as he remarks in his Memoir, the same reason which had influenced him on a previous occasion of the same kind, "obliged him still to decline." This was the health of his wife. Mrs. Jefferson had borne her fifth child in the preceding November. When it was two months old, she had fled with it in her arms as Arnold approached Richmond. It was a fine healthy infant, but it had sickened and died in April. The constant liability of her husband to capture, and her necessary separation from him as he hovered about the enemy, added to the distressing anxieties of the wife and mother. Then, to shatter all her remaining strength and courage, came the sudden flight before Tarleton, and the horrors of Elkhill. The groans and ghastly forms of her dying servants haunted her by day and by night. The conduct of the Legislature, and an accident which befell her husband (presently to be named), brought new shocks, and it required but a breath more to extinguish the feeble taper of life.

Mr. Jefferson nowhere, that we are aware, intimates such a thing—for reasons which will by and by be more apparent—but there is not a doubt that he would have been compelled to decline a reëlection as Governor, on account of the state of his wife's health, if for no other reason. It demanded immediate quiet, and freedom from excitement, and the soothing attentions of her husband, to even briefly prolong her life.[1]

There was another reason which would have prevented Mr. Jefferson from leaving Virginia at this period, had the previous one not existed. Letters from him to Lafayette and Edmund Randolph, show that he regarded it as incumbent on his honor to remain at home until the Legislative inquiry into his conduct was formally disposed of; though if he imagined it would end in a serious attempt to *prove* anything against him, he imagined

---

[1] To have *desired* Mrs. Jefferson at this period to expose herself and her two remaining children "to the dangers of the sea and of capture by British ships then covering the ocean," or to have *desired* her to remain at home, separated from her husband for an indefinite period (and she had not a male blood-relative living), while Cornwallis and Tarleton were still roaming like beasts of prey over the State—and one or the other of these alternatives merely to enable her husband to *hold an office* (when his country had three *acting* Plenipotentiaries in Europe to appear at the Congress of Vienna of the stamp of Franklin, Jay and Adams), would have been, in our judgment, about as *becoming* as the gratuitous taunt insinuated by the biographer of another and rival statesman, in commenting on Mr. Jefferson's reasons for declining!

what probably no other intelligent man in the State did. But the truth is, concurring circumstances had given a morbid tone to his feelings on this subject. We shall see more of this hereafter.

It has been stated that he repaired to his estate of Poplar Forest, in Bedford county, during the agitation of the Dictator scheme. The election of General Nelson relieved him of the necessity of leaving that retreat until the health of his wife should become sufficiently improved to make a return to Monticello desirable. On the last day of the month (June), he was thrown from his horse, and received contusions which, though they did not prove serious enough to confine him for any considerable length of time to his bed, or even strictly to his house, prevented him from horseback-riding, or from long journeys in a carriage, for a number of weeks.[1]

Mr. Jefferson employed this confinement in preparing replies to a set of inquiries which had been propounded to him by the learned Marquis of Barbé-Marbois, nominally Secretary of the French Legation in Philadelphia, but perhaps as much or more than his principal, De la Luzerne, the confidential agent of his government in the United States. Marbois's inquiries were made in consequence of orders to collect the important statistics of the American States; and furnishing them to him, therefore, was rather gratifying the wishes of a national ally than those of a mere individual. Mr. Jefferson's answers, with some additions and corrections made principally in the winter of 1782, constitute the work subsequently published under the title of "Notes on Virginia."

The rapidity with which a production betraying such an amount of research, and more particularly, such a vast amount of personal observation, was dashed off, would seem a curious fact in the life of a man who had hitherto appeared so constantly engaged in public affairs. But his habits of microscopic observation—of putting the minutest discoveries on paper—and of collecting and preserving all the facts, of any interest to him, found floating in the oral statements or transient publications of

---

[1] The doctor was called in twice, and it is a good illustration of the *currency* to say his fee for the two calls was £600! But what particular sum *in specie* this represented, at the moment, it would be difficult to say! To relieve the doctor from all suspicion of *extortion*, we will proclaim that among the entries in the account book of the same week, we find the following: "Pd. for chickens £30." "Pd. Mosely for 3 quarts brandy £71 2s." "Pd. for chickens to Judy £40 10s.," and the *same day*, to three o'her of his slaves, for *chickens*, £50 8s!

the day—have been mentioned. And the busiest public man who ever lived, has found time to garner up an immense amount of knowledge on any chosen topic—to actually make important achievements in science—provided he has adopted the practice of making them the amusements of his spare hours. This practice *rests* the mind, as a change of movement rests the tired muscle, about as readily as complete inaction; and certainly it provides surer amusement to an active and grasping intellect. There is more substance in a pleasure which tends incidentally in a useful direction;[1] and the horse that has strained every ligament in the severe race, will suffer less soreness and stiffening if walked gently about, than if suffered to sink down without further movement, in his stable!

This train of remark applies better to the naturalist (that is, naturalist in his amusements) than perhaps to any other person. When he escapes from his business office, from his study, from the legislative hall, from the thick and eager crowd, and goes forth to look on nature, he gazes not around in the listlessness of ignorance, or superficial and soon-satisfied curiosity. For him all nature is a glorious museum of exhaustless and never-palling wonders. For him there is not an animated existence that does not fill some fitting chink in the space from God to the worm. For him there is not one solitary plant that is not an object of beauty in itself, and that would not detract something from the perfect whole if removed. For him every rocky fossil is a medal[2] struck by Omnipotent hand to perpetuate the history of dead ages. For him the greater and lesser lights of the heavens, as they wheel on mystically in their eternal orbits, utter such harmonies as Zoroaster and the Magi heard them uttering, in the dawn of the ages.

Not a step can the true naturalist take, not a sound can he hear, not a glance can he give with his eye, without discovering some more or less revealed part of a wondrous and connected machinery, indissoluble in every part, perfect in every part, marvellous and beautiful in every part. The knowledge which

---

[1] Far be it from us to offer disrespect to that very sage aphorism (if not uttered by Solon or Confucius, wise enough for either of them!) that "all work and no play makes Jack a dull boy"—albeit we cling tenaciously to our proposition in the text. We would like to know if the speckled trout or the woodcock for supper does not give *substance* to the day's sport in fishing or hunting! *Verb. sap.*

[2] We forget who first conceived the fine idea of comparing fossils to medals.

drinks in these things sees order, and purpose, and unity, and a glorious framing hand, where ignorance, or that poor knowledge which grasps only the practical concerns of life, finds only confusion, or chance, or sources of lamentation, or worthless shards to be trodden upon.

The character of Mr. Jefferson's Notes on Virginia is too well known to require very extended comment. As a well digested general exposition of the natural history, statistics, and important systems of a State, we know of no preceding work, within the same compass, that compares with it. The Virginian who should now seek the best description of the physical characteristics of his country, and of at least the *foundation* of all its systems, would probably still turn to this work, written between seventy and eighty years ago, when there were no railroads—when scarcely turnpike-roads or highways of any kind penetrated vast regions of the State—when Indians yet possessed extensive portions of it—when no newspapers were published out of capitals or large cities—when it was about as serious an undertaking to surmount the most westerly of those chains of mountains which are in the *middle* of Virginia and to reach the banks of the two Kenhawas and the other eastern affluents of the Ohio, as it would now be for a Virginian to surmount the Rocky Mountains, and penetrate to the vales where "rolls the Oregon."

The style of the Notes is concise, vigorous, and simple, occasionally rising, where the topic solicits it, into passages of great beauty. The descriptions of the passage of the Potomac through the Blue Ridge, of the Big Buffalo of Indian tradition, and some others, are instances of this, which have been familiarized to American readers by innumerable publications. Of compact argument presented in language having the freshness of narration, and set off now and then by felicitous and absolutely clinching illustrations, there are numerous examples. As a whole, perhaps, no book of statistics was ever more pleasingly or vigorously written.

It now raises a smile to peruse the earnest and long array of facts and arguments with which Buffon's then recent theory of animal degeneracy in America, and the Abbé Raynal's super-added one of the degeneracy of the man of Europe transplanted to America, are combated. Raynal's assertion that America has not produced " one good poet, one able mathematician, one man of genius in a single art or a single science," [1] is met with the following animated rejoinder :

" ' America has not yet produced one good poet.' When we shall have existed as a people as long as the Greeks did before they produced a Homer, the Romans a Virgil, the French a Racine and Voltaire, the English a Shakspeare and Milton, should this reproach be still true, we will inquire from what unfriendly causes it has proceeded, that the other countries of Europe and quarters of the earth shall not have inscribed any name in the roll of poets. But neither has America produced ' one able mathematician, one man of genius in a single art or a single science.' In war we have produced a Washington, whose memory will be adored while liberty shall have votaries, whose name shall triumph over time, and will in future ages assume its just station among the most celebrated worthies of the world, when that wretched philosophy shall be forgotten which would have arranged him among the degeneracies of nature. In physics we have produced a Franklin, than whom no one of the present age has made more important discoveries, nor has enriched philosophy with more, or more ingenious solutions of the phenomena of nature We have supposed Mr. Rittenhouse second to no astronomer living; that in genius he must be the first, because he is self-taught. As an artist he has exhibited as great a proof of mechanical genius as the world has ever produced. He has not indeed made a world; but he has by imitation approached nearer its Maker than any man who has lived from the creation to this day.[2] As in philosophy and war, so in government, in oratory, in painting, in the plastic art, we might show that America, though but a child of yesterday, has already given hopeful proofs of genius, as well as of the nobler kinds, which arouse the best feelings of man, which call him into action, which substantiate his freedom, and conduct him to happiness, as of the subordinate, which serve to amuse him only.   *   *   *   *

We therefore suppose, that this reproach is as unjust as it is unkind : and that, of the geniuses which adorn the present age, America contributes its full share. For, comparing it with those countries where genius is most cultivated, where are the most excellent models for art, and scaffoldings for the attainment of science, as France and England for instance, we calculate thus : The United States contains three millions of inhabitants; France twenty millions; and the British islands ten.

---

[1] This remark occurs in Raynal's " *Histoire Philosophique des Etablissemens et du Commerce des Européens dans les deux Indes,*" published about 1774, and which when the Notes were written, continued to attract considerable notice.

A number of humorous encounters took place between the learned Abbé and Dr. Franklin on the subject of this disparaging theory. Jefferson thus (long afterward) gave an account of one of them:

" Dr. Franklin had a party to dine with him one day at Passy, of whom one half were Americans, the other half French, and among the last was the Abbé. During the dinner he got on his favorite theory of the degeneracy of animals, and even of man, in America, and urged it with his usual eloquence. The Doctor at length noticing the accidental stature and position of his guests, at table, ' Come,' says he, ' M. l'Abbé, let us try this question by the fact before us. We are here one half Americans, and one half French, and it happens that the Americans have placed themselves on one side of the table, and our French friends are on the other. Let both parties rise, and we will see on which side nature has degenerated.' It happened that his American guests were Carmichael, Harmer, Humphreys, and others of the finest stature and form; while those of the other side were remarkably diminutive, and the Abbé himself particularly, was a mere shrimp. He parried the appeal, however, by a complimentary admission of exceptions, among which the Doctor himself was a conspicuous one."

[2] In the construction of his orrery.

We produce a Washington, a Franklin, a Rittenhouse. France then should have half a dozen in each of these lines, and Great Britain half that number, equally eminent."

This arithmetical style of argument is highly characteristic of its author, and perhaps was as well put as any other would have been as an answer to the impudent Frenchman; but, we confess, we have great doubts whether it was very sound in logic. We think it more than probable that our country will never produce a Shakspeare or a Milton, and certainly never a Homer. There is very small chance that Europe will produce a Washington. But this, should it be so, we apprehend, will furnish no proof of intellectual inferiority on either side. It will only show that those ethnologic and other circumstances —those peculiar phases in civilization—which develop Homers, and Shakspeares, and Miltons, and Washingtons, are not at work, while minds of quite as "broad and ample pinion" may still be active in other realms of thought or action. While England has produced such names as the above, and her Bacons and Newtons in addition, she never has produced one really transcendent orator. She has produced unrivalled debaters like Fox, splendid declaimers like Chatham, and magnificent oratorical *writers* like Burke. But she has made no approach to a Demosthenes, nor scarcely, in our opinion, to a Mirabeau. She has had ten thousand parliamentary speakers who excelled Patrick Henry in information, wisdom, logic, nearly everything— but if she has had one such truly lyrical orator, one man capable like him of sweeping along the feelings of his hearers as the tempest sweeps along the forest leaves on its wing, we know not who that man was. Yet Patrick Henry would be a good deal more misplaced, a good deal more, in nautical phrase, out of his latitude, in the English Parliament, than would Red Jacket or Logan in the American Congress! America has had no gradual growth in civilization, from a barbaric origin, presenting those varying stages or phases of development favorable to certain exhibitions of mind. We are inclined to subscribe to Mr. Macaulay's theory (if the theory was original with Mr. Macaulay), that poetry is the peculiar fruit of a middle point between barbarism and cultivation—that it breaks out like springs from hill-sides, when mind first begins to feel and assert its superiority over thews and sinews, and before after-training has shorn away its wild, native vigor, in shearing away its redundancies. We shall never, then, have a Homer. Patrick Henry's lost productions were our nearest approach to the Iliad! Yet, if our nation sprouted from the side of another, after its great poetic age had passed—if our utilitarianism is even more complete (because more necessary)—there are imaginative traces in the offshoot which are not found in the parent stem. The utilitarianism of England is that of one fixedly ordered workshop, where each man works for his particular wages and expects no more. Ours is the struggle of a people, each craving opulence, each expecting to beget Governors and Presidents. Our scramble, instead of being carried on amidst the clang of trip-hammers and the buzz of spinning-jennies, and within factory walls, is carried on by the shores of great inland seas, on which the armadas of England might ride—by rivers, single ones of which would cross and recross England more than ten, more than twenty times from ocean to ocean—under mountains on the sides of which the loftiest of England would barely form the usual cones and knobs of great mountains. As these surroundings impressed the mental structure of the Iroquois and Algonquin—as they impressed the mental structure of Logan and Red Jacket—so have they in some part impressed the mental structure of the Anglo-American. Perhaps a strong infusion of Celtic blood has helped along the change. At all events, the Anglo-American is a very different animal from his English ancestors. He is less staid and plodding, more excitable. Anglo-American writers and speakers appeal oftener to the feelings and to the imagination. They aspire oftener to the picturesque and the grand, and failing to find the last in the subject, or in *themselves*, they sometimes attempt to supply its place by exaggerations of language.

Our orators and writers of every stamp differ, then, from those of England. This divergence may increase; we believe it will never diminish. Our material and psychological wants call for exertions in different fields of intellectual labor. Our tones of thought, our modes of expression, and even our languages are coming to vary. Our political exigencies, our social structures, call for different kinds of talent, or, at least, different modes of mental activity. It cannot be just, then, to make either nation the standard to judge the other by, in greatness or even in good taste. Each must, ultimately, be a law unto itself. We had a colonial political party long after our final political separation from England. We yet have, and are likely to have, for an age to come, a colonial literary party, a colonial class of ideologists generally. With such, to change from the olden standards—to cease, for example, to use the language of Shakspeare and Milton, is, if in England, "improvement," or, at all events, the necessary change wrought by the advance of human affairs; in America, it is provincialism and vulgarity. A new word added to the language in England (a thing of constant occurrence) is, if the authority be pretty good, a mere growth of the "English undefiled ;" in America, introduced by abler and better authority—it is an "Americanism" —to be shunned with horror by the literary purists! To go but a little way back, England has changed as much from the poetry of Dryden and Pope, as much from the prose of Swift and Addison, as much from the parliamentary style of Chatham and Burke, as we have; indeed, in parliamentary style, they have changed far *most*. We are not throwing away our literary birthright any more, then, than England. Whether we are making a worse exchange is another question. Every nation, out of its intellectual swaddling clothes, must be its own standard and its own judge. The tastes of England and France do not correspond. Neither of these correspond with those of Germany. Italy presents still another national taste. The Orient still another. Men might as well fall disputing which is inherently the most beautiful color, the green of the leaves, the blue of the sky, the crimson of the flowers, or the gold tint of the sunset! In this view, Mr. Jefferson's arithmetical rule seems to us inapplicable and preposterous.

To return from this long digression. There are other ethnological remarks contained in the Notes on Virginia—such as comparisons between the European, Indian, and Negro races —which possess much interest. Distinctions between the white and red race are clearly pointed out; but the author considers the Indian originally, or under equal circumstances, equal to the European, intellectually and physically. The African he considers inferior "in the endowments both of body and mind ;" but he hazards this opinion "with great diffidence," and hazards it as a "suspicion only." [1]

---

[1] These views are repeated by Mr. Jefferson in a letter to the Marquis de Chastellux, June 7th, 1785. He says : "I believe the Indian to be in body and mind equal to the

His hostility to African slavery is earnestly, vehemently expressed; and he avows the opinion embodied in the "kept back" plan of the Law Revisers' in 1779 (and which he reiterated forty years after writing these Notes, in his Memoir), that it was impossible for the two races to live equally free in the same government—that "nature, habit, opinion, had drawn indelible lines of distinction between them"'—that, accordingly, emancipation and "deportation" (colonization) should go hand in hand—and that these processes should be gradual enough to make proper provisions for the blacks in their new country, and fill their places in this with free white laborers.'

Some views are advanced on the subject of religious toleration, which have been frequently misconstrued into an open and direct attack on religion. After describing the terrible penalties denounced by the English and Virginia laws against Atheists, Unitarians, Polytheists, etc. (and in evident allusion to the *phraseology* of the Virginia Act of 1705, c. 30), he says:

"The error seems not sufficiently eradicated, that the operations of the mind, as well as the acts of the body, are subject to the coercion of the laws. But our rulers can have no authority over such natural rights, only as we have submitted to them. The rights of conscience we never submitted, we could not submit. We are answerable for them to our God. The legitimate powers of government *extend to such acts only as are injurious to others. But it does me no injury for my neighbor to say there are twenty gods, or no God. It neither picks my pocket nor breaks my leg.* If it be said his testimony in a court of justice cannot be relied on, reject it then, and be the stigma on him. Constraint may make him worse by making him a hypocrite, but it will never make him a truer man. It may fix him obstinately in his errors, but will not cure them. Reason and free inquiry are the only effectual agents against error. Give a loose to them, they will support the true religion, by bringing every false one to their tribunal, to the test of their investigation. They are the natural enemies of error, and of error only."

The sentences placed in italics—and which contain the sup-

---

white man. I have supposed the black man, in his present state, might not be so; but it would be hazardous to affirm, that, equally cultivated for a few generations, he would not become so."

¹ Jefferson, Wythe and Pendleton.
² This is the language of the Memoir. The following is from the Notes:
"It will probably be asked, Why not retain and incorporate the blacks into the State, and thus save the expense of supplying by importation of white settlers. the vacancies they will leave? Deep-rooted prejudices entertained by the whites; ten thousand recollections, by the blacks, of the injuries they have sustained; new provocations: the real distinctions which nature has made; and many other circumstances, will divide us into parties, and produce convulsions, which will probably never end but in the extermination of the one or the other race. To these objections, which are political, may be added others, which are physical and moral."
³ See Chap. vi. p. 227, of this volume.

posed attack on religion—most obviously mean, in their connection, simply that my neighbor's irreligion will do me no injury in a legal or political sense, and that consequently, it is not a proper subject of legislative penalties. It was to clearly take this distinction between a *moral* wrong and a *legal* wrong, that Mr. Jefferson used the illustration which has provoked so much criticism. He meant to say, and only to say, that a neighbor's religious error does me no injury that law can properly take cognizance of, as for example, such physical injuries as breaking my leg or stealing my purse.

Other religious criticisms, some of them specious at first blush, and others baldly ridiculous—not one of them making an approach to convicting the author of any *intended* attack on religion, or of a covert sneer exhibiting (after the meaner fashion of Gibbon), malevolence without courage—were levelled at the "Notes," in various publications. We will allude to these fully at a subsequent stage of this narrative.

While the Notes disclose great familiarity with a large range of sciences, they touch others where the author, not being in advance of his own times, is necessarily far behind the present ones. In geology especially, it is amusing to observe this keen-sighted observer, groping about, blundering and puzzled, among the nascent theories of that science.[1]

Our limits do not permit us to extend comments on this work ; and we dismiss it with the remark, that though superseded in some departments by the further advance of knowledge, it will yet richly repay perusal—will always remain a monument of industry and vigorous thought—and a model for a compact description of a commonwealth.

The latter part of 1781, Mr. Jefferson remained in strict retirement, watching over the health of his wife, and, it must be confessed, brooding gloomily over the indignity which had been offered him in the Legislature. To Lafayette, who had been

---

[1] Rejecting the reference of the palæontological phenomena witnessed in mountains to a Noachian or other deluge, or the inference, based on Voltaire's false facts, that shells are generated and grow in rocks disconnected from animal bodies—he also condemned that theory of upheaval which the learned world have since (from vastly more extended opportunities of investigation) settled upon as the true one. In a letter to Mr. Rittenhouse in 1786, and in another to Charles Thomson in 1787, he appears as incredulous and bewildered as ever, and so, we doubt not, he always remained. Indeed, besides a few general inquiries in the infancy of the science, we do not find that he ever paid much attention to it. He seems to have been disgusted with the boldness of its unsupported theories, and therefore not to have kept up with that development of facts which has finally, in the judgment of the learned, established those theories.

made the channel of conveyance to communicate to him his late appointment as a foreign minister, and who had accompanied that communication with some obliging offers of personal service in France, he wrote August 4th:

"I lose an opportunity, the only one I ever had, and perhaps ever shall have, of combining public service with private gratification, of seeing countries whose improvements in science, in arts, and in civilization, it has been my fortune to admire at a distance, but never to see, and at the same time of lending some aid to a cause, which has been handed on from its first organization to its present stage, by every effort of which my poor faculties were capable. These, however, have not been such as to give satisfaction to some of my countrymen, and it has become necessary for me to remain in the State till a later period in the present year, than is consistent with an acceptance of what has been offered me. The independence of private life under the protection of republican laws will, I hope, yield me the happiness from which no slave is so remote as the minister of a commonwealth."

He wrote Edmund Randolph, September 16th:

"Were it possible for me to determine again to enter into public business, there is no appointment whatever which would have been so agreeable to me. But I have taken my final leave of everything of that nature. I have returned to my farm, my family and books, from which I think nothing will ever more separate me. A desire to leave public office with a reputation not more blotted than it has deserved, will oblige me to emerge at the next session of our Assembly, and perhaps to accept a seat in it. But as I go with a single object, I shall withdraw when that shall be accomplished."

Soon after the battle of Yorktown, he addressed General Washington in terms expressing his continued warm respect and affection:

MONTICELLO, *October 28th*, 1781.

SIR,—I hope it will not be unacceptable to your Excellency to receive the congratulations of a private individual on your return to your native country, and, above all things, on the important success which has attended it. Great as this has been, however, it can scarcely add to the affection with which we have looked up to you. And if, in the minds of any, the motives of gratitude to our good allies were not sufficiently apparent, the part they have borne in this action must amply evince them. Notwithstanding the state of perpetual *decrepitude* to which I am unfortunately reduced, I should certainly have done myself the honor of paying my respects to you personally; but I apprehend these visits, which are meant by us as marks of our attachment to you, must interfere with the regulations of a camp, and be particularly inconvenient to one whose time is too precious to be wasted in ceremony.

I beg you to believe me among the sincerest of those who subscribe themselves, your Excellency's most obedient, and most humble servant.[1]

---

[1] This letter appears first published in the Congress Edition of his Works.

The word " decrepitude," in the preceding, must be a misprint. Mr. Jefferson was laboring under no *decrepitude ;* his health was perfectly good. But his wife's health gave him perpetual *solicitude,* and this, we conjecture, was the word intended.

In the spring of 1782, the learned and accomplished Major-General, the Marquis de Chastellux—one of the commanders of the French army in America, one of the forty members of the French Academy, etc.—paid a visit to Monticello. In his subsequently published Travels in North America, the Marquis thus describes his observations and impressions at Mr. Jefferson's residence :

* * " The conversation continued, and brought us insensibly to the foot of the mountains. On the summit of one of them, we discovered the house of Mr. Jefferson, which stands preëminent in these retirements ; it was himself who built it, and preferred this situation ; for, although he possessed considerable property in the neighborhood, there was nothing to prevent him from fixing his residence wherever he thought proper. But it was a debt nature owed to a philosopher, and a man of taste, that in his own possessions he should find a spot where he might best study and enjoy her. He calls his house *Monticello* (in Italian, *Little Mountain*), a very modest title, for it is situated upon a very lofty one, but which announces the owner's attachment to the language of Italy ; and, above all, to the fine arts, of which that country was the cradle, and is still the asylum. As I had no further occasion for a guide, I separated from the Irishman ; and after ascending by a tolerably commodious road, for more than half an hour, we arrived at *Monticello.* This house, of which Mr. Jefferson was the architect, and often one of the workmen, is rather elegant, and in the Italian taste, though not without fault ; it consists of one large square pavilion, the entrance of which is by two porticos, ornamented with pillars. The ground floor consists chiefly of a very large, lofty saloon which is to be decorated entirely in the antique style ; above it is a library of the same form ; two small wings with only a ground floor and attic story, are joined to this pavilion, and communicate with the kitchen, offices, etc., which will form a kind of basement story, over which runs a terrace. My object in this short description is only to show the difference between this and the other houses of the country ; for we may safely aver, that Mr. Jefferson is the first American who has consulted the fine arts to know how he should shelter himself from the weather. But it is on himself alone I ought to bestow my time. Let me describe to you a man, not yet forty, tall, and with a mild and pleasing countenance, but whose mind and understanding are ample substitutes for every exterior grace. An American, who without ever having quitted his own country, is at once a musician, skilled in drawing, a geometrician, an astronomer, a natural philosopher, legislator, and statesman. A senator of America, who sat for two years in that famous Congress which brought about the Revolution ; and which is never mentioned without respect, though unhappily not without regret,[1] a governor of Virginia, who filled

[1] This obviously alludes to Mr. Jefferson's feelings in regard to the attack made on him in the Legislature.

this difficult station during the invasions of *Arnold*, of *Phillips*, and of *Cornwallis;* a philosopher, in voluntary retirement from the world, and public business, because he loves the world, inasmuch only as he can flatter himself with being useful to mankind; and the minds of his countrymen are not yet in a condition either to bear the light, or to suffer contradiction. A mild and amiable wife, charming children, of whose education he himself takes charge, a house to embellish, great provisons to improve, and the arts and sciences to cultivate; these are what remain to Mr. Jefferson, after having played a principal character on the theatre of the New World, and which he preferred to the honorable commission of Minister Plenipotentiary in Europe. The visit which I made him was not unexpected, for he had long since invited me to come and pass a few days with him in the centre of the mountains; notwithstanding which, I found his first appearance serious; nay, even cold; but before I had been two hours with him, we were as intimate as if we had passed our whole lives together; walking, books, but above all, a conversation always varied and interesting, always supported by that sweet satisfaction experienced by two persons, who in communicating their sentiments and opinions, are invariably in unison, and who understand each other at the first hint, made four days pass away like so many minutes.

"This conformity of sentiments and opinions on which I insist because it constitutes my own eulogium (and self-love must somewhere show itself), this conformity, I say, was so perfect, that not only our taste was similar, but our predilections also, those partialities which cold methodical minds ridicule as enthusiastic, whilst sensible and animated ones cherish, and adopt the glorious appellation. I recollect with pleasure that as we were conversing one evening over a bowl of punch, after Mrs. Jefferson had retired, our conversation turned on the poems of *Ossian*. It was a spark of electricity which passed rapidly from one to the other; we recollected the passages in those sublime poems which particularly struck us, and entertained my fellow-travellers, who fortunately knew English well, and were qualified to judge of their merits, although they had never read the poems. In our enthusiasm the book was sent for, and placed near the bowl, where, by their mutual aid, the night far advanced imperceptibly upon us. Sometimes natural philosophy, at others, politics or the arts were the topics of our coversation, for no object had escaped Mr. Jefferson; and it seemed as if from his youth he had placed his mind, as he has done his house, on an elevated situation, from which he might contemplate the universe."—*Vol. II. From page 40 to 46.*

"Mr. Jefferson amused himself by raising a score of these animals [deer] in his park; they are become very familiar, which happens to all the animals of America; for they are in general much easier to tame than those of Europe. He amuses himself by feeding them with Indian corn, of which they are very fond, and which they eat out of his hand. I followed him one evening into a deep valley, where they are accustomed to assemble towards the close of the day, and saw them walk, run, and bound; but the more I examined their paces, the less I was inclined to annex them to any particular species in Europe. Mr. Jefferson being no sportsman, and not having crossed the seas, could have no decided opinion on this part of natural history; but he has not neglected the other branches. I saw with pleasure that he had applied himself particularly to meteorological observation, which, in fact, of all the branches of philosophy, is the most proper for Americans to cultivate, from the extent of their country and the variety of their situations, which gives them in this point a great advantage over us, who, in other respects, have so many over them. Mr. Jefferson has made, with *Mr.*

Madison, a well-informed professor of mathematics, some correspondent observations on the reigning winds at *Williamsburg* and Monticello."—*Vol. II., page* 48 to —.

"But I perceive my journal is something like the conversation I had with Mr. Jefferson; I pass from one object to another, and forget myself as I write, as it happened not unfrequently in his society. I must now quit the friend of nature, but not nature herself, who expects me in all her splendor at the end of my journey; I mean the famous *Bridge* of *Rocks*, which unites two mountains, the most curious object I ever beheld, as its construction is the most difficult of solution. Mr. Jefferson would most willingly have conducted me thither, although this wonder is upwards of eighty miles from him, and he had often seen it,[1] but his wife being expected every moment to lie in, and himself being as good a husband as he is an excellent philosopher and a virtuous citizen, he only acted as my guide for about sixteen miles, to the passage of the little river *Mechum*, where we parted, and, I presume to flatter myself, with mutual regret."—*Vol. II., page* 55.

It is to be regretted that our author did not give oftener *what* he actually saw and heard, instead of his *impressions*. A Boswellian narrative of a few of those conversations where the amiable and somewhat enthusiastic Frenchman experienced such "sweet satisfaction," actually "forgot himself," would be worth a good deal more than all his general descriptions. A daguerreotype, for example, of the "punch-bowl" scene, where the inspiring beverage probably warmed up the prevailing cloudy and mist-covered scenery of Ossian—of the book "near the bowl"—of Jefferson and De Chastellux alternately spouting "passages in those sublime poems" amidst (we fancy) stamping Frenchmen brimful of punch and sentiment, until the small hours were "imperceptibly" reached—would be priceless!

De Chastellux saw little of Mrs. Jefferson, and he saw her now again laboring under increasing depression and debility—and to this, or to his delicacy, we owe the loss of a description of one of the most beautiful and engaging women of her time The little children, as he states, were taught by their father, and with them his orphaned wards, the Carrs.

The house as here described was but a part of the completed Monticello of after years, and was far less perfect in its appointments. The remark that Mr. Jefferson was "often one of the workmen" in constructing it, is to be taken with some qualification. He had long used one of its rooms as a private workshop. This was fitted up with a variety of tools, and he

---

[1] Doubtless he had pretty often seen it. He had *owned* it and 157 surrounding acres, since 1774.

frequently spent his hours of exercise in it, especially in bad weather, making some small article, like a case for books, a simple instrument, or the like. He may have also made architectural models, but this was about all. Those political painters who have represented him as a Cincinnatus, engaged in manual labor as his chief and favorite occupation, except when dragged forth by the exigencies of the State, have painted a purely fancy sketch. If this is a statesman's merit, he is not entitled to claim it. With him manual labor was the amusement, mental labor the occupation. He had, however, a decided fondness for nearly all mechanical pursuits (as well as agricultural ones) and great handiness in acquiring their manipulations. He could turn off his bits of cabinet ware with neatness and dispatch, and tradition is disposed to claim that he could have successfully aspired to the mystery of shoeing his horse, had occasion demanded.

Mr. Jefferson, though remaining a member, did not attend the spring session of the General Assembly in 1782. This furnished a topic of criticism to opponents, and was sincerely regretted by his truest friends. It was felt that his counsels were needed, and that no personal wrongs could excuse a son of the State from declining its service in a period of difficulty and danger. Mr Madison wrote Edmund Randolph, June 11th, 1782:

"Great as my partiality is to Mr. Jefferson, the mode in which he seems determined to revenge the wrong received from his country does not appear to me to be dictated either by philosophy or patriotism. It argues, indeed, a keen sensibility and strong consciousness of rectitude. But this sensibility ought to be as great towards the relentings as the misdoings of the Legislature, not to mention the injustice of visiting the faults of this body on their innocent constituents." [1]

This is strong language for the gentle, and usually cautious speaking Madison to apply to his dearest, most admired friend; and, if we judge right, *most manly* language too!

Colonel Monroe (the future President) was a member of the Virginia House of Delegates. He was also an *élève* of Mr Jefferson—had studied under his direction—was his ardent friend and admirer. With the blunt, downright sincerity which ever marked Monroe's character, he plainly apprised Mr. Jeffer

[1] Madison Papers. vol. i. p. 141.

son of the murmurs his conduct was occasioning. He was but a rough surgeon, and drew a groan from his patient.[1] Jefferson's reply is dated May 20th, and the following are passages from it:

"Before I ventured to declare to my countrymen my determination to retire from public employment, I examined well my heart to know whether it were thoroughly cured of every principle of political ambition, whether no lurking particle remained which might leave me uneasy, when reduced within the limits of mere private life. I became satisfied that every fibre of that passion was thoroughly eradicated. I examined also, in other views, my right to withdraw. I considered that I had been thirteen years engaged in public service—that, during that time, I had so totally abandoned all attention to my private affairs as to permit them to run into great disorder and ruin—that I had now a family advanced to years which require my attention and instruction—that, to these, was added the hopeful offspring of a deceased friend, whose memory must be forever dear to me, and who have no other reliance for being rendered useful to themselves or their country—that by a constant sacrifice of time, labor, parental and friendly duties, I had, so far from gaining the affection of my countrymen, which was the only reward I ever asked or could have felt, even lost the small estimation I had before possessed.

"That, however I might have comforted myself under the disapprobation of the well-meaning but uninformed people, yet that of their representatives was a shock on which I had not calculated. That this, indeed, had been followed by an exculpatory declaration. But, in the meantime, I had been suspected in the eyes of the world, without the least hint then or afterwards being made public, which might restrain them from supposing that I stood arraigned for treason of the heart, and not merely weakness of the mind; and I felt that these injuries, for such they have been since acknowledged, had inflicted a wound on my spirit which will only be cured by the all-healing grave. If reason and inclination unite in justifying my retirement, the laws of my country are equally in favor of it."

After arguing at considerable length against the *legal* right of the government to perpetually command the official services of the citizen, and showing that contrary precedents had prevailed in the State, he added:

"Nothing could so completely divest us of that liberty as the establishment of the opinion, that the State has a perpetual right to the services of all its members. This, to men of certain ways of thinking, would be to annihilate the blessings of existence, and to contradict the Giver of life, who gave it for happiness and not for wretchedness. And certainly, to such it were better that they had never been born. However, with these, I may think public service and private misery inseparably linked together, I have not the vanity to count myself among those whom the State would think worth oppressing with perpetual service. I have received a sufficient memento to the contrary. I am persuaded that, having hitherto dedicated

[1] Monroe's letter (of May 11th, 1782) will be found in the Congressional edition of Mr. Jefferson's Works, vol. i. p. 316.

to them the whole of the active and useful part of my life, I shall be permitted to pass the rest in mental quiet. I hope, too, that I did not mistake modes any more than the matter of right when I preferred a simple act of renunciation, to the taking sanctuary under those disqualifications (provided by the law for other purposes indeed but) affording asylum also for rest to the wearied."

Nor were these feelings wholly transient. In the Preface to the Notes on Virginia, dated February 27, 1787, he said:

" The subjects are all treated imperfectly, some scarcely touched on. To apologize for this by developing the circumstances of the time and place of their composition, would be to open wounds which have already bled enough."

We have here neither the misanthropy of Timon nor the rage of Coriolanus, but we clearly have keen sensibilities so severely wounded that they have become morbid in their action. The inflictions which a proud and sensitive man will often bring upon himself, under such circumstances, by magnifying the blame imputed to him—by trying to fancy himself only half acquitted—are here well illustrated. If we construe one passage in the letter to Monroe aright, he would seem to intimate that the exculpatory resolution of the Legislature had not sufficiently exonerated his *motives*. This was obviously the waywardness of wounded feeling; his motives had never been attacked. If they had, the legislative resolution most fully and explicitly vindicated them by paying the highest compliment to his impartiality, uprightness, rectitude, and integrity—and this was passed without a word of objection, and without an opposing vote. Never was reparation more ample! If he means to say that the resolution should have contained an affirmation in terms that the original complaint or accusation imputed to him no " treason of the heart," all we have to say is, we think the Legislature judged more wisely and in better taste than he, what was demanded in the premises. It is generally time enough to vindicate the innocent from charges, when those charges have been made. And Mr. Jefferson himself lived to view the subject in this healthier light, as clearly appears by the general tenor of his writings.

Keen sensibilities seem peculiar to the individual—and not to necessarily pertain to weak or to strong minds—to the innocent or to the guilty. The weakest often exhibit the least—the strong the most. There was not, for example, a more sensitive

man to personal defamation—originally sensitive and to the last
sensitive—connected with the events of our whole Revolutionary
history, than General Washington. Mr. Jefferson began, we
think, deeply sensitive, but he gradually schooled his mind,
first, to refuse to see or hear personal attacks unless they were
forced on his attention; secondly, to regard them with a quiet
feeling allied to indifference; and, finally, to meet them with
contemptuous defiance and scorn. The very circumstance
under narration materially helped, we have no doubt, to commence this change. It was a wholesome lesson never again to
rely on smooth sailing at all times—never again, when the contrary ensued, to so yield up the mastery to wounded feeling.

It is due, however, to Mr. Jefferson to say, that this first and
last display of so excessive a sensibility in regard to public censures, was not in keeping with his true character at *any* period.
Circumstances had thrown a particular trait of the mind, as disease occasionally does a particular function of the body, into a
violent and disproportioned activity. He had undergone that
constant overwork and excitement of body and mind, which is
so shattering to the tone—to the nerves (if we may be excused
the metaphor) of both—when quiet and reaction supervene.
He had been hunted from place to place by pursuing soldiery.
His property had been wantonly destroyed under circumstances
of peculiar and brutal barbarity. His slaves had died horrid
deaths. His farm had been turned into a hospital, while his
crops, as if in a plague-stricken land, had fed wild birds or been
scattered and wasted on the ground where they grew. Last,
and worst of all, his wife, crushed by sorrow and misfortune,
had sunk into what seemed a hopeless decline. This was the
moment which neighbors, gentlemen, men of political standing,
legislators, had chosen to make an assault on his official character and reputation! They had not, it is true, known anything
of the peculiarity of his personal circumstances, at the time.
They had but acted on the spur of the moment, when they were
mad with excitement and panic. Their indignity was of little
real account, because it was sure to be soon wiped off—sure to
finally stain only its perpetrators, unless averted (as it *was*
averted) by their candid confession and retraction of their mis-
conduct. But grant all this, and still we leave it to any high
minded and high-spirited man to say, whether Mr. Jefferson

acted or felt any differently from what he himself would have
been likely to feel—whether his morbid sensitiveness and his determination to be no longer *used* by those who, to say the least
of it, had so inconsiderately and precipitately placed a stigma
on even his capacity to serve them, were or were not, under *all*
the circumstances, and for the period to which Mr. Jefferson
adhered to his determination, entirely excusable.

Another phase in the tragedy was drawing on when Monroe's missive was sent and answered. " A darker departure was
near." Mrs. Jefferson had rallied towards the close of 1781.
Her last child was born May 8th, 1782. Greater apprehensions
than usual had preceded the event, and they were fatally verified. The delicate constitution was irrevocably sapped. A
momentary hope for her might sometimes flutter in the bosom
of her lonely husband, but it was in reality a hope against hope
—a hope against reason—and he *knew* it to be so. That association which had been the first joy of his life—which blent itself
with all his future visions of happiness—which was to be the
crowning glory of that delightful retreat he was forming—and
which was to shed mellow radiance over the retirement to which
he was fondly looking forward—was now to end ; and it was only
a question of weeks, or possibly months, how soon it would end.
Mrs. Jefferson had returned her husband's affection, with not
only the fervor of a woman whose dream of love and pride (for
what woman is not proud of the world's estimation of her husband?) had been more than gratified, but with the idolatrous
gratitude of a wife who knew how often that husband had cast
away the most tempting honors without a sigh, when her own
feeble health had solicited his presence and attentions. And
now as the dreadful hour of parting approached, her affection
became painfully, almost wildly absorbing. The faithful daughter of the Church had no dread of the hereafter, but she yearned
to remain with her husband with that yearning which seems to
have power to retard even the approaches of death. Her
eyes ever rested on him, ever followed him. When he spoke,
no other sound could reach her ear or attract her attention.
When she waked from slumber, she looked momentarily
alarmed and distressed, and even appeared to be frightened, if
the customary form was not bending over her, the customary
look upon her.

For weeks Mr. Jefferson sat at that bedside, only catching brief intervals of rest. There Monroe's letter found him. Stung by its blunt but well-meant home-thrusts—like the bray of the trumpet summoning him back to the rough conflicts of public life—he left the darkling sick chamber to write the first letter he had penned for weeks, the last one he penned for months.[1] Will any one who has watched over the last moments of the loved and dying—who has stood in that dread presence in which the things of earth dwindle into insignificance, in which fame sounds but a word of mockery, in which abashed self-love confesses to the highest that he is but a drop in the great rushing stream of life; scarcely felt while he remains, and not missed beyond an instant when he is gone—we say, will any one with such recollections wonder at Mr. Jefferson's refusal to obey the summons? Are they not surprised rather that he condescended to give reasons for his refusal?

But in the existing state of facts, if Mr. Jefferson condescended to give reasons at all, why did he not allude to the health of his family? He had declined a seat in Congress, and repeated his refusal on that ground. He had more than once before absented himself from the Legislature for that avowed reason. He had twice refused a mission to Europe for that avowed reason. He had but to repeat it now to satisfy all. He had but to let the extent of the danger of his wife be known, to excite the respectful sympathy of every gentleman of Virginia, in and out of the Legislature. It may be difficult to show to the satisfaction of all, why he did not do so, but not, we think, difficult to show it to the satisfaction of proud and high-spirited men, who have been themselves injured and wounded from quarters where they felt they had a right to expect an exemption from all injury, whether of reckless or whether of deliberate injury. It is hard for anybody to render *excuses* to those who are felt to have no right to ask even *reasons!* Especially is it hard to ask, or look like asking, the sympathy of such. He could not state the fact to Madison or Monroe, under an injunction of silence, for that would appear like puerility. It does not appear, indeed, that either of these confidential friends *asked him* his reasons. Madison remained silent, and Monroe told

---

[1] It was about six months before he wrote another letter which has found a record and *six months* more elapsed before he wrote another.

him how much people blamed him, without hinting that he or any other person imagined there could be a satisfactory excuse for his course.   This is not the way to melt the proud reserve of a wronged man!

Mrs. Jefferson died on the 6th of September. Her eldest daughter, Mrs. Randolph, thus, many years afterwards, recorded her recollections of the sad scene: [1]

"During my mother's life, he [Mr. Jefferson] bestowed much time and attention on our education—our cousins the Carrs and myself—and after her death, during the first month of desolation which followed, I was his constant companion, while we remained at Monticello.   *   *   *   *   *   *   *
As a nurse, no female ever had more tenderness or anxiety. He nursed my poor mother in turn with Aunt Carr and her own sister—sitting up with her and administering her medicines and drink to the last. For four months that she lingered, he was never out of calling; when not at her bedside, he was writing in a small room which opened immediately at the head of her bed. A moment before the closing scene, he was led from the room almost in a state of insensibility by his sister Mrs. Carr, who, with great difficulty, got him into his library, where he fainted, and remained so long insensible that they feared he never would revive. The scene that followed I did not witness; but the violence of his emotion, when almost by stealth I entered his room at night, to this day I dare not trust myself to describe. He kept his room three weeks, and I was never a moment from his side. He walked almost incessantly night and day, only lying down occasionally, when nature was completely exhausted, on a pallet that had been brought in during his long fainting fit. My aunts remained constantly with him for some weeks, I do not remember how many. When at last he left his room, he rode out, and from that time he was incessantly on horseback, rambling about the mountain, in the least frequented roads, and just as often through the woods. In those melancholy rambles, I was his constant companion, a solitary witness to many a violent burst of grief, the remembrance of which has consecrated particular scenes of that lost home beyond the power of time to obliterate."

In that wooded inclosure, amidst surrounding forest, on the carriage-way from the Milton and Charlottesville road to the summit of Monticello, which forms the burial place of Mr. Jefferson's family, is *now* a cluster of monuments pointing out the last resting-place of two generations, and a part of the third generation of that family. By the side of the small granite

[1] These recollections were written in answer to some inquiries of Professor Tucker when writing his Life of Mr. Jefferson, and are published by him (except the first sentence) in that work, vol. i. p. 158. The above copy, however, differs from Mr. Tucker's in several small particulars, in language; and once in the sense—he accidentally substituting the words "*his* own sisters" for "*her* own sister," in the sixth line—which *latter* version corresponds with the *facts*. We follow the original draft, and the copy sent to Mr. Tucker may have received changes which were not inserted in it. But we do not think they improved the original.

obelisk which rests on Mr. Jefferson's grave, is a plain horizontal slab of white marble, bearing the following inscription:

> To the memory of
> Martha Jefferson,
> Daughter of John Wayles;
> Born October 19th, 1748, O. S.
> Intermarried with
> Thomas Jefferson
> January 1st, 1772;
> Torn from him by death
> September 6th, 1782:
> This monument of his love is inscribed.

> Εἰ δὲ θανόντων περ καταλήθοντ' εἰν Ἀΐδαο,
> Αὐτὰρ ἐγὼ κἀκεῖθι φίλη μεμνήσομ' ἑταίρη.[1]

On a leaf of Mr. Jefferson's prayer-book, in his handwriting, is the following family register:

Thomas Jefferson was born April 2, 1743, old stile.
Martha Wayles was born October 30, N. S., or October 19, O. S., 1748.
　　　They intermarried January 1, 1772.

Martha Jefferson was born September 27, 1772, at 1 o'clock A.M.
Jane Randolph Jefferson, born April 3, 1774, at 11 o'clock A.M.
　　　She died September, ——, 1775.
A son, born May, 28, 1777, at 10 o'clock, P.M.
　　　Died June 14, at 10 o'clock and 20 minutes P.M.
Mary Jefferson, born Aug. 1, 1778, at 1 o'clock and 30 minutes A.M.
　　　Died April 17, 1804, between 8 and 9 A.M.
A daughter, born in Richmond, Nov. 3, 1780, at 10 o'clock and 45 minutes P.M.
　　　Died April 15th, 1781, at 10 o'clock A.M.
Lucy Elizabeth Jefferson, born May 8, 1782, at 1 o'clock A.M.
　　　Died —— 1784.

Martha Wayles Jefferson died September 6, 1782, at 11 o'clock 45 minutes A.M.

---

[1] These lines occur in the 22d book of the Iliad, in the apostrophe of Achilles to Patroclus, over the dead body of Hector.　Pope thus paraphrases them (losing the compact simplicity of the original) in the four last of the following lines:

> "But what is Troy, or glory what to me?
> Or why reflects my mind on aught but thee,
> Divine Patroclus! Death has sealed his eyes;
> Unwept, unhonored, uninterr'd he lies!
> Can his dear image from my soul depart,
> Long as the vital spirit moves my heart?
> If in the melancholy shades below,
> The flames of friends and lovers cease to glow,
> Yet mine shall sacred last; mine undecay'd
> Burn on through death and animate my shade."

"A Greek epitaph [very well remarks Mr. Tucker] wears the appearance, at first sight, of an ostentation of learning, on a most inappropriate occasion; but such a censure is inconsistent not only with Mr. Jefferson's general character, but also with the

On Mr. Jefferson's own decease, forty-four years after that of his wife, in the most secret drawer of a private cabinet which he constantly resorted to, were found locks of hair, and various other little souvenirs of his wife, and of each of his living and lost children—down to those of the latter who died youngest—" with words," says a member of his family in describing the fact to us, " of fond endearment, written in his own hand upon the envelopes of the little mementos." They were all arranged in perfect order, and the envelopes indicated their frequent handling.

These were unusual occupations for a grey-haired statesman, for a man who had filled great positions, who had for years been divided from his home and from these associations by an ocean. But Mr. Jefferson's family affections had the softness and the tenderness of a woman's, while they borrowed unchangeableness from his whole mental structure. " My father never gave up a friend or an opinion," was a thousand times repeated remark of Martha Jefferson!

The first occupation which Mr. Jefferson entered upon after the decease of his wife, was to carry his children and his wards, the Carrs, to be inoculated for small pox at Ampthill, the residence of Colonel Archibald Cary, who had lent it to him for that purpose. He remained with the children, and acted, says his daughter, Mrs. Randolph, as their "chief nurse." While thus occupied, he received a notification that Congress had again—for the third time—appointed him a Plenipotentiary to Europe.

The English nation were becoming tired of the American war. In February, 1782, General Conway carried an address against its further prosecution, in the House of Commons. The royal answer was considered evasive, and Conway therefore moved "that all of those who should advise, or by any means attempt the further prosecution of offensive war in America should be considered as enemies to their king and country."[1] This resolution passed March 4th, and was that constitutional expression which no British ministry, since the reign of Wil-

fact, that few persons of his day to whom the classics were familiar, quoted them sc seldom. We may, therefore, with more probability refer the singularity to some refinement of delicacy, which in paying a tribute to the memory of the deceased, sought to veil the expression of his feelings from indiscriminate observation."
[1] Pitkin's Pol. Hist. vol. i. p. 122.

liam III., could disregard but at the cost of their lives, and no monarch, without imminent peril to his throne. Nothing short of this could overcome the sullen animal obstinacy of George III. The North Ministry retired, and that of the Marquis of Rockingham succeeded. The latter opened those negotiations with the United States, which after the necessary amount of higgling and shuffling on the part of England (so clearly described in Sparks's Life of Franklin, and in Lord Russel's Memoirs of Fox) led to peace.

It was in view of these negotiations that Congress had appointed Mr. Jefferson a plenipotentiary on the 12th of November. Mr. Madison, in his record of the debates of Congress, under that date, said:

"The reappointment of Mr. Jefferson as Minister Plenipotentiary for negotiating peace, was agreed to unanimously, and without a single adverse remark. The act took place in consequence of its being suggested, that the death of Mrs. Jefferson had probably changed the sentiments of Mr. Jefferson with regard to public life; and that all the reasons which led to his original appointment still existed, and, indeed, had acquired additional force from the improbability that Mr. Laurens would actually assist in the negotiation." [1]

He now accepted the appointment for the reasons anticipated by Mr. Madison, and which, on the day of his acceptance, he thus mentioned in a letter to the Marquis de Chastellux:

AMPTHILL, *November* 26, 1782.

DEAR SIR:

I received your friendly letters of —— and June 30th, but the latter not till the 17th of October. It found me a little emerging from the stupor of mind which had rendered me as dead to the world as was she whose loss occasioned it.

*   *   *   *   *   *   *   *

Before that event, my scheme of life had been determined. I had folded myself in the arms of retirement, and rested all prospects of future happiness on domestic and literary objects. A single event wiped away all my plans, and left me a blank which I had not the spirits to fill up. In this state of mind an appointment from Congress found me, requiring me to cross the Atlantic. [2]

Before Mr. Jefferson reached Philadelphia, to proceed on his mission, Robert R. Livingston, of New York, who so ably

[1] Madison Papers.
[2] He says, on the same subject as his Memoir:
"I had two months before that, lost the cherished companion of my life, in whose affections, unabated on both sides, I had lived the last ten years in unchequered happiness. With the public interests, the state of my mind concurred in recommending the change of scene proposed; and I accepted the appointment."

discharged the duties of United States Secretary of Foreign
Affairs, tendered his resignation to Congress (December 2d).
He had notified Mr. Madison of his intention, a short time previously, and suggested the appointment of Mr. Jefferson as his
successor, or that Mr. Jay succeed to the Foreign Department,
and Mr. Jefferson take Mr. Jay's place in the Spanish mission.
Mr. Madison doubted Jefferson's acceptance of either, "but
promised to sound him on these points by the first opportunity."[1]
Whether he did sound him on the subject we are not informed.
Before Mr. Livingston's resignation was sent in, Mr. Jefferson
received his appointment as a plenipotentiary, to negotiate
peace.[2]

He left Monticello, on the 19th of December, to enter upon
his official duties. He repaired to Philadelphia, and remained
there a month, awaiting the sailing of the French frigate Romulus, in which the French Minister, De la Luzerne, had offered
him a passage, and which now lay blocked in the ice below
Baltimore. He spent the time in examining the papers in the
office of the Secretary of Foreign Affairs, "to possess himself
of the general state of our foreign relations."

During this period, he wrote an affectionately respectful
letter to General Washington, in which he said:

"I cannot leave the continent without separating myself for a moment from the
general gratitude of my country, to offer my individual tribute to your Excellency
for all you have suffered and all you have effected for us. Were I to indulge myself
in those warm effusions which this subject forever prompts, they would wear
an appearance of adulation very foreign to my nature; for such is become the pros-
titution of language, that sincerity has no longer distinct terms in which to express
her own truths. Should you give me occasion, during the short mission on which
I go, to render you any service beyond the water, I shall, for a proof of my gratitude, appeal from language to the zeal with which I shall embrace it."

He then informed the General that he should keep him
apprised of the progress of the negotiations, should they be
protracted.

Washington replied (February 10th), in a corresponding
tone, and we give a few sentences of his letter, as it is not
included in Sparks's edition of his writings:

[1] Madison Papers, vol. i. p. 212.
[2] Mr. Livingston's resignation was temporarily recalled, Congress not being able to
agree on his successor.

" I feel myself much flattered by your kind remembrance of me in the hour of your departure from this continent, for the favorable sentiments you are pleased to entertain of my services for this our common country. To merit the approbation of good and virtuous men is the height of my ambition, and will be a full compensation for all my toils and sufferings in the long and painful contest in which we have been engaged. It gave me great pleasure to hear that the call upon you from Congress to pass the Atlantic in the character of one of their ministers for negotiating peace had been repeated; but I hope you will have found the business already done.   *   *   *   *   *   *   *   *   * You will please to accept my grateful thanks for your obliging offer of services during your stay in France. To hear from you frequently will be an honor and very great satisfaction to, dear sir, your most obedient, and most humble servant." [1]

There being a prospect that the Romulus would get to sea, Mr. Jefferson went to Baltimore (January 30th, 1783), but further detentions occurred, and it was ascertained that the number of British cruisers watching the capes of the Chesapeake, rendered the capture of the vessel, should the attempt be made, next to certain. Another frigate, the Guadelupe, was placed at Mr. Jefferson's disposal, if he chose to make the adventure. But he did not feel at liberty to risk the loss of the vessel, without consulting the government. He accordingly wrote the Foreign Secretary, asking his advice, and informing him that any course he recommended would be adopted, " without regard to personal risk or trouble." Mr. Livingston, conceiving it " hardly possible" for either of the French frigates to elude the enemy, while their " cruisers retained their present station," withheld his reply, to take the sense of Congress on the subject.[2] That body obtaining, meanwhile, intelligence that a provisional treaty of peace was probably agreed on, ordered (February 14th):

" That the Secretary for Foreign Affairs inform Mr. Jefferson that it is the pleasure of Congress, considering the advices lately received in America and the probable situation of affairs in Europe, that he do not proceed on his intended voyage until he shall receive their further instructions."

The news of a provisional treaty being soon after confirmed, Mr. Jefferson returned to Philadelphia, and again addressed the Secretary of Foreign Affairs a letter (March 13th), in which he supposed the last advices would enable Congress to decide

[1] The letter entire will be found in the Congress edition of Mr. Jefferson's Works vol. i. p. 328.
[2] See letter entire in Jefferson's Works, Congress Ed. vol. i. p. 329.

definitely whether it was expedient for him to go or remain,
and he asked such decision. That body accordingly, on the 1st
of April, passed the following resolution :

"*Resolved*, That the Secretary for Foreign Affairs inform the Hon. Thomas Jefferson, in answer to his letter of the 13th of March, that Congress consider the
object of his appointment so far advanced as to render it unnecessary for him to
pursue his voyage, and that Congress are well satisfied with the readiness he has
shown in undertaking a service which from the present situation of affairs they
apprehend can be dispensed with." [1]

Mr. Jefferson set out for home a few days afterward, and
reached Monticello on the 15th of May.

On the 6th of June, the General Assembly of Virginia
elected Thomas Jefferson, Samuel Hardy, John F. Mercer,
Arthur Lee, and James Monroe, Delegates in Congress from the
ensuing 1st of November. During the summer months of 1783,
we find few traces of Mr. Jefferson's employments. He appears
to have written no letters which he considered worthy of preservation. Before his departure from Philadelphia in the spring,
he had (April 11th) written Mr. Jay congratulating him on the
terms of the Treaty of Peace, and expressing the hope that he
would continue "at some one of the European Courts most
agreeable to himself, that we might still have the benefit of his
talents." This is the last letter published in his Correspondence
until April 16th, 1784. The entries in his pocket account-books
show that he was most of the time at home. Those in the farm
and garden books, exhibit none of his former activity in these
directions. In the former, excepting three inconsiderable items,
the gloomy death-roll of 1781 closes the record for several years
—until his return from France. There is but a solitary memorandum for 1783 in the garden book, as follows : "September
2d and 3d. White frosts which killed vines in the neighborhood
—hills of tobacco in the north garden—fodder and later corn in
Augusta—and forward corn in Greenbrier." This then closes
until his return from France. Frost, too, had fallen on the life
and happiness of Monticello!

Mr. Jefferson repaired to Trenton where Congress was sitting,
and took his seat November 4th. But that body adjourned the
same day to meet in Annapolis on the 26th.

[1] For two letters written by Mr. Jefferson to his brother-in-law, Francis Eppes,
January 14th and March 4th, 1783, see APPENDIX, No. 5.

At this period commences a series of Mr. Jefferson's family letters, addressed to his daughters, and afterwards to his sons-in-law and grandchildren, extending, where the parties were separated, through their common lives. The list includes some hundreds of letters, and a considerable portion of it has been kindly placed at our disposal by his family. Of Mr. Jefferson's family letters, properly speaking,[1] not beyond two or three probably (if even so many), have ever been published. But one addressed to either of his daughters, appears in Mr. Randolph's or in the Congress edition of his works.[2] Believing that these private familiar letters will give a better view of private character—of the man as contradistinguished from the politician, the official, or the mere literary, or other correspondent—than is obtainable from any other indisputable memorials he has left behind him, we shall quote from them much more largely than their intrinsic importance would demand. Very many of them will be given not for their talent, their originality, their excellence of thought, or their felicity of expression, but simply to show how their author, under every variety of circumstances, and at many different periods of his age, was wont to habitually address those he most loved and from whom he had the fewest personal reserves. Some new political letters will also be from time to time given, to show how his expressions to his family on that subject corresponded with those addressed to other persons. A portion of all the letters will be withheld, as mere repetitions. They would be expected, of course, in many instances, to be very similar in tenor, as they were written contemporaneously to the scattered members of the same family, who would be naturally interested in the same class of facts and the same expressions of feeling. Some details of mere family arrangements will be omitted, and delicacy may, in a few instances, call for the suppression of a name—but in no single instance from prudential considerations towards *the writer*. There is not a bitter, there is not a censorious word in these long files of confidential communications, extending over all the most exciting periods of his life! In his family, he sought alone the atmosphere of peace

[1] That is to say, exclusive of the *political* letters addressed to his sons-in-law, both of whom were in public life.
[2] We do not at this moment remember but one, but perhaps one or two more, *not of a family character*, to his oldest daughter, Mrs. Randolph, appear *without address* in the Congress edition.

and love. Even foes were there unnamed, or named respectfully. His personal conflicts or misunderstandings were generally not even known to his daughters. Whatever other omissions we make in Mr. Jefferson's family letters, we pledge ourselves, not to keep back a sentence, or line, or word, which would in the least degree throw light on his mind, or opinions, or character, or on any single exceptional exhibition (should there be such) of that character.[1]

Martha Jefferson, whom her father had intended to take with him to Europe, had been left at school in Philadelphia, when Congress determined that he need not proceed; and she was just turned eleven years of age when the following letter was written:

MR. JEFFERSON TO MARTHA JEFFERSON.

ANNAPOLIS, Nov. 28th, 1783.

MY DEAR PATSY:

After four days' journey, I arrived here without any accident and in as good health as when I left Philadelphia. The conviction that you would be more improved in the situation I have placed you than if still with me, has solaced me on my parting with you, which my love for you has rendered a difficult thing. The acquirements which I hope you will make under the tutors I have provided for you will render you more worthy of my love; and if they cannot increase it, they will prevent its diminution. Consider the good lady who has taken you under her roof, who has undertaken to see that you perform all your exercises, and to admonish you in all those wanderings from what is right, or what is clever, to which your inexperience would expose you; consider her, I say, as your mother, as the only person to whom, since the loss with which Heaven has been pleased to afflict you, you can now look up; and that her displeasure or disapprobation, on any occasion, will be an immense misfortune, which should you be so unhappy as to incur by any unguarded act, think no concession too much to regain her good will. With respect to the distribution of your time, the following is what I should approve:

> From 8 to 10, practise music.
> From 10 to 1, dance one day and draw another.
> From 1 to 2, draw on the day you dance, and write a letter next day.
> From 3 to 4, read French.
> From 4 to 5, exercise yourself in music.
> From 5 till bed-time, read English, write, etc.

Communicate this plan to Mrs. Hopkinson, and if she approves of it, pursue it. As long as Mrs. Trist remains in Philadelphia, cultivate her affection. She has been a valuable friend to you, and her good sense and good heart make her valued by all who know her, and by nobody on earth more than me. I expect you will write me by every post. Inform me what books you read, what tunes you learn, and inclose me your best copy of every lesson in drawing. Write also one letter every week,

---

[1] Extracts will be designated as such, and when the body of the letter is given and only sentences omitted, the omission will be marked by asterisks.

either to your Aunt Eppes, your Aunt Skipwith, your Aunt Carr, or the little lady from whom I now inclose a letter, and always put the letter you so write under cover to me. Take care that you never spell a word wrong. Always before you write a word, consider how it is spelt, and, if you do not remember it, turn to a dictionary. It produces great praise to a lady to spell well. I have placed my happiness on seeing you good and accomplished; and no distress which this world can now bring on me would equal that of your disappointing my hopes. If you love me, then, strive to be good under every situation, and to all living creatures, and to acquire those accomplishments which I have put in your power, and which will go far towards ensuring you the warmest love of your affectionate father,

TH. JEFFERSON.

P. S.—Keep my letters and read them at times, that you may always have present in your mind those things which will endear you to me.[1]

EXTRACT FROM SAME TO SAME.

ANNAPOLIS, December 11, 1788.

I hope you will have good sense enough to disregard those foolish predictions, that the world is to be at an end soon. The Almighty has never made known to any body, at what time he created it; nor will he tell any body when he will put an end to it, if he ever means to do it. As to preparations for that event, the best way is for you to be always prepared for it. The only way to be so is, never to do or say a bad thing. If ever you are about to say anything amiss, or to do anything wrong, consider beforehand. You will feel something within you which will tell you it is wrong, and ought not to be said or done. This is your conscience, and be sure to obey it. Our Maker has given us all this faithful internal monitor; and if you always obey it, you will always be prepared for the end of the world; or for a much more certain event, which is death. This must happen to all: it puts an end to the world as to us; and the way to be ready for it is, never to do a wrong act

---

EXTRACT FROM SAME TO SAME.

ANNAPOLIS, Dec. 22, 1788.

I omitted in that letter to advise you on the subject of dress, which I know you are a little apt to neglect. I do not wish you to be gaily clothed at this time of life, but that what you wear should be fine of its kind. But above all things, and at all times, let your clothes be clean, whole, and properly put on. Do not fancy you must wear them till the dirt is visible to the eye. You will be the last who will be sensible of this. Some ladies think they may, under the privileges of the dishabille, be loose and negligent of their dress in the morning. But be you from the moment you rise till you go to bed, as cleanly and properly dressed as at the hours of dinner or tea. A lady who has been seen as a sloven or slut in the morning, will never efface the impression she has made, with all the dress and

---

[1] A copy of this letter has appeared in Griswold's "Republican Court" since it was transcribed for these pages. The original is in the possession of the Queen of England. When Mr. Aaron Vail was Chargé d'Affaires of the United States at London, he was requested by the Princess Victoria to procure for her an autograph of Mr. Jefferson. Mr. Vail applied to a member of Mr. Jefferson's family, and this letter was transmitted to him for the Princess.

pageantry she can afterwards involve herself in. Nothing is so disgusting to our
sex as a want of cleanliness and delicacy in yours. I hope, therefore, the moment
you rise from bed, your first work will be to dress yourself in such style, as that
you may be seen by any gentleman without his being able to discover a pin amiss,
or any other circumstance of neatness wanting.

A quorum of Congress, necessary even for minor business (a
majority of the States), did not assemble at Annapolis before the
13th of December. About a week afterwards, General Washington came to the city to resign his command of the army, and
with habitual modesty he sought the directions of Congress as
to the manner of laying down his commission—of joyfully
rendering up that sword which those unacquainted with his
character and that of his countrymen, had expected to see
yielded only for a sceptre. Mr. Jefferson was chosen Chairman
of the Committee[1] to arrange the ceremonies of the occasion,
and he drew up that simple but dignified and impressive order
of proceedings which has since been so universally admired.
The beautiful answer of the President of Congress to General
Washington's address, has always also, and without denial, been
ascribed to Mr. Jefferson's pen.

The Treaty of Peace having been received and laid before
Congress, it was referred to a committee of which Mr. Jefferson
was chairman. But seven States were yet represented, and it
required nine to enter into treaties. So remiss at this period
was even personal attendance in this body, that it was often
compelled to adjourn from day to day, and sometimes for a
week,[2] for want of the attendance of the members of the States
nominally represented. The further proceedings on the Treaty
we will give in the language of Mr. Jefferson, in his Memoir:

" On the 23d of December, therefore, we addressed letters to the several Governors, stating the receipt of the definitive treaty; that seven States only were in
attendance, while nine were necessary to its ratification; and urging them to press
on their delegates the necessity of their immediate attendance. And on the 26th,
to save time, I moved that the agent of Marine (Robert Morris) should be instructed
to have ready a vessel at this place, at New York, and at some Eastern port, to
carry over the ratification of the treaty when agreed to. It met the general sense
of the House, but was opposed by Dr. Lee, on the ground of expense, which it
would authorize the Agent to incur for us; and, he said, it would be better to ratify
at once, and send on the ratification. Some members had before suggested, that
seven States were competent to the ratification. My motion was therefore post-

[1] His associates were Messrs. Gerry, Ellery, Read and Hawkins.
[2] See Journal of Congress, 1783-4, vol. iv.

poned, and another brought forward by Mr. Read, of South Carolina, for an immediate ratification. This was debated the 26th and 27th. Read, Lee, William-son and Jeremiah Chase, urged that ratification was a mere matter of form, that the treaty was conclusive from the moment it was signed by the ministers; that, although the Confederation requires the assent of *nine States* to *enter into* a treaty, yet, that its conclusion could not be called *entrance into it;* that supposing nine States requisite, it would be in the power of five States to keep us always at war; that nine States had virtually authorized the ratification, having ratified the pro-visional treaty, and instructed their ministers to agree to a definitive one in the same terms, and the present one was, in fact, substantially, and almost verbatim, the same; that there now remain but sixty-seven days for the ratification, for its pas-sage across the Atlantic, and its exchange; that there was no hope of our soon having nine States present; in fact, that this was the ultimate point of time to which we could venture to wait; that if the ratification was not in Paris by the time stipulated, the treaty would become void; that if ratified by seven States, it would go under our seal, without its being known to Great Britain that only seven had concurred; that it was a question of which they had no right to take cognizance, and we were only answerable for it to our constituents; that it was like the ratification which Great Britain had received from the Dutch, by the negotiations of Sir William Temple."

Against a construction of powers based on a verbal quibble, more worthy of a debating-school than a Legislature, and against a deliberate fiction of legislation on the ground that Great Britain would not know it, or could not take cognizance of it, Jefferson, Monroe, Gerry, Howell, and Ellery, took decided ground, and their arguments are given in the Memoir. Mr. Jefferson con-tinues his narration:

"Mr. Read gave notice he should call for the yeas and nays; whereon those in opposition prepared a resolution, expressing pointedly the reasons for their dissent from his motion. It appearing, however, that his proposition could not be carried, it was thought better to make no entry at all. Massachusetts alone would have been for it; Rhode Island, Pennsylvania and Virginia against it; Delaware, Mary-land and North Carolina would have been divided.

"Those who thought seven States competent to the ratification, being very rest-less under the loss of their motion, I proposed, on the third of January, to meet them on middle ground, and therefore moved a resolution, which premised, that there were but seven States present, who were unanimous for the ratification, but that they differed in opinion on the question of competency; that those, however, in the negative, were unwilling, that any powers which it might be supposed they possessed, should remain unexercised for the restoration of peace, provided it could be done, saving their good faith, and without importing any opinion of Congress, that seven States were competent, and resolving that the treaty be ratified so far as they had power; that it should be transmitted to our ministers, with instructions to keep it uncommunicated; to endeavor to obtain three months longer for exchange of ratifications; that they should be informed, that so soon as nine States shall be present, a ratification by nine shall be sent them: if this should get to them before the ultimate point of time for exchange, they were to use it, and not the other; if not, they were to offer the act of the seven States in exchange, informing them the treaty had come to hand while Congress was not in session, that but seven States were as yet assembled, and these had unanimously concurred in the ratification. This was debated on the third and fourth; and on the fifth, a vessel being to sail for England, from this port (Annapolis), the House directed the President to write to our ministers accordingly.

"*January* 14.—Delegates from Connecticut having attended yesterday, and another from South Carolina coming in this day, the treaty was ratified without a dissenting voice; and three instruments of ratification were ordered to be made out, one of which was sent by Colonel Harmer, another by Colonel Franks, and the third transmitted to the Agent of Marine, to be forwarded by any good opportunity."

Thus it was Mr. Jefferson's fortune, seven years after reporting to Congress the memorable instrument by which the British American Colonies declared themselves free and independent States, to report to the same body, and officially assist in ratifying another instrument, by which that independence was formally admitted by the unnatural parent who first forced on the struggle, and then made it one of such deep and long protracted inflictions on one side, and sufferings on the other.

The inconveniences resulting from the present construction of the federal government were severely felt. Congress exercised both legislative and executive functions, and consequently, when not in session, there was no head to the government, whatever the exigency. The extreme remissness of this body in meeting at its appointed times, has been seen. The plan of a permanent Congress would be attended with great difficulty and expense, and was very obnoxious to some of the States. To remedy these evils, Mr. Jefferson proposed, in April, 1784, that a committee be appointed, consisting of one member from each State, to be designated the "Committee of the States," whose duty it should be to remain in session during the recesses of Congress, and who should be vested during that period with the executive powers of the government. This proposition prevailed, but it proved a total failure in practice. Mr. Jefferson says, in his Memoir:

"A Committee was appointed, who entered on duty on the subsequent adjournment of Congress, quarrelled very soon, split into two parties, abandoned their post, and left the government without any visible head, until the next meeting of Congress." [1]

[1] In a letter to the Count de Tracy, Jan. 26, 1811, Mr. Jefferson says of this event: "This was then imputed to the temper of two or three individuals; but the wise ascribed it to the nature of man."

And he adds :

"We have since seen the same thing take place, in the Directory of France; and I believe it will forever take place in any Executive consisting of a plurality. Our plan, best, I believe, combines wisdom and practicability, by providing a plurality of Counsellors, but a single Arbiter for ultimate decision."

The experiment, however, was necessary, to prepare the minds of the American people for the plan finally adopted. Before that, the memory of George III. would have been too fresh to permit them to accept any form, which placed the interests and happiness of mankind so much under the control of one man, even though his tenure was more limited in power and duration, and held by popular election.

The disruption of the Committee of States took place when Mr. Jefferson was in France; and Dr. Franklin, who, if he did not precisely merit the appellation "Derider" (γελασινος) applied to the laughing philosopher of Thrace, yet always had a good story to illustrate an absurd event, on this occasion brought to bear the humorous one of the two keepers of the Eddystone lighthouse, "who divided into two parties," which is repeated in Jefferson's Memoir.

Congress had, at preceding sessions, given considerable attention to the subject of the coinage and of a money unit; and Mr. Morris, the Financier, had made an able report on that subject. He had proposed as the money unit what he had found would be the common measure, without leaving a fraction, of a penny of every State except South Carolina—namely, the fourteen hundred and fortieth part of a dollar. Various delays had taken place on the subject, and in 1784 it was referred to a committee of which Mr. Jefferson was a member. He at once saw "that the general views of the Financier were sound, and the principle was ingenious on which he proposed to found his unit;" but he considered that unit "too minute for ordinary use, and too laborious for computation either by the head or in figures." He gave the following examples:

"The price of a loaf of bread, 1-20 of a dollar, would be 72 units.
"A pound of butter, 1-5 of a dollar, 288 units.
"A horse or bullock, of eighty dollars value, would require a notation of six figures, to wit, 115,200, and the public debt, suppose of eighty millions, would require twelve figures, to wit, 115,200,000,000 units. Such a system of money arithmetic would be entirely unmanageable for the common purposes of society."

He therefore suggested instead of it, to adopt the dollar as the

unit of account and payment, making its divisions and subdivisions in the decimal ratio. He proposed four coins, a gold
piece of ten dollars, a silver dollar, a silver tenth of a dollar,
and a copper hundredth of a dollar. He embodied these views
in an elaborate and clearly drawn up paper, and submitted them
to Mr. Morris.[1] Morris, however, adhered to his former views,
except that he increased his first proposed unit one hundred
times. Mr. Jefferson replied, and published both his papers on
a flying sheet, to place his views before the individual members
of Congress. The Committee agreed to report his plan, and it
was adopted the next year. He and Mr. Morris, therefore, share
in the honor of founding a far simpler and more easily computed
money system than before existed. The latter, or rather his
assistant, the able Governeur Morris, is entitled to the credit of
proposing the decimal system of computation,[2] and Jefferson of
proposing the unit and present coinage of the United States,
with the exception of a late and incongruous addition.[3]

Mr. Morris being desirous of retiring from the Treasury, it
was thought a good occasion for revising the structure of that
department, and a " grand Committee " (that is, a committee of
one from each State) was appointed for that object, Mr. Jefferson being chairman. Desirous of obviating the great inconvenience arising from appointing an inexperienced person on every
occurrence of a vacancy, he reported an ordinance for appointing three Commissioners in the place of the Financier, and this
passed Congress. This was introducing the plural feature into
another administrative department of the government, and here at
least there would seem to be excellent reasons for it in theory.
The difficulty apprehended from a single head of department is
now, however, obviated, in practice, by the financial officers of the
General and State Governments keeping the experienced deputies and clerks of their predecessors in office. But apart from
this resort to subordinates (personal appointees and not responsible to Nation or State) what would this class of officers do?
Without such help, the ablest business-man in the United States
would find it impossible, entering suddenly upon the National

---

[1] This paper is published in the Appendix to the Memoir in both editions of Mr. Jefferson's Works.

[2] This has often been ascribed to Jefferson, but it is clearly an error. (See Sparks's
Life and Writings of Governeur Morris, vol. i. p. 273.

[3] The silver three cent piece. Perhaps we do not do right in saying he proposed the
present coinage, as he says nothing of the half and quarter eagle, the gold dollar, etc.
But these merely carry out his *plan* a little further.

Treasury, or even that of some large State, to properly carry on its complicated machinery. And until experience had demonstated its inutility, men of republican tendencies would be expected to favor a distribution over a concentration of power in all the great administrative offices of the State.

Mr. Jefferson was also chairman of a " grand Committee " to ascertain and report the arrears of interest on the Public Debt, with the expenses of the current year, and to apportion the sum among the States. His report on the subject was adopted.

The cession of the Northwestern Territory by Virginia to the United States, offered some years before, had not yet been consummated, for reasons which we will not here stop to explain. The Virginia delegates now tendered a deed of cession. A motion was made to qualify the acceptance by a declaration that it should not be construed as an admission of the claim to previous ownership by Virginia, and three States voted for such an amendment. The acceptance was then made unconditional, and the Virginia delegates, headed by Mr. Jefferson, executed the deed, which bore date March 1st, 1784.[1]

A few days afterwards, a committee, consisting of Mr. Jefferson, Mr. Chase of Maryland, and Mr. Howell of Rhode Island, was appointed to prepare a plan for the temporary government of the Western Territory. The draft of the Committee's report, in the handwriting of Mr. Jefferson, is yet preserved among the archives in the State Department at Washington. This being the original of the famous "Ordinance of the Northwestern Territory," so often referred to in modern political discussions, and being in some respects a very curious paper in itself, we have concluded to give it entire :

The Committee appointed to prepare a plan for the temporary government of the Western Territory, have agreed to the following resolutions :

Resolved, That the territory ceded or to be ceded by individual States to the United States, whensoever the same shall have been purchased of the Iudian inhabitants, and offered for sale by the United States, shall be formed into distinct States, bounded in the following manner, as nearly as such cessions will admit— that is to say : northwardly and southwardly by parallels of latitude, so that each State shall comprehend, from south to north, two degrees of latitude, beginning to

[1] This was not quite the end of this long matter. Some stipulations in the deed relating to the division of this territory into States not meeting the approbation of Congress, that body referred back the deed to Virginia, recommending alterations. These were assented to December 30th. 1788.

count from the completion of thirty-one degrees north of the equator; but any territory northwardly of the forty-seventh degree shall make part of the State next below; and eastwardly and westwardly they shall be bounded, those on the Mississippi by that river on one side, and the meridian of the lowest point of the rapids of Ohio on the other; and those adjoining on the east by the same meridian on their western side, and on their eastern by the meridian of the western cape of the mouth of the Great Kanawha; and the territory eastward of this last meridian, between the Ohio, Lake Erie, and Pennsylvania, shall be one State.

That the settlers within the territory so to be purchased and offered for sale, shall, either on their own petition, or on the order of Congress, receive authority from them, with appointments of time and place for their free males, of full age, to meet together for the purpose of establishing a temporary government, to adopt the constitution and laws of any one of these States, so that such laws nevertheless shall be subject to alteration by their ordinary legislature; and to erect, subject to a like alteration, counties or townships for the election of members for their legislature.

That such temporary government shall only continue in force in any State until it shall have acquired twenty thousand free inhabitants; when, giving due proof thereof to Congress, they shall receive from them authority, with appointments of time and place, to call a convention of representatives to establish a permanent constitution and government for themselves: *Provided,* That both the temporary and permanent governments be established on these principles as their basis: 1. [That they shall forever remain a part of the United States of America;] 2. That, in their persons, property, and territory, they shall be subject to the Government of the United States in Congress assembled, and to the Articles of Confederation in all those cases in which the original States shall be so subject; 3. That they shall be subject to pay a part of the federal debts contracted or to be contracted, to be apportioned on them by Congress according to the same common rule and measure by which apportionments thereof shall be made on the other States; 4. That their respective governments shall be in republican forms, and shall admit no person to be a citizen who holds any hereditary title; 5. That after the year 1800 of the Christian era there shall be neither slavery nor involuntary servitude in any of the said States, otherwise than in punishment of crimes, whereof the party shall have been duly convicted to have been personally guilty.

That whensoever any of the said States shall have, of free inhabitants, as many as shall then be in any one of the least numerous of the thirteen original States, such State shall be admitted by its delegates into the Congress of the United States on an equal footing with the said original States; after which the assent of two-thirds of the United States in Congress assembled shall be requisite in all those cases wherein, by the Confederation, the assent of nine States is now required: *Provided,* The consent of nine States to such admission may be obtained according to the eleventh of the Articles of Confederation. Until such admission by their delegates into Congress, any of the said States, after the establishment of their temporary government, shall have authority to keep a sitting member in Congress, with right of debating but not of voting.

That the territory northward of the forty-fifth degree, that is to say, of the completion of forty-five degrees from the equator, and extending to the Lake of the Woods, shall be called SYLVANIA.

That of the territory under the forty-fifth and forty-fourth degrees, that which lies westward of Lake Michigan, shall be called MICHIGANIA; and that which is eastward thereof, within the peninsula formed by the lakes and waters of Michigan,

Huron, St. Clair, and Erie, shall be called CHERRONESUS, and shall include any part of the peninsula which may extend above the forty-fifth degree.

Of the territory under the forty-third and forty-second degrees, that to the westward, through which the Assenisipi or Rock River runs, shall be called ASSENISIPIA; and that to the eastward, in which are the fountains of the Muskingum, the two Miamies of the Ohio, the Wabash, the Illinois, the Miami of the Lake, and Sandusky rivers, shall be called METROPOTAMIA.

Of the territory which lies under the forty-first and fortieth degrees, the western, through which the river Illinois runs, shall be called ILLINOIA; that next adjoining to the eastward, SARATOGA; and that between this last and Pennsylvania, and extending from the Ohio to Lake Erie, shall be called WASHINGTON.

Of the territory which lies under the thirty-ninth and thirty-eighth degrees, to which shall be added so much of the point of land within the fork of the Ohio and Mississippi as lies under the thirty-seventh degree, that to the westward, within and adjacent to which are the confluences of the rivers Wabash, Shawanee, Tanissee, Ohio, Illinois, Mississippi, and Missouri, shall be called POLYPOTAMIA; and that to the eastward, further up the Ohio, otherwise called the Pelisipi, shall be called PELISIPIA.

That the preceding articles shall be formed into a charter of compact, shall be duly executed by the President of the United States in Congress assembled, under his hand and the seal of the United States, shall be promulgated, and shall stand as fundamental constitutions between the thirteen original States and those newly described, unalterable but by the joint consent of the United States in Congress assembled, and of the particular State within which such alteration is proposed to be made.

On the 19th of April Congress took the report into consideration, and Mr. Spaight of North Carolina moved to strike out the following clause: "that after the year 1800 of the Christian era, there shall be neither slavery nor involuntary servitude in any of the said States, otherwise than in punishment of crimes, whereof the party shall have been duly convicted to have been personally guilty." The motion was seconded by Mr. Read of South Carolina, and on the question, "shall the words moved to be struck out stand?" the yeas and nays (called by Mr. Howell of Rhode Island) stood as follows:

N. Hampshire,	Mr. Foster	ay	ay	Pennsylvania,	Mr. Mifflin	ay	ay
	" Blanchard	ay			" Montgomery	ay	
Massachusetts,	" Gerry	ay	ay		" Hand	ay	
	" Patridge	ay		Maryland,	" McHenry	no	no
Rhode Island,	" Ellery	ay	ay		" Stone	no	
	" Howell	ay		Virginia,	" Jefferson	ay	
Connecticut,	" Sherman	ay	ay		" Hardy	no	no
	" Wadsworth	ay			" Mercer	no	
New York,	" DeWitt	ay	ay	N. Carolina,	" Williamson	ay	div
	" Paine	ay			" Spaight	no	
New Jersey,	" Dick	ay		S. Carolina,	" Read	no	no
					" Beresford	no	

Thus six States voted to retain the clause; three voted against it; one lost its vote by being equally divided; one lost its vote by having but one delegate present; and two [1] lost their votes by having no delegates present. A majority of all the States not voting in the affirmative, the clause was stricken out.[2] The clauses declaring that the governments formed out of the territory "shall admit no person to be a citizen who holds any hereditary titles," those bounding and naming the new States and one or two others not further affecting the material principles of the bill, were stricken out, and then Congress, on the 23d of April, adopted the resolutions.

Mr. Jefferson was made chairman of a committee [3] to report an ordinance for regulating the manner of locating and disposing of the public lands. The plan presented, though palpably enough the source from which many of the best parts of the present system were derived, then found so little favor that but one State (North Carolina) voted for it. Virginia and Rhode Island were equally divided; and six States voted against it.

Congress deemed it expedient to propose commercial treaties to the principal nations of Europe, with the double object of securing commercial advantages, and of procuring from them that virtual recognition " of our independence and of our reception into the fraternity of nations," which, in terms, the United States "would not condescend to ask."[4] Mr. Jefferson was made chairman of a committee to draft instructions for the ministers to be charged with these negotiations. They are too long for insertion here, but as a part of their author's political history, we will place a running synopsis of them in the appendix.[5]

Mr. Jefferson left Congress on the 7th day of May, having been appointed by that body to a post presently to be mentioned.

He had been the chairman of some committees and a member of various others, which we have not named. In point of fact, he had headed nearly all the most important ones during his stay in the House. He was twice elected President pro tempore, in the absence of the President. But one measure, of

[1] Delaware and Georgia.
[2] Journals of Congress, 1784, vol. iv. p. 373. (Way and Gideon's edition.)
[3] His associates were Messrs. Williamson of N. C.; Howell of R. I.; Gerry of Mass.; and Read of S. C.
[4] Memoir, p. 48; Jefferson to J. Q. Adams, March 30th, 1826.
[5] See APPENDIX, No. 6.

any consequence, we believe, brought forward by him (that in relation to the location and sale of the public lands) was defeated, and but one other (the plan of government for the Western Territory) changed in essential particulars.

Neither the talents nor the temper of the House made this entire and undisputed leadership a thing to be cheaply secured. Congress contained several members of distinguished ability. No one will deny this rank to Gerry, Sherman, Monroe, and some others who might be named. And it contained a still larger number of highly respectable and experienced legislators. As a whole, it would compare favorably, in point of ability, with any House which assembled during most of the years subsequently to 1776. Of its temper Mr. Jefferson has left a graphic description; and he has interspersed that description with some other remarks which will be read with interest:

"Our body was little numerous, but very contentious. Day after day was wasted on the most unimportant questions. A member, one of those afflicted with the morbid rage of debate, of an ardent mind, prompt imagination, and copious flow of words. who heard with impatience any logic which was not his own, sitting near me on some occasion of a trifling but wordy debate, asked me how I could sit in silence, hearing so much false reasoning, which a word should refute? I observed to him, that to refute indeed was easy, but to silence was impossible; that in measures brought forward by myself, I took the laboring oar, as was incumbent on me; but that in general, I was willing to listen; that if every sound argument or objection was used by some one or other of the numerous debaters, it was enough; if not, I thought it sufficient to suggest the omission, without going into a repetition of what had been already said by others: that this was a waste and abuse of the time and patience of the House, which could not be justified. And I believe, that if the members of deliberate bodies were to observe this course generally, they would do in a day, what takes them a week; and it is really more questionable, than may at first be thought, whether Bonaparte's dumb legislature, which said nothing, and did much, may not be preferable to one which talks much, and does nothing. I served with General Washington in the Legislature of Virginia, before the Revolution, and, during it, with Dr. Franklin in Congress. I never heard either of them speak ten minutes at a time, nor to any but the main point, which was to decide the question. They laid their shoulders to the great points, knowing that the little ones would follow of themselves. If the present Congress errs in too much talking, how can it be otherwise, in a body to which the people send one hundred and fifty lawyers, whose trade it is to question everything, yield nothing, and talk by the hour? That one hundred and fifty lawyers should do business together, ought not to be expected."

Though what are termed "silent members" often, as in the instances cited, have great influence in deliberative bodies, it is very rare to find them possessed of that paramount influence

which Mr. Jefferson evidently exerted in the Congress of
1783–4, and in the Legislatures of Virginia after 1776. On
account of his learning and love of science, on account of his
acting on political theories, new to the practices and oftentimes
to the understandings of his contemporaries (but so hackneyed
now in our country, that it is difficult to convince the present
generation that contrary ones ever existed), it became the
fashion of his opponents, a few years afterwards, to represent
him as that especial bugbear to men of English descent—an
"unpractical" or visionary man!—a man without executive force
—a man who yielded, and trimmed, and swam with the current,
but who did not really control, or even lead public affairs. To
the first great charge, to which the rest were but necessary
corollaries, that he was an "unpractical" man, there were certainly some proofs which are usually regarded as pretty conclusive. In the first place, he was a man of learning; and men of
learning must needs be theorists and visionaries! And it must
be confessed, that Mr. Jefferson presented some of the suspicious
indications of such characters. He did love to arrange practical matters by theoretical standards—he did sometimes carry
out system to almost amusing lengths—and, most dangerous of
all, he did sometimes make use of most scientifically "hard
words!" We know no so good an illustration of all these traits
brought together, as his proposed plan for the temporary government of the Western Territory, and it was in part to furnish
this illustration that we gave that document verbatim. Then,
secondly, Mr. Jefferson was a brilliant man—clearly the most
brilliant political writer in the nation—guilty, sometimes, of
making even legislative enactments readable, if not eloquent!
Brilliancy is, in the judgment of the dull gentlemen who compose the majority of most deliberative bodies, the natural anti-
pode of soundness of mind; and it is not to be denied that in
about three cases out of four, the dull gentlemen are in the right
in this. Nature seems jealous of allowing *all* her choicest
favors to be monopolized by one. It is an incontrovertible fact,
of daily exhibition, that the dull, plodding, slow-thinking man,
who can neither speak nor write with the least degree of effect,
often possesses a sounder and every way more reliable understanding, and also more energy and executive force, than the
man who can rain down words like those curious meteor

showers which have sometimes been observed in physical nature. We are not sure that a suspicion of brilliant men, is not a suspicion on the wholesome side. But nothing can be surer than that nature sometimes permits the union of these qualities —that the ponderous glaive comes as highly finished and keen and glittering, as the slender rapier—and when that happens, few things can resist its edge.

The question whether Mr. Jefferson united the sound to the showy, we waive for the present. We also waive the question whether he was a practical man. Accumulating facts will bring better testimony than any other on those points. But we can already decide sufficiently, whether he *led* or *followed*.

We have sometimes thought that an impression caught up by some of Mr. Jefferson's hostile contemporaries—by men who met him in society and saw him occasionally in official attitudes, but who were not in his confidence, and who really knew nothing of him—that he merely led men because he fell in with their wishes, arose (so far as it was a genuine impression) from the peculiarity of his manners. The peculiarities alluded to are thus described in a letter to us from one who knew him longer and more intimately than any individual now living—his oldest grandson, Colonel Randolph :

"He [Mr. Jefferson] never indulged in controversial conversation, because it often excited unpleasant feeling, and illustrated its inutility by the anecdote of two men who sat down candidly to discuss a subject and each converted the other. His maxim was, that every man had a right to his own opinion on all subjects, and others were bound to respect that right. Hence, in conversation, if any one expressed a decided opinion differing from his own, he made no reply, but changed the subject. Unreserved and candid himself, he was a listener, encouraging others to converse.   *   *   .*   *   *   *   *

¹ How far Jefferson's avowed theories corresponded with the practices here ascribed to him in these particulars, and the grounds on which his theories were based, will appear from a letter to the same grandson who wrote the above, and will be found published in both editions of Mr. Jefferson's Works. The following is an extract :

"But in stating prudential rules for our government in society, I must not omit the important one, of never entering into dispute or argument with another. I never yet saw an instance of one of two disputants convincing the other by argument. I have seen many, of their getting warm, becoming rude, and shooting one another. Conviction is the effect of our own dispassionate reasoning, either in solitude, or weighing within ourselves, dispassionately, what we hear from others, standing uncommitted in argument ourselves. It was one of the rules, which, above all others, made Doctor Franklin the most amiable of men in society, 'never to contradict anybody.' If he was urged to announce an opinion, he did it rather by asking questions, as if for information, or by suggesting doubts. When I hear another express an opinion which is not mine, I say to myself, he has a right to his opinion, as I to mine; why should I question it? His error does me no injury, and shall I become a Don Quixote, to bring all men by force of argument to one opinion? If a fact be misstated, it is probable he is gratified by a belief of it, and I have no right to deprive him of the gratification. If he wants information, he will ask it, and

"His tact in the management of men was great. He inquiringly followed out adverse opinions to their results, leaving it to their friends to note the error into which it led them, taking up their doubts as important suggestions, never permitting a person to place himself upon the defensive, or if he did, changing the subject, so as not to fix him in a wrong opinion by controverting it. With men of fertile and ingenious minds, fond of suggesting objections to propositions stated, he would sometimes suggest the opposite of the conclusion to which he desired them to come, then assent to the force of their objections, and thus lead them to convert themselves. * * * If information was sought, he gave it freely; if doubts were suggested, he explained them without reserve, never objecting to the scrutiny or canvass of his own opinions. As a public man, his friends complained that he spoke too freely, communicating more than they thought prudent."

This strongly reminds us, in some particulars, of Clarendon's description of John Hampden:

"He was of that rare affability and temper in debate, of that seeming humility and submission of judgment, as if he brought no opinion of his own with him, but a desire of information and instruction; yet he had so subtle a way of interrogating, and under the notion of doubts insinuating his objections, that he infused his own opinions into those from whom he pretended to learn and receive them." "He was, indeed, a very wise man, and of great parts, and possessed of the most absolute spirit of popularity, and the most absolute faculties to govern the people, of any man I ever knew."

A joke used to be told by Mr. Madison to this effect. Some years after the period of which we have been writing, a new

---

then I will give it in measured terms; but if he still believes his own story, and shows a desire to dispute the fact with me, I hear him and say nothing. It is his affair, not mine, if he prefers error. There are two classes of disputants most frequently to be met with among us. The first is of young students, just entered the threshold of science, with a first view of its outlines, not yet filled up with the details and modifications which a further progress would bring to their knowledge. The other consists of the ill-tempered and rude men in society, who have taken up a passion for politics. (Good humor and politeness never introduce into mixed society, a question on which they foresee there will be a difference of opinion.) From both of those classes of disputants, my dear Jefferson, keep aloof, as you would from the infected subjects of yellow fever or pestilence. Consider yourself, when with them, as among the patients of Bedlam needing medical more than moral counsel. Be a listener only, keep within yourself, and endeavor to establish with yourself the habit of silence, especially on politics. In the fevered state of our country, no good can ever result from any attempt to set one of these fiery zealots to rights, either in fact or principle. They are determined as to the facts they will believe, and the opinions on which they will act. Get by them, therefore, as you would by an angry bull: it is not for a man of sense to dispute the road with such an animal. You will be more exposed than others to have these animals shaking their horns at you, because of the relation in which you stand with me. Full of political venom, and willing to see me and to hate me as a chief in the antagonist party, your presence will be to them what the vomit grass is to the sick dog, a nostrum for producing ejaculation. Look upon them exactly with that eye, and pity them as objects to whom you can administer only occasional ease. My character is not within their power. It is in the hands of my fellow citizens at large, and will be consigned to honor or infamy by the verdict of the republican mass of our country, according to what themselves will have seen, not what their enemies and mine shall have said. Never, therefore, consider these puppies in politics as requiring any notice from you, and always show, that you are not afraid to leave my character to the umpirage of public opinion."

member of Congress called on Mr. Jefferson, then President of the United States. After an hour's interview, the gentleman was asked by some of his friends how he liked the President. He replied he was greatly pleased with him, but found him very different from what he expected in one particular. " What was that ?" " Why," exclaimed Mr. ———, " he is the most pliable *great* man I ever met with. I brought him to my views on the * * * * question, and I verily believe I could change his mind on almost any point." The exquisite comedy of the affair was, that Mr. ———'s associates were not long in discovering that he had been completely converted out of his own and into Mr. Jefferson's views on this very * * * * question ! This was an accident which happened to a good many such well meaning gentlemen who went proselyting in the same quarter.

These were manners born with Mr. Jefferson—which had distinguished him from his earliest childhood. They resulted, doubtless, from the same causes they did in Mr. Hampden. They were the fruits of natural modesty and amiability coöperating with tact. Both men had learned that they could do more with mankind, and therefore more *for* mankind, by " taking things by the smooth handle." These manners were natural to to them, and not assumed for special occasions. Arrogant and overbearing men are apt to condemn this as cunning. When this natural smoothness degenerates into sinuosity or duplicity, it is time enough, we think, to pronounce its condemnation. Whether Hampden and Jefferson were earnest men, steadfast in their cause, and ready to risk life and property on it, or whether they were mere party tricksters (like not a few of that bluff sort who do "a saucy roughness entertain "), we will leave others to decide.

Some time before Mr. Jefferson's retirement from Congress, he and General Washington corresponded with much interest in regard to the furtherance of a plan, then under the auspices of a joint stock company created by the Virginia Legislature, for opening a communication between the Potomac and Ohio rivers. This had long been a favorite plan of General Washington ; and Jefferson seems to have entered into it with equal zeal. It continued henceforth a subject of more or less intercommunication between them for many years. Both seemed to fancy that the struggle for the trade of the West lay between

Virginia and New York, and that the one which acted first effectually would secure the prize.[1]

Another subject, and one in which public feeling was deeply enlisted, occupied their correspondence. In 1783 the officers of the army established the "Society of the Cincinnati." It was to include the principal officers of the American army, and the French ministers and officers down to the rank of Colonels, who had served in America during the Revolution. Each member was to contribute a month's pay. The members were to wear a decoration consisting of a golden eagle, suspended by a ribbon of deep blue, edged with white. Membership was to be hereditary, descending to the oldest of the male line, or in default of male issue, to the oldest in the collateral male line. The members in each State were to constitute a separate society, and triennially to appoint delegates to a national meeting. The funds, after defraying necessary expenses, were to be devoted to the aid of needy members and their families. General Washington had been chosen temporary President, and the first national meeting of the Society called in Philadelphia in May, 1784.

This organization was not looked upon with favor by the civilians, who were the friends of a decidedly popular form of government. The day of State and national voluntary societies for a thousand objects great and little, following each other like the soap-bubbles which children blow from a pipe—expanding, glittering, and bursting in like manner—had not yet arrived. The events which had taken place in the army on the publication of the "Newburgh Letters," the year before (March, 1783), and which will be found very distinctly described by a distinguished apologist of the Cincinnati, Judge Marshall, in his Life of Washington,[2] had not tended to allay jealousies, which the supposed monarchical views of *some* distinguished army officers had already created.

An attack made on the Society by Judge Burke, of South Carolina, in a pamphlet in which he directly accused it of aiming at the foundation of an hereditary order in the State, was the signal for a general onslaught. The Governor of South Carolina

---

[1] For an interesting letter (of March 29th, 1784) from General Washington to Jefferson on this subject, and alluding to the efforts of "the Yorkers," will be found in Sparks's edition of Washington's Works, vol. ix. p. 30.

[2] Q. v. vol. ii. pp. 44–54.

condemned it in an address. The legislatures of at least three
States (Massachusetts, Pennsylvania, and Rhode Island) passed
resolutions of censure. Our plenipotentiaries in Europe wrote
home expressing mortified regrets that all our previous doctrines
of government were thus repudiated. The friends of popular
freedom in Europe generally, who had sympathized with the
cause in America, joined in these mortifications and regrets.
Four out of five probably of the entire population of the United
States took the same view of the subject.[1]

General Washington was pained and somewhat perplexed at
this state of things. We find him writing various letters on the
subject, urging a full attendance at the May meeting in 1784,
that the affairs of the Society may be fully and discreetly considered, and the proper steps taken to obviate the public objections. We find him asking but one man's *advice* on the subject, and that man was Jefferson. To the latter he wrote,
April 8th :

"This pamphlet [Judge Burke's] has, I am told, had its effect. People are
alarmed, especially in the Eastern States; how justly, and how contrary to the
avowed principles of the Society, and the purity of their motives, I will not declare,
lest it should appear that I wish to bias your judgment, rather than to obtain an
opinion; which, if you please, might be accompanied with sentiments, under the
information here given, respecting the most eligible measures to be pursued by the
Society at their next meeting. You may be assured, sir, that to the good opinion
alone, which I entertain of your abilities and candor, this liberty is to be attributed."[2]

To this appeal, Mr. Jefferson replied, eight days afterwards, in an equally frank and respectful spirit. He said he
had wished to see his correspondent standing on ground separated from the Society, "that the character which would be
handed to future ages as the head of our Revolution, might, in
no instance, be compromitted in subordinate altercations." He
said this subject had been "at the point of his pen in every
letter," but he had been "restrained by the reflection that he
[General Washington] had among his friends more able coun-

---

[1] Judge Marshall makes the following statements :
"The Ministers of the United States too in Europe, and the political *theorists* who cast
their eyes *towards the West for support to favorite systems*, having the privileged order
constantly in view, were loud in their condemnations of an institution from which a race
of nobles was expected to spring. The alarm was spread *throughout every State*, and
a high degree of *jealousy* pervaded the *mass of the people*."—*Life of Washington*,
vol. ii. p. 73.
[2] This is all of the letter published by Mr. Sparks, q. v. vol. ix. p. 28—note.

sellors, and, in himself, one abler than them all." After as
liberally as beautifully sketching the causes and the motives
which led to the organization of the Society, he first attempted
to show its inability to secure its proposed objects, and then, in
this wise, the objections to it:

"The objections of those who are opposed to the institution shall be briefly
sketched. You will readily fill them up. They urge that it is against the Confederation—against the letter of some of our constitutions—against the spirit of all
of them; that the foundation on which all these are built, is the natural equality
of man, the denial of every preëminence but that annexed to legal office, and, particularly, the denial of a preëminence by birth; that, however, in their present dispositions, citizens might decline accepting honorary installments into the order, but
a time may come, when a change of dispositions would render these flattering, when
a well directed distribution of them might draw into the order all the men of
talents, of office and wealth, and in this case, would probably procure an ingraft-
ment into the government; that in this they will be supported by their foreign
members, and the wishes and influence of foreign courts; that experience has shown
that the hereditary branches of modern governments are the patrons of privilege
and prerogative, and not of the natural rights of the people, whose oppressors they
generally are; that besides these evils, which are remote, others may take place
more immediately; that a distinction is kept up between the civil and military,
which it is for the happiness of both to obliterate; that when the members assemble they will be proposing to do something, and what that something may be will
depend on actual circumstances; that being an organized body, under habits of
subordination, the first obstruction to enterprise will be already surmounted; that
the moderation and virtue of a single character have probably prevented this Revolution from being closed as most others have been, by a subversion of that liberty
it was intended to establish; that he is not immortal, and his successor, or some of
his successors, may be led by false calculation into a less certain road to glory."

He stated that after receiving General Washington's letter, he
had taken occasion to hold private conversations pretty generally with all but the military gentlemen in Congress, whom, as
members of the Society, "delicacy forbade" him to approach
on the subject, and that "he had found as yet but one who was
not opposed to the institution, and that with an anguish of mind,
though covered under a guarded silence, which he had not seen
produced by any circumstance before." He stated that the preceding Congress had entertained the same impressions. For the
solicited advice in regard to "the most eligible measures to be
pursued by the Society at the next meeting," and for other interesting remarks, we must refer the reader to Mr. Jefferson's
Correspondence.[1]

[1] Randolph's edition, vol. i. p. 223; Congress edition, vol. i. p. 333.

General Washington called on Mr. Jefferson, at Annapolis, on his way to and from the Society meeting; and the latter thus describes what took place at their first and then at their subsequent interview :

"It was a little after candle-light, and he sat with me till after midnight, conversing almost exclusively on that subject. While he was feelingly indulgent to the motives which might induce the officers to promote it, he concurred with me entirely in condemning it; and when I expressed an idea that if the hereditary quality were suppressed, the institution might perhaps be indulged during the lives of the officers now living, and who had actually served; 'no,' he said, ' not a fibre of it ought to be left, to be an eye-sore to the public, a ground of dissatisfaction, and a line of separation between them and their country;' and he left me with a determination to use all his influence for its entire suppression. On his return from the meeting, he called on me again, and related to me the course the thing had taken. He said that from the beginning he had used every endeavor to prevail on the officers to renounce the project altogether, urging the many considerations which would render it odious to their fellow citizens, and disreputable and injurious to themselves; that he had at length prevailed on most of the old officers to reject it, although with great and warm opposition from others, and especially the younger ones, among whom he named Colonel W. S. Smith as particularly intemperate. But that in this state of things, when he thought the question safe, and the meeting drawing to a close, Major L'Enfant arrived from France, with a bundle of eagles, for which he had been sent there, with letters from the French officers who had served in America, praying for admission into the order, and a solemn act of their King permitting them to wear its ensign. This, he said, changed the face of matters at once, produced an entire revolution of sentiment, and turned the torrent so strongly in an opposite direction that it could be no longer withstood; all he could then obtain, was a suppression of the hereditary quality. He added, that it was the French applications, and respect for the approbation of the King, which saved the establishment in its modified and temporary form."

In a letter written two or three years after these events, to the editor of the *Encyclopédie Méthodique*, in France, Mr. Jefferson thus more fully stated what was done at this general meeting of the Society :

"The Society was to retain its existence, its name, its meetings, and its charitable funds: but these last were to be deposited with their respective legislatures. The order was to be no longer hereditary; a reformation, which had been pressed even from this side the Atlantic; it was to be communicated to no new members; the general meetings, instead of annual, were to be triennial only. The eagle and ribbon, indeed, were retained; because they were worn, and they wished them to be worn, by their friends who were in a country where they would not be objects of offence; but themselves never wore them. They laid them up in their bureaus, with the medals of American Independence, with those of the trophies they had taken, and the battles they had won."

FROM MR. JEFFERSON TO MARTHA JEFFERSON.

(Extract.)

ANNAPOLIS, *Jan.* 15, 1784.

MY DEAR MARTHA:

I am anxious to know what books you read, what tunes you play, and to receive specimens of your drawing. With respect to your meeting Mr. Simitiere at Mr. Rittenhouse's, nothing could give me more pleasure than your being much with that worthy family, wherein you will see the best examples of rational life, and learn to esteem and copy them. But I should be very tender of intruding you on the family; as it might perhaps be not always convenient to them for you to be there at your hours of attending Mr. Simitiere. I can only say, then, that if it has been desired by Mr. and Mrs. Rittenhouse, in such a way as that Mrs. Hopkinson shall be satisfied they will not consider it inconvenient, I would have you thankfully accept it; and conduct yourself with so much attention to the family as that they may never feel themselves incommoded by it. I hope Mrs. Hopkinson will be so good as to act for you in this matter with that delicacy and prudence of which she is so capable. I have much at heart your learning to draw, and should be uneasy at your losing this opportunity, which probably is your last.

EXTRACT FROM SAME TO SAME.

ANNAPOLIS, *Feb.* 18th, 1784.

I am sorry Mr. Simitiere cannot attend you; because it is probable you will never have another opportunity of learning to draw, and it is a pretty and pleasing accomplishment. With respect to the payment of the guinea, I would wish him to receive it; because if there is to be a doubt between him and me, which of us acts rightly, I would wish to remove it clearly off my own shoulders. You must thank Mrs. Hopkinson for me for the trouble she gave herself in this matter; from which she will be relieved by paying Mr. Simitiere his demand.

The Mr. Simitiere, or Du Simitiere, here mentioned, was a West India Frenchman settled in Philadelphia, who painted miniatures and other objects in water colors. He was well informed, an ardent patriot, and a man of no little consideration, corresponding (in a small, cramped, microscopic hand, long familiar to our eye) with some of the most eminent men of his day. The "worthy family" held up by Mr. Jefferson to the special admiration and attention of the daughter whose mind and manners he was devoted to moulding, was the plain industrious family of a practical mechanic, who constructed clocks, and, sometimes, orreries! That mechanic was David Rittenhouse!

CHAPTER XI.

1784—1786.

On the 7th day of May (1784), Congress resolved that a
Minister Plenipotentiary be appointed to act in conjunction with
Mr. Adams and Dr. Franklin, in negotiating treaties of commerce with foreign nations; and Mr. Jefferson received that
appointment.

He took immediate measures for his departure; and on the 11th of the same month left Annapolis for Philadelphia, for his oldest daughter, whom he determined to carry with him to Europe. His other two daughters, being too young for such a journey,[1] were left with their maternal aunt, Mrs. Eppes, wife of Francis Eppes, Esquire, of Eppington, Chesterfield county, Virginia.

Having completed his preparations, he set out for Boston, from whence he was to sail, "making it a point" in his way through New Jersey, New York, Connecticut, and Rhode Island, "of informing himself of the state of the commerce of each."[2] He reached New York the 30th, and, it appears from his pocket account-book, paused there a week, for the above purpose, and then proceeded leisurely through Connecticut and Rhode Island, reaching Boston June 18th. Making a short trip from this point to New Hampshire and Vermont, he returned, and sailed for Europe on the 5th of July, in the merchant ship Ceres, Captain St. Barbe, bound to Cowes, England. The voyage was rapid and pleasant. The account-book just mentioned, contains a minute diary of its events, arranged with the customary exact precision; and his daughter afterwards gave her recollections, in a paper lying before us; but one voyage to Europe is too much like another to make these particulars interesting. Nathaniel Tracy, the owner of the vessel, was a passenger; and everything went off exceedingly pleasantly until the little Martha became so dreadfully sea-sick that she was confined to her bed. On the 24th of July, soundings were reached off the mouth of the British Channel, and two days later the passengers landed at West Cowes. The continued illness of his daughter detained Mr. Jefferson at Portsmouth until the 30th. He then embarked for Havre, and on the 6th of August reached Paris.[3]

[1] Mary, the second of his surviving children, was six years old, and Lucy Elizabeth, the third, was two years old. The latter died before the close of 1784. The child of sorrow and misfortune, her organization was too frail and too intensely susceptible to last long. Her sensibilities were so precociously acute, that she listened with exquisite pleasure to music—and *wept* on hearing a false note !

[2] Memoir.

[3] We think one of the above trifling details (merely where Martha's illness detained him) differs from the statements of the Memoir. We only mention it to say that where we add to his statements, we write from the minute daily record which he kept at the time—and the same from which he gleaned the dates and minor facts of his Memoir. After habitually collating his statements, sometimes public and sometimes private—sometimes made near to each other and sometimes a half a century apart—we come with a sort of surprise on even so trivial an error as that above mentioned.

He took lodgings at the Hôtel d'Orléans, *Rue Petits Augus-tins*, but soon removed to a handsome house in the *Cul-de-sac Tétebout*, which he furnished and occupied his first year. We may as well here remark, that Colonel David Humphreys, Secretary of Legation, and Mr. Short, his private secretary, were members of his family; and that Martha, after enjoying a proper period of sight seeing, was placed at a convent school, *à l'Abbaye Royale de Panthemont*, the most fashionable and dif-ficult of access in France.

Immediately after reaching Paris, Mr. Jefferson had called on Dr. Franklin, at Passy, and they had written Mr. Adams, then at the Hague, to join them. He soon did so, and the Ministers drew up the form of a commercial treaty, based on the late instructions of Congress,[1] to be offered to such nations as should be found ready to treat with them.

One of Mr. Jefferson's early occupations in France, was to superintend the printing of his Notes on Virginia. Before leaving America, various of his friends had solicited copies of the work. To make these in manuscript was out of the ques-tion, and he had accordingly inquired the price of printing a few copies, but had found that it would " exceed the importance of the object." Ascertaining that he could get it printed at one-fourth of the American price in France, he ordered two hundred copies. A portion of these were distributed among the learned men of Europe, and a larger number sent to his friends in America; but publication was carefully guarded against, for the following reasons, expressed in a letter to Colonel Monroe (June 17, 1785):

" I have taken measures to prevent its publication. My reason is, that I fear the terms in which I speak of slavery, and of our Constitution, may produce an irritation which will revolt the minds of our countrymen against reformation in these two articles, and thus do more harm than good. I have asked of Mr. Madison to sound this matter as far as he can, and if he thinks it will not produce that effect, I have then copies enough printed to give one to each of the young men at the college, and to my friends in the country."[2]

The same reasons against publication are repeated to various other correspondents; but a European copy, by the death of

[1] Drafted by Jefferson while in that body.
[2] Mr. Madison, it appears, replied that the publication would not do the injury appre-hended. " but on the contrary, might do some good." (See Jefferson to Wythe; Aug. 13th, 1786.)

its owner, a Mr. Williams, found its way into the hands of a
French publisher (M. Barrois), who procured it to be translated
into French, and then very coolly sent the manuscript to Mr.
Jefferson for correction, "without asking any other permission
for the publication." The latter remarks in his Memoir:

"I never had seen so wretched an attempt at translation. Interverted,
abridged, mutilated, and often reversing the sense of the original, I found it a
blotch of errors, from beginning to end. I corrected some of the most material,
and, in that form, it was printed in French. A London bookseller, on seeing the
translation, requested me to permit him to print the English original. I thought it
best to do so, to let the world see that it was not really so bad as the French translation had made it appear."

This London bookseller was Stockdale, of Piccadilly, and
his edition made the work common to English readers on both
sides of the Atlantic.

The commercial negotiations of the American ministers
made slow progress, and their history is thus carried down
through 1784, and, indeed, for some subsequent period, by Mr.
Jefferson, in his Memoir:

"In a conference with the Count de Vergennes, it was thought better to leave
to legislative regulation, on both sides, such modifications of our commercial intercourse, as would voluntarily flow from amicable dispositions. Without urging, we
sounded the ministers of the several European nations, at the court of Versailles,
on their dispositions towards mutual commerce, and the expediency of encouraging
it by the protection of a treaty. Old Frederic, of Prussia, met us cordially, and
without hesitation, and, appointing the Baron de Thulemeyer, his minister at the
Hague, to negotiate with us, we communicated to him our *projet*, which, with
little alteration by the King, was soon concluded. Denmark and Tuscany entered
also into negotiations with us. Other powers appearing indifferent, we did not
think it proper to press them. They seemed, in fact, to know little about us, but
as rebels, who had been successful in throwing off the yoke of the mother country.
They were ignorant of our commerce, which had been always monopolized by
England, and of the exchange of articles, it might offer advantageously to both
parties. They were inclined, therefore, to stand aloof, until they could see better
what relations might be usefully instituted with us. The negotiations, therefore,
begun with Denmark and Tuscany, we protracted designedly, until our powers had
expired; and abstained from making new propositions to others having no colonies; because our commerce being an exchange of raw for wrought materials, is a

[1] It would *seem* from letters of Mr. Jefferson's to W. F. Dumas (February 2, 1786),
and to Dr. Bancroft (February 26, 1786), that this pirated edition was *not* published, up
to the dates of those letters: and *then* Mr. Jefferson did not apprehend it would be published, the Abbé Morrelet having stopped it by promising to furnish Barrois with a
translation by himself. Whether the pirated edition was *afterwards* published, or
whether Mr. Jefferson accidentally conveys an erroneous impression in the text, we are
unable to say.

competent price for admission into the colonies of those possessing them; but were we to give it, without price, to others, all would claim it, without price, on the ordinary ground of *gentis amicissimæ.*"

In January, 1785, Mr. Jefferson received a letter from Mr. Eppes, of Virginia, informing him of the death of his youngest daughter. His reply will be found in the Appendix.[1]

In the spring of the same year, Dr. Franklin, now old and infirm, obtained his long sought permission to return home, and on the 10th of March, Congress appointed Mr. Jefferson to succeed him as Minister Plenipotentiary to the Court of France. Mr. Adams had received a similar commission to the British Court, in February, and left France, in June, to enter upon his duties.

Dr. Franklin bade adieu to Passy, on the 12th of July, and his journey to the coast was accompanied with the attentions of every class of the French people. With all, indeed, he was unboundedly popular. His statesmanship had attracted the admiration of the government, his wisdom that of the philosophers, his learning that of the savans, his wit that of society, his *bonhomie* that of all Frenchmen. Such a combination of qualities, and such a rivalry in admiration, had swelled the general tide of feeling in his favor to one of enthusiasm.

To fill the place of such a man in the lively, impressible, and sharply discriminating society of France, was not an easy task; and of this Mr. Jefferson was very sensible. But his beginning was good, for it was with a *bon-mot,* by no means badly turned. "You replace M. Franklin, I hear," said the Count de Vergennes, the celebrated French Minister of Foreign Affairs, to him. " I *succeed,* no one can *replace* him," was the prompt reply.

Jefferson's popularity grew apace. He had the advantage of starting with Franklin's mantle on his shoulders. There were a few strong points of similarity in their characters, and their friendship had early reached the pitch even of affection. Jefferson revered Franklin, and Franklin admired and had full confidence in Jefferson. Then, Jefferson started, too, with the unbounded good will and applause of the French officers who had served in America. It was his fortune throughout his whole life, without apparent effort, perhaps more than any other American, besides Washington or Franklin, to win the

[1] APPENDIX, No. 7.

admiration of the *Continental* foreigners who visited America; and he seems to have formed strong personal friendships with more such than even Washington or Franklin. De Chastellux's picture of the young "Senator of America" combining so many solid attainments and polite accomplishments—"the musician, the geometrician, the astronomer, the natural philosopher, in voluntary retirement," looking down from his elegant mountain home amidst vast trans-Atlantic solitudes, was well calculated to impress French imagination. Jefferson's house in Paris became a central point and a common rendezvous, for all that glittering train of brilliant young French officers, with Lafayette at their head, who in those solitudes, and associated with the Americans, had, in the minds of their enthusiastic countrymen, hunted the British lion, if not to his death, at least to his grievous wounding and to his ignominious overthrow. In those solitudes, the disgraces and disasters of Cape Breton, Guadaloupe, Ticonderoga, Cape Lagos, and Quebec, had been wiped off, and avenged on the head of the inflicter. America was "the rage" in France, and the American Minister, if he possessed proper personal qualifications, would be sure to have them all heightened, in the national regard, by the prestige of his country.

Jefferson's public and private appearance did not disappoint general expectation. Like Franklin, his claims to regard were varied, and appealed to different and to the most influential classes in the State. His Notes on Virginia gave the philosophers and savans a hint of what he could do in their line, should he give his time and efforts to philosophy and science. The tone and tenor of this work brought it extraordinary popularity in France. The *littérateurs* and men of taste were not long in discovering that he was an infinitely finer classical scholar than Franklin—possessed a far higher appreciation of Art. Resembling Franklin in various practical qualities and attainments, Jefferson excelled him generally in the purely æsthetic. They belonged to the same political school. Both loved France. Neither began, like some of their countrymen, to relapse into a colonial veneration for England and a colonial hate for France, before the wounds of the Revolution were even well skinned over. Then, Jefferson's ardor and hopefulness were unchilled by age. He was naturally more sanguine and daring than Franklin. We will not say that he was a more earnest man, but he had a more earnest manner. He had not been so ground and triturated among the conventionalisms of political society, that all the sharp native points of his character had been worn away—succeeded by a glossy, uniform round-ness and polish. He talked, at times, with deep natural feeling, and with what, in a diplomatist, appeared startling unreserve. If his conversation did not lack adroitness—if he intuitively took the measure of his auditor and somewhat proportioned the size of his weapons to his game—if he condescended to turn natty sentences for delicate ears—still, he was essentially an earnest man. He had a few great objects, and of these he never for an instant lost sight. The lightest and gayest listeners generally were gradually drawn from the shallow waters where they were accustomed to sport towards a deep central current, down which they oftentimes unexpectedly found themselves drifting vehe-mently enough! If there was an earnest spark in the soul, Jef-ferson always knew how to find it, and how to blow it into a flame. And then he knew exquisitely well how to appropriate the heat to his own or rather his country's objects. There was not an influential young officer who had served in America, there was not a glittering leader of female fashion, who claimed to be in Mr. Jefferson's list of friends (and it soon became unfashionable not to be in that list), who was not a sturdy adherent of the United States, in all things. If the United States had an object to accomplish, or a favor to ask, Ministers' doors were at once besieged by young colonels, and generals, and marquises, the rising young men of France, all vehemently interceding for it; and in every salon and boudoir of Paris, all those voices were at once heard on the same side, which rarely, in France (if anywhere else), plead in vain!

Franklin had sparkled preëminent, with his diamond pointed wit, in the court of *old* France. But, imperceptibly, the scene was shifting. The day of the wits—the day when gilded court ceremonials were the chief occupations, and a rose-scented vo-luptuousness the chief object, of life (pleasantly termed by Mr. Burke, the ": the age of chivalry"), was "passing away," and a day of earnest—terribly earnest—men and women, was already sending up lurid harbingers of its approach.

We cannot understand our subject, because we cannot understand the real position of Jefferson, without a brief glance at the surroundings of the period.

France had lain supine under the inherited evils of Pompadourism and Du Barryism—the wars of Louis XIV., and the vices of Louis XV. But the American War had brought the diseases of the State to a crisis, by sweeping away the last vestige both of its funds and its credit. The mild virtues of an inefficient prince, while they rescued the State councils from the dictation of open courtesans, and while they brought back some personal respect to the throne, were wholly incompetent to restore vitality to a worn-out, effete despotism. Even the chivalric and blind loyalty of the past could no longer shut its eyes and ears to the degradation of the higher classes, and the abject misery of the lower. It could no longer hide from its view the portentous facts that in a country of as genial soil and climate as any the sun shone upon, agriculture was deplorably depressed; that in a country of city-engirded ports, and noble rivers to transport products and propel machinery, there was neither commerce nor manufactures; in a word, that in a country where every element of material prosperity had been showered down in unsparing profusion, paralysis and death pervaded every department of material activity.

While the brilliant Calonne reigned and revelled as if in a perpetual holiday—while he apparently overleapt all difficulties, and scattered doubts and objections to the winds by a flight of eloquence, or a stroke of wit, the few political wise men saw (or should have seen) that all this display was but the dying flash of the taper. They saw a land exhausted by wars which shook the four quarters of the globe, and which had been undertaken for as good objects as to gratify the hate or the partialities of a mistress.[1] They saw a land not only drained by ages of taxation to support the licentious splendor of the court and privileged classes, but every opening to future wealth, every avenue to gain, every chance for invigoration farmed out in advance for the same objects, so that to acquire more, was only to be robbed of more. To meet these unending exactions, the

---

[1] France took part in the Seven Years' War for Austria and against her natural ally, Prussia, because the Empress Maria Theresa condescended to write a friendly letter to Madame Pompadour, addressing her as her "dear cousin!"

middle classes of France had been reduced to the condition of peasants, and the peasants to that of starved and overworked helots. There was but one deeper abyss of physical misery—starvation ; and starvation was at hand.

There comes a time when hopeless submission is suddenly changed into wild ferocity—when the abjectly weak start up in the strength of despair. There comes a time when the march of civilization, God ordained, must be hindered no longer—when nations or governments which have sinned away every germ of renovation, and filled up the cup of their abomination, must be swept away by the bloody sword of conquest or revolution. Extinction is then the only remedy. Thus Rome perished under the Gothic sword, and was succeeded by the Gothic kingdoms. Every sign was imminent that France stood on the verge of some such dread catastrophe.

The unvenerating and audacious spirit of moral and intellectual inquiry which marked the nation at this period—not the cause, as has been idly pretended, of the French Revolution, but only an earlier effect of the same causes ; the fierce and uncontrollable reaction against the moral and intellectual oppressions of ages—was sternly conning the political and social problems submitted to its examination.

The example of America was having its weight—was daily having more weight—on the political mind of France. France judged the fruit of the American Revolution more favorably, perhaps, as she had contributed to its production. She felt partial to a nation which had stood successfully in arms with her, and aided her to humble her old hereditary foe. Her soldiers, glorious with the scars of Savannah and the laurels of Yorktown, brought back strange, and, to an oppressed people, bewitching maxims, learned of simple and august chiefs, who had left the plow and the workshop to guide the armed squadrons of war. They gave wondrous accounts of a comparatively weak and rural people surrendering up their quiet and plentiful homes to the ravages and insults of a long war of invasion and attempted subjugation from the most formidable nation in Europe, rather than submit to exactions which were trifles—which were as nothing to those that France had endured for ages. This seed fell not on the rock of indifference, or amidst the tares of ignorance. The French officers were generally nobles in rank. They were placed by their birth in the privileged class, or on its outskirts. They were now the "lions" of Paris. Thus liberalism commenced in high places. A "Patriotic party" was formed. Outside of the nobility and clergy, interest brought thinking men to its support. Within those orders, there were multitudes, especially of the young, willing to prefer their country to their caste. And as it always happens in the inception of great moral movements, the kindly and just instincts of the female heart came warmly to the aid of the proposed reforms. Beautiful young Duchesses and Marchionesses— in whose veins flowed the blood of Condés and Montmorencis —began to talk liberalism! Thus, fashion, more despotic in the gay metropolis of France than the throne, more powerful than its armies, adopted the patriotic movement. For a time, counter sentiments could scarcely be heard. Debauched young nobles grew sentimental in descanting on the beauties of equality and fraternity; and painted women pondered on remedies for the vices of the State. But under the froth and garbage, ran the currents of honest and patriotic national feeling. Every class gave its best intellects, its most magnanimous hearts, to the cause. The philosophers, the savans, the nobility, the clergy, the army, the professions, and the world of fashion, agreed in this. And never in the world was more intellect or more sincerity combined in a national movement.

It was at the first glimmering dawn of such an epoch, that Jefferson was brought into close contact with French society, as the Ambassador of that Republic to which so many eyes and sympathies were turned. He had acted one of the most prominent, as well as one of the most showy civic parts in the great trans-Atlantic drama. He had preceded the French patriots in their present class of ideas. He had acted a high part where they were only commencing to speculate. He had reported the Declaration of Independence itself, and was generally supposed to be its author. He had overthrown and reconstructed the legal systems of a chief member of the Confederacy. He had seen the practical workings of his labors. He was profoundly versed in the theories of government. With the same knowledge of the ancient ones possessed by the best educated Frenchman, he was far more deeply read in the legal and constitutional system and precedents of England than any man who could be found in France. So diligent and systematic had been his investigations in this direction, that few persons not English, and no great number of Englishmen, could so clearly and readily trace every minute step—its causes and bearings—in the growth of the British Constitution. In respect to American systems, there was, of course, no one in France who could pretend to vie in knowledge with this actual builder of those systems. And it was to England and America alone that the French Patriotic Party looked for precedents and for examples.

Mr. Jefferson's intellectual and physical habits were of a kind to produce favorable impressions among the French people. The tendency of his mind was towards those philosophic generalizations, and those bold speculations in regard to political and social problems, which characterized the leading French minds of the day. His habit of expressing important ideas in the form of resounding abstractions, was in the French taste. His manners had the grace, finish, suavity and unpresumingness, if they had not the freedom in some un-English particulars,[1] of a well-bred Frenchman. He had none of those abrupt angularities and inequalities of temper and demeanor, which had embroiled Mr. Adams with the people and government, almost as soon as he set his foot in France, and made his entire stay there a series of torments and misunderstandings. Finally, even Jefferson's appetites were French. He ate delicately and sparingly of light materials, and chose the lightest wines of the French vintage. His physical, and in some particulars his mental constitution, seems to us to have more resembled the man of Southern than the man of Northern Europe.

Rather singularly as it might seem at a first view, Jefferson stood as well with the Government as with the people of France. The old celebrated statesman, the Count de Vergennes, at this period controlled the foreign policy of France. Jefferson had

---

[1] Hon. Edward Coles, of Philadelphia (ex-Governor of Illinois, etc.), a lifelong acquaintance of Mr. Jefferson and of his private Secretary Mr. Short, informs us that Short very often diverted himself in after years with relating laughable anecdotes of Jefferson's fastidious adherence to American ideas of decorum in those particulars where American and French standards differ. He not only could never enter upon any freedoms in manners or conversation himself, but any approach to a *broad* one in his presence, always made him, literally, "*blush* like a boy."

Mrs. Adams draws a somewhat different picture of Franklin—but she was not much more partial to him than was her husband; nor could she tolerate the least deviation from the austere standard of New England manners. And the Massachusetts Juno, when roused, understood the art of expressing her feelings *very pointedly!* Her profound friendship for Jefferson (of which we shall presently see the evidence) was undoubtedly greatly heightened by the fact stated by Mr. Short.

the good fortune to secure his regard from the outset. One of the means through which he did so, may be surmised from the following passage from his Memoir:

"The Count de Vergennes had the reputation, with the diplomatic corps, of being wary and slippery in his diplomatic intercourse; and so he might be with those whom he knew to be slippery and double-faced themselves. As he saw that I had no indirect views, practised no subtleties, meddled in no intrigues, pursued no concealed object, I found him as frank, as honorable, as easy of access to reason, as any man with whom I had ever done business; and I must say the same for his successor, Montmorin, one of the most honest and worthy of human beings."

This view will be found corroborated by all the official intercourse and diplomatic papers which passed between the parties.

Next, Mr. Jefferson's abilities as a diplomatist were not less conspicuous than his straightforwardness. We shall find this abundantly conceded by all—by even personal, political, and national enemies—before we dismiss the history of this part of his life.

Jefferson had the ready good sense and knowledge of the world, which taught him not only when and how to ask, but what to ask of our national ally. He did not expect that an ancient and powerful monarchy would instantly and radically change its habits, overturn its commercial laws, or reform its abuses of administration, to meet either his wishes or demands. He did not make such demands, and then, on their refusal, work himself into a passion, quarrel with the heads of departments, write home flaming letters, and get laughed at for his pains. We shall find him throughout calmly, dexterously, and perseveringly pushing after the attainable, and making each attainment a step to another and generally a more important one.

In saying above, that he "meddled in no intrigues," he probably referred to ordinary diplomatic intrigues, but he might have extended the remark to another class, the avoidance of which did still more to secure the confidence of the government. Long before he left France, it was filled with active opponents of the existing order of things—men who were seeking radical political changes. Among these were those chiefs of the Patriotic Party, who so much frequented his house and society—who had his personal sympathies, and his personal concurrence in their general views and objects. But his idea of an ambassador's privilege in a foreign country did not extend to personal privity, much less complicity in political plots against existing institutions. We shall presently have a strong specimen of his scrupulousness in this particular.

Mr. Jefferson had the rare good fortune not only to steer clear of those painful misunderstandings which occurred between Adams and Franklin, but to even steer clear of the jealousy of either party. This was easy enough, if not a matter of course, as far as Franklin was concerned. But to remain on terms of confidential intercourse and warm friendship with him, and at the same time with the impetuous and always (when irritated) morbidly jealous Mr. Adams, was an achievement requiring tact and good sense. It was readily undertaken, however, by Jefferson, for the "Colossus of Independence," always, in spite of foibles and follies, held a high place in his respect, and a warm place in his affections. This wise and proper effort completely succeeded. Adams's early attachment for Jefferson ripened and deepened. More scrupulous regard to the rights, more gentlemanly consideration for the feelings of a colleague and associate, were never exhibited, than Mr. Adams uniformly exhibited towards Jefferson during their common stay in France, and throughout all their subsequent intercourse as co-ambassadors. Indeed, towards Jefferson, Adams always (with an unfortunate exception or two) seems to us to have laid aside the imperiousness, the pugnacity, the dogmatism, and the jealousy of his nature, and to have exhibited the same beautiful traits that he uniformly did in his domestic circle. No finer passage occurs in his personal history, than his habitual treatment of Jefferson; and it serves to show how this lion, generally rampant, could be the lamb, if he was considerately dealt with, and some little grains of allowance made for his foibles. Adams treated Jefferson like a younger brother—the next younger and near to his own age. Jefferson, as much from real feeling as from tact, took the younger brother's place. He always asked Mr. Adams's opinion first, and always urged him to take the post of honor. He felt that this was due to Mr. Adams's seniority in years and public services. This unusual modesty melted the stormy New England chief. He was sharp-sighted enough

to recognize profound talent; he loved decision, though it did
not take the demonstrative form of his own; and this personal
respect paid to him by the courtly Virginian (are not powerful
rough men prone to admire powerful smooth men?) and by a
man ten times as popular as himself in the country where they
had acted together, superadded affection to esteem. Perhaps
we should rather say it increased his " affection," for by his own
showing, Mr. Adams's " heart " " had been seized upon by Jefferson " years before this.

This friendly tableau would not be quite complete without
the introduction of another figure. Mrs. John Adams was (if
we may be excused a trite, and, ordinarily, a very exaggerated
designation) a magnificent woman. Of her peculiarities of
character we may hereafter find occasion to speak. Suffice it
now to say, that she was an admirable specimen of New
England intelligence and firmness—as unbending to the semblance as to the reality of a departure, to a hair's breadth, from
any of those rigid observances which had always been practised
in New England society, and which would have solicited the
grim approbation of John Calvin and John Knox! Mrs. Adams
was little pleased with the society of France. Her letters to
her correspondents at home give some piquant sketches, and it
must be confessed that she succeeds in making a good deal that
she saw sufficiently ridiculous. Her picture of the table scene
at Franklin's, of Madame Helvetius, of the little dog, etc., will
always be laughed at by the best friends of the ridiculed
" philosopher." One man, however, Mrs. Adams found in
France, to respect and admire. She wrote home to her sister
that he was " the chosen of the earth." She sincerely lamented
that Mr. Adams's departure for England would separate them
from his society. She kept up no sentimental correspondence
with him, after that departure, because that was not the way
that " Abigail Adams " had been brought up to feel or act—
that was not according to the New England standard; but she
did, from time to time, address him friendly letters, and she
honored him with the execution of her little orders on shop-
keepers in Paris, as if he had been a member of her family.
That man was Jefferson, and he thoroughly reciprocated her
respect and admiration.

The year 1785 made no important changes in the relations

between the United States and the European nations. Mr. Adams accomplished nothing in England, Mr. Jefferson but little in France. Europe had not yet settled itself into a new commercial system in regard to America, on which it was prepared to act. Jefferson thus specifies the prominent immediate objects in his field of diplomacy:

"My duties at Paris were confined to a few objects; the receipt of our whale-oils, salted fish, and salted meats, on favorable terms; the admission of our rice on equal terms with that of Piedmont, Egypt, and the Levant; a mitigation of the monopolies of our tobacco by the Farmers-General, and a free admission of our productions into their islands, were the principal commercial objects which required attention."

And in this connection, he pays the following handsome tribute to Lafayette and to the French government:

"On these occasions, I was powerfully aided by all the influence and the energies of the Marquis de Lafayette, who proved himself equally zealous for the friendship and welfare of both nations; and, in justice, I must also say, that I found the government entirely disposed to befriend us on all occasions, and to yield us every indulgence, not absolutely injurious to themselves."

But the close of the year, as already remarked, found little accomplished. The influence of the Farmers-General was too strong to be yet shaken. So far from attaining a free admission of American products into the French West Indies, the qualified one of the year before (which had always been bitterly opposed by the French commercial classes) was now threatened with stoppage, in retaliation for commercial restrictions injurious to the interests of France, imposed by two or three of the American States.

A subject of difficulty and solicitude to Mr. Adams and Mr. Jefferson, sprung up also with the piratical Barbary powers who held the keys of the Mediterranean, and even sometimes extended their depredations into adjacent portions of the Atlantic. A Morocco cruiser captured an American vessel and crew, and, as usual, confiscated the former, and held the latter to an enormous ransom. The only alternatives were tribute, war continued captures, or a cessation of American commerce in and adjacent to the Mediterranean. The first maritime powers of Europe, England, France, Spain, and the States-General, condescended to submit to the first degrading expedient. The impoverished treasury of the United States rendered it a very inconvenient one to them; and the first cost of a war would be still more onerous. A cessation of commerce was out of the question, if union was to be preserved between the maritime and agricultural American States.

Mr. Adams and Mr. Jefferson took exactly the opposite sides on this question from what would be expected, by cursory observers, from their subsequently developed theories and practices in regard to redressing national wrongs. Mr. Adams was for tribute, Mr. Jefferson for war! Congress agreed with the former, and those negotiations were entered upon which dragged their slow length along during the stay of these ministers in Europe—accomplishing little—and not preventing the annual increase of American captives in the prisons and slave marts of Barbary. Few middle-aged Americans of the present day will fail to remember seeing in their childhood haggard mendicants passing from door to door, soliciting money, to ransom fathers or brothers who were "slaves in Algiers," and narrating betimes, as wild and pathetic tales of suffering and adventure— of attempted escapes, in which dark-eyed Moorish maidens acted the usual part—of grim pachas, hideous jailers, dire imprisonments and other inflictions—as are to be found on the same fruitful theme in the drama and in the lyrics of Spain. Whatever the imaginary embellishments, sooth to say, the reality was hard enough! Not a few Americans spent the best part of their lives in that dreary bondage. "Commodore O'Brien," whom we have named as the commander of a Virginia brig, destroyed during Arnold's and Phillips's invasion of that State, was, we think, ten or fifteen years a prisoner on the Barbary coast.

Mr. Adams and Mr. Jefferson had written home for instructions in regard to negotiations with these States. After waiting for a good deal more than a reasonable time for an answer, they determined, in virtue of their general powers, to dispatch an agent to negotiate; and Jefferson drew up instructions for the guidance of that agent. Before the latter started, the tardy messenger of Congress arrived in Paris (September, 1785). It was curious that the instructions transmitted by Congress so closely coincided with Jefferson's, that no changes were required in the latter, beyond a few of form.

In Jefferson's correspondence home, this year, he several times speaks favorably of establishing a "little navy." He thought it necessary to protect our country from the aggressions of the Barbary powers, and also to hold "as a bridle" in the mouths of the powerful European nations who had West India possessions, or fisheries on the American coast. But he urged this only as a necessity, growing out of the United States making themselves a commercial and maritime nation. Individually, he was opposed to it, but he thought it a duty to acquiesce in the decided wishes of the nation. His entire ideas on these subjects, and some kindred ones, are succinctly expressed in a letter to John Jay, then Secretary of Foreign Affairs, August 23d. An inner view of his early political theories demands a careful perusal of the letter:

"I shall sometimes ask your permission to write you letters, not official, but private. The present is of this kind, and is occasioned by the question proposed in yours of June the 14th: 'whether it would be useful to us, to carry all our own productions, or none?'

"Were we perfectly free to decide this question, I should reason as follows. We have now lands enough to employ an infinite number of people in their cultivation. Cultivators of the earth are the most valuable citizens. They are the most vigorous, the most independent, the most virtuous, and they are tied to their country, and wedded to its liberty and interests, by the most lasting bonds. As long, therefore, as they can find employment in this line, I would not convert them into mariners, artisans, or anything else. But our citizens will find employment in this line, till their numbers, and of course their productions, become too great for the demand both internal and foreign. This is not the case as yet, and probably will not be for a considerable time. As soon as it is, the surplus of hands must be turned to something else. I should then, perhaps, wish to turn them to the sea in preference to manufactures; because, comparing the characters of the two classes, I find the former the most valuable citizens. I consider the class of artificers as the panders of vice, and the instruments by which the liberties of a country are generally overturned. However, we are not free to decide this question on principles of theory only. Our people are decided in the opinion, that it is necessary for us to take a share in the occupation of the ocean, and their established habits induce them to require that the sea be kept open to them, and that that line of policy be pursued, which will render the use of that element to them, as great as possible. I think it a duty in those intrusted with the administration of their affairs, to conform themselves to the decided choice of their constituents: and that, therefore, we should, in every instance, preserve an equality of right to them in the transportation of commodities, in the right of fishing, and in the other uses of the sea.

"But what will be the consequence? Frequent wars without a doubt. Their property will be violated on the sea, and in foreign ports, their persons will be insulted, imprisoned, etc., for pretended debts, contracts, crimes, contraband, etc, etc. These insults must be resented, even if we had no feelings, yet to prevent their eternal repetition; or, in other words, our commerce on the ocean ar 1 in other countries, must be paid for by frequent war. The justest dispositions possible in ourselves, will not secure us against it. It would be necessary that all other nations were just also. Justice, indeed, on our part, will save us from those wars which would have been produced by a contrary disposition. But how can we prevent those produced by the wrongs of other nations? By putting ourselves in a condition to punish them. Weakness provokes insult and injury, while a condition to punish, often prevents them. This reasoning leads to the necessity of some naval force; that being the only weapon by which we can reach an enemy. I think it to our interest to punish the first insult; because an insult unpunished is the parent of many others. We are not, at this moment, in a condition to do it, but we should put ourselves into it, as soon as possible. If a war with England should take place, it seems to me that the first thing necessary would be a resolution to abandon the carrying trade, because we cannot protect it. Foreign nations must, in that case, be invited to bring us what we want, and to take our productions in their own bottoms. This alone could prevent the loss of those productions to us, and the acquisition of them to our enemy. Our seamen might be employed in depredations on their trade. But how dreadfully we shall suffer on our coasts, if we have no force on the water, former experience has taught us. Indeed I look forward with horror to the very possible case of war with an European power, and think there is no protection against them, but from the possession of some force on the sea. Our vicinity to their West India possessions, and to the fisheries, is a bridle which a small naval force, on our part, would hold in the mouths of the most powerful of these countries. I hope our land office will rid us of our debts, and that our first attention then will be, to the beginning a naval force of some sort. This alone can countenance our people as carriers on the water, and I suppose them to be determined to continue such."

These ideas in regard to commerce are now as obsolete in the United States as is that primitive and austere simplicity of republican government which was also advocated by Jefferson! As the United Sates rush along with headlong velocity in their career of material prosperity—as their commerce and wealth grow to fabulous limits—as their navies and armies necessarily extend—as their wars and expenditures constantly increase—as their resemblance in all particulars to the colossal nations of the past becomes more and more apparent, God grant that our "Tyre of the further West" may not find, like those dead nations of the past, the sources of their precocious and extravagant splendor, the sources, too, of an equally premature corruption, decline, and fall! God grant that the hopes of mankind in liberty and self-government, may not be wrecked by our too successful pursuit of national wealth.

Mr. Jefferson's remarks about "the class of artificers," judged by the standards of the present day, would betray a very uncharacteristic illiberality and prejudice. They would sound much more like the diatribes of his kinsman, the atrabilarious cynic of Roanoke,[1] than like the philanthropic and liberal Jefferson. He spoke in reference to a state of things learned purely from books, or seen transiently in the festering suburbs of Paris, before the French Revolution. America then had no manufactories, filled with the sons and daughters of its agricultural yeomanry, to show that vice or virtue is not dependent on occupation—to banish the absurd hypothesis, the libel on Heaven, that any proper and necessary department of human industry necessarily, or even naturally, leads to vice! Mr. Jefferson never ceased to believe that simple rural life—moderation in living, daily toil, and no greater aggregation of human beings than is to be found in the family on each farm—is more conducive to virtue than any other social state: and probably no one will dispute him in this. Prose Georgics sprinkle all his writings, from the earliest to the latest. But he lived to entirely change his mind in regard to "the class of artificers"—to give up all the prejudices against them expressed in the letter to Mr. Jay. We suppose, indeed, that he never actually believed that mechanical occupations, *per se*, led to vice. If so, he was amazingly inconsistent, for he always, as we have seen, had a particular fondness for that class of occupations himself; and not one planter in a hundred, or a thousand, fostered them so carefully on his farm! He only meant, then, we imagine, that great aggregations of ignorant, abjectly poor, hungry, squalid factory operatives, completely under the power of their employers—a thing which he had read of in books, and which still existed in Europe—would be a very undesirable and dangerous class of American population.

We find his opinions on many of the contemporaneous questions before Congress and the American people very freely expressed in his correspondence. He was opposed to the building of a "Federal town" by Congress for the seat of government. He disapproved of dividing the public lands between the States, and approved of the plan subsequently adopted of selling them at auction to the highest bidder, above a fixed minimum, and receiving the public certificates of debt in payment, at their par value. He approved of investing Congress with the regulation of trade—of free trade in the abstract; but he thought the latter then impracticable. Disapproving of the

[1] John Randolph.

basis of equal imposts as disadvantageous to our country, he saw
no alternative but in adopting that " of the most favored nation."
He "trusted," if the reports of the aggressive conduct of our
people against the Spaniards at Natchez were true, that Congress would not protect them. To a lady applying to him in
behalf of her son, a Virginia "Tory," he expressed the hope that
the latter might recover his property, declaring the following
just and liberal views on a subject in regard to which many
good men differed from him :

" I suppose him to have taken side with the British, before our Declaration of
Independence ; and, if this was the case, I respect the candor of the measure,
though I do not its wisdom. A right to take the side which every man's conscience
approves in a civil contest, is too precious a right, and too favorable to the preservation of liberty, not to be protected by all its well-informed friends."

The interests of his native State were keenly looked after,
whenever occasion offered. He entered with particular relish
into all the preparatory arrangements for procuring for that
State a statue of General Washington; selected and employed
Houdon to execute it; and watched every succeeding step until
it was completed and sent home,[1] with unremitting attention.
He consulted architects, and furnished plans for a State House.
He executed all sorts of commissions in France for his private
friends. He corresponded with General Washington about the
Potomac improvements, and a canal through the Dismal Swamp.
He informed the General that he should " continue uneasy, till
he knew that Virginia had assumed her ultimate boundary to the
westward." Two months after, however, he had become satisfied that the separation of Kentucky was expedient, " whenever
the people of Kentucky should have agreed among themselves."

To his various correspondents in the United States he communicated a vast mass of information in regard to the condition
of things, and on subjects of interest, in Europe. To different
persons he sent new astronomical discoveries and calculations;
improvements in musical instruments; fresh explorations in
natural history; descriptions of fine specimens of architecture;
his opinion of statues and paintings; agricultural and mechanical
inventions; accounts of climate, scenery, and products; ethnological, political, and statistical disquisitions, etc., etc. We

[1] It now stands in the Virginia capitol.

have had our eye on particular instances of all throughout
the preceding enumeration, and they probably do not embrace
a tithe of the topics handled by him every year during his stay
in France. In nearly all, he displays a sharpness of observation,
and uses a vigor of language which, to an intelligent person
interested in the topics treated, make his letters fresh and readable to this day.

It would be inexcusable not to give with some fullness the
impressions formed of Europe, by so sharp an observer occupying Mr. Jefferson's peculiar stand-point. A good many who
dread and denounce European institutions, at a distance, find
their views not a little modified by familiarity. This was undeniably the case with Mr. Adams, though one would think he
found little in the demeanor of the people towards himself, as a
whole, to propitiate him. Jefferson, on the other hand, found
everything which ordinarily propitiates vanity ; and that which
oftentimes secures the affection of the modest, and dazzles the
judgment of the honest, and even the wise. Genius, learning,
official authority, rank, fashion, wealth, beauty—every element
which sways society and individuals—spread their blandish-
ments around him, united to honor him. In that splendid circle
of philosophy, wit, and beauty, for example, which collected constantly at Madame Houdetot's—pronounced by Jefferson the
most agreeable in Paris—where D'Alembert and Diderot had
shone, where St. Lambert was always found, and where De
Grignon uttered his exquisite criticisms and pleasantries, there
was not a more conspicuous figure than the American Ambassador. And if there was a distinguished personage of Paris or
visiting Paris who did not frequent that Ambassador's hotel, it
would be difficult to say who it was. Every class in France
reëchoed his praises, and it is not probable that any American
Minister was ever so caressed, abroad, besides Franklin. We
have seen from an early letter to the latter, how much pleasure
Jefferson anticipated from association with " literati of the first
order," and a " polite court." This association had now come.
Were his anticipations realized ?

It appears that the physical country of France, the natural
character of its people, its culture and its arts, met his highest
expectations. Its genius and learning did not disappoint him,
but there was something—a good deal—yet wanting ! Let him

say himself what it was.   He wrote Colonel Monroe, June 17th, 1785 :

"I sincerely wish you may find it convenient to come here ; the pleasure of the trip will be less than you expect, but the utility greater. It will make you adore your own country, its soil, its climate, its equality, liberty, laws, people, and manners. My God! how little do my countrymen know what precious blessings they are in possession of, and which no other people on earth enjoy. I confess I had no idea of it myself. While we shall see multiplied instances of Europeans going to live in America, I will venture to say no man now living, will ever see an instance of an American removing to settle in Europe, and continuing there. Come, then, and see the proofs of this, and on your return add your testimony to that of every thinking American, in order to satisfy our countrymen how much it is their interest to preserve, uninfected by contagion, those peculiarities in their governments and manners, to which they are indebted for those blessings."

To Mrs. Trist,[1] August 18th :

"I am much pleased with the people of this country. The roughnesses of the human mind are so thoroughly rubbed off with them, that it seems as if one might glide through a whole life among them without a jostle. Perhaps, too, their manners may be the best calculated for happiness to a people in their situation, but I am convinced they fall far short of effecting a happiness so temperate, so uniform, and so lasting, as is generally enjoyed with us. The domestic bonds here are absolutely done away, and where can their compensation be found ? Perhaps they may catch some moments of transport above the level of the ordinary tranquil joy we experience, but they are separated by long intervals, during which all the passions are at sea without rudder or compass. Yet, fallacious as the pursuits of happiness are, they seem on the whole to furnish the most effectual abstraction from a contemplation of the hardness of their government. Indeed, it is difficult to conceive how so good a people, with so good a King, so well-disposed rulers in general, so genial a climate, so fertile a soil, should be rendered so ineffectual for producing human happiness by one single curse—that of a bad form of government. But it is a fact, in spite of the mildness of their governors, the people are ground to powder by the vices of the form of government. Of twenty millions of people supposed to be in France, I am of opinion there are nineteen millions more wretched, more accursed, in every circumstance of human existence, than the most conspicuously wretched individual of the whole United States. I beg your pardon for getting into politics. I will add only one sentiment more of that character, that is, nourish peace with their persons, but war against their manners. Every step we take towards the adoption of their manners is a step to perfect misery."

To the Baron De Geismer, September 6th :

"I am now of an age which does not easily accommodate itself to new manners and new modes of living: and I am savage enough to prefer the woods, the

---

[1] The excellent lady under whose care Martha Jefferson had been during her stay in Philadelphia. She was the mother of Hore Browse Trist, Esquire, who was sent, afterwards, by President Jefferson as first Collector of the port of New Orleans, and who died of yellow fever at the age of twenty-eight. Hore Browse Trist was the father of Nicholas P. Trist, who married a grand-daughter of Mr. Jefferson.

wilds, and the independence of Monticello, to all the brilliant pleasures of this gay capital. I shall therefore, rejoin myself to my native country, with new attachments, and with exaggerated esteem for its advantages; for though there is less wealth there, there is more freedom, more ease, and less misery."

To M. Bellini,' September 30th:

"Behold me at length on the vaunted scene of Europe! It is not necessary for your information, that I should enter into details concerning it. But you are, perhaps, curious to know how this new scene has struck a savage of the mountains of America. Not advantageously, I assure you. I find the general fate of humanity here, most deplorable. The truth of Voltaire's observation, offers itself perpetually, that every man here must be either the hammer or the anvil. It is a true picture of that country to which they say we shall pass hereafter, and where we are to see God and his angels in splendor, and crowds of the damned trampled under their feet. While the great mass of the people are thus suffering under physical and moral oppression, I have endeavored to examine more nearly the condition of the great, to appreciate the true value of the circumstances in their situation, which dazzle the bulk of spectators, and, especially, to compare it with that degree of happiness which is enjoyed in America, by every class of people. Intrigues of love occupy the younger, and those of ambition, the elder part of the great. Conjugal love having no existence among them, domestic happiness, of which that is the basis, is utterly unknown. In lieu of this, are substituted pursuits which nourish and invigorate all our bad passions, and which offer only moments of ecstasy, amidst days and months of restlessness and torment. Much, very much inferior, this, to the tranquil, permanent felicity with which domestic society in America blesses most of its inhabitants; leaving them to follow steadily those pursuits which health and reason approve, and rendering truly delicious the intervals of those pursuits.

"In science, the mass of the people is two centuries behind ours; their literati, half a dozen years before us. Books, really good, acquire just reputation in that time, and so become known to us, and communicate to us all their advances in knowledge. Is not this delay compensated by our being placed out of the reach of that swarm of nonsensical publications, which issues daily from a thousand presses, and perishes almost in issuing? With respect to what are termed polite manners, without sacrificing too much the sincerity of language, I would wish my countrymen to adopt just so much of European politeness, as to be ready to make all those little sacrifices of self, which really render European manners amiable, and relieve society from the disagreeable scenes to which rudeness often subjects it. Here, it seems that a man might pass his life without encountering a single rudeness. In the pleasures of the table, they are far before us, because, with good taste they unite temperance: They do not terminate the most sociable meals by transforming themselves into brutes. I have never yet seen a man drunk in France, even among the lowest of the people. Were I to proceed to tell you how much I enjoy their architecture, sculpture, painting, music, I should want words. It is in these arts they shine. The last of them, particularly, is an enjoyment, the deprivation of which, with us, cannot be calculated. I am almost ready to say, it

- A Florentine gentleman, who was Professor of Modern Languages in William and Mary College.

is the only thing which from my heart I envy them, and which, in spite of all the authority of the Decalogue, I do covet. But I am running on in an estimate of things infinitely better known to you than to me, and which will only serve to convince you, that I have brought with me all the prejudices of country, habit, and age."

To a young Virginia friend, J. Bannister, Jr., who had consulted him in regard to the best European institution for the completion of an education, Mr. Jefferson wrote (October 15th) a reply, which deserves the attentive consideration of all his countrymen. After mentioning the relative merits of the different universities, he proceeds to discuss the utility (to Americans) of going to Europe at all for an education :

"Let us view the disadvantages of sending a youth to Europe. To enumerate them all, would require a volume. I will select a few. If he goes to England, he learns drinking, horse-racing, and boxing. These are the peculiarities of English education. The following circumstances are common to education in that, and the other countries of Europe. He acquires a fondness for European luxury and dissipation, and a contempt for the simplicity of his own country ; he is fascinated with the privileges of the European aristocrats, and sees, with abhorrence, the lovely equality which the poor enjoy with the rich, in his own country ; he contracts a partiality for aristocracy or monarchy ; he forms foreign friendships which will never be useful to him, and loses the season of life for forming, in his own country, those friendships which, of all others, are the most faithful and permanent ; he is led by the strongest of all the human passions, into a spirit for female intrigue, destructive of his own and others' happiness, or a passion for whores, destructive of his health, and, in both cases, learns to consider fidelity to the marriage bed as an ungentlemanly practice, and inconsistent with happiness ; he recollects the voluptuary dress and arts of the European women, and pities and despises the chaste affections and simplicity of those of his own country ; he retains through life, a fond recollection, and a hankering after those places, which were the scenes of his first pleasures and of his first connections ; he returns to his own country, a foreigner, unacquainted with the practices of domestic economy, necessary to preserve him from ruin, speaking and writing his native tongue as a foreigner, and therefore unqualified to obtain those distinctions, which eloquence of the pen and tongue ensures in a free country ; for I would observe to you, that what is called style in writing and speaking, is formed very early in life, while the imagination is warm, and impressions are permanent. I am of opinion, that there never was an instance of a man's writing or speaking his native tongue with elegance, who passed from fifteen to twenty years of age, out of the country where it was spoken. Thus, no instance exists of a person's writing two languages perfectly. That will always appear to be his native language, which was most familiar to him in his youth. It appears to me, then, that an American coming to Europe for education, loses in his knowledge, in his morals, in his health, in his habits, and in his happiness. I had entertained only doubts on this head before I came to Europe : what I see and hear, since I came here, proves more than I had even suspected. Cast your eye over America : who are the men of most learning, of most eloquence, most beloved by their countrymen, and most trusted and promoted by them? They are those who have been educated among them, and whose manners, morals, and habits, are perfectly homogeneous with those of the country.

"Did you expect, by so short a question, to draw such a sermon on yourself? I dare say you did not. But the consequences of foreign education are alarming to me, as an American. I sin, therefore, through zeal, whenever I enter on the subject. You are sufficiently American to pardon me for it."

The following letter on a different class of topics, was addressed to a favorite nephew, Peter Carr—the oldest of that family of children of this name, whom Mr. Jefferson had brought up as members of his own household. It is long, but he who is anxious to study closely the mind and character of the writer, would not excuse the omission of a word of it.

DEAR PETER: PARIS, *August*, 19, 1785.

I received, by Mr. Mazzei, your letter of April the 20th. I am much mortified to hear that you have lost so much time; and that, when you arrived in Williamsburg, you were not at all advanced from what you were when you left Monticello. Time now begins to be precious to you. Every day you lose will retard a day your entrance on that public stage whereon you may begin to be useful to yourself. However, the way to repair the loss is to improve the future time. I trust, that with your dispositions, even the acquisition of science is a pleasing employment. I can assure you, that the possession of it is, what (next to an honest heart) will above all things render you dear to your friends, and give you fame and promotion in your own country. When your mind shall be well improved with science, nothing will be necessary to place you in the highest points of view, but to pursue the interests of your country, the interests of your friends, and your own interests also, with the purest integrity, the most chaste honor. The defect of these virtues can never be made up by all the other acquirements of body and mind. Make these your first object. Give up money, give up fame, give up science, give the earth itself and all it contains, rather than do an immoral act. And never suppose, that in any possible situation, or under any circumstances, it is best for you to do a dishonorable thing, however slightly so it may appear to you. Whenever you are to do a thing, though it can never be known but to yourself, ask yourself how you would act were all the world looking at you, and act accordingly. Encourage all your virtuous dispositions, and exercise them whenever an opportunity arises; being assured that they will gain strength by exercise, as a limb of the body does, and that exercise will make them habitual. From the practice of the purest virtue, you may be assured you will derive the most sublime comforts in every moment of life, and in the moment of death. If ever you find yourself environed with difficulties and perplexing circumstances, out of which you are at a loss how to extricate yourself, do what is right, and be assured that that will extricate you the best out of the worst situations. Though you cannot see, when you take one step, what will be the next, yet follow truth, justice, and plain dealing, and never fear their leading you out of the labyrinth, in the easiest manner possible. The knot which you thought a Gordian one, will untie itself before you Nothing is so mistaken as the supposition, that a person is to extricate himself from a difficulty by intrigue, by chicanery, by dissimulation, by trimming, by an untruth, by an injustice. This increases the difficulties tenfold; and those who pursue these methods, get themselves so involved at length, that they can turn no way but their infamy becomes more exposed. It is of great importance to set a resolution, not to be shaken, never to tell an untruth. There is no vice so mean, so pitiful, so contemptible; and he who permits himself to tell a lie once, finds it much easier to do it a second and third time, till at length it becomes habitual; he tells lies without attending to it, and truths without the world's believing him. This falsehood of the tongue leads to that of the heart, and in time depraves all its good dispositions.

An honest heart being the first blessing, a knowing head is the second. It is time for you now to begin to be choice in your reading; to begin to pursue a regular course in it; and not to suffer yourself to be turned to the right or left by reading any thing out of that course. I have long ago digested a plan for you, suited to the circumstances in which you will be placed. This I will detail to you, from time to time, as you advance. For the present, I advise you to begin a course of ancient history, reading every thing in the original and not in translations. First read Goldsmith's history of Greece. This will give you a digested view of that field. Then take up ancient history in the detail, reading the following books, in the following order: Herodotus, Thucydides, Xenophontis Hellenica, Xenophontis Anabasis, Arrian, Quintus Curtius, Diodorus Siculus, Justin. This shall form the first stage of your historical reading, and is all I need mention to you now. The next will be of Roman history.[1] From that, we will come down to modern history. In Greek and Latin poetry, you have read or will read at school, Virgil, Terence, Horace, Anacreon, Theocritus, Homer, Euripides, Sóphocles. Read also Milton's Paradise Lost, Shakspeare, Ossian, Pope's and Swift's works, in order to form your style in your own language. In morality, read Epictetus, Xenophontis Memorabilia, Plato's Socratic dialogues, Cicero's philosophies, Antoninus, and Seneca. In order to assure a certain progress in this reading, consider what hours you have free from the school and the exercises of the school. Give about two of them, every day, to exercise; for health must not be sacrificed to learning. A strong body makes the mind strong. As to the species of exercise, I advise the gun. While this gives a moderate exercise to the body, it gives boldness, enterprise and independence to the mind. Games played with the ball, and others of that nature, are too violent for the body, and stamp no character on the mind. Let your gun, therefore, be the constant companion of your walks. Never think of taking a book with you. The object of walking is to relax the mind. You should, therefore, not permit yourself even to think while you walk; but divert your attention by the objects surrounding you. Walking is the best possible exercise. Habituate yourself to walk very far. The Europeans value themselves on having subdued the horse to the uses of man; but I doubt whether we have not lost more than we have gained, by the use of this animal. No one has occasioned so much, the degeneracy of the human body. An Indian goes on foot nearly as far in a day, for a long journey, as an enfeebled white does on his horse; and he will tire the best horses. There is no habit you will value so much as that of walking far without fatigue. I would advise you to take your exercise in the afternoon: not because it is the best time for exercise, for certainly it is not, but because it is the best time to spare from your studies; and habit will soon reconcile it to health, and render it nearly as useful as if you gave to that the more precious hours of the day. A little walk of half an hour in the morning.

---

[1] Livy, Sallust, Cæsar, Cicero's epistles, Suetonius, Tacitus, Gibbon.

when you first rise, is advisable also. It shakes off sleep, and produces other good effects in the animal economy. Rise at a fixed and an early hour, and go to bed at a fixed and early hour also. Sitting up late at night is injurious to the health, and not useful to the mind. Having ascribed proper hours to exercise, divide what remain (I mean of your vacant hours) into three portions. Give the principal to History, the other two, which should be shorter, to Philosophy and Poetry. Write to me once every month or two, and let me know the progress you make. Tell me in what manner you employ every hour in the day. The plan I have proposed for you is adapted to your present situation only. When that is changed, I shall propose a corresponding change of plan. I have ordered the following books to be sent to you from London, to the care of Mr. Madison: Herodotus, Thucydides, Xenophon's Hellenics, Anabasis and Memorabilia, Cicero's works, Baretti's Spanish and English Dictionary, Martin's Philosophical Grammar, and Martin's Philosophia Britannica. I will send you the following from hence: Beyzout's Mathematics, De Lalande's Astronomy, Muschenbroek's Physics, Quintus Curtius, Justin, a Spanish Grammar, and some Spanish books. You will observe that Martin, Beyzout, De Lalande, and Muschenbroek, are not in the preceding plan. They are not to be opened till you go to the University. You are now, I expect, learning French. You must push this; because the books which will be put into your hands when you advance into Mathematics, Natural philosophy, Natural history, etc., will be mostly French, these sciences being better treated by the French than the English writers. Our future connection with Spain renders that the most necessary of the modern languages, after the French. When you become a public man, you may have occasion for it, and the circumstance of your possessing that language, may give you a preference over other candidates. I have nothing further to add for the present, but husband well your time, cherish your instructors, strive to make everybody your friend; and be assured that nothing will be so pleasing as your success to, Dear Peter,

Yours affectionately.

In the fall, Mr. Jefferson exchanged the house he had hitherto occupied, for one belonging to the Count de Langeac, at the corner of the Grande Route des Champs Elysées and the Rue Neuve de Berry, which he continued to occupy during his further stay in France. The house was a fine one even for Paris, with a large court and outbuildings, and an extensive garden. He also, subsequently, kept rooms in the Carthusian Monastery on Mount Calvary, to the unbroken solitude of which he could retire when he desired to be out of the reach of interruption. "Whenever he had a press of business," says a manuscript of Martha Jefferson, lying before us, "he was in the habit of taking his papers and going to this hermitage, where he sometimes spent a week or more till he had finished what he had in hand." The author of Anacharsis, and some other of Jefferson's talented literary friends, spent a portion of their time at the same place.

Mr. Jefferson's official correspondence of 1786 opened with

a letter to Mr. Jay, American Secretary of Foreign Affairs, communicating to Congress the substance of various oral and written communications between himself and the Count de Vergennes concerning the commercial regulations between France and the United States. The particular points discussed between them have long since lost all practical interest, but we will name two or three. The French Minister made the common complaint that American trade continued to centre in England and did not come to France. Jefferson demonstrated that this resulted from the laws of trade—that France could not expect America to come to her to purchase, when she did not take American commodities in return. He then showed that of various American exports, such as rice, indigo, flour, fish, and provisions, France produced her own supply, except in the article of rice, and of that she could procure a cheaper though inferior article in the Mediterranean. America could not export peltry and furs so long as the northwestern posts were held by the English; whether she could export potash and naval stores, was yet a matter of experiment. There seemed to be but two articles that she could send to France with a certainty of profit—whale-oil and tobacco. On both there were still very injurious restrictions. Of tobacco, France annually consumed the value of ten million livres, but instead of making it advantageous for it to come directly to her own ports to be paid for on the spot with French merchandise, she now purchased eight-tenths of it in London, paying the money for it. De Vergennes's candid answer to this last proposition presents an admirable specimen of the political economy of the day:

"The Count observed, that my proposition contained what was doubtless useful, but that the King received on this article, at present, the revenue of twenty-eight millions, which was so considerable, as to render them fearful of tampering with it; that the collection of this revenue by way of Farm, was of very ancient date, and that it was always hazardous to alter arrangements of long standing, and of such infinite combinations with the fiscal system."

The renewal of the contract with the Farmers-General[1] being

---

[1] A company which, on condition of paying a stipulated sum annually into the Treasury, was allowed to levy enormous taxes on certain articles and pursuits. Thus they had the monopoly of salt, tobacco, the impost duties at Paris, inland tolls, etc. Sully asserted that when he assumed the direction of the finances, that for the 30 millions paid into the treasury by the Farmers-General, they collected 150 millions! Men destitute of all character, ability, or even knowledge of business—the basest favorites of mistresses and those minions of every shade and degree who grow up under despotism—found places in this association, to be inflated into instant wealth. As would be expected from

then in progress, the American Minister earnestly pressed the idea of leaving tobacco out of it, showing, in his *arithmetical* way, how easily, and with what a vast saving of revenue to the government, the duties on it might be collected by a few direct government officials in half a dozen ports, to which the import could be confined. Vergennes saw the force of this, but he could " make no promises." The clear-sighted old minister was disinclined by nature and habit to " tamper " with " arrangements of long standing." The Farmers-General were a body which could not be induced, by a ministerial nod, to relinquish one of their best monopolies. And they were powerful enough to overthrow a minister not as firmly seated as Vergennes, and to offer a resistance formidable to any minister, if not to the government itself. If Vergennes was willing to come in conflict with them, it might not be so with his principal, Calonne, the Comptroller-General. In short, a thousand difficulties lay in the way.

But Vergennes acquitted himself of his duty as an honest and able statesman, by favoring Jefferson's proposition. Calonne extricated himself characteristically. His uniform policy was to make no reforms, to cry all was well, to keep up appearances at all hazards, and to support this display by any expedients, however degrading and desperate. How and where he expected this policy would end, it is impossible to say. Probably he expected, like Louis XV., that *after him* " would come the deluge." It was no part of his plan to provoke internal opposition and investigation. He avoided Jefferson's clinching argument that it would be immensely profitable to the government, as well as the manufacturers of France (whose goods would thus find a new market) to exempt tobacco from the contract with the Farmers-General, by saying that the contract had already proceeded too far to admit of honorable retraction.

Vergennes had several times complained to the American Minister of the conduct of the American States, severally and

---

the constitution of the body, they executed their power with inhuman and oftentimes with gratuitous severity. They proceeded against the country people for their salt duties, inland tolls, etc., oftentimes when they were engaged in their harvests, distraining, con fiscating and selling their property at the most ruinous sacrifices. Lamentation was met with insult, attempts at evasion with a prison, and a shadow of opposition with the swords and bullets of the ready soldiery. This was one of the enormous grievances in France which cried to Heaven for the avenging besom of the Revolution.

collectively. In a formal interview he now recapitulated his complaints. He urged that Massachusetts and New Hampshire had violated the United States treaty with France, by their navigation acts; that Georgia had done the same thing by its treatment of the French heirs of General Oglethorpe; that, in consequence of this separate action, arrangements with the American States could not be sufficiently depended upon; that their administration of civil justice was so tardy that French merchants looked upon American debts as desperate; that the American commercial regulations were difficult to observe, and "disgusting" to Frenchmen. On the two last heads, Jefferson says he did not choose to "hazard himself" to reply in French in which they were then talking. Possibly, too (though he intimates nothing of the kind), the calm temper was a little ruffled! He therefore prepared a written answer, which will be found published in his correspondence.[1] It is too long even for analysis here. As a specimen of terse, calm narration—unanswerable argument—proper respect for the dignity of his nation —and yet an avoidance of boastful grandiloquence—it will still well repay perusal.

Mr. Jefferson had, the preceding year, rather urgently suggested to General Washington, that he decline to accept, as a gratuity, certain shares of the Potomac and James River Companies, voted to him by the Virginia General Assembly.[2] General Washington informed him, in reply, that he purposed to devote the proceeds to the foundation of charity schools. Jefferson's answer (Jan. 4, 1786) is worthy of notice:

"The institutions you propose to establish, by the shares in the Potomac and James River Companies, given you by the Assembly, and the particular objects of those institutions, are most worthy. It occurs to me, however, that if the bill ' for the more general diffusion of knowledge,' which is in the revisal, should be passed, it would supersede the use, and obscure the existence of the charity schools you have thought of. I suppose, in fact, that that bill, or some other like it, will be passed. I never saw one received with more enthusiasm than that was, in the year 1778, by the House of Delegates, who ordered it to be printed. And it seemed afterwards, that nothing but the extreme distress of our resources prevented its being carried into execution, even during the war. It is an axiom in my mind that our liberty can never be safe but in the hands of the people themselves, and that, too, of the people with a certain degree of instruction. This it is the business of the State to effect, and on a general plan. Should you see a probability of this, how-

[1] See his dispatch to Mr. Jay, Jan. 2, 1786, Randolph edition; not in Cong. edition.
[2] Jefferson to Washington, July 10, 1785.

ever, you can never be at a loss for worthy objects of this donation. Even the remitting that proportion of the toll, on all articles transported, would present itself under many favorable considerations, and it would, in effect, be to make the State do in a certain proportion, what they ought to have done wholly: for I think they should clear all the rivers, and lay them open and free to all. However, you are infinitely the best judge, how the most good may be effected with these shares."

In the early part of 1786 (Jan. 13), Mr. Jefferson replied to a series of questions propounded to him by M. de Meusnier, author of that part of the *Encyclopédie Méthodique* included under the heads "Political Economy" and "Diplomacy." The questions involved many important points in the history and the past and present civil systems of the United States; and they received elaborate answers. The whole article on the "United States," prepared for the same work, was submitted to Mr. Jefferson's corrections; and it drew out numerous ones. These last, and the communication to M. Meusnier,[1] contain statements of facts and opinions in regard to the constitutional, commercial, and civil history of the United States, and of several separate States, of great abstract value (we doubt whether many of these facts have any other contemporarily attesting and indisputably authentic record) and possessing the additional interest of disclosing, in a strong light, many of Jefferson's opinions, where he differed widely from the mass of his contemporaries. Our plan does not allow us to include these long papers.

A ruinous system of American overtrading in Europe, and particularly in England, had followed the peace of 1782. Commercial speculation ran mad, and wide-spread bankruptcy was the speedy result. The facts were bad enough in themselves, and they were seized upon by the British press to brand the whole American people as cheats and swindlers. All Europe rung with accounts of American parvenues living in gaudy splendor, on means almost literally filched from British manufacturers and traders. There was no end to the variety and rancor of these statements; and they engendered a constantly growing animosity in Great Britain, and scorn and disgust elsewhere. France was perhaps the only foreign country where kindly or even respectful feelings towards the United States, were anything like generally entertained; and we have

---

[1] They are published, without date, in Randolph's edition of his Correspondence vol. i. pp. 398-430; in the Congress edition, vol. ix. p. 244-304.

already had a hint that the French merchants partook some-what of the feelings of the British ones. But in England, the commercial class was one of paramount influence—in France, it was a cipher.

Both Jefferson and Adams were called upon to experience bitter mortifications on this subject. The correspondence of both gives ample evidence of their divided indignation—indignation at the real swindlers in America, and indignation that the folly and baseness of a comparative handful of our population (and a heavy proportion of these rotten traders were English) should thus throw disgrace on the whole. We shall, from time to time, give expressions of Jefferson on the subject, and here is one, in a letter to A. Stewart (January 25th):

"American reputation, in Europe, is not such as to be flattering to its citizens. Two circumstances are particularly objected to us; the non-payment of our debts, and the want of energy in our government. These discourage a connection with us. I own it to be my opinion, that good will arise from the destruction of our credit. I see nothing else which can restrain our disposition to luxury, and to the change of those manners which alone can preserve republican government. As it is impossible to prevent credit, the best way would be to cure its ill effects, by giving an instantaneous recovery to the creditor. This would be reducing purchases on credit, to purchases for ready money. A man would then see a prison painted on everything he wished, but had not ready money to pay for."

This was surely proposing a radical remedy for the disease!

In the same letter occurs Mr. Jefferson's first expression (so far as we remember) in regard to the safety of including large territories within a republic, and in regard to what is now termed "Annexation" doctrines.

"I fear from an expression in your letter, that the people of Kentucky think of separating, not only from Virginia (in which they are right), but also from the confederacy. I own I should think this a most calamitous event, and such a one as every good citizen should set himself against. Our present federal limits are not too large for good government, nor will the increase of votes in Congress produce any ill effect. On the contrary, it will drown the little divisions at present existing there. Our confederacy must be viewed as the nest, from which all America, North and South, is to be peopled. We should take care, too, not to think it for the interest of that great continent, to press too soon on the Spaniards. Those countries cannot be in better hands. My fear is, that they are too feeble to hold them till our population can be sufficiently advanced, to gain it from them, piece by piece. The navigation of the Mississippi we must have. This is all we are, as yet, ready to receive."

In a letter to Madison, February 8th, we catch a slight, low rumbling of the coming revolution. Urging a gift of lands by Virginia to Rochambeau and Lafayette, Jefferson prophetically says, in regard to the latter:

> "Nor, am I sure that the day will not come, when it might be an useful asylum to him. The time of life at which he visited America, was too well adapted to receive good and lasting impressions, to permit him ever to accommodate himself to the principles of monarchical government; and it will need all his own prudence, and that of his friends, to make this country a safe residence for him."

An Austrian prison proved Lafayette's best "asylum!" Rochambeau escaped about as narrowly. D'Estaing went to the guillotine. Other French officers who served in America perished on the guillotine, in the dungeon, or in exile. They all had imbibed "impressions" which unfitted them equally for the tyranny of a single despot, or the tyranny of a bloody and licentious rabble. Some phase of the Revolution, therefore, proved fatal to the life or the prospects of nearly all of them who had not the good fortune to die before it opened.

John Ledyard, the American traveller, described by Jefferson as "a man of genius, of some science, and of fearless courage and enterprise," was in Paris in February, in the hope of forming a company to embark in the fur trade on the west coast of America. Failing in this, and "being out of business, and of a roaming, restless character," Jefferson suggested to him a geographical exploration of the same region, making his journey thither eastward through the territories of Russia. Jefferson undertook to have the permission of the Empress solicited, furnished Ledyard with some funds, and introduced him to those who furnished him with more. The Empress at once refused her permission, but the sanguine traveller pushed on to St. Petersburg, trusting that he should be able to secure it by his personal representations. Catharine II. had gone to the Crimea, and he ventured to proceed without her approbation. Having traversed Europe and the frozen regions of Northern Asia to within two hundred miles of Kamtschatka, he was overtaken by an arrest, carried back to the borders of Poland, and there set at liberty, to reflect on the consequences of trusting to the forbearance of absolute power. Before he reached London again, he underwent sufferings and degradations too great "to be dis closed" by one who, on his other journeys, has revealed so much that was both humiliating and distressing.[1]

Towards the close of February, Colonel Smith, Mr. Adams's Secretary of Legation (and then, or subsequently, his son-in-law), arrived in Paris with a letter from Mr. Adams, pressing Jefferson's immediate attendance in London, as a Minister was there from Tripoli, authorized to negotiate with them, and as the Portuguese Ambassador had received instructions which would probably make a satisfactory treaty with his government, readily attainable were the negotiators of it "all on the spot together." "A third motive had also its weight" with Jefferson. "He hoped his attendance there [in London], and the necessity of shortening it, might be made use of to force a decisive answer from that [the British] Court."[2]

He got his arrangements made for his departure on the 6th of March, and before starting sent another and a written adieu to Martha, from which the following is an extract:

To Martha Jefferson.

Paris, *March* 6, 1786.

MY DEAR MARTHA:

*   *   *   *   *   *   *   *

I need not tell you what pleasure it gives me to see you improve in everything agreeable and useful. The more you learn, the more I love you; and I rest the happiness of my life on seeing you beloved by all the world, which you will be sure to be, if, to a good heart, you join those accomplishments so peculiarly

---

[1] To the point of his dismissal from the Russian dominions, we have substantially followed Jefferson's statements in his Memoir, except that he there makes no mention of aiding Ledyard in the way of funds. Jefferson's pocket account-book shows that he *did* so aid him. And we find the following curious entries: "February 20th. Received of M. de Lafayette to be paid to Ledyard, *on account of Empress of Russia*, 600 francs." "Feb. 21. Paid Ledyard, as above, 600 francs." The only explanation we can offer of this, is, that Lafayette may have advanced the money, on some understanding with the Russian Ambassador, M. de Sémoulin, or, more likely still, with the Empress's special correspondent, Baron Grimm. Neither of these seems to have anticipated a refusal from the Empress; and from the wording of the above entry (worded, too, by the, in business matters, mathematically exact Jefferson), we cannot help partly conjecturing that they anticipated she would give something besides her consent.

A Life of Ledyard, by J. A. St. John, lying before us, states that he actually had a pass from the Empress, but this is clearly a mistake, as were Jefferson's declarations of the same kind, contained in his Notes of the Life of Captain Lewis. These he corrects, as already mentioned, in his Memoir.

The stories narrated of poor Ledyard's simplicity and daringness, sound fabulous. On this trip just spoken of to St. Petersburg, he reached Stockholm when the Baltic opposite there was not yet free enough from ice to be navigable, and accordingly, with characteristic precipitation, he immediately set about going on foot round the whole Gulf of Bothnia, at the northern extremity of which the Arctic winter yet reigned—and a distance of about twelve hundred miles, to attain what a few weeks' delay would enable him to attain by passing considerably less than one hundred miles by water, in a ship! He was seven weeks on his journey, and thus, doubtless, lost as much in time, as he did in distance!

[2] Letter to Mr. Jay, March 12, 1786.

pleasing in your sex. Adieu, my dear child ; lose no moment in improving your head, nor any opportunity of exercising your heart in benevolence.

Yours affectionately.

He reached London on the 11th of March. The Tripolitan Minister asked the modest sum of thirty thousand guineas for a peace with his particular Court, and as much more for Tunis, for which he also claimed authority to act. "Calculating on this scale," said Jefferson, " Morocco should ask sixty thousand, and Algiers one hundred and twenty thousand." The American Ministers, authorized to offer no approach to such sums, spun out the negotiation, merely in the hope of obtaining information.

With Portugal a treaty was promptly concluded, but a clause was inserted in relation to the introduction of ground breadstuffs into that country, which its minister believed would lead his government to reject the treaty ; and so it resulted.

Adams and Jefferson agreed on a summary form of a commercial treaty to be offered to England. It proposed " an exchange of citizenship for our citizens, our ships, and our productions generally, except as to office."[1] Jefferson thus described the reception of himself and colleague by the Court, and of their proposed treaty by the Ministry :

" On my presentation, as usual, to the King and Queen, at their levées, it was impossible for anything to be more ungracious, than their notice of Mr. Adams and myself. I saw, at once, that the ulcerations of mind in that quarter left nothing to be expected on the subject of my attendance ; and, on the first conference with the Marquis of Caermarthen, the Minister for foreign affairs, the distance and disinclination which he betrayed in his conversation, the vagueness and evasions of his answers to us, confirmed me in the belief of their aversion to have anything to do with us. We delivered him, however, our *Projet*, Mr. Adams not despairing as much as I did, of its effect. We afterwards, by one or more notes, requested his appointment of an interview and conference, which, without directly declining, he evaded, by pretences of other pressing occupations for the moment. After staying there seven weeks, till within a few days of the expiration of our commission, I informed the minister, by note, that my duties at Paris required my return to that place, and that I should, with pleasure, be the bearer of any commands to his ambassador there. He answered, that he had none, and wishing me a pleasant journey, I left London the 26th, and arrived at Paris the 30th of April."

Neither Mr. Adams's Diary, nor his diplomatic letters, we believe, give any particulars of this presentation scene.[2] His

[1] Memoir.

[2] Since writing the above, Mr. Adams's Life, by his grandson, has been published : and in it (p. 420) we find the following :

usual accounts of his interviews with the King and Minister of
Foreign Affairs, are somewhat differently colored. He represents them as exhibiting quite sufficient personal courtesy; and
George III. became, in the remembrances of after years, a very
amiable and good sort of an old gentleman, in his eyes. It has
been conjectured, therefore, that Jefferson received a "colder
shoulder" than Mr. Adams, from Royalty—or else that he
looked through jaundiced eyes. But they do not seem to have
differed at the time in any important view of the case. In
the joint dispatch home on the above occasion, signed by both,
and probably written by Mr. Adams, they speak of clauses that
ought to be added to their *projet* of a treaty, "if there was the
smallest symptom of an intimation [on the part of Great Britain]
to treat at all." And the dispatch proceeds:

"But there is not. There is no party nor individual here in favor of a treaty,
but upon the principle that the United States will retaliate, if there is not one. All
agree that if America will suffer England to pocket all her navigation, England
would be unwise not to avail herself of the advantage."[1]

"Mr. Jefferson, who soon joined Mr. Adams in London, for the purpose of carrying
out, in the case of the British government, the powers vested in the commission to
negotiate commercial treaties, has left his testimony of the treatment he met with at
court. The King turned his back upon the American Commissioners, a hint which, of
course, was not lost upon the circle of his subjects in attendance."
[1] Diplomatic Correspondence of the U. S. from 1783 to 1789, vol. ii. p. 337.
  Mr. Adams wrote Mr. Jay, December 15, 1785:
"So much of his [the King's] time is, and has been consumed in this [small talk],
that he is in all the great affairs of society and government as *weak*, as far as I can judge,
as we ever understood him to be in America. He is also as *obstinate* . . . . *He has
a pleasure in his own will and way, without which he would be miserable*, which seems to be
the true principle upon which he has always chosen and rejected ministers. *He has an
habitual contempt of patriots and patriotism*, at least for what are called in this country by
those names, and takes a delight in mortifying all who have any reputation for such
qualities, and in supporting those who have a counter character. Upon this principle
only can I account for the number of Tories which were forced into the administration
of the Earl of Shelburne, the Duke of Portland and Mr. Pitt, and for the immoderate
attachment to American refugees which has appeared in all of them."—*Dip. Corr.*,
vol. iv. p. 468.
"Lord Caermarthen is rich and of high rank, very civil and obliging, but is not enough
of a man of business to have influence in the Cabinet, or to project or conduct anything."
—*Ib.* p. 471.
"I am like to be as insignificant here as you can imagine. I shall be treated as I have
been, with all the civility that is shown to other foreign Ministers, but shall do nothing;
I shall not even be answered, at least this is my opinion."—*Ib.* p. 474.
"If the ministry really are desirous of an equitable settlement, I am well persuaded
they cannot yet carry it in Parliament; so I hope the States will persevere in their own
measures, and that even all the Southern States will at least lay heavy duties upon the
tonnage of such nations as have not treaties with us." (Jan. 4, 1786.)—*Ib.* p. 477.
"This nation would now crouch to France for the sake of being insolent to us."
(Jan. 21.)—*Ib.* p. 480.
  The following is from Mr. Adams's Diary, during Mr. Jefferson's stay in England:
"*April 30th, Thursday.*—Presented Mr. Hamilton to the Queen at the drawing-room.
Dined at Mr. Paradise's, Count Woronzow and his gentleman and chaplain, M. Soderini,
the Venetian Minister, Mr. Jefferson, Dr. Bancroft, Colonel Smith, and my family. Went
at nine o'clock to the French Ambassador's ball, where were two or three hundred people, chiefly ladies. Here I met the Marquis of Lansdowne and the Earl of Harcourt. These
two noblemen ventured to enter into conversation with me, so did Sir George Young. But
there is an awkward timidity in general. These people cannot look me in the face; there

Mr. Jefferson's general impressions of physical England were thus summed up in a letter written after his return to France (May 4th), to his early friend Page:

"I returned but three or four days ago, from a two months' trip to England. I traversed that country much, and own, both town and country fell short of my expectations. Comparing it with this, I found a much greater proportion of barrens, a soil, in other parts, not naturally so good as this, not better cultivated, but better manured, and therefore more productive. This proceeds from the practice of long leases there, and short ones here. The laboring people here are poorer than in England. They pay about one half their produce in rent; the English, in general, about a third. The gardening in that country is the article in which it surpasses all the earth. I mean their pleasure gardening. This, indeed, went far beyond my ideas. The city of London, though handsomer than Paris, is not so handsome as Philadelphia. Their architecture is in the most wretched style I ever saw, not meaning to except America, where it is bad, nor even Virginia, where it is worse than in any other part of America which I have seen. The mechanical arts in London are carried to a wonderful perfection."

And he energetically added, on another subject:

is conscious guilt and shame in their countenances when they look at me. They feel that they have behaved ill, and that I am sensible of it."—*Life and Works*, vol. iii. p. 393.

The particular motive assigned for the inability of the English people to look Mr. John Adams "in the face"—that they felt that they had behaved ill, and that "*he* was sensible of it," is deliciously and most laughably characteristic of the writer. But it shows pretty plainly whether Jefferson was mistaken in regard to the state of things and the feeling towards America, when he visited England.

It would not be quite fair to George the Third to omit Mr. Adams's picture of his personal virtues and *accomplishments!*

"The King, I really think, is the most accomplished courtier in his dominions; with all the affability of Charles the Second, he has all the domestic virtues of Charles the First!!"—*Dip. Corr.* vol. iv. p. 467.

That George III. possessed some of the leading domestic virtues, there is no doubt. His palace was not a bagnio—and he was generally respectable in his private character. His deportment towards his son, the Prince of Wales, was, however, harsh and injudicious. He was everywhere, *where he encountered the slightest opposition*, to the last degree arbitrary and stubborn. The American War was prolonged *for years* to gratify his dull, sullen obstinacy. If it is necessary to apotheosize a king, because, as far back as the eighteenth century, he respected the decencies of private life, we certainly have no objections! We are willing that one of the plainest and most ungraceful men in mind and person in his dominions—as plain as his Hanoverian predecessors, who were the laughing-stocks of old Jacobite songs—should be compared with the two most accomplished princes of the Stuart race, though probably the latter would have thought their *dethronement* by the "wee, wee German Lairdies," *bad enough!* We should not have objected if Mr. Adams's prurient fancy had clothed Charlotte Sophia of Mecklenburg-Strelitz (also indisputably correct and decorous in personal character) with the graces of a Mary of Modena, if not of a Mary of Scotland! Mr. Adams, with his sturdy puritanism of character, and his *bitter and open dislike of France*, was rather a favorite, we think, with the royal pair—and it is hard to resist any approach to graciousness from such quarters! But if Mr. Adams found, in his Brunswick Apollo, the ruler of a nation willing to crouch even to France, "*for the sake of being insolent to us*"—himself always heading the most violent anti-American party—we submit that it is rather hard to hold another American minister, on whom never shone the "grace" of the royal face, guilty of prejudice, personal hostility to England, and bitter malevolence towards kings in general, and George III. in particular, for averring no more than Mr. Adams himself repeatedly did!

[Since writing the preceding, it would appear, however (see last note), that Mr Adams *did* join in this particular statement of Jefferson—that their common reception was as "ungracious" as possible.]

" But of these I need not speak, because, of them my countrymen have unfortunately too many samples before their eyes. I consider the extravagance which has seized them, as a more baneful evil than Toryism was during the war. It is the more so, as the example is set by the best and most amiable characters among us. Would a missionary appear, who would make frugality the basis of his religious system, and go through the land, preaching it up as the only road to salvation, I would join his school, though not generally disposed to seek my religion out of the dictates of my own reason, and feelings of my own heart. These things have been more deeply impressed on my mind, by what I have heard and seen in England. That nation hate us, their ministers hate us, and their King, more than all other men. They have the impudence to avow this, though they acknowledge our trade important to them. But they think, we cannot prevent our countrymen from bringing that into their laps. A conviction of this determines them to make no terms of commerce with us. They say, they will pocket our carrying trade as well as their own. Our overtures of commercial arrangements have been treated with a derision, which shows their firm persuasion, that we shall never unite to suppress their commerce, or even to impede it. I think their hostility towards us is much more deeply rooted at present, than during the war."

These views of the feelings of Great Britain towards America, are repeated to Richard H. Lee, and a number of other correspondents.

During his stay in England, Mr. Jefferson visited such of its classic localities as were most accessible, and also its most celebrated country seats and gardens. Mr. Adams generally accompanied him, and sometimes Colonel Smith. He kept a brief journal—principally confined, however, to gardens, and to those described in Whateley's work on gardening. He says his " inquiries were directed chiefly to such practical things as might enable him to estimate the expense of making and maintaining a garden in that style." [1] He mentions Chiswick, Hampton Court, Twickenham, Esher Place, Claremont, Paynshill, Woburn, Caversham, Wotton, Stowe, Leasowes, Hagley, Blenheim, Enfield Chase, Moor Park, and Kew.

It must be confessed that his comments are usually " practical " enough ! He speaks often, it is true, of the beautiful, the merely beautiful, and his taste, we doubt not, will be found sufficiently correct. His language is graceful. But he looked, even at the beautiful, with a sort of " arithmetical " eye. Beauty, with him, was a utility, and he therefore sought it. But he apparently kindled into no fine imaginings as he gazed on it. He measured its height and depths—duly estimated its

[1] This whole paper will be found in the Congress edition of his Works, commencing at vol. ix. p. 367.

components—counted its accessories. We do not mean to say that he was one of those men who would have applied a pocket measure to the nose, or the mouth, of the Venus de Medici—but he was equally not one of those who

> ———" gaze and turn away, and know not where,
> Dazzled and drunk with beauty, till the heart
> Reels with its fullness."

He lacked what, in the technology of a new (and not yet undisputed) science, is termed ideality,[1] and he clearly lacked sentiment. The creative imagination did not accompany an eye which was attuned to the simple perception of beauty or grandeur. He wandered amidst scenes linked with a thousand memories which would have come sweeping in notes of joy or dirge-like wailings, through the mind of a half as well read man as himself, who possessed the quality which we are describing him as lacking; yet if one such memory had power to touch a chord of his feelings, the fact is sedulously disguised! Twickenham does not call out a word in regard to his favorite Pope (precisely the poet to be such a man's favorite); the sigh uttered at the Leasowes, is not for the man or the poet, but for the broken-hearted debtor; no legends of the mouldering towers of Woodstock, or the " Dædalian labyrinth " of the fair Rosamond Clifford, stole over him while gazing on the magnificence of Blenheim. Nay, more; the Journal does not mention (but the pocket account-book does) that on the 6th of April, leaving Banbury (famous in nursery rhyme) he took a post-chaise to Kineton, and from there to *Stratford-upon-Avon!* There, says the last named chronicle, he "paid postillion 3*s.*; for seeing house where Shakspeare was born, 1*s.*; seeing his tomb-stone, 1*s.*; entertainment, 4*s.* 2*d.*; servants, 2*s.*; horses to Hockley, 12*s.* This is the only allusion to his visit to this place, that we remember in all of Mr. Jefferson's writings, published or unpublished. On the fields of Edgehill and Worcester—amidst the memorials of Westminster Abbey—in the classic precincts of Oxford—under the frowning bastions of Dover—he is equally mute.

This is worse than Mr. Adams! *He* declares that " we

---

[1] Not to be confounded with *ideology,* as used by French and some English (or American) writers.

[himself and Jefferson] cut a chip, according to custom," from Shakspeare's chair; and his emotions prompt *him* to this very original declaration: "Paintings and sculpture would be thrown away upon his [Shakspeare's] fame. His wit, fancy, his taste and judgment, his knowledge of nature, of life and character, are immortal!" A brighter scintillation still broke from the "Colossus," on the battle-field of Worcester. "The people in the neighborhood appeared so ignorant and careless " " that he was provoked," and exclaimed: "And do Englishmen so soon forget the ground where liberty was fought for? Tell your neighbors and your children that this is holy ground; much holier than that on which your churches stand. All England should come in pilgrimage to this hill once a year." This speech, says Mr. Adams, " animated them [the rustics], and they seemed much pleased with it." We dare say they were, and it would have been worth a little to watch the workings of Jefferson's eyebrows during this interesting scene!

Again we say that Jefferson did not belong wholly to the Utilitarian School. That he records nothing, does not prove that he felt nothing. It perhaps shows that sentimental views were not uppermost in his mind—that they were entirely secondary to the practical. At all events, such was the fact. But he could talk interestingly, if not exactly poetically, of the associations suggested by viewing memorable scenes—as many of his living auditors can yet testify. His conversations showed that such recollections flowed in placid and quiet currents through his mind. And his house, his grounds, his gardens, his love of architecture and other arts, all show that he could feel and act apart from the standard of dry, rigid utility—that he was possessed of an æsthetic as well as an intellectual taste and cultivation. We do not know how to describe the æsthetic side of his character any better than by saying he loved and culti-vated the beautiful—but possessed no romance of character. If " a primrose by a river's brim," was nothing to him but a " yel-low primrose," it required no associations, no sentimentality, to make it an object of sweet and simple beauty. If the ancient was no holier to him than the present—if he saw the footsteps of human progress pointing forward instead of backward—we have yet to learn where, in a single instance, the iron mace of the iconoclast shattered anything because it was ancient, or because it was beautiful. It was the false *faith* that was uprooted—the *fane*, with its antique carvings, and frescoed walls, and mediæval gloom, was left undisturbed.

One of Mr. Jefferson's first occupations after his return to France, was to forward to Mr. Drayton, for the Agricultural Society of South Carolina, seeds of the St. Foin (Sanfoin) grass, and some other seeds, for experiment in that State. During his stay abroad, he thus forwarded to different parts of the United States, in numerous parcels, and with particular care, plants or seeds of the olive, upland rice, various kinds of grasses, cork oak, etc., etc. There were few agricultural productions of value, or new agricultural implements, in Europe, which gave the least promise of being valuable in any part of his own country, which were not carefully examined by him, sent to their appropriate destinations, and minute directions for their management sent with them.

The new contract with the French Farmers-General was finished during Jefferson's absence in England. It contained a clause allowing the King to withdraw the article of tobacco from the effect of the contract when he chose—a marked concession to the force of Jefferson's suggestions on that point. To procure such withdrawal, as soon as the preceding lease should expire (about the close of 1786), Jefferson now bent his efforts. Lafayette volunteered his aid on the same side. A committee was appointed to investigate the question. Jefferson did not consider it appropriate for him to act on it, but Lafayette did—well supplied by Jefferson with all the necessary argumentative ammunition. Two of the Farmers-General represented the opposing interest. Both sides prepared memorials. De Vergennes, after the examination of these, was decidedly for the withdrawal. Calonne hesitated, and here the matter came to another stand for a time.

Various other negotiations took place between Jefferson and the Foreign Bureau, during the summer, all conducted in the most amicable spirit on the part of France. Jefferson also, having ascertained that France would not interfere to protect the Barbary States against a combination of the lesser maritime powers, nor permit England to do so, if disposed, set himself busily about maturing such a combination—in pursuance of his favorite idea that it would be cheaper and vastly more respectable to conquer than purchase a peace of them. His plan was to have a dozen frigates, and as many tenders, jointly and proportionately furnished by the interested powers, and to have half of these kept in perpetual cruise off the Barbary coast.[1] Portugal, Naples, the Two Sicilies, Venice, Malta, Denmark, and Sweden, evinced an inclinationn to make the arrangement, and nothing was lacking but the action of the American Government, which was expected to furnish one frigate. Congress had not energy enough to do this, and so the whole thing fell through. The United States paid for their remissness, by being compelled, subsequently, to carry on this war alone.

We get another vivid view of European political civilization, after a *year more* of observation, in a letter to Mr. Wythe, dated August 13th :

"Our act for freedom of religion is extremely applauded. The ambassadors and ministers of the several nations of Europe, resident at this court, have asked of me copies of it, to send to their sovereigns, and it is inserted at full length in several books now in the press; among others in the new Encyclopedia. I think it will produce considerable good even in these countries, where ignorance, superstition, poverty, and oppression of body and mind, in every form, are so firmly settled on the mass of the people, that their redemption from them can never be hoped. If all the sovereigns of Europe were to set themselves to work, to emancipate the minds of their subjects from their present ignorance and prejudices, and that, as zealously as they now endeavor the contrary, a thousand years would not place them on that high ground on which our common people are now setting out. Ours could not have been so fairly placed under the control of the common sense of the people, had they not been separated from their parent stock, and kept from contamination, either from them, or the other people of the Old World, by the intervention of so wide an ocean. To know the worth of this, one must see the want of it here. I think by far the most important bill in our whole code, is that for the diffusion of knowledge among the people. No other sure foundation can be devised for the preservation of freedom and happiness. If anybody thinks that kings, nobles, or priests are good conservators of the public happiness, send him here. It is the best school in the universe to cure him of that folly. He will see here, with his own eyes, that these descriptions of men are an abandoned confederacy against the happiness of the mass of the people. The omnipotence of their effect cannot be better proved, than in this country, particularly, where, notwithstanding the finest soil upon earth, the finest climate under heaven, and a people of the most benevolent, the most gay and amiable character of which the human form is susceptible; where such a people, I say, surrounded by so many blessings from nature, are loaded with misery, by kings, nobles, and priests, and by them alone. Preach, my dear sir, a crusade against ignorance; establish and improve the law for educating the common people. Let our countrymen know, that the people alone can protect us against these evils, and that the tax which will be paid for this

[1] The plan entire will be found in the Congress edition of his Works, vol. ix. p. 387.

purpose, is not more than the thousandth part of what will be paid to kings, priests, and nobles, who will rise up among us if we leave the people in ignorance. The people of England, I think, are less oppressed than here. But it needs but half an eye to see, when among them, that the foundation is laid in their dispositions for the establishment of a despotism. Nobility, wealth, and pomp, are the objects of their admiration. They are by no means the free minded people, we suppose them in America. Their learned men, too, are few in number, and are less learned, and infinitely less emancipated from prejudice, than those of this country."

In September, Mr. Jefferson furnished an extensive series of answers to questions, and corrections of submitted statements, for a French work on America by M. Soulés. The paper is in the Congress edition of his Works,[1] and we shall here transcribe but a single paragraph, giving the writer's opinion on a somewhat mooted point—whether the United States would have secured their independence without the aid of France:

"Their [the Americans'] main confidence was in their own resources. They considered foreign aid as probable and desirable, but not essential. I believe myself, from the whole of what I have seen of our resources and perseverance, that had we never received any foreign aid, we should not have obtained our independence. But that we should have made a peace with Great Britain on any terms we pleased short of that, which would have been a subjection to the same king, a union of force in war, etc. 2. That had France supplied us plentifully with money, suppose about four millions of guineas a year, without entering into the war herself at all, we should have established our independence, but it would have cost more time and blood, but less money. 3. That France, aiding us as she did, with money and forces, shortened much the time, lessened the expense of blood, but at a greater expense of money to her than would have otherwise been requisite."

On the 27th of September, Jefferson, in behalf of the Commonwealth of Virginia, addressed a communication to the principal civil functionaries of Paris, requesting them to accept a bust of Lafayette, and "to place it where, doing most honor to him, it would most gratify the feelings of an allied nation." The bust was accepted, and inaugurated, with appropriate forms, in the *Hôtel de Ville*.

This event was not without significance. By French usage, the King was the sole fountain of honor. The ready waiver of this objection on the part of an old punctilious monarchy (which had never before waived it), and the willingness evinced to give an important prominence to Lafayette, showed the influence of the American government, or rather of its Minister, at this period. Lafayette's American sympathies were so strong and

[1] Commencing vol. ix. p. 393.

undisguised that he was the avowed champion of the United
States on all questions, and an open actor for them in all their
negotiations. It would be unjust to him to say that he was
under the influence of Jefferson, to an extent in any degree im-
plicating the independence of his judgment—but we deem it as
honorable to him as to Jefferson, to declare, what we believe to
be the truth, that he looked to the latter with unbounded confidence and respect—as his senior in the school of politics towards
which the Marquis was rapidly drifting—and as an almost infallible political adviser. On the other hand, Jefferson had the
greatest respect and attachment for Lafayette, found him most
useful to the United States, and took good care to throw him
into the foreground in France and America on every practicable
occasion. Jefferson has been severely censured for saying, in a
private confidential letter, that Lafayette had a "*canine* thirst
for popularity." If the word "canine" was used in any invi-
dious sense, every American would assuredly regret the application of it to this national benefactor. That it could not have
been so intended Jefferson's uniform and constant way of warmly
lauding his acts, his motives, and his character, would be sufficient proof. And then we find that Jefferson applied the same
word to himself, speaking of his own "canine" appetite or
thirst for reading.[1] It was one of his favorite *strong* adjectives,
borrowed, very likely, from Lord Bolingbroke's remarks on
the "Absurdity of Useless Learning." His lordship, in these,
says : "All history is not an object of curiosity for any man.
He who improperly, wantonly, and absurdly makes it so, indulges a sort of canine appetite," etc. Jefferson was familiar
with Bolingbroke, and hence, probably, the derivation of a
rather disagreeably sounding adjective. He meant by it merely
a very strong, or an inordinate desire. If he was to blame for
saying thus much of Lafayette, he was to blame for telling a
notorious truth to a friendly *private* correspondent.

The committee already spoken of as acting to some degree as
an umpire between France and the United States—or rather
to advise the French Ministry what course to pursue towards
the United States—drew from Mr. Jefferson a letter on the subject of the commercial intercourse between the countries,[2] and
they agreed to report in favor of various of his proposed modi-

[1] In a letter dated May 17, 1818.   [2] Q. v. in Dip. Corr., vol. iii. p. 154

fications. Their report was adopted by the Ministry, and Jefferson remarks on it:

"It furnished a proof of the disposition of the King and his ministers to produce a more intimate intercourse between the two nations. Indeed, I must say that, as far as I am able to see, the friendship of the people of this country towards us is cordial and general, and that it is a kind of security for the friendship of ministers who cannot in any country be uninfluenced by the voice of the people. To this we may add, that it is their interest, as well as ours, to multiply the bans of friendship between us."

He also hinted immediately to Congress that their thanks to Lafayette would be very appropriate.[1]

The new regulations (called the order of Bernis) granted the Americans four free ports in France, instead of the two stipulated by treaty; suppressed the duties on the exportation of brandy; diminished and consolidated into a single one, the several duties payable by American vessels arriving in French ports; abolished for ten years the duty of fabrication on whale oil and spermaceti imported in French and American bottoms (so that they should pay no other duties than 7 *livres* 10*d.*, and 10 *sols* per *livre*, this last augmentation to cease in 1790); suppressed all duties on pot and pearl ashes, beaver skins and hair, raw leather, all kinds of wood fit for ship-building, shrubs, trees, and seed, the growth of the United States and imported therefrom in French or American vessels; suppressed the duty on the purchase of ships built in the United States; suppressed the prohibitions and duties on the exportation of arms and gunpowder to the United States (except a nominal one to facilitate the calculation of exports), also on the exportation of books and papers, in French or American vessels. In regard to tobacco, it was declared:

"It has been resolved not to break the agreement with Mr. Morris; but that after the expiration of this contract, no similar one shall be made, and that in the meanwhile the Farmers-General should be obliged to purchase annually about fifteen thousand hogsheads of American tobacco, imported directly from the United States in French or American vessels, at the same price or on the same conditions which have been stipulated by the contract with Mr. Morris."

It was promised that inquiries should be instituted to ascertain the best means for encouraging the importation of Ameri

[1] Jefferson to Jay, October 22d.

can rice; and attention was called to general *arrêts* temporarily reducing the duty on the exportation of wines to all countries. Thus some very important advantages were secured to American commerce, and concessions made in the gross in its favor, which were made, we think, to no other country in the world at the time.

On the 4th day of September, Mr. Jefferson met with an accident thus described by his daughter Martha:

"At one o'clock he always rode or walked. He frequently walked as far as seven miles in the country. Returning from one of those rambles, he was joined by some friend, and being earnestly engaged in conversation he fell and fractured his wrist. He said nothing at the moment, but holding his suffering limb with the other hand, he continued the conversation till he arrived near to his own house, when, informing his companion of the accident, he left him to send for the surgeon. The fracture was a compound one, and probably much swollen before the arrival of the surgeon; it was not *set*, and remained ever after weak and stiff. While disabled by the accident, he was in the habit of writing with his left hand, in which he soon became tolerably expert, the writing being well formed, but stiff."

He was four or five miles from his lodgings when the disaster occurred. Grasping the fractured wrist tightly with his left hand, he continued the conversation so quietly and with so little alteration of countenance, that his companion, as his daughter intimates, had no suspicion of the extent of the accident until they were on the point of parting—though he was suffering the most intense pain. This was a good illustration of the calm and silent fortitude which always characterized him, where his own bodily suffering or danger was alone concerned. The extremest bodily agony hardly ever drew from him a groan or a complaint. And we have another familiar trait conspicuously developed. The pocket account-book contains several entries written in his ordinary hand on the forenoon of the day of the accident. In the afternoon there is an entry of the purchase of some "buttons" and "gloves," in the cramped, stiff, perpendicular characters of a man writing for the first time with his left hand—yet made so slowly and carefully that they are as legible as print! The pain of a badly fractured limb, and of an unsuccessful attempt to set it, was not sufficient to stop, for a single afternoon, his inflexible system in keeping his accounts!

The letter of M. de Calonne to Mr. Jefferson will be found in the Dip. Corr. of U. S. vol. iii. p. 160.

2. pd French & nephew, a bill drawn on me by Mr Barc.
— mistake ―― for 240f which charge to Bannister.
pd Goldsmith for books 6f.10
pd do for 19th livraison of Encyclopedie. viz

    for myself —— 24
    J. Madison   24
    Dr Franklin   24
    F. Hopkinson —   24
    La. Monroe   23
    Dr Currie — — 23
                     ―――
                      142

3. pd seeing gallery, St Cloud 6f
4. pd Petit viz.

	Aug. 21―25.	Aug. 26 — 31.
Kitchen exp	234N (29)	213. 2 - 6 (20) = 49
office	120. 9-6	72. 14.
little depences . .	54.18	32. 15
postage	41. 1	4
washing	. . . .	36 - 14
wagon & harness . .	. . . .	86
servant's acc . . .	. . . .	40. 9
marshal's acct . . .	―――	17. 19
	450 - 8 - 6	504. 19-6

1786.
Sep. 4. pd for buttons 22f.10. gloves 4f.6
5 pd seeing the king's library 3f. Madrid 6f
7. pd seeing machine of Marly. 6f. the Chateau 6f
   pd Petit towards dinner at Marly 12f pd at Louveciennes 6f
8 paid at Concert Spirituel 6f
9. paid seeing Gardes meubles 12f — for books 3f.10.
   pd Mlle Guyard ―――――― for picture. 240f
   gave Patsy 6f pd at Italians 6f
10. pd Valade for a picture 96f
13. pd hire of Piano forte 12f
14. pd Charpentier for a press for M.de Lafayette 96f — for clamps. 12f
    pd seeing machine 3f
15. pd seeing Desert 6f
18. pd two Surgeons 12f
19. pd Petit on acc 160f
21. pd clothes for Patsy 64f.10 — lent Mazzei 36f
22. pd postage 106f.17 — Petit on acct 93 f.3
Oct. 1. pd Corneillon engraving 27f do for picture 48f
2. state of expences of September.

	Sep 4-9	10 — 16	17-23	24-30	
Kitchen exp	266.6.6	206-11	172.10	116-4-6	(28)(26/12)(13)
office	107-16	88-2-6	56-10	107-8.	
Pet: depences	206-15	. . .	57.4	128-14	
Postage	49-3	. . .	19.0	28-17	
	614 - 0-6	294-13-6	305.4	381-8-6	1611. 6-6

ACCOUNT KEPT WHILE Mr JEFFERSON'S RIGHT WRIST WAS BROKEN.

This left-hand chirography continues to the middle of November; and it, for some time after, alternates with the other. He never again wrote rapidly or easily with his right hand.

On the 14th of November, Mr. Jefferson wrote General Washington a letter, explaining his agency in furnishing or correcting the remarks on the Cincinnati Society, in the *Encyclopédie Méthodique,* and it shows his increasing jealousy of that institution, and his increasing (if that was possible) hostility to monarchical and aristocratic government.

We shall begin, from this period, to get occasional expressions from Mr. Jefferson on a point becoming one of paramount interest at home—the formation of a more solid national government. He thus alludes to the Annapolis Convention, and the then coming one at Philadelphia, which framed the present United States Constitution. We get a clear view of what Jefferson thought in advance—thought originally—should be the *general* form and construction of the federal government:

"I find by the public papers, that your commercial convention failed in point of representation. If it should produce a full meeting in May, and a broader reformation, it will still be well. To make us one nation as to foreign concerns, and keep us distinct in domestic ones, gives the outline of the proper division of powers between the general and particular governments. But to enable the federal head to exercise the powers given it, to best advantage, it should be organized, as the particular ones are, into legislative, executive, and judiciary. The first and last are already separated. The second should be. When last with Congress, I often proposed to members to do this, by making of the committee of the States an executive committee during the recess of Congress, and during its sessions, to appoint a committee to receive and dispatch all executive business, so that Congress itself should meddle only with what should be legislative. But I question if any Congress (much less all successively) can have self-denial enough to go through with this distribution."

He thus, in the same letter, spoke of the final passage of the act for religious freedom (his own) by the Virginia Legislature:

"It is comfortable to see the standard of reason at length erected, after so many ages, during which the human mind has been held in vassalage by kings, priests, and nobles: and it is honorable for us to have produced the first legislature who had the courage to declare, that the reason of man may be trusted with the formation of his own opinions."

In a letter to Monroe (December 18th), he mentioned that "some symptoms" had given him reason to suspect that his opposition to the monopoly of importing tobacco by the Far mers-General, had given offence to Robert Morris of Philadelphia, who was "profiting from the abuse." He added:

"I have done what was right, and I will not so far wound my privilege of doing that, without regard to any man's interest, as to enter into any explanations of this paragraph with him. Yet I esteem him highly, and suppose that hitherto he had esteemed me."

He alluded, in the same, to a contemplated journey:

"I am now about setting out on a journey to the south of France, one object of which is to try the mineral waters there, for the restoration of my hand; but another is, to visit all the seaports where we have trade, and to hunt up all the inconveniencies under which it labors, in order to get them rectified. I shall visit, and carefully examine too, the canal of Languedoc."

And here is a dream, more and more henceforth recurring—but yet long and weary years from its realization:

"On my return, which will be early in the spring, I shall send you several livraisons of the Encyclopedia, and the plan of your house. I wish to heaven, you may continue in the disposition to fix it in Albemarle. Short will establish himself there, and perhaps Madison may be tempted to do so. This will be society enough, and it will be the great sweetener of our lives. Without society, and a society to our taste, men are never contented. The one here supposed, we can regulate to our minds, and we may extend our regulations to the sumptuary department, so as to set a good example to a country which needs it, and to preserve our own happiness clear of embarrassment."

Receiving the honorary degree of Doctor of Laws from the *Senatus Academicus* of Yale College, Mr. Jefferson acknowledged the honor in a letter to Dr. Stiles, the President of the institution, December 24th; and he subjoined the following characteristic remarks in relation to "Shay's insurrection," information of which had lately reached him:

"The commotions that have taken place in America, as far as they are yet known to me, offer nothing threatening. They are a proof that the people have liberty enough, and I could not wish them less than they have. If the happiness of the mass of the people can be secured at the expense of a little tempest now and then, or even of a little blood, it will be a precious purchase. 'Malo libertatem periculosam quam quietem servitutem.' Let common sense and common honesty have fair play, and they will soon set things to rights."

According to our floating recollections, Mr. Jefferson here substituted "periculosam" for "inquietam," in the original—willing to declare that he preferred a dangerous—instead of a mere quiet—liberty to a quiet slavery. We know nothing specially of President Stiles—but assuming that he was one of the staid, conservative kind of gentlemen who usually fill such positions, in New England, it is amusing to imagine what must have been his consternation on receiving this missive from the new Doctor of Laws! A day or two afterwards Jefferson wrote Mr. Carmichael :

" These people are not entirely without excuse. Before the war, these States depended on their whale oil and fish. The former was consumed in England, and much of the latter in the Mediterranean. The heavy duties on American whale oil, now required in England, exclude it from that market: and the Algerines exclude them from bringing their fish into the Mediterranean. France is opening her ports for their oil, but in the meanwhile, their ancient debts are pressing them, and they have nothing to pay with. The Massachusetts Assembly, too, in their zeal for paying their public debt, had laid a tax too heavy to be paid in the circumstances of their State. The Indians seem disposed, too, to make war on us. These complicated causes, determined Congress to increase their forces to two thousand men. The latter was the sole object avowed, yet the former entered for something into the measure. However, I am satisfied the good sense of the people is the strongest army our governments can ever have, and that it will not fail them."

The insurrectionary movements in Massachusetts and New Hampshire, known as "Shay's insurrection"—in which no battle or skirmish even was fought, and for which no one suffered death subsequently by the acts of the civil magistracy—had a very different influence on other minds. A good many who had hitherto been friends of popular government, were now nearly or quite discouraged. Forgetting that their own example had just proved that serious, bloody, and successful rebellions might occur in monarchies, and in the best administered and most firmly established monarchies—they now talked deprecatingly of the rule of the " ever fickle and inconstant mob," and reasoned themselves speedily into the belief that strong government, monarchical in spirit if not in form, was absolutely necessary to keep society within the safe and healthy limits of political action!

It was a favorite charge or taunt of Mr. Jefferson's disparagers, in after years, that his " democracy " was " French democracy "—that it was " caught " in the French Revolution, and of a body of men who were opposed to all human, if not divine government, etc. The expressions of his we have last quoted (and we shall have them stronger in the next chapter), implying a pitch of democracy he never afterwards exceeded—and it is difficult, indeed, to see how they could be exceeded—were made before there was a revolution in France, and before there was a democrat in France. The most extreme member of the patriotic party had not broached such an idea. It is fair enough for those of different views to complain of the excess of Mr. Jefferson's theories on the subject of popular rights. They are entitled to complain, if they see fit, of his daring practical application of his theories to Shay's insurrection. His remarks on that head did carry consternation to the bosoms of some excellent men, who were by no means monarchists. They were brought up against him afterwards when a candidate for the Presidency. But whether the doctrines were good or bad, it is ridiculous to say they were learned in or from France. Every fact goes to show that if there was any learning from each other in political science between him and the French patriots, they were the pupils, not he. Democratic doctrines may not have been born in the man. We cannot say how this was. But a very superficial study of his character shows, from first to last, a constitution or texture of mind which irresistibly impelled him in that direction; and the current had but to meet with forcible resistance to boil and roar with vehemence. All the circumstances which chilled in other bosoms the first democratic glow of *our* revolution, all those foreign flatteries which so often have mollified republicans towards other systems, in him but added combustibles to the early flame. If ever there was a man who was a republican from the necessity of his mental organization, we think it was he.

We should perhaps make a remark in this connection for the benefit of younger readers. Jefferson's declarations on this and parallel occasions, were not (like so many public men's letters now days!) ostensibly written in private letters which were really intended for the public eye—intended, in a cant phrase of our times, "for Buncombe." His letters were addressed to a class who he knew would treat them as too private for the newspapers. More than this, they were a good deal more than half the time addressed to persons who he had every reason to judge would disapprove, if not revolt, at their propositions.

Without assuming that it constitutes a merit or demerit at that point of our national history, the historical fact appears to be certain, that in 1786, and for some period later, there were few, if any, prominent Americans, who avowed themselves in favor of broadly democratic systems. In the Federal Convention of 1787 (which framed our Constitution) not a man could be found who advocated such systems, or was willing to be suspected of at heart favoring them. There were gentlemen in that Convention who avowed themselves monarchists in theory, but not one could be found who would take the name of democrat! Jefferson was the first, and, for a long time, the only very prominent American we know of who was willing to persistently avow that democracy constituted the essence of his system, or the rule of construction which he would apply to the mixed forms of the State and Federal Governments. We doubt whether such doctrines were even popular in our country— whether they attained the approbation of the majority of our then conservative people—until very near the close of the eighteenth century. But it is not time to enter upon speculations on this head.

CHAPTER XII.

1787.

No diplomatic measures of importance between the French and United States governments marked the opening of 1787. The latter had attained everything, by the order of Bernis, that could be immediately expected ; and the former was beginning to be absorbed painfully in its own affairs.

Mr. Jefferson having described, in his Memoir, the state of public opinion in France down to this point—the numbers, influence, and just aims of the Patriotic party—added :

"Happily for the nation, it happened, at the same moment, that the dissipations of the Queen and court, the abuses of the pension-list, and dilapidations in the administration of every branch of the finances, had exhausted the treasures and credit of the nation, insomuch, that its most necessary functions were paralyzed. To reform these abuses would have overset the Minister ; to impose new taxes by the authority of the King, was known to be impossible, from the determined opposition of the Parliament to their enregistry. No resource remained, then, but to appeal to the nation. He advised, therefore, the call of an Assembly of the most distinguished characters of the nation, in the hope, that, by promises of various and valuable improvements in the organization and regimen of the government, they would be induced to authorize new taxes, to control the opposition of the Parliament, and to raise the annual revenue to the level of expenditures."

For the first time, therefore, in more than a century and a half, an Assembly of Notables was called to meet on the 22d of February. It was the Count de Vergennes's peculiar felicity to die at his post (February 13th), before he could have any beyond dim anticipations of what was in store for France. Louis XVI. afterwards vainly believed that the Revolution would not have taken place, had this able minister continued at the helm of affairs.

On the 16th of January, Mr. Jefferson wrote Colonel Edward Carrington, of Virginia, a letter on the text of "Shay's insurrection," which deserves a careful perusal from all who desire a clear and striking exposition of the writer's theories of government.

"The tumults in America, I expected would have produced in Europe an unfavorable opinion of our political state. But it has not. On the contrary. the small effect of these tumults, seems to have given more confidence in the firmness of our governments. The interposition of the people themselves on the side of government, has had a great effect on the opinion here. I am persuaded myself, that the good sense of the people will always be found to be the best army. They may be led astray for a moment, but will soon correct themselves. The people are the only censors of their governors ; and even their errors will tend to keep these to the true principles of their institution. To punish these errors too severely. would be to suppress the only safeguard of the public liberty. The way to prevent these irregular interpositions of the people, is to give them full information of their affairs through the channel of the public papers, and to contrive that those papers should penetrate the whole mass of the people The basis of our governments

being the opinion of the people, the very first object should be to keep that right;
and were it left to me to decide whether we should have a government without
newspapers, or newspapers without a government, I should not hesitate a moment
to prefer the latter. But I should mean that every man should receive those
papers, and be capable of reading them. I am convinced that those societies (as
the Indians) which live without government, enjoy in their general mass an infinitely
greater degree of happiness, than those who live under the European governments.
Among the former, public opinion is in the place of law, and restrains morals as
powerfully as laws ever did anywhere. Among the latter, under pretence of governing, they have divided their nations into two classes, wolves and sheep. I do not
exaggerate. This is a true picture of Europe. Cherish, therefore, the spirit of our
people, and keep alive their attention. Do not be too severe upon their errors, but
reclaim them by enlightening them. If once they become inattentive to the public
affairs, you, and I, and Congress, and Assemblies, Judges and Governors, shall all
become wolves. It seems to be the law of our general nature, in spite of individual
exceptions: and experience declares that man is the only animal which devours his
own kind; for I can apply no milder term to the governments of Europe, and to
the general prey of the rich on the poor."

Some new turns of the same thoughts and an extension of
them, occur in a letter to a more confidential correspondent,
Mr. Madison, January 30th.

The letter contains some plainer sketches of personal character than it is common to find in Mr. Jefferson's writings, and we
give three or four of them, preceded by his reasons for speaking
so freely:

"As you have now returned into Congress, it will become of importance that
you should form a just estimate of certain public characters: on which, therefore,
I will give you such notes as my knowledge of them has furnished me with. You
will compare them with the materials you are otherwise possessed of, and decide on
a view of the whole.

"You know the opinion I formerly entertained of my friend Mr. Adams.
* * * and the Governor were the first who shook that opinion. I afterwards
saw proofs, which convicted him of a degree of vanity, and of a blindness to it, of
which no germ appeared in Congress. A seven months' intimacy with him here,
and as many weeks in London, have given me opportunities of studying him
closely. He is vain, irritable, and a bad calculator of the force and probable effect
of the motives which govern men. This is all the ill which can possibly be said of
him. He is as disinterested as the being who made him: he is profound in his
views, and accurate in his judgment, except where knowledge of the world is
necessary to form a judgment. He is so amiable, that I pronounce you will love
him, if ever you become acquainted with him. He would be, as he was, a great
man in Congress.

"The Marquis de Lafayette is a most valuable auxiliary to me. His zeal is
unbounded, and his weight with those in power, great. His education having been
merely military, commerce was an unknown field to him. But his good sense
enabling him to comprehend perfectly whatever is explained to him, his agency has

been very efficacious. He has a great deal of sound genius, is well remarked by the King, and rising in popularity. He has nothing against him, but the suspicion of republican principles. I think he will one day be of the ministry. His foible is, a canine [1] appetite for popularity and fame ; but he will get above this.

*　　　*　　　*　　　*　　　*　　　*　　　*

"The Count de Vergennes is ill. The possibility of his recovery renders it dangerous for us to express a doubt of it; but he is in danger. He is a great minister in European affairs, but has very imperfect ideas of our *institutions*, and no confidence in them. His devotion to the principles of pure despotism, renders him unaffectionate to our governments. But his fear of England makes him value us as a make-weight. He is cool, reserved in political conversations, but free and familiar on other subjects, and a very attentive, agreeable person to do business with. It is impossible to have a clearer, better organized head ; but age has chilled his heart.

*　　　*　　　*　　　*　　　*　　　*　　　*

"I learn that Mr. Adams desires to be recalled, and that Smith [2] should be appointed Chargé des Affaires there. It is not for me to decide whether any diplomatic character should be kept at a court, which keeps none with us. You can judge of Smith's abilities by his letters. They are not of the first order, but they are good. For his honesty, he is like our friend Monroe ; turn his soul wrong side outwards, and there is not a speck on it. He has one foible, an excessive inflammability of temper, but he feels it when it comes on, and has resolution enough to suppress it, and to remain silent till it passes over."

Mr. Jefferson mentioned in this letter, that he could not make the least use of his fractured wrist except for writing ; that he had great anxieties lest he never should recover any considerable use of it ; that he should, by the advice of his surgeons, set out in a fortnight for the waters of Aix in Provence ; and as in a previous letter to Monroe, he said he should seize the occasion to examine the canal of Languedoc, and " acquire knowledge of that species of navigation which may be useful hereafter," and, more especially, " to make a tour of the ports concerned in commerce with us ; to examine, on the spot, the defects of the late regulations respecting our commerce ; to learn the further improvements which may be made in it ; and, on his return, to get this business finished." He mentioned that he should be absent between two and three months, but should always be where he could be recalled to the capital in ten days, should it become necessary.

Before the close of the preceding year, the American agent dispatched to Morocco had succeeded in forming a treaty with that power, and active negotiations were thenceforth entered upon by Mr. Adams and Mr. Jefferson to procure the liberation

---

[1] See ante, p. 454.　　　[2] Colonel W. S. Smith, Mr. Adams's son-in-law.

of the American captives in Algiers. Jefferson's correspondence, at this period, is full of this subject; and after resorting to various other unsuccessful steps, the aid of the Mathurins, a body of French priests organized for such benevolent projects, was invoked to promote the undertaking. But no important results followed.

Jefferson was present at the opening of the Assembly of Notables on the 22d of February, and on the 27th, had an audience from M. de Montmorin, the successor of De Vergennes in the Foreign Bureau, whose modesty, simplicity of manners, and good dispositions towards the United States, made a most favorable impression on his mind.

He set out on the 28th, on his journey to the south of France, but before going, addressed this noticeable letter to Lafayette who was a member of the Notables:

"I wish you success in your meeting. I should form better hopes of it, if it were divided into two Houses instead of seven. Keeping the good model of your neighboring country before your eyes, you may get on, step by step, towards a good constitution. Though that model is not perfect, yet, as it would unite more suffrages than any new one which could be proposed, it is better to make that the object. If every advance is to be purchased by filling the royal coffers with gold, it will be gold well employed. The King, who means so well, should be encouraged to repeat these Assemblies. You see how we republicans are apt to preach, when we get on politics. Adieu, my dear friend."

He kept a journal of his progress, which is published in both editions of his works;[1] and the pocket account-book, as usual, supplies many minor details. His route lay up the Seine through Champagne and Burgundy, and thence down the Saône and the Rhone through the Beaujolais, Dauphiné, Orange, and Languedoc to Aix. He travelled in his own carriage and with post horses. Reluctant to withdraw Martha so long from her school, he did not take her with him. The first day, he passed through Mélun and reached Fontainebleau. He paused here a day to have changes made in his carriage; and he inspected that famous palace from whose voluptuous retreats Montespan and Du Barry had lavished those countless treasures, wrung pitilessly from the toiling millions, the want of which was now, in the process of a just retribution, hurrying the ancient monarchy of France to its bloody doom. He reached

---

[1] Randolph's edition, vol. ii. p. 115; Congress edition, vol. ix. p. 313.

Sens on the 2d of March, and on his route from thence to Vermanton, the entries in his journal are commenced.

This cannot be republished here. Like his journal in England, it is chiefly occupied with practical descriptions; but in this case, agriculture and wine-making, instead of gardening, receive the principal share of his attention. In regard to these, his information is extensive, and oftentimes almost exact enough for the directions of those about to engage, without previous practice, in the culture of vineyards and the production of the different varieties of wine. Spirited sketches of scenery occur in the journal, but they are brief, and are only intended to show what kind of a country, topographically speaking, is adapted to this or that kind of culture.

He arrived at Lyons on the 11th of March, and remained until the 15th; and his journal dispatches the city in four lines. Nismes was reached on the 19th, and four days were spent here in examining the remains of Roman grandeur—the Maison Quarrée (the plan of which he had previously obtained and sent to Virginia as a model for its capitol), the huge Doric circus, the temple and fountain of Diana, and the various other remains of ancient art. None of these things are mentioned in the journal, but a letter from this place to Madame la Comtesse de Tesse (aunt of Madame Lafayette), shows that not only here, but on the whole route from Paris, he had studied works of art quite as closely as those matters which occupied his journal; but in the latter he was, as usual, recording useful facts to carry home to his countrymen. The letter to the Countess is written playfully, and in the tone of high-flown gallantry of that day. The familiar eye skips along this badinage for the point of the letter, and by and by it comes! "His journey has given him leisure to reflect on the *Assemblée des Notables.*" The result of these reflections are thus given :

"Under a good and a young King, as the present, I think good may be made of it. I would have the deputies then, by all means, so conduct themselves as to encourage him to repeat the calls of this Assembly. Their first step should be, to get themselves divided into two chambers instead of seven; the Noblesse and the Commons separately. The second, to persuade the King, instead of choosing the deputies of the Commons himself, to summon those chosen by the people for the Provincial administrations. The third, as the Noblesse is too numerous to be all of the Assemblée, to obtain permission for that body to choose its own deputies. Two Houses so elected would contain a mass of wisdom which would make the people happy, and the King great; would place him in history where no other act can possibly place him. They would thus put themselves in the track of the best guide they can follow; they would soon overtake it, become its guide in turn, and lead to the wholesome modifications wanting in that model, and necessary to constitute a rational government. Should they then attempt more than the established habits of the people of the ripe for, they may lose all, and retard indefinitely the ultimate object of their aim. These, madam, are my opinions; but I wish to know yours, which I am sure will be better."

The accomplished Countess was an active politician, and a staunch liberal. Governeur Morris more than once, in his diary kept in France, speaks of her reproaching *him* for his want of republicanism. Mr. Jefferson had a zealous friend and admirer in her. Within twenty-four hours of her receipt of the above letter, we dare say, its contents were known to most of the patriotic chiefs in the Assembly of Notables.

Before leaving Nismes, he fulfilled an appointment with an unknown correspondent, who had announced that he had a communication of importance to make. He proved to be a Brazilian anxious to engage the United States in an attempt to revolutionize that country. Mr. Jefferson declined committing himself to him. Those anxious to see the particulars of their interview, will find them in a dispatch to Mr. Jay, dated May 4th.

He reached Aix on the 25th of March. The following letter, written from thence to his oldest daughter, in Paris, contains a good deal of his philosophy of life:

To MARTHA JEFFERSON.

AIX EN PROVENCE, *March* 28, 1787.

I was happy, my dear Patsy, to receive, on my arrival here, your letter, informing me of your good health and occupations. I have not written you sooner because I have been almost constantly on the road. My journey hitherto has been a very pleasing one. It was undertaken with the hope that the mineral waters of this place might restore strength to my wrist. Other considerations also concurred instruction, amusement, and abstraction from business, of which I had too much at Paris. I am glad to learn that you are employed in things new and good, in your music and drawing. You know what have been my fears for some time past —that you do not employ yourself so closely as I could wish. You have promised me a more assiduous attention, and I have great confidence in what you promise. It is your future happiness which interests me, and nothing can contribute more to it (moral rectitude always excepted) than the contracting a habit of industry and activity. Of all the cankers of human happiness, none corrodes with so silent, yet so baneful a tooth, as indolence. Body and mind both unemployed, our being becomes a burthen, and every object about us loathsome, even the dearest. Idleness begets ennui, ennui the hypochondria, and that a diseased body. No laborious person was ever yet hysterical. Exercise and application produce order in our affairs, health of body, cheerfulness of mind, and these make us precious to our friends. It is while we are young that the habit of industry is formed. If not then, it never is afterwards. The fortune of our lives, therefore, depends on employing well the short period of youth. If at any moment, my dear, you catch yourself in idleness, start from it as you would from the precipice of a gulf. You are not, however, to consider yourself as unemployed while taking exercise. That is necessary for your health, and health is the first of all objects. For this reason, if you leave your dancing-master for the summer, you must increase your other exercise.

I do not like your saying that you are unable to read the ancient print of your Livy, but with the aid of your master. We are always equal to what we undertake with resolution. A little degree of this will enable you to decipher your Livy. If you always lean on your master, you will never be able to proceed without him. It is a part of the American character to consider nothing as desperate—to surmount every difficulty by resolution and contrivance. In Europe there are shops for every want: its inhabitants therefore have no idea that their wants can be furnished otherwise. Remote from all other aid, we are obliged to invent and to execute; to find means within ourselves, and not to lean on others. Consider, therefore, the conquering your Livy as an exercise in the habit of surmounting difficulties; a habit which will be necessary to you in the country where you are to live, and without which you will be thought a very helpless animal, and less esteemed. Music, drawing, books, invention, and exercise, will be so many resources to you against ennui. But there are others which, to this object, add that of utility. These are the needle and domestic economy. The latter you cannot learn here, but the former you may. In the country life of America there are many moments when a woman can have recourse to nothing but her needle for employment. In a dull company and in dull weather, for instance, it is ill manners to read; it is ill manners to leave them; no card-playing there among genteel people—that is abandoned to blackguards. The needle is then a valuable resource. Besides, without knowing how to use it herself, how can the mistress of a family direct the works of her servants?

You ask me to write you long letters. I will do it, my dear, on condition you will read them from time to time, and practice what they will inculcate. Their precepts will be dictated by experience, by a perfect knowledge of the situation in which you will be placed, and by the fondest love for you. This it is which makes me wish to see you more qualified than common. My expectations from you are high—yet not higher than you may attain. Industry and resolution are all that are wanting. Nobody in this world can make me so happy, or so miserable, as you. Retirement from public life will ere long become necessary for me. To your sister and yourself I look to render the evening of my life serene and contented. Its morning has been clouded by loss after loss, till I have nothing left but you. I do not doubt either your affection or dispositions. But great exertions are necessary, and you have little time left to make them. Be industrious, then, my dear child. Think nothing unsurmountable by resolution and application, and you will be all that I wish you to be.

You ask me if it is my desire that you should dine at the Abbess's table? It is. Propose it as such to Madame de Frauleinheim, with my respectful compli ments and thanks for her care of you. Continue to love me with all the warmth with which you are beloved by, my dear Patsy,

Yours affectionately,

TH. JEFFERSON.

This is, certainly, line upon line, and precept upon precept, on the subject of industry, to a girl of fifteen, advanced enough to be reading Livy, and occupied in a number of other studies. But Martha had a joyous, serene, contented disposition—taking the world easily ; and it was rather this easiness of temper than any actual symptoms of indolence, which alarmed a parent so easily alarmed, and so exacting on *that* head. He undoubtedly made an effort to produce a deep and a lasting impression on her mind in regard to a virtue ranked so highly by him—and he fully succeeded. In this she became a complete reflection of himself.'

Mr. Jefferson soon became satisfied that the waters of Aix were of no benefit to him, and he accordingly abridged his stay there. He remained several days at Marseilles, prosecuting commercial and several other inquiries, but failing to ascertain satisfactorily whether the difference in American and Piedmont rice consisted in the species or the method of cleaning, he determined to visit the rice fields of the latter to settle the question. He reached Toulon on the 6th of April, and the next day again wrote his daughter :

To MARTHA JEFFERSON.

TOULON, *April* 7, 1787.

MY DEAR PATSY :

I received yesterday at Marseilles your letter of March 25th ; and I received it with pleasure, because it announced to me that you were well. Experience

---

' The person who furnished us the above letter—nearly related to the parties, and entirely familiar with them personally—subjoined the following note, which the writer must excuse us for copying :

" The constant solicitude, the sleepless vigilance, and indefatigable assiduity manifested by him on this point, were crowned with their just reward. In this feature of character, as in many others, hers became but a beautiful reflection of his own—a daguerreotype of the finest stamp. In thinking of him under this aspect, the conviction has often arisen, that never, in any single instance, under any circumstances however fortuitous (since early manhood at least), can he have willingly ' wasted his time,' *even to the extent of one minute.* I feel sure that this never can have happened ; that, when in health, he never can have been for an instant ' listless,' never in the mood of ' whiling away time.'

" Such is my conviction as to him ; and the same conviction exists as to her. She was always employed when her time was at her own disposal. Had her day been 240 hours long instead of 24, not a minute of it would have ' hung heavy' on her hands. She would have had *occupation* for them all—a part of this occupation (in conformity with his scheme of life) consisting in the exercise of the affections, domestic and social ; in recreations of the refining and purifying kind, and in bodily exercise."

learns us to be always anxious about the health of those whom we love. I have not been able to write to you so often as I expected, because I am generally on the road; and when I stop anywhere, I am occupied in seeing what is to be seen. It will be some time now, perhaps three weeks, before I shall be able to write you again. But this need not slacken your writing to me, because you have leisure, and your letters come regularly to me. I have received letters which inform me that our dear Polly [1] will certainly come to us this summer. By the time I return, it will be time to expect her. When she arrives, she will become a precious charge on your hands. The difference of your age, and your common loss of a mother, will put that office on you. Teach her, above all things, to be good—because without that, we can neither be valued by others, nor set any value on ourselves. Teach her to be always true; no vice is so mean as the want of truth, and at the same time so useless. Teach her never to be angry: anger only serves to torment ourselves, to divert others, and alienate their esteem. And teach her industry and application to useful pursuits. I will venture to assure you, that if you inculcate this in her mind, you will make her a happy being in herself, a most inestimable friend to you, and precious to all the world. In teaching her these dispositions of mind, you will be more fixed in them yourself, and render yourself dear to all your acquaintances. Practice them, then, my dear, without ceasing. If ever you find yourself in difficulty, and doubt how to extricate yourself, do what is right, and you will find it the easiest way of getting out of the difficulty. Do it for the additional incitement of increasing the happiness of him who loves you infinitely, and who is, my dear Patsy,

Yours affectionately,
TH. JEFFERSON.

He arrived at Nice on the 9th of April. From this place (April 11th) he wrote General Lafayette :

"In the great cities I go to see, what travellers think alone worthy of being seen; but I make a job of it, and generally gulp it all down in a day. On the other hand, I am never satiated with rambling through the fields and farms, examining the culture and cultivators, with a degree of curiosity which makes some take me to be a fool, and others to be much wiser than I am."

After comparing (in the same letter) the agricultural condition of some of the provinces which he had passed, with each other and with England—complaining that the French laws did not allow leases long enough for the benefit of both the landlord and tenant, he uttered the following noble sentences :

"From the first olive fields of Pierrelatte, to the orangeries of Hieres, has been continued rapture to me. I have often wished for you. I think you have not made this journey. It is a pleasure you have to come, and an improvement to be added to the many you have already made. It will be a great comfort to you, to know, from your own inspection, the condition of all the provinces of your own country, and it will be interesting to them at some future day, to be known to you.

[1] Mary, Mr. Jefferson's youngest daughter.

This is, perhaps, the only moment of your life in which you can acquire that knowledge. And to do it most effectually, you must be absolutely incognito, you must ferret the people out of their hovels as I have done, look into their kettles, eat their bread, loll on their beds under pretence of resting yourself, but in fact, to find if they are soft You will feel a sublime pleasure in the course of this investigation, and a sublimer one hereafter, when you shall be able to apply your knowledge to the softening of their beds, or the throwing a morsel of meat into their kettle of vegetables."

Leaving Nice on the 13th, he proceeded to Coni on mules, the snows on the mountains not yet permitting the passage of carriages. He had expected to reach the country furnishing the " Piedmont rice " of commerce, immediately after crossing the Alps, but found that it was cultivated no nearer than Vercelli and Novarra, a good portion of the way to Milan. He reached Turin on the 16th, and Vercelli on the 20th. He soon ascertained that the machines used here in cleaning rice were the same with the American ones—that the breaking of the Carolina rice was owing to its inferior quality. The Government of Turin, aware of the superiority of its variety, even over those of the rest of Italy, prohibited the exportation of rough rice, as Mr. Jefferson was informed, under pain of death. He seems to have regarded this a state of things where smuggling was justifiable, so he crammed his coat and surtout pockets with the precious product, and also, though very doubtful of ever seeing any return for his money, hired a muleteer to run a couple of sacks across the Apennines to Genoa—his object being, of course, to send the seed to the rice-producing regions of the United States.[1]

He was at Milan on the 20th, Pavia on the 23d, Genoa on the 25th, and back again at Nice May 1st—so that he was a little over three weeks in Italy. His journal there contains the usual minute practical details, and little besides. He thus, a few months afterwards,[2] spoke of this trip to Mr. Wythe:

"My time allowed me to go no further than Turin, Milan, and Genoa: consequently, I scarcely got into classical ground. I took with me some of the writings, in which endeavors have been made to investigate the passage of Annibal over the Alps, and was just able to satisfy myself, from a view of the country, that the descriptions given of his march are not sufficiently particular, to enable us at this day, even to guess at his track across the Alps. In Architecture, painting, sculpture, I found much amusement: but more than all, in their agriculture, many

<hr>

[1] Letter to Edward Rutledge, July 14, 1787.   [2] September 16th.

objects of which might be adopted with us to great advantage. I am persuaded, there are many parts of our lower country where the olive tree might be raised, which is assuredly the richest gift of heaven. I can scarcely except bread. I see this tree supporting thousands among the Alps, where there is not soil enough to make bread for a single family. The caper, too, might be cultivated with us. The fig we do raise."

And he added this very memorable opinion, as the result of his investigations, in regard to making the grape a staple of national industry :

"I do not speak of the vine, because it is the parent of misery. Those who cultivate it are always poor, and he who would employ himself with us, in the culture of corn, cotton, etc., can procure, in exchange for them, much more wine, and better, than he could raise by its direct culture."

In the principal Italian, as in the French towns, Mr. Jefferson was received with marked attention by the officials and prominent inhabitants. Here, too, he conferred with the leading merchants in regard to the best steps for increasing their commerce with the United States. He satisfied himself that this part of Italy might be supplied with American whale-oil ; and he put matters in train to induce the Italian merchants to purchase their tobacco directly from the United States, instead, as hitherto, from England.

Some letters to Martha describe his further progress, and give other particulars :

TO MARTHA JEFFERSON.

MARSEILLES, *May* 5, 1787.

MY DEAR PATSY :

I got back to Aix the day before yesterday, and found there your letter of the 9th of April—from which I presume you to be well, though you do not say so. In order to exercise your geography, I will give you a detail of my journey. You must therefore take your map and trace out the following places : Dijon, Lyons, Pont St. Esprit, Nismes, Arles, St. Remis, Aix, Marseilles, Toulon, Hieres, Fréjus, Antibes, Nice, Col de Tende, Coni, Turin, Vercelli, Milan, Pavia, Tortona, Novi, Genoa, by sea to Albenga, by land to Monaco, Nice, Antibes, Fréjus, Brignolles, Aix and Marseilles. The day after to-morrow, I set out hence for Aix, Avignon, Pont du Gard, Nismes, Montpellier, Narbonne, along the canal of Languedoc to Toulouse, Bordeaux, Rochefort, Rochelle, Nantes, L'Orient, Nantes, Tours, Orléans, and Paris—where I shall arrive about the middle of June, after having travelled something upwards of a thousand leagues.

From Genoa to Aix was very fatiguing, the first two days having been at sea, and mortally sick—two more clambering the cliffs of the Apennines, sometimes on foot, sometimes on a mule, according as the path was more or less difficult—and two others travelling through the night as well as day without sleep. I am not yet rested, and shall therefore shortly give you rest by closing my letter, after mentioning that I have received a letter from your sister, which, though a year old, gave me great pleasure. I inclose it for your perusal, as I think it will be pleasing to you also. But take care of it, and return it to me when I shall get back to Paris, for trifling as it seems, it is precious to me.

When I left Paris, I wrote to London to desire that your harpsichord might be sent during the months of April and May, so that I am in hopes it will arrive a little before I shall, and give me an opportunity of judging whether you have got the better of that want of industry which I began to fear would be the rock on which you would split. Determine never to be idle. No person will have occasion to complain of the want of time who never loses any. It is wonderful how much may be done if we are always doing. And that you may be always doing good, my dear, is the ardent prayer of

Yours affectionately,
Th. Jefferson.

To Martha Jefferson.

May 21, 1787.

I write you, my dear Patsy, from the canal of Languedoc, on which I am at present sailing, as I have been for a week past—cloudless skies above, limpid waters below, and on each hand, a row of nightingales in full chorus. This delightful bird had given me a rich treat before, at the fountain of Vaucluse. After visiting the tomb of Laura, at Avignon, I went to see this fountain—a noble one of itself, and rendered forever famous by the songs of Petrarch, who lived near it. I arrived there somewhat fatigued, and sat down by the fountain to repose myself. It gushes, of the size of a river, from a secluded valley of the mountain, the ruins of Petrarch's château being perched on a rock two hundred feet perpendicular above. To add to the enchantment of the scene, every tree and bush was filled with nightingales in full song. I think you told me that you had not yet noticed this bird. As you have trees in the garden of the Convent, there might be nightingales in them, and this is the season of their song. Endeavor, my dear, to make yourself acquainted with the music of this bird, that when you return to your own country you may be able to estimate its merit in comparison with that of the mocking-bird. The latter has the advantage of singing through a great part of the year, whereas the nightingale sings but about five or six weeks in the spring, and a still shorter term, and with a more feeble voice, in the fall.

I expect to be at Paris about the middle of next month. By that time we may begin to expect our dear Polly. It will be a circumstance of inexpressible comfort to me to have you both with me once more. The object most interesting to me for the residue of my life, will be to see you both developing daily those principles of virtue and goodness which will make you valuable to others and happy in yourselves, and acquiring those talents and that degree of science which will guard you at all times against ennui, the most dangerous poison of life. A mind always employed is always happy. This is the true secret, the grand recipe, for felicity. The idle are the only wretched. In a world which furnishes so many employments which are useful, and so many which are amusing, it is our own fault if we ever know what ennui is, or if we are ever driven to the miserable resource of gaming, which corrupts our dispositions, and teaches us a habit of hostility against all mankind.

We are now entering the port of Toulouse, where I quit my bark, and of course must conclude my letter. Be good and be industrious, and you will be what I shall most love in the world. Adieu, my dear child.

Yours affectionately,

TH. JEFFERSON.

The following is the conclusion of a hitherto unpublished letter to his brother-in-law, Mr. Eppes, dated Bordeaux, May 26, accompanying a present of wine:

* * * "Much hurried by my departure hence, I cannot enter into details of news, etc. I must beg you, however, to deliver my love to Jack,[1] to tell him that his letter which he wrote near a year ago, came to my hands but a few days ago at Marseilles, and that it shall be among the first I answer on my arrival at Paris, which will not be till the middle of next month. He will have more claims to every service of mine than I can possibly find opportunities of rendering them. Recall me to the affectionate remembrance of Mrs. Eppes and the family. I say nothing of my dear Poll, hoping she is on her passage, yet fearing to think of it. Adieu, my dear sir, and be assured of the warmest esteem of your affectionate friend and servant."

TO MARTHA JEFFERSON.

(Extract.)

NANTES, June 1, 1787.

*   *   *   *   *   *   *   *   *   *   *

I forgot, in my last letter, to desire you to learn all your old tunes over again perfectly, that I may hear them on your harpsichord, on its arrival. I have no news of it, however, since I left Paris, though I presume it will arrive immediately, as I have ordered. Learn some slow movements of simple melody, for the Celestini stop, as it suits such only. I am just setting out for L'Orient, and shall have the happiness of seeing you at Paris about the 12th or 15th of this month, and assuring you in person of the sincere love of

Yours affectionately,

TH. JEFFERSON.

The passage in the letter of May 5th, about returning to him the " precious " few words of child's scrawl, written by the little " Polly " (or Mary), calls to mind the drawer of mementos, " covered with fond words of endearment," found in Mr. Jefferson's cabinet after his death !

We are also reminded of a manuscript[2] letter, forgotten by us in passing from Mr. Jefferson to Mr. Eppes (with whom

---

[1] John W. Eppes, the future husband of Mary or Maria Jefferson, the "dear Poll" of this letter.
[2] We have not supposed it necessary to continue to repeat to the reader with each of Mr. Jefferson's letters to his daughters and family, that they are from manuscripts, not heretofore published, and placed in our possession by Mr. Jefferson's grandchildren. The remark applies to this entire class of letters.

" Polly " had been left) written the year before (July 22d, 1786),
from which we will now clip but the following passage, to show
the yearning of the father's heart for his absent child. He said:
" Your letters of April 11th, and Mr. Lewis's of March 14th,
came to hand the 29th of June. ·I perceive they were to have
come by Colonel Le Maire, but I hear nothing of his arrival. I
had fondly flattered myself to receive my dear Polly with him,
an idea which I cannot relinquish whatever be the difficulties."

We might as well here include another letter to Martha,
exceedingly characteristic in its contents, written four days after
his return to Paris:

To Martha Jefferson.

Paris, June 14, 1787.

I send you, my dear Patsy, the 15 livres you desired. You propose this to
me as an anticipation of five weeks' allowance ; but do you not see, my dear, how
imprudent it is to lay out in one moment what should accommodate you for five
weeks ?—that this is a departure from that rule which I wish to see you governed
by, thro' your whole life, of never buying anything which you have not money in
your pocket to pay for ? Be assured that it gives much more pain to the mind to
be in debt, than to do without any article whatever which we may seem to want.
The purchase you have made is one of those I am always ready to make for you,
because it is my wish to see you dressed always cleanly and a little more than
decently. But apply to me first for the money before you make a purchase, were
it only to avoid breaking thro' your rule. Learn yourself the habit of adhering
rigorously to the rules you lay down for yourself. I will come for you about eleven
o'clock on Saturday. Hurry the making your gown, and also your reding-cote.
You will go with me some day next week to dine at the Marquis Fayette's. Adieu
my dear daughter.

Yours affectionately,

Th. Jefferson.

It may be scarcely necessary to say that the aim of this
letter (like that of a former one) was to impress a *rule*. He
knew the vigorous and sensible, but at the same time, ductile
mind to which he was addressing himself. He knew the quiet,
reasoning Martha would weigh well his words both for themselves, and because they were his. It was his practice, as we
have just seen, to make a particular and earnest appeal to her
where he feared her easy disposition, not prone to " borrow
trouble," might lead, or was leading her into careless habits.
After that earnest appeal, and perhaps two or three subsequent
finishing blows, the work was done, and forever. Herein
Martha resembled her father when he was at the same age.
The mind seemed as impressible as the heated wax, yet tho

Paris June 14. 1787.

I send you, my dear Patsy, the 15 livres you desired. you propose this to me as an anticipation of five weeks allowance. but do you not see my dear how imprudent it is to lay out in one moment what should accomodate you for five weeks? that this is a departure from that rule which I wish to see you governed by. had you a watch like ... I never traverse any thing which you have

understanding must be convinced to make any permanent impression. That done, the wax took the form of the seal, and held it sharp and clear ever after. Wax does not, however, furnish us a proper illustration; neither would rock nor iron. Wax is too easily re-molten and re-impressed—iron and granite too rough and rigid. Martha, like her father, had not a pharasaical feature. She did not carry her virtues catalogued on her front, nor was she given to returning thanks in public or private for not being as other people. Hers was one of those sweet, gentle, and thoroughly womanly natures every day met with—seemingly too pliant and unselfish to entertain a feeling that would contravene another's—and actually ready to gratify others by yielding everything immaterial; yet when a principle, or an established maxim of conduct became involved, unobtrusively exhibiting *impressions* as clear as those marked on the wax, and more ineffaceable than those wrought in the granite or iron. Granite and iron may be shattered by overwhelming force. The calm resolve of a gentle, virtuous, and truly elevated mind, no force on earth can bend or shatter.

We turn to the never-failing pocket account-book, and we find the identical entry of the "fifteen livres," named in the letter of June 14th. Twelve days after comes the entry of the liberal sum paid for the "reding-cote." Running our eye backward and forward, there is scarcely a page which does not contain from two or three to a half a dozen records of sums paid for necessaries or luxuries (some of the last elegant) "for Patsy." When little "Polly" arrived, these thicken. The first teachers in Paris attended them in certain branches, besides their regular attendance at vastly the most expensive boarding-school at Paris. Mr. Jefferson's liberality to his daughters, in money matters, would have been censurable in a man of narrow means. But none the less were they taught such lessons as those contained in the letter of June 14th:

Soon after Mr. Jefferson's return to the capital, he thus (in a dispatch to Mr. Jay, June 21st) mentions the political changes which had taken place in his absence:

"The new accessions to the ministry are valued here. Good is hoped from the Archbishop of Toulouse, who succeeds the Count de Vergennes as *Chef d* Conseil de Finance. Monsieur de Villedeuil, the Controller-General, has been approved by the public in the offices he has heretofore exercised. The Duke de

Nivernois, called to the Council, is reckoned a good and able man; and Monsieur de Malesherbes, called also to the Council, is unquestionably the first character in the kingdom, for integrity, patriotism, knowledge, and experience in business. There is a fear that the Maréchal de Castries is disposed to retire."

Some further sketches are furnished [1] to a private correspondent, Mr. Madison:

"The late changes in the ministry here, excite considerable hopes. I think we gain in them all. I am particularly happy at the reëntry of Malesherbes into the Council. His knowledge and integrity render his value inappreciable, and the greater to me, because while he had no views of office, we had established together the most unreserved intimacy. So far, too, I am pleased with Montmorin. His honesty proceeds from the heart as well as the head, and therefore may be more surely counted on. The King loves business, economy, order, and justice, and wishes sincerely the good of his people; but he is irascible, rude, very limited in his understanding, and religious bordering on bigotry. He has no mistress, loves his queen, and is too much governed by her. She is capricious like her brother, and governed by him; devoted to pleasure and expense; and not remarkable for any other vices or virtues. Unhappily the King shows a propensity for the pleasures of the table. That for drink has increased lately, or, at least, it has become more known."

The American Minister immediately set himself to work, with the new cabinet, to produce the meliorations in or additions to the Order of Bernis, of which his recent journey had suggested the propriety. These included a considerable list of American imports which he claimed could be properly made free, or placed at lower rates of duty, and also regulations which would prevent future evasions on the part of the Farmers-General.[2]

Several interesting letters, answers to those of friends, that had accumulated during his absence, appear in his correspondence at this period. Most of them, however, must be passed, as usual, without notice. In one to Madison, commences his comments on the propositions before, and the proceedings of, the Convention of the American States, sitting in Philadelphia, to form a Federal Constitution. He thus speaks of the proposal to give the General Government a negative on State laws:

[1] June 20th.
[2] He asked an entire suppression of duties on pitch, tar and turpentine; that all other fish oils be placed on the same footing with whale oil, as had been intended in the Order of Bernis: that duties levied in contravention of that order at Rouen, be henceforth stopped; that the order itself be formed into an *Arrêt*, and dated back; and some other things. See (in Jefferson's Works) Observations addressed to Count de Montmorin, July 6, 1787. Letter to John Adams, July 1. He also renewed his attack on the contract with the Farmers-General—attempting to procure the unqualified withdrawal of tobacco from it. Letter to Jay, August 6th.

"*Primâ facie*, I do not like it. It fails in an essential character; that the hole and the patch should be commensurate. But this proposes to mend a small hole by covering the whole garment. Not more than one out of one hundred State acts concerns the confederacy. This proposition, then, in order to give them one degree of power, which they ought to have, gives them ninety-nine more, which they ought not to have, upon a presumption that they will not exercise the ninety-nine."

He also complains that the sale of the Western lands of the United States is not commenced for the immediate extinction of their debts; and that on the subject of the navigation of the Mississippi, Congress had shown itself "capable of hesitating on a question which proposed a clear sacrifice of the Western to the maritime States."[1]

Here is the favorite arithmetical argument, applied to a familiar topic, in a letter to David Hartley, of England; and the closing sentences are worth remembering, as giving the length and breadth of Jefferson's "democracy:"

"An insurrection in one of thirteen States in the course of eleven years that they have subsisted, amounts to one in any particular State, in one hundred and forty-three years, say a century and a half. This would not be near as many as have happened in every other government that has ever existed. So that we shall have the difference between a light and a heavy government, as clear gain. I have no fear, but that the result of our experiment will be, that men may be trusted to govern themselves without a master. Could the contrary of this be proved, I should conclude, either that there is no God, or that he is a malevolent being."

On the 6th of July, he replied to a letter from Thomas Mann Randolph, Jr., of Virginia, then at the University of Edinburgh; and three weeks later, to another, from John Wayles Eppes, of the same State, in the College of William and Mary, by both of whom he had been solicited to give his advice in regard to a proper pursuit and a proper line of studies, after the writers should have completed their collegiate education. It is probable that ten such applications were made to Mr. Jefferson by the eminent young men of the day, where one was made to any other of the public men of Virginia, if not of the United States The letters to young Randolph and young Eppes possess the usual interest of all such communications written by the same author, and the additional one, in this case, of being letters of

[1] Jefferson to Madison, June 20.

advice to the future husbands of his daughters, though at the time such a thing was probably very little anticipated.

During this month (July), the long expected " Polly " (Mary, called Marie in France, and thenceforth through life, Maria) reached London. She had crossed the Atlantic with simply a servant girl, though doubtless they were both intrusted to the charge of some passenger friend, or some known and trusted ship commander, whom we do not find named. They were received by Mrs. Adams, and awaited an expected opportunity of crossing the Channel with a party of French friends of Mr. Jefferson. These continued to defer their return, and Mr. Jefferson became too impatient to await their movements. Accordingly his steward, the favorite and trusty Petit, was sent to London after Marie, and she reached her father's hotel in Paris on the 29th of July, just three days before her ninth birth-day.

Mrs. Adams thus described her little guest, immediately after her departure, in a letter to her sister, Mrs. Cranch, of Massachusetts:

"I have had with me for a fortnight a little daughter of Mr. Jefferson's, who arrived here with a young negro girl, her servant, from Virginia. Mr. Jefferson wrote me some months ago that he expected them, and desired me to receive them I did so, and was amply repaid for my trouble. A finer child of her age I never saw. So mature an understanding, so womanly a behavior, and so much sensibility, united, are rarely to be met with. I grew so fond of her, and she was so attached to me, that, when Mr. Jefferson sent for her, they were obliged to force the little creature away. She is but eight years old. She would sit, sometimes, and describe to me the parting with her aunt, who brought her up,[1] the obligations she was under to her, and the love she had for her little cousins, till the tears would stream down her cheeks; and how I had been her friend, and she loved me. Her papa would break her heart by making her go again. She clung round me so that I could not help shedding a tear at parting with her. She was the favorite of every one in the house. I regret that such fine spirits must be spent in the walls of a convent. She is a beautiful girl, too."[2]

Maria (for so we shall henceforth call her, unless when adopting her father's *sobriquet* of Polly) was soon placed with Martha in the school of the Abbaye de Panthemont.

Martha had now grown into a tall, graceful girl, with that calm, sweet face, stamped with thought and earnestness, which, with the traces of many more years on it, and the nobler dignity of the matron superadded, beams down from the speaking can-

----

[1] Mrs. Francis Eppes, of Eppington, Va.   [2] Mrs. Adams's Letters, vol. ii. p. 179.

vas of Sully. The most dutiful of daughters, the most attentive of learners, possessing a solid understanding, a judgment ripe beyond her years, a most gentle and genial temper, and an unassuming modesty of demeanor which neither the distinction of her position, nor the flatteries that afterwards surrounded her, ever wore off in the least degree, she was the idol of her father and family, and the delight of all who knew her.

The little Maria has been sufficiently described by Mrs. Adams. She remarks that she was "beautiful." Slighter in person than her sister, she already gave indications of a superior beauty. It was that exquisite beauty possessed by her mother —that beauty which the experienced learn to look upon with dread, because it betrays a physical organization too delicately fine to withstand the rough shocks of the world.

The relations which Mr. Jefferson bore to his daughters were not the usual ones of a father. We have mentioned the feminine softness and feminine general cast of his feelings in a few particulars—especially where his family was concerned. Then, the early death of his wife devolved maternal as well as paternal duties on him towards his orphaned children. Neither his inclinations nor his habits made the former irksome. He was naturally fond of children ; he was cautious and painstaking; his eye and ear were quick to watch over them and note their little wants ; he had the feminine dexterity and delicacy of manipulation ; he had the feminine loving patience ; he appreciated their feelings and decided instantly and correctly what was under all circumstances appropriate to them, with a feminine instinct. No child or grandchild of his (we make these assertions on full authority) ever received a harsh or angry word from him, on one solitary occasion. Nay, no member of his family ever saw him exhibit passion but barely twice, during his whole life. What those occasions were we shall not fail to relate. No child or grandchild ever complained, even momentarily, of an injustice, great or small, received at his hands. Often and often have those grandchildren heard their mother, Martha Jefferson (Mrs. Randolph), declare, that though her dear and excellent mother died when she was ten years old, she could remember trifling, unintentional errors on her part, but "never, never," she would emphatically add, "had she witnessed a *particle* of injustice in her father—never had she heard

him say a word, or seen him do an act, which she at the time,
or afterwards, regretted." We have heard the same declaration
in respect to him from several of his grandchildren who lived
from ten to thirty years under the same roof.[1]

We seriously doubt whether Mr. Jefferson, in any instance, allowed his most confidential servant—even Petit—
to buy so much as a pair of shoestrings for his daughters
while in Paris. To provide for all their wants was his own
especial and favorite task, either alone or in their company.
He chose thus to let them know his solicitude for their gratification—and they, on the other hand, were not willing to
purchase the most trifling thing until their father's supposed
infallible taste was consulted. "They venerated him," Martha
was wont to say, "as something wiser and better than other
men ; he seemed to them to know everything, even the thoughts
in their minds, all their untold wishes ; they wondered they
did not fear him, yet they did not any more than they did
companions of their own age." "To do anything that he
thought was wrong, in the most trivial thing, they thought not
only wrong, but ungrateful and unaffectionate. They desired
that he might think differently from them, so they could have
the chance of surrendering up their wishes to his. They longed
to do something to serve him—to add, if but in the least degree,
to his comfort and happiness." These feelings were entertained,
as we shall have occasion to see, quite as strongly by the next
generation of his descendants.

If Mr. Jefferson supplied the place of a mother to his two
daughters, they treated him, in some particulars, more as
daughters are wont to treat a mother, than as they often do a
father. Neither had a serious feeling which they did not communicate to him. He was their confident and counsellor in
every girlish doubt—they ran to him with their joys, and fled
to him to weep out their childish griefs on his bosom. And
never, in after life, were these tender and beautiful relations for
a moment broken in upon, or interrupted by a passing shadow.

On the 6th of August, Mr. Jefferson "received an intimation that it would be agreeable [to the French Government] not
to press our commercial regulations at that moment, the Ministry being too much occupied with the difficulties surrounding

---

[1] *All* of his grandchildren most emphatically concur in this declaration.

them to spare a moment on any subject which would admit of delay."[1]

Indications threatening to public tranquillity were now rife in several parts of Europe. In Holland, those fatal convulsions had commenced which destroyed popular freedom. In France, the low rumbling of the earthquake was increasing to an angry roar, and the ground was beginning to heave and to rock under the foundations of society. The meeting of the Assembly of Notables had been the means of exposing the national bankruptcy to every eye. A few timely reforms, and promises of retrenchment, had lulled the public mind into a temporary hope of extrication. It soon became apparent, however, that no serious retrenchments were meditated. On the contrary, the King issued edicts for new taxes, and ordered the Parliament of Paris to enregister them. That body refused. Finally it was summoned to Versailles to hold a " bed of justice," and the King personally, and, in harsh terms, ordered them to enregister two edicts. They stood out, it being their object to compel a resort to a meeting of the States-General, which it was hoped would limit expenses and dictate a constitution. On their final refusal, the King (Aug. 15th) exiled them to Troyes.

Paris was now in commotion. Mobs gathered in the streets and caricatures and inflammatory placards, attacking or ridiculing the Government, were seen in every direction. Some regiments were ordered into the neighborhood of the city; arrests were made; the streets were patrolled by strong military parties; and the places of public amusement were shut up. This apparently restored order—but indications of seated and sullen discontent became daily more apparent. The unfortunate King, " long in the habit of drowning his cares in wine, plunged deeper and deeper. The Queen cried, but sinned on."[2] The reform party daily became stronger, and soon embraced nearly all the young and middle-aged men of France.[3] Finally, the government yielded. The Parliament of Paris was recalled; the obnoxious taxes were given up; and others substituted which fell in proper proportion on the wealthy. The national feelings were again appeased for a time. But the worn-out monarchy had exhibited to the world a fatal indication of its weakness. Mr. Jefferson wrote Mr. Jay:

---

[1] Jefferson to Jay.   [2] Jefferson to Adams, August 30.   [3] Ib

"There can be no better proof of the revolution in the public opinion, as to the powers of the monarch, and of the force, too, of that opinion. Six weeks ago, we saw the King displaying the plenitude of his omnipotence, as hitherto conceived, to enforce these two acts.[1] At this day, he is forced to retract them by the public voice; for as to the opposition of the Parliament, that body is too little esteemed to produce this effect in any case, where the public do not throw themselves into the same scale."

During this lull, the American Minister again urgently pressed the claims of his country. The principal modifications recently solicited by him, in the duties, were made.[1] He then urged the exception of the United States from a recent general *Arrêt* in regard to whale oils, which would operate severely on Massachusetts—insisting that the commerce of a nation which brought nothing but raw materials in exchange, was entitled to privileges over those which brought manufactured products.[2] He pressed his former proposition to reduce all temporary orders and regulations in regard to American commerce into a formal *Arrêt*. This was assented to, and the Comptroller-General and the American Minister worked several days together, aided by General Lafayette and M. Dupont, in settling and arranging its provisions. It was finally passed; and tobacco was, in a separate instrument, made the subject of favorable modifications.[4] The *Arrêt* met with an unsuccessful opposition in the Council. Except in regard to tobacco, nearly every commercial advantage which the United States could, at this period, reasonably expect from France, was now attained.

The complications, and indications of a general war, growing out of the difficulties in Holland, and the interference of Prussia in them, drew from Mr. Jefferson the following reflections on the influence of such a war on the interests of the United States (in a letter to General Washington, August 14th):

"A war, wherein France, Holland, and England should be parties, seems, *primâ facie*, to promise much advantage to us. But in the first place, no war can be safe

[1] The stamp tax and land tax.   [2] See Jefferson to Jay, September 22d.
[3] Letter to Montmorin, October 23d.
[4] Letters to Mr. Jay, November 3d and December 31. We have not the Arrêt before us, but the order of Bernis was the basis of its provisions as far as that went. Then the duties on tar, pitch and turpentine, asked by Jefferson on his return from his journey, were reduced to two and a half per cent. This was but a fourth to a sixth of the former duties on these articles, and was retained as the articles were produced in the South of France. A right of *entrepôt* was thenceforth given to American commerce in all the ports of France. American citizens were given the privileges and advantages of native subjects in all the French possessions in Asia and in the "scales leading thereto," i. e. the isles of France and Bourbon.

for us which threatens France with an unfavorable issue.[1] And in the next, it will probably embark us again into the ocean of speculation, engage us to over-trade ourselves, convert us into sea-rovers, under French and Dutch colors, divert us from agriculture, which is our wisest pursuit, because it will in the end contribute most to real wealth, good morals, and happiness. The wealth acquired by speculation and plunder is fugacious in its nature, and fills society with the spirit of gambling. The moderate and sure income of husbandry begets permanent improvement, quiet life, and orderly conduct both public and private. We have no occasion for more commerce than to take off our superfluous produce, and the people complain that some restrictions prevent this; yet the price of articles with us, in general, shows the contrary. Tobacco, indeed, is low, not because we cannot carry it where we please, but because we make more than the consumption requires. Upon the whole, I think peace advantageous to us, necessary for Europe, and desirable for humanity. A few days will decide, probably, whether all these considerations are to give way to the bad passions of kings, and those who would be kings."

His king-phobia increased ! After commenting (in a letter to Colonel Humphreys, August 14th) on the unfortunate and threatening condition of Europe, he added :

"So much for the blessings of having kings, and magistrates who would be kings. From these events our young Republic may learn useful lessons, never to call on foreign powers to settle their differences, to guard against hereditary magistrates, to prevent their citizens from becoming so established in wealth and power, as to be thought worthy of alliance by marriage with the nieces, sisters, etc., of kings, and, in short, to besiege the throne of heaven with eternal prayers, to extirpate from creation this class of human lions, tigers, and mammoths called kings; from whom, let him perish who does not say, 'good Lord deliver us.'"

He wrote to Mr. Hawkins, August 4th :

"I look up with you to the federal Convention, for an amendment of our federal affairs. Yet I do not view them in so disadvantageous a light at present, as some do. And above all things, I am astonished at some people's considering a kingly government as a refuge. Advise such, to read the fable of the frogs who solicited Jupiter for a king. If that does not put them to rights, send them to Europe, to see something of the trappings of monarchy, and I will undertake, that every man shall go back thoroughly cured. If all the evils which can arise among us, from the republican form of our government, from this day to the day of judgment, could be put into a scale against what this country suffers from its monarchical form in a week, or England in a month, the latter would preponderate. Consider the contents of the Red Book in England, or the Almanach Royal in France, and say what a people gain by monarchy. No race of kings has ever presented above one man of common sense in twenty generations. The best they

---

[1] His belief was that nothing but the fear of France would prevent England from holding on permanently to the portion of our territory she yet forcibly held, and from extending her aggressions.

can do is, to leave things to their ministers; and what are their ministers but a committee, badly chosen? If the king ever meddles, it is to do harm."

To Joseph Jones, August 14th:

"I am anxious to hear what our federal Convention recommends, and what the States will do in consequence of their recommendation. * * * * With all the defects of our Constitution, whether general or particular, the comparison of our governments with those of Europe, is like a comparison of heaven and hell. England, like the earth, may be allowed to take the intermediate station. And yet, I hear there are people among you who think the experience of our governments has already proved that republican governments will not answer."

The view here expressed, that the present American General Government (under the Articles of Confederation), combined with the action of the State Governments, was entirely preferable to any European plan or model, is repeated to many correspondents. To one, he utters the strong language "that it is without comparison the best existing, or that ever did exist." [1]

To John Adams, he wrote, September 28th:

"What a crowd of lessons do the present miseries of Holland teach us! Never to have an hereditary officer of any sort: never to let a citizen ally himself with kings: never to call in foreign nations to settle domestic differences: never to suppose that any nation will expose itself to war for us, etc."

In regard to the proper attitude of the United States in the event of a general war, he thus wrote Mr. Adams, in the same letter:

"We, I hope, shall be left free to avail ourselves of the advantages of neutrality; and yet, much I fear the English, or rather their stupid King, will force us out of it. For thus I reason: By forcing us into the war against them, they will be engaged in an expensive land war, as well as a sea war; common sense dictates, therefore, that they should let us remain neuter: *ergo*, they will not let us remain neuter. I never yet found any other general rule for foretelling what they will do, but that of examining what they ought not to do"

These sentiments are repeated to various other correspondents.

Commenting on the shameless desertion of the patriots of Holland by France, contrary to the most solemn stipulations, he remarked to Mr. Jay:

"It conveys to us the important lesson, that no circumstances of morality, honor, interest, or engagement, are sufficient to authorize a secure reliance on any

[1] Letter to E. Carrington, August 4th.

nation, at all times, and in all positions. A moment of difficulty, or a moment of error, may render forever useless the most friendly dispositions in the King, in the major part of his ministers, and the whole of his nation."

The action of England, its arming to re-establish the Stadtholder, and the present acrimony of all classes of its inhabitants towards the United States, lead to the following suspicions:

"Yet it is possible, that having found that this court will not make war in this moment for any ally, new views may arise, and they may think the moment favorable for executing any purposes they may have, in our quarter. Add to this, that reason is of no aid in calculating their movements. We are, therefore, never safe till our magazines are filled with arms. The present season of truce or peace should, in my opinion, be improved without a moment's respite, to effect this essential object, and no means be omitted, by which money may be obtained for the purpose."

Mr. Jefferson's earlier impressions of the Federal Constitution, and of the expediency of its adoption by the States, has been made a point of some interest in his political history. He expressed great regret that the Convention sat with closed doors, but had a profound respect for the character of that body. He wrote Mr. Adams, August 30th:

"I am sorry they began their deliberations by so abominable a precedent as that of tying up the tongues of their members. Nothing can justify this example, but the innocence of their intentions, and ignorance of the value of public discussions. I have no doubt that all their other measures will be good and wise. It is really an assembly of demigods."

The Constitution, at first view, filled him with disappointment. He wrote Mr. Adams (November 13th), "that there were things in it which staggered all his dispositions to subscribe to what such an assembly had proposed;" to Colonel Smith (the same day), "that there were good articles in it and very bad, he did not know which preponderated." His first elaborate statement of the parts he approved and disapproved, accompanied by his reasons, is contained in a letter to Mr. Madison of December 20th. To give a very rapid synopsis of these: he liked a government which could go on without a recurrence to the State legislatures—the organization into departments—the power of Congress to levy taxes—the election of the greater house by the people directly—the " compromise of the opposite claims of the great and little States, of the latter to equal, and the former to proportional influence "—the substitution of voting in Congress by persons instead of States—the negative given to the Executive conjointly with a third of either house'—and "other good things of less moment," provided for by the Constitution.

What he disliked was: first, "the omission of a bill of rights, providing clearly, and without the aid of sophism, for freedom of religion, freedom of the press, protection against standing armies, restriction of monopolies, the eternal and unremitting force of the habeas corpus laws and trials by jury in all matters of fact triable by the laws of the land, and not by the laws of nations." He declared "that a bill of rights was what the people were entitled to against every government on earth, general or particular—and what no just government should refuse or rest on inference." The second feature he disliked, and strongly disliked, was "the abandonment, in every instance, of the principle of rotation in office, and most particularly in the case of the President."

These objections are supported with great force—particularly that against the perpetual reëligibility of the President. He suggested that after the Constitution had been duly weighed and canvassed by the people, and the parts they disliked and those they approved ascertained, the Convention should reassemble, and again act upon it. "At all events, he hoped" the people "would not be discouraged from making other trials if the present one should fail."

He, however, soon abandoned this idea of having the Convention reassembled, and subscribed heartily to the course proposed by Massachusetts. To bring his views on this subject before the reader connectedly, we will anticipate in the presentation of some later declarations. He wrote Colonel Carrington, May 27th, 1788:

"I learn with great pleasure the progress of the new Constitution. Indeed I have presumed it would gain on the public mind, as I confess it has on my own. At first, though I saw that the great mass and groundwork was good, I disliked many appendages. Reflection and discussion have cleared off most of these. You have satisfied me as to the query I had put to you about the right of direct taxation. My first wish was that nine States would adopt it in order to ensure what was good in it, and that the others might, by holding off, produce the necessary amendments. But the plan of Massachusetts is far preferable, and will, I hope, be

---

¹ But he would have liked it better had the judiciary been associated for that purpose, or invested separately with a similar power.

followed by those who are yet to decide. There are two amendments only which I am anxious for: 1. A bill of rights, which it is so much the interest of all to have, that I conceive it must be yielded. The first amendment proposed by Massachusetts will in some degree answer this end, but not so well. It will do too much in some instances, and too little in others. It will cripple the Federal Government in some cases where it ought to be free, and not restrain in some others where restraint would be right. The 2d amendment which appears to me essential is the restoring the principle of necessary rotation, particularly to the Senate and Presidency: but most of all to the last. Reëligibility makes him an officer for life, and the disasters inseparable from an elective monarchy, render it preferable if we cannot tread back that step, that we should go forward and take refuge in an hereditary one. Of the correction of this article, however, I entertain no present hope, because I find it has scarcely excited an objection in America. And if it does not take place ere long, it assuredly never will. The natural progress of things is for liberty to yield and government to gain ground. As yet our spirits are free. Our jealousy is only put to sleep by the unlimited confidence we all repose in the person to whom we all look as our President. After him inferior characters may perhaps succeed, and awaken us to the danger which his merit has led us into. For the present, however, the general adoption is to be prayed for, and I wait, with great anxiety, for the news from Maryland and South Carolina, which have decided before this, and with that Virginia, now in session, may give the ninth vote of approbation. There could then be no doubt of North Carolina, New York, and New Hampshire. But what do you propose to do with Rhode Island? as long as there is hope we should give her time. I cannot conceive but that she will come to rights in the long run. Force, in whatever form, would be a dangerous precedent."

He wrote E. Rutledge, of South Carolina, July 18, 1788:

"I congratulate you on the accession of your State to the new federal Constitution. This is the last I have yet heard of, but I expect daily to hear that my own has followed the good example, and suppose it to be already established. Our government wanted bracing. Still we must take care not to run from one extreme to another; not to brace too high. I own, I join those in opinion, who think a bill of rights necessary. I apprehend, too, that the total abandonment of the principle of rotation in the offices of President and Senator, will end in abuse But my confidence is, that there will, for a long time, be virtue and good sens} enough in our countrymen to correct abuses. We can surely boast of having set the world a beautiful example of a government reformed by reason alone, without bloodshed. But the world is too far oppressed, to profit by the example. On this side of the Atlantic, the blood of the people is become an inheritance, and those who fatten on it, will not relinquish it easily."

The Constitution, with the amendments adopted in 1789–90, substantially, then, met all of Mr. Jefferson's views, with the single exception of the perpetual reëligibility of the President. And most fortunately (in our judgment) the examples of the first and third Presidents added the desired amendment, in practice, in that particular.

We find Mr. Jefferson, in 1787, as attentive as at previous periods to his miscellaneous correspondence, to those minor official duties which are not of sufficient importance for record, to executing private commissions for friends, and to looking out for everything new, and which promised advantage to his country in any branch of utility. On considering all his occupations, and how much he accomplished, we are inclined to ask ourselves where and when this machine-like industry could have ever paused for rest or sleep? But his secret, in this particular, has been told. "It is wonderful," as he wrote Martha, "how much may be done, if we are always doing."[1] He who turns amusement, relaxation, rest, every waking moment, into some channel of necessary endeavor, will, even though his pace be that of the tortoise, accomplish much in a life—nay, in a single year. And if this unremitting effort is accompanied by the swiftness of the hare, what broad fields of labor will not a single year find passed over—what towering Alps on Alps will not a life-time overcome!

Among a few of his most prominent miscellaneous correspondents of the year (that is, on topics neither diplomatic nor political), we may mention the Count de Buffon, Mr. Rittenhouse, Rev. James Madison, Mr. Vaughan (of England), and Charles Thompson, on scientific topics; Mr. Wythe, Mr. Hopkinson, Dr. Ramsay, and the Count del Vermi, on literary ones; General Washington, on internal improvements; Mr. Drayton and Mr. Rutledge, on the subject of introducing better varieties of rice, the culture of olives, and various other South-of-Europe products into the Southern States of America, etc., etc.

An amusing anecdote is preserved of the subject of his correspondence with the celebrated Buffon. The story used to be so well told by Daniel Webster—who probably heard it from the lips of the New Hampshire party to it—that we will give it in his words, as we find it recorded by an intelligent writer, and one evidently very familiar with Mr. Webster, in an article in Harper's Magazine, entitled Social Hours of Daniel Webster:

"Mr. Webster, in the course of his remarks, narrated a story of Jefferson's overcoming Buffon on a question of Natural History. It was a dispute in relation

[1] Letter to Martha, May 5th, 1787, ante, p. 474.

to the moose—the moose-deer, as it is called in New Hampshire—and in one of the circles of *beaux esprits* in Paris, Mr. Jefferson contended for certain characteristics in the formation of the animal, which Buffon stoutly denied. Whereupon Mr. Jefferson, without giving any one notice of his intention, wrote from Paris to General John Sullivan, then residing in Durham, New Hampshire, to procure and send him the whole frame of a moose. The General was no little astonished at a request he deemed so extraordinary; but well acquainted with Mr. Jefferson, he knew he must have sufficient motive for it; so he made a hunting party of his neighbors and took the field. They captured a moose of unusual proportions, stripped it to the bone, and sent the skeleton to Mr. Jefferson, at a cost of fifty pounds sterling. On its arrival, Mr. Jefferson invited Buffon and some other *savans* to a supper at his house, and exhibited his dear-bought specimen. Buffon immediately acknowledged his error, and expressed his great admiration for Mr. Jefferson's energetic determination to establish the truth. 'I should have consulted you, monsieur,' he said, with usual French civility, 'before publishing my book on Natural History, and then I should have been sure of my facts.'" [1]

This has the advantage of most such anecdotes of eminent men, of being accurate nearly to the letter as far as it goes. The box of President Sullivan (he was the President of New Hampshire) containing the bones, horns, and skin of a moose, and horns of the caribou, elk, deer, spiked-horned buck, etc., reached Mr. Jefferson on the 2d of October. They were the next day forwarded to Buffon—who, however, proved to be out of town.[2] On his return, he took advantage of a supper at Jefferson's, to make the handsome admissions mentioned by Mr. Webster.[3]

As a specimen of the old Federal (using the word in its partisan sense) *ideal* of Mr. Jefferson, we cannot forbear to give some other remarks attributed to Mr. Webster, in the same connection, by the same writer:

"Jefferson rather preferred scientific or literary discussions. He was addicted to French tastes, French manners, and French principles. Often unjustly attacked by them, the Federalists yet did him no injustice in charging upon him a preference for French opinions, whether in politics, morals, or religion.

"He used to dwell with pleasure upon his acquaintance with D'Alembert, Condorcet, and others of the Liberal Philosophy; and often spoke of the *conversazioni* of Madame Deffand, at which he was a frequent and not undistinguished guest. His 'Notes on Virginia' had been published, and were known and admired at Paris; while his conversational powers, no less than his diplomatic ability, confirmed the impression of his intellectual eminence."

[1] Harper's Magazine of July, 1856.
[2] See Jefferson to Monsieur le Comte de Buffon, October 3d; and to his Excellency President Sullivan, October 5th.
[3] Since the above was written, the Private Correspondence of Daniel Webster, edited by Fletcher Webster (his son), has appeared, and in a memorandum of conversations held with Mr. Jefferson at Monticello, in December, 1824, Mr. Webster gives some additions to the preceding statements, but they are not material.

To show how extremely easy it is for distinguished conversationalists to slide into errors of fact, we may remark that death had closed the doors of Du Deffand's "conversazioni" some years before Jefferson arrived in France! And we think D'Alembert died in 1783.

How far Jefferson borrowed his political views from France we have been showing in this and the preceding chapter. We think we have shown how applicable also is the remark in respect to his "morals." But we will not press that head now, as evidence on it will continue to accumulate to the end of his life. On the declaration that Jefferson gave a preference to "French opinions" in "religion," we propose to bestow some notice.

An assertion of this kind, especially connected with the allusion to the "liberal philosophy," and coming from the lips of a New Englander, will be generally understood as implying the charge of atheism. D'Alembert, and most of the propagators of the "liberal philosophy," were, as we understand it, unqualified Atheists.[1] Those who stopped short of this miserable abyss, and who were what are technically called Deists, were usually scoffers and railers. There was a class of early English Deists, who, like Milton's evil angels, were stately enemies of the truth, and who, like them, hurled mountains in combat. Voltaire's private correspondence with D'Alembert gives us an inside picture of French infidelity (whether atheism or deism) towards the close of the last century; and the difference is enormous. It is Faust's Mephistopheles to Milton's Lucifer. It is Thersites against Agamemnon and Ulysses. It is a leering, sneering, petty devil, that scolds like a drab, and seeks to raise a laugh like a buffoon. There is a cold-blooded selfishness in Voltaire's letters that disgusts any large-hearted man, whatever his faith, or want of faith. For example, with what an icy contempt he repeatedly expresses his willingness that "cooks," "chambermaids," and "butlers" should cling to a system which he affects to regard as not only wholly untruthful, but pernicious to all the best interests of society! The spirit of French infidelity, as exhibited by this its great champion, was malignant and cow-

---

[1] Priestley, in his sixth "Letter to the Philosophers of France," says that, "when I was in your country [in 1774] then, excepting Mr. Necker, who was a Protestant, every person of eminence to whom I had access, and, as I saw reason to think, *every man of letters, almost without exception, was a professed Atheist, and an unbeliever in a future state on any principle whatever.*"

ardly. It snatched the last plank from the sinking wretch, and then offered him no shadow of a substitute. It dodged, and equivocated, and falsified, even on the death-bed, to escape temporal punishments, or disgraces inflicted after death.¹ There were better-hearted men doubtless than Voltaire—some noble-hearted men—who adopted his ideas in religion. But in giving his character, we have given what has generally been regarded in this country, and particularly in New England, as the personal type of French infidelity. We have shown what idea a New Englander, professing Calvinistic tenets, is generally understood to hold out, when he charges French opinions in religion. Nay, if Mr. Webster did not do so, thousands of others did charge Mr. Jefferson with atheism, and with a truly Voltairean bitterness and hate towards Christianity. Pulpit and press rung with these charges.

It is proper that we frankly apprise the reader how far we propose to discuss Mr. Jefferson's religious views. Let us say at once, that we do not propose, in any event, to make up an individual issue with Mr. Webster, on this topic. If he said what is imputed to him, he only repeated a common charge of Mr. Jefferson's foes. His remarks but incidentally attracted our attention to a topic to which we should otherwise have been immediately brought by a letter in Mr. Jefferson's correspondence in 1787.

Whether we have any right to inquire into and discuss another man's individual opinions in religion, depends, in our judgment, upon one circumstance. The simple holding of an opinion, deemed by others erroneous, ought not to entitle any one to denounce the holder of it for so doing. If he attempts to propagate his faith, then most clearly, those who consider it a pernicious one, have full right to attack it and expose its tendencies, whatever may be the influence of that exposure on the public estimation of the holder. It is a sickly and overstrained sentiment which would protect the individual who turns proselyter, at the

---

¹ "See, I pray you [Voltaire wrote D'Alembert], a *pious fraud*. I receive in my bed the viaticum, brought me by my curé, attended by the heads of my parish" (vol. ii. p. 236). "There are eleven Jesuits at Marseilles, and one who says mass for me" (vol. i. p. 313). D'Alembert wrote back: "You are in the right, my dear master, people of condition can only combat *by hiding themselves behind hedges*; but thence they may fire with effect on the wild beasts that infest the country." "You reproach us with indifference; but I think I told you that the fire of the fagots is very refreshing," etc. etc.

expense of society ; which would prevent the manly lover of the truth from assailing untruth, come when or from whom it may.

The only question, then, in respect to the propriety of examining into and pronouncing on Mr. Jefferson's religious opinions, is this. Did he, by publication or any other means, attempt to propagate those opinions? Strictly speaking, he did not, as we shall abundantly show at the proper time. But yet there are reasons which we believe ought still to deprive him of the immunity which that circumstance usually confers. Mr. Jefferson left all his papers to a grandson. He made him the owner of the papers without any restrictions or directions. He therefore confided them to the judgment of his descendant, and made himself answerable for the manner in which that judgment should be exercised. The grandson published the papers after Mr. Jefferson's death. They thus came legitimately before the world, and the world has an undeniable right to judge and speak of them according to its opinion of their merits.

We are attempting to give the history of the *mind* as well as of the public career of a statesman. If he has by himself, or by another, admitted the public to a knowledge of his religious views, it is far too important a subject to be passed in silence or slurred over in a few general or vague phrases. We esteem it our duty to give his opinions on this as on other important topics, so far as they are in our possession. We shall not do so yet, for his expressions concerning religion are, at the point of his life now reached, but commencing. The importance and delicacy of the topic, and its utter disconnection with any of the incidents of his public career, will induce us to depart from our usual course of giving or alluding to his declarations as they are from time to time made, and to reserve them for a connected view at the end of his Life.

We shall have occasion, however, to earlier examine a related, but nevertheless essentially different question. Mr. Jefferson did not become responsible to the world for the utterances of what we shall show to have been a few deeply confidential letters, until those letters were made public. But long before their publication, during the last twenty-five or thirty years of his life, his religious opinions were made a free topic of discussion. He was charged with being an active and aggressive foe of Christianity. Thousands are yet alive who recollect the furious tempest which burst on his head, on this subject, from press and pulpit, pending both his elections to the Presidency. The Christian church of our country was declared to be in danger if he succeeded. It was popularly said at the time, that in parts of New England, timid females hid their Bibles in the clefts of rocks, and enthusiastic disciples girded up their loins to encounter terrible persecutions, when it was understood that he was elected.

What had he done to give rise to such impressions of his religious character? Had he published, or permitted the publication of anything which avowedly, or by fair implication, was intended as an attack on Christianity? All that was adduced to prove this was a sentence or two from the Notes on Virginia, declaratory of the fact that the religious beliefs of one man do not inflict on any other man that physical or other legal injury, which it is the province of law to punish; and by certain geological and ethnological speculations which do not, as we understand it, deny anything in the Scriptures, or require an interpretation of them different from that adopted by men whom Mr. Jefferson's assailants would be ready to concede of the most eminent ability and piety.[1]

Was Mr. Jefferson in the habit of arguing against, or sneering at, Christianity in conversation? We remember only to have seen a single remark of such a tenor attributed to him (said to have been made to Mazzei—see Appendix 18), which was too manifestly ridiculous to call for a denial; yet Mr. Jefferson did, in his private correspondence, indignantly deny it. But whether one or twenty such stories got afloat, we feel perfectly authorized to say that they were false, and were not supported by any proof which really justified cool and rational men in giving them temporary credit.

We will give our reasons fully for so unhesitatingly declaring their falsity. We will attempt to show, by as satisfactory proof as the nature of the case admits of—as nearly as a negative can ever be shown—that Mr. Jefferson never, at any period of life, made himself an aggressive assailant of Christianity; that he

---

[1] The most distinguished *writer*, perhaps—certainly the most distinguished *ecclesiastical* writer who found intentional attacks on Christianity in the Notes on Virginia—was the Rev. John M. Mason, D.D., of New York, and his pamphlet on the subject is *republished* in his collected writings by his son. Those who are desirous to see what were the Rev. gentleman's positions, and what was the character of his strictures, will find them hereafter stated.

never, in a solitary instance, sought directly or indirectly to proselyte a human being to unchristian views, or to shake his conviction in Christian ones. Looking at the naked facts now, it would seem a matter of astonishment that he could have been so misunderstood and misrepresented· on this subject by a portion of his contemporaries, on the strength of evidence which, before a tribunal accustomed to pay any attention to sound and just rules of evidence, would fail to command serious notice. But if we look into the surrounding circumstances impartially —with that spirit of liberality towards his opponents which it must be confessed they never showed to him, we believe some excuses can be found for the conduct of the great portion, and particularly the religious portion of them. We do not propose to defer this question—the religious issue between the *living* Jefferson and his antagonists—like the preceding one, to the conclusion of his history. The facts will be required to furnish contemporaneous explanations of several important circumstances in his public and private career. We shall probably enter upon their examination while narrating the events of the year 1800—when he was first publicly assaulted on this subject on an extensive and imposing scale.

CHAPTER XIII.

1788—1789.

First Official Acts in 1788—Paul Jones—Pecuniary Difficulties of United States—Jefferson repairs to Holland—With Adams effects Loans—Tour up the Rhine—Mathematical Formula for shaping a Plow—State of Paris at his Return—Letter to General Washington—Proposes transferring French Debts to Holland—Gives Brissot Letters of Introduction—Outfit—New Consular Convention—Annoyed by French Creditors of United States—Repulses Impertinence of General Armand—Asks Leave of Absence—Nobody to grant it—Miscellaneous Correspondence of the Year—Questions a Theory of Newton—Disregard of mere Authority in Science—Newton, Buffon, and Lavoisier—Blunders of the Learned—Curtain drops on Poor Ledyard—His Warm Affection for Jefferson—Jefferson declines joining Society for Abolition of Slave Trade—English Judicial Decisions in America—Letter to General Washington—Inside Views—Opinion on Female Influence in French Politics—Further History of French Affairs—Famine in the Winter of 1788-9—Relief from America—Recall of French Minister in America asked—Governeur Morris's Secret—Extracts from Letters and Diary of Morris—Speculations—France on Morris's Shoulders—Jefferson's Views of Proper Objects of the Patriots—Sack of Reveillon's House—Opening of States-General—Disputes between Orders—Lafayette's Instructions and Jefferson's Advice—Progress of Events—Jefferson's Letter to St. Etienne—Proposes a Charter of Rights—Patriots demand too much and lose all—Character of Necker—Jefferson and Mirabeau—Further Events—"Let the People eat Grass"—The Issue of Blood made up—Jefferson between the Military and the People—Different Accounts of the Fray—Attack on the Bastile—Another Chance for Compromise thrown away—Jefferson's Opinion of the King and Queen—He is invited to Assist in forming a Constitution—His Reasons for declining—Constitution Settled at his House—The Parties in the National Assembly—Explanations between Jefferson and Montmorin—Personal Affairs—Jefferson neither Federalist nor Anti-Federalist—Made LL.D. by Harvard University—His Answer—Family Incidents—Martha wishes to enter a Convent—Letter to General Washington—Views on Titles of Honor in United States—Views on Neutrality between France and England—Past and Present Course of these Nations towards the United States—English Sympathisers in United States—This Party existed before the French Revolution—Jefferson averse to entering President's Cabinet—"Can one Generation of Men bind another?"—He receives Leave of Absence—Particulars of Journey until final Sailing—His Valedictory to France—Some Review of his Diplomatic Labors—Discharge of Minor Duties—Attentions to Americans Abroad—His Course towards Young Travellers—His Strong Partiality for Young Men—Other Unofficial Duties—Ability of his Dispatches—Political Prophesying—His Diplomatic Career commands Universal Applause—Mr. Jay's Testimony on the Subject—Judge Marshall's—Daniel Webster's—English Expressions—Martha Jefferson's Narrative of Journey Home—Danger at Norfolk—Reception at Home—Old Wormley's Version of the Reception—An African Ovation.

ONE of Mr. Jefferson's first official acts, in 1788, was to dispatch a special agent to Denmark to obtain reparation for prizes captured by Commodore John Paul Jones from the English, during the recent war; and which having put into Bergen in distress, were, by the orders of the Danish Court, taken from their captors and delivered back to the English. Congress having intrusted our Minister to France with the negotiation, and with the appointment of an agent, he very properly selected Jones himself. Jefferson always entertained a favorable opinion of this remarkable man, and had employed his services on several previous occasions. Thus, three years earlier, he had sent him to Brest to observe Laperouse's ill-fated expedition then fitting out—as it had been reported that it was designed to plant a colony or trading factories on the west coast of North America.[1] Jefferson seems to have entertained these suspicions for a long time, and indeed until they were dispelled by a full knowledge of the facts. He always spoke of Jones in his correspondence, and always treated him personally as a discreet and intelligent man, whose honor and whose patriotism to his adopted country were entirely above suspicion. Very soon after the mission of the latter to Denmark, a circumstance occurred which illustrated his character in these particulars. Received as a Vice-Admiral into the Russian service, he annexed as a condition of his acceptance, that he should be permitted to withdraw whenever the United States required his services.

Another subject now began "to press upon" Jefferson's "mind," to use his own words, "like a mountain."[2] The position of affairs between the United States and their European creditors had always been a source of great annoyance to our Ministers. Not even the interest of the French debt, so peculiarly one of honor, and the repayment of which was so pressingly needed, was met. And the Treasury Board had recently announced that they could not possibly make further remittances to Europe within a year—indeed, until the new Government established under the federal Constitution (of 1787) should go into operation and should make provisions for raising the money. In the meantime, the American Ministers in Europe were expected to sustain the credit of their country by meeting the demands against it, from the proceeds of a loan which had been opened in Holland, but which, after being but in small part filled, had ceased to be taken up. Two hundred and

[1] Jefferson to Jay. August 14, 1785.   [2] Letter to John Adams, March 2d, 1788.

seventy thousand florins would be requisite to meet interest, in the coming June. The holders of the former bonds offered to take all the remaining ones, provided they might receive out of them the interest of a part of the United States domestic debt, of which they were also the holders. Jefferson had no authority to accept this proposal.[1] He writes in his Memoir :

"Mr. Adams, while residing at the Hague, had a general authority to borrow what sums might be requisite for ordinary and necessary expenses. Interest on the public debt, and the maintenance of the diplomatic establishment in Europe, had been habitually provided in this way. He was now elected Vice-President of the United States, was soon to return to America, and had referred our bankers to me for future counsel, on our affairs in their hands. But I had no powers, no instructions, no means, and no familiarity with the subject. It had always been exclusively under his management, except as to occasional and partial deposits in the hands of Mr. Grand, banker in Paris, for special and local purposes.   *   * *   *   Mr. Adams had received his appointment to the court of London while engaged at Paris, with Dr. Franklin and myself, in the negotiations under our joint commissions. He had repaired thence to London, without returning to the Hague, to take leave of that government. He thought it necessary, however, to do so now, before he should leave Europe, and accordingly went there. I learned his departure from London, by a letter from Mrs. Adams, received on the very day on which he would arrive at the Hague. A consultation with him, and some provision for the future, was indispensable, while we could yet avail ourselves of his powers ; for when they would be gone, we should be without resource. I was daily dunned by a company who had formerly made a small loan to the United States, the principal of which was now become due ; and our bankers in Amsterdam had notified me that the interest on our general debt would be expected in June ; that if we failed to pay it, it would be deemed an act of bankruptcy, and would effectually destroy the credit of the United States, and all future prospect of obtaining money there."

Two days after receiving Mrs. Adams's letter (March 4th), Jefferson set out for Amsterdam, travelling as usual in his own carriage by post horses. He went by the way of Valenciennes, Bruxelles, Antwerp, Rotterdam, and the Hague, where he found Mr. Adams, and they proceeded together to Amsterdam, which they reached on the 10th.

Both Ministers concurred in the belief that it would be better at once, by a new and sufficient loan, to provide for the demands against the government for the current and two succeeding years, for the purpose of placing the latter at its ease, and its credit in security, during what they foresaw would be a very trying period. Bonds for a new loan of a million of florins

---

[1] Jefferson to Jay, March 16th.

were accordingly executed—but the American bankers were instructed not to sell them, until Congress should give its approbation to the action of the Ministers.

Nothing urgent demanding Jefferson's immediate presence in Paris, he determined to proceed up the Rhine as far as Strasbourg on his return route. He kept a journal of his journey. It is as dry and utilitarian in its tone and topics as his previous productions of the same class. It gives precise and oftentimes minute details in regard to the topography, agriculture, population, architecture, mechanical arts, etc., of the country passed through, and will be found entire in the ninth volume of the Congress edition of his works.[1]

The pocket account-book, as usual, throws a good deal of additional light on the journal—but we can devote but little space to either. He left Amsterdam March 30th, and reached Nymegen on the 31st. Crossing the Prussian frontier the next morning, he saw, without any change of soil or climate, a sudden transition from opulence to poverty, and the "fear of slaves visible in the faces of the Prussian subjects." Dusseldorf was reached on the 2d of April, and he paid *exactly* "two florins one stiver" for seeing its famous gallery. He arrived at Cologne the next day, and Bonn and Coblentz on the 4th. Entering Nassau, he passed up the Maine to Frankfort and Hanau, and the difference in the agriculture and commercial stir in the republic and the landgravate, suggests the customary political comparisons. Remaining three days at Frankfort, he returned down the Maine to Mayence on the 11th. He next passed through Oppenheim and Worms, and reached Manheim. He paused here two days, making excursions to Heidelburg, and to points where celebrated German wines were made, such as Hocheim, Johansberg, and Rudesheim. At Heidelburg, we have a very brief description of the ruins of the Château, as he terms it—(the huge palace of the Electors of the Palatinate, one of the vastest and most magnificent wrecks of mediæval grandeur in Germany)—in less than a dozen lines; and about an *equal number* are devoted to the "ton of Heidelburg!" The Drachenfels, Ehrenbreitstein, Rheinfels, etc., are not, we believe, even named.

He left Manheim on the 15th of April, reached Carlsruhe

----
[1] Pp. 373-403.

the same day, and Strasbourg on the next. On the 17th, he struck across the northwest part of France, by the way of Nancy, to St. Dizier on the Marne, and followed the banks of that river to Paris, which he reached on the 23d of April.

It has been claimed that Mr. Jefferson was the first who laid down a *rule*—a mathematical formula—for shaping the mould-board of a plow. The first notice of this which we have met in his writings, occurs in his journal of his progress from Strasbourg to Nancy, dated April 19th. The following quotation contains all he there said on the subject (though we shall have more of it subsequently):

"Oxen plough here with collars and hames. The awkward figure of their mould-board leads one to consider what should be its form. The offices of the mould-board are to receive the sod after the share has cut under it, to raise it gradually, and to reverse it. The fore-end of it, then, should be horizontal to enter under the sod, and the hind end perpendicular to throw it over; the intermediate surface changing gradually from the horizontal to the perpendicular. It should be as wide as the furrow, and of a length suited to the construction of the plough. The following would seem a good method of making it: Take a block, whose length, breadth, and thickness, is that of your intended mould-board, suppose two and a half feet long, and eight inches broad and thick. Draw the lines *a d* and

Fig. 1.　　Fig. 2.

c d, figure 1; with a saw, the toothed edge of which is straight, enter at *a* and cut on, guiding the hind part of the saw on the line *a b*, and the fore part on the line *a d*, till the saw reaches the points *c* and *d*, then enter it at *c* and cut on, guiding it by the lines *c b* and *c d* till it reaches the points *b* and *d*. The quarter, *a b c d*, will then be completely cut out, and the diagonal from *d* to *b* laid bare. The piece may now be represented as in figure 2. Then saw in transversely at every two inches till the saw reaches the line *c e*, and the diagonal *b d*, and cut out the pieces with an adze. The upper surface will thus be formed. With a gauge opened to eight inches, and guided by the lines *c e*, scribe the upper edge of the board from *d b*, cut that edge perpendicular to the face of the board, and scribe it of the proper thickness. Then form the under side by the upper, by cutting transversely with the saw, and taking out the piece with an adze. As the upper edge of the wing of the share rises a little, the fore end of the board, *b c*, will rise as much from a strict horizontal position, and will throw the hind end, *e d*, exactly as much beyond the perpendicular, so as to promote the reversing of the sod."

Mr. Jefferson thus sums up and comments on the situation of affairs as he found them in the French capital on his return from his seven weeks' absence:

"On my return from Holland, I found Paris as I had left it, still in high fermentation. Had the Archbishop, on the close of the Assembly of Notables, immed'.

ately carried into operation the measures contemplated, it was believed they would all have been registered by the Parliament; but he was slow, presented his edicts, one after another, and at considerable intervals, which gave time for the feelings excited by the proceedings of the Notables to cool off, new claims to be advanced, and a pressure to arise for a fixed constitution, not subject to changes at the will of the king. Nor should we wonder at this pressure, when we consider the monstrous abuses of power under which this people were ground to powder; when we pass in review the weight of their taxes, and the inequality of their distribution; the oppressions of the tythes, the tailles, the corvées, the gabelles, the farms and the barriers; the shackles on commerce by monopolies; on industry by guilds and corporations; on the freedom of conscience, of thought, and of speech; on the freedom of the press by the Censure, and of the person by Lettres de Cachet; the cruelty of the Criminal Code generally; the atrocities of the Rack; the venality of Judges, and their partialities to the rich; the monopoly of military honors by the Noblesse; the enormous expenses of the Queen, the Princes and the Court; the prodigalities of pensions; and the riches, luxury, indolence, and immorality of the Clergy. Surely under such a mass of misrule and oppression, a people might justly press for thorough reformation, and might even dismount their rough-shod riders, and leave them to walk on their own legs." [1]

The first letter written after his return, was a very long reply to a recent one from General Washington. It discussed numerous topics, and is distinguished for its frankness. After detailing very fully the existing political relations of Europe, and alluding to the causes of his journey to Holland, he took occasion to press the idea on his correspondent that the United States ought to adopt "the English plan" of never opening a loan "without levying and appropriating taxes for the payment of its interest." It is noticeable that a project of Mr. Jefferson, afterwards denounced by a fellow member of General Washington's cabinet (Colonel Hamilton), as both a dishonest and dishonorable one, is pressed upon the notice of the General, in this letter, as if the writer was too dull to discern his own criminality, or else expected his correspondent to be so. This was the expediency of transferring all the United States French debts, public and private, to Holland. The object of this, and its alleged unfairness, will be hereafter examined. Jefferson strongly urged his objections to the new Constitution—particularly to the perpetual reëligibility of the President—though, trusting to the good sense of the people for the necessary amendments, he expressed a decided hope for its adoption.

M. Brissot (or Brissot de Warville), subsequently so celebrated in the French Revolution, being about to set out on that

[1] Memoir.

tour in the United States, of which he has left a printed account, received a letter of introduction from Mr. Jefferson to Mr. Madison, dated May 3d, under the name of "Mr. Warville"—and Jefferson's impression of his much disputed character will be found in the statement to Madison that he was a "truly estimable" man, "and a great enthusiast for liberty."

Jefferson wrote Mr. Jay in May, asking in lieu of the actual expense of his outfit (as provided for by act of Congress) an additional year's salary ($9,000), stating that his outfit, though plain, had exceeded that cost; but that he had found it impracticable to separate his private and official expenses, and have each minute item of the latter regularly vouched. Congress assented to this, and the same rule was subsequently adopted in all cases.

On the 20th of June, the American Minister addressed the Count de Montmorin on the subject of the existing Consular Convention between France and the United States. The causes and result of the application are thus stated in the Memoir:

"A Consular Convention had been agreed on in '84, between Dr. Franklin and the French government, containing several articles, so entirely inconsistent with the laws of the several States, and the general spirit of our citizens, that Congress withheld their ratification, and sent it back to me, with instructions to get those articles expunged, or modified so as to render them compatible with our laws. The Minister unwillingly released us from these concessions, which, indeed, authorized the exercise of powers very offensive in a free State. After much discussion, the Convention was reformed in a considerable degree, and was signed by the Count Montmorin and myself, on the 14th of November, '88, not, indeed, such as I would have wished, but such as could be obtained with good humor and friendship."[1]

Nothing further of importance took place, during the year, in the diplomatic affairs of the two countries. Towards the close of it, we find Mr. Jefferson proposing some further concessions in the French tariff on American productions. The concerns of the American prisoners among the Barbary powers were, as heretofore, most assiduously cared for, and every effort, compatible with the Minister's instructions, made for their release. Many other diplomatic affairs received attention, which, though of importance at the time of their occurrence, would now possess no interest to the general reader.

· The amended convention is published in Mr. Jefferson's Works (Randolph's edition), vol. ii. p. 375. Congress edition, vol. ii. p. 498.

There was no more vexatious part of the Minister's duty than to meet and parry, as well as he could, the demands of the private creditors of the United States in France. Many of these were officers who had served in America, and who, doubtless, sorely needed the sums due them. Their complaints were loud, and unfortunately they were just. But the Minister was in no way accountable for this, and when, in a single instance, importunity assumed the tone of insolence, the offender received a lesson which taught him, if it did not others, the inutility of that course. After explaining to this person, the Marquis de la Rouerie (General Armand), exactly how the matter of his debt stood, in a business point of view, Jefferson quietly added :

"Finding that my interference, which was friendly only, and avowed to be inofficial, has given occasion to your letter of yesterday, in a style which I did not expect, and to which I can have no motive for further exposing myself, I must take the liberty of desiring that the correspondence between us on this subject may cease. I presume that the certificate given you, points out the person, here or elsewhere, to whom your applications are to be made, and that he will inform you when he receives orders on your subject."

This is the only letter we remember to have seen in Jefferson's voluminous correspondence, replying to a personally offensive communication.

About the middle of November, he solicited Congress for a leave of absence, extending, including his journey to and from America, to five or six months, and that, in the meantime, Mr. Short might be named Secretary of Legation, which would enable him to act as *Chargé des Affaires*. Mr. Jay replied, the next spring, that "since the 13th day of September [1788] nine States had not been represented in Congress, and since the 10th of October last, a sufficient number for ordinary business had not convened."[1] There was no one, therefore, officially authorized to grant the Minister's request. The Secretary of Foreign Affairs, at the same time, informed Mr. Jefferson that "his conduct was greatly and deservedly commended."[2]

The scientific and miscellaneous correspondence of the year betrays the usual activity in those directions. A remark in the former, in a letter to the Rev. James Madison, of William and Mary College, is somewhat characteristic of a trait of Mr. Jef-

---

[1] Jay to Jefferson, March 9, 1789; Diplomatic Correspondence of the U. S., vol. iv p. 43.
[2] Ib.

ferson's mind. He says: "an abbé here has shaken, if not destroyed, the theory of De Dominis, Descartes, and Newton, for explaining the phenomenon of the rainbow." During Mr. Jefferson's whole life, we find that his regard for mere authority, however weighty, was next to nothing. He particularly respected the character, the abilities, and, we may add, the scientific achievements of Newton. He was wont to name him as one of his "trinity" of truly great men. Yet one of Newton's theories would be thrown into the scale against any glib-tongued French abbé's, or new English or American professor's, as if Newton's mere name did not weigh a feather in the argument. Nay, such was the boldness and ardor of Jefferson's mind, that we have sometimes thought he possessed a sort of credulity or partiality towards a new proposition, because it was new. But further observation satisfies us of the injustice of this criticism. He was a rapid and a bold thinker—and, as it always happens with such (especially where they are bold in expressing as well as forming impressions) his first ones were often erroneous. If he settled down into any scientific heresies, we do not happen to know what they were, unless it was in geology, and there he adopted no false theory, but only from omitting to keep up with investigation, refused to accept what is generally received as the right one.[1] These off-hand, bold expressions of his are not perhaps oftener erroneous than those of other men, who dare, like him, to think out loud. If the transient vagaries of the learned and the great were all fairly recorded, we should find these "sceptered monarchs of mankind" very human sort of beings after all. We should find each of them possessed of his wisdom and his folly—his credulities and his incredulities—his whims, vagaries, and weaknesses, as well as his great parts. Their characters, as publicly received, are generally at least half manufactured by fancy and fiction. How the world, for example, repeats with pleased wonder the stereotyped tale of this same majestic Newton, that when his priceless papers were destroyed by fire (in 1692) he only calmly turned to his *dog*, and exclaimed, "Ah, Diamond! little dost thou know what thou hast done!"[2] Yet indisputable facts would seem to make it appear, that instead of displaying any such marvellous and unnatural equanimity, that majestic

[1] See page 371, note.   [2] Or some about equivalent expression.

mind tottered long on the dark confines of madness. And facts
would seem to show that even Newton was not always right
and always great, because out of upwards (so Dr. Hutton states)
"four thousand sheets in folio, or eight reams of foolscap paper,
besides the bound books, of which the number of sheets is not
mentioned," which he spent years in writing, but two inconsiderable articles were thought worth publication,[1] and neither of
these added anything to his fame.

We have a nearer case in point, recorded in the very letter
of Jefferson to Madison, under consideration. He says:

"Speaking one day with Monsieur de Buffon, on the present ardor of chemical
inquiry, he affected to consider chemistry but as cookery, and to place the toils of
the laboratory on a footing with those of the kitchen. I think it, on the contrary,
among the most useful of sciences, and big with future discoveries for the utility
and safety of the human race. It is yet, indeed, a mere embryo. Its principles
are contested; experiments seem contradictory; their subjects are so minute as to
escape our senses; and their result too fallacious to satisfy the mind. It is probably an age too soon, to propose the establishment of a system. The attempt, therefore, of Lavoisier to reform the chemical nomenclature, is premature. One single
experiment may destroy the whole filiation of his terms, and his string of sulphates,
sulphites, and sulphures, may have served no other end, than to have retarded the
progress of the science, by a jargon, from the confusion of which, time will be
requisite to extricate us. Accordingly, it is not likely to be admitted generally."

We have here another hasty judgment of Jefferson's on
Lavoisier's[2] system; but the point to which we would call
attention is that Buffon considered chemistry (in 1788) as a
science on a par with *cookery!* This extract shows (like a multitude of others that might be quoted) that Jefferson, like other
men, great and small, sometimes formed wise and shrewd judgments, and sometimes very crude ones; and it shows that not
only active business men like him who are compelled to run as
they read, may sometimes blunder in their scientific impressions
and conjectures, but that professed savans, of the first magnitude, may and do fall into most absurd errors. A decent sized
library would be required to contain all the instances of this,
which could be collected in the lives of really great and really
learned men.

We catch two or three glimpses of poor Ledyard this year—

---

[1] Art. *Newton*—Hutton's Mathematical Dictionary.
[2] Jefferson was a personal acquaintance of Lavoisier's, and was present at some of his
scientific *conversazioni*. It is somewhat singular to think of this celebrated man in the
world of science as one of the obnoxious Farmers-General of France! And this cost him
his life in the Revolution. He was guillotined in 1794.

before the curtain fell on his brief and rough career. Regarding Jefferson as a particular benefactor and friend, he kept him apprised of his movements. Before starting on his last fatal expedition to the Niger, he called on the former at Paris, and promised, "if he escaped through his journey," to renew his old endeavor to explore the west coast of America. He wrote Mr. Jefferson several times from Egypt. The following passage from one of his letters, shows that if he did not possess high breeding, he certainly did high and acute feelings:

"I shall never think my letter an indifferent one, when it contains the declaration of my gratitude and affection for you; and this, notwithstanding you thought hard of me for being employed by an English Association, which hurt me much while I was at Paris. You know your own heart, and if my suspicions are groundless, forgive them, since they proceed from the jealousy I have, not to lose the regard you have, in time past, been pleased to honor me with. You are not obliged to esteem me, but I am obliged to esteem you, or to take leave of my senses, and confront the opinions of the greatest and best characters I know."

Jefferson showed great solicitude about Ledyard's fate, when rumors of his death began to reach France and England. We find inquiries, new rumors, hopes and fears on the subject in various of his letters.

The following passage from a letter from Mr. Jefferson to A. Donald, shows with what ready fondness he recurred to and renewed the attachments of early life. The letter was accompanied by a present of books:

"Your letter has kindled all the fond recollections of ancient times; recollections much dearer to me than anything I have known since. There are minds which can be pleased by honors and preferments; but I see nothing in them but envy and enmity. It is only necessary to possess them, to know how little they contribute to happiness, or rather how hostile they are to it. No attachments soothe the mind so much as those contracted in early life; nor do I recollect any societies which have given me more pleasure, than those of which you have partaken with me. I had rather be shut up in a very modest cottage, with my books, my family and a few old friends, dining on simple bacon, and letting the world roll on as it liked, than to occupy the most splendid post, which any human power can give. I shall be glad to hear from you often. Give me the small news as well as the great."

He declined to become a member of a European Society for the Abolition of the Slave Trade, on the ground that being a "public servant" it would be "decent for him" to await the action of those he served, and that a different course, without promoting the object in Europe, might render him less able to do so in America.[1]

Here is an early remark on a topic which often occupied his pen in later years (addressed to Mr. Cutting, October 2d):

> "I am now to acknowledge the receipt of your favors of the 16th and 23d ultimo, and to thank you for the intelligence they conveyed. That respecting the case of the interrogatories in Pennsylvania, ought to make noise. So evident a heresy in the common law, ought not to be tolerated on the authority of two or three civilians, who happened, unfortunately, to make authority in the courts of England. I hold it essential, in America, to forbid that any English decision which has happened since the accession of Lord Mansfield to the bench, should ever be cited in a court: because, though there have come many good ones from him, yet there is so much sly poison instilled into a great part of them, that it is better to proscribe the whole."

His first and contemporaneous opinion of the Federalist, is disclosed in a letter to Mr. Madison, November 18th:

> "With respect to the Federalist, the three authors had been named to me. I read it with care, pleasure and improvement, and was satisfied there was nothing in it by one of those hands, and not a great deal by a second. It does the highest honor to the third, as being, in my opinion, the best commentary on the principles of government, which ever was written. In some parts, it is discoverable that the author means only to say what may be best said in defence of opinions, in which he did not concur. But in general, it establishes firmly the plan of government. I confess it has rectified me on several points."

A letter to General Washington (December 4th) contains several interesting remarks, and an inside view of the writer's opinion on some important domestic and foreign questions; and it furnishes a key to a good deal of his commercial diplomacy in France. But we must content ourselves with referring the reader to it in his published works. We will quote but a single paragraph, giving Mr. Jefferson's very noticeable views of the influence of WOMEN in French politics:

> "In my opinion, a kind of influence, which none of their plans of reform take into account, will elude them all; I mean the influence of women in the government. The manners of the nation allow them to visit, alone, all persons in office, to solicit the affairs of the husband, family, or friends, and their solicitations bid defiance to laws and regulations. This obstacle may seem less to those, who, like our countrymen, are in the precious habit of considering right, as a barrier against all solicitation. Nor can such a one, without the evidence of his own eyes, believe in the desperate state to which things are reduced in this country, from the

---

[1] Jefferson to Mr. Warville (Brissot), February 12.

omnipotence of an influence, which, fortunately for the happiness of the sex itself, does not endeavor to extend itself, in our country, beyond the domestic line."

It may be doubted whether any clearer view is to be found of the history of France through 1788 (and, indeed, we might extend the remark to Mr. Jefferson's entire stay in that country), than is contained in his official dispatches to the American Foreign Secretary, Mr. Jay. Nothing escaped his attention or solution. He afterwards condensed these, without change, in the rapid synopsis of events embraced in his Memoir. From this last we will bring down the history of France from the period of his return from Germany, about the close of April. It will be remembered that he had already stated that, on his return, he found Paris in a great ferment owing to the Prime Minister not carrying promptly into effect the measures contem plated on the dissolution of the Assembly of Notables—but procrastinating each step until the glow of good feeling wore off, and until new claims began to be advanced—and particularly a claim for a fixed or written Constitution. Then, after glowingly reciting the abuses which rendered that claim a most just one, Mr. Jefferson thus takes up the narrative of the struggle between the Ministry and the Parliaments, and the general one of parties:

"The edicts relative to the corvées and free circulation of grain, were first presented to the Parliament and registered; but those for the impôt territorial, and stamp tax, offered some time after, were refused by the Parliament, which proposed a call of the States-General, as alone competent to their authorization. Their refusal produced a bed of justice, and their exile to Troyes. The advocates, however, refusing to attend them, a suspension in the administration of justice took place. The Parliament held out for awhile, but the ennui of their exile and absence from Paris began at length to be felt, and some dispositions for compromise to appear. On their consent, therefore, to prolong some of the former taxes, they were recalled from exile, the King met them in session Nov. 19, '87, promised to call the States-General in the year '92, and a majority expressed their assent to register an edict for successive and annual loans from 1788 to '92; but a protest being entered by the Duke of Orleans, and this encouraging others in a disposition to retract, the King ordered peremptorily the registry of the edict, and left the Assembly abruptly. The Parliament immediately protested, that the votes for the enregistry had not been legally taken, and that they gave no sanction to the loans proposed. This was enough to discredit and defeat them. Hereupon issued another edict, for the establishment of a cour plénière, and the suspension of all the Parliaments in the kingdom. This being opposed, as might be expected, by reclamations from all the Parliaments and Provinces, the King gave way, and by an edict of July 5th, '88, renounced his cour plénière, and promised the States-

General for the first of May of the ensuing year; and the Archbishop, finding the
times beyond his faculties, accepted the promise of a Cardinal's hat, was removed
[September, '88] from the Ministry, and M. Necker was called to the department
of finance. The innocent rejoicings of the people of Paris on this change provoked
the interference of an officer of the city guards, whose order for their dispersion
not being obeyed, he charged them with fixed bayonets, killed two or three, and
wounded many. This dispersed them for the moment, but they collected the next
day in great numbers, burnt ten or twelve guardhouses, killed two or three of the
guards, and lost six or eight more of their own number. The city was hereupon
put under martial law, and after awhile the tumult subsided. The effect of this
change of ministers, and the promise of the States-General at an early day, tran-
quillized the nation. But two great questions now occurred. 1st. What proportion shall the number of deputies of the Tiers Etat bear to those of the Nobles and
Clergy? And 2d. Shall they sit in the same or in distinct apartments? M.
Necker, desirous of avoiding himself these knotty questions, proposed a second
call of the same notables, and that their advice should be asked on the subject.
They met, Nov. 9, '88; and, by five bureaux against one, they recommended the
forms of the States-General of 1614; wherein the Houses were separate, and voted
by orders, not by persons. But the whole nation declaring at once against this,
and that the Tiers Etat should be, in numbers, equal to both the other orders, and
the Parliament deciding for the same proportion, it was determined so to be, by a
declaration of December 27th, '88. A Report of M. Necker, to the King, of about
the same date, contained other very important concessions. 1. That the King
could neither lay a new tax, nor prolong an old one. 2. It expressed a readiness
to agree on the periodical meeting of the States. 3. To consult on the necessary
restriction on Lettres de Cachet; and 4. How far the press might be made free.
5. It admits that the States are to appropriate the public money; and 6. That
ministers shall be responsible for public expenditures. And these concessions came
from the very heart of the King. He had not a wish but for the good of the
nation; and for that object, no personal sacrifice would ever have cost him a
moment's regret; but his mind was weakness itself, his constitution timid, his
judgment null, and without sufficient firmness even to stand by the faith of his
word. His Queen, too, haughty and bearing no contradiction, had an absolute
ascendency over him; and around her were rallied the King's brother, D'Artois,
the court generally, and the aristocratic part of his ministers, particularly Breteuil,
Broglio, Vauguyon, Foulon, Luzerne, men whose principles of government were
those of the age of Louis XIV. Against this host, the good counsels of Necker,
Montmorin, St. Priest, although in unison with the wishes of the King himself,
were of little avail. The resolutions of the morning, formed under their advice,
would be reversed in the evening, by the influence of the Queen and court. But
the hand of Heaven weighed heavily indeed on the machinations of this junto;
producing collateral incidents, not arising out of the case, yet powerfully co-excit-
ing the nation to force a regeneration of its government, and overwhelming, with
accumulated difficulties, this liberticide resistance."

These " collateral incidents "—carrying the narration through
the winter of 1788–89, may as well be here given :

"While laboring under the want of money for even ordinary purposes, in a government which required a million of livres a day, and driven to the last ditch by the universal call for liberty, there came on a winter of such severe cold, as was without example in the memory of man, or in the written records of history. The Mercury was at times 50° below the freezing point of Fahrenheit, and 22° below that of Réaumur. All out-door labor was suspended, and the poor, without the wages of labor, were, of course, without either bread or fuel. The government found its necessities aggravated by that of procuring immense quantities of fire-wood, and of keeping great fires at all the cross streets, around which the people gathered in crowds, to avoid perishing with cold. Bread, too, was to be bought, and distributed daily, gratis, until a relaxation of the season should enable the people to work; and the slender stock of breadstuff had for some time threatened famine, and had raised that article to an enormous price. So great, indeed, was the scarcity of bread, that, from the highest to the lowest citizen, the bakers were permitted to deal but a scanty allowance per head, even to those who paid for it; and, in cards of invitation to dine in the richest houses, the guest was notified to bring his own bread. To eke out the existence of the people, every person who had the means was called on for a weekly subscription, which the Curés collected, and employed in providing messes for the nourishment of the poor, and vied with each other in devising such economical compositions of food as would subsist the greatest number with the smallest means."

America, during the months of March, April, and May, sent to the Atlantic ports of France alone, about twenty-one thousand barrels of flour, and also great amounts to the French West Indies, which had been drained to supply the parent country. Another idea is obtained of the extent of the scarcity by a letter from Jefferson to the Count de Moustier (the French Minister in the United States), dated March 13th, in which he declares " that the supplies from America have already reduced the price of flour at Bordeaux, from 36l. to 33l. the barrel!" [1]

The conduct of the Count de Moustier being regarded " as politically and morally offensive," in the United States, Jefferson was directed to attempt to amicably obtain his recall. To ask this, without specifying any charges against him, was a matter of some delicacy—and Jefferson had recourse to Lafayette, who, as a Frenchman, could utter explanations which would greatly embarrass the diplomatic representative of the United States. Montmorin at once assented to the propriety of the recall, but desired delay, as it would be a violation of established

---

[1] He wrote the next day to Madame de Brehan (a sister of the Count de Moustier), residing temporarily in the United States:

" We have had such a winter, madam, as makes me shiver yet, whenever I think of it. All communications, almost, were cut off. Dinners and suppers were suppressed, and the money laid out in feeding and warming the poor, whose labors were suspended by the rigor of the season. Loaded carriages passed the Seine on the ice, and it was covered with thousands of people from morning to night, skating and sliding. Such sights were never seen before, and they continued two months."

custom to order a minister home, against whom no complaints
were specified, without giving him another mission; and no
other mission was now vacant. Montmorin's proposed method
of solving the difficulty, and some particulars in regard to De
Moustier's successor, are mentioned in a dispatch from Mr.
Jefferson to Mr. Jay (February 4th, 1789):

> "There was a loose expression in one of De Moustier's letters, which might be
> construed into a petition for leave of absence; that he [Montmorin] would give
> him permission to return to France; that it had been before decided, on the request
> of the Marquis de la Luzerne, that Otto should go to him to London; that they
> would send a person to America as Chargé des Affaires in place of Otto, and that if
> the President (General Washington) approved of him, he should be afterwards
> made minister. He had cast his eye on Colonel Ternant, and desired the Marquis
> to consult me whether he would be agreeable. At first I hesitated, recollecting to
> have heard Ternant represented in America as an hypochondriac, discontented
> man, and paused for a moment between him and Barthelemy, at London, of whom
> I have heard a great deal of good. However, I concluded it safer to take one
> whom we knew, and who knew us. The Marquis was decidedly of this opinion.
> Ternant will see that his predecessor is recalled for unconciliatory deportment, and
> that he will owe his own promotion to the approbation of the President. He
> established a solid reputation in Europe, by his conduct when Generalissimo of one
> of the United Provinces, during their late disturbances; and it is generally thought
> that if he had been put at the head of the principal province, instead of the Rhin-
> grave de Salm, he would have saved that cause. Upon the whole, I believe you
> may expect that the Count de Moustier will have an immediate leave of absence,
> which will soon after become a recall in effect."

After reading this, it produces a broad smile to peruse the
following knowing passage in a letter from Paris, from Governeur Morris to General Washington, written upwards of five
months after Mr. Jefferson's to Mr. Jay.

> "I will also communicate a matter *which Mr. Jefferson was not yet informed of
> and which I could not tell him, because I was forbidden to mention it to any person
> here.* You know, I dare say, that the Count de Moustier has his *congé.* His suc-
> cessor will be Colonel Ternant. At first, in the character of Chargé des Affaires,
> and when M. de Moustier is otherwise placed, it is highly probable that Ternant
> may be made Minister; but that will depend on the situation of the court at the
> time, so that there I only state probability. As to the other you may rely upon it,
> because my intelligence I know to be good. The important trait in this appoint-
> ment is, that he is named as a person who will be agreeable to *us.*" [1]

How the French Ministry had ascertained that Ternant
"would be agreeable to *us,*" Jefferson not having been yet

---

[1] Morris to Washington, July 31, 1789. Life and Writings of Governeur Morris, by
J. Sparks, vol. ii. p. 78.

informed of the matter, does not appear; but the inference would be very strong from the above that the Ministry had consulted Mr. Governeur Morris on the subject, in preference to the Ambassador !

The high official positions held by this gentleman before and after this period, the fact that he was ultimately appointed Mr. Jefferson's successor as Minister to France, his clear, brilliant capacity, his great knowledge of society, and supposed knowledge of men, and the perfect and beautiful intellectual bravery with which he always formed and expressed an opinion, give a degree of interest to his intercourse with Jefferson, and his impressions of him, during their common stay at Paris. We will, therefore, quote what we find on this subject, in a rapid turning over of his writings.

This to Mr. Jay, March 4th (1789) does not wear quite so knowing an air, as the letter to General Washington :

"I will not have the assurance, with his [Mr. Jefferson's] dispatches in my hand, to say a word about politics. And more especially as he has not only the advantage, by frequent access to the ministers, of seeing more distinctly those movements which others contemplate at a distance, but also because he is very much in the confidence of the patriotic party here, and consequently well informed of their views and intentions."

This to Mr. Carmichael, July 4th, exhibits delightful *naïveté :*

" You seem surprised that our minister here does not mention me in his letters ; but *cui bono !* He knows that we correspond together. You suppose that he has introduced me to the *Corps Diplomatique.* In this you are mistaken. I hinted that matter to him shortly after my arrival. He told me they were not worth my acquaintance. I did not press the matter, and I am persuaded he assigned his real reason."

The following are excerpts from Mr. Morris's Diary :

"*April 3d.—*   *   * Call on Mr. Jefferson and sit an hour with him, which is, at least, fifty minutes too long, for his daughters had left the room on my approach, and waited only my departure to return. At least, I think so."

" *May 30th.*—Call on Mr. Jefferson and sit a good while. General conversation on character and politics. I think he does not form very just estimates of character, but rather assigns too many to the humble rank of fools, whereas, in life, the gradations are infinite, and each individual has his peculiarities of fort and feeble."

" *June 3d.*—Go to Mr. Jefferson's. Some political conversation. He seems to be out of hope of anything being done to purpose by the States-General. This comes from having sanguine expectation of a downright republican form of government. The literary people here, observing the abuses of their monarchical form, imagine that everything must go the better in proportion as it recedes from the present establishments, and in their closets they make men exactly suited to their systems ; but unluckily they are such men as exist nowhere else, and least of all in France."

" *June 6th.*—Dine with Mr. Jefferson. He has just received some news from America, where all is going on well. Sit pretty long at the table and stay tea."

" *June 12th.*—Mr. Jefferson has been to Versailles. The Tiers have called on the nobles and clergy to join them and proceed to business, which has thrown the former into a rage. He considers the affairs of this country as being in a very critical situation. They are so ; but the royal authority has yet great weight, and, if brought to the aid of the privileged orders, may yet prevent their destruction. However, he and I differ in our political systems. He, with all the leaders of liberty here, is desirous of annihilating distinctions of order. How far such views may be right, respecting mankind in general, is, I think, extremely problematical. But, with respect to this nation, I am sure it is wrong, and cannot eventuate well."

" *July 4th.*—Go to Mr. Jefferson's to dinner. A large party of Americans, and among them Monsieur and Madame de Lafayette. Some political conversation with him after dinner, in which I urge him to preserve, if possible, some constitutional authority to the body of nobles, as the only means of preserving any liberty for the people. The current is setting so strong against the Noblesse that I apprehend their destruction, in which will, I fear, be involved consequences most pernicious, though little attended to in the present moment."

" *September 17th.*—Go to Mr. Jefferson's. The Duc de la Rochefoucauld comes in from the States-General, and at half past four Lafayette, when we sit down to dinner. He tells us that some of his troops under his command are about to march to-morrow to Versailles, to urge the decisions of the States-General. This is a rare situation, for which they must thank themselves. I ask him if his troops will obey him," etc.

These extracts would, of themselves, furnish significant hints of a very notorious fact—that Mr. Jefferson and Mr. Morris belonged to different sets, politically, and that if they mingled in the same general society, their intimacies and confidences were with a wholly different class of persons. While the Minister kept up the forms of social courtesy, and did not perform the process of what is termed " tipping the cold shoulder " to a distinguished countryman who was personally a gentleman, he took no pains, probably, to push his attentions beyond the limits which a gentleman had a right to expect from the representative of his country at a foreign court.

It would, in truth, be difficult to name an American of any approach to Mr. Morris in talents, and, in some respects, in elevation of character, more likely to be thoroughly distasteful to Mr. Jefferson than he ; and that he was so, and that Jefferson had as little confidence in as liking for him, appears occasionally throughout his writings, though he very rarely makes allusion to him. On one point, we cannot but think he carried this prejudice too far. The mention and discussion of that point we will reserve for a special occasion, where Jefferson's beliefs take the form of a special allegation.

Mr. Morris was one of that gigantic breed of financial speculators, whom Jefferson could scarce refrain from abhorring, *per se.* He had the reputation of being extensively implicated in Robert Morris's great pecuniary schemes, and it was to push claims against the Farmers-General for a violation of their tobacco contract with the latter (which Jefferson had labored so long and assiduously to overthrow), that Governeur Morris now appeared in France. In regard to all such transactions, Jefferson had a standard very different from that of most of the commercial world, and from that of multitudes of most honorable men in nearly all the occupations of life. The period that succeeded our Revolution was peculiary one of speculations. They took nearly every form. Buying vacant lands, was one of the favorite ones, and it was an enormous and unprecedented attempt of this kind (aided by palace building) that consigned the last days of a man who had been so deservingly honored by his country as Robert Morris, to a prison. He died in jail.

Jefferson (as we shall have abundant occasion hereafter to see) believed that all these classes of financial transactions were seriously hurtful to the public interest—that they superseded legitimate commerce by a wild spirit of gambling—that they uprooted the elements of moral order, and converted society into an association of swindlers and dupes, the one living in vicious splendor on the earnings of the other. Precisely where in theory he drew the line between " speculation " and legitimate business, we cannot say. Where he drew that line in practice, we do know. He never in his life bought a dollar's worth of property of any kind on the principle of forestalling—that is, in commercial phrase, " to take advantage of the rise "—in other words, for the purpose of selling it again at an enhanced price without having in any way added to its value. He would not buy an acre of vacant land for this purpose, because he felt that the real settler who needed it and who was prepared to improve and make it useful, was entitled to it at its lowest cost. He equally eschewed stockjobbing, on any scale, or under any circumstances. Far be it from us to pass judgment upon the theories or acts of others, in this regard. We but state Mr. Jefferson's lifelong theory and practice.

This was but one of a numerous train of causes calculated to disgust Jefferson with Governeur Morris. The latter was "a high-flying monarchist,"[1] at least while in France. His scorn was lofty to find the Revolutionary spirit had already placed "booksellers," "woollen drapers," "goldsmiths," "venders of skins," and "grocers," in the civil offices which the prosecution of his business brought him first in contact with !" His luxury, hauteur, and imperious abruptness of manners, exceeded those of the proudest old English noble. They, perhaps, rather resembled those of that later animal, an English East Indian nabob, counting his lacs of rupees as a beggarly French Count would enumerate the barren arpents of his exhausted patrimony ; and who had come to Paris to find new objects to inflict himself upon. He had hardly set his foot in the country, before he placed himself in avowed opposition to the Patriotic party and movement. But he soon condescendingly took upon himself the part of an umpire between the old and new régime— between the government and the people. He read lectures to Lafayette—he whispered portentous words of warning in the ear of Rochefoucauld-Liancourt—he hurried off to Mirabeau with an all-important hint—he laid down programmes for Montmorin—he was closeted with old marquises and marchionesses —he memorialized the King—he sent letters of advice to Maria Antoinette. Never was so busy a man ; never a man so deep in secrets five months old. He could read Sphinx riddles. France seemed pretty nearly on his shoulders. A mere duke or marquis was sometimes annihilated, by a flash of supercilious sarcasm, for venturing on terms of too much equality with him.

Mr. Morris was not very young, and he had but one leg, but he was a good-looking man—a gallant of the first water—one of those lords of the female heart against whom resistance is presumption. He *records*[3] that in their very first interview,

---

[1] These are Jefferson's words. General Miranda, whose prejudices were all with the Federal party in America. wrote a member of that party from Paris afterwards, that Morris had been an *exaggerated* monarchist, and that Monroe was now an *exaggerated* Republican—or words implying this idea.

[2] Life and Works, by Sparks, vol. i. pp. 308, 309.

[3] See his Diary in Mr. Sparks's Life and Works of Morris, vol. i. pp. 326-7

Madame de Staël fell into fulsome personal flatteries, and gave
him, if not the "leer of invitation," what "amounted to the
same thing." At this interesting point, a letter was placed in
her hand from "her lover Narbonne," which "brought her to a
little recollection;" but he "thought a little time would again
banish" it. In short, Mr. Morris was one of those "admirable
Crichtons" that turn up once in a century, and who are born to
conquer or captivate all man and womankind!

Jefferson evidently did not appreciate him. He considered
such political views, so offensively and pretentiously advanced,
intolerable in an American. He probably construed his bust-
ling activity into the fruits of vanity and officiousness. The
manners, habits, and moral maxims of the two men went to that
point of divergence which is apt to produce personal aversion
and disgust. Jefferson, so far as we can form an opinion from
his casual expressions, did not give Morris any credit for that
intellectual integrity which (to our eye) shines out like a
diamond among many disagreeable and some positively repulsive traits of character. This is, this must be (taken in connection with his estimate of Morris's ability) the key to that
confidence which General Washington felt in a man so different
from himself in almost every particular.

Hamilton once wrote Morris that he was "an exotic" in the
United States. This was true. He was not only an exotic but
a misplaced one. If he had been a British peer, he would have
been admired not only for his brilliancy, but we have no doubt
our "high-flying monarchist" (he was rather, to be precise in
terms, an aristocrat than a monarchist) would have been one of
the foremost to resist the encroachments of a court. In that
position we believe he would, too, have been a just and kind
protector of the people. We discover nothing trickish or servile
in him. In some places he might have proved a hero. Nowhere was he contemptible, except when he sat down to pen
such records as that in regard to Madame de Staël.

How completely Jefferson parried all confidential communication with him[1] appears from Mr. Morris's already quoted
entry in his journal of June 3d. Jefferson and the "literary

[1] We have no idea that Morris failed to see and perfectly understand this—but he was
a cool, wary man of the world, who also perfectly understood that he had all to lose and
nothing to gain by a rupture. His naïve communication to Carmichael we put in the
same category. Vanity, too, might have conspired with interest in the matter.

people" are there spoken of as in favor of a "downright republican form of government" for France. This was merely the writer's conjecture, or rather inference. Jefferson never entertained such a thought while in France. We suspect that Mr. Morris's inferences in regard to the views of the patriotic chiefs, on various occasions, were about as well founded. That they all distrusted and disliked him would be a matter of course.' He was attacked in the leading Girondist papers, and stigmatized as an emissary of the court.' General Washington very freely hinted to him that more circumspection would be necessary when he received the appointment of Minister.'

To show more fully Jefferson's real views of the proper and attainable aims of the French Revolution, we must go a little back. We have seen him advising Lafayette to make the English Constitution the model of the French Reformers. He wrote Mr. Madison, November 18th, 1788:

"Here, things internally are going on well. The Notables now in session have, indeed, passed one vote which augurs ill to the rights of the people; but if they do not obtain now so much as they have a right to, they will in the long run. The misfortune is, that they are not yet ripe for receiving the blessings to which they are entitled. I doubt, for instance, whether the body of the nation, if they could be consulted, would accept of a habeas corpus law, if offered them by the King. If the *Etats Généraux*, when they assemble, do not aim at too much, they may begin a good constitution. There are three articles which they may easily obtain: 1. Their own meeting periodically; 2. The exclusive right of taxation; 3. The right of registering laws and proposing amendments to them, as exercised now by the parliaments. This last would be readily approved by the court, on account of their hostility against the parliaments, and would lead immediately to the origination of laws; the second has been already solemnly avowed by the King; and it is well understood, there would be no opposition to the first. If they push at much more, all may fail."

To Mr. Jay, November 19th (1788), after enumerating the same three attainable objects:

"If the States stop here, for the present moment, all will probably end well, and they may, in future sessions, obtain a suppression of *lettres de cachet*, a free press, a civil list, and other valuable mollifications of their government. But it is to be feared, that an impatience to rectify everything at once, which prevails

---

¹ He records in his Diary, June 23d, that Lafayette told him that day at dinner that "he injured the cause, for that his sentiments were continually quoted against the good party." He mentions, the same day, that the Comtesse de Tessé "complained" to him of "his politics."—*Life and Works*, vol. i. p. 314.
² Ib. p. 367.   ³ Ib. p. 370.

in some minds, may terrify the court, and lead them to appeal to force, and to depend on that alone."

These views are also expressed to General Washington, December 4th, to Dr. Currie, December 20th, and to other correspondents up to the meeting of the States-General.

The States-General opened on the 5th of May. Four days afterwards Jefferson wrote Jay:

"The progress of light and liberality in the order of the Noblesse, has equalled expectation in Paris only and its vicinities. The great mass of deputies of that order, which come from the country, show that the habits of tyranny over the people are deeply rooted in them. They will consent, indeed, to equal taxation; but five-sixths of that chamber are thought to be, decidedly, for voting by orders; so that, had this great preliminary question rested on this body, which formed heretofore the sole hope, that hope would have been completely disappointed. Some aid, however, comes in from a quarter whence none was expected. It was imagined the ecclesiastical elections would have been generally in favor of the higher clergy; on the contrary, the lower clergy have obtained five-sixths of these deputations. These are the sons of peasants, who have done all the drudgery of the service for ten, twenty, and thirty guineas a year, and whose oppressions and penury, contrasted with the pride and luxury of the higher clergy, have rendered them perfectly disposed to humble the latter. They have done it in many instances, with a boldness they were thought insusceptible of. Great hopes have been formed that these would concur with the Tiers Etat in voting by persons. In fact, about half of them seem as yet so disposed; but the bishops are intriguing, and drawing them over with the address which has ever marked ecclesiastical intrigue. The deputies of the Tiers Etat seem, almost to a man, inflexibly determined against the vote by orders. This is the state of parties, as well as can be judged from conversation only, during the fortnight they have been now together."

This voting by the various orders, or by persons, had become the test question between the reformers and anti-reformers—for it was known that otherwise a decided majority in the nobles (to look no further) would defeat all effectual improvements. Jefferson, too, doubtless looked upon this body as what is termed in the United States a convention, to organize or alter a constitution—always a single chamber voting by persons. As an independent question, he never considered it desirable, in any country, that the ordinary parliamentary body consist of one chamber. Indeed, he wrote Lafayette the next day after the meeting of the States-General, that "for good legislation two houses were necessary."

Lafayette occupied a peculiar position. His feelings were

with the Tiers Etat, but he had received his election from the
nobility of Auvergne, and he had been instructed by them to
support the vote by orders. Jefferson correctly anticipated the
uncompromising temper of the different orders, and his whole
correspondence shows that he anticipated a scission most likely
to eventuate in civil war. He therefore advised Lafayette not
take sides against the "nation"—to propose a compromise of
two houses (equivalent to Lords and Commons)—and having
failed in that, to disobey his instructions, and act with the Tiers
Etat. This last was so singular a position to be taken by one
ordinarily so sensitive to the obligations of the representative to
his constituency, that it ought to be placed before the reader
fully and in Mr. Jefferson's own words:

TO THE MARQUIS DE LAFAYETTE.

PARIS, May 6, 1789.

MY DEAR FRIEND,

As it becomes more and more possible that the Noblesse will go wrong, I
become uneasy for you. Your principles are decidedly with the Tiers Etat, and
your instructions against them. A complaisance to the latter on some occasions,
and an adherence to the former on others, may give an appearance of trimming
between the two parties, which may lose you both. You will, in the end, go over
wholly to the Tiers Etat, because it will be impossible for you to live in a constant
sacrifice of your own sentiments to the prejudices of the Noblesse. But you would
be received by the Tiers Etat at any future day, coldly, and without confidence.
This appears to be the moment to take at once that honest and manly stand with
them which your own principles dictate. This will win their hearts forever, be
approved by the world, which marks and honors you as the man of the people, and
will be an eternal consolation to yourself. The Noblesse, and especially the
Noblesse of Auvergne, will always prefer men who will do their dirty work for
them. You are not made for that. They will therefore soon drop you, and the
people, in that case, will perhaps not take you up. Suppose a scission should take
place. The priests and nobles will secede, the nation will remain in place, and,
with the King, will do its own business. If violence should be attempted, where
will you be? You cannot then take side with the people in opposition to your own
vote, that very vote which will have helped to produce the scission. Still less can
you array yourself against the people. That is impossible. Your instructions are
indeed a difficulty. But to state this at its worst, it is only a single difficulty, which
a single effort surmounts. Your instructions can never embarrass you a second
time, whereas an acquiescence under them will reproduce greater difficulties every
day, and without end. Besides, a thousand circumstances offer as many justifica-
tions of your departure from your instructions. Will it be impossible to persuade
all parties, that (as for good legislation two houses are necessary) the placing the
privileged classes together in one house, and the unprivileged in another, would be
better for both than a scission? I own I think it would. People can never agree
without some sacrifices; and it appears but a moderate sacrifice in each party to

meet on this middle ground. The attempt to bring this about might satisfy your instructions, and a failure in it would justify your siding with the people, even to those who think instructions are laws of conduct. Forgive me, my dear friend, if my anxiety for you makes me talk of things I know nothing about. You must not consider this as advice. I know you and myself too well to presume to offer advice. Receive it merely as the expression of my uneasiness, and the effusion of that sincere friendship with which I am, my dear sir, yours affectionately,

TH. JEFFERSON.

Four days afterwards, Jefferson wrote General Washington :

"I am in great pain for the Marquis de Lafayette. His principles, you know, are clearly with the people ; but having been elected for the Noblesse of Auvergne, they have laid him under express instructions to vote for the decision by orders, and not persons. This would ruin him with the Tiers Etat, and it is not possible he could continue long to give satisfaction to the Noblesse. I have not hesitated to press on him to burn his instructions, and follow his conscience as the only sure clue which will eternally guide a man clear of all doubts and inconsistencies."

This is plausible reasoning, and it was, it must be confessed, in this particular case, arraying democracy in the substance against a mere democratic theory. But it will not, in our judgment, bear the test of cold and unexcited examination. Lafayette acted indiscreetly, not to say improperly, in accepting a position where his obligations to his direct constituents required him to violate his convictions of right. But having voluntarily entered upon a trust, thus hampered, it is our clear impression that good faith—which even the wild waves of revolution cannot wash a voluntary stain from—required him to discharge the conditions, or resign his place. Gloomy anticipations, the excitement of a perilous hour, the intense solicitude which Jefferson felt for Lafayette, not only as a man, but as the proper warlike leader of the people, should convulsion ensue, and that preference of substance to form, already mentioned, prompted him, we think, to give advice contrary to the just theories and to the sound practice of the whole of his own life. And to show the danger of applying the argument of necessity, in anticipation of the future, things took a different turn from Mr. Jefferson's expectations. Lafayette obeyed his instructions ; and his scruples were respected by the Tiers Etat and Patriotic Party of France.

Mr. Jefferson thus describes the tone of the debates in the States-General, and succinctly sketches the further progress of events :

" The objects for which this body was convened being of the first order of importance, I felt it very interesting to understand the views of the parties of which it was composed, and especially the ideas prevalent as to the organization contemplated for their government. I went, therefore, daily from Paris to Versailles, and attended their debates, generally till the hour of adjournment. Those of the Noblesse were impassioned and tempestuous. They had some able men on both sides, actuated by equal zeal. The debates of the Commons were temperate, rational, and inflexibly firm. As preliminary to all other business, the awful questions came on—Shall the States sit in one, or in distinct apartments? And shall they vote by heads or houses? The opposition was soon found to consist of the Episcopal order among the clergy, and two-thirds of the Noblesse; while the Tiers Etat were, to a man, united and determined. After various propositions of compromise had failed, the Commons undertook to cut the Gordian knot. The Abbé Siéyès, the most logical head of the nation (author of the pamphlet ' Qu'est ce que le Tiers Etat?' which had electrified that country, as Paine's Common Sense did us), after an impressive speech on the 10th of June, moved that a last invitation should be sent to the nobles and clergy, to attend in the hall of the States, collectively or individually, for the verification of powers, to which the Commons would proceed immediately, either in their presence or absence. This verification being finished, a motion was made, on the 15th, that they should constitute themselves a National Assembly, which was decided on the 17th, by a majority of four-fifths. During the debates on this question, about twenty of the Curés had joined them, and a proposition was made, in the chamber of the clergy, that their whole body should join. This was rejected, at first, by a small majority only; but being afterwards somewhat modified, it was decided affirmatively by a majority of eleven. While this was under debate, and unknown to the court, to wit, on the 19th, a council was held in the afternoon, at Marly, wherein it was proposed that the King should interpose, by a declaration of his sentiments, in a *séance royale*. A form of declaration was proposed by Necker, which, while it censured, in general, the proceedings both of the Nobles and Commons, announced the King's views, such as substantially to coincide with the Commons. It was agreed to in council, the *séance* was fixed for the 22d, the meetings of the States were till then to be suspended, and everything, in the meantime, kept secret. The members, the next morning (the 20th), repairing to their house, as usual, found the doors shut and guarded, a proclamation posted up for a *séance royale* on the 22d, and a suspension of their meetings in the meantime. Concluding that their dissolution was now to take place, they repaired to a building called the ' Jeu de paume ' (or Tennis Court), and there bound themselves by oath to each other, never to separate, of their own accord, till they had settled a constitution for the nation, on a solid basis, and if separated by force, that they would reassemble in some other place. The next day they met in the church of St. Louis, and were joined by a majority of the clergy. The heads of the aristocracy saw that all was lost without some bold exertion. The King was still at Marly. Nobody was permitted to approach him but their friends. He was assailed by falsehoods in all shapes. He was made to believe that the Commons were about to absolve the army from their oath of fidelity to him, and to raise their pay. The court party were now all rage and desperation. They procured a committee to be held, consisting of the King and his ministers, to which Monsieur and the Count d'Artois should be admitted. At this committee, the latter attacked Mr. Necker personally, arraigned his declaration, and proposed one, which some of his prompters had put into his hands. Mr. Necker was brow-beaten and intimidated, and the King shaken. He determined that the two plans should be deliberated on the next day, and the *séance royale* put off a day longer. This encouraged a fiercer attack on Mr. Necker the next day. His draft of a declaration was entirely broken up, and that of the Count d'Artois inserted into it. Himself and Montmorin offered their resignation, which was refused, the Count d'Artois saying to Mr. Necker, 'No, sir, you must be kept as the hostage; we hold you responsible for all the ill which shall happen.' This change of plan was immediately whispered without doors. The Noblesse were in triumph; the people in consternation." [1]

He goes on to mention what his own feelings and views were in this fearful crisis, and also a proposition which he urged on some of the leaders of the Patriotic party:

"I was quite alarmed at this state of things. The soldiery had not yet indicated which side they should take, and that which they should support would be sure to prevail. I considered a successful reformation of government in France as insuring a general reformation through Europe, and the resurrection, to a new life, of their people, now ground to dust by the abuses of the governing powers. I was much acquainted with the leading patriots of the Assembly. Being from a country which had successfully passed through a similar reformation, they were disposed to my acquaintance, and had some confidence in me. I urged, most strenuously, an immediate compromise; to secure what the government was now ready to yield, and trust to future occasions for what might still be wanting." [2]

The "compromise" he proposed, and his reasons for it, will be found in the following communication to a distinguished member of the Tiers Etat:

To Monsieur de St. Etienne.[3]

PARIS, *June* 3, 1789.

SIR:

After you quitted us yesterday evening, we continued our conversation (Monsieur de Lafayette, Mr. Short, and myself) on the subject of the difficulties which environ you. The desirable object being, to secure the good which the King has offered, and to avoid the ill which seems to threaten, an idea was suggested, which appearing to make an impression on Monsieur de Lafayette, I was encouraged to pursue it on my return to Paris, to put it into form, and now to send it to you and him. It is this: that the King, in a *séance royale*, should come forward with a Charter of Rights in his hand, to be signed by himself and by every member of the three orders. This charter to contain the five great points which the

---

[1] Memoir.   Ib.

[3] As we understand it, this was the same "bookseller" whose occupation is italicized at the end of his name so piquantly by Mr. Morris, when describing the magistrates he called upon, on his arrival in Paris. See ante, page 516.

Résultat of December offered, on the part of the King; the abolition of pecuniary privileges offered by the privileged orders, and the adoption of the national debt, and a grant of the sum of money asked from the nation. This last will be a cheap price for the preceding articles; and let the same act declare your immediate separation till the next anniversary meeting. You will carry back to your constituents more good than ever was effected before without violence, and you will stop exactly at the point where violence would otherwise begin. Time will be gained, the public mind will continue to ripen and to be informed, a basis of support may be prepared with the people themselves, and expedients occur for gaining still something further at your next meeting, and for stopping again at the point of force. I have ventured to send to yourself and Monsieur de Lafayette a sketch of my ideas of what this act might contain, without endangering any dispute. But it is offered merely as a canvas for you to work on, if it be fit to work on at all. I know too little of the subject, and you know too much of it, to justify me in offering anything but a hint. I have done it, too, in a hurry: insomuch, that since committing it to writing, it occurs to me that the fifth article may give alarm; that it is in a good degree included in the fourth, and is, therefore, useless. But after all, what excuse can I make, sir, for this presumption? I have none but an unmeasurable love for your nation, and a painful anxiety lest despotism, after an unaccepted offer to bind its own hands, should seize you again with tenfold fury. Permit me to add to these, very sincere assurances of the sentiments of esteem and respect, with which I have the honor to be, sir, your most obedient and most humble servant,

TH. JEFFERSON.

The annexed is the Charter accompanying the preceding letter :

A Charter of Rights, solemnly established by the King and Nation.

1. The States-General shall assemble, uncalled, on the first day of November, annually, and shall remain together so long as they shall see cause. They shall regulate their own elections and proceedings, and until they shall ordain otherwise, their elections shall be in the forms observed in the present year, and shall be triennial.

2. The States-General alone shall levy money on the nation, and shall appropriate it.

3. Laws shall be made by the States-General only, with the consent of the King.

4. No person shall be restrained of his liberty, but by regular process from a court of justice, authorized by a general law. (Except that a Noble may be imprisoned by order of a court of justice, on the prayer of twelve of his nearest relations) On complaint of an unlawful imprisonment, to any judge whatever, he shall have the prisoner immediately brought before him, and shall discharge him, if his imprisonment be unlawful. The officer in whose custody the prisoner is, shall obey the orders of the judge ; and both judge and officer shall be responsible, civilly and criminally, for a failure of duty herein.

5. The military shall be subordinate to the civil authority.

6. Printers shall be liable to legal prosecution for printing and publishing false facts, injurious to the party prosecuting; but they shall be under no other restraint.

7. All pecuniary privileges and exemptions, enjoyed by any description of persons, are abolished.

8. All debts already contracted by the King, are hereby made the debts of the nation; and the faith thereof is pledged for their payment in due time.

9. Eighty millions of livres are now granted to the King, to be raised by loan, and reimbursed by the nation; and the taxes heretofore paid, shall continue to be paid to the end of the present year, and no longer.

10. The States-General shall now separate, and meet again on the 1st day of November next.

Done, on behalf of the whole nation, by the King and their representatives in the States-General, at Versailles, this —— day of June, 1789.

Signed by the King, and by every member individually, and in his presence.

This was written the same day with Mr. Morris's statement in his Diary that Jefferson had "sanguine expectation of a downright republican form of government," and a little more than a week before Mr. Morris declared (in the same record), that Jefferson was "desirous of annihilating distinctions of order."

Speaking, more than thirty years afterwards of the rejection by the Patriots of his proposed compromise of June 3d, Mr. Jefferson said:

"They thought otherwise, however, and events have proved their lamentable error.—For, after thirty years of war, foreign and domestic, the loss of millions of lives, the prostration of private happiness, and the foreign subjugation of their own country for a time, they have obtained no more, nor even that securely. They were unconscious of (for who could foresee?) the melancholy sequel of their well-meant perseverance; that their physical force would be usurped by a first tyrant to trample on the independence, and even the existence of other nations: that this would afford a fatal example for the atrocious conspiracy of kings against their people; would generate their unholy and homicide alliance to make common cause among themselves, and to crush, by the power of the whole, the efforts of any part to moderate their abuses and oppressions."

In a letter to Mr. Jay (June 17th), Mr. Jefferson thus expressed his contemporaneous opinion of Necker:

"It is a tremendous cloud, indeed, which hovers over this nation, and he at the helm [Necker] has neither the courage nor the skill necessary to weather it. Eloquence in a high degree, knowledge in matters of account, and order, are distinguishing traits in his character. Ambition is his first passion, virtue his second. He has not discovered that sublime truth, that a bold, unequivocal virtue is the best handmaid even to ambition, and would carry him further, in the end, than the temporizing, wavering policy he pursues. His judgment is not of the first order scarcely even of the second; his resolution frail; and upon the whole, it is rare to meet an instance of a person so much below the reputation he has obtained."

The waves of the Revolutionary whirlpool now rushed on swifter and darker—but it is not our province to give beyond that very slight historical sketch, which is necessary to show the occasionally visible connection between the American Minister and the public events which were taking place about him. The National Assembly received important accessions from the nobles and the clergy. With respect to the utility or inutility of the minority of the nobles joining themselves with the Tiers Etat, in that body, Lafayette consulted Jefferson, and received for answer that he was then (June 12) unable to form an opinion —that he "knew too little of the subject to see what might be its consequences"—but he promised to see the former personally. On the 25th, Jefferson wrote Jay, that "forty-eight of the nobles had joined the Tiers," but that "the Marquis de Lafayette could not be of the number, being restrained by his instructions"—that "he was writing his constituents to change his instructions or accept his resignation."

Early in July a circumstance took place which Jefferson thus communicated to Mr. Jay (July 19th):

"Monsieur de Mirabeau, who is very hostile to Mr. Necker, wished to find a ground for censuring him, in a proposition to have a great quantity of flour furnished from the United States, which he supposed me to have made to Mr. Necker, and to have been refused by him; and he asked time of the States-General to furnish proofs. The Marquis de Lafayette immediately gave me notice of this matter, and I wrote him a letter to disavow having ever made any such proposition to Mr. Necker, which I desired him to communicate to the States. I waited immediately on Mr. Necker and Monsieur de Montmorin, satisfied them that what had been suggested was absolutely without foundation from me; and indeed they had not needed this testimony. I gave them copies of my letter to the Marquis de Lafayette, which was afterwards printed. The Marquis, on the receipt of my letter, showed it to Mirabeau, who turned then to a paper from which he had drawn his information, and found he had totally mistaken it. He promised immediately that he would himself declare his error to the States-General, and read to them my letter, which he did. I state this matter to you, though of little consequence in itself, because it might go to you misstated in the English papers."

Jefferson's letter of explanation to Lafayette, which Mirabeau read in the National Assembly, and some others on the same subject, will be found in his published correspondence (July 6th to 10th, et passim).

This is almost the only, if not the only occasion, where we find Mirabeau and Jefferson brought into official or public political contact. The former, we think, very soon after the event just mentioned, owing to the death of his father, retired for a time from the stormy theatre of the Assembly; and he did not return to it during Jefferson's subsequent stay in France. It would seem remarkable that so little mention is made of this most extraordinary man in Jefferson's writings. He gives, in his Memoir, Mirabeau's celebrated reply to the Marquis de Brezé, when (June 23d) he ordered the National Assembly in the King's name to disperse;[1] and he elsewhere speaks of the Address to the King to remove the troops (July 8th), as a "piece of masculine eloquence." His is but a cold description of the affair of the 23d, of which he was an eye and ear witness. His colloquial accounts of it in after years were occasionally striking. He entertained an exalted estimate of Mirabeau's genius and power as an orator, but a poor one of his integrity.[2]

Mr. Jefferson's *hôtel* having been robbed three times, he asked the Minister of Foreign Affairs for suitable protection. A guard was immediately set over it.

The Aristocratic party, headed by the Queen and the Count d'Artois, persuaded the weak King to come to the fatal resolution of putting down the Revolution by force. Thirty thousand troops, a considerable portion of them foreign mercenaries, were ordered to march on Paris. The Marshal de Broglio, "a high-flying aristocrat, cool and capable of anything," was named to the command. Strong positions were occupied and fortified in the environs of the city. Cannon were pointed from the Queen's Mews on the Hall where the National Assembly met. Some French Guards were arrested for favoring the national cause. The people liberated them. The Assembly urged the people to keep the peace, and at the same time solicited the

---

[1] Mr. Jefferson gives his words as follows: "Tell those who sent you that we shall not move hence but at our own will, or the point of the bayonet."

[2] Mr. Wirt, in a letter to Benjamin Edwards, dated May 6th, 1806, referring to descriptions *he* had heard from Mr. Jefferson's mouth of Mirabeau, says:

"He [Jefferson] spoke of him [Mirabeau] as uniting two distinct and perfect characters in himself, whenever he pleased: the mere logician, with a mind apparently as sterile and desolate as the sands of Arabia, but reasoning at such times with a Herculean force, which nothing could resist; at other times, bursting out with a flood of eloquence more sublime than Milton ever imputed to the cherubim and seraphim, and bearing all before him."—*Kennedy's Life of Wirt*, vol. i. p. 137.

The late Henry Clay informed us that he had heard Mr. Jefferson speak in strong and glowing terms of Mirabeau's matchless power over the minds every class of men.

Some of Mr. Jefferson's family entertain similar recollections.

King to pardon the offending Guards. It also voted (July 8th) Mirabeau's address, already mentioned, asking the removal of the troops. The King refused; and he said the Assembly "might remove themselves, if they pleased, to Noyons or Sossions." On the 11th, Lafayette moved his celebrated Declaration of the Rights of Man. On the same day, Necker was secretly dismissed by the Court, and sent into exile. On the 12th, the whole Ministry were removed, and their places filled with men, to use Jefferson's words, "the principal among whom had been noted through their lives for the Turkish despotism of their characters." In the afternoon of the same day, bodies of German cavalry and Swiss artillery were marched to the Place of Louis XV. The news of these events spread over the city. Foulon, the new Minister of War, when, not long before, informed that the people of the provinces were in the extremity of the famine (which did not end until the new crops began to be harvested in July), subsisting on substances unheard of as the food of man, fiercely exclaimed, "Then let the people eat grass."

When an impious wretch like this was intrusted with the sword of the State, every man, every woman, and every child old enough to feel the instinct of self-preservation, knew that their old oppressors—their oppressors through ages—had determined to yield nothing, but to exterminate reform by the sword. The question, thenceforth, was whether their sons should, as in times past (as in Mr. Burke's splendid "age of chivalry"), be sent to manure Europe with their bodies in wars undertaken at the nod of a courtesan—whether their wives and daughters, cursed with beauty enough to excite a transient emotion of sensuality, should be lured or torn from them and debauched—whether every man who dared to utter a manly political thought or to assert his rights against rank, should be imprisoned at pleasure without a hearing—whether the toiling masses, for the purpose of supporting lascivious splendor, of building *Parcs aux Cerfs*, of pensioning discarded mistresses,' of swiftly enriching corrupt favorites and minions of every stamp, should be so taxed that the light and air of heaven hardly came to them untaxed, and they should be so sunk by

---

¹ The Memoirs of Madame du Hausset will furnish the curious with some light on these subjects.

exactions of every kind in the dregs of indigence that a short crop compelled them to live on food that the hounds, if not the swine, of their task-masters would reject; and, finally, whether when in the bloody sweat of their agony they asked some mitigation of their hard fate, they should be answered by the bayonets of foreign mercenaries; and when a people—stout manhood, gentle womanhood, grey-haired age and tender infancy—turned their pale faces upward and shrieked for food, fierce, licentious nobles should scornfully bid them "eat grass."

The Court and Nobility of France, driven yet to no disgraceful or perilous extremity—unassailed yet by the red hand of warlike Revolution—deliberately inaugurated a war between castes—deliberately chose the sword as the final arbiter—deliberately made up the issue, where they should have known, if they possessed common intelligence as to either the passions or the interests of mankind, that the alternative *they* staked against was extermination. When, on Sunday, July 12th, the people of Paris suddenly heard the sound of artillery carriages rolling forward towards the *Place Louis Quinze*, and the comparatively silent streets echoing with the clang of Prince Lambesc's advancing cavalry, that issue, for weal or woe, was finally made up. It mattered not which side chanced to do the first act of physical violence—to shed the first drop of blood, any more than whether any other robber or foe, contemplating slaughter in case of resistance, gives or receives the first shot. One side understood that they were to forcibly put down all opposition to the Government, and they took an open and direct step to effect that object, by pouring mercenary troops into the heart of an unarmed city, not even in a state of insurrection. The other side understood they must submit tamely, or assert their rights by the sword.[1]

[1] Carlyle, in his History of the French Revolution, describes with wild picturesqueness the scene in Paris when the troops poured into the city:
"But see Camille Desmoulins, from the Café de Foy, rushing out, sibylline in face; his hair streaming, in each hand a pistol! He springs to a table: the Police satellites are eying him; alive they shall not take him, not they alive him alive. This time he speaks without stammering:—Friends! shall we die like hunted hares? Like sheep hounded into their pinfold; bleating for mercy, where is no mercy, but only a whetted knife? The hour is come: the supreme hour of Frenchman and Man; when Oppressors are to try conclusions with Oppressed: and the word is swift Death or Deliverance for ever. Let such hour be *well*-come! Us, meseems, one cry only befits: To arms! Let universal Paris, universal France, as with the throat of the whirlwind, sound only: To arms!—'To arms!' yell responsive the innumerable voices; like one great voice, as of a Demon yelling from the air: for all faces wax fire-eyed, all hearts burn up into

Mr. Jefferson was an eyewitness of the first collision—the first bloodshed of the Revolution proper. It was an interesting fact that respect for his person and his country for a moment stayed the uplifted arm of civil, we cannot call it fratricidal, war. He narrates the facts (in his Memoir) in his usual quiet and unexaggerated, not to say rather impassive way, when recording historical events:

"The news of this change [in the Ministry] began to be known at Paris, about one or two o'clock. In the afternoon, a body of about one hundred German cavalry was advanced, and drawn up in the Place Louis XV. and about two hundred Swiss posted at a little distance in their rear. This drew people to the spot, who thus accidentally found themselves in front of the troops, merely at first as spectators; but, as their numbers increased, their indignation rose. They retired a few steps, and posted themselves on and behind large piles of stones, large and small, collected in that place for a bridge, which was to be built adjacent to it. In this position, happening to be in my carriage on a visit, I passed through the lane that had formed, without interruption. But the moment after I had passed, the people attacked the cavalry with stones. They charged, but the advantageous position of the people, and the showers of stones, obliged the horse to retire, and quit the field altogether, leaving one of their number on the ground, and the Swiss in their rear, not moving to their aid. This was the signal for universal insurrection, and this body of cavalry, to avoid being massacred, retired towards Versailles. The people now armed themselves with such weapons as they could find in armorers' shops, and private houses, and with bludgeons; and were roaming all night, through all parts of the city, without any decided object."

This first fray is differently described by the author[1] just

madness. In such, or fitter words, does Camille evoke the Elemental Powers, in this great moment. Friends, continues Camille, some rallying-sign! Cockades; green ones; —the color of Hope! As with the flight of locusts, these green tree-leaves; green ribbons from the neighboring shops; all green things are snatched, and made cockades of. Camille descends from his table; 'stifled with embraces, wetted with tears;' has a bit of green ribbon handed him: sticks it in his hat. And now to Curtius' Image-shop there; to the Boulevards; to the four winds, and rest not till France be on fire!"

[1] Carlyle says:

"However, Besenval, with horse and foot, is in the Place Louis Quinze. Mortals promenading homewards, in the fall of the day, saunter by from Chaillot or Passy, from flirtation and a little thin wine, with sadder step than usual. Will the Bust-Procession pass that way? Behold it; behold also Prince Lambesc dash forth on it, with his Royal Allemands! Shots fall, and sabre-strokes; busts are hewed asunder; and, alas, also heads of men. A sabred procession has nothing for it but to *explode*, along what streets, alleys, Tuileries Avenues it finds; and disappear. One unarmed man lies hewn down; a Garde Française by his uniform: bear him (or bear even the report of him) dead and gory to his barracks—where he has comrades still alive!

"But why not now, victorious Lambesc, charge through that Tuileries Garden itself, where the fugitives are vanishing? Not show the Sunday promenaders, too, how steel glitters, besprent with blood; that it be told of, and men's ear tingle? Tingle, alas, they did; but the wrong way. Victorious Lambesc, in this his second or Tuileries charge, succeeds but in overturning (call it not slashing, for he struck with the flat of his sword) one man, a poor old schoolmaster, most pacifically tottering there: and is driven out, by barricades of chairs, by flights of 'bottles and glasses,' by execrations in bass-voice and treble. Most delicate is the mob-queller's vocation; wherein Too-much may be as bad as Not-enough. For each of these bass-voices, and more each treble voice, borne to all parts of the city, rings now nothing but distracted indignation; will ring all night. The

quoted (Carlyle), but Mr. Jefferson's accuracy is sustained by another cool eyewitness, Mr. Governeur Morris.[1]

Mr. Jefferson thus describes the progress of events:

"The next day (the 13th), the Assembly pressed on the King to send away the troops, to permit the Bourgeoisie of Paris to arm for the preservation of order in the city, and offered to send a deputation from their body to tranquillize them; but their propositions were refused. A committee of magistrates and electors of the city were appointed by those bodies, to take upon them its government. The people, now openly joined by the French guards, forced the prison of St. Lazare, released all the prisoners, and took a great store of corn, which they carried to the corn-market. Here they got some arms, and the French guards began to form and train them. The city-committee determined to raise forty-eight thousand Bourgeois, or rather to restrain their numbers to forty-eight thousand. On the 14th they sent one of their members (Monsieur de Corny) to the Hôtel des Invalides, to ask arms for their Garde Bourgeoise. He was followed by, and he found there, a great collection of people. The Governor of the Invalids came out, and represented the impossibility of his delivering arms, without the orders of those from whom he received them. De Corny advised the people then to retire, and retired himself; but the people took possession of the arms. It was remarkable, that not only the Invalids themselves made no opposition, but that a body of five thousand foreign troops, within four hundred yards, never stirred.[2] M. de Corny, and five others, were then sent to ask arms of M. de Launay, Governor of the Bastile. They found a great collection of people already before the place, and they immediately planted a flag of truce, which was answered by a like flag hoisted on the parapet. The deputation prevailed on the people to fall back a little, advanced themselves to make their demand of the Governor, and in that instant, a discharge from the Bas-

cry, To arms, roars tenfold; steeples with their metal storm-voice boom out, as the sun sinks; armorers' shops are broken open, plundered; the streets are a living foam-sea, chafed by all the winds."

[1] He says in his Diary, July 12th:

"Having set him [Abbé Bertrand] down, I depart for Mr. Jefferson's. In riding along the Boulevards, all at once the carriages, horses and foot passengers turn about and pass rapidly. Presently after, we meet a body of cavalry, with their sabres drawn, and coming at half speed. After they had passed on a little way, they stop. When we come to the Place Louis Quinze, I observe the people, to the number, perhaps, of one hundred, picking up stones, and, looking back, find that the cavalry are returning. Stop at an angle to see the fray, if any. The people take post among the stones, which lie scattered about the whole place, being there hewn for the bridge now building. The officer at the head of this party is saluted by a stone, and immediately turns his horse in a menacing manner towards the assailant. But his adversaries are posted on ground where the cavalry cannot act. He pursues his route, therefore, and the pace is soon increased to a gallop, amid a shower of stones. One of the soldiers is either knocked from his horse, or the horse falls under him. He is taken prisoner, and at first ill treated. They had fired several pistol shots, but without effect. Probably they were not even charged with ball. A party of Swiss guards are posted in the Champs-Elysées with cannon."—Life and Works, vol. i. p. 317.

Mr. Morris's conjecture that the pistols of the Royal Germans were not loaded with ball, is, we believe, purely gratuitous; though perhaps it was so, and perhaps it was hoped that the people would submit without a massacre, and if so, it was certainly far safer to avoid forcing them into resistance. The comparative moderation and speedy retreat of the troops were evidently dictated by considerations for their own safety. Benseval had had a little experience how the Parisian populace would bear skin-cutting at the sack of Reveillon's house; and the wild roar of the increasing multitude now taught him he was in the lion's mouth.

[2] Commanded, we believe, by Benseval. The Government was paralyzed, and issued no orders.

tile killed four persons of those nearest to the deputies. The deputies retired. I
happened to be at the house of M. de Corny, when he returned to it, and received
from him a narrative of these transactions."

The leader of the people on this occasion, M. Ethys de
Corny, King's Procureur (attorney), was the husband of that
Madame de Corny to whom a number of letters are addressed in
Jefferson's Correspondence.

Jefferson describes the attack on the Bastile—the execution of its governor and lieutenant-governor, and of the *Prevôt
des Marchands*—the deputations of the National Assembly to
the King—his "dry and hard answers"—the Duke de Liancourt's forcing himself into the King's bedchamber in the night,
and disclosing to him the real state of affairs—the alarm of the
Court and of the aristocrats—the King's proceeding to the Assembly, and, in effect, surrendering at discretion—the appointment of Lafayette as Commander-in-Chief of the *Milice Bourgeoise*—the demolition of the Bastile—the ordering off of the
foreign troops—the resignation of the Ministry—the recall of
Necker—the first emigration of nobles—the King's return to
Paris escorted by Lafayette, and the Bourgeois Guards and the
people—the address of the King at the Hôtel de Ville, and his
assumption of the popular cockade—and his return to Versailles
escorted as he came.

Jefferson says in his Memoir, that this was "such an
amende-honorable as no sovereign ever made and no people
ever received," and he indulges in the following train of reflections on these and succeeding events:

"And here again was lost another precious occasion of sparing to France the
crimes and cruelties through which she has since passed, and to Europe, and finally
America, the evils which flowed on them also from this mortal source. The King
was now become a passive machine in the hands of the National Assembly, and had
he been left to himself, he would have willingly acquiesced in whatever they should
devise as best for the nation. A wise constitution would have been formed, hereditary in his line, himself placed at its head, with powers so large as to enable him to
do all the good of his station, and so limited as to restrain him from its abuse.
This he would have faithfully administered, and more than this, I do not believe,
he ever wished. But he had a Queen of absolute sway over his weak mind and
timid virtue, and of a character the reverse of his in all points. This angel, as
gaudily painted in the rhapsodies of Burke, with some smartness of fancy, but no
sound sense, was proud, disdainful of restraint, indignant at all obstacles to her
will, eager in the pursuit of pleasure, and firm enough to hold to her desires, or
perish in their wreck. Her inordinate gambling and dissipations, with those of the

Count d'Artois, and others of her *clique*, had been a sensible item in the exhaustion of the treasury, which called into action the reforming hand of the nation; and her opposition to it, her inflexible perverseness, and dauntless spirit, led herself to the guillotine, drew the King on with her, and plunged the world into crimes and calamities which will forever stain the pages of modern history. I have ever believed, that had there been no Queen, there would have been no revolution. No force would have been provoked, nor exercised. The King would have gone hand in hand with the wisdom of his sounder counsellors, who, guided by the increased lights of the age, wished only, with the same pace, to advance the principles of their social constitution. The deed which closed the mortal course of these sovereigns I shall neither approve nor condemn. I am not prepared to say, that the first magistrate of a nation cannot commit treason against his country, or is unamenable to its punishment; nor yet, that where there is no written law, no regulated tribunal, there is not a law in our hearts, and a power in our hands, given for righteous employment in maintaining right and redressing wrong. Of those who judged the King, many thought him willfully criminal; many that his existence would keep the nation in perpetual conflict with the horde of kings who would war against a generation which might come home to themselves, and it were better that one should die than all. I should not have voted with this portion of the Legislature. I should have shut up the Queen in a convent, putting harm out of her power, and placed the King in his station, investing him with limited powers, which I verily believe he would have honestly exercised, according to the measure of his understanding In this way no void would have been created, courting the usurpation of a military adventurer, nor occasion given for those enormities which demoralized the nations of the world, and destroyed, and is yet to destroy, millions and millions of its inhabitants."

Whether it was Burke or whether it was Jefferson that best appreciated the real character of Maria Antoinette, history must decide. A witness whose prejudices and feelings were generally opposite enough to Jefferson's—who was a professed friend and admirer of the Queen—records that she spent the fatal 14th of July in "tampering with" the troops, intoxicating them, inducing the King to make them promises, the plan being to "reduce Paris by famine and to take two hundred members of the National Assembly prisoners;" and that she and those about her took care not to inform the King of the state of affairs, until the Duke de Liancourt made his way to his sleeping apartment, and undeceived him.[1] The latter was struck

---

[1] The following is from Governeur Morris's Diary:

"*July 15th.* The Duc d'Aiguillon and Baron Menon are at club, both of them deputies of the Noblesse. I learn through and from them, the secret history of the Revolution of this day. Yesterday evening an address was presented by the Assembly, to which his Majesty returned an answer by no means satisfactory. The Queen, Count d'Artois, and Duchess de Polignac had been all day tampering with two regiments, which were made almost drunk, and every officer was presented to the King, who was induced to give promises, money, etc., to these regiments. They shouted *Vive la Reine, Vive le Comte d'Artois, Vive la Duchesse de Polignac,* and their music came and played under her Majesty's window. In the meantime, the Maréchal de Broglio was tampering in person

with consternation. Necker was invited to resume his former office. Montmorin and St. Priest were reinstated. A liberal ministry was formed, and all things moved on for a time in perfect harmony. On the 4th of August, the National Assembly, on the motion of the Viscount de Noailles, the brother-in-law of Lafayette, abolished all the privileges of class in the State. Thus went down, says Jefferson, at one sweeping blow, "all titles of rank, all the abusive privileges of feudalism, the tithes and casuals of the clergy, all provincial privileges, and, in fine, the feudal regimen generally." Laws to carry out these changes were rapidly matured and passed. The Declaration of Rights was adopted. The House then appointed a committee to draft a Constitution, at the head of which was the Archbishop of Bordeaux, one of the Ministry.

This committee paid Mr. Jefferson an extraordinary, if not an unprecedented compliment, when addressed to a foreign citizen and foreign ambassador. They, by their chairman, addressed him a letter, July 20th, "requesting him to attend and assist in their deliberations." Jefferson "excused himself on the obvious considerations, that his mission was to the King as chief magistrate of the nation—that his duties were limited to the concerns of his own country, and forbade him to intermeddle with the internal transactions of that in which he had been received under a specific character only." [1]

The committee reported their Constitution by sections as they were agreed upon. The first grand feature of a constitutional system, that the government should be divided into Executive, Legislative, and Judiciary departments, was readily agreed on by the Assembly. It was also agreed, without any open opposition, that the government should be monarchical and hereditary. But on the points whether the Executive should have a veto on laws; whether the veto should be absolute, or merely suspensive; whether there should be one or two houses of the legislature; whether, if two, one of them should be

with the artillery. The plan was to reduce Paris by famine, and to take two hundred members of the National Assembly prisoners. But they found the troops would not serve against their country. Of course these plans would not be carried into effect. They took care, however, not to inform the King of all the mischiefs. At two o'clock in the morning, the Duc de Liancourt went into his bedchamber and waked him. Told him all. Told him that he pledged his life on the truth of his narration, and that unless he changed speedily, all was lost. The King took his determination." etc.   *   *   *
—*Life and Works*, vol. i. p. 319.
[1] Memoir, Randolph's edition, p. 84 ; Congress edition, p. 103.

hereditary, for life, for a fixed term, appointed by the Crown, or elective ; and some other questions, says Mr. Jefferson, " found strong differences of opinion, and produced repulsive combinations among the Patriots." The aristocracy clung together, always voting in mass for the plan which would make the least change in the existing order of things. The features of the Constitution thus began to assume " a fearful aspect," and the honest Patriots of all shades became alarmed at the consequences of their divisions. Mr. Jefferson having reached this point of the narration, says :

" In this uneasy state of things, I received one day a note from the Marquis de Lafayette, informing me, that he should bring a party of six or eight friends, to ask a dinner of me the next day. I assured him of their welcome. When they arrived, they were Lafayette himself, Duport, Barnave, Alexander la Meth, Blacon, Mounier, Maubourg, and Dagout. These were leading Patriots, of honest but differing opinions,[1] sensible of the necessity of effecting a coalition by mutual sacrifices, knowing each other, and not afraid, therefore, to unbosom themselves mutually. This last was a material principle in the selection. With this view, the Marquis had invited the conference, and had fixed the time and place inadvertently, as to the embarrassment under which it might place me. The cloth being removed, and wine set on the table, after the American manner, the Marquis introduced the objects of the conference, by summarily reminding them of the state of things in the Assembly, the course which the principles of the Constitution were taking, and the inevitable result, unless checked by more concord among the Patriots themselves. He observed, that although he also had his opinion, he was ready to sacrifice it to that of his brethren of the same cause ; but that a common opinion must now be formed, or the Aristocracy would carry everything, and that, whatever they should now agree on, he, at the head of the National force, would maintain. The discussions began at the hour of four, and were continued till ten o'clock in the evening ; during

[1] Jefferson thus classified the parties in the National Assembly :
" The Assembly now consists of four distinct parties. 1. The Aristocrats, comprehending the higher members of the clergy, military, nobility, and the parliaments of the whole kingdom. This forms a head without a body. 2. The moderate Royalists, who wish for a constitution nearly similar to that of England. 3. The Republicans, who are willing to let their first magistracy be hereditary, but to make it very subordinate to the Legislature, and to have that Legislature consist of a single chamber. 4. The faction of Orleans. The second and third descriptions are composed of honest, well-meaning men, differing in opinion only, but both wishing the establishment of as great a degree of liberty as can be preserved. They are considered together as constituting the patriotic part of the Assembly, and they are supported by the soldiery of the army, the soldiery of the clergy, that is to say, the Curés and monks, the dissenters, and part of the nobility which is small, and the substantial Bourgeois of the whole nation."—*Jefferson to Jay, September* 19th.
The fourth party is more particularly spoken of in another letter :
" The lees, too, of the patriotic party, of wicked principles and desperate fortunes, hoping to pillage something in the wreck of their country, are attaching themselves to the faction of the Duke of Orleans : that faction is caballing with the populace, and intriguing at London, the Hague, and Berlin, and have evidently in view the transfer of the crown to the Duke of Orleans. He is a man of moderate understanding, of no principle, absorbed in low vice, and incapable of extracting himself from the filth of that, to direct anything else. His name and his money, therefore, are mere tools in the hands of those who are duping him."—*Jefferson to Madison, August* 28.

which time, I was a silent witness to a coolness and candor of argument, unusual in
the conflicts of political opinion ; to a logical reasoning, and chaste eloquence, dis-
figured by no gaudy tinsel of rhetoric or declamation, and truly worthy of being
placed in parallel with the finest dialogues of antiquity, as handed to us by Xeno-
pt.on, by Plato and Cicero. The result was, that the King should have a suspensive
veto on the laws, that the legislature should be composed of a single body only,
and that to be chosen by the people. This Concordat decided the fate of the Constitution. The Patriots all rallied to the principles thus settled, carried every
question agreeably to them, and reduced the Aristocracy to insignificance and
impotence."

The American Minister felt that his hotel was not exactly
the fit place for the assemblage of makers of political concordats
for France. To relieve himself from the consequences of the
false position in which he had been thus placed, he immediately
decided on the step mentioned below :

"But duties of exculpation were now incumbent on me. I waited on Count
Montmorin the next morning, and explained to him, with truth and candor, how it
had happened that my house had been made the scene of conferences of such a
character. He told me, he already knew everything which had passed, that so far
from taking umbrage at the use made of my house on that occasion, he earnestly
wished I would habitually assist at such conferences, being sure I should be useful
in moderating the warmer spirits, and promoting a wholesome and practicable
reformation only. I told him, I knew too well the duties I owed to the King, to
the nation, and to my own country, to take any part in councils concerning their
internal government, and that I should persevere, with care, in the character of a
neutral and passive spectator, with wishes only, and very sincere ones, that those
measures might prevail which would be for the greatest good of the nation. I have
no doubt, indeed, that this conference was previously known and approved by this
honest minister, who was in confidence and communication with the Patriots, and
wished for a reasonable reform of the Constitution."

Here drops Mr. Jefferson's connection, even to the extent of
being a looker-on, with the stupendous drama of the French
Revolution. He soon left for home with the expectation of
returning in a few months to France—but his adieu to that
country proved to be a final one.

We have not, for a period, interrupted the narration of these
important national events, with personal affairs connected with
other topics. We now go back to bring down the history of the
latter.

In a letter to Francis Hopkinson (March 13th, 1789), Mr.
Jefferson thus, for the first time, we think, stated his position
and feelings towards the two political parties which had sprung

up in the United States, on the adoption of the federal Constitution.

"You say that I have been dished up to you as an anti-Federalist, and ask me if it be just. My opinion was never worthy enough of notice, to merit citing: but since you ask it, I will tell it to you. I am not a Federalist, because I never submitted the whole system of my opinions to the creed of any party of men whatever, in religion, in philosophy, in politics, or in anything else, where I was capable of thinking for myself. Such an addiction, is the last degradation of a free and moral agent. If I could not go to heaven but with a party, I would not go there at all. Therefore, I protest to you, I am not of the party of Federalists. But I am much farther from that of the anti-Federalists."

He then detailed the history of his views in regard to the character of the United States Constitution and in regard to its adoption, as they have already been fully and repeatedly shown. Speaking of his objections to the reëligibility of the President, he added :

"And, indeed, since the thing is established, I would wish it not to be altered during the life of our great leader, whose executive talents are superior to those, I believe, of any man in the world, and who, alone, by the authority of his name and the confidence reposed in his perfect integrity, is fully qualified to put the new government so under way, as to secure it against the efforts of opposition. But, having derived from our error all the good there was in it, I hope we shall correct it, the moment we can no longer have the same name at the helm.

"These, my dear friend, are my sentiments, by which you will see I was right in saying I am neither Federalist nor anti-Federalist ; that I am of neither party, nor yet a trimmer between parties."

Mr. Jefferson lived to learn that the idea of no partyism among the intelligent and patriotic in a free republic, is a Utopian dream.

In the preceding September, the University of Harvard had conferred on him the degree of Doctor of Laws. His acceptance is addressed to Dr. Willard, March 24th, and is accompanied with a very full account of the recent discoveries in science and the domestic arts, and the recent publications in literature in Europe. The letter closes in this fine strain :

"What a field have we at our doors to signalize ourselves in ! The Botany of America is far from being exhausted, its Mineralogy is untouched, and its Natural History or Zoology totally mistaken and misrepresented. As far as I have seen, there is not one single species of terrestial birds common to Europe and America, and I question if there be a single species of quadrupeds. (Domestic animals are to be excepted.) It is for such institutions as that over which you preside so worthily, sir, to do justice to our country, its productions and its genius. It is the work to

which the young men, whom you are forming, should lay their hands. We have
spent the prime of our lives in procuring them the precious blessing of liberty.
Let them spend theirs in showing that it is the great parent of science and of virtue ; and that a nation will be great in both, always in proportion as it is free."

In April, an incident of an interesting character occurred in
Mr. Jefferson's family. His oldest daughter, as has been seen,
had been educated in the views and feelings of the Church of
England. Her mother had zealously moulded her young mind
in that direction. Her father had done nothing certainly by
word or act to divert it from that channel ; and it had flowed
on, for aught Martha knew or suspected to the contrary, with his
full approbation. If she had then been called upon to state
what were her father's religious beliefs, she would have declared
that her impressions were that he leaned to the tenets of the
church to which his family belonged. The daring and flippant
infidelity now rife in French society, disgusted the earnest,
serious, naturally reverential girl. The calm seclusion of Panthemont, its examples of serene and holy life, its intellectual
associations, wooed her away from the turmoil, and glare, and
wickedness, and emptiness without. After meditating on the
subject for a time, she wrote her father for his permission to
remain in the convent, and to dedicate herself to the duties of a
religious life.

For a day or two she received no answer. Then his carriage
rolled up to the door of the Abbaye, and poor Martha met her
father in a fever of doubts and fears. Never was his smile more
benignant and gentle. He had a private interview with the
Abbess. He then told his daughters he had come for them. They
stepped into his carriage—it rolled away—and Martha's school
life was ended.[1] Henceforth she was introduced into society—
and presided, so far as was appropriate to her age, as the mistress of her father's household. But sums paid " to Balbatre
for lessons on the harpsichord," to the " guitar master," to the
" dancing master," to " Polly's Spanish master," etc., continue
to find their record in the account-book, during Mr. Jefferson's
further stay in France.

Neither he nor Martha ever, after her first letter on the subject, made the remotest allusion, to each other, to her request
to enter a convent. She spoke of it freely, in after years, to

[1] This happened April 22d, 1789.

her children—and always expressed her full approbation of her father's course on the occasion. She always spoke of her early wish as rather the dictate of a transient sentiment, than a fixed conviction of religious duty; and she warmly applauded the quiet and gentle way which her father took to lead her back to her family, her friends, and her country.

Mr. Jefferson became satisfied that the period had arrived when it would be better for his daughters to be habituating themselves to the associations among which they were to spend their lives. He wrote General Washington, May 10th:

"In a letter to Mr. Jay, of the 19th of November, I asked a leave of absence to carry my children back to their own country, and to settle various matters of a private nature, which were left unsettled, because I had no idea of being absent so long. I expected that letter would have been received in time to be decided on by the government then existing. I know now that it would arrive when there was no Congress, and consequently that it must have awaited your arrival at New York. I hope you found the request not an unreasonable one. I am excessively anxious to receive the permission without delay, that I may be able to get back before the winter sets in. Nothing can be so dreadful to me as to be shivering at sea for two or three months, in a winter passage. Besides, there has never been a moment at which the presence of a minister here could be so well dispensed with, from certainty of no war this summer, and that the government will be so totally absorbed in domestic arrangements as to attend to nothing exterior." [1]

---

[1] Since this part of our work was written, we have received from Mr. Eppes, of Florida, the following letter addressed to his grandmother, by Mr. Jefferson, which will be read with interest in this connection:

"MR. JEFFERSON TO MRS. FRANCIS EPPES.

"PARIS, *December* 15, 1788.

"DEAR MADAM:

"In my last, of July 12, I told you that in my next I would enter into explanations about the time my daughters would have the happiness to see you. Their future welfare requires that this should be no longer postponed. It would have taken place a year sooner, but that I wished Polly to perfect herself in her French. I have asked leave of absence of Congress for five or six months of the next year, and if I obtain it in time I shall endeavor to sail about the middle of April. As my time must be passed principally at Monticello during the two months I destine for Virginia, I shall hope that you will come and encamp there with us a while. He who feedeth the sparrow must feed us also. Feasting we shall not expect, but this will not be our object. The society of our friends will sweeten all. Patsy is just recovered from an indisposition of some days. Polly has the same, it is a slight but continual fever, not sufficient, however, to confine her to her bed. This prevents me from being able to tell you that they are absolutely well. I inclose a letter which Polly wrote a month ago to her aunt Skipwith, and her sickness will apologize for her not writing to you or her cousins; she makes it up in love to you all, and Patsy equally, but this she will tell you herself, as she is writing to you. I hope you will find her an estimable friend as well as a dutiful niece. She inherits stature from her father, and that you know is inheriting no trifle. Polly grows fast. I should write to Mrs. Skipwith also, but that I rely on your friendship to repeat to her the assurance of my affection for her and Mr. Skipwith. We look forward with impatience to the moment when we may be all reunited, though but for a little time. Kiss your dear children for us, the little and the big, and tender them my warmest affections, accepting yourself of assurances of the sincere esteem and attachment, with which I am,

"My dear madam,

"Your affectionate and humble servant,

"TH. JEFFERSON."

In this same letter Mr. Jefferson said:

"Though we have not heard of the actual opening of the new Congress, and consequently, have not official information of your election as President of the United States, yet, as there never could be a doubt entertained of it, permit me to express here my felicitations, not to yourself, but to my country. Nobody who has tried both public and private life, can doubt but that you were much happier on the banks of the Potomac than you will be at New York. But there was nobody so well qualified as yourself to put our new machine into a regular course of action; nobody, the authority of whose name could have so effectually crushed opposition at home, and produced respect abroad. I am sensible of the immensity of the sacrifice on your part. Your measure of fame was full to the brim; and therefore you have nothing to gain. But there are cases wherein it is a duty to risk all against nothing, and I believe this was exactly the case. We may presume, too, according to every rule of probability, that after doing a great deal of good, you will be found to have lost nothing but private repose."

He wrote Mr. Carmichael (August 9th) on a topic which in its day attracted no little notice, and caused no little feeling in the United States:

"The Senate and Representatives differed about the title of the President. The former wanted to style him 'His Highness George Washington, President of the United States, and Protector of their liberties.' The latter insisted and prevailed, to give no title but that of office, to wit, 'George Washington, President of the United States.' I hope the terms of Excellency, Honor, Worship, Esquire, forever disappear from among us, from that moment: I wish that of Mr. would follow them."

He wrote Mr. Madison (August 28th) in relation to the proposition then urged [1] and always urged by a strong party in the United States, that policy and duty required those States, as a neutral power, to make no distinction in their commercial and international legislation generally, as between France and England—that all idea of national gratitude to the former for her aid in the Revolution was not only an absurdly preposterous, but a most mischievous fallacy. He said:

"It is impossible to desire better dispositions towards us, than prevail in this Assembly. Our proceedings have been viewed as a model for them on every occasion; and though in the heat of debate, men are generally disposed to contradict every authority urged by their opponents, ours has been treated like that of the Bible, open to explanation, but not to question. I am sorry that in the moment of such a

[1] In the debate on the import and tonnage bills, which passed the U. S. House of Representatives with a clause making a discrimination in favor of such nations as had formed commercial treaties with the United States. The Senate struck out the clause. The House disagreed to the amendment, but after some conferences, reluctantly yielded its ground.

disposition, anything should come from us to check it. The placing them on a mere footing with the English, will have this effect. When of two nations, the one has engaged herself in a ruinous war for us, has spent her blood and money to save us, has opened her bosom to us in peace, and received us almost on the footing of her own citizens, while the other has moved heaven, earth, and hell, to exterminate us in war, has insulted us in all her councils in peace, shut her doors to us in every part where her interests would admit it, libelled us in foreign nations, endeavored to poison them against the reception of our most precious commodities; to place these two nations on a footing, is to give a great deal more to one than to the other, if the maxim be true, that to make unequal quantities equal, you must add more to one than the other. To say, in excuse, that gratitude is never to enter into the motives of national conduct, is to revive a principle which has been buried for centuries, with its kindred principles of the lawfulness of assassination, poison, perjury, etc. All of these were legitimate principles in the dark ages which intervened between ancient and modern civilization, but exploded and held in just horror in the eighteenth century. I know but one code of morality for men, whether acting singly or collectively. He who says, I will be a rogue when I act in company with a hundred others, but an honest man when I act alone, will be believed in the former assertion, but not in the latter, I would say with the poet, '*hic niger est, hunc tu Romane cavato.*' If the morality of one man produces a just line of conduct in him, acting individually, why should not the morality of one hundred men produce a just line of conduct in them, acting together? But I indulge myself in these reflections because my own feelings run me into them; with you they were always acknowledged. Let us hope that our new government will take some other occasion to show, that they mean to proscribe no virtue from the canons of their conduct with other nations. In every other instance, the new government has ushered itself to the world as honest, masculine, and dignified. It has shown genuine dignity, in my opinion, in exploding adulatory titles; they are the offerings of abject baseness, and nourish that degrading vice in the people."

These early and vigorously expressed views on this subject will, we suspect, be read with peculiar satisfaction by the venerators of Mr. Jefferson's political principles and fame. It became afterwards the fashion to ascribe such views as these to a sympathy with all the mad excesses of the French Revolution, and with a rancorous and unfounded animosity towards England. The opponents of these views afterwards justified themselves not only on the ground that national gratitude was a sham—that France had acted only for her own interest, and therefore deserved no gratitude—but that the character of the French Revolution justified all civilized and Christian nations in setting their faces against a people guilty of such enormities. It here appears that the issue was distinctly taken too early to be effected by the latter consideration, between what, for convenience, may be termed English and French sympathizers. Up to this point, the French Revolution had committed no excesses

—unless the American Revolution was itself an excess from the first moment of its inception. The people of France were attempting to throw off a multitude of political evils, some of the lightest of which were far more onerous than any or all which had caused the people of America to unfurl the standard of rebellion. And down to the time of Jefferson's departure from France, nothing had occurred in the progress of the French Revolution to shock the moral sense of any portion of mankind, who are not believers in legitimacy. The friends of even a moderate freedom throughout the world drew a deep breath of satisfaction when they learned that the mercenaries had been driven away from Paris—when they learned the accursed Bastile—accursed at the bar of God and man by the tears, and groans, and blood of the innocent who had perished in its stony dungeons for ages—had sunk under the avenging hand of the people. And if a few officials had been beheaded who had fired upon the people when flags of truce were flying on both sides [1] —who were engaged in treacherous correspondences [2]—who, amidst the horrors of famine, had scornfully said, let the people eat grass, and who had urged on the resort to mercenary troops to put down the people; [3] it was but a mild meting out of revolutionary justice when deep wrongs, otherwise incurable, required men to put aside for a time the sword of the civil law and gird on that of rebellion; and where, as in France, no ocean three thousand miles wide separated the aggressor and the avenger—but where they were brought face to face to act out the first impulses of mutual rage.

We aver that to this point (and to a later one) the French Revolution carried with it the sympathies of the wise and good, and even moderately conservative friends of free government throughout the earth—such men as Washington in America—such men as Fox, Mackintosh, and even Burke, in England. And yet at this moment, when France, in addition to her aid to us in the Revolution, had exhibited the greatest leniency in pressing her debts against us—had conceded to us every commercial privilege which it was in her power then to make or modest in us to ask—had evinced towards us every mark of comity and respect which it was possible for one nation to

[1] This was true of De Launay, the Governor, and of the deputy Governor of the Bastile.
[2] This was true of De Flesselles, the *Prévôt des Marchands.*
[3] This was true of Foulon, the Minister of War.

show to another—at this moment was the idea of showing her the least preference, even commercially, over England, just as much scouted at by a party in the United States, as ever afterwards. England at that time forcibly and menacingly held occupation of thousands and thousands of square miles of territory, admitted to be ours by the treaty of peace. Her flags floated over fortresses planted south of the St. Lawrence and the great lakes, from Lake Champlain to the peninsula of Michigan. These fortresses, if not quite near enough to each other to mingle the roar of their morning guns, were near enough together to constitute an effective, forcible occupation of our whole northern frontier. England was seducing the Indians within our own territory from their friendship to the United States—was protecting them in aggressions on us—was inciting them to what proved a bloody war on us. She had haughtily refused all commercial negotiation, and treated our ministers with official, if not personal, contempt. She had, as Mr. Jefferson remarks, libelled us over Europe as a nation of swindlers, if not miscreants. She had not, since the close of her war with us, shown us a solitary act of good will; permitted herself to be guilty of a national comity; or evinced any desire for anything looking towards a restoration of amicable feeling. From the King on her throne to the beggar in her streets, nothing but scorn and loathing towards America moved every heart and tongue.

Yet, as already said, there was even now a strong party in America who pronounced all those who desired to show any commercial or other preference to France over England a "French party"—an "anti-English party"—inflamed with bitter and unreasonable prejudices against England—and not long afterwards, a party of "Jacobins and infidels!"

The same letter to Mr. Madison from which the foregoing extract was taken (that of August 28th), contained a very decided expression in regard to Jefferson's accepting an "appointment" in the United States:

"You ask me if I would accept any appointment on that side of the water? You know the circumstances which led me from retirement, step by step, and from one nomination to another, up to the present. My object is to return to the same retirement. Whenever, therefore, I quit the present, it will not be to engage in any other office, and most especially any one which would require a constant residence from home."

We make no doubt that the appointment referred to was a place in the President's cabinet, and that Mr. Madison consulted him on this point, at the suggestion of General Washington. To suppose otherwise (if we are right as to the office) would be to suppose that the former gratuitously intermeddled in a matter which might (if Jefferson answered "yes") prove very embarrassing to the volunteer interrogator. Such officiousness was entirely foreign to Mr. Madison's habits, and his relations with General Washington at the period would have pointed him out as the person most likely to be intrusted with a confidential inquiry of this nature.

In another letter to Mr. Madison (September 6th) he discussed, at considerable length, a new question, arising from reflections on the elementary principles of society, which the course of affairs in France had suggested. He broached the subject in this wise: "The question whether one generation of men has a right to bind another, seems never to have been started either on this or our side of the water. Yet it is a question of such consequences as not only to merit decision, but place also among the fundamental principles of every government." He arrived at the negative conclusion. His intellectual history would not be complete without a full and fair view of his radical positions on this subject, especially as they became the persistent ones of his life. They are too long for insertion here, and a synopsis would not do entire justice to them. They will therefore be presented entire in the Appendix.[1]

Mr. Madison, in his reply, dissented from these views with his habitual force of logic, but with his habitual candor and modesty. The letter is given by Professor Tucker, and we place it before the reader with Jefferson's, in the Appendix.

Ninety-nine out of nearly every hundred well educated persons in the United States, we doubt not, would have concurred with the conclusions of Mr. Madison, at the period when these letters were written. Nay, we can readily fancy the "hard names" that would have been showered upon Jefferson then had his views found publication. But it has happened in this instance, as with most of his political "radicalisms." But little over half a century has passed away and they are now adopted and practised theories among men, constantly spread-

[1] See Appendix, No. 8.

ing over and controlling larger portions of human society—and where they have not been adopted by the majority, they are no longer met as frightful innovations, but as open questions where men have a right to doubt and discuss. The principal practical application which Mr. Jefferson proposed to make of the above theory—the limitation of the power of governments to contract debts beyond the life of a generation, and a provision, in all instances, simultaneous with the contracting for the payment of annual interest—has been engrafted with the happiest effects into the constitution of several American States. The radicalism of the eighteenth century becomes conservatism in the nineteenth.

President Washington informed the Senate of the United States, June 16th (1789), that he had given Mr. Jefferson a leave of absence, and he the next day nominated Mr. Short Chargé des Affaires during that absence. The Senate confirmed the appointment on the 18th. Information of these facts reached Mr. Jefferson towards the close of August, but considering October the best autumn month for a passage across the ocean, he did not leave Paris to return home until the 26th of September. He received the attentions of a vast circle of friends before his departure; but that departure not being understood as a final one, he, most agreeably for his own feelings, escaped the public and imposing demonstrations which his unbounded popularity in France would have otherwise called forth.

He reached Havre on the 28th, where he was detained by contrary winds until the 8th of October. He then passed over in a packet to Cowes, at which place Colonel Trumbull had chartered a vessel bound from London to Norfolk, to stop for him. Here again he was detained by contrary winds until the 22d; but he spent the intermediate time very pleasantly with his daughters, exploring all that was worth seeing in the Isle of Wight. They visited Carisbrook Castle, the scene of the confinement of Charles I., and various other places of interest, especially to the young ladies. A narrative of Martha's, lying before us, says that Colonel Trumbull had applied to Mr. Pitt to have Mr. Jefferson's baggage exempted from all Custom House examinations—and that the Minister, though informed that Mr. Jefferson was unapprised of the request, promptly and courteously issued the order. On the 23d the Clermont put to sea with favoring breezes, and Mr. Jefferson soon saw for the last time the shores of Europe.

His Memoir contains the following warm valedictory to France:

"I cannot leave this great and good country, without expressing my sense of its preëminence of character among the nations of the earth. A more benevolent people I have never known, nor greater warmth and devotedness in their select friendships. Their kindness and accommodation to strangers is unparalleled, and the hospitality of Paris is beyond anything I had conceived to be practicable in a large city. Their eminence, too, in science, the communicative disposition of their scientific men, the politeness of the general manners, the ease and vivacity of their conversation, gave a charm to their society, to be found nowhere else. In a comparison of this, with other countries, we have the proof of primacy, which was given to Themistocles, after the battle of Salamis. Every general voted to himself the first reward of valor, and the second to Themistocles. So, ask the travelled inhabitant of any nation, in what country on earth you would rather live?—Certainly, in my own, where are all my friends, my relations, and the earliest and sweetest affections and recollections of my life. Which would be your second choice? France."

A full history of Jefferson's diplomatic labors and achievements in France, has not been attempted in the preceding pages. We have but sketched important or characteristic facts. There was an every day filling up of minor details and duties, which though not entitled to separate narration, in the aggregate had perhaps as much to do with his usefulness and his popularity as a minister, as those we have given. In a country so hedged about by a complication of old and not easily changed commercial regulations as France before the Revolution, and in the first opening of its commerce and trade with a country wholly unfamiliar with those forms, there were necessarily frequently occurring difficulties requiring diplomatic interposition. Mr. Jefferson's correspondence shows that he firmly declined improper interferences for his countrymen—but his zeal, tact, and success on other occasions, were the theme of admiration to all seafaring Americans. His promptitude was especially admired. He took up every proper case brought to his notice, not like an official who was doing a favor and who was therefore entitled to consult his own leisure, but like an active agent or attorney, or rather like a deeply interested friend. The consequences of this and of his popularity at the French Court were, that it was generally understood that what he undertook would not only be successfully but quickly accomplished. Such an officer always wins the golden opinions of business men of every rank and description.

We might have cited a strong and very characteristic instance of his tact and perseverance in the case of some American prisoners, seized for a violation of the revenue laws. They had a part cargo of tobacco, and alleged they were driven into a prohibited French port, by stress of weather. The revenue officers, on the other hand, accused them of an attempt to smuggle. They were in the gripe of the inexorable Farmers-General, and the Government scarcely dared to interfere to show mercy. Jefferson supported them in prison. It is curious to note his appeals for these unfortunate men. If the Ministry granted him any favor, he said, "Fill the cup of gratitude full by releasing my countrymen." If the Ministry refused anything, he immediately said, "At least sweeten refusal by liberating my countrymen." On the point of leaving for England to aid in negotiating a treaty with her (not a bad time to ask a favor from France), his last parting note to the Minister of Foreign Affairs of the latter mentioned, "what a satisfaction it would be to him to see his poor countrymen set at liberty before his departure."[1] Such skillful and iron pertinacity is not to be resisted.

He discharged most gracefully another class of duties regarded as semi-official ones in the Ministers of civilized nations —namely, proper social and personal attentions to countrymen visiting foreign lands. To every American in France, Mr. Jefferson gave the full measure, and a little more, of those civilities which he had a right to expect, in the way of introductions, letters, and official countenance in other respects. These attentions to young persons on their travels, were often delightful to them. He entered into their plans with all the warmth of a comrade. He sketched routes for them—gave them letters to his friends—bade them draw on him if accidents happened to their remittances[2]—and during their stay at Paris, by his marked but wholly unpatronizing courtesy in society, gave them a position which they had not usually dreamed of attaining.

[1] We are not here quoting his precise language, but giving the spirit of many of his letters.

[2] This remark is suggested by a frank letter of this kind under our eye, and by the account-book, which shows that Mr. Jefferson's purse was more than once drawn upon by young American travellers. We dare say, however, that he never put his purse to a more agreeable use to himself; and that there was not an instance where the borrower's drafts would not have been cheerfully (and safely) answered to ten times their amounts.

Mr. Jefferson was, indeed, always fond of young men. To the last day of his life, no society could be possibly more acceptable to him than that of intelligent, ingenuous, well-bred, and especially scholarly young men—though he could well overlook the last qualification, where gallantry or elevation of character atoned for the loss. It was with such, that his conversation always took its most captivating tone and range. It was with such, that the usually carefully repressed enthusiasm of his nature gradually infused itself into his conversation, and burning words, and tones that lingered for years in the ears, and that indefinable expression in his eye of earnestness and human lovingness, spell-bound and captivated. We do not believe that a candid and unprejudiced man was ever admitted to half an hour's free conversation with Jefferson, who did not leave him with the undoubting conviction that he was a throughly earnest man. When this quality is united with a warm humanity, and a generous pecuniary liberality—when talent burns below, and a graceful refinement sparkles above—when to all this is added cordial attentions to others, and a frank desire to please—what young man ever refused to be pleased?

We may here add he was remarkably tolerant to the foibles of young men. He could, if he saw the *man* underneath, very readily excuse many things in them, which are apt to excite the indignation, or at least the contemptuous ridicule, of mature persons. He could, for instance (under the saving clause just named) goodnaturedly tolerate any moderate display of foppishness, heedlessness, exuberant levity, and all those other transient mental diseases, which, like chicken-pox, measles, and other youthful disorders of the body, most must have once. The cases, we are inclined to think, present another parallel. Is it not those who have these maladies most " dangerously " themselves, who ever after exhibit the greatest dread and aversion for them in others?

Mr. Jefferson (as we happen to know from the proof furnished by several specific instances[1]) could look not only with indul-

---

[1] We know one sad instance where the qualities of which we are about to speak led to most disastrous consequences—to exile—and to early death. The feelings of fervent love and gratitude of the gifted and unfortunate young man towards Mr. Jefferson, find an expression in some poetry which is under our eye. We had thought to quote it, as a specimen of the impressions which he produced on minds of this class. But it is not necessary to the vindication of any truth—it would probably bring back most painful memories to some living persons—and would raise the curtain of oblivion from a

gence, but with a sort of pleasure, on youthful idiosyncrasies and mental qualities, which had never belonged to himself. Thus, a romantic disposition, displaying itself in Quixotic acts, if but the effervescence of a manly and true character, seemed to interest him rather favorably; and his daughters Martha and Maria more than once heard him repeat, after a conversation or interview with such a person, the fine soliloquy of Don Quixote as he set forth on his adventures. And as he did this, his expression was not one of sarcasm, but of a man who felt for a generous fallacy. If he utterly lacked romance, he, in truth, possessed a quality sufficiently akin to it in some particulars to call forth his sympathy for it. This was HOPE—radiant and superabounding hope. If his card castles were different from those of the sentimental dreamer, he did his share in building up brilliant structures for the future, just as little likely to be realized. But we are wandering wide of our subject.

We do not propose here a formal analysis of Mr. Jefferson's Ambassadorial career; and we shall allude to but a few more of its marked points.

His dispatches home have been generally admired equally for their breadth and clearness of view, and for their minute accuracy in details. No excitement or confusion of the moment misled him as to substantial facts, or just conclusions. He possessed an intuitive faculty for reading the hidden motives of men, the wiles of diplomacy, and the secrets of statecraft. His Memoir, containing the matured views of his life in regard to French affairs and French politicians, is, on this subject, but a compilation made up of extracts taken almost without change from his contemporaneous letters.

It has been said he did not accurately foresee the results of the French Revolution. He foresaw them, it would be easy to show, quite as well as those whose sympathies were all the other way. But the discussion of this question here would be premature. Whether he persistently gave as prudent and in all respects as sound advice to the French Patriotic party as any other man in or out of France did, or could have done, the facts we have given will show. Whether the acceptance of his conservative advice by the Patriotic chiefs, and a faithful attempt to

tragedy produced by no crime of the heart. We will, then, let the sleeper sleep on forgotten in his foreign grave.

carry it out, would have saved France from the horrors in store
for her, we cannot decide. "Man proposes but God disposes."
We confess it is our individual opinion that nothing could have
averted the catastrophe—that it was as much the inevitable
effect of causes which had been ages in accumulating, as is the
pestilence of long permitted filthy conditions of the physical
world—that no remedy could have reached to the foundation
of the disease but extirpation—that extirpation was necessary
to save the moral civilization of the continent of Europe. In
fact, we do not believe Lafayette and his compatriots could
have followed Jefferson's advice, had they made the attempt.
Had they sought to pause midway, a new and deeper eruption
of the volcano would have sooner overwhelmed them. As with
Egypt, Assyria, Carthage, Greece, and Rome, the French political and social structure had finally reached that point, where
the inevitable next step was destruction. The avenging arm
that smote the thoroughly and hopelessly corrupted organizations of the early world was now stretched forth again to smite
—and the philosophy of the sage and the fury of the sans-
culotte, the wisdom of the Senate and the lawlessness of the
mob, could only tend to the inevitable result.

Mr. Jefferson's diplomatic conduct received the hearty
approbation of all classes at home, and the unconcealed admiration of the liberal and intelligent in Europe. The testimony
of the clear and profound Jay, who was then United States
Secretary for Foreign Affairs, has already been quoted. Judge
Marshall, always peculiarly "faint" in his "praise" of Jefferson,
wrote in the very height of the after party heats, that "in that
station he acquitted himself much to the public satisfaction."
As we have incidently quoted Mr. Webster's rather adverse
remarks on another topic connected with Jefferson's stay in
France, it is but fair to do so on this. He said in one of his
ablest and best known productions:

"Mr. Jefferson's discharge of his diplomatic duties was marked by great ability,
diligence, and patriotism; and while he resided at Paris, in one of the most interesting periods, his character for intelligence, his love of knowledge and of the
society of learned men, distinguished him in the highest circles of the French
capital. No court in Europe had at that time in Paris a representative commanding
or enjoying higher regard, for political knowledge or for general attainments, than
the minister of this then infant republic."

The Edinburgh Review, in an article betraying anything but partiality for Jefferson, thus reflected the sentiment of Europe in regard to his diplomatic career in France:

"His watchfulness on every subject which might bear on the most favorable arrangement of their new commercial treaties, his perseverance in seeking to negotiate a general alliance against Algiers, the skill and knowledge with which he argued the different questions of national interest that arose during his residence, will not suffer even in comparison with Franklin's diplomatic talents. Everything he sees seems to suggest to him the question, whether it can be made useful in America. Could we compare a twelvemonth's letters from our Ambassador's bags at Paris, Florence, or elsewhere, we should see whether our enormous diplomatic salaries are anything else than very successful measures for securing our business being ill and idly done."

We left Mr. Jefferson on the Atlantic. His homeward passage was speedy for the times, and not an unpleasant one until the Clermont arrived off the Capes of the Chesapeake, where she encountered so thick a fog that it was impossible to see a pilot boat, if any were out. Martha Jefferson's narrative says:

"After beating about three days, the captain, a bold as well as an experienced seaman, determined to run in at a venture, without having seen the Capes. The ship came near running upon what was conjectured to be the middle ground, when anchor was cast at ten o'clock, P.M. The wind rose, and the vessel drifted down, dragging her anchors one or more miles. But she had got within the Capes, whilst a number which had been less bold were blown off the coast, some of them lost, and all kept out three or four weeks longer. We had to beat up against a strong head wind, which carried away our topsails; and we were very near being run down by a brig coming out of port, which, having the wind in her favor, was almost upon us before we could get out of the way. We escaped, however, with only a loss of a part of our rigging. My father had been so anxious about his public accounts that he would not trust them to go until he went with them. We arrived at Norfolk in the forenoon, and in two hours after landing, before an article of our baggage was brought ashore, the vessel took fire and seemed on the point of being reduced to a mere hull. They were in the act of scuttling her, when some abatement in the flames was discovered, and she was finally saved. So great had been the activity of her crew, and of those belonging to other ships in the harbor who came to their aid, that everything in her was saved. Our trunks, and perhaps also the papers, had been put in our state rooms and the doors incidentally closed by the captain. They were so close that the flames did not penetrate, but the powder in a musket in one of them was silently consumed, and the thickness of the travelling trunks alone saved their contents from the excessive heat. • • Norfolk had not recovered from the effects of the war, and we should have found it difficult to obtain rooms but for the politeness of the gentlemen at the hotel (Lindsay's), who were kind enough to give up their own rooms for our accommodation. There were no stages in those days. We were indebted to the kindness of our friends for horses, and visiting all on the way homeward, and spending more or less time with them all in turn, we reached Monticello on the 23d of December.

"The negroes discovered the approach of the carriage as soon as it reached Shadwell, and such a scene I never witnessed in my life. They collected in crowds round it and almost drew it up the mountain by hand. The shouting, etc., had been sufficiently obstreperous before, but the moment it arrived at the top, it reached the climax. When the door of the carriage was opened, they received him in their arms and bore him to the house, crowding round and kissing his hands and feet—some blubbering and crying—others laughing. It seemed impossible to satisfy their anxiety to touch and kiss the very earth which bore him. These were the first ebullitions of joy for his return after a long absence, which they would of course feel; but perhaps it is not out of place to add here that they were at all times very devoted in their attachment to him. They believed him to be one of the greatest, and they knew him to be one of the best of men and kindest of masters. They spoke to him freely, and applied confidingly to him in all their difficulties and distresses: and he watched over them in sickness and in health—interested himself in all their concerns—advising them, showing esteem and confidence in the good, and indulgence to all. I believe I have said nothing that they would not unhesitatingly confirm, if asked."[1]

Wormley, the aged slave already referred to in this work, was between nine and ten years old when Mr. Jefferson returned from France, and when we talked with him in 1851, had a distinct recollection of the reception scene described above, and he gave us, partly from recollection and partly from the statements of his fellows, several minor touches of the story.

Two or three days before reaching home, Mr. Jefferson had sent an express directing his overseer to have his house made ready for his reception by a specified day. The overseer mentioned this, and the news flew like wildfire over the different farms which it is customary to mention collectively as Monticello. The slaves could hardly attend to their work. They asked leave to make his return a holiday and of course received permission. Bright and early were all up on the appointed day, washed clean of the stains of labor, and attired in their "Sunday best." They first determined to receive him at the foot of the mountain; and the women and children refusing to be left behind, down they marched in a body. Never dragged on hours so slowly! Finally, the men began to straggle onward—the women and children followed—and the swarm did not settle again until they reached the confines of the estate, perhaps two miles from the house. By and by a carriage and four horses

---

[1] The last paragraph of this quotation (with the exception of the last sentence) has already appeared in Professor Tucker's Work.

was seen rapidly approaching. The negroes raised a shout. The postillions plied their whips, and in a moment more, the carriage was in their midst. Martha's description of what ensued is sufficiently accurate until the summit of the notch between Monticello and Carter's Mountain was attained. She says, the carriage was almost drawn up by hand. We consider old Wormley's authority the best on this point! He pointed out the very spot soon after the carriage had turned off from the highway, when in spite of the entreaties and commands (not however, we imagine, very sternly uttered!) of the "old master," the horses were detached and the shouting crowd pushed and dragged the heavy vehicle at no snail's pace up the further ascent, until it reached the lawn in front of the house. Mr. Jefferson had no idea whatever of being "toted" (Africanice for "carried") from the carriage door into his house—riding on men not being to his taste. But who can control his destiny? Not a word could be heard in the wild uproar, and when he stepped from the carriage he unexpectedly landed on a cluster of swarthy arms, and amidst the oriental salutations described by Martha, was borne once more under his own roof-tree. The crowd respectfully broke apart for the young ladies, and as the stately, graceful Martha and the little fairy-like Maria advanced between the dark lines, escorted by "Jack Eppes," shouts rent the sky and many a curly-headed urchin was held aloft to catch a look of what their mothers and sisters were already firmly persuaded could not be paralled in the Ancient Dominion!

CHAPTER XIV.

1789—1790.

WHILE Mr. Jefferson was at the seat of his brother-in-law, Mr. Eppes, at Eppington, on his way from Norfolk to Monti-cello, he received the following letters from General Washington, tendering him the appointment of Secretary of State; the second being accompanied by a commission for that office:

NEW YORK, *October* 13, 1789.

SIR,

In the selection of characters to fill the important offices of Government, in the United States, I was naturally led to contemplate the talents and dispositions which I knew you to possess and entertain for the service of your country; and

554

without being able to consult your inclination, or to derive any knowledge of your intention from your letters, either to myself or to any other of your friends, I was determined, as well by motives of private regard, as a conviction of public propriety, to nominate you for the department of State, which, under its present organization, involves many of the most interesting objects of the Executive authority. But grateful as your acceptance of this commission would be to me, I am, at the same time, desirous to accommodate your wishes, and I have, therefore, forborne to nominate your successor at the court of Versailles, until I should be informed of your determination.

Being on the eve of a journey through the Eastern States, with a view to observe the situation of the country, and in a hope of perfectly reëstablishing my health, which a series of indispositions has much impaired, I have deemed it proper to make this communication of your appointment, in order that you might lose no time, should it be your *wish* to visit Virginia during the recess of Congress, which will probably be the most convenient season, both as it may respect your private concerns, and the public service.

Unwilling, as I am, to interfere in the direction of your choice of assistance, I shall only take the liberty of observing to you, that, from warm recommendations which I have received on behalf of Roger Alden, Esq., assistant Secretary to the late Congress, I have placed all the papers thereunto belonging, under his care. Those papers which more properly appertain to the office of Foreign Affairs, are under the superintendence of Mr. Jay, who has been so obliging as to continue his good offices, and they are in the immediate charge of Mr. Remsen.

With sentiments of very great esteem and regard,

I have the honor to be, sir,

Your most obedient servant,

GEORGE WASHINGTON.

The Honorable Thomas Jefferson.

I take this occasion to acknowledge the receipt of your several favors, of the 4th and 5th of December of the last, and 10th of May of the present year, and to thank you for the communications therein.   G. W.

———

NEW YORK, *November* 30, 1789.

DEAR SIR,

You will perceive by the inclosed letter (which was left for you at the office of Foreign Affairs, when I made a journey to the Eastern States), the motives on which I acted with regard to yourself, and the occasion of my explaining them at that early period.

Having now reason to hope, from Mr. Trumbull's report, that you will be arrived at Norfolk before this time (on which event I would most cordially congratulate you), and having a safe conveyance by Mr. Griffin, I forward your commission to Virginia; with a request to be made acquainted with your sentiments as soon as you shall find it convenient to communicate them to me.

With sentiments of very great esteem and regard,

I am, dear sir,

Your most obedient humble servant,

GEORGE WASHINGTON.

The Honorable Thomas Jefferson.

Mr. Jefferson, as his letter to Mr. Madison from France would prepare us to expect, received this proffer with "real regret."[1] He replied to it as follows:

CHESTERFIELD, *December* 15, 1799.

SIR,

I have received at this place the honor of your letters of October the 13th and November the 30th, and am truly flattered by your nomination of me to the very dignified office of Secretary of State, for which, permit me here to return you my humble thanks. Could any circumstance seduce me to overlook the disproportion between its duties and my talents, it would be the encouragement of your choice. But when I contemplate the extent of that office, embracing as it does the principal mass of domestic administration, together with the foreign, I cannot be insensible of my inequality to it; and I should enter on it with gloomy forebodings from the criticisms and censures of a public, just indeed in their intentions, but sometimes misinformed and misled, and always too respectable to be neglected. I cannot but foresee the possibility that this may end disagreeably for me, who, having no motive to public service but the public satisfaction, would certainly retire the moment that satisfaction should appear to languish. On the other hand, I feel a degree of familiarity with the duties of my present office, as far, at least, as I am capable of understanding its duties. The ground I have already passed over enables me to see my way into that which is before me. The change of government, too, taking place in the country where it is exercised, seems to open a possibility of procuring from the new rulers some new advantages in commerce, which may be agreeable to our countrymen. So that as far as my fears, my hopes, or my inclination might enter into this question, I confess they would not lead me to prefer a change.

But it is not for an individual to choose his post. You are to marshal us as may be best for the public good; and it is only in the case of its being indifferent to you, that I would avail myself of the option you have so kindly offered in your letter. If you think it better to transfer me to another post, my inclination must be no obstacle; nor shall it be, if there is any desire to suppress the office I now hold, or to reduce its grade. In either of these cases, be so good only as to signify to me by another line your ultimate wish, and I shall conform to it cordially. If it should be to remain at New York, my chief comfort will be to work under your eye, my only shelter the authority of your name, and the wisdom of measures to be dictated by you and implicitly executed by me. Whatever you may be pleased to decide, I do not see that the matters which have called me hither will permit me to shorten the stay I originally asked; that is to say, to set out on my journey northward till the month of March. As early as possible in that month, I shall have the honor of paying my respects to you in New York. In the meantime, I have that of tendering you the homage of those sentiments of respectful attachment with which I am, sir, your most obedient and most humble servant,

TH. JEFFERSON.

This was as strong an expression of unwillingness to accept the office as Mr. Jefferson's sense of duty and his very strong

[1] Memoir.

feelings of reverence and affection towards General Washington would permit him to make.

On receiving this letter, the President deferred his reply until he should hear from Mr. Madison, who had been on a visit to Monticello, and who was able to correct some of Mr. Jefferson's impressions in regard to the duties of the proffered office. Receiving Madison's information,[1] the President again wrote Jefferson January 21st. He very kindly declined to oppose the personal inclinations of the latter if they should continue adverse to an acceptance of the appointment, after being made "acquainted with the light" in which the President "viewed the office of Secretary of State;" and he also stated that "he did not know that any alteration was likely to take place in the commission from the United States to the Court of France." The letter was long, and the following is the only paragraph in it which seems to require quotation:

"I consider the successful administration of the general government as an object of almost infinite consequence to the present and future happiness of the citizens of the United States. I consider the office of Secretary for the Department of State very important on many accounts, and I know of no person who, in my judgment, could better execute the duties of it than yourself. Its duties will probably be not quite so arduous and complicated in their execution as you may have been led at the first moment to imagine. At least, it was the opinion of Congress that, after the division of all the business of a domestic nature between the Departments of the Treasury, War, and State, those which would be comprehended in the latter might be performed by the same person who should have the charge of conducting the department of foreign affairs. The experiment was to be made, and if it shall be found that the fact is different, I have little doubt that a further arrangement or division of the business in the office of the Department of State will be made in such manner as to enable it to be performed, under the superintendence of one man, with facility to himself, as well as with advantage and satisfaction to the public. These observations, however, you will be pleased to remark, are merely matters of opinion. But in order that you may be better prepared to make your ultimate decision on good grounds, I think it necessary to add one fact, which is this, that your late appointment has given very extensive and very great

[1] Mr. Madison wrote the President after his visit to Monticello:
"A few days before I was allowed to set out for New York, I took a ride to Monticello. The answer of Mr. Jefferson to the notification of his appointment will no doubt have explained the state of his mind on the subject. I was sorry to find him so little biased in favor of the domestic service allotted to him, but was glad that his difficulties seemed to result chiefly from what I take to be an erroneous view of the kind and quantity of business annexed to that, which constituted the foreign department. He apprehends that it will far exceed the latter, which has of itself no terrors to him. On the other hand, it was supposed, and I believe truly, that the domestic part will be very trifling, and for that reason improper to be made a distinct department. After all, if the whole business can be executed by any one man, Mr. Jefferson must be equal to it. All whom I have heard speak on the subject, are remarkably solicitous for his acceptance, and I flatter myself, that they will not in the event be disappointed."—*January 4th*, 1790

satisfaction to the public. My original opinion and wish may be collected from my nomination."

This was an obvious intimation of the writer's continued wishes; and Jefferson felt there was no other course left which would be satisfactory to his own feelings, or consistent with his duty, but to promptly signify his acceptance.

On the 23d of February (1790) Martha Jefferson was married[1] to Thomas Mann Randolph, Jr., eldest son of Colonel Thomas Mann Randolph, of Tuckahoe, who had been, during his minority, the ward of Mr. Jefferson's father. The young people were second-cousins, and had been attached to each other from childhood. During Martha's stay in France, young Randolph had completed his education at the University of Edinburgh, and visited Paris, in 1788, where he spent a portion of the summer.[2] He had just shot up into manhood, and in person and mind exhibited marked traces of both his parent stocks.[3] He was tall, lean, with dark expressive features and a flashing eye, commanding in carriage, elastic as steel, and had that sudden sinewy strength which it would not be difficult to fancy he inherited from the forest monarchs of Virginia.[4] He was brilliant, versatile, eloquent in conversation when he chose to be, impetuous and imperious in temper, chivalric in generosity, a Knight-Errant in courage, in calm moments a just, and at all times a high-toned man. He possessed a restless and vehement energy—though after years disclosed that this was not sufficiently accompanied with that perseverance which is the basis of important and continued success. His education was a

---

[1] By the Rev. Mr. Maury of the Episcopal church.

[2] He, his brother William, and their cousin, Archibald Cary Randolph, went to Edinburgh in 1785. William and Archy returned home in the spring of 1788. Thomas Mann spent the summer on the Continent, and returned home in autumn.

[3] His mother was Ann Cary, daughter of Colonel Archibald Cary, of Ampthill. The families were closely interwoven, as Col. Archibald Cary's wife was Mary Randolph, a daughter of Richard Randolph, of Curles.

Since writing the preceding, we find the Cary pedigree given with some fullness in Mr. Grigsby's Discourse on The Virginia Convention of 1776. He mentions that the family are the same with the Carys of Fullerton given in Burke's Commoners—that Col. Archibald Cary, of Ampthill, was a descendant of Henry Lord Hunsdon, and was himself, at the time of his death, the heir apparent of the barony. The family emigrated to Virginia in 1640, and Miles Cary sat in the House of Burgesses more than a century before the passage of the Stamp Act.

Mr. Grigsby says, Colonel Cary was popularly designated by the sobriquet of "Old Iron"—an expressive one, certainly, when applied to this lion-hearted man. We find all of our favorable views of Cary fully confirmed by this careful investigator of Virginia History. The iron lay in his determination; he was characterized neither by violence nor by roughness. He died in 1786.

He was descended, by several different strains of blood, from Pocahontas.

finished one.   His reading was extensive and varied.   His
fortune was ample in prospect, and it would have been immense
but for the change effected in the Virginia statutes of descent
by the efforts of his father-in-law.   Few young Americans had
attracted more notice abroad.   He received those marked
attentions in the Scottish capital, which, it used to be said, were
lavished only on such young gentlemen of the University as in
point of rank, wealth (and possibly we should add, parts and
appearance), were considered prizes worth playing for by the
prudent mammas of daughters who unfortunately could not
inherit the family property—as they did the family pedigree
and pride—undiminished by use, or by the number of the
sharers!   Young Randolph, too, made friends among the grave
and the learned.   Professor Leslie returned with him to Virginia, and was about eighteen months (so family tradition preserves the period) a guest of the family at Tuckahoe.[1]   Few
young men in Virginia, or in the United States, were starting
life, in all respects, with greater promise of future honor and
usefulness.

On the 1st of March, Mr. Jefferson set out for New York,
the seat of government, to take his place in President Washington's Cabinet.   Stopping at Richmond to arrange some private
affairs, he resumed his journey on the 8th.   Two days afterwards, he reached Alexandria, where the Mayor and citizens
gave him a public reception.   Here his horses and carriage met
him, but a snow of eighteen inches deep falling over night, he
took the stage, having his horses led, and sending round the
carriage by water.   His progress through the snow and mud
did not exceed two or three miles an hour by day, and a mile
an hour by night, so that he was a fortnight in getting from
Richmond to New York.   He somewhat relieved the intolerable tedium of the route by occasionally mounting his led saddle-
horse.[2]

He reached Philadelphia on the 17th, and immediately

---

[1] We rather think (to go more into detail) that Leslie took his passage to America
with William and Archy, in the spring of 1788 (see two notes back).   It has often been
said, in repeating Virginia colloquial traditions, that Leslie was a tutor in the Tuckahoe
family of Randolphs.   This is a mistake.   Dr. Elder was the family tutor at the period ;
and Leslie bore no other relation to it, but that of a guest and friend.
[2] An entry in the account-book about this saddle-horse shows the old taste was not
yet extinct :

"*Alexandria, March* 11.   Recd. here Mr. W. Fitzhugh's horse Tarquin, 9 or 10 years
old, got by Eclipse out of Peyton Randolph's roan mare, who was of the blood of
Monkey, Othello, etc.   I am to pay 75 pounds sterling.   Excels in two-mile heats.

repaired to the bedside of the "venerable and beloved Franklin," now in his last illness.   During their interview, the latter
intrusted him with a historical paper, which Jefferson returned
to William Temple Franklin, about a month afterwards, on the
death of his grandfather.   Subsequent events led Mr. Jefferson
to believe that Dr. Franklin had intended this as a "confidential
deposit" with him, and that he had "done wrong in parting
from it."   His account of his interview with Franklin, and his
singular impressions concerning this paper, will be found at the
close of his Memoir.

He arrived at New York on the 21st, and took lodgings at
the City Tavern.   He looked for a house in "the Broadway,"
but finding none vacant, rented and occupied a small one, in
Maiden Lane (No. 57, owned by Robert and Peter Bruce), until
he could get "time to look about him."   Congress was in session, and as "much business had been put by for his arrival,"
he "found himself all at once involved under an accumulation
of it." [1]

He had hinted to a French traveller, a year or two before,
than an "imitation of European manners" prevailed in the
American cities; but he seems to have been utterly unprepared
for finding that this imitation extended to much more serious
things.   Giving an account of New York society at the time of
his arrival, he some years afterwards said:

"Here, certainly, I found a state of things which, of all I had ever contemplated, I the least expected.   I had left France in the first year of her revolution, in
the fervor of natural rights, and zeal for reformation.   My conscientious devotion to
these rights could not be heightened, but it had been aroused and excited by daily
exercise.   The President received me cordially, and my colleagues and the circle of
principal citizens, apparently with welcome.   The courtesies of dinner parties given
me, as a stranger newly arrived among them, placed me at once in their familiar
society.   But I cannot describe the wonder and mortification with which the table
conversations filled me.   Politics were the chief topic, and a preference of kingly
over republican government, was evidently the favorite sentiment.   An apostate I
could not be, nor yet a hypocrite; and I found myself, for the most part, the
only advocate on the republican side of the question, unless among the guests
there chanced to be some member of that party from the legislative Houses."

This has been thought a very highly colored picture.   As a
New Yorker by birth and affections, we should be very glad to

---

[1] Account-book.   Letter to his son-in-law, T. M. Randolph (misprinted M. Randolph
in Congress edition).   March 28.

think it so, did we suppose the present character of the State, or of its inhabitants, in any wise depended on the facts asserted. Mr. Sabine, the historian of the American Loyalists, records that "New York was undeniably the Loyalists' stronghold in America," and "contained more of them than any other colony." He declares that "in some counties a Whig was a man rarely met with "—that "Documents are extant to show that in 1776 no less than twelve hundred and ninety-three persons acknowledged allegiance, and professed themselves well affected subjects [of Great Britain] in the single county of Queens "—that eight hundred of the militia appeared in a body in another county and swore to be faithful to the Crown, etc. Mr. Sabine thinks it "beyond all doubt " that the royal party had the preponderance in the entire State.[1] The Documentary History of New York (published by its Legislature), Onderdonk's Revolutionary Incidents of Long Island, and various other minute publications,[2] exhibit an abundance of original documentary proof on this subject.

That a large portion of the wealthy and aristocratic families of the city of New York, who, when Jefferson came north in 1790, led in the fashionable world and gave "dinner parties " to government officers, had been quite as attentive to the British officials, during their long occupation of the city, no one, we presume, will doubt, that has seriously inquired into the (mostly unwritten) history of the British occupation.[3] Some of those families publicly proclaimed their loyalism. Others were saved the necessity of such avowals, because, living within the British lines during most of the war, their Whig countrymen could not reach them to compel them to take sides ; and when the struggle was over, they chose to remain where their property was, and became good Whigs ! Perhaps this is a harsh judgment of people who did nothing to aid their country—who constantly and freely mingled in society with British officers—who habitually invited them to their houses—who met with them at parties, balls, etc.—whose wives and daughters danced and flirted with dashing colonels and baronets—when a minute's

[1] See the American Loyalists, by Lorenzo Sabine, p. 17.
[2] Among which we would name Stone's Life of Brant, Campbell's Annals of Tryon County, Life of Hale, etc. etc. And there are sundry unpublished records (letters) on the subject in the office of the N. Y. Secretary of State.
[3] It will not be understood, of course, that we apply this remark promiscuously The New York aristocracy furnished a portion of the most decided Whigs in the State.

drive, or a five minutes' walk, would have carried them where
the groans of their countrymen, perishing for food, for air, for
the common decencies of life, pierced the thick walls of the
Sugar-House—where the earth was steaming rankly with the
fresh blood of the daily martyrs slaughtered by the fiendish
Cunningham—or whose moans and screams of maniacal anguish
were wafted on the night air from those pestilence dens and
floating hells, the prison-ships in the East River ! [1]

We have ever regarded the choice between Loyalism or
Whiggism, at the breaking out of the American Revolution, as
fairly an open question. We believe the Loyalist deeply mis-
judged ; but to say that he had not the same right to pursue his
conscientious convictions that the Whig had, would be to strike
at the root of every just or democratic theory. If he openly
took his side with England, and waged honorable warfare, he
could only properly be treated like any other foe. Again, when
thousands and thousands of Loyalists at heart, and even by
avowal, in the southeastern counties of New York, and elsewhere, driven to take sides, decided to act with their relatives,
neighbors, and countrymen, and did faithfully so act, their error
of private opinion ceased to be a just ground of subsequent
imputation against them by their countrymen.

Every well informed man understands that the American
Revolution began as a war against the aggressions, and not
against the form, of the British government. There was not a reason why a man might not at its beginning have been a true Whig,
and at the same time a decided friend of constitutional monarchy.
There is little doubt, however, that if the direct question of
monarchism or republicanism was not necessarily involved
between the Whig and the Tory, each was generally influenced
by a mental tendency, by education, or by other circumstances,
which, to a considerable extent, exerted what has been commonly regarded as a corresponding effect on his opinions on
that question. The friend of strong government was disposed
to be a Tory—the friend of popular government was disposed
to be a Whig. These terms are vague, but their import is well
understood. But while, probably, nearly every thorough Tory

[1] In regard to the treatment of the American prisoners in the city of New York, a good deal of minute and curious documentary information will be found in Onderdonk's Revolutionary Incidents, etc.

was also a decided monarchist, it did not as certainly follow
that all Whigs were republicans. Patriotism, too, might, for
some subsequent period, triumph over moderately monarchical
biases. Thousands were in a great measure neutrals or middle
men on that question, ready to drift with the current of circumstances. The general current, during the Revolution, was, past
all doubt, decidedly against monarchy.

When peace came, the weakness and inadequacy of the
existing federal pact became more and more manifest. The
general Congress had not power to pass laws necessary to preserve the public faith, to protect and develop the most important
national interests, or really to carry on efficiently and regularly
the common concerns of government. The States often declined
or neglected to supply this deficiency, so far as it depended on
their action. The lapse of time did not help this situation of
affairs ; the rope of sand, instead of cementing, continued to drop
asunder. Looser ideas of the force of public if not of private
obligations began to prevail. Some of the States passed stay-
laws against the collection of private debts. Never in the world
perhaps, was there as valid an excuse for such laws, as during
the first few years after the American Revolution; but they
were regarded, and perhaps justly regarded, as not only dangerous innovations on the established order of things, but as
symptoms of a state of feeling which might lead to more radical
disorganizations.

Then came on "Shay's Insurrection"—produced by an
attempt on the part of Massachusetts to raise taxes which, at
that particular juncture, fell very onerously on its people. For
a time, it rapidly spread, and seemed to threaten a formidable
civil war. The rioters proclaimed various Agrarian-sounding
doctrines. If that class of writers whom Judge Marshall so well
represents, are to be implicitly credited on this subject, " twelve
or fifteen thousand " citizens of New England, " chiefly of the
young and active part of the community," " desperate and
unprincipled," banded themselves together against the government, without any real grievance, or even serious hardship to
complain of, acting and avowing just about such a code of
political and social principles as Shakspeare puts into the mouth
of Jack Cade and his followers.[1] We confess we never have,

---

[1] See Marshall's Washington, vol. ii. p. 116, *et seq.*

for a moment, believed that these representations were accurate, or approached accuracy, in regard to twelve or fifteen thousand, or even twelve or fifteen hundred of the young and active men of New England—themselves participators in the Revolution, or the sons of Revolutionary and Pilgrim sires. A few ignorant or ruffianly men, we suppose, seized upon an occasion of great popular excitement to proclaim wild and disorganizing views. It was a feverish and unsettled time, and political alarmists— the men who never witness the slightest popular outbreak without fancying the end of social and moral order has come—were seized with their usual panic. And if such statements as we have quoted, could creep into deliberately written history—history written years afterwards—the fact furnishes some data for conjecturing what must have been the wild exaggerations which prevailed during the consternation of the moment. We have already intimated that "Shay's Insurrection" suddenly changed the views of government entertained by not a few persons Superadded to preceding political difficulties, its anti-republican and more especially its anti-democratic influence was profound and almost universal throughout the United States.

Nothing could be more natural than for all reflecting men, at a period of so little experience, and of such unsettledness in our affairs, to cast their eyes back to the example of the government from which we had so recently separated. There, the man of property saw the rights of property jealously and securely guarded; the man of business, all business obligations rigorously enforced; the public creditor, every government engagement punctually met; the man of position, rank sedulously protected; the alarmist, executive strength to at once crush disorder; the enemy of despotism, power prescribed within fixed limits. Was it strange that a good many of these several classes, educated in monarchy in their own youth, attributed the differences they observed between the two countries in these particulars to the difference in their form of government? Was it strange that a good many men, who started as republicans in 1776, and who yet would have preferred republicanism, had they considered it adequate to our national exigences—now relapsed into monarchists, in the name or in the substance?

In our judgment, it was not at all strange. And where it was the result of a conscientious conviction, it would be absurd to pronounce it criminal. It is remarkable that it is those American writers who most evidently lean towards strong consolidated government themselves, that have been the first to assume that the imputation of American monarchism (since 1776) is equivalent to the imputation of a crime; that he who "charges" it upon any body of American citizens, subsequently to that period, is guilty of a most heinous calumny.

Thus Jefferson's statements in regard to the tone of fashionable society in New York in 1790, have been pronounced deliberate misrepresentations, or else the ravings of a disordered fancy. This is by no means the only instance where he imputes monarchical views to bodies of our citizens, and to very prominent citizens, by name. He had scarcely taken his seat in President Washington's Cabinet, before he declared that some of his colleagues in that Cabinet avowed such views to him or in his hearing. It became, indeed, one of the settled dogmas of his political creed that there was such a party in the United States, and that it was constantly at work, openly or secretly, to overthrow republicanism. He carefully perpetuated documentary evidence to establish this fact. He died with such allegations on his lips.

Volumes have been written to prove that these assertions were unfounded, and consequently where they rest on personal testimony, false. There can be but three theories on the subject. Either Mr. Jefferson uttered the truth; or he was a monomaniacal fanatic, like Balfour Burleigh, fiercely hewing and stabbing at the phantoms conjured up by a distempered imagination; or he was, what was infinitely more detestable, a cold-blooded demagogue attempting to excite popular prejudices against adversaries by deliberate falsehood. And as he repeatedly adduces the evidence of his own senses—of his own ears—for his assertions, it would be very difficult to shelter him under the second plea, unless we should suppose the distemper of his imagination extended to actual insanity. Neither friend nor enemy pretends this. The question comes then so far as his personal testimony goes to a naked one of veracity.

Such an issue cannot be properly shunned by a biographer of Mr. Jefferson. That issue is already fully opened by the declarations we have quoted. It involves facts which color almost every subsequent political transaction we shall be called

upon to record. It cannot, therefore, be treated of more season-
ably than now. A separate outline of the facts, presented connectedly and without reference to their chronological connection
with the general events of this narration, it is believed will lead
to a clearer understanding of the subject. We do not propose,
by any means, to exhaust the testimony. It would require a
volume to do this. We shall but aim to so far " make out a
case," as to enable candid men to settle in their own minds the
question of Mr. Jefferson's veracity.

We will begin our view at the period of the Annapolis Convention in 1786. In regard to that Meeting, we find this declaration in Mr. Jefferson's Memoir :

> " Although at this meeting, a difference of opinion was evident on the question
> of a republican or kingly government, yet, so general through the States was the
> sentiment in favor of the former, that the friends of the latter confined themselves
> to a course of obstruction only, and delay, to everything proposed; they hoped,
> that nothing being done, and all things going from bad to worse, a kingly govern-
> ment might be usurped, and submitted to by the people, as better than anarchy and
> wars internal and external, the certain consequences of the present want of a
> general government. The effect of their manœuvres, with the defective attendance
> of Deputies from the States, resulted in the measure of calling a more general
> convention, to be held at Philadelphia."

These views receive confirmation from several quarters never
suspected, we believe, of any partiality for Mr. Jefferson's person
or political ideas. Judge Marshall says in his Life of Washington (vol. ii., p. 116) :

> " Among those who were disinclined to a convention [that called at Philadelphia
> in 1787], were persons who were actuated by different, and even by opposite
> motives. There were, probably, some who believed that a higher toned government
> than was compatible with the opinions generally prevailing among the friends of
> order, of real liberty, and of national character, was essential to the public safety.
> They believed that men would be conducted to that point only through the road
> of misery into which their follies would lead them, and that 'times must be worse
> before they could better.' "

We find General Knox, Colonel Humphreys, and other distinguished men in New England dissuading General Washington from attending the Convention, on the ground that the
people of the United States were not yet prepared to adopt a
proper Constitution. They solicit him to reserve himself for
some subsequent " solemn occasion," for " the united call of a
Continent entire." They carry the idea that the Eastern States

will not send delegates, unless it is understood that he purposes to attend.[1]

John Jay wrote General Washington, January 7th, 1787:

"Shall we have a king? Not in my opinion while other expedients remain untried. Might we not have a Governor-General limited in his prerogative and duration? Might not Congress be divided into an upper and a lower House; the former appointed for life, the latter annually? And let the Governor-General (to preserve the balance) with the advice of a council, formed for that only purpose, of the great judicial officers, have a negative on their acts. Our government should in some degree be suited to our manners and circumstances, and they, you know, are not strictly democratical."[2]

Mr. Madison, in a paper which is prefixed to his Debates in the Federal Convention of 1787, after reciting clearly and fully the difficulties in the form and administration of the Government prior to that Convention,[3] says:

"As a natural consequence of this distracted and disheartening condition of the Union, the Federal authority had ceased to be respected abroad, and dispositions were shown there, particularly in Great Britain, to take advantage of its imbecility, and to speculate on its approaching downfall.   *   *   *   *   *
It was found, moreover, that those least partial to popular government, or most distrustful of its efficacy, were yielding to anticipations, that from an increase of the confusion, a government might result more congenial with their taste or their opinions; whilst those most devoted to the principles and forms of Republics were alarmed for the cause of liberty itself, at stake in the American experiment, and anxious for a system that would avoid the inefficacy of a mere confederacy, without passing into the opposite extreme of a consolidated government. It was known that there were individuals who had betrayed a bias towards monarchy, and there had always been some not unfavorable to a partition of the Union into several confederacies; either from a better chance of figuring on a sectional theatre, or that the sections would require stronger governments, or by their hostile conflicts lead to a monarchical consolidation."[4]

General Washington seems to have had no doubt of the existence of a monarchical party at this period, or in what part

---

[1] See General Knox to General Washington, January 14th, 1787. Sparks's Washington, vol. ix. Appendix, p. 513.
It has often been claimed that Knox, in this letter, declared himself for a government substantially like our present one. The correctness of this pretence may be estimated by two features of his plan. He desired the complete extinction of the State governments, and he proposed a permanent standing army to enforce the laws of the general government!
For some of Humphreys' Letters, see Marshall's Washington, vol. ii. p. 115, and Sparks's Washington, vol. ix. p. 238, et seq. and notes.
[2] See letter entire in Sparks's Washington, vol. ix. p. 510.
[3] Our own sketch of these was necessarily very general and meagre. He who would have a full and fair view of them, would do well to turn to this paper of Mr. Madison's, in "The Madison Papers," commencing at vol. ii. p. 685.
[4] Ib. vol. ii. p. 713.

of the United States it was to be principally found. He wrote Mr. Madison, March 31, 1787:

"I am fully of opinion that those who lean to a monarchical government, have either not consulted the public mind, or that they live in a region which (the levelling principles in which they were bred being entirely eradicated) is much more productive of monarchical ideas, than is the case in the Southern States, where, from the habitual distinctions which have always existed among the people, one would have expected the first generation and the most rapid growth of them. I am also clear that, even admitting the utility, nay, necessity of the form, the period is not arrived for adopting the change, without shaking the peace of this country to its foundation. That a thorough reform of the present system is indispensable, no one, who has a capacity to judge, will deny; and with hand and heart I hope the business will be essayed in a full convention. After which, if more powers and more decision are not found in the existing form; if it still wants energy and that secrecy and dispatch (either from the non-attendance or the local views of its members), which are characteristic of good government; and if it shall be found (the contrary of which, however, I have always been more afraid of than of the abuse of them) that Congress will, upon all proper occasions, exert the powers which are given, with a firm and steady hand instead of frittering them back to the States, where the members, in place of viewing themselves in their national character, are too apt to be looking——I say, after this essay is made, if the system proves inefficient, conviction of the necessity of a change will be disseminated among all classes of the people. Then, and not till then, in my opinion, can it be attempted without involving all the evils of civil discord."[1]

The final meeting and splendid success of the Convention for the formation of a Constitution, in 1787, are matters of universal knowledge. But the auspicious result was not obtained without severe struggles. The instrument, as completed, did not meet the first views or choice of many of the members. The avowed monarchists formed but a small fragment of the whole number, but they were represented, and by men conspicuous for their abilities.

On the 18th day of June, Colonel Alexander Hamilton proposed, in the Convention, a plan of government, by which the Chief Magistrate and Senate were to be elected to serve "during good behavior;" the State Governments were to be reduced to mere shadows, their Executives being appointed by the National Executive, and having a veto on laws, and their legislatures being allowed to enact nothing contrary to the Constitution or laws of the United States; and besides a national Judiciary, something on the basis of the existing one, the National Legis

[1] For the letter entire, see Sparks's Washington, vol. ix. p. 247.

lature was to have powers to institute Courts in each State, "for the determination of all matters of general concern." [1]

In the speech with which Colonel Hamilton introduced his plan, he frankly avowed that it did not come up to his own ideas of what would constitute the best form of government— but he was sensible that it would be unwise to propose any other.

James Madison kept, so far as he was able, "an exact account " of what transpired in the Convention. He occupied a seat immediately "in front of the presiding member," in the most "favorable position for hearing all that passed." He noted "in terms legible, and in abbreviations and marks intelligible to himself" (a short-hand), " what was read from the chair or spoken by the members; and losing not a moment unnecessarily between the adjournment and reassembling of the Convention, he was enabled to write out his daily notes during the session, or within a few finishing days after its close, in the extent and form preserved in his own hand on his files." In this labor and in its correctness, " he was not a little aided by practice," etc. [2]

Mr. Madison, in the record thus preserved, gave Colonel Hamilton's speech of June 18th. He represents him as sketching, at considerable length, the impracticable features of a federative government—the impossibility of two sovereignties coexisting within the same limits, etc., and as then proceeding to say :

" This view of the subject almost led him [Hamilton] to despair that a republican government could be established over so great an extent. He was sensible, at the same time, that it would be unwise to propose one of any other form. In his private opinion, he had no scruple in declaring, supported as he was by the opinion of so many of the wise and good, that the British Government was the best in the world; and that he doubted much whether any thing short of it would do in America. He hoped gentlemen of different opinions would bear with him in this, and begged them to recollect the change of opinion on this subject which had taken place, and was still going on. It was once thought that the power of Congress was amply sufficient to secure the ends of their institution. The error was now seen by every one. The members most tenacious of republicanism, he observed, were as loud as any in declaiming against the vices of democracy.[3] This progress of the public mind led him to anticipate the time when others as well as himself, would join in the

[1] Journal of Convention: Hamilton's Life by his son, vol. ii. p. 492, et seq. The Madison Papers, vol. ii. p. 890.
[2] See Madison Papers, vol. ii. p. 716.
   This confirms the views advanced by us at p. 461.

praise bestowed by Mr. Necker on the British Constitution, namely. that it is the only government in the world ' which unites public strength with individual security.' " [1]   *   *   *   *   *   *   *

" Their [the British] House of Lords is a most noble institution. Having nothing to hope by a change, and a sufficient interest, by means of their property, in being faithful to the national interest, they form a permanent barrier against every pernicious innovation, whether attempted on the part of the Crown or of the Commons. No temporary Senate will have firmness enough to answer the purpose "
    *   *   *   *   *   *   *

" As to the executive, it seemed to be admitted that no good one could be established on republican principles. Was not this giving up the merits of the question ; for can there be a good government without a good executive ? The English model is the only good one on this subject. The hereditary interest of the King was so interwoven with that of the nation, and his personal emolument so great, that he was placed above the danger of being corrupted from abroad, and at the same time was both sufficiently independent and sufficiently controlled to answer the purpose of the institution at home. One of the weak sides of republics was their being liable to foreign influence and corruption. Men of little character, acquiring great power, became easily the tools of intermeddling neighbors."

Mr. Madison, in addition to his usual precautions for securing accuracy, says that this speech, " as above taken down and written out, was seen by Mr. Hamilton, who approved of its correctness, with one or two verbal changes, which were made as he suggested." [2]

[1] This accords with the view that we have taken, that monarchical sentiments in the United States were not the dying-out vestiges of a few old men's opinions, but a growing reactionary idea, which had been spreading for two or three years prior to the federal Convention, and especially after Shay's Insurrection.

[2] Mr. Hamilton's filial biographer (Mr. John C. Hamilton), states (vol. ii. p. 481) that " no report approaching to accuracy has been given of this memorable speech "—speaks (p. 486) of " Madison's very imperfect report of this speech "—imputes (p. 492) intentional suppressions to Mr. Madison—and finally, explicitly declares (p. 490), that " it is not possible to give credence to his [Madison's] statement," that the report of the speech was submitted to Hamilton, who approved its correctness after making some verbal changes ! Mr. John C. Hamilton proceeds to aver : " neither in the general outline, nor in the subdivisions, does it approach so near to accuracy as by possibility to have received the sanction of its author !"

This unqualified charge, for it can be construed nothing less, of deliberate falsehood against Mr. Madison, is alone supported, so far as we discover, by exhibiting certain supposed discrepancies between Mr. Madison's report of the speech, and a " brief " of it, found among Hamilton's manuscripts; secondly, by showing discrepancies between that report and a much more limited one, or rather some Notes kept by another member of the Convention, Mr. Yates of New York; and, thirdly, by pointing out errors of fact in statements attributed by Madison to Hamilton, which the writer supposes his father could neither have made nor overlooked in the report of his speech, if it had been, as Mr. Madison asserts, submitted to him.

We are to infer from this, that if an undated " brief " is found among a dead man's papers to differ from a reported speech by him—if one of the most accurate and painstaking. and we may add practised, reporters of parliamentary proceedings of his times, is found to differ slightly from the comparatively rough notes of another gentleman—if an error of fact is found in a reported speech which the speaker ought not to have made, or ought to have corrected on seeing it—then it is both decorous and proper to assume that James Madison has been guilty of a falsehood purely deliberate, and especially atrocious, because levelled at the dead (for it was not published during Hamilton's lifetime)—and partaking of all the character and spirit of a forgery ! Arguments or assertions like these are not entitled to an answer.

The main object of Mr. J. C. Hamilton seems to be to clear his father from the impu-

Governeur Morris addressed the Convention July 2d. His theory of government now, as through life, differed from Hamilton's, being, in the technical sense of the word, more aristo-

tation of being a monarchist—or rather, perhaps, of "contemplating a monarchy." Yet in that "brief," so authoritatively quoted against Mr. Madison, we find among others the following heads of arguments:

"Here I shall give my sentiments of the best form of government—not as a thing attainable by us, but as a model which we ought to approach as near as possible.

"British Constitution best form.

"Aristotle—Cicero—Montesquieu—Necker.

"Society naturally divides itself into two political divisions—the few and the many, who have distinct interests.

"If government is in the hands of the few, they will tyrannize over the many.

"If (in) the hands of the many, they will tyrannize over the few. It ought to be in the hands of both; and they should be separated.

"This separation must be permanent.

"Representation alone will not do.

"Demagogues will generally prevail.

"And if separated, they will need a mutual check.

"This check is a monarch.

    *   *   *   *   *   *   *

"The monarch must have proportional strength. He ought to be hereditary and to have so much power, that it will not be his interest to risk much to acquire more.

"The advantage of a monarch is this—he is above corruption—he must always intend, in respect to foreign nations, the true interest and glory of the people.

"Republics liable to foreign corruption and intrigue—Holland—Athens.

"Effect of the British Government.

"A vigorous execution of the laws, and defence of the people will result.

"Better chance for a good administration.

"It is said a Republican Government does not admit a vigorous execution.

"It is, therefore, bad; for the goodness of a government consists in a vigorous execution.

"The principle intended to be established is this—that there must be a permanent will.

"Gentlemen say we need to be rescued from the Democracy. But what the means proposed?

"A Democratic Assembly is to be checked by a Democratic Senate, and both these by a Democratic chief magistrate.

"The end will not be answered—the means will not be equal to the object.

"It will, therefore, be feeble and inefficient." (See Life of Hamilton, vol. ii. pp. 486–488.)

Mr. J. C. Hamilton assumes that these were but the "theoretical opinions" of his father, and quotes, in proof of it, and to disprove Madison's assertions, a letter *afterwards* written to General Washington. These often quoted words were as follows:

"That the republican theory ought to be adhered to in this country, as long as there was any chance of its success—that the idea of a perfect equality of political rights among citizens, exclusive of all permanent or hereditary distinctions, was of a nature to engage the good wishes of every man, whatever might be his theoretic doubts; that it merited his best efforts to give success to it in practice; that hitherto, from an incompetent structure of the government, it had not had a fair trial, and that the endeavor ought then to be to secure to it a better chance of success by a government more capable of energy and order."

Now, had Colonel Hamilton's biographer further shown that Hamilton never changed his views or expressions—and that, consequently, to prove that he made a certain declaration to General Washington at one time, was tantamount to proving that such were his real views and his expressions for all time afterwards—then the distinction between his "theoretical" opinions, and practical wishes or efforts would be pretty well established by the letter just quoted.

We shall have constant and abundant occasion to see whether this uniformity marked the declarations of Hamilton.

Judge Yates's minutes of Hamilton's speech of June 18th, will be found in Elliot's Debates on the Federal Constitution, vol. i, p. 417. The passages corresponding to those we have quoted, in the text, from Mr. Madison, are on pages 421 and 422. In the main substance (so far as the speaker's preference for monarchy is concerned) we discover no serious discrepancy. A discrepancy supposed by Mr. J. C. Hamilton to be important, consists in the following sentences attributed by Yates to Hamilton: "I [said

cratic than monarchical. Hamilton found the "check" between all the conflicting elements of a State in a King, Morris
in a permanent Senate. The latter, in the speech under consideration, declared for a Senate for life, appointed by the
Chief Magistrate; and he said that it "must have great personal property, it must have the aristocratic spirit, it must love
to lord it through pride."

The speech contained a number of other equally salient
points. It is difficult to say which are most contemptuous, its
assaults on democracy, or on the idea that men can be well
governed except through interest and corruption. It will be
found in Madison's Report of the Debates, commencing at page
1017. As in Hamilton's case, Mr. Madison showed his report
of the speech to the maker of it, who, "when the thing stared

Colonel Hamilton] despair that a republican form of government can remove the difficulties. Whatever may be my opinion, I would hold it, however, unwise to change
that form of government." Mr. J. C. Hamilton, while apparently partly admitting (certainly not denying) that these sentences occurred in a subsequent speech (or in Mr.
Madison's words, in "explanatory observations which did not immediately follow"), insinuates that Mr. Madison omitted them from an unworthy motive! (See Life of Hamilton,
vol. ii. p. 491, and note to 492.) He appears to think that if Mr. Madison reported the
first speech, he was bound to report the last, though the latter expressly mentions as the
reason for not so doing that they (the "explanatory observations" made afterwards)
"were to have been furnished by Mr. H. [Hamilton] who did not find leisure at the time
to write them out, and they were not obtained," (Madison papers, vol. ii. p. 893, note).
After waiting some weeks, or only days, for the promised copy of the second speech,
was it Mr. Madison's business to attempt to report it from memory? Would these recollections have properly found a place in such a record of the Convention as that which he
was aiming to make, and which he says he did make?

Mr. J. C. Hamilton, while affecting to discredit the accuracy, and even the honesty,
of Mr. Madison's reports, and to lean so confidingly on Judge Yates's notes, affords a
lively idea of his manner of estimating accuracy. He does not venture to deny that
there were two speeches, and that the "omitted" words occurred in the last one. He
does not deny Mr. Madison's explanation that Judge Yates "consolidated" the two
speeches into one! We do not understand that Judge Yates himself pretended to *report*
the speeches made in the Convention. (For a little fuller explanation of the facts by Mr.
Madison, when he understood this attack was to be made on him in Hamilton's Life, see
APPENDIX, No. 9.)

Having disposed of these disagreeable but necessary explanations, we may now be
permitted to say that we regard the whole issue manufactured out of the "omitted"
words above quoted, as one purely about nothing. Nobody pretends that Hamilton
proposed, in the federal Convention, to change the form of our government from a
republican to a monarchical one; or that he did not say, in substance, that a proposition
or attempt of that kind would *then* be unwise. Let the reader compare the two "omitted" sentences with the two opening ones of Madison's report of his speech, given by us
(p. 569), and he will see what this imaginary suppression amounts to. Yates, just as
strongly as Madison (and just as strongly as the "brief" quoted by Mr. J. C. Hamilton),
exhibits the fact that Hamilton had no confidence in that Republican experiment, which
he yielded to for the time for the excellent reason that there was no other alternative.

But were there all the important explanatory matter in the "omitted" sentences
which Mr. J. C. Hamilton supposes, still (Mr. Madison's conduct having been vindicated)
we should not now regard it as a matter of any importance, except in one light—as a
test of Colonel Hamilton's sincerity. The history of his life must speak for itself. If he
clung sincerely and faithfully to the Republican "experiment" against the avowed convictions of his mind, we need no assertions of his, in advance, to prove it. If he did not,
his own assertions (adopting that theory of their meaning advanced by his son) would
but convict him of deceit or vacillation. The real issue is one of facts, not of declarations.

him in the face, as written down," "laughed while he acknowledged its truth."[1]

We have probably said enough to show whether there were monarchists in the federal Convention, eleven years after our permanent separation from Great Britain, and four years after the close of the Revolutionary war.

During the session of the Convention, a report appeared in a New York city paper (Daily Advertiser, August 18th, 1787), that a project was in contemplation for the establishment of a Monarchy; at the head of which it was proposed to put the Bishop of Osnaburg, a brother of the King of England. The report was traced to a letter which had been circulated in Connecticut. Hamilton immediately wrote to Colonel Wadsworth for information on the subject. Wadsworth referred the inquiry to Colonel Humphreys, who replied to Hamilton September 1st, that the letter had been printed in a Fairfield paper, July 25th, that it had been first found in the hands of "one Jared Manshfield, a reputed loyalist"—that it had "been received and circulated with avidity by that class of people"—that "the quondam Tories had undoubtedly conceived hopes of a future union with Great Britain"—that the "ultimate practicability of introducing the Bishop of Osnaburg was not a novel idea among those who were formerly termed Loyalists"—that "ever since the peace, it had been occasionally talked of and wished for"—that "yesterday, where he [Humphreys] dined, half jest half earnest, he [the Bishop of Osnaburg] was given as the first toast." We draw these facts from Hamilton's Life (vol. ii. p. 534 *et seq.*), and his son says: "It appears from a subsequent memorandum of Hamilton's, that though there was little to fear from the project, that he did not consider it entirely destitute of reality."

We have personal reasons for knowing that both Madison and Monroe equally believed in this Bishop of Osnaburg affair, and considered it one of some seriousness, for a time.

We have never heard those who declared themselves believers in monarchy in the Convention of 1787, and their set— those who may be termed the Whig monarchists—accused, on any respectable testimony, of complicity in these projects of the

Tory monarchists. But the Osnaburg project (and we might name some kindred later ones) aids to show whether the idea that American citizens could have contemplated monarchy after the close of the Revolution is so monstrous and absurd, as some writers have assumed.

It has been usually claimed by the apologists of the strong-government party, and of its ultra leaders, like Hamilton and Morris, that after the federal Constitution was framed and adopted, they thenceforth wholly abandoned their "theoretical" positions in favor of monarchy, and went "heart and soul" for the republican structure as reared, both in the substance and the form—nay, that they became the special champions and protectors of the Constitution in what they believed to be its true intended import and spirit.

And more recently Mr. Hamilton's political sympathizers—those who would deify the man to sanctify some relics of the doctrine—have made further discoveries. Pickering, and other followers, ascertained before his death, that he carried our country safely through the Revolution by generously sacrificing his reputation to uphold Washington's! It since has been made as clearly to appear that he was the guiding and controlling spirit in the Convention of 1787, and really principally gave its form and spirit to the Constitution!

Assertions like these, if true, are fatal to Jefferson's hypothesis and to his veracity. It was after the adoption of the federal Constitution, and when its machinery was in full motion, that he declared he saw machinations, and heard declarations against Republicanism. The above assertions then require our examination. As Jefferson placed Hamilton at the head of the alleged monarchical party—as all the world placed him there, provided there was such a party—it is incumbent on us to first and most particularly investigate his conduct.

In this, as in all other cases of important controverted questions affecting the character of individuals, we will not rely on the testimony of political enemies. We will not call Jefferson to the witness-stand against Hamilton, or Hamilton against Jefferson. We should be entirely willing to see even Madison's Debates of the Convention "ruled out" as testimony in respect to Hamilton, if that is asked—though no formal division of parties, and certainly no alienation between the two men, had then taken place; and although the former was acting in a capacity that would have rendered an intentional misrepresentation of the moral nature of a forgery.[1] There are men whose personal testimony to facts can be relied on as much in respect to enemies as to friends. We believe this was emphatically true of both Jefferson and Madison. But the rule of exclusion we have named is, on the whole, a wholesome and safe one; and should we anywhere in the progress of this work involuntarily trench on it, the reader is requested to judge without reference to the hostile testimony introduced.

Governeur Morris played an important part in the federal Convention. His attendance was, we believe, much steadier than Hamilton's. He was by far too prominent, and observing, and trusted a man not to know what was going on among at least those of his own side. When the terms of the Constitution were finally settled, to his clear vigorous pen was assigned the honor of drafting the instrument. He was one of the earliest and latest—and unquestionably, taken all in all, was the most deeply confidential political correspondent of Hamilton's whole life. The published letters of the latter show that he wrote to Morris secret views and feelings, which he *wrote* to no other man. Morris was selected by the relations and friends of Hamilton to deliver the funeral oration over his corpse.

Morris wrote Robert Walsh, February 5th, 1811:

"General Hamilton had little share in forming the Constitution. He disliked it, believing all republican government to be radically defective. *   * He heartily assented, nevertheless, to the Constitution, because he considered it a band which might hold us together for some time, and he knew that national sentiment is the offspring of national existence. He trusted, moreover, that in the changes and chances of time, we should be involved in some war which might strengthen our union and nerve the executive."[2]

What the last singular-sounding intimation meant, we shall very soon have occasion to see more distinctly.

[1] Nor is this the worst, if the hypothesis of Hamilton's biographer is true. According to that hypothesis, Madison in cold blood perpetrated this crime against a man with whom he had, at the time, no personal misunderstanding, and left it to stand when he afterwards professed to be a personal and political friend—as during that period when the two were writing the Federalist together! Or else, the original record was a fair one, and Madison went back and deliberately mutilated it, to injure Hamilton after the period of their subsequent alienation!
[2] Life and Works, vol. iii. p. 260.

If Mr. Morris was mistaken in the above estimate of Hamilton's services in framing the Constitution, neither the Journals of the Convention, nor any of the various published statements of its members, serve to correct his error. Hamilton was absent for a considerable period, and his letters in the interim would go to show that he had left in discouragement if not disgust, and that he proposed to return only "for the sake of propriety and public opinion."[1] Among a multiplicity of records on the subject, there chances to be none, we believe, to show that he either proposed or carried any of the great important features of the Constitution. That it bore some general resemblance to his "plan" as it did to Jefferson's, and perhaps five hundred other men's, so far as the arrangement of the departments into Executive, Legislative and Judiciary, and some general definition of their powers in relation to each other was concerned, was most true. Nobody who knew the outlines of the British Constitution, could fail to think of these. But Hamilton's "plan" after striking out his "good behavior" Chief Magistrate and Senate, his proposal to substantially obliterate State Sovereignties, by making their governors appointable by the National Chief Magistrate, their laws entirely controllable by the National Legislature, and all their "general concerns" subject to the jurisdiction of the National Courts, was about as near the substance and spirit of the original, as, to use the familiar illustration, would be the play of Hamlet with the part of Hamlet struck out! Mr. Jefferson not only proposed in advance the same division of governmental departments and of their powers in reference to each other, but we have seen him proposing substantially the same division of powers between them and the State authorities, which received the ultimate sanction of the Convention. His plan, as a whole, came vastly nearer, then, to the adopted instrument than Hamilton's—yet we never have heard any claim advanced that he originated or shaped the Constitution.[2]

<hr/>

[1] Hamilton to Washington, July 3d; to Rufus King, Aug. 20; to the same, Aug. 28th.

[2] One of the most exquisite specimens we have seen of the kind of laudation heaped upon Hamilton, by the class of American politicians we have mentioned, is to be found in his Life. His biographer gravely says, that Dr. Johnson (William S. Johnson of Connecticut), a member of the Convention, and one of the final committee of revisal, remarked:

"If the Constitution did not succeed on trial, Hamilton was less responsible for the result than any other member, for he fully and frankly pointed out to the Convention what he apprehended were the infirmities to which it was liable. And if it answered the fond expectations of the public, the community would be more indebted to Hamilton than to any other member; for after its essential outlines were agreed to, he labored

That Colonel Hamilton did abandon his "theoretical opinions" and cordially assent to the spirit and letter of the Constitution, there would appear to be some strong proofs. He was one of the three authors of the Federalist, which most earnestly and cogently urged the adoption of that instrument—ably defending all its principal features and provisions. We have had a great abundance of assertions to the same effect from friends who professed to intimately know his secret views. And, lastly, we have had what the public accepted as positive declarations from his own lips to that effect.

The joint authorship of the Federalist does not clash with Mr. Morris's theory; for it was necessary to tone up the public mind to procure the adoption of even this temporary "band" which was to "hold us together" until "war" should strengthen it into something better. We pass over the second-hand evidence of friends, where the party himself has testified, and we are content to take *his* testimony.

Colonel Hamilton certainly did carry the idea, more than once, which has been advanced by his apologists—that he abandoned earlier "theoretical opinions," or, at all events, abandoned all attempts to introduce them into practice—and that he both approved of the Constitution as adopted, and gave it his faithful and zealous subsequent support. Nay, we shall find him making it the subject of newspaper attacks on Jefferson that *he* at first hesitated or doubted in regard to that instrument! It was always the climax of his charge against the Republican leaders and party that they were openly or covertly assailing "the Constitution!" We have seen his unequivocal pledge to General Washington.[1] During the Presidential campaign of 1803, he actually wrote a long letter for the eye of partisans, carrying the idea,[2] not only that he became suited

---

most indefatigably to heal those infirmities, and to guard against the evils to which they might expose it." (Vol. ii. p. 537.)

In a little more direct English, this would seem to mean that if the Constitution failed, Hamilton was to be praised, for he opposed nearly everything in it—if it succeeded, he was to be praised, because his opposition was unsuccessful. The only thing that was fixed and unconditional in the matter was, that Hamilton was to be praised.

Another equally interesting specimen of the apotheosizing process—of the thorough belief that if Hamilton did not literally "make " the American "world " he clearly did nearly "all things in it," will be found in Geo. T. Curtis's History of the American Constitution.

[1] See his letter in note on p. 571.

[2] We are obliged to use this form of expression on account of a remarkable peculiarity in this and in some other letters of Hamilton. They convey an obvious impression throughout, and appear, at first view, frank and unstudied. Yet on close examination,

with the Constitution as adopted, but that his earlier propositions in the Convention were among a class of " suggestions for
consideration," thrown out " with a view to free investigation,"
and not even understood at the time to be " evidences of a definitive opinion in the proposer."

Are there any reasons for supposing that we must look
further or elsewhere for Hamilton's real sentiments and feelings ?
In a letter to Governeur Morris, February 2d, 1802—a year
before the letter to Pickering just cited—he said :

"Mine is an odd destiny. Perhaps no man in the United States has sacrificed
or done more for the present Constitution than myself; and contrary to all my
anticipations of its fate, as you know from the very beginning. I am still laboring to
prop *the frail and worthless fabric.* Yet I have the murmurs of its friends no
less than the curses of its foes for my reward. What can I do better than withdraw from the scene ? Every day proves to me more and more, that this American
world was not made for me.   *   *   *   *   *   *   *

"You, friend Morris, are by birth a native of this country, but by genius an
exotic. You mistake, if you fancy that you are more of a favorite than myself, or
that you are in any sort upon a theatre suited to you."[1]

This discouragement did not last long. He wrote Morris
again, April 6, 1802 :

*   *   " But, my dear sir, we must not content ourselves with a temporary effort to oppose the approach of evil. We must derive instruction from the
experience before us ; and learning to form a just estimate of the things to which
we have been attached, there must be a systematic and persevering endeavor to
establish the fortune of a great empire on foundations *much firmer than have yet
been devised.* What will signify a vibration of power, if it cannot be used with
confidence or energy, and must be again quickly restored to hands which will
prostrate, much faster than we shall be able to rear, under so frail a system ?
Nothing will be done until the structure of our national edifice shall be such as
naturally to control eccentric passions and views, and keep in check demagogues
and knaves in the disguise of patriots."

These views sprung naturally from Hamilton's estimate of
the virtue and intelligence of the American people. He wrote
James A. Bayard, April, 1802 :

"Nothing is more fallacious than to expect to produce any valuable or perma-

they do not make a tangible declaration in support of their ostensible meaning. They
could on occasion be made to show something entirely different. The particular letter
under consideration (addressed to Timothy Pickering, and to be found in Hamilton's
Works, vol. vi. p. 556), is a specimen of this parrying, or special pleading, or whatever
else it should be called, well worth the curious study of political letter writers, and
political casuists !
[1] See Hamilton's Works, vol. vi. p. 530.

nent results in political projects by relying merely on the reason of men. Men are rather reasoning than reasonable animals, for the most part governed by the impulse of passion. This is a truth well understood by our adversaries, who have practised upon it with no small benefit to their cause." [1]

To Rufus King, June 3, 1802 :

"I as yet discover no satisfactory symptoms of a revolution of opinion in the mass—'*informe ingens cui lumen ademptum.*' Nor do I look with much expectation to any serious alteration until inconveniences are extensively felt, or until time has produced a disposition to coquet it with new lovers." [2]

Quotations of a similar tenor, and extending to the period of Hamilton's death, might be indefinitely multiplied.

In Judge Yates's version of Hamilton's speech in the federal Convention, June 18th, 1787, after giving a remark to which much importance has been attached, that he (Hamilton) "would hold it unwise" to change the republican "form of government," the latter is represented as adding in the *next* sentence:

"I believe the British Government forms the best model the world ever produced; and such has been its progress in the minds of the many, that *the truth gradually gains ground.*" Three sentences later he added: "All communities divide themselves into the few and the many. The first are the rich and well-born, the other the mass of the people. The voice of the people has been said to be the voice of God; and, however generally this maxim has been quoted and believed, it is not true in fact. The people are turbulent and changing; they seldom judge or determine right. Give, therefore, to the first class a distinct, permanent share of government. * * * Nothing but a permanent body can check the imprudence of democracy. Their turbulent and uncontrollable disposition requires checks." And he thus closed: "*But the people are gradually ripening in their opinions of government*—they begin to be tired of an excess of democracy—and what even is the Virginia plan but pork still, with a little change of the sauce?"

Whenever we penetrate to Hamilton's secret views subsequently, we find that he never for a moment abandoned his wishes or efforts to favor that reaction towards monarchy, under the expectation of which he accepted the Constitution as the best "temporary band" of which the temper of the times admitted.

The inner circle of his confidential friends perfectly understood this. And it would seem, from some terrible words in the second of the following extracts, that they also understood that

[1] Hamilton's Works, vol. vi. p. 540.   [2] Ib. vol. vi. p. 547.

he anticipated and desired an appeal to the sword when reaction had proceeded far enough to promise success to his "favorite form."

The following is from Morris's letter to Walsh (February 5th, 1811), already quoted from:

"General Hamilton hated republican government, because he confounded it with democratical government, and he detested the latter, because he believed it must end in despotism, and be, in the meantime, destructive to public morality. ⁎ ⁎ ⁎ In short, his study of ancient history impressed on his mind a conviction that democracy ending in tyranny is, while it lasts, a cruel and oppressive domination.

"One marked trait of the General's character was the pertinacious adherence to opinions he had once formed. ⁎ ⁎ ⁎ ⁎ He never failed on every occasion to advocate the excellence of, and avow his attachment to, monarchical government. By this course he not only cut himself off from all chance of rising into office, but singularly promoted the views of his opponents, who, with the fondness for wealth and power, which he had not, affected a love for the people, which he had and they had not." [1]

In a letter to Aaron Ogden, of New Jersey, December 28th, 1804, about five months after Hamilton's death, Morris wrote:

"Our poor friend Hamilton bestrode his hobby to the great annoyance of his friends, and not without injury to himself. More a theoretic than a practical man, he was not sufficiently convinced that a system may be good in itself, and bad in relation to particular circumstances. He well knew that his favorite form was inadmissible, unless as the result of civil war; and I suspect that his belief in that which he called an approaching crisis arose from a conviction that the kind of government most suitable, in his opinion, to this extensive country, could be established in no other way. When our population shall have reached a certain extent, his system may be proper, and the people may then be disposed to adopt it; but under present circumstances they will not, neither will it answer any valuable purpose.

⁎   ⁎   ⁎   ⁎   ⁎   ⁎

"When a general question is raised, as to the best form of government, it should be discussed under the consideration that this best being presupposed is, if unable to preserve itself, good for nothing; wherefore, permanency is an essential object, to which minor advantages must be sacrificed. But an absolute, that is, an unmixed monarchy, would hardly last three lives. Perhaps, on impartial inquiry, it may appear that a country is best governed (taking for a standard any long period such as half a century) when the principal authority is vested in a permanent Senate. But there seems little probability that such a body could be established here. Let it be proposed by the best men among us, and it would be considered as a plan for aggrandizing themselves. Experience alone can incline the people to such an institution. That a man should be born a legislator, is now, among unfledged witlings, the frequent subject of ridicule. But experience, that

[1] See Sparks's Life and Works of Morris, vol. iii. p. 260.

wrinkled matron whom genius contemns and youth abhors, experience, the mother
of wisdom, will tell us that men destined from the cradle to act an important part
will not, in general, be so unfit as those who are objects of popular choice. But
hereditary senators could not long preserve their power. In order to strengthen
the body, it might be needful to weaken the members, and fixing the office for life,
fill up vacancies from, but not by, the people.

" When a general abuse of the right of election shall have robbed our government of respect, and its imbecility have involved it in difficulties, the people will
feel what your friend once said, that they want something to protect them against
themselves. And then, excess being their predominant quality, it may be a
patriotic duty to prevent them from going too far the other way." [1]

We now have had ample proof of Hamilton's secret political
doctrines, carried down to the period of his death, from his own
lips and those of his nearest friend. It is not necessary to pause
here to show how well his conduct corresponded with his doctrines. The history of parties, which is indispensable in presenting a history of Mr. Jefferson's life, will necessarily contain this
information. Facts abundant and unanswerable will continue
to accumulate (after the period of General Washington's retirement from the Presidency) to show that Hamilton practically
acted on all the views ascribed to him by Morris, and that he
played his game boldly, if not desperately, in that direction,
until he overwhelmed himself and his party with ruin, and was
completely banished from public life. Were all the written
evidence of his monarchical views we have presented struck out
of existence, the evidence of facts which it will be our duty to
record, would alone be conclusive in establishing the fact.

Morris's own ideas of government have been made sufficiently to appear; and it is not necessary to cite further specimens of them from his writings.

But Jefferson's imputation of monarchical views did not stop
with two or three men; it extended to a party, or rather the
leaders of a party, namely, the ultra or Hamiltonian Federalists.
He was wont to say, if ever their hoards of private letters should
be broken up and come before the world, no further proofs
would be needed of his assertions. We have seen in two
instances how well his prediction has been verified. All the
other publications which have been made of the confidential
correspondence of the same class of politicians, have more or

---

[1] For letter entire, see Sparks's Life and Correspondence of Morris, vol. iii. p. 215

less (in proportion to their apparent completeness) distinctly corroborated the same view.

Hamilton's Works by his son, daguerreotype (by publishing their letters) not a few of his political intimates.' Some of them show the whole face, some half, some but a feature, in proportion to that caution with which different men write confidential letters. There is abundance of the conventional expressions usual among men. who hold dangerous and proscribed opinions to guard against accidental disclosures—abundance of professions of devotion, for example, to something which is termed "the Constitution," but obviously not the "frail and worthless fabric" framed in 1787! The pervading spirit of the writers, however, is everywhere manifest; if the reader pauses to collate, and gather the true meaning, that spirit is unmistakable. John Quincy Adams afterwards scorchingly remarked of these men: "Like the priests of Egypt, they had a revelation for the multitude, and a secret for the initiated." And he added: "The holders of these tenets, like the Dutch traders of Japan, wherever traffic is to be obtained by denial of their Lord, will trample upon his cross to disprove their religion." *

Hamilton's works do not apparently contain any complete correspondences. There are frequent chasms even in his own series of letters, and at points where the world would have given most for his confidential ones. But we get in all of them unmistakable glimpses of the "secret" which was divulged only to the "initiated." If the temple and shrine are not entire, some of the apartments, some of the secret altars, some of the pontifical instruments and machinery, some of the robes worn in public and private, are sufficiently preserved to show the nature of the worship. The high-priest's creed is found, nearly entire, written out by his own hand.

Whether the lower priests precisely concurred in that creed, we cannot in every instance say. They concur, in the essence, so far as they have left traces of their opinions. They sat in the conclave. They knew their leader's views and designs, and they steadily sustained him, and so far as circumstances would permit, attempted to sustain his plans. We cannot catch their

---

' There may be some question about the good taste or even the propriety of a member of Hamilton's family publishing confidential letters to him; but there can be no question about the value of the contribution thus made to history.
' Adams's Review of the Writings of Fisher Ames.

minor shades of opinion. We cannot tell how many of them leaned to the views of Hamilton and how many to those of Morris—how many looked to a change in the form of our government or how many proposed to content themselves with a change in the spirit. There is but one uniform and apparently irrepressible manifestation. They all detested popular government. They spurned the intelligence and the virtue of the mass of the American people. They consequently secretly contemned that "frail and worthless" Constitution which derived every power and every tenure from the people. They did not, however, like the "Dutch traders of Japan," insult the symbol in *public*. Like disguised infidels, they affected to revere it in public, and "trampled" upon it in private. Those who dared not, like Hamilton, spit upon the name, spit upon the thing. Those who did not consider it safe to name the substitute which they desired, acted out their partialities by a constant and ultra-colonial adulation of England.

Fisher Ames wrote Hamilton, January 26th, 1797 :

"Our proceedings smell of anarchy. We rest our hopes on foolish and fanatical grounds—on the superior morals and self-supporting theories of our age and country; on human nature being different from what it is, and better here than anywhere else. We cannot think it possible our government should stop, or that there is the least occasion to provide the means for it to go on." * * *

"We are formed but of late for independent sovereignty. Experience has not laid on her lessons with birch, and we forget them. Our whole system is but little removed from simple democracy." [1]

He wrote Christopher Gore, October 3d, 1803 :

"Two causes might make a government in principle, tranquil in operation and stable in existence ; *separate orders in the State*, each possessing much, and therefore pledged to preserve all ; or secondly, the pressure of an external foe. The latter would produce the most exalted patriotism—the former would provide the most adequate substitute for it. But democracy is only the isthmus of a middle state ; it is nothing of itself. Like death, it is only the dismal passport to a more dismal hereafter. Such is our State." [2]

He wrote Thomas Dwight, October 26, 1803 :

"Our country is too big for union, too sordid for patriotism, too democratic for liberty. What is to become of it, he who made it best knows. Its vice will govern it by practising on its folly. This is ordained for democracies, and if morals as

---

[1] For the letter entire, see Hamilton's Works, vol. vi. p. 198.
[2] Works of Fisher Ames, edited by his son, Seth Ames, Boston, 1854, vol. i. p. 324.

pure as Mr. —— ascribes to the French Republic, did not inspire the present administration [Jefferson's], it would have been our lot at this day." [1]

He wrote Christopher Gore (then in England), November 16th, 1803 :

"In England I behold a real people, patriotism broad awake, and holding authority over all the passions and prejudices of the nation. This at least is the outside look of the thing; I well know how deceptive this often is. You are behind the scenes, and, probably enough, discover the measures of those who seem to play the great parts so well." [2]

He wrote Thomas Dwight, November 29, 1803 :

"Suppose an attack on property, I calculate on the 'sensibilities' of our nation. There is one sensorium. Like a negro's shins, there our patriotism would feel the kicks, and twinge with agonies that we should not be able so much as to conceive of, if we only had our faces spit in. In this case, we could wipe off the ignominy, and think no more of the matter." [3]

He said in his Laocoön : [4]

"In that enslaved [5] country [Great Britain] every executive attempt at usurpation has been spiritedly and perseveringly resisted, and substantial improvements have been made in the constitutional provisions for liberty. Witness the habeas corpus, the independence of the judges, and the perfection, if anything human is perfect, of their administration of justice, the result of the famous Middlesex election, and that on the right of issuing general search warrants. Let every citizen who is able to think, and who can bear the pain of thinking, make the contrast at his leisure."

He wrote Josiah Quincy, February 3d, 1807 :

"I often dare to think our nation began self-government without education for it. Like negroes freed after having grown up to man's estate, we are incapable of learning and practising the great art of taking care of ourselves. We must be put to school and whipped into wisdom." [6]

He said in Laocoön : [7]

"For our part we deem her [Great Britain's] grandeur intrinsic, the fair fruit of her constitution, her justice, her arts, and her magnanimity."

He wrote Timothy Pickering, February 4th, 1807 :

"We are abject and base, people as well as government, and nothing could save us but energy and magnanimity. We have none of these. Our great democracy cannot remain where it is. Ipsa moles nocet." [8]

---

[1] Ames's Works, vol. i. pp. 327-8.
[2] Ib. vol. i. p. 332.
[3] Ib. p. 335.
[4] Page 429.
[5] This word is obviously used ironically
[6] Ames's Works, vol. i. p. 393.
[7] Page 376.
[8] Ames's Works, vol. i. p. 395.

He said in Laocoön : [1]

"Great Britain, by being an island, is secured from foreign conquest; and by having a powerful enemy within sight of her shore, is kept in sufficient dread of it to be inspired with patriotism. That virtue, with all the fervor and elevation that a society which mixes so much of the commercial with the martial spirit can display, has other kindred virtues in its train; and these have had an influence in forming the habits and principles of action, not only of the English military and nobles, but of the mass of the nation."

He wrote Timothy Pickering, November 6th, 1807 :

"I am ready to believe that we, as great boasters as the ancient Greeks, are the most ignorant nation in the world, because we have had the least experience. Fresh from the hands of a political mother who would not let us fall, we now think it impossible that we should fall. Bonaparte will cure us of our presumption; or if that task should be left to some other rough teacher, we shall learn at last the art, that is, the habits, manners, and prejudices of a nation, especially the prejudices which are worth more than philosophy, without which I venture to consider our playing government a sort of free negro attempt. It is probably necessary that we should endure slavery for some ages, till every drop of democratic blood has been got rid of by fermentation or bleeding." [2]

This admirer of England gives us to understand which of the political parties even in that country had his sympathies and those of his associates. He wrote Josiah Quincy, March 19th, 1806 :

"The death of Mr. Pitt fills me with grief and terror—with grief that so great a statesman and patriot should sink under his labors—and with terror that Fox, Erskine, and Sheridan, should come into power." [3]

We might continue to quote a volume of extracts of a kindred tenor from the writings of a man who, for a long time, led one of the great parties of the United States, in the House of Representatives; and who was politically the bosom and confidential coadjutor and friend of Alexander Hamilton. But we will turn to other associates.

Theodore Sedgwick, of Massachusetts (then Speaker of the United States House of Representatives), wrote Hamilton, January 10, 1801 :

"For myself, I declare I think it impossible to preserve the honor of our country or the principles of our Constitution, by a mode of election which was intended to secure to prominent talents and virtues the first honors of our country, and for ever to disgrace the barbarous institutions by which executive power is to be trans-

---

[1] Page 427.   [2] Ames's Works, vol. i. p. 398.   [3] Ib. p. 371.

mitted through the organs of generation. We have at one election placed at the head of our government a semi-maniac, and who, in his soberest senses, is the greatest marplot in nature ;[1] and at the next a feeble and false enthusiastic theorist,[2] and a profligate without character and without property, bankrupt in both."[3]

He wrote the same, January 27, 1803 :

" What think you of democracy ? Will it not progress successfully until its evils are felt ? For myself I have no doubt that it will. Even in this State [Massachusetts] great sacrifices are made to popular passions and prejudices, and they are deemed necessary to retain the power of our government in Federal hands. There is one consolation under all the humiliation which we endure from a sense of the degradation of our national character. This state of things cannot long exist. The disorganization which is the inevitable effect of the enfeebling policy of democracy, will produce such intolerable evils as will necessarily destroy their cause."[4]

Oliver Wolcott, Sen., wrote his son, of the same name, November 21st, 1796 :

" I never believed our present system of government or union would be very permanent ; but I never could have believed that a people who had so recently gone through the distresses of a revolution, and risen from a state of almost extreme poverty, into an affluence more real than that of any other nation, could so soon have forgot their sufferings as wantonly to sport with the enjoyment of the greatest social happiness, and expose the continuance of it to the utmost hazard. The conduct of these States for some time past exhibits a melancholy proof of the folly and depravity of mankind.   *   *   *   *   If the French arms continue to predominate, and a governing influence of this nation shall continue in the southern and western countries, I am confident, and indeed hope, that a separation will take place ; and I am very sure that the northern people will never submit (but by the event of a war) to the domination of a foreign power, whether open or insidious.

*   *   *   *   *   *   *   *   *

" This mode of electing a president will probably operate finally, pretty much like a Polish election, and produce the same effects."[5]

John Adams was included by Jefferson among the believers in monarchy. The following are a few sentences from his Defence of the Constitutions of Government of the United States of America, which we take in preference to a multitude of others, simply because we find them already selected for our hand.[6]

---

[1] John Adams.   [2] Jefferson.
[3] Burr; for this letter entire see Hamilton's Works, vol. vi. p. 511.   [4] Ib. p. 552.
[5] The letter entire will be found in Gibbs's Administrations of Washington and Adams, vol. i. p. 398.[6]
[6] In Remarks on the Hon. J. Q. Adams's Review of Mr. Ames's Works, Pamphlet, Boston, 1809.

"The proposition that the people are the best keepers of their own liberties, is not true; they are the worst conceivable; they are no keepers at all; they can neither judge, act, think, or will, as a political body.

"If it is meant by our author a representative assembly, they are not still the best keepers of the liberties of the people: at least the majority would invade the liberty of the minority sooner and oftener than an absolute monarchy."

*   *   *   *   *   *   *

"A great writer has said, that a people will never oppress themselves, or invade their own rights. This compliment, if applied to any nation or people, in being or memory, is more than has been merited."

*   *   *   *   *   *   *

"Aristides, Fabricius, and Cincinnatus are always quoted, as if such characters were always to be found in sufficient numbers to protect liberty; and a cry and show of liberty is set up by the profligate and abandoned, such as would sell their fathers, their country, and their God, for profit, place, and power. Hypocrisy, simulation, and finesse, are not more practised in the courts of princes than in popular elections, nor more encouraged by kings than people."

*   *   *   *   *   *   *

"The real merit of public men is rarely known and impartially considered. When men arise, who to real services add political empiricism, conform to the errors of the people, comply with their prejudices, gain their hearts, and excite their enthusiasm, then gratitude is a contagion—it is a whirlwind."

It has been asserted that " single passages " have been " torn from the context of this work," to misrepresent Mr. Adams, and the idea has been conveyed that he did not advocate in it an essentially different government from our existing one.[1] If the general theory advanced in the preceding extracts can be reconciled with a belief in the theory of real and thorough republicanism, then perhaps Mr. Adams's Defence was written to advocate precisely such a Government in frame or spirit as that of the United States. No unbiased man can possibly, it seems to us, arrive at any such conclusion on a perusal of the work. He was evidently a believer in a " mixed " government, essentially analogous to that of England. And we judge from his correspondence that he *never* abandoned this theoretical opinion. But there is a broad distinction observable in his course and Hamilton's. During his Presidency Mr. Adams lost his balance. Excitement and the goadings of those about him impelled him into some violent (though generally half reluctant) excesses against what he ought to have known was the spirit and true intent of the Constitution. But there was no deliberate system and design in this. He was, we believe, willing in his heart

---

[1] See his Life and Works, vol. iv. p. 277.

that the republican experiment should have a fair trial, and to leave the American people to be the judges of the duration and the result of that experiment. If he exhibited gross inconsistencies, he practised no deliberate deception. His "revelation for the multitude" substantially comported with his "secret for the initiated."

We could cite declarations from many more of the early Ultra-Federal leaders, which with an explanation of the circumstances under which they were written, would substantially imply the same belief with that more directly avowed by the Hamiltons, the Morrises, the Ameses, etc. These explanations would require too much space. And we cannot conceive how such proofs can be really necessary, with the already stated fact that knowing Hamilton's ultimate designs they sustained all his preparatory measures. He who fights voluntarily under a standard makes himself responsible for the cause in which that standard is displayed. This remark, however, demands qualification. The common soldier and the inferior officer are not always admitted to the secrets of the general. The follower is not always placed among the "initiated." As this narrative progresses we shall have occasion to see, in a good many instances, who comprised the latter.

Strict fairness requires another admission. We do not believe that all Hamilton's leading associates and apparent confidants—not even all those who were to be found muttering against democracy, really partook of his ultimate designs. They were frightened by democratic excesses in other parts of the world; they wanted to give a conservative direction to our Constitution; they got in the habit of following Hamilton while he was under the close eye of Washington, and before his subsequent schemes blossomed forth; and we think some kept along even after they understood the latter, because they believed that those schemes could not be possibly carried out. They hoped that between this exaggerated action on their own side, and the extreme of democratic sentiment on the other, a middle line of action would practically result, which would just about meet their views. Such men were really misplaced among the followers of Hamilton. They belonged more properly to the moderate Federalists—a class of men who were republicans, but whose republicanism was far more conservative and less democratic than that of Jefferson and his followers. Yet it is obvious that incidental circumstances placed not a few of this class of men among the apparent coadjutors of Hamilton.

The idea has often been advanced that Jefferson stands alone among our earlier and eminent statesmen in the assertion that a monarchical party existed. The same fact has been tacitly assumed by writers too intelligent to risk the allegation. They have done this by taking up his assertions, pronouncing them false, attempting to show them malicious, treating them as strange and monstrous, and not alluding to the fact that multitudes of other eminent statesmen have *deliberately* made the same assertions. It is an undeniable fact, however, that the same belief in the existence of a powerful faction of monarchists, made up of the very men Jefferson always designated as such, was a common belief, indeed the common one, among every class of persons in the early Republican party. Their political haranguers, their newspapers, their pamphlets constantly asserted this. The State papers and the public and private correspondences of their chiefs unhesitatingly declare the same fact. It cannot be necessary to cite numerous examples of this. We will select a few, where the prominence of the individuals will not be denied; and for this purpose will confine ourselves to the Presidents of the United States.

The *seven* first Presidents, all who were contemporaneous actors on the political stage with the generation of the Revolution, have (without respect to party) placed on record their belief in the existence of a monarchical party in our country after our separation from England and after our creation of republican governments in the States and over the Confederation.

General Washington's opinion has been cited. He seems, however (unlike the succeeding six), to have believed on the declarations made to him, that the monarchical party gave up their designs on the adoption of the federal Constitution. Jefferson quotes him as saying this while President. If he changed his mind during the short subsequent period of his life, we have no information of the fact.

John Adams wrote a letter to Jefferson, December 16th, 1816, in which, stating the " chaos " of opinions in the United States on religion, politics, and all other subjects, he declared that Aristocrats, Monarchists, " the Despotists of all denominations," and "every *emissary* of every one of these sects" would "find a party here already formed to give him a cordial reception." This appears as a casual expression in one of its author's usual rambling letters, but none the less, we suppose, does it express his real belief.

Mr. Jefferson's opinions require no citation.

Mr. Madison was chary of unnecessarily putting offensive declarations on paper. He is well known to have concurred in Jefferson's opinion on this subject, and that fact could now, were it necessary, be amply proved by the evidence of his surviving friends. If his private political letters to Jefferson were extant, we should undoubtedly have abundant written evidence of that fact. He drafted the Virginia Resolutions of 1798, which declared that the "inevitable" result of the measures against which those resolutions were directed was to "transform the present Republican system of the United States into an absolute or at best a mixed monarchy." He has already been quoted (in Appendix 9) as saying that Hamilton "made no secret" of his monarchical views in the Convention of 1787, "or afterwards."

The fifth President, Mr. Monroe, has left a long and deliberate expression on this topic. His conceded coolness and candor, his moderation towards opponents, and his speaking on the evidence of facts occurring within his own knowledge and observation, entitle his testimony to transcription at considerable length. He wrote General Jackson, December 14th, 1816:

"We have heretofore been divided into two great parties. That some of the leaders of the Federal party entertained principles unfriendly to our system of government, I have been thoroughly convinced; and that they meant to work a change in it by taking advantage of favorable circumstances, I am equally satisfied. It happened that I was a member of Congress under the Confederation, just before the change made by the adoption of the present Constitution; and afterwards of the Senate, beginning shortly after its adoption. In the former I served three years, and in the latter rather a longer term. In these stations I saw indications of the kind suggested. It was an epoch at which the views of men were most likely to unfold themselves, as, if anything favorable to a higher toned government was to be obtained, that was the time. The movement in France tended, also, then, to test the opinions and principles of men, which was disclosed in a manner to leave no doubt on my mind of what I have suggested. No daring attempt was ever made, because there was no opportunity for it. I thought that Washington was opposed to their schemes, and not being able to take him with them, that they were forced to work, in regard to him, under-handed, using his name and standing with the nation, as far as circumstances permitted, to serve their purposes. The opposition, which was carried on with great firmness, checked the career of this party, and kept it within moderate limits. Many of the circumstances on which my opinion is founded, took place in debate and in society, and therefore find no place in any public document. I am satisfied, however, that sufficient proof exists, founded on facts and opinions of distinguished individuals, which became public to justify that which I had formed.

"The contest between the parties never ceased from its commencement to the present time, nor do I think it can be said now to have ceased. You saw the height to which the opposition was carried in the late war; the embarrassment it gave the Government; the aid it gave to the enemy. The victory at New Orleans, for which we owe so much to you, and to the gallant freemen who fought under you, and the honorable peace which took place at that time, have checked the opposition, if they have not overwhelmed it. I may add that the daring measure of the Hartford Convention, which unfolded views which had been long before entertained, but never so fully understood, contributed, also, in an eminent degree, to reduce the opposition to its present state.

*   *   *   *   *   *   *

"My candid opinion is that the dangerous purposes I have adverted to, were never adopted, if they were known, especially in their full extent, by any large portion of the Federal party, but were confined to certain leaders, and they principally to the Eastward. The manly and patriotic conduct of a great proportion of that party in the other States, I might perhaps say all who had an opportunity of displaying it, is a convincing proof this fact."

John Quincy Adams was born and brought up among, and was long the associate of, those Federal leaders in New England who rested particularly under the imputation of being monarchists. Mr. Adams ought to have known the New England character and modes of exhibiting opinion too well to be deceived. In his review of the Works of Fisher Ames (1809), he said:

"He [Ames's biographer] tells us that Mr. Ames was emphatically a Republican —but that he considered a republic and a democracy as essentially distinct and opposite. Probably this was the state of his opinions at one period of his life— but in his latter days, when the English fascinations and the French antipathies had attained their uncontrolled ascendency over his mind, he appears to have had as little esteem for a republican government as for the American people. It is not to a democracy, but to a republic, that he compares the essential rottenness of the white birch stakes, in one of the above extracts. In short, he was too thoroughly Britonized to preserve a relish for anything republican; and in the paper last published before his decease, contained in this volume, he says in express terms, that 'the immortal spirit of the wood-nymph liberty, dwells only in the British oak.'

*   *   *   *   *   *

"There is indeed one point of view in which the publication of these [Mr. Ames's] letters will be serviceable to the public. They have discovered beyond all contradiction and denial, the real fundamental principles of that political sect which has obtained the control of our State administration, and which for the last two years has been driving with such furious zeal to a dissolution of the Union—combined with an alliance, offensive and defensive, with Great Britain.

"The last half of this volume might be denominated. the political bible of the junto.[1] If there be a reflecting man in any of our sister States, not infected with the scab of this political leprosy, who has any doubt what the junto principles really are, let him attentively read that part of this volume which has never before been published. Here he will find those principles which they have heretofore circulated in whispers among themselves, and denied when charged with them in public; which in their secret conclaves they profess as articles of faith, and which in their public manifestoes they repel with indignation as slanderous aspersions.   *   *   *   *

"The floods of sarcasm and invective which have gushed upon him [Jefferson], for his repeated references to the umpirage of reason, are universally known; and this sagacious mirth might be indulged as harmless, were it not inseparably connected with a political system."

*   *   *   *   *

"Had these been merely the errors of Mr. Ames, I would have lamented in silence the indiscretion of his friends, in exposing them to the world, and suffered them to perish by the natural decays of their own absurdity. But they are not the wanderings of Mr. Ames's imagination. They are the principles of a faction which has succeeded in obtaining the management of this commonwealth, and which aspired to the government of the Union. Defeated in this last object of their ambition, and sensible that the engines by which they have attained the mastery of the State are not sufficiently comprehensive, nor enough within their control to wield the machinery of the nation, their next resort was to dismember what they could not sway, and to form a new confederacy, to be under the glorious shelter of British protection. To prepare the public mind for changes so abhorrent to the temper and character of our people, the doctrines with which this volume teems were to be ushered into public view whenever a prospect for their favorable reception might appear."   *   *   *   *

Equally pointed asseverations, by President Adams, of a monarchical party as much in design as in theory, might be extended over pages.

The seventh President, General Jackson, wrote Mr. Monroe, January 6th, 1817, in answer to that letter of the latter which we have already quoted:

"I have read with much satisfaction that part of your letter on the rise, progress, and policy of the Federalists. It is, in my opinion, a just exposition. I am free to declare, had I commanded the military department where the Hartford Convention met, if it had been the last act of my life, I should have punished the three principal leaders of the party. I am certain an independent court-martial would have condemned them under the 2d section of the act establishing rules and regulations for the government of the army of the United States. These kind of men, although called Federalists, are really monarchists and traitors to the constituted government. But I am of opinion that there are men called

[1] Mr. Adams thus charactered the Ultra Federal leaders of Massachusetts.

Federalists that are honest, virtuous, and really attached to our government, and, although they differ in many respects and opinions with the Republicans, still they will risk everything in its defence."

It is not claimed that this array of coinciding testimony and belief (which might be swelled to volumes), impairs any one's right to question the soundness of Jefferson's opinions. Men have the legal right, we suppose, to disbelieve everything, even to the admissions of accused men! But it may at least be hoped that henceforth the impression will not be conveyed, either by direct false statements, or by omissions as false in their object, that Jefferson exhibited eccentricity of views, temper, or conduct, in any particular, in regard to this subject.

CHAPTER XV.

1790—1791.

WHEN Mr. Jefferson took his place in President Washington's Cabinet, in March 1790, as Secretary of State, he found the following colleagues already acting in the other departments:—Colonel Alexander Hamilton, of New York, Secretary of the Treasury; General Henry Knox, of Massachusetts, Secretary of War; Edmund Randolph, of Virginia, Attorney-General.[1]

---

[1] These, we hardly need to say, were all the Executive departments then created, except the Postmaster-General's, and he was not then included in the Cabinet.

President Washington had taken the oath of office and entered upon his duties April 30th, 1789. In selecting his Cabinet, he evidently aimed at the establishment of a balance between parties, or rather between the holders of those conflicting political theories which had disclosed themselves before and in the federal Convention, and which were ultimately to form the grounds of party divisions.

Colonel Hamilton was a West Indian, having been born in the island of Nevis, in 1757, of parents on the father's side Scotch, and on the mother's French, in descent. The indigence of his family threw him at an early age upon the bounty of maternal relatives. His family biographer (from whom we shall draw all these early details) mentions that he attended a school kept by a Jewess; that his education before leaving the West Indies probably embraced little more than the rudiments of the English and French languages; but that he early became a lover of books, and devoted much time to miscellaneous reading. In 1769, he was placed in the counting-house of a Santa Cruz merchant. He betrayed equal precocity in talents and ambition. During his twelfth year he wrote a youthful friend "that he contemned the grovelling condition of a clerk, or the like"— that he "would willingly risk his life, though not his character, to exalt his station"—that "youth excluded him from any hopes of immediate preferment, nor did he desire it, but he meant to prepare the way for futurity." "He should conclude by saying he wished there was a war!"[1]

An article he wrote in a newspaper attracted notice. The governor and some of the principal persons of the island determined that he should be sent to New York to complete his education. He reached that city in 1772, provided with "ample funds" by "his relations." He joined a celebrated grammar school at Elizabethtown, where he remained for a short period[2] studying intensely, and then entered King's (now Columbia) College, in New York, being "received as a private student, and not attached to any particular class." He, to use his own words, entertained in politics, "strong prejudices on the ministerial side, until he became convinced by the superior force of

---

[1] Hamilton's Life, by his son, vol. i. p. 5.
[2] We infer from the statements in his biography, less than a year, though all the particulars of his early life are so vaguely given, that it is difficult to settle upon anything with certainty.

the arguments in favor of the colonial claims." [1] This abandonment of loyalism seems to have occurred during, or by reason
of, a visit to Boston towards the close of 1773, or in the beginning of 1774, and in his seventeenth year; and he soon signal-
ized it, by making an eloquent address at a popular meeting
held to denounce the Boston Port Bill. He then became a frequent newspaper writer on the Whig side, and, soon after, an
able and efficient pamphleteer, in which capacity he attracted
much notice. In 1775, he joined a volunteer corps of militia,
and applied himself to the study of arms. On the 14th of
March, 1776, he was made captain of a provincial company of
artillery, and took an honorable part in the military affairs of
the day, until March, 1777, when he was appointed an aid-de-
camp, by General Washington, with the rank of Lieutenant
Colonel. His published correspondence commences immediately
after this period, and is marked with the same characteristics of
mind which distinguished it through life. [2]

He was now an advocate of the broadest representative
democracy, believing that " from the records of history it would
be found that the fluctuations of governments in which the
popular principle had borne a considerable sway, had proceeded
from its being compounded with other principles, from its being
made to operate in an improper channel." [3]

He remained in the military family of the Commander-in-
Chief, serving with credit, until 1781, when a " breach " occurred
between them, under circumstances which are detailed in a
letter written by Hamilton to General Schuyler, February 18th,
1781; and Hamilton rejecting the overture, made by the General, to an accommodation, declined longer to retain his position. [4]

---

[1] Life of Hamilton, vol. i. p. 25.
[2] Namely, ability, clearness, and unbounded self esteem. His first letters are
addressed to Gouverneur Morris, Robert Livingston, and —— Allison (collectively), and
seem to have been in answer to an invitation from those gentlemen to correspond with
the New York Convention through them. The way in which he signifies to them that
his " sentiments are never to be considered as an echo of those of the General," in his
first letter, and in which, in his second, he " must beg leave to repeat what he had before
observed, that whenever he gave opinions, they were merely his own, and would probably, so far from being a transcript of those of the General, differ widely from them in
many respects," are amusing illustrations of self-complacency in a young gentleman of
twenty! There was a manifest propriety, certainly, in cautioning his correspondents
that General Washington was not to be held in anywise responsible for the views of his
Aid; but the repetition of these cautions, and the phraseology of them, furnish characteristic hints.
[3] Hamilton's Works, vol. vi. pp. 581-2.
[4] For this letter, see Hamilton's Life, vol. i. p. 333 : or his Works, vol. i. p. 211.
Those who would study carefully the character and temper of Hamilton (and judge
how far the lapse of years affected his estimate of himself), should turn to this letter

He subsequently, after considerable difficulty,[1] received the rank of colonel in the line, and led, by his own request, and with great intrepidity, a corps that carried an outwork of the enemy at Yorktown. At the end of the campaign of 1781, he retired from the army and commenced the study of law in Albany, where his father-in-law, General Philip Schuyler (whose daughter he had married in 1780), resided. His political sentiments, some time before leaving the army, had undergone a second change, and acquired that bias they retained through life; and their new tone was probably fostered by his connection with General Schuyler's family. He was admitted, after a few months' study, to the bar, where he rapidly distinguished himself. He was elected to Congress in 1782, held some other offices, was one of the two delegates from New York in the Annapolis Convention in 1786, and was one of the three delegates of that State in the Convention of 1787, which framed the Constitution. His course and his views in the latter body have been sufficiently described.

General Knox, the Secretary of War, requires less prelimi nary space on the canvas. He was born in Boston in 1750. He was a zealous Whig from the beginning of those difficulties with England which more immediately preceded the Revolution. He commanded an independent artillery company in his native city, and rendered himself so conspicuous that when the artillery corps of the army was increased to three regiments in 1776, he was promoted to the command with the rank of Brigadier-General. He was distinguished by bravery and good conduct on numerous occasions, and after the capture of Yorktown, in 1781,

entire, and to his two succeeding ones to General Washington, dated April 27, 1781, and May 2d, 1781 (see his Life, vol. i. pp. 341, 343). We will quote a couple of para· graphs from the letter to Schuyler:

"I always disliked the office of an aid-de-camp, as having in it a kind of personal dependence. I refused to serve in this capacity with two Major-Generals, at an early period of the war. Infected, however, with the enthusiasm of the times, an idea of the General's character overcame my scruples, and induced me to *accept his invitation* [italicized in original] to enter into his family. * * * It has been often with great difficulty I have prevailed upon myself not to renounce it; but while from motives of public utility, I was doing violence to my feelings, I was always determined if there should ever happen a breach between us, never to consent to an accommodation. I was persuaded, that when once that nice barrier, which marked the boundaries of what we owed to each other, should be thrown down, it might be propped again, but could never be restored.

"The General is a very honest man· his competitors have slender abilities, and less integrity. His popularity has often been essential to the safety of America, and is still of great importance to it. These considerations have influenced my past conduct respect ing him, and will influence it in future ; I think it necessary he should be supported !"

The writer of this letter was twenty-four years old !

[1] See his letter to Washington, March 1, 1782.

was made a Major-General. Not ranking perhaps so high as Greene and one or two other generals of the Revolution, who were usually intrusted with the more important separate commands, he was, nevertheless, one of the best and bravest of those able officers to whom General Washington confided the execution of his plans. The latter had great confidence in Knox, and his personal attachment for him was thought to be hardly equalled by that entertained for any other officer under him. Knox was, if we have obtained a correct impression of his character, a fine, frank, amiable, soldierly man, and if without much education or profundity of mind, prompt and effective in execution, and endowed, when he thought for himself, with good sense and liberality of sentiment.

While Hamilton was a pigmy in stature, Knox was a giant; and an intelligent old Revolutionary soldier who had more than once seen the latter in battle, informed us that his carriage was magnificent as he bore down impetuously on a foe; his voice ringing sonorously even above the roar of battle, and his vehemently uttered commands interlarded with expletives which indicated anything but a Puritan ancestry! He succeeded Lincoln in the War Department in 1785. In politics, he was thought by many of his contemporaries (and Jefferson amongst them) to be one of the foremost of that anti-republican reactionary party which had become eagerly and almost openly advocates of monarchy in 1785–6. Knox, certainly, struck the very key note of this party when he advised General Washington to keep aloof from the Convention of 1787 and reserve himself for some "solemn occasion." [1] But in the same letter he proposed a plan for the general government which, though indicating the extreme of consolidation views, and a wish to maintain consolidation by a standing army, went as far to preserve elective forms as did the system afterwards adopted. We doubt whether he was a fixed thinker, or obstinately wedded to his theoretical beliefs. On the contrary, we apprehend his opinions were much influenced by the public tone and by the tone of those about him whom he most trusted.

The Attorney-General, Mr. Randolph, was a second cousin of Jefferson, and was probably some years younger than the latter, as he succeeded to his law business.[2] Like his father and

[1] See p. 566.   [2] We do not remember to have seen Randolph's precise age stated

grandfather before him,[1] he was a man of elegant parts, appearance, and education. He had been a member of Washington's military family in the Revolution, Attorney-General and then Governor of Virginia. He had been a member of the federal Convention; had acted a conspicuous part in it; had introduced what was called the Virginia plan; had opposed and declined to sign the instrument as finally adopted; and had ended, however, by cordially pressing its acceptance on the Virginia Convention. In politics he belonged to the popular school. He seems to have been a marked favorite with his various constituencies, never, we believe, having been beaten in an election. His mind was of a fine analytical order, fertile in its views, and not without an infusion of what may be properly styled genius. He was one of the best and showiest lawyers of his day—a thing impossible without a good share of genius. But his love of analysis was too apt to run into mere refinements, and his very fertility weakened the vigor of his own impressions, and scattered his strength in a multitude of slight blows on his adversary, instead of concentrating them into one overwhelming one. Nor was this the worst result. The consummate hair-splitter saw and considered so many objections, that he not unfrequently ended in converting himself from the position from which he started; or if it did not reach to this, he left the question so nicely balanced, that some little expediency, some fine-spun quirk ultimately induced him to vote against the tenor of his own argument—as Jefferson afterwards significantly expressed it, "giving the oyster to his adversaries, and saving only the shell for his friends."

The President's Cabinet stood thus not unequally balanced between the friends of popular and strong government. Jefferson and Hamilton represented the extremes, and though differing greatly in manners, and in their ways of maintaining or attempting to propagate their opinions, were, when it came to the substance, equally inflexible. Knox and Randolph both probably occupied an inner circle of opinions—both were more likely to be controlled by circumstances and the views of others. Jefferson was the senior in the Cabinet, possessed, indisputably,

---

[1] His father was John Randolph, Attorney-General of Virginia under the Crown (and who went to England on the breaking out of the war), and his grandfather, Sir John, Attorney-General, Speaker, etc. Peyton, the first President of Congress, was his uncle.

far greater personal attainments and public experience than any
other member,[1] was the most conspicuous man in the public
eye,[2] and lastly, held the most important official position. This
last fact has been questioned, and perhaps with some plausi-
bility. In pecuniary circles, the financial bureau is always considered the main spring of a government, and politicians are
disposed to give it the same rank, because it is commonly made
the principal centre of patronage. But important as it really is
—absolutely essential as its good management is to national
success (and of what other department is not this remark equally
true?)—it would be absurd, in our judgment, to assume that,
acting within its legitimate limits, it can exercise any such generally moulding influence on the character and policy of a government, and particularly a new government, as the department
of domestic and foreign affairs. A government may be completely sound and prosperous in its monetary affairs, and yet the
worst government on earth. One wisely and successfully conducted in its foreign and domestic bureaux cannot be a very
bad one.

Hamilton had a personal advantage in the Cabinet, over all
his colleagues. He had been much previously about Washington. He had acted for him; in small matters, and during pres-
sures of business, had both thought and acted for him as a
trusted secretary[3] is always required, on occasion, to think and
act for his principal. Leaning on an inferior in such cases
becomes, to some extent, habitual. It is easier to go to him for
information and advice; and he can present his opinion with
greater freedom, and press it with more importunity.

[1] Colonel Hamilton was a man of remarkable attainments, considering his opportunities, his active and varied course of life, and his present age. Randolph was older,
and had enjoyed far better early advantages. He, perhaps, had lacked the intensity
of Hamilton's application, but his general and particularly his belles-lettres culture, was
undoubtedly far superior at this period. Jefferson had received equal early advantages
with Randolph, and better recent ones—possessed all of Hamilton's intensity of application—and he was the senior of both. He was fourteen years older than Colonel
Hamilton.
On comparing their previous experience in public life and as statesmen, it will be
readily seen that Jefferson's quite or more than equalled Randolph's and Hamilton's, both
put together.
[2] The difference, it will readily be conceded, afterwards became less in this particular,
for a time. Hamilton was already a very conspicuous man in point of abilities. But he
had nearly always been a minority man, and therefore had, as yet, accomplished little.
He never had really controlled affairs for a day in his own State—had appeared always
as a minority representative of his State in the Federal councils, and there, too, he had
fallen into the minority on those great test questions which were to decide the cardinal
principles and spirit of the government. Up to this point, then, his achievements in
civil life had been literally nothing, when compared with Jefferson's.
[3] He had acted as Washington's Military Secretary.

We shall not stop here to ask what was the degree of personal affection which existed between Washington and Hamilton. There were very different theories on that subject among those who knew both the parties well, and we may hereafter allude to them. But it is at least certain that Washington entertained great confidence in the intellectual capacity and fidelity of his former Aid; and he deeply felt the convenience of having near him a subordinate so tireless in the investigation of subjects, so clear in his own class of views, so ready with his pen, and the master of so vigorous and polished a style. Hamilton had entered his family at a very early age, and the stately Commander-in-Chief had become accustomed to his foibles, while he probably regarded them as rather the manifestations of boyhood than anything more important; and having become thus used to them, they never afterwards struck him as they would have done coming first from a middle-aged person. Hamilton's vehemence and pertinacity were accordingly tolerated; nay, they gave him a sort of advantage, for when a superior or an associate has made up his mind to overlook such qualities, he will generally, if he possesses self-respect, go as far as he can to avoid provoking their display.

Between the Secretary of War and Attorney-General, the preponderance of official importance and influence was, we should say, a good deal on the side of the former. Knox did not possess half the ability or knowledge of Randolph on general topics, but he was a stauncher follower. His vote could at least be counted upon.

We perhaps should say here, at the outset, that while the theory of the government would seem to imply an entire separation between the governmental departments, and their entire independence of each other, connecting only through the executive head, such was not the practice under the first President. He had been used to the Executive Council of Virginia, and to councils of war. He was a modest man, and loved advice; and, more than all, he was intent on an amalgamation as well as a balance of parties in his Cabinet. He desired the Cabinet action, or rather its fruits (his own executive action) to be what in mechanics is termed the "resultant," of these opposing forces. To effect this, conference and compromise were necessary between the Cabinet representatives of the different principles

Accordingly, the Cabinet was generally converted into an executive council, and sometimes substantially into a directory or plural executive, for the President allowed questions to be decided by the majority of voices, and counted his own vote but one, or merely reserved a casting vote. This practice has been (with less reason we think) much followed since. It accordingly has happened that the real Executive, legally responsible to the nation for his conduct, has been voted down, actually controlled in his action, by his own appointees, responsible to nobody but himself. And it has much oftener happened that the head of one department, selected with particular reference to his qualifications for it, has been voted down by colleagues selected with no reference to such qualifications. Even the moral responsibility—the responsibility which each might feel in reputation—is lost just so far as this mixing up of department duties renders them undistinguishable. On the other hand, such a course is calculated to secure more deliberation and caution, and to guard against the results of marked weakness or eccentricity in action. It may fairly perhaps be considered a moot-point whether the theory of the Constitution, or the practice which has measurably grown up under it, is productive of most good, and least subject to abuse.

President Washington was probably influenced by several considerations in selecting a Cabinet in which the previous parties were balanced. It was, in the first place, tantamount to a declaration to those parties of amnesty for the past, and neutrality, so far as persons were concerned, for the future. It was also equivalent to inviting both parties to come in and support the administration, on the implied understanding that a moderate and middle course would be pursued.

This programme comported not only with the President's habitual line of policy, but, in truth, it undoubtedly better represented his individual views. He was constitutionally, and by the habits of his whole life, averse to extreme positions or courses—believing fully in the wisdom of that maxim which is often scouted at by radicals, but which, properly interpreted, it must be confessed, oftenest solves well the difficult problems of practical life—" *in medio tutissimus ibis.*" [1] He was sincerely in favor of a republican government, not only in form but in

[1] In the middle path you will go most safely

substance; but the tenor of his past public life had rendered his affections and sympathies decidedly national. He felt that he was the father of his whole country. The firmness which had so signally sustained him in every dark and desperate crisis of the war, shook when insurrection unfurled its standards over the very battle-fields of the Revolution. His great heart then sunk in uncontrollable anguish, and he asked himself whether he would not have chosen to fill a premature grave like Greene, for the purpose of obtaining " such an exit to the scenes which it was more than probable many of his compatriots might live to bemoan." [1] It was in a great measure through his influence, that several of the Eastern States had sent representatives to the federal Convention. The result of that body's deliberations had met his fullest hopes.

It appears, from his letters, and particularly from those to Hamilton, [2] that before hearing the full discussions of the Convention, and before witnessing its final action, he would have preferred a government rather more consolidated in form. He had obviously become deeply disgusted with the conduct of the State governments. But he considered the Constitution, as completed by the Convention, a fair and just compromise between opposing views. He accepted it not as a make-shift, which by latitudinarian constructions or the sword of civil war was to be converted into something else, but as a finality good in itself and fairly agreed upon; and he was unquestionably resolved to carry it out in its real meaning. He judged he would best attain this, and be more likely to induce parties to rally round the Constitution and round his administration, by giving those parties an equal voice in his Cabinet—and where they disagreed, holding the balance firmly and impartially between them. Nothing can be more certain than that the first President entered his office firmly resolved to be a no-party President.

The heterogeneous materials thus brought together coalesced for a period. Jefferson and Hamilton met each other, it would appear, with no unfavorable prepossessions. They were both, personally, attractive men—genial in temper and manner—frank and indisposed to underhandedness among associates. Jefferson

[1] Greene died from a sun-stroke, June 19, 1786, aged 46. These words of Washington occur in one of his letters, the date of which is not now remembered.
[2] Q. v. in Life of Hamilton.

came back from France unfamiliar with some of the domestic questions, and particularly those of finance, which had sprung up during his absence. The selection of the President justified the impression that Hamilton was profoundly familiar with the public finances. They fell within his official department, and no man was more habitually modest than Jefferson, under such circumstances, in forming and thrusting forward his own opinions. For a time, therefore, he seemed disposed to take Hamilton's views upon trust—and his doubts were only expressed with caution and reluctance. Here are his after opinions of the state of affairs, on his arrival in New York:

"Hamilton's financial system had then passed. It had two objects: 1st, as a puzzle, to exclude popular understanding and inquiry; 2d, as a machine for the corruption of the Legislature: for he avowed the opinion, that man could be governed by one of two motives only, force or interest: force, he observed, in this country, was out of the question, and the interests, therefore, of the members must be laid hold of, to keep the Legislature in unison with the Executive. And with grief and shame it must be acknowledged that his machine was not without effect; that even in this, the birth of our government, some members were found sordid enough to bend their duty to their interests, and to look after personal rather than public good.

"It is well known that during the war, the greatest difficulty we encountered, was the want of money or means to pay our soldiers who fought, or our farmers, manufacturers, and merchants, who furnished the necessary supplies of food and clothing for them. After the expedient of paper money had exhausted itself, certificates of debt were given to the individual creditors, with assurance of payment, so soon as the United States should be able. But the distresses of these people often obliged them to part with these for the half, the fifth, and even a tenth of their value; and speculators had made a trade of cozening them from the holders, by the most fraudulent practices, and persuasions that they would never be paid. In the bill for funding and paying these, Hamilton made no difference between the original holders and the fraudulent purchasers of this paper. Great and just repugnance arose at putting these two classes of creditors on the same footing, and great exertions were used to pay the former the full value, and to the latter the price only which they had paid, with interest.[1] But this would have prevented the game which was to be played, and for which the minds of greedy members were already tutored and prepared. When the trial of strength, on these several efforts, had indicated the form in which the bill would finally pass, this being known within doors sooner than without, and especially, than to those who were in distant parts of the Union, the base scramble began. Couriers and relay horses by land, and swift-sailing pilot boats by sea, were flying in all directions. Active partners and agents were associated and employed in every State, town, and country neighborhood, and this paper was bought up at five shillings, and even as low as two shillings in the pound, before the holder knew that Congress had already provided

[1] This was one of the amendments proposed, but it was not the one which received most notoriety from being moved and advocated by Mr. Madison.

for its redemption at par. Immense sums were thus filched from the poor and ignorant, and fortunes accumulated by those who had themselves been poor enough before. Men thus enriched by the dexterity of a leader, would follow of course the chief who was leading them to fortune, and become the zealous instruments of all his enterprises."

Mr. Madison had made an effort to mitigate the injustice of this bill, as between the first holders and the speculating purchasers of the public certificates of debt, by moving an amendment which would have produced a compromise between the interests of the parties. It provided that the present holder should receive the highest cash value that the certificates had borne, and that the residue (up to their par value) should be paid to the original holder. He claimed that inasmuch as the public creditors had suffered solely by the default of the Government, the Government was bound to exercise the highest prerogative of sovereignty to make reparation to them; and he cited cases to show that both the English and French governments had sanctioned departures from the ordinary rules of commercial law, to protect individual rights imperilled by the action of the Government, and that no resulting injury to public credit had ensued. He claimed, what was undoubtedly true, that the United States had already acted on an analogous principle in repudiating and attempting to make compensation otherwise, to the original holders of its paper currency. He thought his proposition a very liberal one to the present holders of certificates, because they had generally purchased them for from a fifth down to a tenth of their nominal value, and the certificates had suddenly risen to half that nominal value on the publication of Hamilton's report to Congress on the subject. His proposition would enable holders still to realize several hundred per centum on the money they had invested.

Mr. Madison's proposition was sustained, on the floor, by several members. Gerry proposed that full payment be made to present holders, and then that compensation be also made to a class of the original ones. This proposition did not meet much favor. The Government was too poor to be so magnanimous. Madison's proposition would defeat what it has been seen Jefferson considered the main object of the bill, and the future leaders of the Ultra-Federalists exerted themselves warmly against it. Fisher Ames poured out his customary amount of invective and pathos on the subject of national credit. Sedgwick admitted that Government might even regulate contracts, where the stability of the social structure required it,[1] but he did not consider this such a case. Smith of South Carolina—popularly accused of sharing largely in the speculations produced by the bill—took the same side. But thirteen members rose for Mr. Madison's amendment.[2] The policy of the Treasury Department was now completely in the ascendant.

The Funding Law produced striking effects. The political ones have been given. The social if not moral ones were not less important. A class of already rich men were suddenly made enormously rich, that is, in comparison with American fortunes generally. The keen, alert, hungry class of adventurers who had ridden " relay horses " and crowded canvas on the " pilot boats," to buy up certificates of battered soldiers, or their needy orphans, suddenly shot up into wealth and splendor. In every part of the country, there were men whose family estates had been ruthlessly devastated by the foe—or who had voluntarily stripped them to meet the imploring calls of Government in the dark straits of the Revolution—or who had grievously burdened them to support the soldiers which those estates had sent forth, the master of the household and his sons, to serve in the army. A nominal reparation had been made for supplies actually furnished, and for personal services. It came, however, in the form of pledges which could not be immediately redeemed, and every succeeding day lowered the value of those evidences of debt. Meanwhile the estate crumbled and its occupants sunk lower and lower from their former scale of opulence and social importance. Men who had entered the Revolution in easy circumstances and the prominent persons of their respective localities— who had fought the battles of their country—who had borne commissions—who held honorable discharges signed by the name of Washington—who were scarred, and maimed, and in some instances wholly broken in constitution by the exposures of the war—were now, in innumerable instances, reduced to the necessity of toiling with their own hands for their daily bread, or to subsist on the charity of relatives only less needy than

---

[1] Perhaps this admission was made in the debate on a previous amendment, and if so, it is none the less german to the matter.
[2] Against thirty-six negatives.

themselves [1]—while had the Government, with its present nice sense of commercial honor,[2] fulfilled its obligations to them, they would have been in affluence, and they and their children would not have been sunk into indigence, and obscurity, and supplanted in public and social consequence by adventurers, who had risen literally on their ruins.

This new class of moneyed men could not often boast of patriotic services to their country.[3] They had been generally trained on other theatres than the camp, the march and the battle-field, to their present ferret-eyed sagacity in politico-commercial speculation. They had been educating during the Revolution, in those places where the little money that was to be made was made by commercial men, from the rank of honorable merchants down to small sutlers, and traders with the enemy, rather than in those places where both money and blood were spent for the country. Now ostentatious upstarts, they rolled in their carriages; took the lead in politics; declaimed about "national obligations" and "national honor;" talked of the country's acquiring "a character;" and spoke with huge disapprobation of the dangerous and agrarian doctrines tolerated by the State governments, by the "common people," and at length advanced even on the floors of Congress by Madison.

Bad as were the individual results we have named, they were not the worst. The example debauched the public mind. The young, the ardent, and the enterprising, seeing fortunes made by the turn of a vote, for the lucky "knowing ones" who

[1] We have never seen the miserable spectacle of a soldier of the Revolution absolutely begging his food from door to door—but we have personally known scores and scores of them, who were compelled to work hard in their old age for subsistence, or to depend on the charity of relatives, eked out by the pensions long after the period of which we write, conferred upon them by the Government—and not a few of them would have been men of substance with their honest claims against the Government paid.

The bounty lands, pensions, etc., were an honorable effort towards late reparation. But the lands lying in deep wildernesses, were immediately available to but few, and they had no market value. Their titles were often transferred, in the expressive popular phrase, "for a song." The annual pension was an excellent device to keep broken down old men from starvation—but to say that in this country where money went so far, soon after the Revolution, that these pensions were a full equivalent for pay, in the commercial sense of the word, for what the recipients had lost by the depreciation of Government paper money and certificates, would be a monstrous perversion of the facts. The speculators received the ready pay and became the men of property—the battered soldier sunk into hopeless indigence, though his country did finally interfere to save him from starvation.

[2] We by no means say that the Government forfeited its commercial honor by omitting to pay its debts, when due, or by repudiating the Continental money. But if so tenacious to pay the certificates to the holders in 1790, to save commercial honor, why on the same principle should not the Continental money have been redeemed to save the commercial honor of the country? Yet the Funding Bill itself, we believe, recognized its repudiation!

[3] We are sorry to say there were some striking exceptions to this remark.

were the hangers-on of Government, were not only in haste to abandon their legitimate avocations to join that corps, but a wild spirit of speculation widened and spread throughout the land, embracing almost every branch of financial operations, and especially stock jobbing and banking. Government was necessarily connected with both. It must give legal authority to these schemes. Consequently round the General Government, and even, before long, round some of the State Governments, a vast army of speculators was congregated striving to obtain wealth by "jobs"—either plundering the government, or selling it their fealty for the privilege of being allowed to plunder others "according to law." These men passed their lives in the lobby of Congress, corrupting legislation at the fountain-head, by dexterously appealing to the party fears and hopes of politicians, and to the palms of the directly venal. Many a Congressman at that day was popularly and directly accused of being a silent partner in speculations, which his vote helped to originate ; and many a Congressman lived and died under such imputations, founded on strongly corroborating circumstances, without making any explanations which tended to relieve his reputation.

Mr. Jefferson's expressions, already quoted, in regard to the Funding Bill, were fruits of after-knowledge. By his own showing (and by his alone), he was himself made to "hold the candle" to one of Hamilton's projects ! He thus proceeds in his Memoir from the point where we dropped the preceding quotation :

"This game [the Funding Bill] was over, and another was on the carpet at the moment of my arrival; and to this I was most ignorantly and innocently made to hold the candle. This fiscal manœuvre is well known by the name of the Assumption. Independently of the debts of Congress, the States had during the war contracted separate and heavy debts ; and Massachusetts particularly, in an absurd attempt, absurdly conducted, on the British post of Penobscot: and the more debt Hamilton could rake up, the more plunder for his mercenaries. This money, whether wisely or foolishly spent, was pretended to have been spent for general purposes, and ought, therefore, to be paid from the general purse. But it was objected, that nobody knew what these debts were, what their amount, or what their proofs. No matter; we will guess them to be twenty millions. But of these twenty millions, we do not know how much should be reimbursed to one State, or how much to another. No matter; we will guess. And so another scramble was set on foot among the several States, and some got much, some little, some nothing But the main object was obtained—the phalanx of the Treasury was reinforced by additional recruits. This measure produced the most bitter and angry contest ever known in Congress before or since the Union of the States. I arrived in the midst of it.

But a stranger to the ground, a stranger to the actors on it, so long absent as to have lost all familiarity with the subject, and as yet unaware of its object, I took no concern in it. The great and trying question, however, was lost in the House of Representatives. So high were the feuds excited by this subject, that on its rejection business was suspended. Congress met and adjourned from day to day without doing anything, the parties being too much out of temper to do business together. The eastern members particularly, who, with Smith from South Carolina, were the principal gamblers in these scenes, threatened a secession and dissolution. Hamilton was in despair. As I was going to the President's one day, I met him in the street. He walked me backwards and forwards before the President's door for half an hour. He painted pathetically the temper into which the Legislature had been wrought; the disgust of those who were called the creditor States; the danger of the secession of their members, and the separation of the States. He observed that the members of the administration ought to act in concert; that though this question was not of my department, yet a common duty should make it a common concern; that the President was the centre on which all administrative questions ultimately rested, and that all of us should rally around him, and support, with joint efforts, measures approved by him; and that the question having been lost by a small majority only, it was probable that an appeal from me to the judgment and discretion of some of my friends, might effect a change in the vote, and the machine of government, now suspended, might be again set into motion. I told him that I was really a stranger to the whole subject; that not having yet informed myself of the system of finance adopted, I knew not how far this was a necessary sequence; that undoubtedly, if its rejection endangered a dissolution of our Union at this incipient stage, I should deem that the most unfortunate of all consequences, to avert which all partial and temporary evils should be yielded. I proposed to him, however, to dine with me the next day, and I would invite another friend or two, bring them into conference together, and I thought it impossible that reasonable men, consulting together coolly, could fail, by some mutual sacrifices of opinion, to form a compromise which was to save the Union. The discussion took place. I could take no part in it but an exhortatory one, because I was a stranger to the circumstances which should govern it. But it was finally agreed, that whatever importance had been attached to the rejection of this proposition, the preservation of the Union and of concord among the States was more important, and that therefore it would be better that the vote of rejection should be rescinded, to effect which, some members should change their votes. But it was observed that this pill would be peculiarly bitter to the Southern States, and that some concomitant measure should be adopted, to sweeten it a little to them. There had before been propositions to fix the seat of government either at Philadelphia or at Georgetown on the Potomac; and it was thought that by giving it to Philadelphia for ten years, and to Georgetown permanently afterwards, this might, as an anodyne, calm in some degree the ferment which might be excited by the other measure alone. So two of the Potomac members (White and Lee, but White with a revulsion of stomach almost convulsive), agreed to change their votes, and Hamilton undertook to carry the other point. In doing this, the influence he had established over the Eastern members, with the agency of Robert Morris with those of the middle States, effected his side of the engagement; and so the Assumption was passed, and twenty millions of stock divided among favored States, and thrown in as a pabulum to the stock-jobbing herd. This added to the number of votaries to the Treasury, and made its chief the master of every vote in the legislature, which might give to the Government the direction suited to his political views.

"I know well, and so must be understood, that nothing like a majority in Congress had yielded to this corruption. Far from it. But a division, not very unequal, had already taken place in the honest part of that body, between the parties styled Republican and Federal. The latter being monarchists in principle, adhered to Hamilton, of course, as their leader in that principle, and this mercenary phalanx added to them, insured him always a majority in both Houses; so that the whole action of the Legislature was now under the direction of the Treasury."[1]

The whole amount of State debt and interest included in "the Assumption," ultimately proved about two and a half millions of dollars more than above named by Mr. Jefferson. Mr. Gallatin, a few years afterwards, it is believed perfectly truthfully, said:

"Had the United States waited to assume the State debt till the accounts had been finally settled, instead of assuming at random before a final settlement had taken place, the very same result which now exists might have been effected; and the amounts of the Union with the individual States might have been placed in the same relative situation in which they now stand, by assuming eleven millions

---

[1] We have been fortunate in recovering the following contemporaneous letter of Mr. Jefferson, which puts him in a more favorable attitude in regard to the Assumption Bill, than he puts himself in the above rapid and general statement of facts made thirty-one years afterwards:

"NEW YORK, *July* 4, 1790.

"DEAR SIR:
   "The business of Congress has proceeded very slowly lately. Two interesting questions have so chafed the members, that they can scarcely go on with one another. One of these is happily getting over. The Senate has passed the bill for transferring the temporary residence of Congress to Philadelphia for 10 years, and the permanent one to Georgetown thenceforward. The other question relative to the assumption of the State debts is still undecided. In the form in which it has been proposed, it can never be admitted, but neither can the proposition be totally rejected without preventing the funding the public debt altogether, which would be tantamount to a dissolution of the Government. I am in hopes it will be put into a just form, by assuming to the creditors of each State in proportion to the census of each State, so that the State will be exonerated towards its creditors just as much as it will have to contribute to the assumption, and consequently no injustice done. The only objection, then, would be that the States could more conveniently levy taxes themselves to pay their debts. I am clearly of this opinion, but I see the necessity of sacrificing our opinions sometimes to the opinions of others for the sake of harmony. There is some prospect of a war between Spain and England. Should this take place, France will certainly be involved in it, and it will be as general a war as has ever been seen in Europe; consequently it will be long patching up a peace which may adjust so many interests. In the meantime, I hope peace and profit will be our lot. I think there is every prospect of a good price for our produce, and particularly our wheat, for years to come. The revolution in France goes on with a slow but steady step. Their West India islands are all in combustion. There is no government in them, consequently their trade is entirely open to us. I shall come to Virginia in September, most probably early in the month, though I had rather make it a little later, if the time to be fixed by the President for removal to Philadelphia will admit it; for I take for granted the bill will pass the House of Representatives when it has been read once or twice, and will be finally decided on the day after to-morrow. Present me most affectionately to Mrs. Eppes and the family. I am, my dear sir,
               "Your affectionate friend and servant,
"Mr. Eppes, Eppington,   "TH. JEFFERSON.
         "Chesterfield, Va."

instead of twenty-two. The additional and unnecessary debt created by that fatal measure amounts, therefore, to $10,883,628 58."

The Assumption had been voted down, April 10th, 1790, by a division of thirty-one to twenty-nine. Mr. Gerry renewed the proposal with a proviso that the amount to be assumed from each State, be first settled. This was rejected without a count. This measure, on which the "Eastern members particularly," and Smith, of South Carolina, "threatened a secession and dissolution," had not, we think, been called for by a Legislative resolution, and scarcely by a petition, from any of the creditor States!

Mr. Jefferson's published correspondence for some period after his arrival in New York—apart from official letters now of little interest—consists mainly of leave-takings of his friends in France. All these indicate his strong attachment to that country, his disappointment in not returning to it, and the continuance of his keen interest in the progress of its Revolution. He had not given up his sympathy in the popular cause there because the Patriots had not followed his prudent advice, nor had he ceased to hope for their success. Violences and excesses had taken place, but he regarded these as not to be deprecated if they were necessary preludes to national freedom. He wrote General Lafayette (April 2d) that "we are not to expect to be translated from despotism to liberty in a feather bed." He still believed that conservative checks would be required to give stability to the French Constitution. He wrote the Duke de la Rochefoucauld, April 3d :

"I find my countrymen as anxious for your success as they ought to be ; and thinking with the National Assembly in all points except that of a single house of legislation. They think their own experience has so decidedly proved the necessity of two houses to prevent the tyranny of one, that they fear that this single error will shipwreck your new Constitution. I am myself persuaded that theory and practice are not at variance in this instance, and that you will find it necessary hereafter to add another branch. But I presume you provide a facility of amending your Constitution, and perhaps the necessity may be altogether removed by a council of revision well constituted."

On the 15th of April, the Secretary of State reported to the House of Representatives on a copper coinage, adverse to the proposition to supply it from abroad. On the 24th, he delivered a written Cabinet opinion against the right of the Senate "to

negative the grade of persons appointed by the Executive to fill
foreign missions." On the 3d of May, he delivered a Cabinet
opinion against "the validity of a grant made by the State of
Georgia to certain companies of individuals of a tract of country
whereof the Indian right had never been extinguished, with
power to such individuals to extinguish the Indian right." He
therein assumed the position that the General Government possessed the sole right of acquiring the Indian titles.

During most of the month of May, Mr. Jefferson was too ill
to attend to much business, from the effect of a malady somewhat peculiar to him—a headache, occurring only at considerable intervals, but when it did occur, lasting for a number of
days, and with such violence that it produced nearly as much
prostration as a severe fit of sickness. Over exertion and the
want of rest rendered the present attack a very protracted one,
and its debilitating effects did not entirely disappear before
July.

On the 3d of June, he delivered a written Cabinet opinion in
favor of the President's approving of resolutions of Congress
(May 21st) "directing that in all cases where payment had not
been already made, the debts due to the soldiers of Virginia and
North Carolina should be paid to the original claimants or their
attorneys, and not to their assignees." He distinctly asserted in
this opinion,[1] that the accounts of these soldiers having been
examined by an officer of the Government, and a list of the
balances due them made out, that list "became known to certain persons before the soldiers themselves had information of
it." This gave an opportunity for the "relay-horse" and
"pilot-boat" scramble on a smaller scale, but under circumstances of even more contemptible and cold-blooded turpitude.[2]
Jefferson did not take the ground (as was done on the Funding
Bill) that the case was sufficiently important, though caused
clearly by the fault of the Government (or some of its officers)
to demand retrospective legislation. He said:

[1] And if the assertion was denied by any of his colleagues, we are not informed of
the fact.
[2] These acts did not amount to technical swindling—"obtaining goods on false pretences." But if it was not, morally, unmitigated swindling—and quite as much worthy
of a State-prison as the technical offence, we confess we do not see the true bearings of
the case. It would seem rather farcical to make "forestalling" "regrating," etc.,
penal, and yet allow this kind of offence against honor and morality to pass for gentlemanly! The pillory and whipping-post, if not branding, would, in our judgment, be well
revived, for this class of "gentlemen!"

"I agree in an almost unlimited condemnation of retrospective laws. The few instances of wrong which they redress are so overweighed by the insecurity they draw over all property and even over life itself, and by the atrocious violations of both to which they lead, that it is better to live under the evil than the remedy.

"The only question I shall make is, whether these resolutions annul acts which were valid when they were done?"

He then contended that at least in Virginia, where the common law on the subject had been changed by no statute, the conveyance of a right to a debt, whereof the party was not in possession, was wholly void;[1] and he proceeded to argue towards the same practical conclusion, on other legal grounds. The Secretary of the Treasury submitted a counter opinion, and in favor of vetoing the resolutions of Congress. His opinion did not prevail.

In a letter to his son-in-law (May 30th) Mr. Jefferson expressed himself in favor of the passage of *a* tonnage bill, and he declared some very radical views in regard to the "natural right" of every nation to trade with others:

"The tonnage bill will probably pass, and must, I believe, produce salutary effects. It is a mark of energy in our Government, in a case, I believe, where it cannot be parried. The French Revolution still goes on well, though the danger of a suspension of payments is very imminent. Their appeal to the inhabitants of their colonies to say on what footing they wished to be placed, will end, I hope, in our free admission into their islands with our produce. This precedent must have consequences. It is impossible the world should continue long insensible to so evident a truth as that the right to have commerce and intercourse with our neighbors, is but a natural right. To suppress this neighborly intercourse is an exercise of force, which we shall have a just right to remove when the superior force."

In the same letter will be found a list of those he considered the best authors on political economy and the science of government, still worthy of the attention of the student in those topics.

During the summer there were decided appearances of a rupture between Great Britain and Spain, growing out of the attack made on the settlement of the former at Nootka Sound. The prompt steps taken by Great Britain to resent the affront, and the strong probability that France would sustain Spain, and thus put her in a condition to hazard a struggle, made a European war appear imminent. This offered a favorable occasion for the United States to press the adjustment of outstanding

[1] He said neither the law-merchant nor statutes of Virginia made any exceptions in this respect but as to bills of exchange, promissory notes and bonds.

differences with both Spain and Great Britain. The Secretary of State accordingly instructed Mr. Carmichael, our *Chargé des Affaires* at Madrid, to urge a full concession to the United States of the navigation of the Mississippi, and certain other resulting rights which will be presently mentioned. Spain was to be warned that any further delay in the matter might lead to war, for that the western citizens of the United States had already been kept quiet with difficulty, and that "in a moment of impatience," they might resort to force, in which event "neither themselves nor their rights would ever be abandoned" by their Government. The claims of Spain to territory north of 31° on the east bank of the Mississippi were pronounced "never to have merited the respect of an answer." Such was to be the leonine diplomatic roar, provided the war had begun, but if "an accommodation had taken place," a lower key was to be struck. In the latter event, the Secretary very quietly says :

" Your discretion will suggest that they [our claims] must be pressed more softly, and that patience and persuasion must temper your conferences, till either these may prevail, or some other circumstance turn up, which may enable us to use other means for the attainment of an object which we are determined in the end to attain at any risk." [1]

But there was another contingency to provide against. Spain, proverbially unpliable and wrong-headed, might choose to take another foe on her hands, even if engaged in hostilities with England. This would not only cost the United States a war, but it would, in all probability, produce some awkward complications between them and their ally, France. It would, in effect, array the United States on the side of England and against France in a European war. To say nothing of gratitude, it would be poor policy to help to cripple France, when her power was believed to be all that prevented England from reopening her own former struggle with America.

Mr. Short, the American representative at the court of France, was therefore written (August 10th):

" This letter, with the very confidential papers it incloses, will be delivered to you by Mr. Barret, with his own hands. If there be no war between Spain and England, they need be known to yourself alone. But if that war be begun, or whenever it shall begin, we wish you to communicate them to the Marquis de

[1] See Jefferson to Carmichael, August 2d, 1790.

Lafayette, on whose assistance we know we can count in matters which interest both our countries. He and you will consider how far the contents of these papers may be communicated to the Count de Montmorin, and his influence be asked with the court of Madrid. France will be called into the war, as an ally, and not on any pretence of the quarrel being in any degree her own. She may reasonably require then that Spain should do everything which depends on her, to lessen the number of her enemies. She cannot doubt that we shall be of that number, if she does not yield our right to the common use of the Mississippi, and the means of using and securing it. You will observe, we state in general the necessity, not only of our having a port near the mouth of the river (without which we could make no use of the navigation at all) but of its being so well separated from the territories of Spain and her jurisdiction, as not to engender daily disputes and broils between us. It is certain, that if Spain were to retain any jurisdiction over our entre-pôt, her officers would abuse that jurisdiction, and our people would abuse their privileges in it. Both parties must foresee this. and that it will end in war. Hence the necessity of a well-defined separation. Nature has decided what shall be the geography of that in the end, whatever it might be in the beginning, by cutting off from the adjacent countries of Florida and Louisiana, and inclosing between two of its channels a long and narrow slip of land, called the Island of New Orleans. The idea of ceding this, could not be hazarded to Spain, in the first step; it would be too disagreeable at first view; because this island, with its town, constitutes, at present, their principal settlement in that part of their dominions, containing about ten thousand white inhabitants of every age and sex. Reason and events, however, may, by little and little, familiarize them to it. That we have a right to some spot as an entrepôt for our commerce, may be at once affirmed. The expediency, too, may be expressed of so locating it as to cut off the source of future quarrels and wars. A disinterested eye, looking on a map, will remark how conveniently this tongue of land is formed for the purpose; the Iberville and Amit channel offering a good boundary and convenient outlet, on the one side for Florida, and the main channel, an equally good boundary and outlet on the other side for Louisiana; while the slip of land between, is almost entirely morass or sandbank; the whole of it lower than the water of the river, in its highest floods, and only its western margin (which is the highest ground) secured by banks and inhabited. I suppose this idea too much even for the Count de Montmorin at first, and that, therefore, you will find it prudent to urge, and get him to recommend to the Spanish court, only in general terms, 'a port near the mouth of the river, with a circumjacent territory sufficient for its support, well defined, and extra-territorial to Spain,' leaving the idea to future growth."

Here we have the extent of the original and resulting claims on Spain, if she was at war. The gradual and lubricous progress of the Secretary until he reaches that "long and narrow slip of land called the Island of New Orleans," creates a smile; and the climax of cool assurance would seem to be reached, when he so quietly points out the "convenience" of this possession to the United States, and affirms that a "disinterested eye, looking on a map, would remark" *that* fact.

To a pure mind, there is something at first revolting in the smooth, glossy pretences of diplomacy! But not only the world at large, but even the best men who have ever filled diplomatic positions, have held it necessary not only to meet artifice by artifice—on the same principle on which spies and ambuscades are resorted to in war—but to assign reasons, and offer assurances habitually, which nobody is even expected to believe. Perhaps this is their best apology, it being held that to perpetrate a falsehood, there must be an intent to deceive. What nation treats with another without asserting its friendship, or assigning a friendly motive for whatever it has resolved to do short of declaring war? These appear to be the stereotyped "white lies" of diplomatic etiquette, meaning about as much as " your very humble servant" at the bottom of a letter.

We will not enter here at large on the character of the relations existing between Spain and the United States in 1791. Suffice it to say they were far from cordial. Spain had helped France in our Revolution and not us; and she had made this indirect benefit a pretext for exorbitant demands. When those demands were not acquiesced in, she superadded malevolence to Spanish hauteur and obstinacy. The United States, on their part, had made up their minds that owning one bank of the Mississippi for upwards of two thousand miles, they were of natural right entitled to its navigation and of egress to the sea. They were determined eventually to vindicate this right by the sword, if it could not be otherwise obtained. General Washington and every member of his Cabinet concurred in the propriety of this view, and they also as unanimously held that to obtain and enjoy the full benefit of the right, it would be necessary to secure under the jurisdiction and control of our Government a place of entrepôt near the mouth of the river. Jefferson then but expressed the views of Washington and his entire Cabinet. By the President's direction the missive was sent, and sent at that particular time. It was but smoothly saying to Spain, concede these things to us, or we will extort them when we can do so most safely.

Great Britain was not left unapproached on this occasion, though the tone to be used to her was not in any event to be quite so round a one. If the war took place she was to be informed by Mr. Morris (now acting by the President's directions as a sort of informal diplomatic agent in England)—that

the United States " wished to be neutral and would be so, if
they [the British Ministry] would execute the treaty fairly and
attempt no conquests adjoining us." The Secretary added to
Morris :

> "If the war takes place, we would really wish to be quieted on these two points,
> offering in return an honorable neutrality. More than this they are not to expect.
> It will be proper that these ideas be conveyed in delicate and friendly terms; but
> that they be conveyed, if the war takes place.   *   *   *   But in no case,
> need they think of our accepting any equivalent for the posts."

None of our foreign diplomatic representatives were called
upon to act on their instructions. France did not evince the
expected readiness to aid Spain, and the latter avoided a contest with England, by making the required concessions.

In July, Mr. Jefferson submitted to the House of Representatives a plan for establishing uniformity in the coinage, weights,
and measures of the United States. We have not room for
even an analysis of this elaborate and able paper. As a standard of measure, he recommended the pendulum, or, as a substitute (to, in a greater degree, avoid the difficulty in practice of
ascertaining its centre of oscillation) a uniform cylindrical rod
of iron, of such length as in latitude 45° (and in the level of
the ocean and in a cellar, or other place of uniform temperature), should perform its vibrations in small and equal arcs, in
one second of mean time. He had originally fixed upon 38°,
the medium latitude of the United States, but receiving the
Bishop of Autun's proposition in the French National Assembly to take 45°, as being the middle term between the equator
and poles, and therefore one in which the nations of both hemi-
spheres might unite, he adopted it, and went to the labor of
changing all his previous calculations to this basis.

As the standard of weight, he proposed the ancient English
avoirdupois one, that an ounce be of the weight of a cube of
rain water of one tenth of a foot, or that it be the thousandth
part of the weight of a cubic foot of rain water, weighed in the
standard temperature.

He recommended that the divisions of measures of length,
capacity and weight be conformed to the decimal standard.[1]

---

[1] This able report will be found entire in his Works, Congress edition, vol. vii. p. 472.
One or two specimens of his proposed decimal divisions of measures are as follows :
Measure of length.—10 points to make 1 line, 10 lines 1 inch, 10 inches 1 foot, 10 feet
1 decad, 10 decads 1 rood, 10 roods 1 furlong, 10 furlongs 1 mile.
Measure of capacity.—10 metres (a cubic inch each) to make 1 demi-pint, 10 demi

Several other Cabinet opinions were delivered by him before the adjournment of Congress, but they were not on topics which specially solicit our attention.

On the 15th of August, Mr. Jefferson accompanied the President on a visit to Rhode Island, undertaken by the latter to recruit his health, shattered by a recent and dangerous illness, and also to complete his late tour through New England. When he made that tour he did not visit Rhode Island, because it had not then adopted the Constitution.[1] Mr. Jefferson returned to New York on the 21st, and he spent the period between this and the close of the month in preparing the business of his department for a visit home. Among these preparatory labors were two or three Cabinet opinions, one of which deserves notice.

On the 27th of August, the President, still laboring under the very decided impression that the dispute between Great Britain and Spain would lead to war, and that in that event, the former would immediately "undertake a combined operation from Detroit" against the Spanish possessions on the Mississippi, asked the opinions of his Cabinet on the proper attitude to be assumed by the United States on the questions likely to arise from such a movement. In his written interrogatories to the Heads of Departments, the President said :

"The *consequences* of having so formidable and enterprising a people as the British on both our flanks and rear, with their navy in front, as they respect our western settlements which may be seduced thereby, as they regard the security of the Union and its commerce with the West Indies, are too obvious to need enumeration.

"What, then, should be the answer of the Executive of the United States to Lord Dorchester, in case he should apply for permission to march troops through the territory of the said States from Detroit to the Mississippi?

"What notice ought to be taken of the measure, if it should be undertaken without leave, which is the most probable proceeding of the two?"

Mr. Jefferson's answer was communicated the next day after

pints 1 pottle, 10 pottles 1 bushel, 10 bushels 1 quarter, 10 quarters 1 last or double ton.

Weights.—10 mites to make 1 minim, 10 minims 1 carat, 10 carats 1 double-scruple, 10 double-scruples 1 ounce, 10 ounces 1 pound, 10 pounds a stone, 16 stones a kental, 10 kentals a hogshead.

We do not understand why the decimal standard was to be departed from in establishing the capacity of a "kental." We therefore are inclined to suspect that "16" is a misprint for 10. We have no copy of this report lying before us but that in the Congress edition of his writings—a work superabounding in typographical errors.

[1] Marshall, vol. ii. p. 198.

receiving the inquiries. He unhesitatingly expressed the belief
that the United States " ought to make themselves parties in the
general war expected to take place, should this be the only
means of preventing " the Spanish possessions from falling into
the hands of England. He thought, however, that this step
should be deferred as long as possible, for although it was
" more easy to prevent the capture of a place than to retake it,"
" the difference between the two operations of preventing and
retaking, would not be so costly as two, three, or four more
years of war." He thought it would be no violation of neutrality to permit the English troops to pass, provided we held ourselves ready to extend the same leave to Spain. If we refused the
English a passage, and they nevertheless took it, he thought
" we must enter immediately into the war, or pocket an acknowledged insult in the face of the world; and [that] one insult pock-
eted soon produced another." The following was his conclusion:

" There is indeed a middle course, which I should be inclined to prefer; that is,
to avoid giving any answer. They will proceed notwithstanding, but to do this
under our silence, will admit of palliation, and produce apologies, from military
necessity; and will leave us free to pass it over without dishonor, or to make it a
handle of quarrel hereafter, if we should have use for it as such. But, if we are
obliged to give an answer, I think the occasion not such as should induce us to
hazard that answer which might commit us to the war at so early a stage of it;
and therefore that the passage should be permitted.

" If they should pass without having asked leave, I should be for expressing
our dissatisfaction to the British court, and keeping alive an altercation on the
subject, till events should decide whether it is most expedient to accept their
apologies, or profit of the aggression as a cause of war."

The Secretary of the Treasury did not give in his answer
until the 15th of September; and it was a long and labored
paper. Some of his reasoning coincided with that of the Secretary of State. If Lord Dorchester marched across our western territory, without asking permission, he advised remonstrance and
procrastination. If the American post on the Wabash was
forced (and without orders to the contrary, he thought it almost
certain that it would oppose Lord Dorchester's progress), or
should Lord Dorchester march after asking permission and having it refused, he thought there would be no honorable alternative
but war. But he dissented entirely from Mr. Jefferson's proposed " middle course."[1] He thought if the British Com-

---

[1] It is obvious that Hamilton wrote after seeing Mr. Jefferson's opinion, or at least
with a full knowledge of its contents.

mander asked consent, he must be answered, and that though "the acquisition of the Spanish territories bordering on the United States by Great Britain, would be dangerous to us," it would, on the whole, be preferable to taking the consequences of refusing a passage to the British troops. He therefore thought the United States ought not to refuse that passage.[1]

It would be difficult to convey the substance of this remarkable paper without devoting a good deal of space to it, and we must therefore refer the reader to it in the Works of its author. But among its positions, are those, which as clearly now as after the great atrocities of the French Revolution commenced, indicated those biases as between England and France, which distinguished the Ultra-Federal school of politicians.[2]

[1] For the paper entire, see Hamilton's Works, vol. iv. pp. 48–69.
[2] The remarks on this subject, which follow, comprise the reasoning on the subject referred to. It is interesting to note the gradual train of argument which soon led the Federalists to the conclusion that we substantially and practically owed no more to France than to England! Here we have the entering wedge of this doctrine:

"It is not to be forgotten that we received from France, in our late Revolution, essential succor, and from Spain valuable countenance, and some direct aid. It is also to be remembered, that France is the intimate ally of Spain, and there subsists a connection by treaty between the former power and the United States.

"It might thence be alleged that obligations of gratitude towards those powers require that we should run some risk, rather than concur in a thing prejudicial to either of them, and particularly in favor of that very nation against which they assisted us. And the natural impulse of every good heart will second the proposition, till reason has taught it that refinements of this kind are to be indulged with caution in the affairs of nations.

"Gratitude is a word, the very sound of which imposes something like respect. Where there is even an appearance upon which the claim to it can be founded, it can seldom be a pleasing task to dispute that claim. But where a word may become the basis of a political system, affecting the essential interests of the State, it is incumbent upon those who have any concern in the public administration to appreciate its true import and application.

"It is necessary, then, to reflect, however painful the reflection, that gratitude is a duty, a sentiment, which between nations can rarely have any solid foundation. Gratitude is only due to a kindness or service, the predominant object of which is the interest or benefit of the party to whom it is performed. Where the interest or benefit of the party performing is the predominant cause of it, however, there may result a debt; in cases in which there is not an immediate adequate and reciprocal advantage, there can be no room for the sentiment of gratitude. Where there is such an advantage, there is not even a debt. If the motive to the act, instead of being the benefit of the party to whom it is done, should be a compound of the interest of the party doing it, and of detriment to some other, of whom he is the enemy and the rival, there is still less room for so noble and refined a sentiment. This analysis will serve as a test of our true situation, in regard both to France and Spain.

"It is not to be doubted, that the parts which the courts of France and Spain took in our quarrel with Great Britain, is to be attributed, not to an attachment to our independence or liberty, but to a desire of diminishing the power of Great Britain by severing the British Empire. This they considered as an interest of very great magnitude to them. In this their calculations and their passions conspired. For this they united their arms with ours, and encountered the expenses and perils of war. This has been accomplished; the advantages of it are mutual; and so far the account is balanced.

"In the progress of the war * they lent us money, as necessary to its success, and during our inability to pay, they have foreborne to press us for it. The money we ought to exert ourselves to repay with interest, and as well for the loan of it, as for the forbearance to urge the repayment of the sums which have become due, we ought always to be ready to make proportionate acknowledgments, and when opportunities shall offer, returns answerable to the nature of the service.

"Let it be added to this, that the conduct of France in the manner of affording her

* France has made us one loan since the peace.

The President, it appears, also consulted the Vice-President
on this subject. His questions, marked as secret, are to be found
in Mr. Adams's Works, with the replies of the latter (vol viii.
pp. 496–500). Mr. Adams advised neutrality as long as practicable—a distinct refusal to Lord Dorchester if he asked the
permission alluded to—and if he crossed our territory without
leave, or after refusal, that we should send a minister to England expressly to remonstrate against the act, and directed to
withdraw unless England would send a minister in exchange.
He added:

> "As it is, God knows where the men are to be found who are qualified for such
> missions, and would undertake them. By an experience of ten years, which made
> me too unhappy at the time to be ever forgotten, I know that every artifice which
> can deceive, every temptation which can operate on hope or fear, ambition or
> avarice, pride or vanity, the love of society, pleasure, or amusement, will be
> employed to divert and warp them from the true line of their duty and the impar-
> tial honor and interests of their country."

As has been seen, the threatened difficulties between Great
Britain and Spain passed over without calling for any final
determination on the President's questions, and his views cannot
therefore, so far as we are informed, be known with absolute
certainty. But the form of his interrogatories, his recent instructions to Mr. Morris (in England), and many subsequent facts,
leave little doubt on our minds, that he would not have assented
to Hamilton's propositions, or Jefferson's "middle course," but
would in all probability have adopted Mr. Adams's view, and
peremptorily refused under any circumstances to sanction by his
own act a humiliation, to which there would be no excuse for
submitting but downright, and almost avowed, fear.

On the 1st of September, Mr. Jefferson set out for home,
travelling leisurely with Mr. Madison, who occupied a seat in
his carriage. They stopped two days at Mount Vernon, where
the President had already arrived. Mr. Jefferson reached Monticello on the 19th.

We shall, at this point, go back and bring down his unpub-

aid, bore the marks of a liberal policy. She did not endeavor to extort from us, as the
price of it, any disadvantageous or humiliating concessions. In this respect, however,
she may have been influenced by an enlightened view of her own interest. She entitled
herself to our esteem and good will. These dispositions towards her ought to be cher
ished and cultivated; but they are very distinct from a spirit of romantic gratitude, call
ing for sacrifices of our substantial interests, preferences inconsistent with sound policy,
or complaisances incompatible with our safety "

lished correspondence with his daughters, during his recent six months' absence from home. There are some objections to this manner of presenting this class of letters in mass; but except where particular reasons may appear for a different course, we, on the whole, prefer it to scattering them in chronological order, amidst a recital of events with which they have so little connection as with politics and general history.

To Martha Jefferson Randolph.

(Extract.)

New York, *April 4th*, 1790.

I am anxious to hear from you of your health, your occupations, where you are, etc. Do not neglect your music. It will be a companion which will sweeten many hours of life to you. I assure you mine here is triste enough. Having had yourself and dear Poll to live with me so long, to exercise my affections and cheer me in the intervals of business, I feel heavily the separation from you. It is a circumstance of consolation to know that you are happier; and to see a prospect of its continuance in the prudence and even temper both of Mr. Randolph and yourself. Your new condition will call for abundance of little sacrifices. But they will be greatly overpaid by the measure of affection they secure to you. The happiness of your life depends now on the continuing to please a single person. To this all other objects must be secondary; even your love for me were it possible that that could ever be an obstacle. But this it never can be. Neither of you can ever have a more faithful friend than myself, nor one on whom you can count for more sacrifices. My own is become a secondary object to the happiness of you both. Cherish, then, for me, my dear child, the affection of your husband, and continue to love me as you have done, and to render my life a blessing by the prospect it may hold up to me of seeing you happy. Kiss Maria for me if she is with you, and present me cordially to Mr. Randolph: assuring yourself of the constant and unchangeable love of

Yours affectionately.

To Maria Jefferson.[1]

New York, *Apr. 11th*, 1790.

Where are you, my dear Maria? how do you do? how are you occupied? Write me a letter by the first post, and answer me all these questions. Tell me whether you see the sun rise every day? how many pages a day your read in Don Quixote? how far you are advanced in him? whether you repeat a grammer lesson every day? what else you read? how many hours a day you sew? whether you have an opportunity of continuing your music? whether you know how to make a pudding yet, to cut out a beefsteak, to sow spinach? or to set a hen? Be good, my dear, as I have always found you; never be angry with anybody, nor speak harm of them; try to let everybody's faults be forgotten, as you would wish yours to be; take more pleasure in giving what is best to another than in having it yourself, and then all the world will love you, and I more than all the world. If your sister is with you, kiss her and tell her how much I love her also, and present my

---

[1] Now lacking between three and four months of being twelve years of age.

affections to Mr. Randolph. Love your aunt and uncle and be dutiful and obliging to them for all their kindness to you. What would you do without them and with such a vagrant for a father? Say to both of them a thousand affectionate things for me; and adieu, my dear Maria.

TH. JEFFERSON.

To MARTHA JEFFERSON RANDOLPH.

(Extract.)

NEW YORK, Apr. 26th, 1790.

I write regularly once a week to Mr. Randolph, yourself, or Polly, in hopes it may induce a letter from one of you every week also. If each would answer by the first post my letter to them, I should receive it within the three weeks so as to keep up a regular correspondence with each.   *   *   *   *

I long to hear how you pass your time. I think both Mr. Randolph and yourself will suffer with ennui at Richmond. Interesting occupations are essential to happiness. Indeed the whole art of being happy consists in the art of finding employment. I know none so interesting, and which crowd upon us so much as those of a domestic nature. I look forward, therefore, to your commencing housekeepers in your own farm, with some anxiety. Till then you will not know how to fill up your time, and your weariness of the things around you will assume the form of a weariness of one another. I hope Mr. Randolph's idea of settling near Monticello will gain strength; and that no other settlement will, in the meantime, be fixed on. I wish some expedient may be devised for settling him at Edgehill. No circumstance ever made me feel so strongly the thralldom of Mr. Wayles's debt. Were I liberated from that, I should not fear but that Colonel Randolph and myself, by making it a joint contribution, could effect the fixing you there, without interfering with what he otherwise proposes to give Mr. Randolph. I shall hope when I return to Virginia in the fall, that some means may be found of effecting all our wishes.[1]

To MARIA JEFFERSON, EPPINGTON.

NEW YORK, May 2d, 1790.

MY DEAR MARIA:

I wrote to you three weeks ago, and have not yet received an answer. I hope, however, that one is on the way, and that I shall receive it by the first post I think it very long to have been absent from Virginia two months, and not to have received a line from yourself, your sister, or Mr. Randolph, and I am very uneasy at it. As I write once a week to one or the other of you in turn, if you would answer my letter the day or the day after you receive it, it would always come to my hand before I write the next to you. We had two days of snow about the beginning of last week. Let me know if it snowed where you are. I send you some prints of a new kind for your amusement. I send several to enable you to be generous to your friends. I want much to hear how you employ yourself.

---

[1] It will be seen by this that Mr. Randolph, sen., had not yet made a disposition of his property among his children—but this in no wise conflicts with what we have already said of his son's legitimate expectations on that head.

Present my best affections to your uncle, aunt, and cousins,[1] if you are with them, or to Mr. Randolph and your sister, if with them; be assured of my tender love to you, and continue yours to

Your affectionate,
TH. JEFFERSON.

—————

To MARIA JEFFERSON, EPPINGTON.

NEW YORK, May 28d, 1790.

MY DEAR MARIA:

I was glad to receive your letter of April 25th, because I had been near two months without hearing from any of you. I hope you will now always write immediately on receiving a letter from me. Your last told me what you were not doing: that you were not reading Don Quixote, not applying to your music. I hope your next will tell me what you are doing. Tell your uncle that the President, after having been so ill as at one time to be thought dying, is now quite recovered. I have been these three weeks confined by a periodical headache. It has been the most moderate I ever had: but it has not yet left me. Present my best affections to your uncle and aunt. Tell the latter I shall never have thanks enough for her kindness to you, and that you will repay her in love and duty. Adieu, my dear Maria.

Yours affectionately,
TH. JEFFERSON.

—————

To MARIA JEFFERSON, EPPINGTON.

NEW YORK, June 18th, 1790.

MY DEAR MARIA:

I have received your letter of May 23d, which was in answer to mine of May 2d, but I wrote you also on the 23d of May, so that you still owe me an answer to that, which I hope is now on the road. In matters of correspondence as well as of money, you must never be in debt. I am much pleased with the account you give me of your occupations, and the making the pudding is as good an article of them as any. When I come to Virginia I shall insist on eating a pudding of your own making, as well as on trying other specimens of your skill. You must make the most of your time while you are with so good an aunt who can learn you everything. We had not peas nor strawberries here till the 8th day of this month. On the same day I heard the first whip-poor-will whistle. Swallows and martins appeared here on the 21st of April. When did they appear with you? and when had you peas, strawberries, and whip-poor-wills in Virginia? Take notice hereafter whether the whip-poor-wills always come with the strawberries and peas. Send me a copy of the maxims I gave you, also a list of the books I promised you. I have had a long touch of my periodical headache, but a very moderate one. It has not quite left me yet. Adieu, my dear; love your uncle, aunt, and cousins, and me more than all. •

Yours affectionately,
TH. JEFFERSON.

—————

[1] That is, Francis Eppes, of Eppington, and his family.

To Maria Jefferson, Eppington.

New York, *July 4th,* 1790.

I have written you, my dear Maria, four letters since I have been here, and I have received from you only two. You owe me two, then, and the present will make three. This is a kind of debt I will not give up. You may ask how I will help myself? By petitioning your aunt, as soon as you receive a letter, to make you go without your dinner till you have answered it. How goes on the Spanish? how many chickens have you raised this summer? Send me a list of the books I have promised you at different times. Tell me what sort of weather you have had, what sort of crops are likely to be made, how your uncle and aunt and the family do, and how you do yourself. I shall see you in September for a short time. Adieu, my dear Poll.

> Yours affectionately,
> TH. JEFFERSON.

To Martha Jefferson Randolph.

New York, *July 17th,* 1790.

My dear Patsy:

I received two days ago yours of July 2d, with Mr. Randolph's of July 3d. Mine of the 11th to Mr. Randolph, will have informed you that I expect to set out from hence for Monticello about the 1st of September. As this depends on the adjournment of Congress, and they begin to be impatient, it is more probable that I may set out sooner than later. However, my letters will keep you better informed as the time approaches.

Col. Randolph's marriage was to be expected. All his amusements depending on society, he cannot live alone. The settlement spoken of may be liable to objections in point of prudence and justice. However, I hope it will not be the cause of any diminution of affection between him and Mr. Randolph and yourself. That cannot remedy the evil, and may make it a great deal worse. Besides your interests, which might be injured by a misunderstanding, be assured that your happiness would be infinitely affected. It would be a canker-worm corroding eternally on your minds. Therefore, my dear child, redouble your assiduities to keep the affections of Col. Randolph and his lady (if he is to have one) in proportion as the difficulties increase. He is an excellent good man, to whose temper nothing can be objected, but too much facility, too much milk. Avail yourself of this softness, then, to obtain his attachment. If the lady has anything difficult in her dispositions, avoid what is rough, and attach her good qualities to you. Consider what are otherwise as a bad stop in your harpsichord, and do not touch on it, but make yourself happy with the good ones. Every human being, my dear, must thus be viewed, according to what it is good for; for none of us, no not one, is perfect; and were we to love none who had imperfections, this world would be a desert for our love. All we can do is to make the best of our friends, love and cherish what is good in them, and keep out of the way of what is bad; but no more think of rejecting them, than of throwing away a piece of music for a flat passage or two. Your situation will require peculiar attentions and respects to both parties. Let no proof be too much for either your patience or acquiescence. Be you, my dear, the link of love, union and peace for the whole family. The world will give you the more credit for it, in proportion to the difficulty of the task, and your own happiness will be the greater as you perceive that you promote that of others. Former acquaintance and equality of age will render it the easier for you to cultivate and gain the love of the lady. The mother, too, becomes a very necessary object of attentions.

This marriage renders it doubtful with me whether it will be better to direct our overtures to Col. R. or Mr. H. for a farm for Mr. Randolph. Mr. H. has a good tract of land on the other side of Edgehill, and it may not be unadvisable to begin by buying out a dangerous neighbor. I wish Mr. Randolph could have him sounded to see if he will sell, and at what price; but sounded through such a channel as would excite no suspicion that it comes from Mr. Randolph or myself. Col. Monroe would be a good and unsuspected hand, as he once thought of buying the same lands. Adieu, my dear child. Present my warm attachment to Mr. Randolph.[1]

Yours affectionately,

TH. JEFFERSON.

———

To MARTHA JEFFERSON RANDOLPH.

(Extract.)

NEW YORK, August 8, 1790.

Congress being certainly to rise the day after to-morrow, I can now, my dear Patsy, be more certain of the time at which I can be at Monticello, and which, I think, will be from the 8th to the 15th of September: more likely to be sooner than later. I shall leave this about a fortnight hence, but must stay some days to have arrangements taken for my future residence in Philadelphia. I hope to be able to pass a month at least with you at Monticello. I am in hopes Mr. Randolph will take dear Poll in his pocket. Tell him I have sent him the model of the mould-board[2] by Mr. David Randolph, who left this place yesterday.

Mr. Jefferson on his return to Monticello had found his entire family assembled under its roof. His health, as well as the calls of his long neglected private business, required that his stay be of some continuance. He remained therefore among the delights of home, daily acquiring more health and elasticity of spirits, until the 8th of November, when he commenced his return. Mr. Madison again occupied a seat in his carriage, and they again visited Mount Vernon, where the President yet remained.

---

[1] The reader will understand that by "Mr. Randolph," Mr. Jefferson alludes to his son-in-law; by "Col. Randolph," to his son-in-law's father. The marriage which is made the topic of this letter took place. Col. Randolph married a lady about the age of his daughter-in-law, and consequences ensued which the further progress of our narrative will require us to mention. But, owing to the discretion, dignity, and affectionate deportment of the younger Mrs. Randolph (Martha Jefferson), no breach, as we understand it, ever occurred between the families, though the younger Randolph never had it "objected" to his temper that it had "too much facility, too much milk," where his rights or feelings were invaded. Martha Jefferson acted on her father's advice to make herself the "link of love, union and peace for the whole family."

[2] This was the mould-board "of least resistance," the form for which he proposed to himself as a physico-mathematical problem. In acknowledgment of this service to agricultural science, a gold medal was awarded him by the *Société d'agriculture de la Seine*. (Note by one of Mr. Jefferson's family.)

Mr. Jefferson's first Cabinet paper of importance, after resuming his duties, was a "report" made to the President, December 15th, on the facts disclosed by Mr. Morris's dispatches from England. The President appears to have referred the correspondence to the Secretary of State alone.[1] The tenor of Mr. Morris's information was—1. That Great Britain was determined not to surrender the American posts in any event; 2. that as to indemnification for the negroes carried off contrary to the Treaty of Peace, the precautions taken to conceal the number had been so successful that it could not, even approximately, be made to appear; 3. that the British Government equivocated on every proposal for a treaty of commerce, and would only relax its regulations on the United States entering also into a treaty of alliance; 4. that the British Secretary of State for Foreign Affairs was disposed to exchange a minister, but that he met with an opposition in his Cabinet, which rendered the issue very uncertain.[2]

The substance of Mr. Jefferson's recommendations, under this state of affairs, is comprised in the following extracts from his report:

"The Secretary of State is of opinion that Mr. Morris's letters remove any doubts which might have been entertained as to the intentions and dispositions of the British Cabinet.

"That it would be dishonorable to the United States, useless and even injurious, to renew the propositions for a treaty of commerce, or for the exchange of a minister; and that these subjects should now remain dormant, till they shall be brought forward earnestly by them.

"That the demands of the posts, and of indemnification for the negroes, should not be again made till we are in readiness to do ourselves the justice which may be refused.

"That Mr. Morris should be informed that he has fulfilled the object of his agency to the satisfaction of the President, inasmuch as he has enabled him to judge of the real views of the British Cabinet, and that it is his pleasure that the matters committed to him be left in the situation in which the letter shall find them."

This advice was promptly acted upon, and Mr. Morris's agency discontinued.

[1] This is only an inference, but we think there is little doubt of its accuracy. Cabinet opinions were uniformly, we believe, headed by Mr. Jefferson as "Opinions, etc.," but when he was separately asked for statements and opinions in regard to matters coming under his particular department, he entitled them "Reports." The paper of Dec. 15th is headed as a report. We find no trace of this subject among Hamilton's published Cabinet opinions, an omission we should not expect, considering the importance of the topic, if he had been consulted.

[2] See Jefferson's Report, etc., in his Works, Congress edition, vol. vii. pp. 517-519.

Not long after the opening of Congress (in December) the Secretary of the Treasury renewed his recommendation of an additional impost on foreign distilled spirits, and an excise on domestic ones, to meet the calls on the treasury created by the Assumption. The bill introduced into Congress to carry out his views was warmly resisted by the class of members which was accustomed to act against the plans of this officer.

An incipient opposition was already forming. Resolutions strongly reprobating the Assumption Bill had passed the Legislatures of three of the States. The Virginia House of Delegates had, by a vote of seventy-five to fifty-two, declared it "repugnant to the Constitution of the United States." So much of the Funding Bill as prevented the United States from redeeming at any time, any portion of the Continental debt, was, by the same body, pronounced "dangerous to the rights and subversive to the interests of the people." This restriction was regarded as the first step towards creating a permanent national debt. The North Carolina Legislature refused to take an oath to support the Constitution of the United States. The Pennsylvania Legislature passed resolutions against the Excise Bill. The Virginia, Pennsylvania, New York, North and South Carolina Legislatures recommended that the United States Senate abandon its practice of sitting with closed doors, so that the public should understand the reasons of its proceedings, and be able to hold its members to a political accountability.

Notwithstanding these growing indications of public dissatisfaction, the Impost and Excise Bill (after an attempt to strike out the excise was voted down by more than two to one) was pressed through the House by the full strength of what, in England, would be termed the "Treasury benches." In the sequel, this proved the cockatrice's egg which hatched sedition, and what, at the time, received the name of "civil war."

Singularly enough, as would seem at first view, Mr. Madison supported this Treasury measure. He saw the country driven to raise money to meet its positive engagements (though he had opposed making those engagements), and he was given the alternative of voting for no other practicable expedient for that purpose. Mr. Madison, too, it is obvious, fell into anything like a regular opposition to the Government (or one of its departments) with exceeding reluctance. He belonged to neither of the extreme schools in politics—was, like the President, rather a middle man both by principle and the natural temper of his mind. Indeed, we believe no two members, at the close of the federal Convention, would have more closely coincided in their interpretation of the Constitution, and of the duty of those who would be called upon to administer it, than Washington and Madison. The latter began, at once, when the new government was put in motion, to dissent from the constitutional interpretations of Hamilton. His profound respect and affection for the President, and earnest desire to sustain his government—to say nothing of his unquestionable friendship for Hamilton—led him never to oppose "ministerial measures" where he felt that he could avoid it; and when he did oppose them, his conduct and language were marked with great moderation. He rarely advocated the extreme antagonistic view. Instead of aiming to create an opposition, he faithfully labored to reconcile the extremes, and to bring them on some middle and defensible ground of compromise. In these respects, he was fairly emulated by a New England leader, who, when the regular organization of parties took place, fell to the other side—but who, at heart, never nursed any of the consolidating or "propping" schemes of his associates. We allude to Elbridge Gerry of Massachusetts.

The Secretary of the Treasury also warmly renewed his recommendation for the establishment of a United States Bank. A bill based on these views passed the Senate January 20th (1791). In the House of Representatives, it encountered a determined opposition. A part of this opposition was to the utility or policy of such an institution, independently of the question of its constitutionality; and a part, to its constitutionality. Madison, Giles of Virginia, Jackson of Georgia, and other prominent chiefs of the anti-consolidation school, took the floor against it. Ames, Sedgwick, Smith of South Carolina, Sherman, Boudinot, and even Gerry, gave it their support. It finally prevailed by a vote of thirty-nine to twenty.

Before giving his sanction to this important measure, the President consulted his Cabinet. He first took the opinion of the Attorney-General, as the law adviser of the Executive, and Randolph pronounced the charter of the institution unconstitutional. The Secretary of State was then applied to, and his views coincided with those of the Attorney-General. Lastly, the Secretary of the Treasury was called upon to defend his project, and the opinions of the two preceding officers were submitted to his inspection.[1]

Mr. Jefferson's opinion, like most of those written by him merely for Cabinet or Executive deliberations, was brief; consisting rather of heads of arguments, than elaborated arguments, like those which are prepared for a legislative or popular body. His opinion covers about six printed octavo pages—Hamilton's thirty-four. No synopsis will be given here of these papers, the arguments of which have since become thoroughly hackneyed, by means of newspapers and Congressional speeches; and they can always be found entire by referring to the works of their respective authors. The President signed the Bank Bill, but not without misgivings and deep reluctance. But as Hamilton was the financial officer of the Government, and made the bank almost an indispensable portion of his system, the President finally yielded to his views.

It will be found a pretty uniform habit of the first President, on a question pertaining especially to the affairs of one of the Government departments, that he made it a point to ultimately defer to the opinions of the head of that department— particularly where the latter had deeply staked his policy, his reputation, or his feelings on the issue.

Herein, we think, we discover the reason, not at first obvious, why the President, so nearly converting his Cabinet into a Directory on a class of questions, on others of equal importance and as purely political, consulted but one head of department. In the first case, the questions were general; in the last, departmental. No Cabinet consultation was called in respect to the Assumption or Excise Bills. They were held to fall particularly within the scope of the Treasury bureau. No consultation was called to settle the line of action in regard to Mr. Morris's last dispatches. That appertained to the State department. Yet the Bank, although a financial measure, was too general in its bearings, and too important, perhaps, to be left to the discretion or settled on the advice of a single Secretary. The answer to

---

[1] Washington's letter to Hamilton, on this occasion, will be found in the Works of the former, vol. iv. p. 103. It is not given in Sparks's Washington. Knox does not appear to have been consulted.

Lord Dorchester presents a similar instance of a question taken from the exclusive coaction of the State department.

We cannot say that the rule we have attempted to deduce from the facts, was observed in every instance. It would, in truth, be impossible to say precisely what classification that rule, rigorously carried out, would have given to many questions; whether it would have made them Cabinet or departmental questions. There were surrounding facts or incidents in many cases, which cannot now be accurately known. Our opinion is that President Washington aimed to act on such a general rule, reserving to himself, however, the exercise of his own discretion, in view of all the facts, in making the classification. This theory affords a key to a harmonious and consistent line of action, and establishes the first President's claims to system, consistency, and impartiality in his Cabinet measures, without any drafts on a venerating credulity.

On the subject of President Washington's feelings on the Bank Bill, we find the following entry in Mr. Trist's memoranda:

MONTPELLIER, *Friday, May 25th*, 1827.

*   *   *   *   *   *   *   *   *

Mr. Madison: "General Washington signed Jay's treaty, but he did not at all like it. He also signed the Bank. But he was *very* near not doing so; and if he had refused, it would, in my opinion, have produced a crisis." "I will mention to you a circumstance which I have never imparted, except in strict confidence. You know by the Constitution, ten days are allowed for the President's veto to come in. If it does not appear within that time, the bill becomes a law. I was conversing with a distinguished member of the Federal party, who observed that according to his computation the time was running out, or indeed *was run* out; when just at this moment, Lear [1] came in with the President's sanction. *I am satisfied that had it been his veto, there would have been an effort to nullify it, and they would have arrayed themselves in a hostile attitude.*" "Between the two parties, General Washington had a most difficult course to steer."

*   *   *   *   *   *

"The foregoing is written immediately after the conversation, which has not lasted half an hour. Mr. Madison having stepped out, and I taking advantage of this interruption to retire to my room and commit the substance to paper. The very words I have retained, as near as I could. In many instances (where I have run a line over the words [2]) I have done this exactly."

The Secretary of State had watched the struggle on the Bank question with painful solicitude. To his old friend George Mason—that great and pure republican statesman whose jea

---

[1] President Washington's private Secretary.   [2] We have italicized these words.

lousy of consolidation had even led him to oppose the adoption of the federal Constitution by Virginia—he wrote, February 4th, 1791:

"What is said in our country of the fiscal arrangements now going on? I really fear their effect when I consider the present temper of the Southern States. Whether these measures be right or wrong abstractedly, more attention should be paid to the general opinion. However, all will pass—the Excise will pass—the Bank will pass. The only corrective of what is corrupt in our present form of government, will be the augmentation of the numbers in the lower House, so as to get a more agricultural representation, which may put that interest above that of the stock-jobbers."

The following extract from the same letter shows, doubtless, that growing political divisions and alienations were not confined to Congress:

"I look with great anxiety for the firm establishment of the new government in France, being perfectly convinced that if it takes place there, it will spread sooner or later all over Europe. On the contrary, a check there would retard the revival of liberty in other countries. I consider the establishment and success of their government as necessary to stay up our own, and to prevent it from falling back to that kind of a half-way house, the English Constitution. It cannot be denied that we have among us a sect who believe that to contain whatever is perfect in human institutions; that the members of this sect have, many of them, names and offices which stand high in the estimation of our countrymen. I still rely that the great mass of our community is untainted with these heresies, as is its head. On this I build my hope that we have not labored in vain, and that our experiment will still prove that men can be governed by reason."

Among those whose "names and offices stood high," it would be impossible to imagine that the Secretary of the Treasury, and probably Vice-President Adams, were not particularly alluded to—or that the "untainted head," did not mean President Washington. The language of this letter is that of a man whose position demanded some reserve, even though writing for confidential and prudent eyes; but it betrays the writer's fixed impression that something besides casual differences already divided the parties in the Cabinet and in Congress—in a word, that there already existed in both these bodies, a well-defined and well-understood party which idolized the British Constitution and was energetically seeking to "prop" (to use Hamilton's word) our own Constitution into a counterpart of it.

Without expressly saying so, Mr. Jefferson would seem to lead to the inference, in the introduction to his Ana, that he

considered the Bank question as that on which parties finally
formed into avowed and permanent organization—though it is
certain that the body of the "Republicans" continued long
afterwards to vote for Government measures, when not of a particular class. In other words, the opposition was to the schemes
of the Treasury Department—of Colonel Hamilton—not to the
Government as a whole, or to the President. The following is
Mr. Jefferson's history of the events of that period, immediately
after giving the account of the Funding and Assumption schemes,
already copied:

"Still the machine was not complete. The effect of the Funding system, and of
the Assumption, would be temporary; it would be lost with the loss of the individual members whom it has enriched, and some engine of influence more permanent must be contrived, while these myrmidons were yet in place to carry it
through all opposition. This engine was the Bank of the United States. All that
history is known, so I shall say nothing about it. While the Government remained
at Philadelphia, a selection of members of both Houses were constantly kept as
directors, who, on every question interesting to that institution, or to the views of
the Federal head, voted at the will of that head; and, together with the stock-
holding members, could always make the Federal vote that of the majority. By
this combination, legislative expositions were given to the Constitution, and all the
administrative laws were shaped on the model of England, and so passed. And
from this influence we were not relieved, until the removal from the precincts of the
Bank, to Washington.

"Here, then, was the real ground of the opposition which was made to the
course of administration. Its object was to preserve the legislature pure and
independent of the executive, to restrain the administration to republican forms
and principles, and not permit the Constitution to be construed into a monarchy, and
to be warped, in practice, into all the principles and pollutions of their favorite
English model. Nor was this an opposition to General Washington. He was true
to the republican charge confided to him; and has solemnly and repeatedly protested to me, in our conversations, that he would lose the last drop of his blood in
support of it; and he did this the oftener and with the more earnestness, because
he knew my suspicions of Hamilton's designs against it, and wished to quiet them.
For he was not aware of the drift, or of the effect of Hamilton's schemes. Unversed
in financial projects and calculations and budgets, his approbation of them was bottomed on his confidence in the man.

"But Hamilton was not only a monarchist, but for a monarchy bottomed
on corruption. In proof of this, I will relate an anecdote, for the truth of
which I attest the God who made me. Before the President set out on his
Southern tour in April, 1791, he addressed a letter of the fourth of that month
from Mount Vernon, to the Secretaries of State, Treasury, and War, desiring that
if any serious and important cases should arise during his absence, they should
consult and act on them. And he requested that the Vice-President should also be
consulted. This was the only occasion on which that officer was ever requested to
take part in a Cabinet question. Some occasion for consultation arising, I invited

those gentlemen (and the Attorney-General as well as I remember) to dine with me, in order to confer on the subject. After the cloth was removed, and our question agreed and dismissed, conversation began on other matters, and, by some circumstance, was led to the British Constitution, on which Mr. Adams observed: 'Purge that Constitution of its corruption, and give to its popular branch equality of representation, and it would be the most perfect Constitution ever devised by the wit of man.' Hamilton paused and said: 'Purge it of its corruption, and give to its popular branch equality of representation, and it would become an *impracticable* government: as it stands at present, with all its supposed defects, it is the most perfect government which ever existed.' And this was assuredly the exact line which separated the political creeds of these two gentlemen. The one was for two hereditary branches and an honest elective one: the other, for an hereditary King, with a House of Lords and Commons corrupted to his will, and standing between him and the people."

And here, in continuation, was Jefferson's matured conclusion (in 1818) of the political character of these two rivals and opponents, written when one of them had long been removed by death, and when he was on the most cordial terms of personal friendship with the other:

"Hamilton was, indeed, a singular character. Of acute understanding, disinterested, honest, and honorable in all private transactions, amiable in society, and duly valuing virtue in private life, yet so bewitched and perverted by the British example, as to be under thorough conviction that corruption was essential to the government of a nation. Mr. Adams had originally been a Republican. The glare of royalty and nobility, during his mission to England, had made him believe their fascination a necessary ingredient in government; and Shay's rebellion, not sufficiently understood where he then was, seemed to prove that the absence of want and oppression, was not a sufficient guarantee of order. His book on the American Constitutions having made known his political bias, he was taken up by the monarchical Federalists in his absence, and on his return to the United States, he was by them made to believe that the general disposition of our citizens was favorable to monarchy. He here wrote his Davila, as a supplement to a former work, and his election to the presidency confirmed him in his errors."

The different political theories and aims of the Secretary of State and of the Secretary of the Treasury, as soon as they were mutually understood, necessarily destroyed their political confidence in each other. Their friendly personal relations, however, survived for a period. Their sense of what was due to themselves, and to the President, led to circumspection in personal deportment. But even this state of things was not likely to last long. Neither had a spark of tolerance for the cardinal political doctrines of the other. Each probably saw in the other the strongest and most influential champion of a detested faith.

Jefferson was modest and unofficious, even to the point of retiringness, in manner[1]—had not a trace of dogmatism in his way of stating or defending a proposition—said very little in discussion—yielded quietly when outvoted—never intermeddled uninvited in the affairs of another department—and never, even in his own, assumed any airs or tone of leadership over colleagues. Yet, under this modest decorum, he was quite as independent as any of his colleagues in forming an opinion, and when his opinion was deliberately formed, it was as firm as adamant. If it was never advanced aggressively—after being voted down a hundred times in succession, it presented precisely the same degree of resistance as at first.

Hamilton probably never directly transcended the manners which gentlemen tolerate from each other in the heat of discussion. He possessed, however, not only that iron pertinacity ascribed to him by Morris both in regard to the substance and letter of his plans, but his natural imperiousness of temper fostered by rapid success and unceasing adulation, exhibited itself very plainly in his manners and conduct. He advanced his opinions dictatorially. When doubtful of success, he argued his side of the question in the President's Cabinet at the length, and with the vehemence of a jury lawyer. He did not scruple to intermeddle with even the direct conduct of important and delicate affairs belonging to the departments of colleagues, and, as we shall have occasion to see, he did this without their solicitation, and in some instances undoubtedly without their supposed knowledge. He obviously aimed at a sort of premiership in the Cabinet—to guide its general policy. To secure this, he trusted to his influence with the President, and to the very important weight he secured in public affairs by carrying along with his views majorities in the early Congresses. Congress was deeply influenced by the fact that Hamilton's views were supposed to represent the spontaneous ones of the Executive; and the support which Congress gave those views, appeared to represent the popular will, and consequently reacted on the Executive.

Jefferson was never tenacious in respect to forms of official etiquette, and had the least possible degree of the jealousy of official or personal consequence. We shall not deny that he

---

[1] Hamilton himself so described him in the first attacks he made on him in the newspapers, as we shall hereafter see.

was intolerant towards ideas, but towards persons he was peculiarly tolerant—towards them his temper was always well regulated and placable. We shall abundantly show, as the history of his life progresses, that he never had a foe or a persecutor so bitter, that he was not ready to drop the personal quarrel on the first overture to conciliation. In Hamilton's case, there is no doubt that for some time before their open breach, he felt his assumption and resented his encroachments. But he was not unwise enough to let vanity or petulance precipitate the explosion. He waited calmly and patiently for the development of events, shunning any issue but an issue of principle.

Another circumstance protracted the seeming calm in the Cabinet. While Hamilton mixed constantly and actively in the affairs of Congress, which his departmental duties at this period brought him perhaps necessarily considerably more in contact with—while he, without concealment, marshalled and led a party—Jefferson, partly from taste, and partly from circumstances, scarcely interfered in any business before Congress, and none in active party arrangements. He never, at any period of his life, possessed an inclination to bustle about in caucuses—to act either as captain or drill-sergeant in the disciplinary labors of partisanship. In this respect he resembled the Republican leader in Congress, Mr. Madison. Besides, as Hamilton's schemes had, after their presentation to Congress, the ostensible sanction of the President, no other Cabinet officer could feel himself at liberty to engage in avowed or active opposition to them outside of the Cabinet. The two secretaries, therefore, were not brought into collision on this theatre.

For a period, Hamilton's political star was to shine broadly and luminously in the ascendant. He had the support of Congress, partly from the important reason already named, and partly because his schemes agreed with the real views, or appealed to the interests of a large number of that body. He had a devoted follower in every man enriched by the Funding Bill, the Assumption, the Bank, etc., or hoping to be enriched by any treasury scheme in future. The mercantile interest was on his side, especially the British merchants, because they believed that his measures had restored public credit, furnished a reliable circulating medium, and again given life to the currents of trade and commerce. The Consolidationists of every grade, from pure

Monarchists down to anti-State-right Republicans (believers in one great consolidated republic), rallied about him as a chief who was rapidly "propping" the Constitution to a substantial concurrence with their views. Those weak men, with unsettled political ideas, whose chief anxiety is to be on the winning side, were of course now on the side of Hamilton. And, finally, there was no inconsiderable class wholly separate from all of these, disinterested and intelligent men and true republicans in the constitutional sense of the term, who, for a considerable period, yet clung to him, because they believed in so doing they were clinging to the individual plans and wishes of the revered President.

Hamilton's last scheme, the bank, was, in the eye of his followers, even more brilliantly successful than any of its predecessors. Before the close of 1791 its scrip had risen to nearly one hundred per cent. above par, and such was the tendency to further inflation, and such the madness that ruled the hour, that Hamilton himself became alarmed, and besought his friends to pause and not convert the whole thing into a "bubble," and make final shipwreck of their "purses" and "reputations."[1] Prices rose so high, and public and private credit rose so high, that the country, yesterday miserably depressed in pecuniary affairs, suddenly overflowed with wealth. The transcendent genius of one man (such was the cry) turned all he touched into gold, so that the dreams of the alchemists stood visibly realized. What varied attainments and great qualities centered in that man! His genius to plan did not exceed his practical power to execute. He grasped the general and the detail, theory and fact, with the same undeviating accuracy. His nerve was equal to his foresight. The tide of deification even set backwards. The eagle eye and the indomitable will flashing along the ranks of war, had been so conspicuous that but one fame had eclipsed his, and the genuine Hamiltonians whispered, *sotto voce*, that the warlike fame of one had eclipsed his, only by borrowing from it. And now that same eagle eye was flashing along and through all the elements of national prosperity that the statistician could array for its inspection—quickly grouping their ordinary rules of action into theories, and on these founding

---

[1] See his letter to King of August 7, 1791; to Duer, August 17th, etc. Hamilton's Works vol. v. pp. 476, 478, *et passim.*

stupendous projects of financial improvement. Wealth must always have an idol, and it now found a brilliant one in Hamilton. Nor was this all. A great party, rich in intellect and Revolutionary renown, had found at once its idol, its champion, its ruler.

Jefferson, as well as Madison, was in the habit of averring, that had a split taken place between Washington and Hamilton, on the financial schemes of the latter, the thorough Federalists would have followed Hamilton! It would be difficult, in truth, to conjecture where weaker and more obsequious men would stop, when Fisher Ames was in the habit of expressing himself as in the following letter to Hamilton (July 31, 1791). He was speaking of the effects of the United States Bank:

"'People' here [Boston] are full of exaltation and gratitude. They know who merits the praise of it, and they are not loth to bestow it.   *   *   * The success of the Government of the United States, and especially of the measures proceeding from your department, has astonished the multitude; and while it has shut the mouths, it has stung the envious hearts of the State leaders."

Hints of the avowed partisan uses to which Hamilton's financial projects were put, gleam clearly enough through the covering of conventional phrases, in the correspondences of the day. We take it for granted that in the following extract from the same letter of Ames to Hamilton, no one will understand the word "Union" to mean anything more or less than the general or federal Government:

"The Bank and the United States Government at this moment possess more popularity than any institution or government can maintain for a long time. Perhaps no act of power can be done to destroy the State banks, but if they are willing to become interested, I mean the State stockholders, and to establish sub banks, so as to absorb the funds and contract the business of the local banks, why should any measures be adopted to support the local banks to the prejudice of my hypothesis? or why should cold water be thrown upon the plan of sub-banks?
   *   *   *   *   *
"All the influence of the moneyed men ought to be wrapped up in the Union, and in one bank. The State banks may become the favorites of the States. They, the latter, will be pressed to emulate the example of the Union, and to show their sovereignty by a parade of institutions, like those of the nation." [1]

Hamilton's correspondence at this period with prominent men of nearly every class—politicians, bankers, stock-jobbers,

[1] For the letter entire, see Hamilton's Works, vol. v. p. 473.

speculators of various species, etc.—in one respect uniformly speaks the same language. He and his correspondents seem under the undoubting impression that he is the maker and the dispenser; that in financial affairs, there is no other Cabinet, or President, or person, entitled to do any more than hear and obey, or, if such be their good luck, to gratefully receive. And both he and his correspondents seem equally under the impression that the control of banks, and stock-markets, and monetary affairs generally, is quite as much within the legitimate province of government—nay, is as much an absolute duty of government, as is the preservation of the peace, or the administration of criminal justice!

We have seen that Jefferson expressly exonerates Hamilton from the charge of personal corruption—of enriching himself by his public schemes—while he was shaking Fortunatus's cap into the laps of others. We suppose the same remark applies to many other Federal leaders—perhaps to a decided majority of the really conspicuous and able ones. While Ames sings pœans in praise of the Treasury department, and talks of appealing to the venality of the " moneyed men," we suppose him to have been himself entirely above being approached by gold. It is even probable that these men would have preferred to rule through higher and better motives. But it was their misfortune to believe that it was impracticable.

Jefferson's phrase, that "Hamilton was not only a monarchist, but for a monarchy bottomed on corruption," has been considered a peculiarly harsh one; and some have professed to be unable to see how this can be reconciled with the idea of his personal integrity. In the abstract, the reconciliation would indeed be a puzzling one. But the world has agreed to consider the two things compatible. It is notorious that a direct appeal to venality has been practised as a part of the undenied, if not unconcealed, machinery of the British Constitution, from the first existence of that Constitution. Without going back to those days of open and shameless profligacy which preceded the reign of William and Mary, it has been perfectly well understood that the wisest and purest ministers have, to a later day than George III.'s, as directly bought political adhesion and votes in Parliament by commissions, titles, sinecures, pensions, and jobs, as butchers buy cattle in the Smithfield market. If the Secretary

of State, like Chatham,[1] is a little addicted to personal squeam-
ishness, there is a premier like the Duke of Newcastle, to man-
age what the historian Macaulay terms the "jobbing department." This is the old convenient arrangement of certain other
business firms. There is the gentleman partner, and the partner
for dirty work. We ought by way of illustration to name another usual addition, or appendage to such "firms." There is
not only the buyer but the *bought!* From the Ministry just
named, from men he had bitterly opposed and abhorred, Fox—
a man of the first mark and rank in politics, and of scarcely less
abilities than his illustrious son, Charles James Fox—received
the wages of adhesion and ignominious silence, in the most lucra-
tive office in the Government.

These illustrations might be swelled to any limits. The fact
that the British administration had always resorted to corruption
as a part of its necessary measures to obtain and secure strength,
is contradicted by no British historian. He who would have
abundance of details on this subject is referred to the pages of
Mr. Macaulay. If he would see the subject treated at some
length, by itself, he is referred to the same author's review[2] of
Thackeray's History of the Earl of Chatham. After inspecting
the testimony of the native witnesses, our liberality, in the preceding remarks, will not be impeached.

No apologist of Alexander Hamilton has denied that " theoretically " he believed the British Constitution was the "best
form "—"a model which we ought to approach as near as possible." [3] This was the life-long burden of that song which Mr.
Morris declares was repeated by him so persistently, and so
much to the annoyance of his more prudent friends. These
laudations involve the administration as well as the written form
—for all know that the Constitution of England exists more in
established practice than in written instruments. But independently of all questions of definition, do we, from the first to the
last, ever hear Hamilton, like John Adams, excepting the system of government corruption when lavishing praises on the
British government? Do we find him attempting to avoid
those corruptions in practice? This question will be better

[1] Then Mr. Pitt.   [2] First published in Edinburgh Review, 1834.
[3] These are his words from the "brief" of a speech in the Convention of 1787,
already cited from his biography.

settled at a later period, but it is not altogether premature now. The circumstances accompanying the Funding Bill, the manner of the Assumption, the history of other bills, the scenes which attended the organization of the United States Bank, furnish evidence which does not demand the hints of Ames and the broad avowals of Morris,[1] for its explanation.

Hamilton's mind was perspicacious, logical, and strong in the wisdom of a beaten circle of precedents. But he never transcended that circle—never was in the least degree inventive—never struck out a new path either in theory or practice—never, in the whole course of his life, proposed an original thought or plan. He adapted and re-combined with promptness; but he who deliberately examines the history of his public career will look in vain for a system or even a marked feature of a system, not as directly and literally transferred from England, as the differences in the structure of the governments, in the condition of those to be acted upon, and in the popular tone, would possibly admit. The highest attribute of the great statesman—to look forward, to adapt his measures to the progress of ideas, to create systems which will stand the test of a broader and deeper civilization—was not vouchsafed to him. His wisdom, to use some one's striking comparison when speaking of another person, was like the stern-lights of a ship. It cast all its light backward, over the course already passed over, and not a ray forward!

As long as the tremendous struggle was going on between the Hamiltonian and Jeffersonian construction of the United States Constitution—between the English theory of it and the democratic theory of it—Hamilton's plans, Hamilton's opinions, Hamilton's resounding name were on every tongue. When the outworks, all but the citadel of the seemingly massive structure, fell in 1801—when the citadel (the Supreme Court) was some years after carried over to the assailants by the death of a majority of its original defenders, what of Hamilton's remained? And now what great political truth, what important maxim in the science of government, what broad and benevolent view of human affairs, traces back to him as either its originator, or its practical developer, or its introducer on that part of the human theatre where his lot was cast? If there is one such, we confess

---

[1] We mean Morris's avowals of his own views. See page 572.

it has eluded our scrutiny.   To make a somewhat different application from the usual one of the often quoted words of Lucan: "Stat magni nominis umbra"—he stands but the shadow of a mighty name—apotheosized, as already remarked, by the American enemies of democratic theories, as the great type-man, the symbol of their idea.

A degree, and no inconsiderable degree, of "greatness" is here willingly conceded to Hamilton.   It was not the greatness of a profoundly wise man in practice, who chances to entertain certain erroneous or inapplicable theories.   He cannot be called wise in practice, all of whose structures, which could be rooted from our system without a breach of public faith, have already perished, as it were, in a night.   Practical wisdom in the states man requires measures not only good in themselves, but suffi ciently adapted to existing circumstances to command something like permanent success.   He certainly cannot be called wise in practice who "props" his edifice till he crushes it with the buttresses he builds against it—in other words, who, in his immoderate efforts to strengthen his system, provokes, nay, compels the opposition, which sweeps away much of it that might otherwise have been permitted to stand.

It is not to be denied that there were fair grounds for different constructions of the American Constitution.   Nay, it did not prescribe, but left to the States a multitude of details, the settlement of which would virtually control that construction. Among the people of the States were three parties, the monarchical, the democratic, and the conservative republican. After the adoption of the federal Constitution, our opinion is that for a considerable period the two first were but handfuls—that the last comprised the body of both leaders and people.   Hamilton, Jefferson, and Washington were the representatives of these three parties.   The rapid tendency of all popular governments in theory, is towards practical democracy. But our people were naturally and habitually cautious, and inclined to conservatism.   They left beaten roads with reluctance.   The opponents of pure democracy had the vantage ground, not only in numbers and the weight of names, but in the feelings of the people.

Had Hamilton understood the temper and character of the American people—had he identified himself with and prudently fostered the conservative feeling—our government might have kept that track until it became fixed in it; and now we might have that mild mixed government in spirit which was the ideal of the middle men. But as Morris truly said, " meaning very well, he acted very ill, and approached the evils he apprehended by his very solicitude to keep them at a distance." [1] In plainer words, Hamilton upbuilt democracy by his over-action against it. He forced the people to choose between it and a consolidated system having all the spirit of monarchy, and which the people believed he ultimately (in some " crisis ") intended to give the *form* of monarchy. He thus rashly and unnecessarily threw all into the scale, and he lost all.

Finally, Hamilton was not a great or a wise man in practice, in the sense in which the words are used to mark the distinction between the efficient performer and the visionary theorist. With the terms " projector," " speculative dreamer," " philosopher," etc., often tauntingly on his lips in respect to opponents, none in all the number formed half so many purely chimerical schemes, or half so often failed in them, as himself. The figures cast on the wall by a magic lantern are scarcely more evanescent, and considering the people and circumstances among whom they were formed, scarcely more unsubstantial than those which swiftly followed each other through his teeming brain. When his authority became full blown, each year brought a new grand scheme from him, embracing public affairs generally, and it would now be difficult to believe that they were the propositions of an American statesman—that they were not forgeries to impeach his common sense—did we not find them in an authorized and family edition of his works.

But Hamilton, in addition to remarkably clear and vigorous intellectual capacities, possessed one kind of practical greatness —that of execution. Whether his theory was sound, or his practice wise, the executive process was marked by promptness and strength. His mental operations were rapid and lucid. His best judgment, if not his only judgment, came to maturity on the investigation of minutes or hours, instead of days or weeks. He could give a fertile display of reasons for his opinion, always fortified by a plausible, and when he was in the

---

[1] Letter to Walsh, Feb. 5, 1811.

right, by a piercing logic. He had at ready command a store
of apt and sonorous words. Whether it was his business to do,
to speak, or to write, he was ready on the instant; and his activity and industry never flagged until his cause was won or lost.

Hamilton had that superlative confidence in himself, that
unbounded self-esteem which in the weak provokes derision, in
the able, inspires confidence. In his party he assumed the tone
of an absolute and undisputed dictator. The position was conceded to him for a time, partly from his real ability and partly
because those were the only terms on which his coöperation could
be secured. Circumstances gave him a weight possessed by no
other man in that party. None liked to provoke his hostility by opposition or disobedience. Mr. Adams ventured to
do so and it proved fatal to him. Morris softens these characteristics of his friend by giving them the name of "a pertinacious adherence to opinions he had once formed." This pertinacity extended from things of prime importance down to' almost
inconsiderable details, and it was evinced as freely in matters
where other men were by law or custom intrusted with the sole
decision, and compelled to assume the sole responsibility, as in
those where he was properly a principal sharer in both. The
boy who at twelve years old "wished there was a war" to
enable him to "exalt his station;" who at twenty thought it was
a sacrifice to become an aid-de-camp of Washington; who always "did violence to his feelings" while he remained in that
post; and who at twenty-four refused to "consent to an accommodation" with the latter for a hasty word followed by an ample
apology, would never be expected, in after life, to doubt his
own infallibility and right to command, or that the world was
"his oyster" made specially for his opening and for his disposition of its contents.

All these traits added to that executive power which we
have said Hamilton possessed. To act with the greatest velocity and intensity, the mind of the actor must be troubled with
no misgivings about the accuracy of its own conclusions. Nor
must it pause to ask too scrupulously whether the rights of
opinion, the feelings or the delicacies of others are to be
.invaded. The most efficient political executive is a despot.
The most efficient actor elsewhere is he who acts on the principles of a despot.

We believe Hamilton was earnest and honest in his political principles. If he stooped, when his inner views were publicly sought, to

—— " with a tricksy word,
Defy the matter;"

if he attempted to induce the public to take the substance by disguising the name, it was because he thought such resorts were necessary to induce the multitude he scorned to submit to that good government which he verily believed he was preparing for them. Clothed with supreme power, he would probably have made a just prince. Under a tyranny, he might have proved a conspirator. The features of Hampden and the features of Strafford blend strangely in his political physiognomy. But those of the latter largely predominate. If he had none of the originating power of a Franklin or Jefferson, he would probably have rendered himself conspicuous in any age or under any government. Such minds as Franklin's and Jefferson's come but once in a century. Such minds as Hamilton's are common in every generation. They belong to the ambitious, energetic, talented class who push their way upward to high office, who wield authority with success, who perhaps fill fame's trumpet with their reputations as generals or prime ministers, who receive honorable mention on the historic page, but who pass away without having contributed a new thought, or a meliorating fact to the currents of human civilization.

We have thought it would tend to a clearer view of affairs in the Cabinet, and subsequently, to present an outline of Hamilton's character in advance of the facts on which much of our view rests. No one will be asked to receive that view, or any part of it, except so far as it is supported by unsuspected and decisive testimony. We certainly will ask no credit for a line of the latter from unfriendly or prejudiced quarters; and, indeed, almost the only testimony offered will be Hamilton's own, and in his own words.

END OF VOL. I.